The Augustinian
of St Mary Mert

Excavations 1976–90

MoLAS Monograph Series

For more information about these titles and other MoLAS publications visit the publications page at www.molas.org.uk

1 Excavations at the priory and hospital of St Mary Spital, London

2 The National Roman Fabric Reference Collection: a handbook

3 The Cross Bones burial ground, Redcross Way, Southwark, London: archaeological excavations (1991–8) for the London Underground Limited Jubilee Line Extension Project

4 The eastern cemetery of Roman London: excavations 1983–90

5 The Holocene evolution of the London Thames: archaeological excavations (1991–8) for the London Underground Limited Jubilee Line Extension Project

6 The Limehouse porcelain manufactory: excavations at 108–116 Narrow Street, London, 1990

7 Roman defences and medieval industry: excavations at Baltic House, City of London

8 London bridge: 2000 years of a river crossing

9 Roman and medieval townhouses on the London waterfront: excavations at Governor's House, City of London

10 The London Charterhouse

11 Medieval 'Westminster' floor tiles

12 Settlement in Roman Southwark: archaeological excavations (1991–8) for the London Underground Limited Jubilee Line Extension Project

13 Aspects of medieval and later Southwark: archaeological excavations (1991–8) for the London Underground Limited Jubilee Line Extension Project

14 The prehistory and topography of Southwark and Lambeth

15 Middle Saxon London: excavations at the Royal Opera House 1989–99

16 Urban development in north-west Roman Southwark: excavations 1974–90

17 Industry in north-west Roman Southwark: excavations 1984–8

18 The Cistercian abbey of St Mary Stratford Langthorne, Essex: archaeological excavations for the London Underground Limited Jubilee Line Extension Project

19 Material culture in London in an age of transition: Tudor and Stuart period finds c 1450–c 1700 from excavations at riverside sites in Southwark

20 Excavations at the priory of the Order of the Hospital of St John of Jerusalem, Clerkenwell, London

21 Roman and medieval Cripplegate, City of London: archaeological excavations 1992–8

22 The royal palace, abbey and town of Westminster on Thorney Island: archaeological excavations (1991–8) for the London Underground Limited Jubilee Line Extension Project

23 A prestigious Roman building complex on the Southwark waterfront: excavations at Winchester Palace, London, 1983–90

24 Holy Trinity Priory, Aldgate, City of London: an archaeological reconstruction and history

25 Roman pottery production in the Walbrook valley: excavations at 20–28 Moorgate, City of London, 1998–2000

26 Prehistoric landscape to Roman villa: excavations at Beddington, Surrey, 1981–7

27 Saxon, medieval and post-medieval settlement at Sol Central, Marefair, Northampton: archaeological excavations, 1998–2002

28 John Baker's late 17th-century glasshouse at Vauxhall

29 The medieval postern gate by the Tower of London

30 Roman and later development east of the forum and Cornhill: excavations at Lloyd's Register, 71 Fenchurch Street, City of London

31 Winchester Palace: excavations at the Southwark residence of the bishops of Winchester

32 Development on Roman London's western hill: excavations at Paternoster Square, City of London

33 Within these walls: Roman and medieval defences north of Newgate at the Merrill Lynch Financial Centre, City of London

34 The Augustinian priory of St Mary Merton, Surrey: excavations 1976–90

The Augustinian priory of St Mary Merton, Surrey

Excavations 1976–90

Pat Miller and David Saxby

MoLAS Monograph 34

Museum of London Archaeology Service

Published by the Museum of London Archaeology Service
Copyright © Museum of London 2007

A CIP catalogue record for this book is available from the British Library

Production and series design by Tracy Wellman
Typesetting and design by Sue Cawood
Reprographics by Andy Chopping
Copy editing by Wendy Sherlock
Series editing by Sue Hirst/Susan M Wright
Post-excavation and series management by Peter Rowsome

Printed by the Lavenham Press

*Front cover: 12th-century gateway/doorway, found during the demolition of Abbey
House in 1914, as reconstructed in the parish churchyard of St Mary the Virgin,
Merton; gold finger ring <S252> with amatory inscription, recovered from a
demolition deposit in the former infirmary hall; the north transept and nave under
excavation, looking west*
*Back cover: painted, scalloped respond capital <A1> (period M1); wooden bowl
<S292> with carved cross potent mark on base; 14th-century burials [2387]
and (right) [2381] in the Lady chapel*

CONTRIBUTORS

Principal authors	Pat Miller, David Saxby
Documentary evidence	Tony Dyson
Moulded stone and architectural reconstructions	Mark Samuel
Stone roofing and paving, ceramic building material	Ian Betts
Pottery	Roy Stephenson, with John Evans (organic residues)
Non-ceramic finds	Geoff Egan, with Helen Ganiaris and Christie Pohl (?hernia belt)
Plant remains	John Giorgi
Pollen	Rob Scaife
Vertebrate remains	Alan Pipe, with Jane Sidell (eggshell)
Molluscs	Lisa Gray, Alan Pipe
Coleoptera (beetles)	David Smith
Human bone	Jan Conheeney
Dendrochronology	Greta Boswijk, Ian Tyers
Graphics	Peter Hart-Allison, Julia Jarrett, Kikar Singh
Site photography	Penny Bruce, Simon Mason
Studio photography	Edwin Baker, Andy Chopping, Maggie Cox
Project managers	Peter Rowsome, Derek Seeley, Barney Sloane
Editors	Susan M Wright, with Ian Grainger, Julian Hill, Sue Hirst

CONTENTS

FIGURES

TABLES

SUMMARY

The Augustinian priory of St Mary Merton (Surrey) was founded on its present site in 1117 by Gilbert, Sheriff of Surrey. Excavations between 1976 and 1990 uncovered much of the medieval priory which lay c 11.3km to the south-west of London on the banks of the River Wandle. Merton was one of the most influential of all the English houses of regular canons; during the 13th century it was favoured by Henry III, who visited frequently.

The investigations allowed elements of the layout and development of the priory to be traced from the 12th century to the Dissolution (Chapters 2 and 3). Excavation revealed the remains of a stone church begun in c 1170 and possibly completed by c 1200, sited on a platform above the flood plain and marsh. However, ex situ architectural fragments, together with some stratigraphic and documentary evidence, suggest this was not the first stone church built, and that an earlier one existed in the vicinity, constructed in the mid 12th century. The late 12th-/early 13th-century church was rebuilt in the 13th century, probably after the documented fall of the tower in 1222. Buildings identified as constructed to the south of the new church in the 13th century included parts of the cloister and east and south ranges, including a square-ended chapter house (with mosaic paving formed of large, plain-glazed and decorated tiles), separated from the south transept by a slype or possibly a vestiarium, and a reredorter undercroft, together with, to the south-east, a large monastic infirmary complex with its own cloister and chapel. The main cloister to the south of the church was apparently separated from the nave by an open space, an unusual feature in an Augustinian house. A gatehouse, a mill and possibly a large aisled guest hall were also identified within the precinct. In the 14th century a new presbytery and Lady chapel extended the church to c 110m long, while the chapter house was rebuilt with an apsidal end. The infirmary hall was subdivided at that time, to provide private accommodation. Subsidiary buildings close to the infirmary could have fulfilled related domestic and medical functions. Some of the priory buildings, particularly the church, were extensively demolished following the Dissolution and large quantities of salvaged stone were used to build Henry VIII's palace at Nonsuch, near Ewell (Surrey). Building materials – notably architectural mouldings, window glass and tiles – recovered from the demolition deposits in particular enable a more detailed reconstruction of the appearance of the priory buildings.

A number of thematic essays (Chapter 4) address key research topics. The foundation and early history of the priory, and the developed monastic layout are described. A reconstruction is attempted of the changing form of the chapter house and of the priory church which culminated in the 14th-century eastern extension, a major lost work of the Decorated period in south-east England. The Merton infirmary complex was extensively excavated and is of particular interest. Intended for the care of the monastic personnel, the infirmary hall, chapel, cloister and ancillary buildings formed a self-contained complex where servants, corrodians and other laity might sometimes be admitted, with buildings paralleling the functions of the main claustral complex. Evidence for medical care and treatment (including a possible hernia belt and medicinal plants), food and diet, material culture and daily life, and the monastic economy is considered, as is the identity of the priory's inhabitants and of those buried within different parts of the precinct. The large number of burials excavated (721 inhumations, not including charnel pits and large amounts of residual human bone, with of those 664 analysed), from the external cemetery, the church, cloister and chapter house, is of national significance. A variety of burial customs, together with evidence of the demographic profile, health and disease, are considered. 'The priory in its wider context' looks at Merton's role and its place in the Augustinian Order, and the significance of royal patronage.

The impact of the Dissolution and the history of the site up to the 19th century are summarised in Chapter 5. The leasing of surviving buildings, the garrisoning of troops there in the Civil War and the development from the 1660s of 'Merton Abbey' as a manufacturing centre, especially of textiles, are discussed. Conclusions and future research form Chapter 6. Supporting specialist data and the finds catalogues make up the final Chapter 7.

ACKNOWLEDGEMENTS

The funding for the first two phases of excavation between 1976 and 1983 came from the Department of the Environment, with funding for the post-excavation work on this provided by English Heritage. The third and largest phase of excavation was undertaken between 1986 and 1990 with funding for this, and subsequent post-excavation work, provided by J Sainsbury plc. The publication costs were generously funded by English Heritage. The project monitor for J Sainsbury plc was Gill Andrews and the English Heritage monitors were Gill Chitty, Ellen Barnes, Brian Kerr and Roger Thomas. Roberta Gilchrist acted as academic referee for the project. The publication work was programmed by Gordon Malcolm at MoLAS.

The authors would like to thank all the excavators and archaeological specialists who worked on the sites and assemblages with special thanks to the volunteers. Particular thanks should go to those people involved in the supervision of the project and the post-excavation (but not the final publication): Penny Bruce, Howard Burkill, Tony Clark, Michael Hammerson, Sue Hurman, Penny MacConnoran, Scott McCracken, Simon Mason, Robin Nielsen, John Nowell, Philip Simmonds, Andrew Skelton, Terence P Smith and Hester White. Museum of London and Specialist Services conservators who worked on material from the site included Helen Ganiaris, Liz Goodman, Will Murray, Gill Nason, Robert Payton, Christie Pohl and Kirsten Suenson-Taylor. Digital drawings, from which the final publication illustrations were created, were produced at MoLAS by Josephine Brown, Mark Burch and Steve Every, while Pete Rauxloh aided the digital analysis of the site.

We are grateful to Terry Ball, Martin Biddle, Richard K Morris, Alan M Rome and David F Williams who helped with the analysis of the MPY86 stonework; Martin Biddle generously gave permission for access to, and publication of material from, Nonsuch Palace. Lionel Green (Merton Historical Society) helped to provenance historic photographs of Abbey House during its demolition. Additional information on the Purbeck marble grave slab was kindly provided by Sally Badham. Lucy Whittingham assisted with the pottery analysis. Thanks also to Cathy Haith, Christopher Knüsel and Mark Redknap for information on hernia belts and to conservators Fleur Sherman (British Museum) and Esther Cameron (Institute of Archaeology, Oxford) for examination of the fibres. John Cherry identified the amatory inscription on the gold finger ring. Many thanks to Tony Waldron for access to his original information in the human bone archive for the 1976–83 excavations and further advice in relation to the complete human bone assemblage; Natasha Powers and William White assisted in the editing of the human bone report.

The authors wish to thank especially John Hawks (Merton Abbey Mills) and Michael Lepper (Priory Park) for access to the archive stored at the site and assistance that was much appreciated.

The summary was translated into French by Elisabeth Lorans and into German by Manuela Struck. The index was compiled by Ann Hudson.

1

Introduction

1.1 Current knowledge of Augustinian houses

The canons of the Augustinian Order, to which St Mary Merton belonged, were unlike other clerics in that they both lived under a communal monastic rule and were ordained priests spending some time in the community looking after the spiritual well-being of lay people (Dickinson 1950, 7–8; Aston 1993, 82). The rule they observed – the so-called rule of St Augustine – was based on a letter by St Augustine of Hippo who died in AD 430. This document was brief and had to be expanded by borrowing from the fuller rule of St Benedict followed by Benedictine houses. The rule was demanding but fell short of the strictness and uniformity of other orders. The daily office was less protracted with more freedom concerning food, drink and movement. The rule of St Augustine was suitable for communities serving priories, collegiate churches, cathedrals and hospitals in both urban and rural settings. Robinson (1980, 349) suggests one reason for its success was its flexibility: many differing ways of life could be based on it, appealing to a variety of patrons. There was a strong contemplative element, which produced some tensions among clergy whose role had been essentially pastoral before they adopted the rule. After adoption however a full common life was the prime consideration, and further clerical responsibilities were avoided (Robinson 1980, 71–7). As clergy in holy orders rather than monks, Augustinian canons were regarded in the 11th and 12th centuries more as clerks with monastic characteristics rather than vice versa, and as clerks they were normally under diocesan authority, their heads of houses preferring the title prior to that of abbot (ibid, 79–80).

The 'canons regular' evolved in the 11th century as a new religious institute in response to the Gregorian reform programme. The rule of St Augustine was first adopted by the movement in north-eastern France in the mid 11th century and spread rapidly in the central, western church during the next 50 years. By the mid 12th century it was widespread although in most cases it is almost impossible to say when individual bodies of canons first adopted the rule. The period of Augustinian settlement within England and Wales was long, from the first foundation, soon after 1100, to at least 1359 when the last house was definitely founded. After 1200, the distribution pattern of houses contracted to mid and eastern England (Robinson 1980, 349).

St Botolph's, Colchester (Essex), is usually regarded as the first English clerical community to adopt the observance and so the first English house of the Order. There was a community of secular canons at Colchester before 1093–1100, but it is unlikely to have adopted a regular life before c 1095 (Robinson 1980, 98–104). However, it had certainly done so before the foundation of Holy Trinity Priory, Aldgate, in London in 1107 by Queen Matilda, wife of Henry I, when some of the Colchester brethren were transferred there. Other communities of regular canons founded in south-east England at this time were St Mary's, Huntingdon (Huntingdonshire), by the middle of the reign of William II (1087–1100); St Gregory's,

Canterbury (Kent), by William de Corbeil; Dunmore (Essex) where a chapel founded in 1104 was converted two years later by Geoffrey Bainard as a house of canons and St Mary Overie, Southwark (Surrey), generally claimed to have been founded in 1106 (Worcester Annals: *Ann Monast*, iv, 374), although there were no regular canons there till some years later (Dickinson 1950, 109). But Colchester, Huntingdon and Canterbury were the only Augustinian communities that could trace their origins to the 11th century (ibid, 104–5).

During the early 12th century the Augustinians expanded further. One of Holy Trinity Aldgate's daughter houses was Llanthony in Monmouthshire, although the foundation details are obscure. An oratory founded and consecrated there in 1108 was set up as a house of regular canons once the first inmates had been instructed by canons from Aldgate, Colchester and Merton, although Merton would not have been in a position to send people until 1117. Other early houses were Bridlington (Yorkshire East Riding) (1113), St Osyth's, Plympton (Devon) (1121), St Frideswide's, Oxford (by 1122), Nostell (Yorkshire West Riding) (1121 or 1122), Bricett (Suffolk) (similar date), St Bartholomew's, Smithfield, London (1123), Kenilworth (Warwickshire) (c 1125), Guisborough (or Gisburne) (Yorkshire North Riding) (c 1129), Oseney (Oxfordshire) (1129; becoming an abbey 1154), and Kirkham (Yorkshire East Riding) a little earlier (Dickinson 1950, 112–16).

In the later 12th century Augustinian canons spread rapidly in England; numbered by foundations the Order became the largest religious institution in the country (Lawrence 1984, 140–1). However, Augustinian foundations varied greatly in type and size: many were extremely small; some were in towns but others, such as Llanthony, were rural. Houses were often endowed with parish churches and expected to serve them or founded in association with hospitals to provide pastoral and practical care. Whether a house was founded on a modest or a grand scale was most often linked to their patronage. Some larger houses might establish their own congregations of daughter houses, linked by common customs and a loose system of surveillance; both Aldgate and Merton had a group of colonies as we have seen. Despite attempts at greater central regulation, the canons regular remained a very disparate collection of establishments (ibid, 141–2).

Robinson's (1980) study of the Augustinian canons in England and Wales in particular provides valuable data on the growth and spread of this disparate order, but there are few published detailed studies of individual sites or of aspects of their art and architecture, with notable exceptions such as Norton Priory (Cheshire) (Greene 1989), Kirkham Priory (Coppack et al 1995), the priory and hospital of St Mary without Bishopsgate, later known as St Mary Spital, London (Thomas et al 1997), and St Gregory's, Canterbury (Hicks and Hicks 2001). Looking at the monastic precinct as a whole has become a prominent theme in monastic archaeological research (eg Aston 2000). Thornholme Priory (Lincolnshire) is an Augustinian example of a study from this perspective (Coppack 1989). However, aspects of Augustinian archaeology such as flexibility towards the monastic layout, possibly reflecting a more practical vocation, have received relatively little attention or remain unpublished.

Together with the publications of the excavations at two urban foundations – the priory and hospital of St Mary Spital (Thomas et al 1997) and Holy Trinity Priory, Aldgate (Schofield and Lea 2005) – and at a suburban foundation – the nunnery of St Mary Clerkenwell (Sloane in prep) – this volume forms part of a study of the Augustinians in the London area, presented in a form designed to make their history and development accessible and easily comparable with that of the London region's other religious houses published in the MoLAS monograph series.

1.2 Location and circumstances of excavation

The former site of the Augustinian priory of St Mary Merton is currently occupied by Sainsbury's supermarket and a hotel, restaurants, sports facilities, residential blocks and Merton Abbey Mills. The centre of the site (Ordnance Survey national grid reference 52662/16989) is crossed by Merantun Way and lies in Colliers Wood, London Borough of Merton (Fig 1). Merton Priory was scheduled in 1980 (SAM 151) but the scheduled area does not cover the whole precinct (a scheduled monument consent condition covered the 1986–90 excavation). The study area covers only part of the priory precinct and is centred on the main priory buildings, the inner precinct and part of the outer precinct. The area covered by the trenches within the study area totals approximately 1 hectare or 10,000m[2] although in some cases the entirety of the trench area was not fully excavated. The full monastic precinct was more extensive and is currently bounded to the north and east by Merton High Street and the River Pickle, to the east by Christchurch Road, to the south by Liberty Avenue, the east bank of the River Wandle and parts of the Merton Industrial Estate, and to the west by Deer Park Road and Abbey Road, forming an enclosure estimated at approximately 17 hectares.

The earliest excavations were carried out by Colonel H F Bidder between 1921 and 1922, and concentrated on the northern part of the church and the chapter house (Bidder and Westlake 1930) (Fig 2). Much of Bidder's excavation was re-exposed by subsequent work.

Further archaeological work on the priory was undertaken from the 1960s onwards. A sewer pipe trench was monitored in 1961. This traversed the high altar and nave and a number of graves were located. In 1962 and 1963 archaeological work was carried out close to Merton Abbey Mills, to the west of the main priory complex, by D J Turner of the Surrey Archaeological Society (Turner 1967). J S McCracken undertook two phases of work on behalf of the Surrey Archaeological Society: in 1976–8, work concentrated on the chapter house and a limited record was also made to the south of the main cloister, during construction of an electricity pylon; in 1983

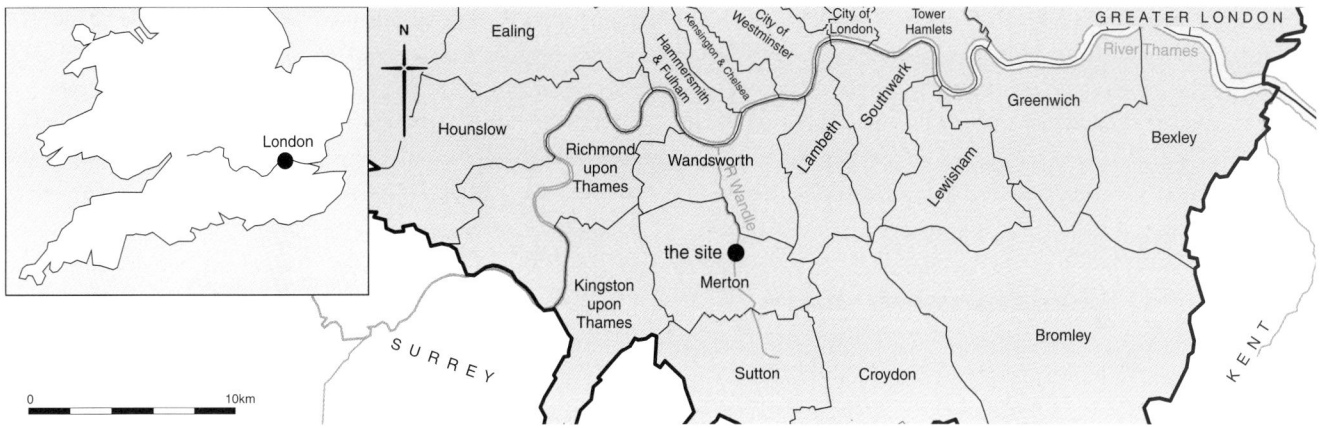

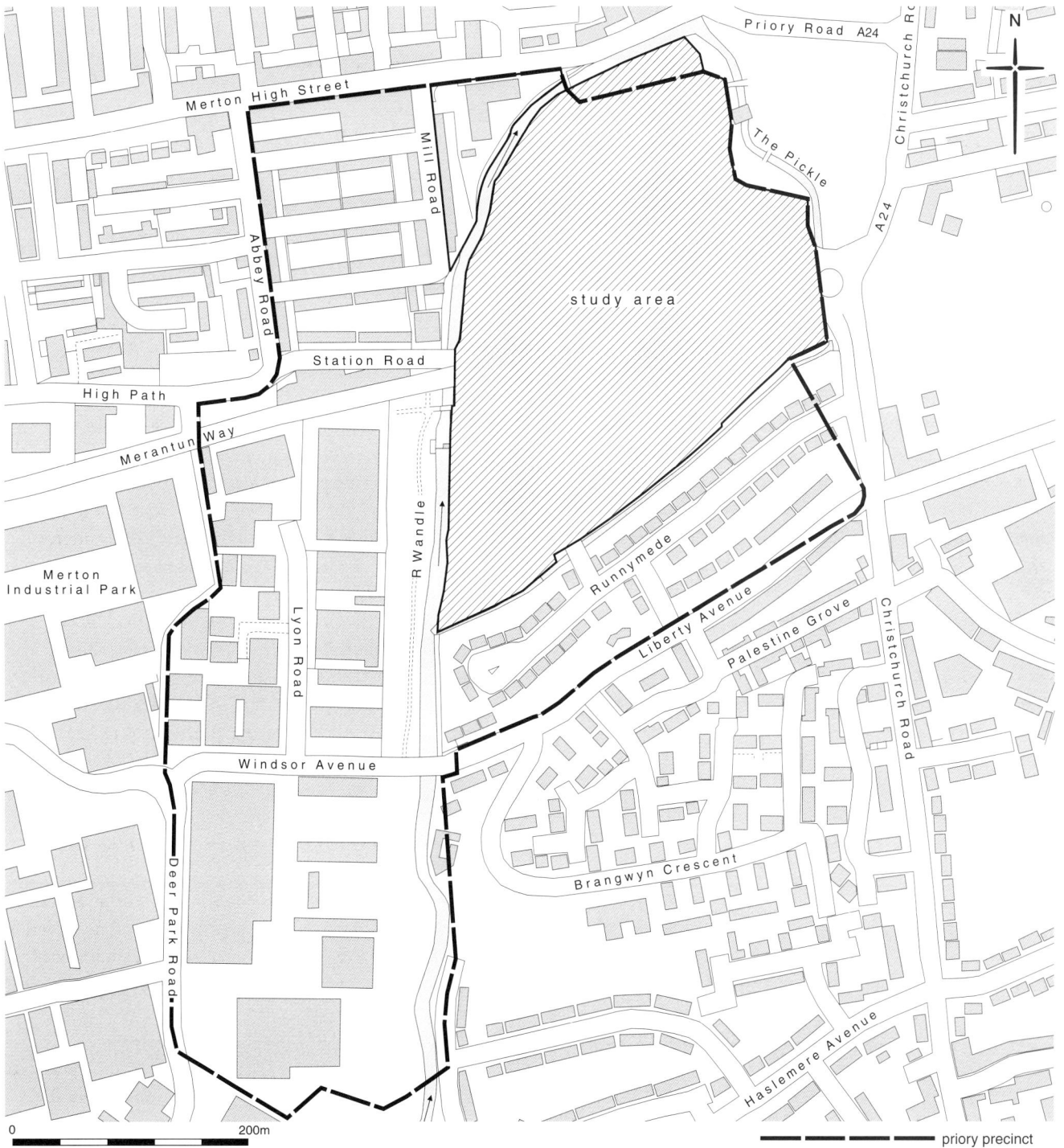

Fig 1 St Mary Merton: location of the priory precinct and study area (scale upper 1:360,000, lower 1:5000)

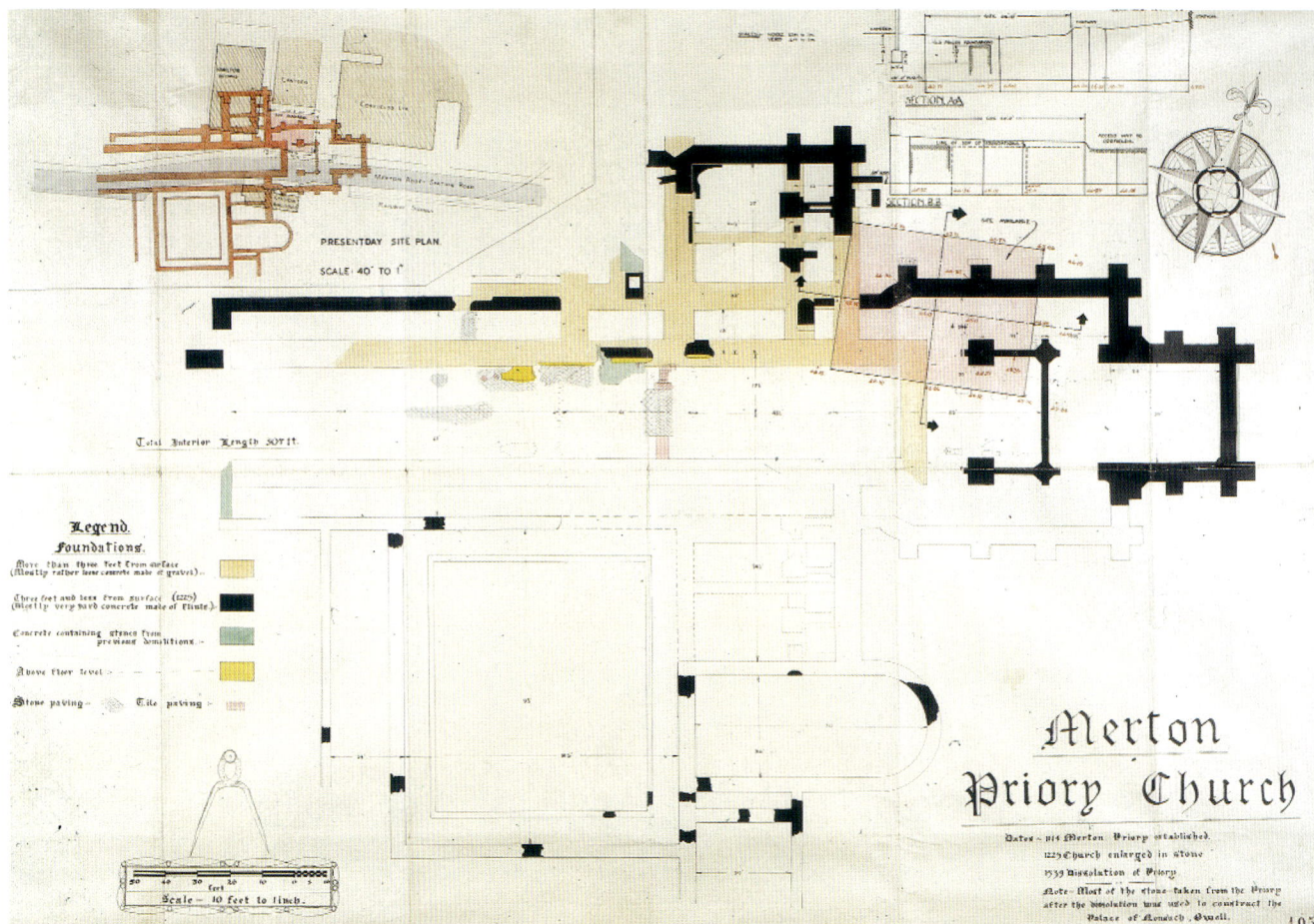

Fig 2 *Bidder's plan of the 1920s excavation of St Mary Merton (drawn at a scale of 10 feet to 1 inch) (courtesy of Merton Library and Heritage Service)*

work continued in the infirmary. Then, between 1986 and 1990, the Museum of London Department of Greater London Archaeology (DGLA) undertook the most extensive work to date as full-scale rescue excavations in advance of redevelopment. This concentrated on the priory church and main cloister, the cemetery areas to the north and south of the church, and the infirmary; the western part of the main cloister (area X on Fig 3) was cleared by machine but not excavated. It also included trial work to the east, and (in more limited form) to the south and south-west of the infirmary.

Details of site codes and archives relating to the site are as follows:

Merton Priory chapter house MPY76, MPY77, MPY78;
Merton Priory infirmary MPY83;
Merton Priory 1986–8 MPY86;
Merton Priory 1988–90 MPY88.

Selected data (moulded stone) from an archaeological excavation at Mill Road, Merton (MIS92, Fig 3), were considered and integrated with other data for this publication. The moulded stone report also refers to moulded stone from the archaeological excavation at Nonsuch Place in Cheam (Surrey) (NON59) and the site of Nonsuch Palace, where much of the building stone from Merton was taken at the Dissolution.

The sites were recorded with different recording systems, although the most recent excavations followed the former DGLA system. Each site was recorded with reasonably

consecutive context numbering and for the purposes of this report all, with the exception of MIS92, are regarded as one site and will not be individually identified. Some burials were planned but could not be precisely located as no grid coordinates were given; thus, not all burials are shown on the published period plans or distribution plots.

More recently, between 1999 and 2004, archaeological investigations were carried out within the southern part of the monastic complex. In some instances the earlier 1986–90 trenches were reopened and extended, providing additional information on the size and location of various monastic buildings. The results of these investigations will be presented in a separate publication (Saxby in prep) although, where the trenches were reopened, in some cases the results have been incorporated here.

Fig 3 locates the 1976–90 excavations within the study area. Excavation across the site was not uniform: some trenches were comprehensively excavated while others were subject to limited investigation. The trenches on the site were labelled alphabetically although not in sequence. The so-called 'trial trenches' excavated in 1986 in the south-east part of the site were identified by double lettering. The chapter house (trench CH) was excavated during 1976 to 1978 and trenches E, F, H and G (the pylon trenches) in 1983. Trenches C, D1 to D7 inclusive, V, X, Z, the trial trenches (trenches AB to AL, and CA to CD, inclusive) and the Wandle Bridge trench were excavated

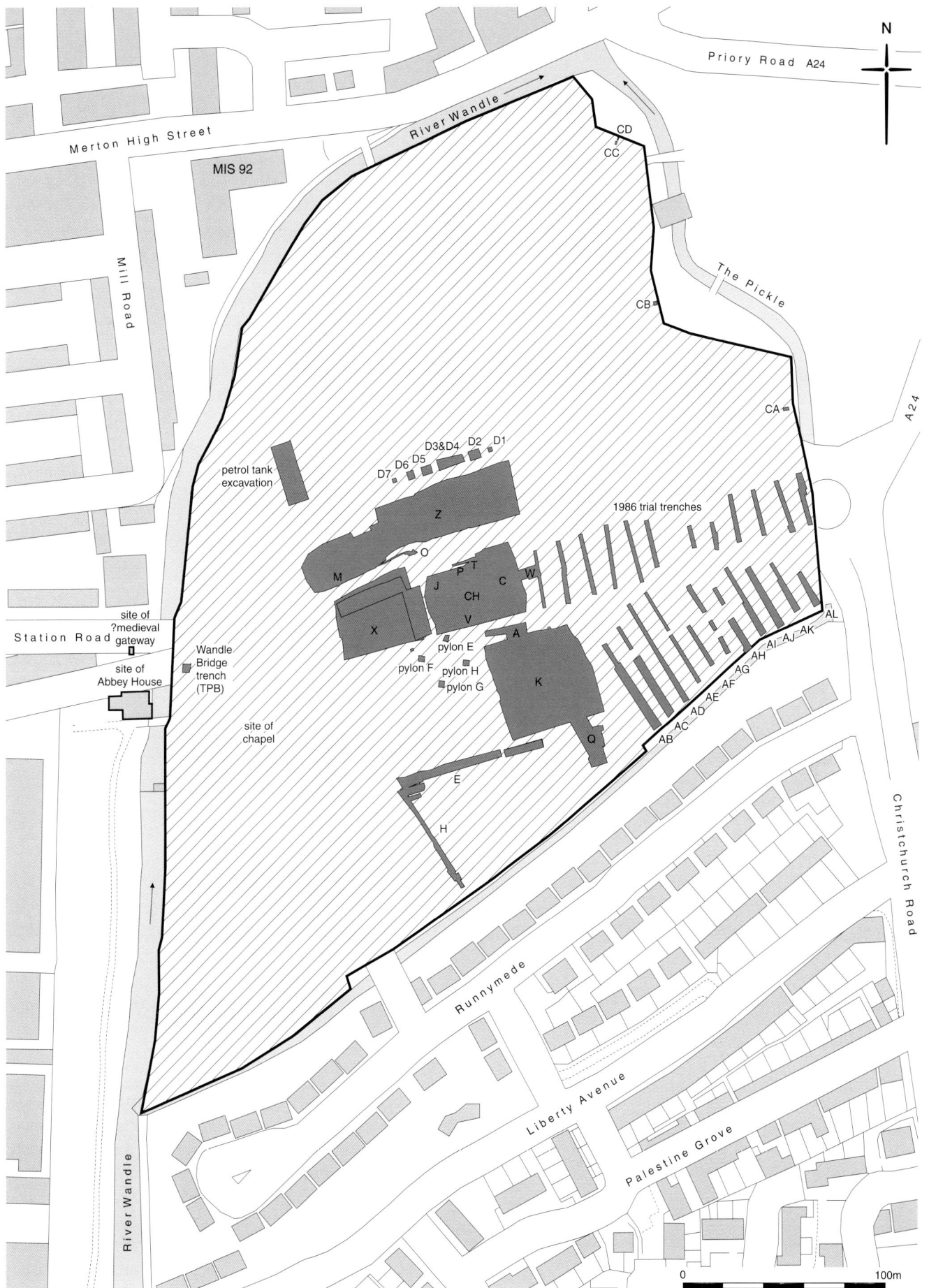

N

Priory Road A24

River Wandle

Merton High Street

MIS 92

Mill Road

CD
CC

The Pickle

CB

A24

CA

petrol tank
excavation

D3&D4   D2   D1
D6 D5
D7

Z

1986 trial trenches

O

M   J   P T
        CH
X   V   C   W

site of
?medieval
gateway

Station Road

Wandle
Bridge
trench
(TPB)

site of
Abbey House

pylon E
pylon F   A
pylon H
pylon G

K

AL

AI AJ AK
AH
AG
AF
AE
AD
AC
AB

site of
chapel

Q

E

H

Christchurch Road

Runnymede

Liberty Avenue

Palestine Grove

River Wandle

0   100m

Fig 3 Location of the 1976–90 excavations within the St Mary Merton study area (scale 1:2500)

in 1986. Trenches A, E, H, J, K, M, O, P, Q, T, W and the petrol tank trench were excavated in 1988.

1.3 Organisation of this report

The nature and extent of the priory of St Mary Merton placed constraints on the level of detail produced in this report. In accordance with *Management of archaeological projects* (English Heritage 1991), analysis resulted in a series of specialist research archives which are lodged with the Museum of London. This report follows the 'integrated' structure adopted by earlier volumes in the MoLAS monograph series (eg Thomas et al 1997). Thus the research and interpretation in this volume are presented in three ways, the chronological narrative, thematic sections and specialist appendices, with a fourth form of data remaining unpublished as outlined below.

The archaeological data are organised chronologically into dated periods grouped into three chapters describing the pre-priory, medieval priory (periods M1–M4) and post-medieval (periods P1–P3), that is Dissolution and later, sequences (Chapters 2, 3 and 5) (Table 1). These periods have been formed from stratigraphic phasing combined with evidence for changes in layout or function and the available dating evidence. The medieval and post-medieval period sections begin with the documentary evidence for that period. Archaeological activity is then described chronologically in terms of land-use elements or units, that is Buildings (B1–B13), Structures (S1–S10), Open Areas (OA1–OA13) and Roads (R1–R2). Artefactual and environmental evidence are described as they relate to a particular land use. Each medieval and post-medieval period narrative concludes with a period discussion and summary. Period plans show major features (Fig 9; Fig 28; Fig 34; Fig 57; Fig 71; Fig 121; Fig 129; Fig 139; Fig 171).

The chronological narrative reveals aspects of the medieval priory throughout its development making it possible to discuss the changing nature of the monastic complex and its inhabitants over time. Chapter 4 comprises a series of essays presenting aspects of the priory, highlighting patterns, comparisons and points of interest. Chapter 6 presents both

general conclusions and research questions resulting from the analysis in this volume. Specialist data are presented separately, where appropriate, in the specialist appendices in Chapter 7.

Thus the major themes and much of the detailed data from each specialist research archive have been integrated into this volume. There remains other material inappropriate for publication in the present format. This includes detailed identification, quantification, measurement and description of the various assemblages, stored in research archives, references for which are detailed in the bibliography. They are publicly accessible in the archive of the Museum of London, and may be consulted by prior arrangement at the Museum's London Archaeological Archive and Research Centre (LAARC), Mortimer Wheeler House, 46 Eagle Wharf Road, London, N1 7ED.

As a major monastic cemetery excavation, Merton data formed part of the database created as part of a research project analysing evidence for demography, burial practice and cemetery use from London's religious houses and elsewhere in the country; differences in criteria, and occasionally interpretation, the result in some cases of subsequent detailed work on the finds, mean that details may vary between the two publications (Gilchrist and Sloane 2005). Subsequent to the analysis reported here, the Merton Priory osteological assemblage has been included in a second research project, the Wellcome Osteological Research Database, funded by the Wellcome Trust and based at the Museum of London.

1.4 Textual and graphical conventions used in this report

The basic unit of cross-reference throughout the research archive for this project is the context number. This is a unique number given to each archaeological event on the site (such as a layer, wall, or grave cut), enclosed within square brackets. For example:

[100] representing context 100 from the site;

[+] representing unstratified and/or unrecorded material.

The broad chronological periods are defined as being pre-priory, M (medieval), or P (post-medieval). The specific periods included are summarised with their date ranges in Table 1. The land-use units are described as Buildings (B), Structures (S), Open Areas (OA) and Roads (R).

There are several categories of finds which have been numbered in the research archive and/or in the volume. Only illustrated architectural fragments, masons' marks, ceramic building material and pottery have been assigned a catalogue number. To indicate to which catalogue reference is being made, a prefix denoting the category appears inside angled brackets. For example:

<A1> refers to (A)rchitectural fragment no. 1;

<MM2> refers to (M)asons' (M)ark no. 2;

<P3> refers to (P)ottery object no. 3;

<S4> refers to (S)mall find no. 4;

<T5> refers to (T)ile no. 5.

Table 1 The chronological periods used in this report

Period	Description	Date range
	pre-priory: prehistoric; Roman; Saxon	
M1	foundation	c 1117–1222
M2	expansion	1222–c 1300
M3	further expansion	c 1300–c 1390
M4	repairs and the final phase	c 1390–1538
Unphased M1–M4	unphased burials	1117–1538
P1	Dissolution activity	1538–c 1550
P2	16th–17th centuries	c 1550–c 1700
P3	18th–19th centuries	c 1700+

For ease of reference back to the original material in the finds archive, site accession numbers (where assigned) are quoted in angled brackets in the catalogues; in the case of the small finds these accession numbers are prefixed by the excavation year because the accessioned material was not treated as a single corpus. Environmental sample numbers appear within curly brackets, for example {4274}.

The two most common building stones were identified on site and are described in the text, without qualification, as 'Reigate stone', meaning stone thought to come from the Upper Greensand of Surrey, and 'Taynton stone', that is an oolitic limestone most probably from the Great Oolite series, in particular the Taynton stone of the Middle Jurassic of Oxfordshire. There are quarry sources other than Reigate (Surrey), such as Gatton and Merstham (both in Surrey), while the Taynton stone formation covers a wide area and medieval quarrying was carried out at several locations (Chapter 7.2, 'Methodology').

The medieval and post-medieval pottery fabric codes used throughout the volume are expanded in Table 37, together with the broadest date range of that fabric. The age groups used to describe individuals are defined in Chapter 7.11.

Weights and measures quoted in the text are where appropriate in the units used before metrication. Documentary evidence and the early 20th-century excavations are reported with imperial measurements (yards, and feet and inches, the latter abbreviated to ft and in), along with conversions when appropriate (1ft equals 0.305m; 12in to 1ft, 3ft to 1 yard). A mile is equivalent to 1.61km. An acre is 0.4 hectare, or alternatively a hectare equals about 2.5 acres. A pound (abbreviated to lb) (1lb equals 0.45kg) comprises 16 ounces (abbreviated to oz) (1oz equals 28g). Eight pints make 1 gallon or 4.55 litres. Sums of money are quoted in the text as cited in £, s and d, where 12 pence (d) made one shilling (s) and 20 shillings (or 240d) a pound (£), since modern equivalents would be misleading. Dyer (1989, xv) provides the following reminder on which to base an approximation to current values: 'a skilled building worker earned 2d per day in 1250, 4d per day in 1400 and 6d in 1500'. County names in the text refer to historic counties.

The graphical conventions used in this report are shown on Fig 4.

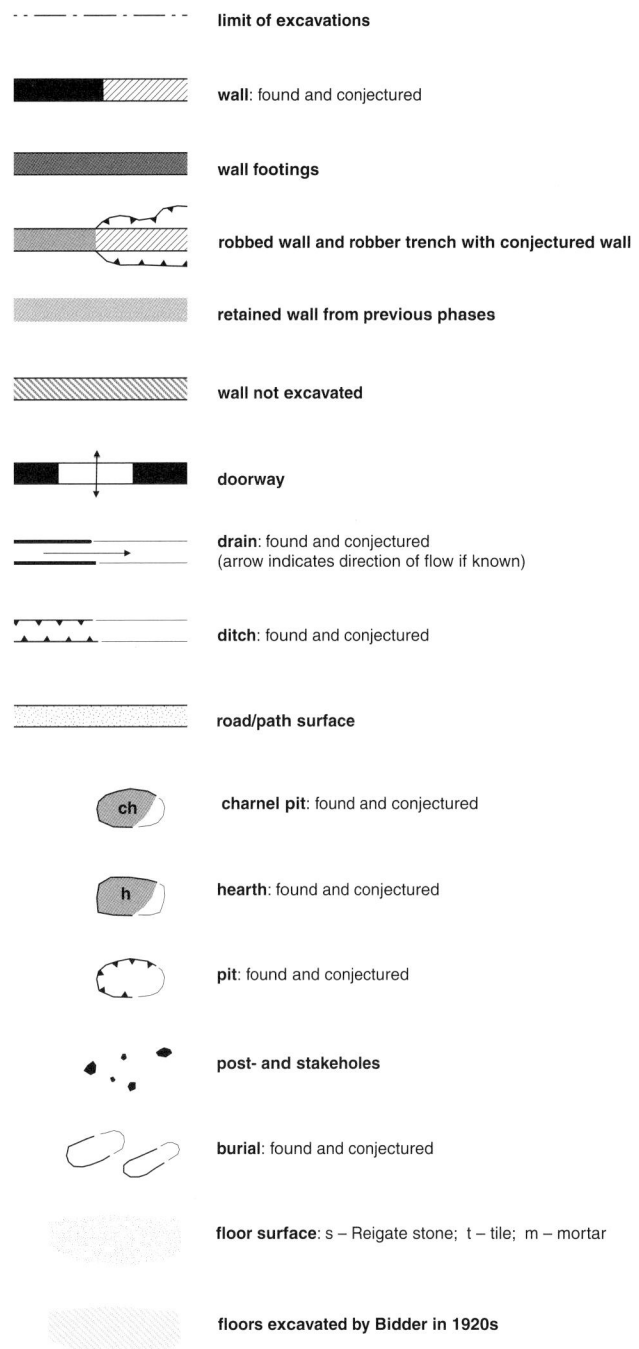

Fig 4 *Graphical conventions used in this report*

1.5 A note on documentary sources

In addition to the standard sources for the history of religious houses, notably Royal Letters Patent, the Close Rolls, and the records of the Court of Augmentations, which administered monastic sites and properties immediately after the Dissolution, Merton Priory has three other valuable documentary sources. The first is an unusually full account of the founder, foundation and early history (College of Arms, MS 28) probably compiled by the canons within two decades of the foundation. Secondly,

an early 13th-century cartulary or register book of charters and deeds (BL, Cotton MS Cleopatra C.vii): the earliest folios, including 38 charters and deeds dating from up to *c* 1150, have not survived, but the remainder contain much detailed material not normally found in a cartulary, including dealings with the secular clergy concerning advowsons (the right to present a clerk to a vacant ecclesiastical benefice) and property. It also records corrodies in unusual detail; these apart, and in common with other monastic cartularies, it contains little material relating to the community itself. Thirdly, there is, unusual in its survival, a late 14th-century miscellany (Bodleian, Laud MS 723) of priory documents and administrative records of the years 1383–93, relating to expenditure, acquisition of property, purchase of stock and the repair of buildings.

Research into Merton Priory is assisted in one further respect: A C Heales's *The records of Merton Priory in the county of Surrey* (1898). A remarkable and comprehensive compilation of materials drawn from a wide range of sources, it includes not only most of the cartulary and the important contents of Laud MS 723, but also feet of fines of relevant counties (largely derived from early antiquarian transcripts in the British Library) and the registers of the bishops of Winchester, Merton's diocesans. Less use seems to have been made by Heales of material in the Public Record Office, apart from ministers' accounts and Patent and Close Rolls, but little of consequence has later been found that does not appear in his *Records*. Much use has been made of this compilation in the present work, but Heales's *Records* present some serious difficulties. Not all his material is particularly illuminating and much, especially that deriving from the British Library transcripts, is repetitious or undiscriminating. Much of that relating to the Merton estates is more relevant to the history and topography of the districts in question than to the priory or the administration of its properties. The chief problem however lies with the presentation of the material: a seamless and strictly chronological narrative with no thematic differentiation or selectivity, difficult to read and poorly indexed.

The availability of information on the topography and fabric of the priory, with a high archaeological value, differs somewhat from that of other religious houses in the MoLAS monograph series. For St Mary Merton, there is conspicuously more information available from the lifetime of the priory, largely from the surviving Merton annals and calendars for the earlier period, and visitations conducted by the bishops of Winchester during the later. Often this relates to the dedication of chapels, such as that in the infirmary. Details of corrodies also throw further light on conditions within the priory precinct.

After the Dissolution the position is reversed. While most of the other monastic precincts were divided up and leased or sold piecemeal creating a wealth of documentation for individual areas and buildings, Merton remained in Crown hands as a quarry for building stone required at Nonsuch, Henry VIII's new palace (Chapter 5.1). Much of the fabric must have survived intact, but Sir Thomas Heneage, to whom the entire site was leased in July 1540 (precluding further detailed description of individual parts), was restricted in the use of some buildings (albeit unspecified) that the king might want demolished and removed. Nevertheless, during the Civil War the priory buildings were still sufficiently substantial to be adjudged, like Farnham Castle, as a Surrey strong point and a threat to parliament, and so garrisoned.

2

Pre-priory land use

2.1 Topography and geology

The site lies on the western side of the valley of the River Wandle, a Thames tributary rising to the south at the foot of the North Downs in Waddon and Carshalton. The valley floodplain consists of the 'Wandle' or 'Mitcham' gravels, dating to c 10,000 BC, overlying the Thames floodplain deposits of the Taplow Terrace and sealed by later local alluvial deposits of fine compact clay silts.

To the south of the study area, excavations at Streatham House (Fig 5, no. 1) showed that during the Mesolithic the Wandle valley was broad and marshy (Saxby 1991). Peat, sealed by later alluvial clays and silts, was radiocarbon dated to 9423±72 BP (UB-339) and probably related to early Flandrian peats and humic clays found in the valley bottoms of a number of Thames tributaries (eg the Colne, the Lea and the Kennet) deposited after the end of the Devensian glaciation when rising sea levels caused the base river levels of these tributaries to rise (Lewis et al 1992, 244). By the Roman period the current of the River Wandle had quickened and, at Streatham House and the High Street, Colliers Wood (Fig 5, no. 2), the peats were cut by chalk and silts carried from the river's source (Saxby 1997, 22–6). During this period the Wandle would have cut many channels in the base of the valley causing localised, sporadic flooding.

The present course of the Wandle, along the western side of the Abbey Mills complex, probably represents a re-routing of the river to power mills after the Dissolution, but, even before this canalisation, the river had followed a number of different channels during its history. The successive channels cannot be mapped precisely but can, generally, be reconstructed from Ordnance Datum heights taken on the surface of the river gravels, either from borehole data or archaeological evaluation. Recent work (Saxby 2001) indicates that the priory occupied higher ground, at approximately 12.5m OD, whereas the 'natural' sand and gravel close to the river to the south was at approximately 10.2m OD. The pre-modern river probably flowed northwards from Phipps Bridge, deviating eastwards to follow a course mirroring that now taken by Bennett's Ditch (named after a calico printer in the 19th century) before again flowing northwards to the east of the present River Pickle, crossing the High Street and passing through Wandle Park until it resumes the course as seen today (Fig 5; see also Fig 144 and Fig 150).

2.2 Prehistoric background

The earliest evidence for human settlement in the Wandle valley has mainly been recovered from gravel pits. Some 1.3km to the south-east of the site at Miles Road (Montague 1992a, 2) a single Lower Palaeolithic (before 38,000 BC) tool of unspecified type was discovered and a single flint flake in

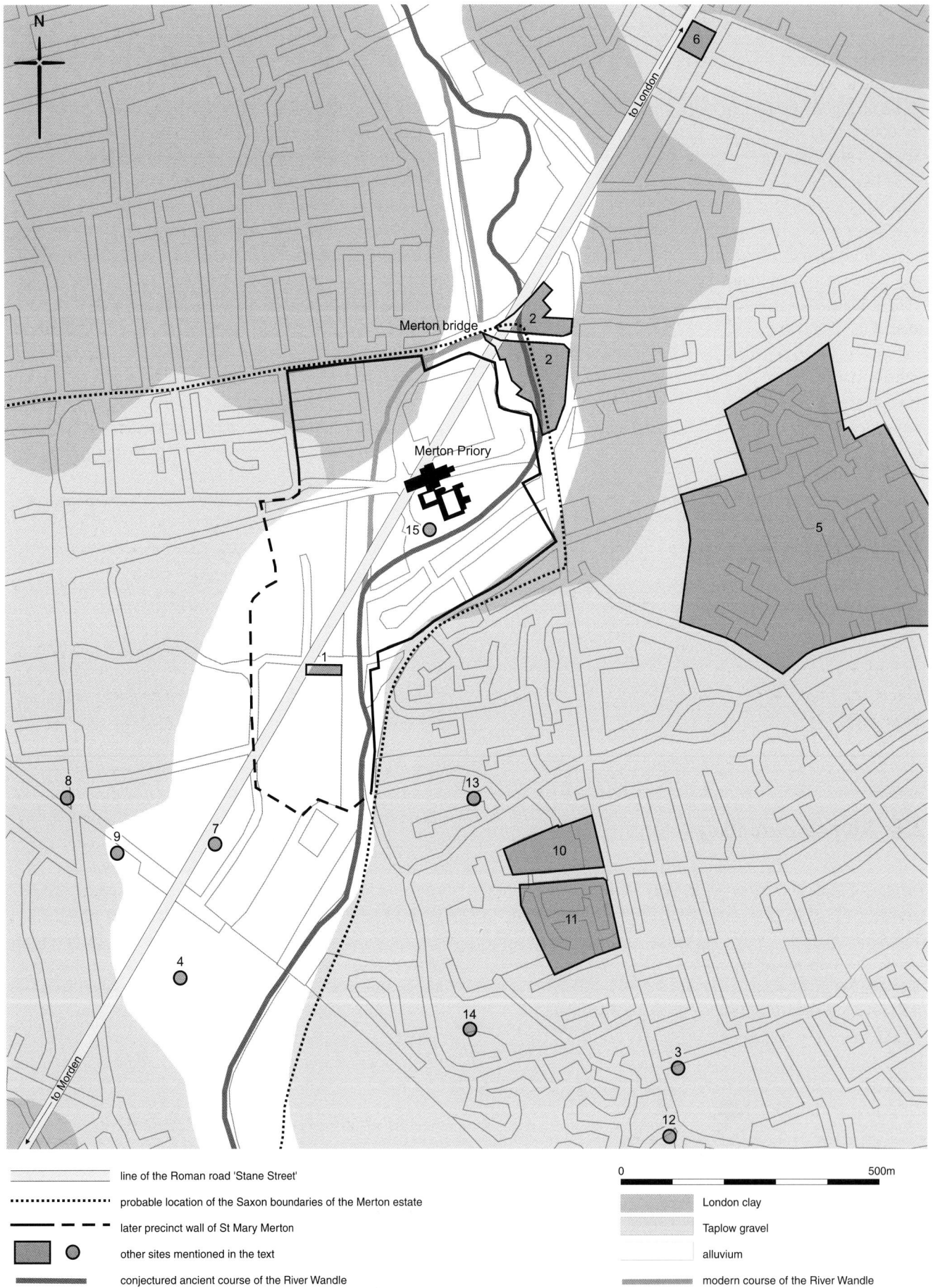

Fig 5 The topography of the Wandle valley showing the River Wandle, the Roman road 'Stane Street', the Saxon estate boundaries and the precinct of Merton Priory, together with sites mentioned in the text (scale 1:10,000)

Morden Hall Park to the south-west (Greater London Sites and Monuments Record (GLSMR) 020008; 030601) (Fig 5, nos 3–4). Other flint artefacts have been found to the south of the site, close to Ravensbury Park (GLSMR 030675; 030602) (not shown on Fig 5). Artefacts from the Upper Palaeolithic (38,000–10,000 BC) and Mesolithic periods are also rare (Wymer 1968, 275–6). The rising base river level after the end of the Devensian glaciation would have forced local populations to seek higher ground. Other traces of Palaeolithic and Mesolithic activity may be sealed beneath the Wandle valley peats.

Neolithic activity, in the form of Ebbsfleet and Mortlake ware pottery, has been found on the eastern fringes of the valley at Kings College Sports Ground (Fig 5, no. 5), although none of the sherds is considered to have been in a primary context. A number of ditches and a possible banjo enclosure with associated Deverel-Rimbury pottery suggest this site was also occupied during the Bronze Age (Bazely 1989a; 1989b). At the former Deen City Farm, Varley Way (Fig 5, no. 11), three ditches dating to the Bronze Age were found (Nielsen 1993). A number of prehistoric flints have been found during recent (2003) excavations at Merton Priory (Saxby 2005a, 51; in prep) (Fig 5, no. 15).

A small group of stray finds of Bronze Age date, including bronze palstaves, have been recovered from the broader Mitcham area to the south of the site since the 1880s (GLSMR 030632; 020181; 020182; 030770) (not shown on Fig 5). No evidence of Iron Age activity has been found yet in the vicinity but further south at Mitcham Grove an Iron Age weaving shuttle and coin have been found (GLSMR 030642; 020207) (not shown on Fig 5).

2.3 Roman summary

The line of Stane Street (Fig 5), the main Roman road from London to Chichester (Sussex), is followed by the modern High Street, Colliers Wood, as far south as Colliers Wood tube station. The Roman road would have crossed the Wandle at this point before continuing across the site of the priory, on a line beneath the north transept and nave of the church, towards the Abbey Mills site and Morden (Surrey) (Saxby 1997, 7).

In the vicinity of the Wandle crossing, to the north-east of the priory site (Fig 5, no. 2), the road has been excavated and shown to be constructed from local gravels and flanked by ditches (Saxby 1998, 9–31). Two phases were revealed. The earliest, probably constructed soon after the Roman invasion, was 12–16m wide (between ditches). First-century coins and pottery have been found elsewhere along the line of Stane Street, for example in Ewell (Surrey) (Abdy and Bierton 1997, 128–40). The road was rebuilt, probably in the second half of the 2nd century AD, when new roadside ditches were cut and two gravel banks added on the inner side of the ditches. The road width between the banks was reduced to c 8–9m.

The second-phase ditches were filling up by the mid 3rd century AD. Pottery sherds from a single 4th-century AD flagon were recovered from the fill of the roadside ditch where it was found further to the north-east along the High Street, Colliers Wood (Saxby 2004) (Fig 5, no. 6).

Gravel-digging in 1922 near Lombard Road, to the south-west of the priory site (Fig 5, no. 7), discovered about 500 Roman coins (of 1st- to 4th-century AD date) and Samian ware (Bidder 1934, 22–4). A brooch was found close by at Morden Road and a coin to the south-east of that (GLSMR 030662; 030653) (Fig 5, nos 8–9).

Excavations by the Merton Historical Society in 1966–8 on the site of the Haselmere First School (Fig 5, no. 10) uncovered evidence of a Romano-British cemetery in the form of three undated burials and two ditches containing pottery dating to the late 1st or 2nd century AD (Montague 1992a, 17). The adjacent site, to the south, at the former Deen City Farm, Varley Way (Fig 5, no. 11), produced further evidence of the same cemetery in the form of 12 more inhumations and a number of ditches (Nielsen 1993).

Further evidence of Roman occupation was found at the Benedict Primary School in the form of ditches containing Roman pottery and on the Windlesham and Sunningdale allotments (CRL89; HMM94) (Fig 5, nos 12–13). A coin of Vespasian was found in 1965 in Belgrave Road (GLSMR ref: 30659) (Fig 5, no. 14).

A small number of features and artefacts of Roman date were found during the excavations at Merton Priory. A possible rubbish pit, filled with clayey silt containing pottery and animal bone, was found beneath the north transept of the priory church, close to the line of the Roman road (OA1). Associated with the pit was a layer of grey-yellow clay, which also contained Roman pottery. A number of residual finds from later monastic features included Roman brick, tile, wall plaster, *opus signinum* (fine Roman concrete), a coin, two glass vessel fragments, an iron rake tine and a stone spindle whorl.

These suggest some Roman activity in the study area but provide limited evidence as to its nature, although the presence of Roman brick may indicate buildings close by. It has been suggested that a *mansio* or post station on the Roman road was situated either close to the site or further south-west, near the Lombard Road coin find (Turner 1965).

2.4 Saxon–early Norman summary

The Anglo-Saxon place-name Merton can be generally translated as 'settlement by the pool' and may date to the 7th century (Montague in prep, 15). The first indisputable reference to Merton appears in a charter of King Edgar, granting 20 cassata (cassatum: equivalent to a hide of 30 acres or 12.14 hectares) of land in Merton in AD 967 to Earl Aelfheah (Watkin 1956, 627–9). The grant includes a recitation of the landmarks by which the Merton estate was bounded (Fig 5) and commences as follows:

> This betz the landmer: erest on southam and on esten
> merkepol on hidebourne and thanen west on slade edichs
> southward thanen on benanberwe thanen on trdmer'
> endlangeridde north bi weste hoppingge over thane mersh
> on the right on ruanmer' and thanne est bi
> wymbedonnyngemerke on ther hop bi north bradenford'
> on hydebourne and thanne south endelangbournyn bi
> michamingemerke thar est on merkepol …

The charter suggests that the boundaries of the Merton estate have changed little in a thousand years. To the east Merton is bounded by Mitcham and Tooting; on the south by Mitcham and Morden; on the north by Wimbledon; and on the west by Kingston and Malden. In more modern times, to the east, the parochial and later district/borough boundary between Merton and Mitcham followed the line of the Pickle (Fig 3), an indication that this stream at one time formed the principal (or only) course of the Wandle in this area.

The Pickle Ditch is located along the approximate line of the former 'hidebourne' (meaning 'loud stream' or less possibly 'steep stream'), which would have been a more substantial watercourse at the time and would have formed a convenient boundary between the Merton estate and Mitcham. The location of a ford or crossing point from the Roman period onwards was found during excavations in 1997 a little to the east of the present Pickle Ditch (Saxby 1997). This would have been the 'Bradenforde' mentioned in the Saxon charter, forming the

eastern estate boundary. The estate ran southwards along the stream by Michammark to the Merkpool or boundary pool. The Merkpool was probably close to the present junction of Christchurch Road and Liberty Avenue. More recent excavations at Merton Priory (Saxby 2004) have revealed that this area was low-lying marshland during the medieval period.

Before the Norman Conquest, the manor of Merton belonged to Harold Godwinson (Heales 1898, 2–5). At the time of the Domesday Survey, in 1086, it was held by William I and remained in the possession of the Crown until Henry I gave the manor to Gilbert 'the Norman' in 1114. In 1086 there were 56 villeins and 13 bordars (peasants, owing agricultural services to their manorial lord) with 18 ploughs. Two mills valued at 60s are also mentioned, which were probably near the site, either along the banks of the present Bennett's Ditch or the Pickle Ditch (the pre-monastic course of the River Wandle), the only stretch of river within the eastern part of the Merton estate.

Some residual evidence of bone- and antler-working waste <S8>, <S10> was recovered from medieval ditches and pits during the excavations at Merton Priory (OA5). Late Saxon/early Norman bone and metal artefacts were recovered from monastic deposits (concentrated, apart from the antler comb <S2>, in the area of the later monastic infirmary cloister), including an ivory 'hipped' pin with a head in the form of a bird with open wings <S1> (Fig 6), a double-sided antler comb <S2>, fragments of an antler comb or comb case <S3> and two antler needles <S5> (Fig 6) and <S6>, and a fragment from a bone bodkin <S7>. A copper-alloy mount <S4> (Fig 6) may be a casket fitting. Saxon pottery included

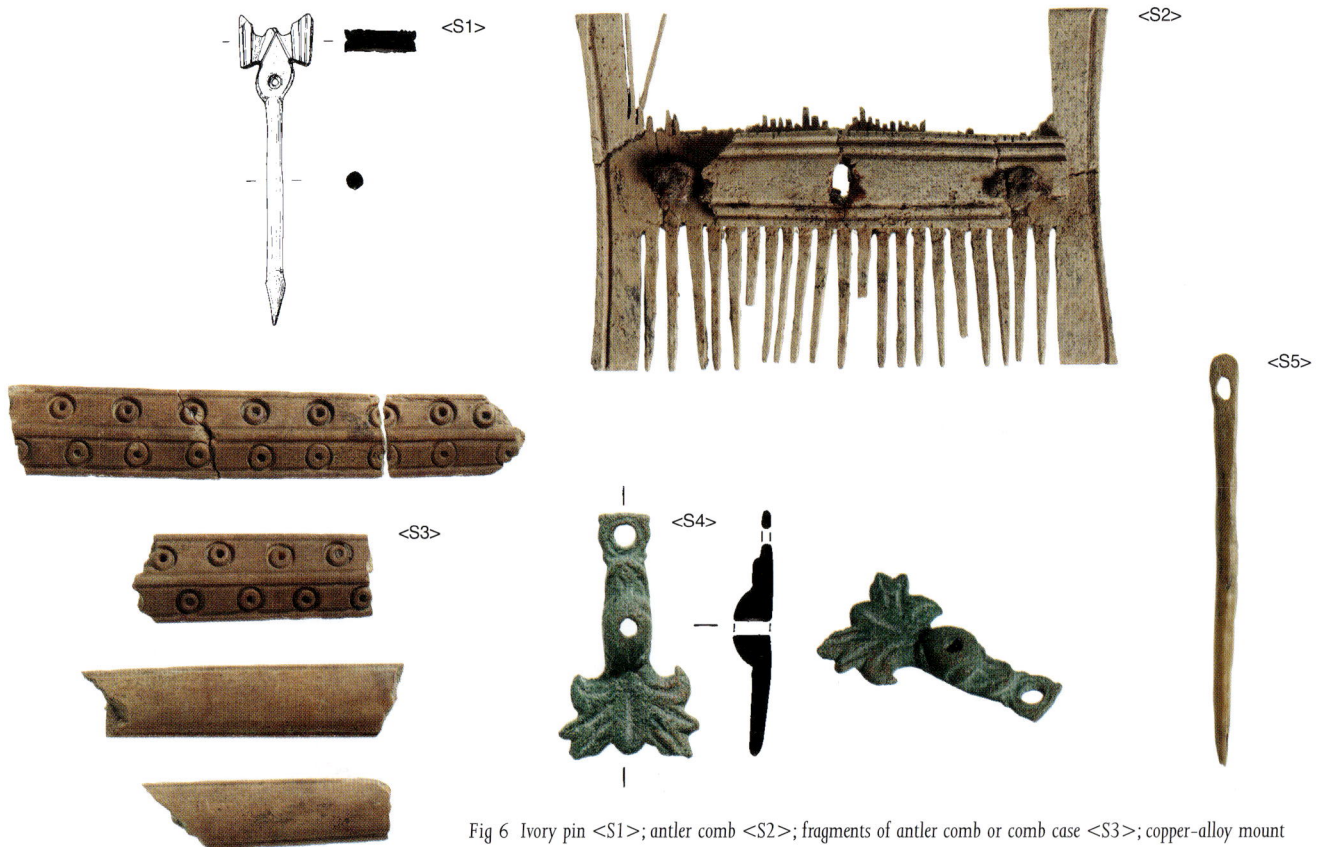

Fig 6 Ivory pin <S1>; antler comb <S2>; fragments of antler comb or comb case <S3>; copper-alloy mount <S4>; and antler needle <S5> (scale 1:1)

late Saxon shelly ware (LSS) and chaff-tempered wares (CHAF), the most significant piece of which was a chaff-tempered ware sprinkling pot, probably used for horticultural purposes and is a form not usually found in this fabric. Much of the Saxon pottery was widely redeposited within 12th-century (period M1) deposits.

Although the excavation identified no features of Saxo-Norman date, the presence of the bone- and antler-working waste and of high-quality items such as the ivory pin <S1> and a piece of fine metalwork <S4> may indicate a relatively affluent late Saxon–early Norman presence and permanent settlement in the vicinity, possibly by the 10th century. Being close to the river, the area was probably used for agriculture or horticulture, as suggested by the presence of the sprinkling pot.

3

The priory of St Mary Merton

3.1 The foundation and early development, c 1117–1222 (period M1)

Documentary evidence

In 1114 King Henry I granted the 'vill' of Merton to Gilbert, Sheriff of Surrey, Huntingdon and Cambridge. Born in Normandy and of relatively humble background, Gilbert was one of Henry I's 'new men' who had risen rapidly in the king's service (Dickinson 1950, 129). At Merton, Gilbert erected a church and wooden huts on two ploughlands (Heales 1898, 2–5). The location of this church is unknown, but is thought to have been close to the present parish church of St Mary the Virgin. Impressed by the canons regular at Huntingdon, a county under his control, Gilbert turned over to Robert Bayle, the subprior there, the church he had built, adding land and a mill returning 60s annually. However, Robert saw the advantages of another site and, with Gilbert's consent, the 'house' and part of the cloister (*nam et domus alique cum parte claustri*) were transported from the earlier site. Queen Matilda, who adopted Gilbert on the death of his mother, visited the construction works and contributed 'pious deeds' before her death in 1118. A wooden chapel was constructed, and William Gifford, Bishop of Winchester, consecrated the cemetery (Heales 1898, 3).

The convent, now numbering 17, was transferred to the new buildings, into which they 'marched festively' on 3 May 1117. This is the foundation date recorded by the Waverley Annals and Matthew Paris but the canons had obviously arrived in Merton some time earlier. The 'Cambridge Calendar' notes that Robert Bayle died in 1150 (Heales 1898, 15, citing [Parker Library] Corpus Christi College, MS 59), and the foundation narrative records that he had served as prior for 35 years, which would date his appointment to 1115 (Colker 1970, 245). According to the foundation narrative, however, the transfer on 3 May 1117 occurred three years and almost five months after Prior Robert had first entered the precinct, giving an alternative date in late December 1113, at least a year earlier. This earlier dating, probably relating to Robert's arrival at the original site, seems preferable given the detail from a source likely to have originated at Merton soon after the events.

Gilbert provided a second, larger, wooden chapel and then, in 1125, according to the foundation narrative, began a most beautiful and sturdy church at Merton. However, Gilbert died that year on 26 July (Heales 1898, 5, citing [Parker Library] Corpus Christi College, MS 59), having arranged the previous March for his burial in the church. The burial of the founder within the church was not atypical: at the Benedictine priory of Sandwell (Staffordshire), founded in the late 12th century, the grave of its founder, William son of Guy de Offeni (or Opheni), was near the high altar (Greene 1992, 91); while at Cistercian Sweetheart Abbey (Kirkcudbrightshire), Devorguilla (or Devorgilla) Balliol, the founder (d 1290), was buried in the abbey church with her husband's heart. The new church at Merton was destroyed after Gilbert's death because it 'seemed too great for certain persons', although the facade, where the founder had laid the first stone, the prior had set the second and the 36 brethren one each in turn, was spared (Colker 1970, 262–3). An alternative claim, that Merton 'abbey' was first built of stone in 1130 and that Gilbert died on the calends of August (1 August) that year, and that the canons entered their new convent in 1136, appears unlikely (*Mon Angl*, vi(1), 245–8). This seems to result from a confusion with the induction of canons by Archbishop William de Corbeil in 1136 on the completion of the cloister and other buildings (*VCH* 1905, 94–5), and the date of 1125 given by the foundation narrative for Gilbert's rebuilding and death is to be preferred (Round 1899, 121; Dickinson 1950, 118). It is also worth noting the foundation narrative's statement that the construction of the priory continued in peace for 15 years after it was first occupied in 1117, that is to say until 1132, seven years after Gilbert's death (Heales 1898, 3–4; Colker 1970, 251).

From very soon after its foundation, Merton began to send out colonies of canons. The first of these was probably c 1120 when Bishop Gifford of Winchester converted the college at Taunton (Somerset) into a house of regular canons. Merton seems to have also supplied canons for the collegiate church of Bodmin (Cornwall), for St Gregory's, Canterbury, for Henry I's great foundation of Cirencester (Gloucestershire) which was among the wealthiest of the Order and one of the few houses of regular canons which ranked as an abbey from the start, and for the short-lived house of regular canons at St Martin's, Dover (Kent) (Dickinson 1950, 118–19).

In 1156–7 King Henry II confirmed the grant of Merton to the priory 'for the welfare of himself and of all his family, as well ancestors as posterity; as freely and absolved from all terrene powers, exactions, vexations and disturbances as it had been in the hands of King Henry his grandfather … and undertaking for himself and for his successors to defend the said Church from damage and disturbance …' (Heales 1898, 18).

Building work at Merton appears to have continued throughout the 12th century. In 1161 the chapel of the infirmary was dedicated (Heales 1898, 21, citing [Parker Library] Corpus Christi College, MS 59) and in 1162–3 Henry II granted £26 13s 4d for the works of the church (ibid). In 1174 the altar of St John Baptist, presumably in the church, was dedicated by Roger, Bishop of Séez, on 24 February (Heales 1898, 26). In 1194 the altars of St Stephen and St Nicholas in the church were dedicated by Godfrey, Bishop of Winchester (ibid, 49), as was the altar of the Holy Cross by Robert, Bishop of Bangor in 1196 (ibid, 50). This church is clearly identified in the archaeological record by foundations and reused stone.

The cartularies of other monastic houses show that Merton was soon involved in the everyday business of a medieval religious house. In the period 1138–57 an agreement was reached between Prior Robert and Abbot Gervase of Westminster by which Merton granted to Westminster land in Wandsworth (Surrey) to facilitate the siting of fulling mills, in exchange for other abbey land in Wandsworth near the granges of Dunsfold (*Westminster Charters*, no. 268). In 1145, Merton's prior, Robert, and subprior, also Robert, witnessed both a grant

by St Paul's of the site of Holy Trinity Caddington (Bedfordshire) and adjacent woodland to Christina, the celebrated anchorite of Markyate, and subsequently its consecration (*Early Charters St Paul*, nos 154, 156). By 1177 Roger I of Wanchy granted the church of his manor of Stanstead (Hertfordshire) to St Mary of Merton, the manor itself being retained and granted to Augustinian Waltham Abbey (Essex) in 1192–3 (*Early Charters Waltham*, nos 356, 360); this was a not uncommon arrangement which could sometimes lead to friction, and which in this case did so in the early 13th century. Henry I's grant to the priory of the manor of Merton itself did not include the parish church, which was given separately by Peter de Talworth (Heales 1898, 26–7). Of perhaps greater significance were mandates sent by Pope Celestine III to the bishop of London, the abbot of Westminster and the prior of Merton. One, possibly dating to 1196, instructed them, or any two of them, to do justice to the abbot and convent of Reading (Berkshire) in the matter of the injury and vexation suffered at the hands of Gilbert Martel and others (*Reading Cart*, no. 157); in 1196 the same three dignitaries were mandated to prevent interference with Reading Abbey in respect of the appropriation of certain chapels and churches for the use of the poor of Reading (ibid, no. 159). In these instances the prior of Merton was clearly considered senior and eminent enough to intervene and mediate effectively in the affairs of this leading Cluniac (later Benedictine) monastery. Something of the prestige and respect which Merton acquired during the first few decades of its existence can also be seen in the note added to the margin of the original text of Matthew Paris's *Historia Minor* relating to the election of Thomas Becket as Archbishop of Canterbury in 1162: 'note that blessed Thomas took up the monk's habit from the pope, and among other things wore a black cowl, which is the dress of the canons of Merton' (*Historia Minor*, i, 316, n 1). As early as 1146–54 William, Earl of Chichester, when founding a religious house at his manor of Buckenham (Norfolk), was advised by William, Bishop of Norwich, to do so according to the Order of St Augustine and the institution of St Mary of Merton (*Cal Chart R, 1300–26*, 368).

Archaeological evidence

Introduction

No evidence was found of the wooden chapels constructed by Gilbert and Prior Robert on the site in 1117. The earliest evidence for a stone church was provided by a small number of carved stones dating to the mid 12th century, and possibly by a building (B2; Fig 9) of uncertain function. Building 1 represents the earliest conclusive evidence for an *in situ* stone church, which dates to c 1170. To the south of the church was a cemetery (OA3) with an open space to the south of the nave (OA4). There was also a large cemetery area to the north and east of the church (OA6) containing a path (R1) and an east–west wall (S3). Further south-east of the church was a garden or orchard (OA5; Fig 9; Fig 28), which produced evidence of nearby food preparation; a timber and daub structure (S1), possibly associated with the garden or orchard, lay within its eastern part. A further open area (OA7) lay between the garden/orchard (OA5) and the River Wandle to the south (Fig 28).

Ex situ evidence for a mid 12th-century stone church

Reused, stylistically early, pieces of moulded stone recovered from later features suggest the presence of a mid 12th-century church on or in the vicinity of the site. No direct archaeological evidence for this, such as wall foundations, was definitely found, although Building 2 may have been part of the early structure. This stonework, identified here as construction phase 1 (CP1), was incorporated into the church (B1), first built in the late 12th/early 13th century (CP2) and subsequently rebuilt and extended. The extant fragments of moulded stone include scalloped capitals and vaulting. Most of this work was in Reigate stone, with the occasional use of spar-prominent oolitic limestone (from the Taynton beds) (Chapters 1.4, 7.2); this contrasts with the following phase where oolitic limestone was used in large quantities alongside Reigate stone.

Vault ribs and wall shafts suggest a destroyed vault of mid 12th-century date. One vault rib <1058> was reused in the (robbed) north nave wall foundation of the late 12th-/early 13th-century (period M1) church (B1); several were found reused in the rebuilding of the north transept post c 1222 (period M2). A wall shaft was recut to form a chamfered quoin (<A2>, Fig 176) used in the later period M1 church. The heavy ribs, probably diagonals, are very much in the 'Anglo-Norman' tradition and form stilted (segmental) arches. The rib form is of a very simple and widespread type, with a hemispherical soffit (ie the underside of an architectural element) roll slightly wider than 8in (203.2mm) on a rectangular dosseret (the detached section placed above a column or pilaster) (eg <837>, <1058>); it is used, for example, at Selby Abbey (Yorkshire West Riding), which Clapham dated to c 1150 (1934, 123, fig 42 no. 9). The moulding is identical to the vault ribs in the crypt of the Knights Hospitaller priory of St John Clerkenwell, constructed in the 1140s (Samuel 2004b, 281–2; Sloane and Malcolm 2004, 36), but the larger scale of the Merton ribs indicates that they derived from significantly larger vault divisions. Fragments of a vault boss in a similar form (but with the soffit roll undercut at the sides) were also recovered (<5474>, <5475>, <5478>); from quadripartite vaulting where the vault compartment was of oblong plan, the boss had a hole drilled through it, showing that lamps or other features were suspended within the building. In the chancel of St Lawrence's, Upton-cum-Chalvey (Buckinghamshire), a quadripartite vault employing a soffit roll is associated with scalloped rectilinear respond (ie half-column or half-pier attached to a wall and supporting an arch) capitals (M Samuel, pers observation). The rib mould is employed for the diagonal ribs (Hoey 1997, 162–3, fig 26). At Upton the dressings are brightly painted with complex patterns, but one rib at Merton was painted in a simple manner with a red soffit roll and white dosseret. On this rather thin evidence, Upton can be seen as a

clue to the appearance of the unlocated church, although no direct link between the two is indicated. The chancel at Upton is thought to date to c 1160 (RCHM 1912, 278).

The scalloped capital forms are comparable to those used in the great northern Cistercian churches of the third quarter of the 12th century, but the decorative motifs (Bilson 1909, 251) were also widespread in south-eastern church architecture such as at Upton. Scalloped capital <A1> (Fig 7) represents the lower part of the capital (or rather technically, corbel) without the abacus (the flat slab on the top of the capital on which the architrave rests); it may have supported a diagonal rib of a quadripartite vault, as at Upton. On capital <A1> the surfaces are very fresh with well-preserved crimson paint on the inverted cones (cover illustration), again suggesting painted decoration within the church. The capital was probably capped by a separate abacus mould (not shown in Fig 7) and could derive from either a wall vault respond or an arcade respond. The 'paper dart' V-shaped fillets between the truncated cones may be a regional peculiarity, occurring also in undated ?nave capitals from the Cluniac priory of Bermondsey (Surrey) (Samuel in prep). The 'outlining' of the scallops by a sunk fillet at Buildwas (Shropshire) (Bilson 1909, fig 5 no. iv) is seen here. This would suggest a date in the second half of the 12th century. It is possible that this respond capital derives from construction phase 2 (CP2), that is from the late 12th/early 13th century (period M1) church (B1).

The various bases (<A3>, Fig 176; <A4>, Fig 8) which might date to the first phase (CP1) are all modified-attic bases of 'reduced upper roll form' (Rigold 1977, fig 4 no. 77) resembling those used in the choir at Chichester Cathedral, after 1114 (ibid, fig 4 no. 116). However, the base moulds can only be treated as an approximate guide to date because variants can often be seen side by side in a single structure, such as in the remaining fragment of the south-west tower at Cluniac Lewes Priory (Sussex). The use of oolitic limestone is more characteristic of construction phase 2 than 1; base <A4>, part of a blind arcade, is in Taynton stone, as is colonnette base <A3>, a form suggested as later 1130s (Chapter 7.2). The square base from

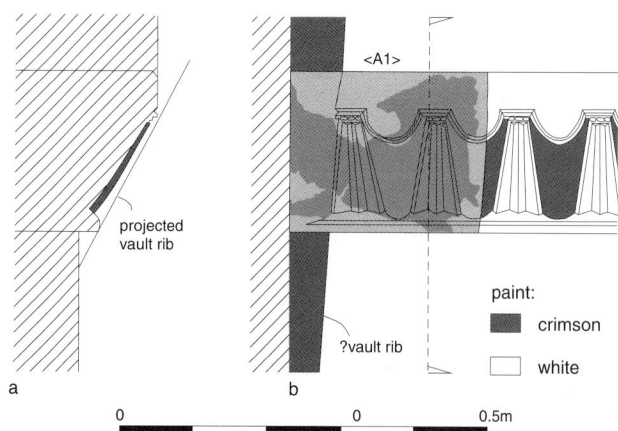

Fig 7 Scalloped respond capital <A1> (period M1): a – in section; b – in elevation (scale 1:10) (on moulded stone figures, dark tone denotes extant surface, lighter tone denotes damaged or lost surface)

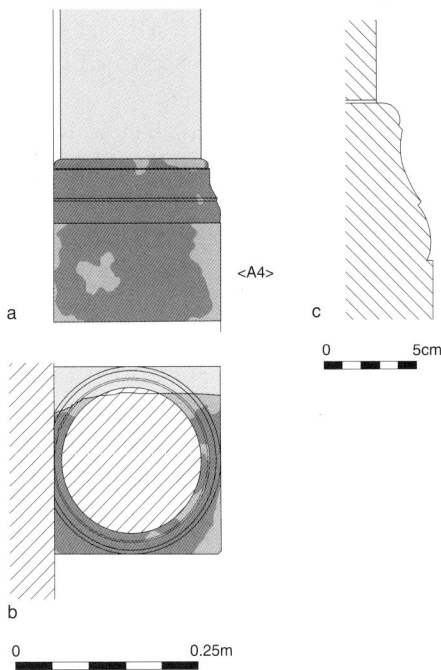

Fig 8 Blind arcade base <A4> (period M1): a – in transverse elevation; b – in plan; c – detailed profile of base moulding (scale: a and b 1:10; c 1:4)

Merton <A4> (Fig 8) closely resembles the blind arcade bases from the south-west tower of Lewes which are dated to after 1147 (F Anderson, pers comm). This Merton base was adapted at the time of setting and this recut allowed the shaft base to be employed in a corner; it was found reused in the later (period M2) foundations.

A possible 12th-century chapel/church (B2)

This building lay to the north-east of, and observed the same alignment as, Building 1 (see right inset in Fig 9) and may be contemporary or pre-date it. The walls had been heavily robbed but the masonry robbing trenches defined a narrow rectangular space with internal measurements of c 7m east–west by c 2m north–south. The apparently wider north wall foundation continued to the east of this rectangular space. The robbed foundation trenches could possibly be read as part of a church, that is, the north wall as the presbytery south wall with corner buttressing and/or north return and the rectangular space as a side chapel; or the north wall and rectangular space could perhaps even be interpreted as a south transept chapel of a small church (cf Holy Trinity Priory, Aldgate: Schofield and Lea 2005, 50, 72). The robbing contained some flint and some chalk fragments suggesting that Building 2, or at least its foundations, may have been constructed from these materials. There was no worked stone in these fills, presumably the result of comprehensive robbing. Alternatively, the building may have been used as a workshop or quarters for construction labourers in the 12th century. Following the demolition and robbing of Building 2, a wall (S3) was built across its former site (OA6). Three burials (in OA6) were also cut by this wall and may be associated with Building 2.

The late 12th-/early 13th-century church (B1)

The most thorough archaeological excavation of deposits associated with clearance and levelling preparatory to the construction of the church, Building 1, occurred in what became the north burial area (OA6) (Fig 9). Clay layers [5609] and other more mixed deposits, containing pottery including sandy shelly-ware (SSW) dated to c 1140–c 1220, formed levelling generally about 0.3m deep. Construction debris, including sand, chalk, Reigate stone and mortar [2720], was also recorded here. Stakeholes within the south-west corner of the north transept and stakeholes/postholes and pits external to the junctions of the nave and transepts suggest scaffolding or supports used during construction or temporary stores and shelters built against the church.

Early deposits to the north and south of the church produced iron slag possibly from small-scale ironworking associated with its construction. There is also a little evidence of copper alloy casting in the form of a bronze runnel <S306> from Open Area 6. No obvious mould fragments or wasters suggest the end product(s) of this metalworking.

The wall foundations were constructed of flint, small amounts of Reigate stone and chalk laid in mortar in trenches. It was difficult to establish the thickness of the foundations because of extensive robbing in the 13th century. However, the north transept foundation trenches generally measured up to 2m wide and 1m deep although the original depth and width of footings could be less (Fig 10).

The church was cruciform in plan with an aisleless nave to the west, transepts and a short presbytery. The foundations and robbing trenches define the internal length of the church as c 64m, although the precise position of the west end is difficult to determine and the building may be slightly longer. The interior of the nave was c 33m long and c 9m wide, whilst the interior width across the transepts was c 38m.

The internal measurements of the main body of the north transept were c 10m east–west by 12m north–south. The east wall of the transept returned eastward some 3m to the north of the line of the north wall of the presbytery, almost certainly to accommodate a side chapel. Although this chapel was generally truncated, by conjecture its internal measurements would have been c 4m north–south by c 9m east–west. Fig 10 shows the foundations of the chapel walls as a sandy fill beneath the later (period M2) north transept foundations. Additional foundation trenches abutting the exterior east wall of the north transept, which may have been either contemporary with the main build or a later addition, defined a second rectangular side chapel, with interior dimensions of c 4m north–south by c 2.5m east–west. A single burial [4359] in the northern chapel of the north transept pre-dates the demolition of this church. This individual was not available for study and only part of the left ribs and humerus survived; it was apparently a relatively plain burial.

Only small areas of the south transept foundations survived later demolition and the layout is unclear. Parts of the east wall may have been built into the later (period M2) church, as occurred in the north transept. In the absence of evidence to

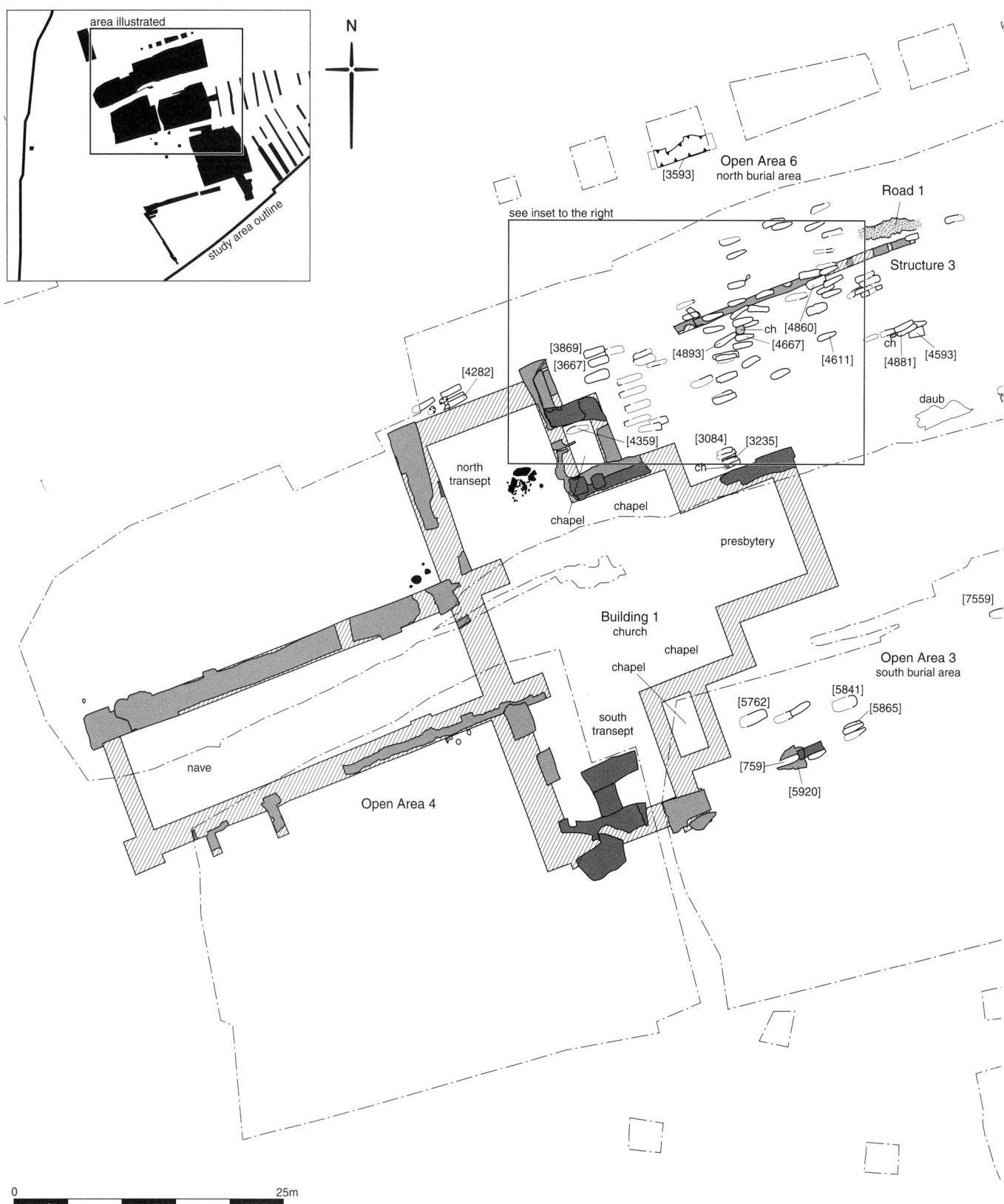

Fig 9 Plan of principal archaeological features in the north part of the precinct, c 1117–1222 (period M1) (scale 1:500)

the contrary, the church is assumed to be symmetrical, with two side chapels flanking the south transept to match the northern arrangement (Fig 9).

A 7.2m length of foundation for the north wall of the presbytery was exposed to the east of the chapels. Later disturbance meant that the junction of the presbytery and adjacent side chapel was missing but the eastern end of this north wall probably represented the east end of the church. On this assumption, the internal length of the presbytery (to the east of the chapels) would have been c 8–9m; its internal width was c 9m.

Building 2

Building 1
church

[5381]

[11318]

[10977]

Open Area 5   ?trellis

daub

Structure 1

[10817]

Structure 2

conjectured. Little ashlar was recovered from the foundations of the church as rebuilt in period M2. This may imply that ashlar was not used much here in the period M1 church and that the walls were largely of rubble faced with flint. Alternatively, ashlar may have been extensively reused in the superstructure of the later church and removed at the Dissolution.

In contrast, a remarkable amount of evidence for the superstructure is represented by mouldings, including fragments of bases, vault ribs, windows and doorways, recovered from later features (Chapter 7.2). Examples of modified-attic bases of 'reduced upper roll form' have already been discussed as possibly derived from a mid 12th-century church (CP1; above, 'Ex *situ* evidence for a mid 12th-century stone church'); because the dating of such base moulds can only be approximate, some may relate to the period M1 church (CP2).

There is evidence that part of the church was vaulted. A finely cut abacus of ?Caen stone <A10> (Fig 178) engaged with a round shaft and scribe lines on the impost indicate that a soffit-roll rib rested on the abacus; the abacus moulding would have run between responds on the wall, forming a string course (a projecting horizontal course or moulding). A similar form was recorded in the southernmost transept chapel at Newark Abbey (Surrey) (Paul 1898, fig 1). Newark was founded as an Augustinian priory in the final decade of the 12th century (*VCH* 1911, 103) and architectural similarities between the two houses are to be expected. Two types of vault rib were identified which may derive from the period M1 church. A heavy triple-roll-in-echelon rib <A52> (Fig 178) is paralleled by the ribs used in the chapter house at Cistercian Buildwas Abbey which dates to the third quarter of the 12th century (Bilson 1909, fig 13 viiiD, 200); however, the tooling marks on <A52> are distinct from the other dressings of the period M1 church and suggest a somewhat later, 13th-century, date. The second rib is on a much smaller scale: a heavy keel forms the soffit of this diagonal rib <A7> (Fig 178) which was originally painted yellow/buff. The use of such keel moulds in ribs is widespread (Bilson 1909, 266), examples being in the chancel at St John Clerkenwell (later 12th century: Samuel in Sloane and Malcolm 2004, 49, 53, fig 39, <A23>, 284–5) and the choir of St Cross, Winchester (Hampshire) (*c* 1160–70: Clapham 1934, fig 42 no. 15). Flanking rolls were also absent in the diagonal ribs of the chapter house at the Cistercian abbey of Kirkstall (Yorkshire West Riding) (Bilson 1909, fig 13 vD). It is possible that the larger rib derived from a presbytery vault. Its apparent early 13th-century date may indicate a time lapse between the construction of the shell of the church and the vault. The rest of the church may have been roofed in timber. Two examples of slight and plain corbels (<990>, <995>, [4260]; not illustrated), which may have taken the feet of timber roof trusses or their wall risers, were found; datable only by the tooling which is characteristic of the first half of the 13th century, these may relate to either this (period M1) church or the post-1222 (period M2) church. The vault from which the smaller rib derived covered a small vaulting compartment, but its position is unknown. Other Augustinian priory churches of this period were sometimes vaulted in part: the central area of

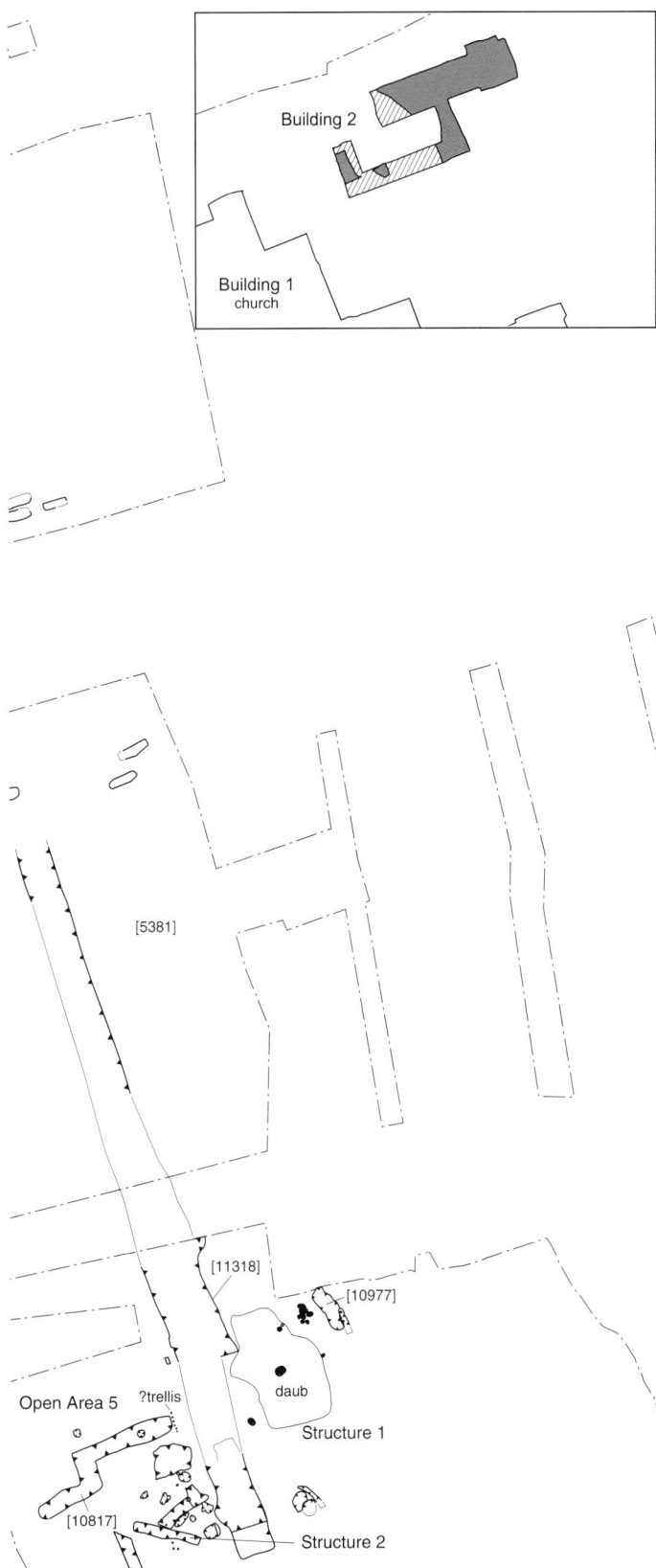

No superstructure survived in *situ* and, consequently, doorways in the church were not defined. Disturbed foundations in the south-west corner of the south transept may be the remains of night stairs but, as no evidence for a contemporary east cloister range was identified, the function can only be

Fig 10 *View of the north transept (B1) showing the much-robbed foundations of the late 12th-/early 13th-century (period M1) walls (indicated by dashed white line), looking north (2.0m scales)*

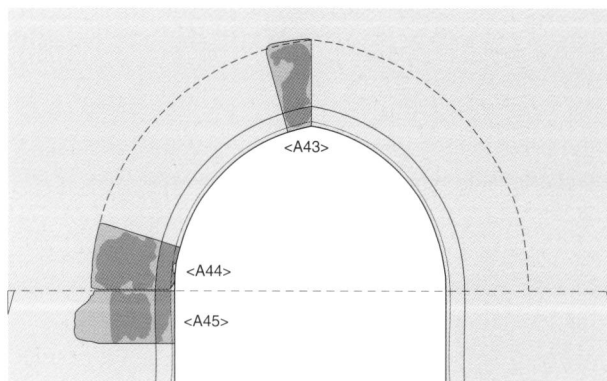

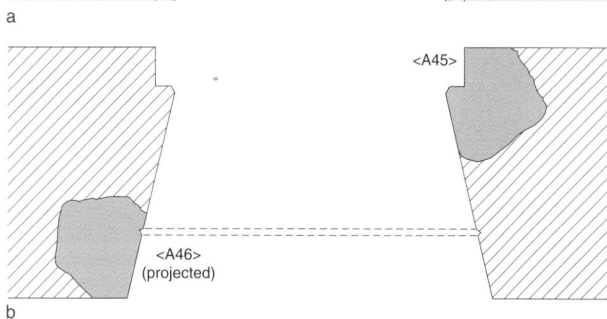

the nave at Holy Trinity Aldgate was vaulted by the late 12th or during the 13th century, and the nave aisles were probably always vaulted, as were the presbytery aisles; there is no evidence as to whether or not the presbytery was vaulted (Schofield and Lea 2005, 83–4, 90–1).

The window mouldings represent tall narrow lancets. Three variants of lancet were being cut contemporaneously. One type, <A43>–<A46> (Fig 11), had a completely plain external reveal. Another was cut in two sizes (<A22>–<A27>, Fig 12; <A28>–<A32>, Fig 13), but with a common mould, hollow-chamfered with a quirk. The majority of the openings had plain

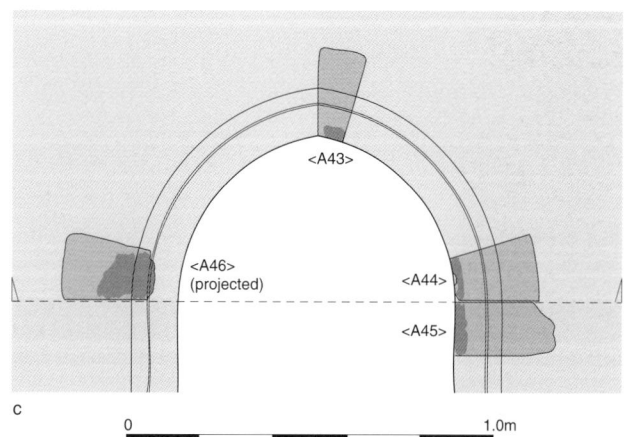

Fig 11 *A reconstruction of a large lancet window with plain rebate <A43>–<A46> (period M1): a – external elevation; b – the moulding at the springing line; c – internal elevation (scale 1:20)*

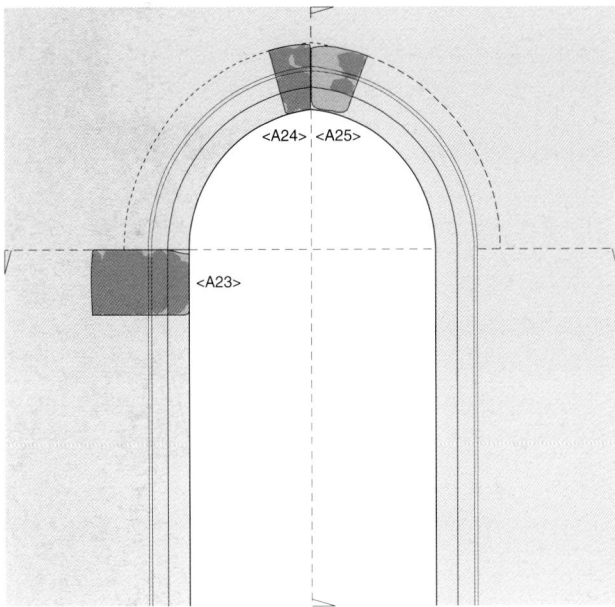

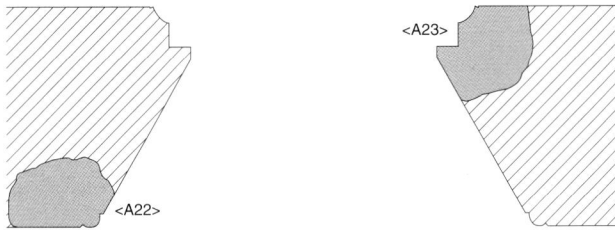

scoinsons (arches that support part of a wall) in their embrasures (ie openings in a wall or parapet, splayed on the inside, typically around a window or door) (Fig 11b) but in some the angle was marked by a shallow roll (Fig 12b; Fig 13c). The windows show no form of glazing, but the deep external rebates common to all the window forms were admirably suited to hold a removable, glazed, timber window frame. Saddlebars at the lip of the internal embrasure would have secured the glass, but only one example can be proven. Many of the windows, and the ?portals, had grooves cut into the rear arches of the embrasures (Fig 11b) which may have held an ephemeral inserted fixture, such as a cloth tympana. It is likely that the smaller thinner lancets illuminated the transepts and the wider lancets lit the main body of the church; there was no clerestory because aisles were absent.

The window moulding is of a common form for this period and can be seen with simple external chamfers in the nave and presbytery at the Augustinian canonesses' house of St Leonard Brewood (Shropshire), commonly called 'White Ladies', a building which is usually dated to the end of the 12th century (Weaver 2001, 35). The White Ladies windows (although they are round) give a good impression of the Merton windows because they share a simple string course to form their common sill (M Samuel, pers observation).

Standardised, polygonal, 5-inch (127mm) chamfered string courses were cut from Taynton and Reigate stone and used in

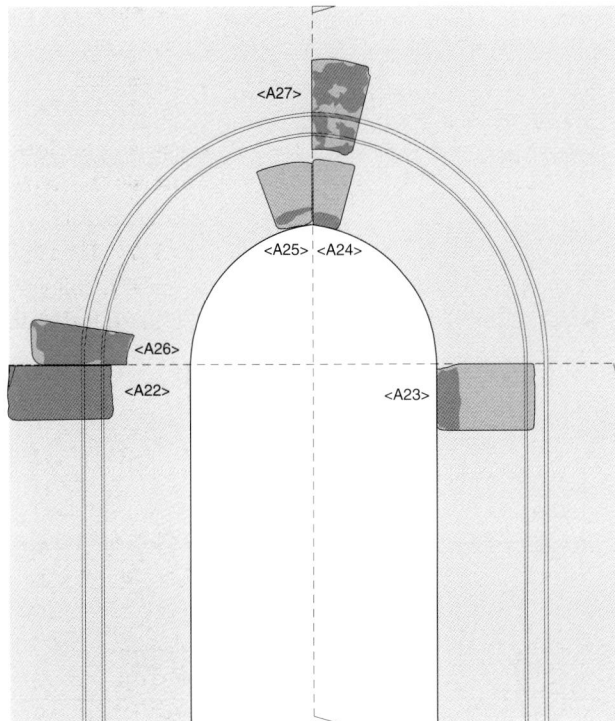

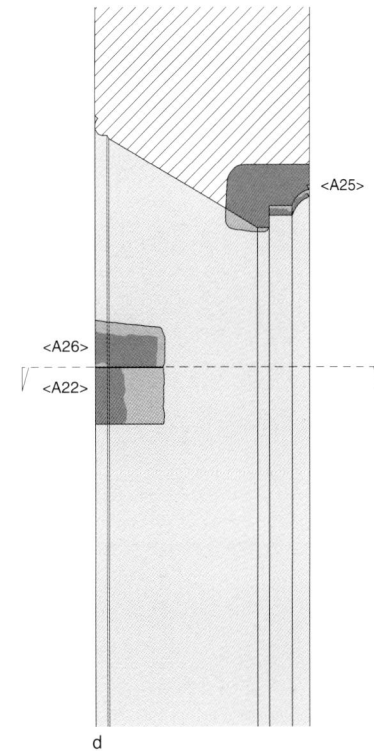

Fig 12 *A reconstruction of a large lancet window with quirk-and-hollow ornament <A22>–<A27> (period M1): a – external elevation; b – the moulding at the springing line; c – internal elevation; d – cross section at the mid point of the arch (scale 1:20)*

21

long (<A50>, Fig 178). A larger version (183mm) of the basic polygonal string existed (<A42>, Fig 178), but the 5-inch string was by far the commonest type. The extant foundations gave no indication of buttresses, but there is some evidence for stair turrets in the later plans of the church. The 'buttress' dressing may have been employed on similar turrets in this church. The foundations hint at the presence of simple clasping buttresses at the north-west corner of the east arm; these are entirely typical of a Cistercian or Augustinian (eg Lilleshall, Shropshire) church of this period. Clasping buttresses may have existed at the west end of the nave.

Fragments were recovered of a fine chevron-ornamented Romanesque portal, which is likely to have originally stood at the west end of the church (<A18>–<A21>, Fig 15; Fig 16). It is stylistically distinct from the gateway/doorway found in 1914 (below, 'An *ex situ*, later 12th-century gateway/doorway'), but roughly contemporary. The inner of the two orders is a variant of saw-tooth chevron, 'an exclusively late phenomenon' dated after *c* 1174 at Broadwell church (Oxfordshire) (Borg 1967, 136). Saw-tooth chevron exists in the triforium (ie the middle storey gallery or arcade above the arches of the nave, choir and transepts of the church) arcade arches of the north-west transept of Peterborough Cathedral (Conway Library, Courtauld Institute of Art, negative no. A94/308).

The chevron-ornamented portal and the windows share chevron-forming-lozenge ornament but differ in other respects. Two other types of voussoir (ie the wedge-shaped component of an arch) were found that have an even closer stylistic resemblance to the windows and must represent a united campaign with them. The larger is probably a portal (<A36>, Fig 17), while a smaller pointed rear arch is probably also a doorway (<A37>–<A40>, Fig 18). There is no door rebate but a socket cut in one of the voussoirs (Fig 18b) might be for a hinge pintle. The jambs were chamfered, while the chevron-forming lozenges decorating the arch were rather irregularly cut to fit each voussoir. This type of ornament, relatively

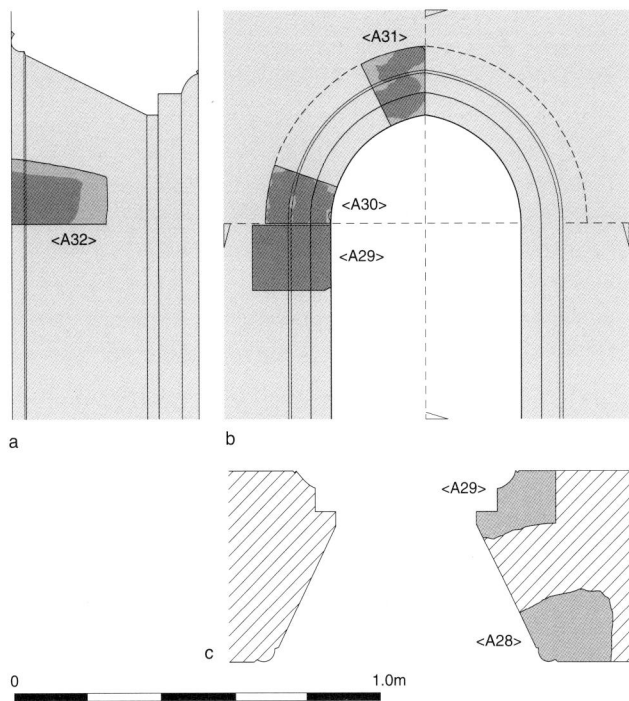

Fig 13 *A reconstruction of a small lancet with quirk-and-hollow ornament <A28>–<A32> (period M1): a – cross section at the mid point of the arch; b – external elevation; c – the moulding at the springing line (scale 1:20)*

both the interior and exterior of the church. The string was customised at the time of setting to form the sills of windows or to hold projecting iron window grills. Fig 14 (<A33>–<A35>) reconstructs the sill and string course of a lancet window. A slightly more ornate version was also used (<A49>, Fig 178). Simple chamfered strings are likewise widely used at the Cistercian abbeys of Kirkstall and Fountains (Yorkshire West Riding) (Bilson 1909, fig 15). A second, heavier (158mm), form of string course used on the exterior to mark offsets was cut in lengths of ?Caen stone 17in and 18in (432–457mm)

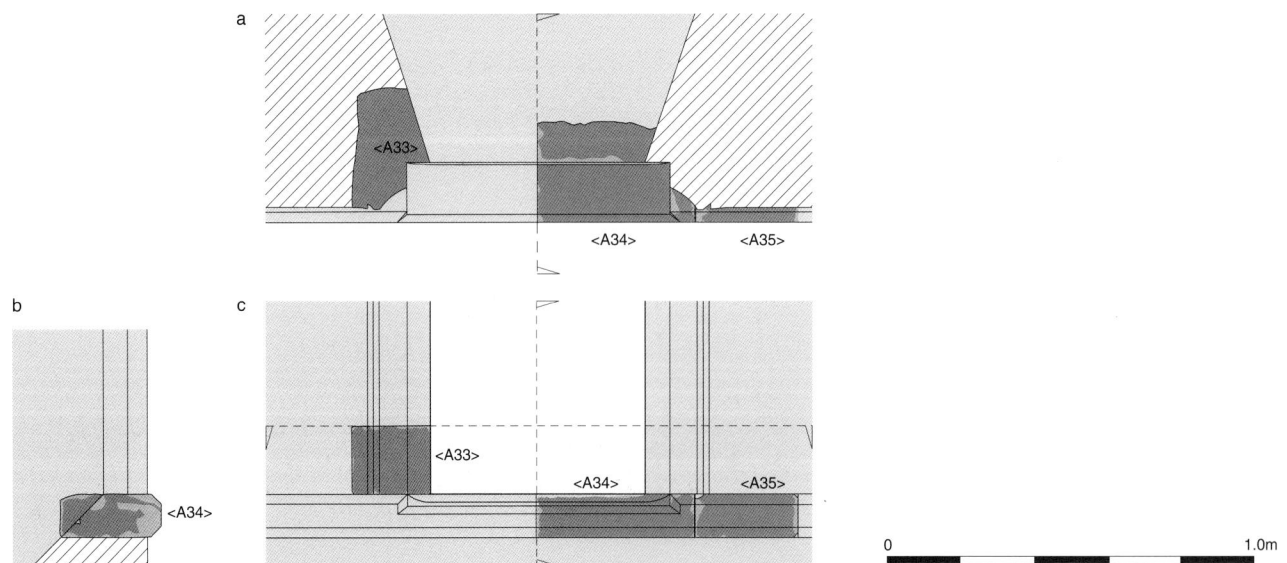

Fig 14 *A reconstruction of a lancet sill and string course <A33>–<A35> (period M1): a – in plan; b – in cross section at the mid point of the sill; c – exterior elevation (scale 1:20)*

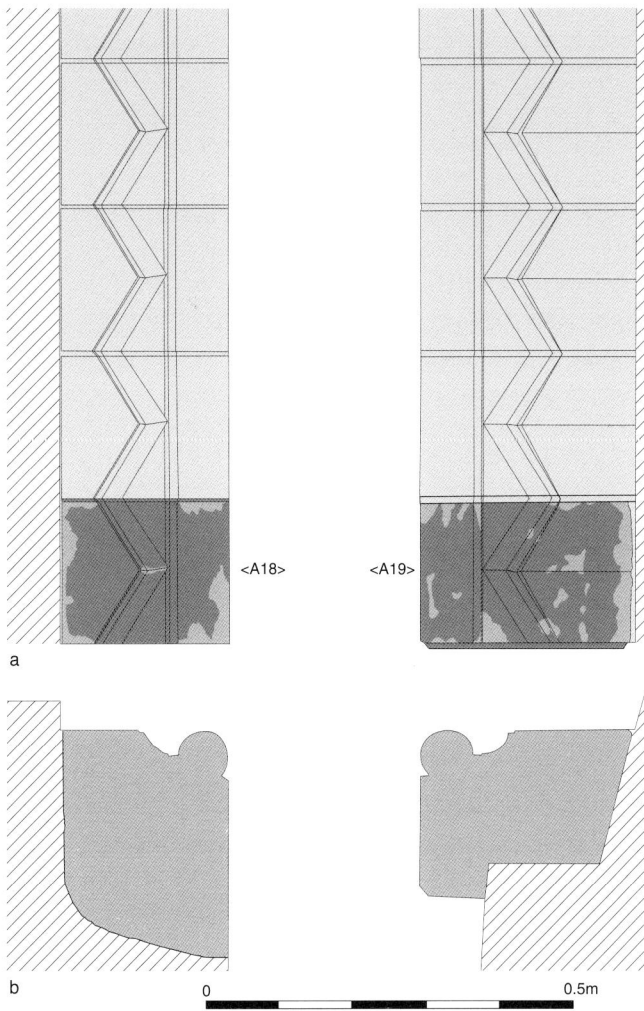

a

b

0   0.5m

<A18>   <A19>

Fig 15 Portal <A18> and <A19> (period M1): a – elevation of details of jambs with chevron ornament; b – moulding in plan (scale 1:10)

unusual, occurs in excavated stonework from St Gregory's, Canterbury (Hicks and Hicks 2001, 162–3).

Isolated spreads of mortar in the north transept have been interpreted as floors although these may be the bedding for tiles or paving, or construction debris from the later (period M2) church. No Reigate stone paving was found *in situ*, but many paviors were reused to line later cist burials suggesting some paving may have been present in this church.

The claustral area (OA4)

With the exception of two walls described below, there is little *in situ* evidence for a formal cloister structure. Open Area 4 is therefore regarded as an open space to the south of the nave.

Levelling and landscaping deposits were cut by two, north–south, flint and mortar foundations *c* 6m apart, which abutted the external face of the south wall of the nave at the western end (Fig 9). The foundations, *c* 1m wide, were only traced for a truncated length of 1.4m. It is unlikely that a monastic church would have had a porch in this position. It is possible that the walls were part of the west claustral range. Work on this structure may have been curtailed and abandoned when part of the church was destroyed in 1222 (below, 3.2).

Further evidence, although tenuous, for the construction of a masonry cloister in the 12th century was found in the form of *ex situ* moulded stone. An early cloister is suggested by a scalloped coupled capital <A5> (Fig 19a–b; Fig 177) and a fragmentary, coupled column base <A6> (Fig 19c–e) with coupled shafts. The nailhead ornament on the capital closely resembles similar decoration on capitals supporting the aisle transverse vault ribs (Conway Library, Courtauld Institute of Art, negative no. 489/9/9a) in the nave at Peterborough. These

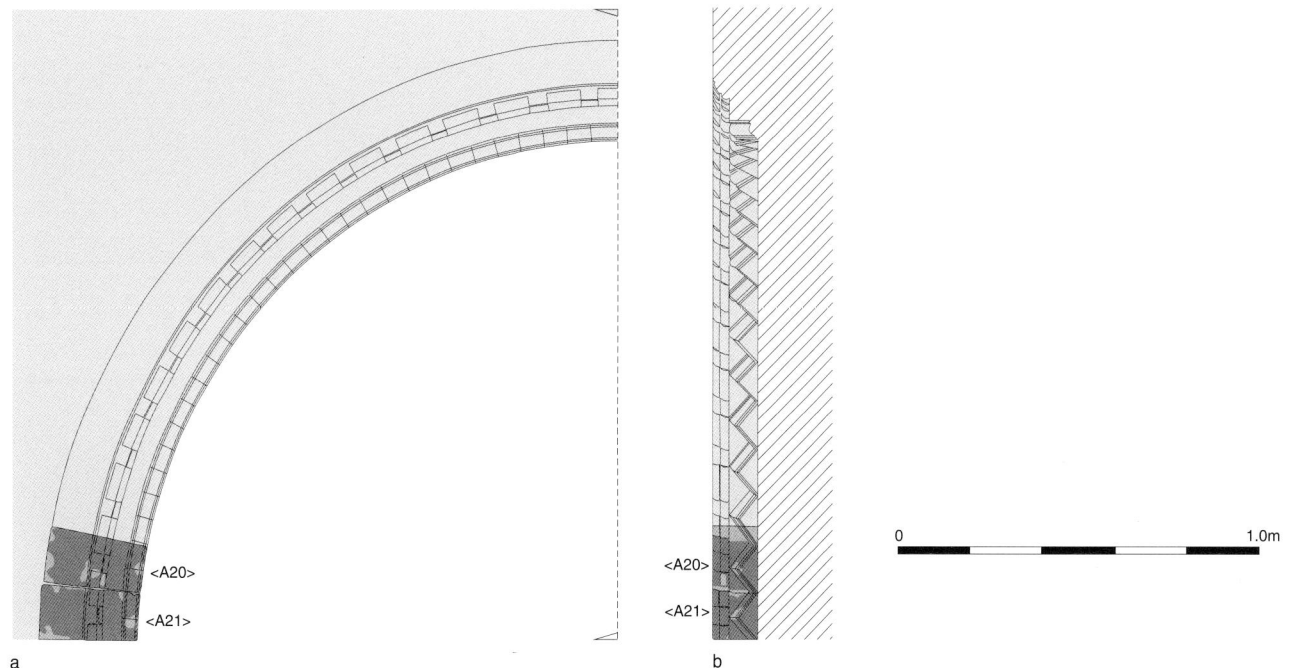

a   b

<A20>   <A20>

<A21>   <A21>

0   1.0m

Fig 16 Portal <A20> and <A21> (period M1): a – suggested external elevation of portal arch with chevron and billet ornament; b – reconstructed section through the portal arch at its mid point (scale 1:20)

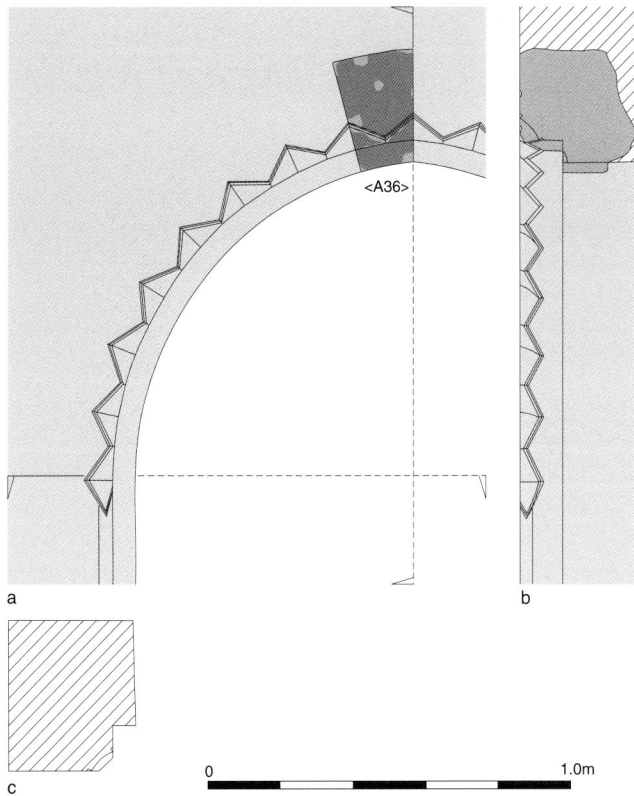

a   b

c

0   1.0m

Fig 17 A reconstruction of a portal with chevron-forming-lozenge ornament <A36>
(period M1): a – internal elevation; b – section at the mid point of the arch; c – the
moulded chamfer stop at the springing line (scale 1:20)

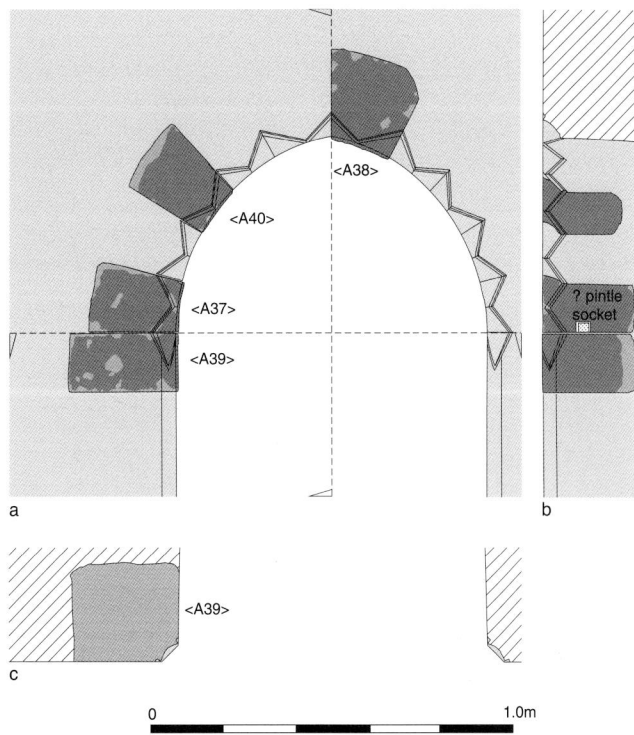

a   b

<A39>

c

0   1.0m

Fig 18 A reconstruction of an embrasure with chevron-forming-lozenge ornament
<A37>–<A40> (period M1): a – internal elevation; b – section at the mid point
of the arch; c – the moulding of the reveal and chamfer stop at the springing line
(scale 1:20)

capitals occur in a part of the nave completed before the
documented additions of two bays in 1177–93 (Cook 1960,
179). This points to a date of the third quarter of the 12th
century for the Merton cloister. The base is paralleled at
Pershore Abbey (Worcestershire) (Rigold 1977, fig 5 no. 99).
This suggests a significantly earlier date of c 1100–30 but
several variations of this basic form can be seen in the south-
west tower of Lewes Priory (after 1147) and they cannot
therefore be treated as precise dating evidence (above, 'Ex situ
evidence for a mid 12th-century stone church'). The coupled
base and capital may derive from a cloister associated either
with (possibly) the postulated mid 12th-century church (CP1;
B2) or with the later, late 12th-/early 13th-century church
(CP2; B1). A further fragmentary, coupled column base
(<A16>, Fig 178) is of similar dimensions to <A6>, but its
'simplified' neo-attic base moulding implies a date in the late
12th/early 13th century.

There is in addition ex situ evidence for both wide and
narrow aumbries, that is stone recesses which acted as
cupboards; they could be closed by timber doors that swung on
iron pintles (<A11> and <A12>, Fig 20; <A13> and <A14>,

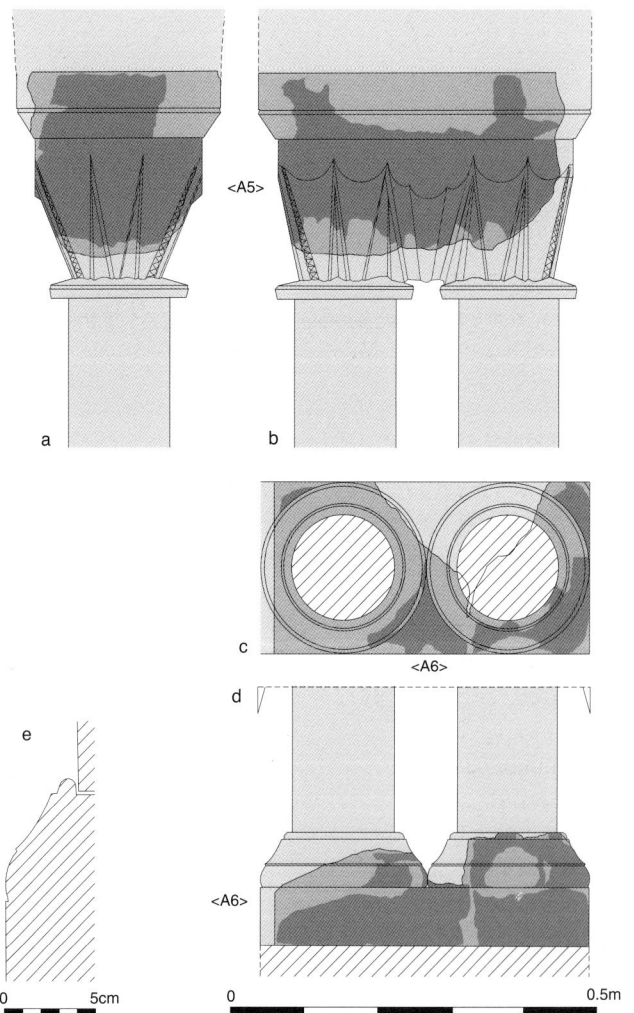

a   b

<A5>

c

<A6>

d

e

<A6>

0   5cm   0   0.5m

Fig 19 Coupled capital <A5> and column base <A6> from a possible cloister
(period M1): a – capital elevation; b – transverse elevation of capital; c – base plan;
d – transverse elevation of base; e – a detail of the base mould (scales: a–d 1:10; e 1:4)

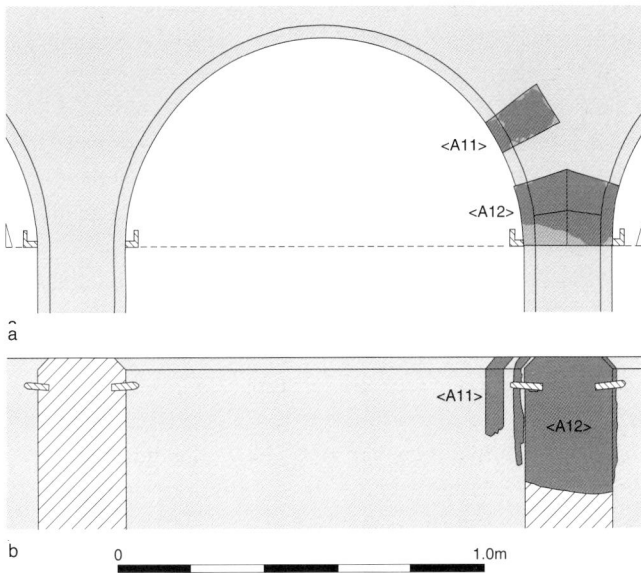

Fig 20 *A reconstruction of the wider type of aumbry <A11> and <A12> with ferramenta restored (period M1): a — arch in elevation; b — arch in inverted plan (scale 1:20)*

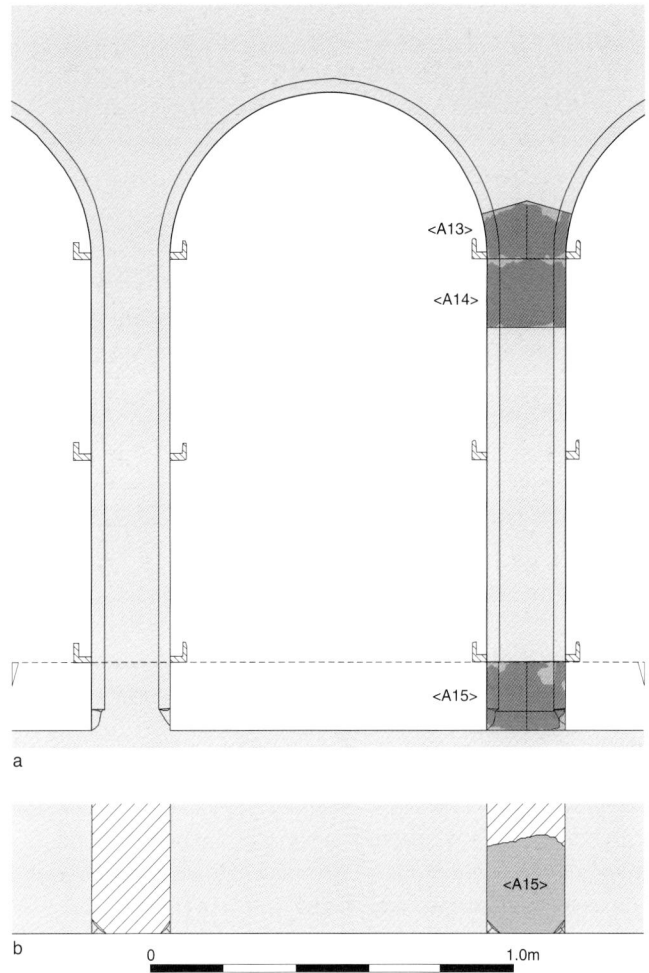

Fig 21 *A reconstruction of the narrower type of aumbry <A13>–<A15> with ferramenta restored (period M1): a — in elevation; b — in plan (scale 1:20)*

Fig 21). This might indicate a cloister or the intention to provide one: for example, at the Augustinian priory church of St Andrews (St Andrews Cathedral, Fife), which is contemporary, two pairs of aumbries occur in the outer wall of the south transept (Cambridge 1977, 278, fig 1), while at Augustinian Lilleshall a 12th-century cupboard with two compartments, interpreted as a book locker, survives in the north-east cloister walk (Ferris 2000, 17–19). However, the aumbries may equally have lain within the church, as at the Premonstratensian house at Bayham Abbey (Sussex) (Rigold 1985, 9).

The monastic cemetery

During this period a number of burials were interred generally to the east of the church but, with a large unexcavated strip dividing excavated areas to the north and south of the short presbytery, these may, with the possible exception of some burials to the north of the line of the north transept, be part of a single cemetery (Fig 9). They are examined here as separate areas, south and north (OA3 and OA6).

SOUTH BURIAL AREA (OA3)

The excavated area measured approximately 26m east–west by 15m north–south. The north-west edge of the cemetery was defined by the (conjectured) south transept and presbytery of the church. The other boundaries are uncertain but interments were not found in the area further south (OA5, below). To the east lay a north–south aligned ditch [5381], possibly an early but short-lived cemetery boundary. Two oyster shell palettes, containing the remains of red pigment <S33> used in mural or manuscript painting, and an iron knife with a decorated turned wooden handle <S262> (Fig 22) were recovered from the northern end of this ditch. The disuse fill was dated to after

c 1230 by Kingston-type ware (KING) pottery. Burials were located to the east and west of the north end of the ditch. This feature extended into the garden (OA5) immediately south. To the east of the south transept was a short length (1.6m) of a shallow, east–west wall footing [5920], formed from flints bonded with orange sand and chalk/lime mortar, sealed by a deposit [5837] containing inclusions of crushed building material and Limpsfield-type ware (LIMP) post-dating c 1150. Further west was an irregular slot [759] measuring 2.2m by 1.2m, possibly a beam slot. These fragmentary foundations represent an early structure to the south of the presbytery, possibly a workshop or masons' shelter.

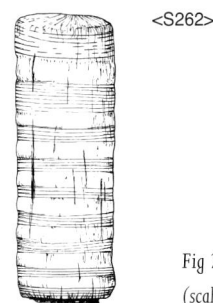

Fig 22 *Wooden knife handle <S262> (scale 1:2)*

Early features which are not illustrated included a ditch or watercourse and a possible robbed-out wall trench beneath the later (period M2) north wall of the chapter house. To the east were two pits containing daub and crushed Reigate stone: one [726] contained traces of vertical wood along one side; the second pit [859] contained Kingston-type ware (KING) dating the backfill to after c 1230.

Thirteen burials were found but one was not analysed. All of the 12 were adults, predominantly males: 6 were mature adult males, 2 older adult males, an adult male otherwise not aged, a mature adult female and 2 adult individuals of indeterminate sex. All were buried supine with their heads orientated to the west, and well spaced, although no true rows were evident.

The 12 burials appeared to be separated into two groups. Nine, including the female [5865], were clustered near the south side of the presbytery, with three further east. The burials in the western group included two in Reigate stone cists, [5841] and [5762], both badly disturbed. Two burials to the east, [7588] (not shown on period plan) and [7559], contained timber remains. In burial [7588], traces of the base and sides of the coffin survived, but burial [7559] (a mature adult male) appears to have been covered by a plank. The remainder of the interments were possibly in undetected coffins; some individuals were probably buried in shrouds or clothing.

NORTH BURIAL AREA (OA6)

The excavated northern area (OA6) covered c 800m² and extended c 40m east of the north transept and c 24m north of the presbytery. Boundaries were not positively identified but the northern limit may have been an east–west aligned ditch [3593] at least c 2m wide and 0.6m deep. The ditch pre-dates a later burial [3592] (period M2) and had silted up by that time.

A total of 84 burials, generally supine with their heads to the west, were interred here. The arms were usually laid out by the side but were occasionally placed over the body, with the hands, sometimes crossed, resting on the pelvis. Men, women and children were present although immature burials were markedly less frequent within the sample. Two small charnel pits are also thought to date to this period.

Most burials lay to the north-east of the north transept and presbytery with the highest density occurring directly north of the presbytery. It is probable that further burials in this area were obscured or destroyed by the later (period M2) church walls. Four outlying burials were close to the north-west corner of the transept. One [4282] was an older adult male interred with his head supported by a Reigate stone 'pillow'. An older adult male [3667], buried to the north of the transept chapels, was presumably dressed when interred as a copper-alloy buckle (<S209>, Fig 23) was positioned on the right hip; this individual also appeared to be associated with an iron spur <S355>, although this was possibly redeposited. One burial of an older adult male [4667] was recorded as having a copper-alloy disc on each arm (<470>, <471>, not catalogued); these may have been medical metal support plates. Two adult male burials lay adjacent to each other but well to the east of the church. Burial [4881] contained a chalice (<S24>, Fig 24) and

paten <S27>, and burial [4593] included a chalice (<S25>, Fig 24), implying the individuals were priests or at least had some religious connection. Six individuals were buried in what appeared to be wooden coffins. Four adult men, [3869], [4611], [4860], [4893], appear to have only been covered by wooden planks; one, covering [4893], was dendrochronologically dated to after 1009 (Table 71).

One of the largest subsamples of analysed skeletons, 82 individuals came from here. These comprised 80 adults and two children (aged 1–6 years). To the north of the presbytery was a group of five burials including three adult males and two children. The two children [3084] and [3235] were in stone cists constructed of Caen stone blocks (Fig 25; Fig 26). These were the only child burials at Merton to lie close to each other but adults buried nearby indicate that this was not a zone used exclusively for the burial of children. Their proximity may, however, indicate a familial relationship. The adults included 64 males and six females. The sex of ten individuals could not be determined. A single female was classified as young adult; three were mature adults and two were older adults. Thirty-one of the

Fig 23 *Copper-alloy buckle <S209> from the right hip of adult male [3667] in the north burial area (OA6, period M1) (scale c 1:1)*

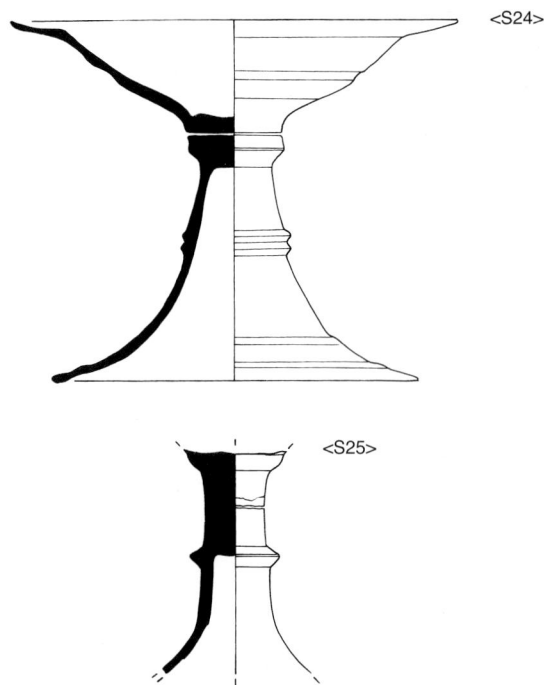

Fig 24 *Lead/tin chalices <S24> and <S25> buried with adult males [4881] and [4593] in the north burial area (OA6, period M1) (scale 1:2)*

Fig 25 *Two children's Caen stone cists (left [3235], right [3084]) (and the legs of an adult) in the north burial area (OA6, period M1), looking west (1.0m scale)*

Fig 26 *Caen stone cist with child [3235], looking west (0.2m scale)*

males were mature adults, 22 were older adults, 10 could only be classified as adult and 1 could not be assigned to an age group. Two of those of indeterminate sex were mature adults and eight could not be aged more precisely than adult.

AN ? EARLY CEMETERY WALL (S3)

Within the north burial area (OA6), an east–west, flint and Reigate stone wall (S3), *c* 1m wide and aligned with the north wall of the north transept, may have been an early boundary or a division within the cemetery. The wall cut three burials and the possible 12th-century chapel/church (B2), which may suggest an association between the burials and Building 2. The alignment suggests the wall was contemporary with the church and probably originally abutted the north transept but the west end was truncated. Structure 3 appears to have been short-lived: the trench robbing the wall was cut by further burials in this period, and by the later north transept (period M2) after *c* 1222. Floor tile of possible 13th-century date found within the robbed wall foundations is presumed to have been intrusive and derived from later cemetery disturbance.

A ? CEMETERY PATH (R1)

Directly north of the wall (S3) and parallel with it lay an east–west pathway (R1) across the north burial area (Fig 27). The path, 1.6m wide, comprised gravel rammed into clay bedding, lined with larger flints along its edges. Although only a *c* 5m length of Road 1 was excavated, it probably continued to the east and west. It was later widened to 2.5m and resurfaced.

A garden or orchard south of the cemetery and east of the cloister/claustral area (OA5)

Open Area 5 was bounded by ditches on the eastern and southern sides (Fig 28). These may also have been used as

Fig 27 *View of the cemetery path (R1) in the north burial area (OA6, period M1), looking north (1.0m scale)*

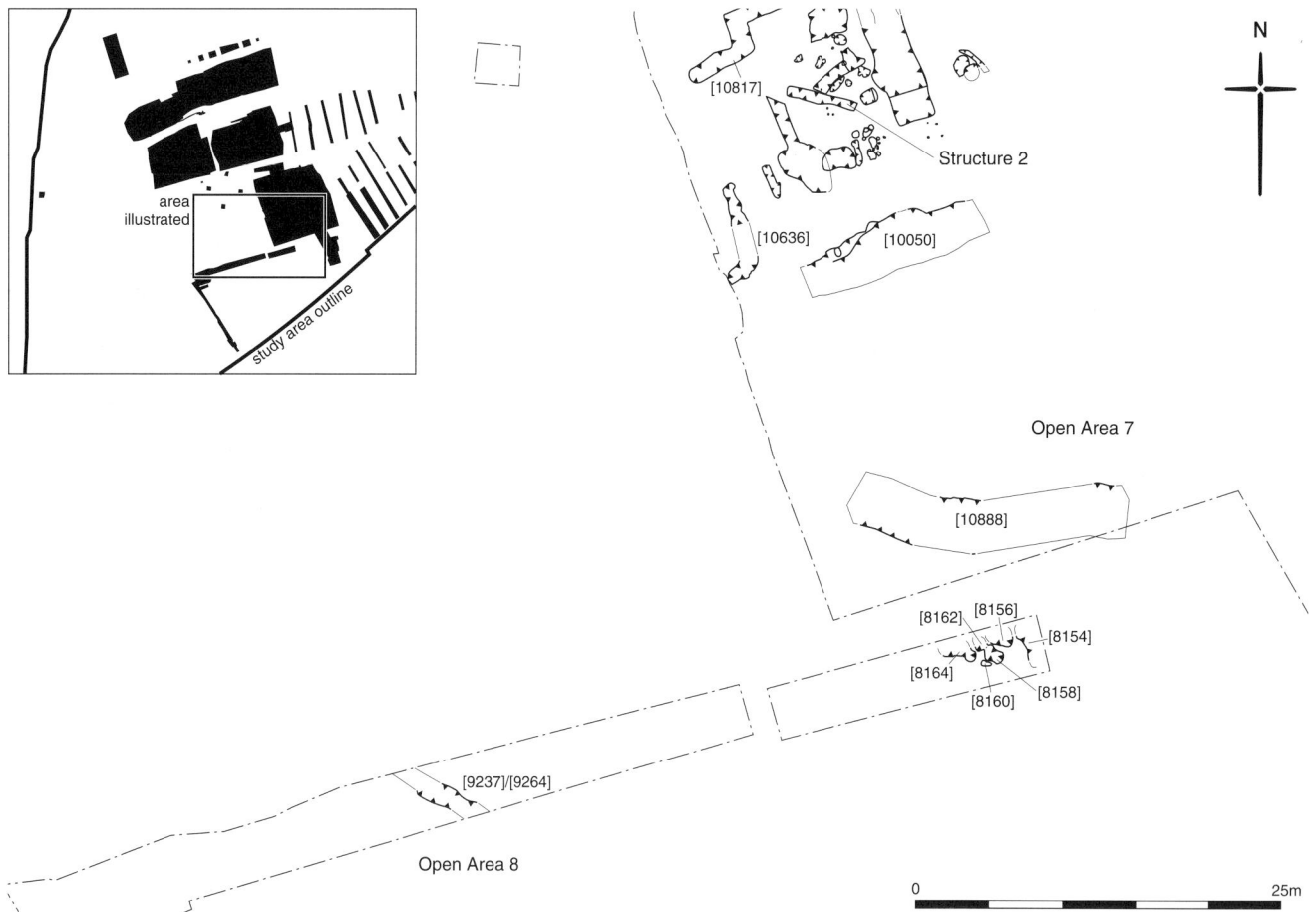

Fig 28 *Plan of principal archaeological features in the south part of the precinct, c 1117–1222 (period M1) (scale 1:500)*

bedding trenches, planting pits or drains. The eastern boundary ditch [11318] (Fig 9) lay immediately west of Structure 1 and could be traced over 50m north, into Open Area 3 as [5381] (above, 'South burial area (OA3)'). The ditch was wide (c 3m) but shallow (c 0.3m) with a flat base. The southern boundary ditch [10050] was also wide and shallow, but steeper sided;

secondary fill [9809] contained Kingston-type ware (KING) pottery, dating to after c 1230. The primary fills of both ditches contained occasional fragments of worked wood, possibly from Structure 1.

To the north-east of the boundary ditches lay other ditches, pits and postholes (Fig 29). A 'dog-leg'-shaped ditch [10817],

Fig 29 Ditch, pit and postholes
within the garden/orchard (OA5,
period M1), looking north (1.0m
scale)

11m by 2m, had vertical sides and a concave base (Fig 30). The
western end contained a timber revetment or lining, that is
vertical timber posts, apparently burnt in situ. At the eastern end
six stakeholes suggested a north–south fence or trellis, possibly
for viticulture. The lower fills, [10344] and [10818], contained
fragments of worked Reigate stone, flint, dumped burnt stakes
and planks, also possibly from Structure 1.

The primary fills [11252] and [10818] of the southern
boundary ditch [10050] and 'dog-leg'-shaped ditch [10817]
contained many freshwater snail shells, indicating the ditches
contained slow-moving or still, well-oxygenated water with a
muddy substrate and abundant vegetation. Terrestrial snails,
including cylindrical whorl snails (Truncatellina cylindrica L) and
grass snails, could have come from the bankside vegetation.
Wetland plants well represented in the fill [10818] of [10817]
may have been growing on or by the margins of the ditch
(Table 41). The fills [10634] and [10635] of another small
curving north–south ditch [10636] (Fig 28) contained
botanical evidence for aquatic and bankside/marshland species
plus freshwater mollusc shells (Table 48).

The 'dog-leg'-shaped ditch also contained the residue of food
and food preparation, including the shells from hatched chicken
eggs, together with pottery and slag from a hearth <S318>.
Eggshell fragments were also present in fills [10634] and
[10635]. Similarly, the organic primary fills of the eastern
boundary ditch [11318] included shells from hatched chicken
(and occasional goose) eggs. The concentration of hatched eggs
may indicate poultry rearing in the close vicinity. Food plants
were well represented in the fill [11252] of southern ditch
[10050], including a small number of charred cereal grains, a
range of fruit seeds and stones, and nutshell fragments suggesting
the disposal of rubbish from food preparation.

Fig 30 'Dog-leg'-shaped ditch in the garden/orchard (OA5, period M1), looking east
(2.0m scale)

Table 2 *Analysis of ceramic groups from fills [9531] and [9889] of eastern ditch [11318] (period M1, OA5) (for fabric codes see Table 37)*

Fabric	Sherd count	Weight (g)	Weight %
Fill [9531]			
EARL	1	12	0.1
EMSH	477	7177	78.7
ESUR	76	1157	12.7
KING	10	74	0.8
LCALC	6	48	0.5
LCOAR	25	415	4.6
LIMP	4	217	2.4
STAM	2	16	0.2
Total	**601**	**9116**	
Fill [9889]			
EMSH	150	2194	61.7
KING	91	144	4.0
KING polychrome decoration	1	14	0.4
LCOAR	10	237	6.7
LIMP	21	524	14.7
LOND	28	444	12.5
Total	**301**	**3557**	

This area (OA5) was probably in use from the mid 12th to the early 13th century. Overlying the natural clay within the southern part were silt deposits; one [10417] produced a silver, 'Watford' type penny <S342> dating to 1134–54. The secondary fills of the eastern ditch [11318] produced a large collection of pottery (Table 2). Fill [9531] contained large quantities of pottery types with a date range of c 1050–c 1150. Early medieval shell-tempered ware (EMSH) and early Surrey ware (ESUR) account for over 90% of the group by weight. The date range is supported by small quantities of Stamford-type ware (STAM) and a medium-sized group of London-type wares – coarse London-type ware (LCOAR) and calcareous London-type ware (LCALC), which both have city date ranges of c 1080–c 1200. However, small quantities of Kingston-type ware (KING), Limpsfield-type ware (LIMP) and a solitary sherd of Earlswood-type ware (EARL) suggest an early 13th-century date for the latest filling. Fill [9889] also probably dated to the 13th century. The ceramic assemblage from the fill of southern ditch [10050] also consisted mainly of mid 12th-century pottery with occasional sherds of KING, suggesting the ditch was finally filled during the first half of the 13th century.

The vertebrate faunal assemblage from Open Area 5 was the largest from this period; it probably represents waste from a nearby kitchen and/or refectory (Table 3; Table 4). The

Table 3 *Recovery of hand-collected vertebrate fauna from Open Area 5 (period M1), by fragment count*

Common name	Latin name	No. of frags	%
Fish			
Fish unidentified		7	0.3
Cod family	Gadidae	3	0.1
Cod	*Gadus morhua*	14	0.6
Cod-sized		7	0.3
Haddock	*Melanogrammus aeglefinus*	6	0.3
Conger eel	*Conger conger*	1	<0.1
Birds			
Bird unidentified		9	0.4
Chicken	*Gallus gallus*	104	4.4
Chicken-sized		4	0.2
Goose, domestic	*Anser anser*	26	1.1
Goose-sized		1	<0.1
Mallard/domestic duck	*Anas platyrhynchos*	3	0.1
Duck unidentified	Anatidae	1	<0.1
Crow	Corvidae	1	<0.1
Mammals			
Mammal unidentified		833	35.2
Cattle	*Bos taurus*	174	7.4
Cattle-sized		191	8.1
Sheep/goat	*Ovis aries/Capra hircus*	177	7.5
Sheep	*Ovis aries*	4	0.2
Sheep-sized		547	23.1
Pig	*Sus scrofa*	229	9.7
Dog	*Canis familiaris*	1	<0.1
Horse	*Equus caballus*	3	0.1
Deer, roe	*Capreolus capreolus*	1	<0.1
Deer, fallow	*Dama dama*	13	0.5
Deer unidentified	Cervidae	2	<0.1
Hare, brown	*Lepus europaeus*	3	0.1
Rabbit	*Oryctolagus cuniculus*	1	<0.1
Total		**2366**	

Table 4 *Recovery of wet-sieved vertebrate fauna from Open Area 5 (period M1), by fragment count*

Common name	Latin name	No. of frags	%
Fish			
Fish unidentified		7	1.1
Thornback ray	*Raja clavata*	2	0.3
Smelt	*Osmerus eperlanus*	97	15.3
Herring family	Clupeidae	85	13.4
Herring	*Clupea harengus*	12	1.9
Carp family	Cyprinidae	21	3.3
Cod family	Gadidae	88	13.9
Cod	*Gadus morhua*	10	1.6
Haddock	*Melanogrammus aeglefinus*	2	0.3
Plaice/flounder	Pleuronectidae	22	3.5
Eel	*Anguilla anguilla*	14	2.2
Birds			
Bird unidentified		27	4.3
Chicken	*Gallus gallus*	20	3.2
Chicken-sized		18	2.8
Duck unidentified	Anatidae	1	0.2
Crow unidentified	Corvidae	1	0.2
Passerine, large		1	0.2
Passerine		4	0.6
Thrush unidentified	Turdidae	5	0.8
Mammals			
Mammal unidentified		89	14.0
Cattle	*Bos taurus*	1	0.2
Cattle-sized		1	0.2
Sheep/goat	*Ovis aries/Capra hircus*	7	1.1
Sheep-sized		63	9.9
Pig	*Sus scrofa*	26	4.1
Hare, brown	*Lepus europaeus*	2	0.3
Mammal, small		8	1.3
Total		**634**	

identifiable fragments derived mainly from cattle and, to a lesser extent, sheep/goat and pig, but domestic poultry, mainly chicken with a little domestic goose and domestic duck/mallard, formed a substantial component. Occasional finds of fallow deer and brown hare, and bones of roe deer and rabbit, represented game species. The marine/estuarine fish species (conger eel, cod and haddock) do occur within the hand-collected group, but analysis of the wet-sieved material, although confirming the dominance of poultry and the major mammalian domesticates, greatly increases the diversity of the dietary assemblage. There is considerable recovery of a range of small passerine bird species, probably including blackbird and/or thrush, and definite evidence for a more diverse fish assemblage including thornback ray, smelt, herring, herring family, eel, and carp family. There was one fragment of dog. The material represents a good-quality diverse diet with some suggestion, from the definite identification of game species, of high-status consumption.

A possible timber and daub building (S1), south of the cemetery and east of the cloister/claustral area (OA5)

To the east of the eastern boundary ditch [11318] were seven postholes sealed by a deposit of daub, additional postholes to the south-west, and one lined with Reigate stone to take a square timber post, which would have been some 270mm thick (S1) (Fig 9; Fig 31). The overlying daub deposit [10537] contained ash and charcoal and filled some of the postholes suggesting destruction by fire. Charred timber planks recovered from two ditches in Open Area 5 may be from the structure. To the east was a north–south ditch [10977], 3.5m long. A shallow pit [10996] was filled with crushed mortar and Reigate stone. The pottery from daub [10537] post-dates c 1230 (KING) and suggests that Structure 1 stood until replaced by the later infirmary complex (period M2).

A ? vine bedding trench (S2), south of the cemetery and east of the cloister/claustral area (OA5, period M1)

In Open Area 5 a north-west to south-east trench (S2), similar to others found there, measured 4.9m by 0.7m by 0.2–0.3m deep (Fig 28; Fig 32); it is interpreted as a possible bedding trench for vines. Numerous sherds of 12th-century pottery recovered from the eastern part of the trench suggest food preparation and serving nearby.

A ?garden (OA7), south of the cemetery and east of the (later) cloister/claustral area

To the south of Open Area 5, in Open Area 7 (Fig 28), was a wide (c 4m), shallow (0.7m), c 18m long east–west drainage ditch [10888] containing a peaty clay. Further south were a series of ?tree bedding pits, [8154], [8156], [8158], [8160], [8162], [8164]. These features are interpreted as the remains of a possible garden or orchard extending from Open Area 5 to the north.

South of the (later) cloister/claustral area in the ? outer court (OA8)

In Open Area 8 (Fig 28), south of the (period M2) cloister/claustral area, two intercutting ditches drained south-eastwards towards the River Wandle. The upper fill of the earlier east–west ditch [9343] contained pottery dating to c 1080–c 1200. This ditch was overlain by a wattle-lined north-west to south-east replacement [9237]/[9264]; this was dated by pottery to c 1150–c 1300, but three dendrochronological dates included one of 1102–?47 from a timber with a possible heartwood/sapwood boundary (Table 71).

Fig 31 Postholes forming part of a possible timber and daub building (S1, period M1) (0.5m scale)

31

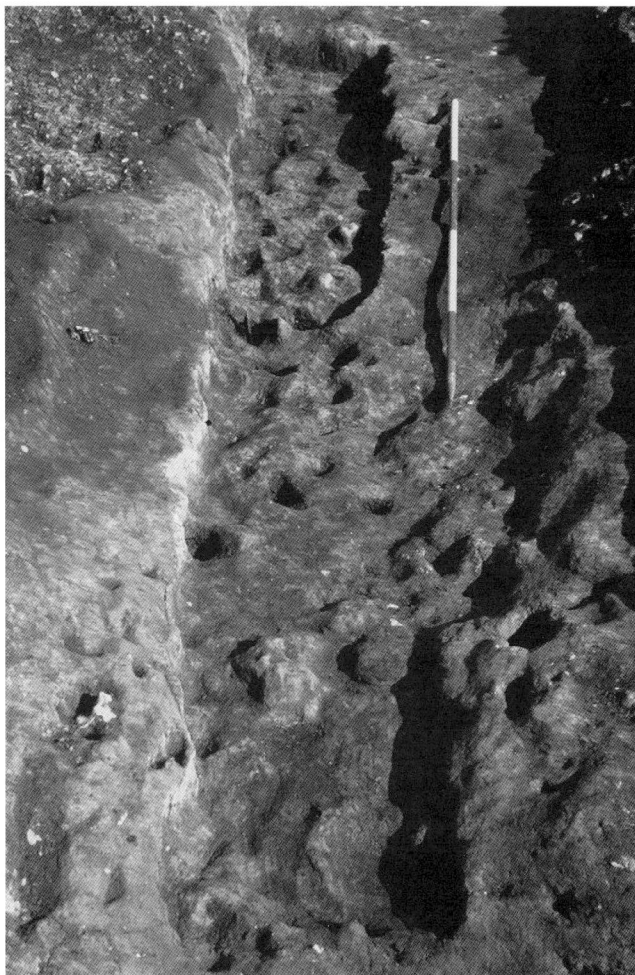

Fig 32 *View of the possible vine bedding trench (S2) within Open Area 5 (period M1), looking south-east (2.0m scale)*

An *ex situ*, later 12th-century gateway/doorway

Ex situ evidence survives for a building constructed during the 1170s or so, possibly to the west of the main church. During the demolition in 1914 of a post-medieval house, Abbey House (for location see Fig 3), an ornately carved entrance was found within the structure (Fig 33). Pevsner dates the entrance to *c* 1175 (Green 1977, 98). Its highly decorated mouldings indicate it was part of an important building and, because of its location when found, it has been interpreted as the entrance to a guest house or *hospitium* (Johnston 1914, 138), but it may have been part of a chapel or other building. The reconstructed entrance stands in the parish churchyard of St Mary the Virgin, Merton (cover illustration).

Discussion *c* 1117–1222 (period M1)

The possible presence of a mid 12th-century stone church in the vicinity of the later priory church (B1) is suggested by *ex situ* worked stone. Building 2 might represent the location of this early church or chapel but its extensively robbed remains are difficult to interpret. It may, alternatively, have been a domestic building or workshop. The chronological relationship

between Building 2 and the *in situ* remains of the late 12th-/early 13th-century priory church (B1) could not be demonstrated. However, Building 2 pre-dated a wall (S3) which was aligned with the north wall of the north transept of the church but was itself redundant before most of this period's burials were dug in the north burial area (OA6). Building 2 is likely to be earlier than the late 12th-/early 13th-century priory church or to have coexisted with it only briefly. The stylistically early, *ex situ* worked stone and Building 2 cannot be equated with either of the documented successive wooden chapels provided by Gilbert in the first half of the 12th century. Conceivably they represent material from and/or the location of Gilbert's first 'most beautiful and sturdy church', begun in 1125 but soon apparently largely demolished, or possibly, and more likely, the church that replaced it.

As none of its superstructure survived, the construction date for Building 1 is also provided largely by *ex situ* worked stone, although levelling deposits to the north indicated a date after *c* 1140. The mouldings undergo some stylistic changes during the building campaign, suggesting a church begun *c* 1170. The dedication of altars recorded in 1174, 1194 and 1196 suggest the completion of parts of the church. It is likely that at least the presbytery and transepts were finished by 1194–6. The church plan reconstructed from the remains is symmetrical and cruciform, with a short square-ended presbytery, aisleless nave, transept chapels, and possibly the foundations for night stairs in the south transept (Chapter 4.3).

Night stairs indicate a two-storey east range, in this case perhaps of timber. For, although in 1136 the cloister and other buildings were described as complete (*VCH* 1905, 94–5), no *in situ* evidence for possible masonry claustral buildings, other than short foundations to the south of the church (B1), was identified. This area (OA4) appears to have remained largely or entirely open throughout the period. Ex situ stonework provides tenuous evidence that a stone cloister may have been started, or at least planned, in the 12th century, probably the later 12th century. It would appear little progress had been made before the end of this period.

A cemetery had been consecrated in the earliest years of the priory's foundation but its location is unknown. By the late 12th century, one existed essentially to the east of the church, with one excavated area to its north and east (OA6) and one to its south and east (OA3). The boundaries probably shifted during the period, as evidenced to the north and east by the construction of the path (R1) and the wall (S3) which was then abandoned, and possibly also to the south by the presence of the eastern ditch [11318] (OA5). Conceivably, the areas immediately to the north of the north transept and/or the wall (S3), where small numbers of interments were made, were not at one or any time regarded as part of the same cemetery. A division may also have existed between all interments to the south (OA3) and those to the north (OA6) (Chapter 4.10, 'The burial areas and population size').

To the south of the cemetery lay a probable domestic timber building (S1), probably associated with a garden/orchard (OA5) to the west. It may have formed early accommodation for the

Fig 33 *The 12th-century gateway/doorway found during the demolition of Abbey House in 1914 (courtesy of Merton Library and Heritage Service)*

canons, but could perhaps have been a private dwelling for a servant or secular person in the precinct. This appears to have burnt down and, significantly, on 26 October 1216 the priory granted to Amicius, nephew of the late archdeacon of Surrey, the garden in their precinct (*curia*) where the houses he had previously built had burnt down, and other gardens with the dwelling that he had since constructed at his own expense (Heales 1898, 71, appendix XLIII). The bedding trenches, planting pits and stakeholes for possible wooden trellises, which could be used for example for viticulture, in Open Area 5, are features known from monastic gardens elsewhere (Coppack 1993, 78–80). These, together with a large quantity of food waste comprising fish, bird and mammal bone, and hatched chicken and goose eggs, reinforce the domestic character of this area to the south of the cemetery and east of the claustral area.

Any discussion of the development of the priory precinct is necessarily limited: only parts were available for excavation. Archaeological evidence was recovered for a priory comprising a stone church to the north with areas of more domestic activity to its south-east. With the exception of the *ex situ*

evidence for a possible guest house or chapel to the west of the church, and perhaps a stone cloister (possibly incomplete or only intended) to the south of the nave, no further evidence for the usual conventual buildings was found. While it is possible that these were not south of the church but elsewhere, and in timber not stone – remaining in use longer than anticipated and only being replaced in stone when the collapse of the church tower in 1222 (period M2; below, 3.2) necessitated a more general rebuilding – the lack of these structures to the south may, perhaps, be the result of truncation and removal by that later rebuild, and of the limited areas excavated.

Topographically this was a near-ideal monastic site, adjacent to a river with a higher platform above the flood plain. The path (R1) immediately to the north of the church lay at 12.2–12.4m OD while the ditches in Open Area 5 were apparently cut from *c* 11.9m OD, suggesting a gentle slope down from the church south-east to the river. Near the River Wandle there was greater risk of flooding; the ditches in Open Area 5 may represent drainage to control this or boundary ditches enclosing the south-eastern precinct.

3.2 Expansion of the priory, 1222– c 1300 (period M2)

Documentary evidence

At Merton Priory, as at many monasteries throughout Britain, the early 13th century was a period of great expansion. The rebuilding programme was probably prompted by severe storm damage suffered by the church in December 1222, when the tower (*corruit turris Mertonie*), probably that over the crossing of the church, collapsed (*Ann Monast*, iii, 76). In December 1225, Henry III granted ten oaks from the forest of Gauct' (Galtres?) to the prior of Merton for the fabric of his church (Heales 1898, 90), which suggests that reconstruction was under way or about to commence. Some of the church was evidently ready in December 1230 when Archbishop Richard of Canterbury consecrated Elias of Radnor as Bishop of Llandaff at Merton (*Ann Monast*, i, 77). In 1232 Hubert de Burgh, chief justiciar, fled to the priory for sanctuary pursued by the king, Henry III, who demanded that he yield and summoned an armed London mob of 20,000. Hubert waited before the high altar until a safe conduct was issued, but was then arrested (*Chron Majora*, iii, 222–6). In 1239, Edmund, Archbishop of Canterbury, also held an ordination at Merton Priory church (Heales 1898, 104, citing [Parker Library] Corpus Christi College, MS 59).

Rebuilding work may have continued until the 1260s. In February 1253 Edward of Westminster was ordered to ensure that the silver image of the Blessed Mary, being made for the prior and convent, should be completed and delivered to them (*Cal Close R*, 1251–3, 317). The following year Peter Chasepore, the Queen's treasurer, bequeathed to Merton 60 marks (£40) to buy land to support a chantry at the priory (*Historia Minor*, iii, 343; *Chron Majora*, v, 484; *Mon Angl*, vi(1), i, 245–8). From 1262 there are several references to the chapel of St Mary but the allusion may be to the chapel of the infirmary for on 14 January 1263 a Henry de Micheham placed himself in the chapel of the hospital of Merton and admitted the theft of a chalice, 'of the alms of Merton' (Heales 1898, 139 and appendix LXXVII). Perhaps the infirmary chapel was the one referred to in 1271–2 in another action in King's Bench, when the prior proceeded against Thomas de Warblinton for a mill and 8 acres (3.24 hectares) of land and an acre (0.4 hectare) of marsh in Tandridge (Surrey), which belonged 'to his chapel of Merton', and where Thomas had been replaced as tenant by Stephen de Crowehurst after the resignation of Walter, the late prior (ibid, 151).

In addition to work on the conventual church, in December 1257 Henry III commanded his mason Master John, 'concerning building operations at Merton' (*de operacionibus apud Merton*), to ensure the repair of the chimneys in the king's chamber (*camera regis*), wardrobe (*garderoba regis*) and in the chamber of the king's chancellor (*camera cancellarie regis*) of Merton Priory, and to have such alterations made as necessary; the costs were to be met by the king and entered under the expenditure at Westminster (*Cal Close R*, 1256–9, 168).

Henry III (1216–72) was a fervent patron of religious orders

and enjoyed a particularly close personal relationship with Merton. He stayed at Merton on 54 occasions. Most such visits took place at the start or end of a royal progress and Merton, only 7 miles (11.3km) from London, made a convenient staging post. Henry clearly had an attachment to Merton Priory. Sometimes his stays were punctuated by short trips to Westminster and, conversely, there were brief visits from Westminster, to which he would return afterwards. These sojourns occurred 18 times: once in the 1220s, on four occasions in the 1240s, nine in the 1250s, one in the 1260s and three in the period 1271–2. The most usual length of stay was four days, but there were also visits of seven days (16–23 April 1259) and ten days (8–18 July 1271). There was little regularity in the number and timing, although post-Christmas visits (27 December–1 January) took place in 1245–6, 1248–9, 1257–8 and 1259–60. Post-Easter visits also occurred in 1247 (4–7 April), 1249 (11–14 April), 1258 (28 March), and 1259 (16–23 April). Other visits took place throughout the year and, like the long stays he made during the course of general progresses, are probably best seen as short holidays. He could easily have stayed instead at his palace at Kennington 5 miles (8km) from Merton and only 3 (4.8km) from Westminster) but evidently preferred to stay in religious houses. The Cistercian abbey of Stratford Langthorne was also regularly patronised by Henry III on his excursions into East Anglia (Barber et al 2004, 17, 33–4). This contrasts with the practice of Edward I, who appears to have stayed at Merton only once, on 24–7 April 1297, and of Edward II.

Merton Priory provided a convenient location, with accommodation, close to London on one of the main routes through Surrey. In July 1235 it was the collection point for the royal aid levied in Surrey (*Cal Close R*, 1234–7, 191) and in January 1236 parliament met there and promulgated the Statutes of Merton (*Ann Monast*, i, 249, iii, 144; *Cal Close R*, 1234–7, 353; *Chron Majora*, iii, 340–3). Other assemblies convened at Merton in this period were a royal council of January 1255 (*Cal Close R*, 1254–6, 158–9), and a convocation of the church on 6 June 1258 (*Ann Monast*, i, 411–12).

Merton developed a reputation for learning. On 23 August 1265 Prior Gilbert granted a charter to Walter de Merton (a former canon of Merton and lord chancellor in 1261–3), quitclaiming the house of scholars of St Mary of Merton, which Walter had founded the previous year at its first home at Malden (Surrey), and placing it in the priory's trusteeship and protection (Heales 1898, 143). By 1274 the house of scholars had moved to its permanent home in Oxford in the shape of Merton College (Martin and Highfield 1997, 11–20). Walter still had connections with St Mary Merton, for in March 1275, while staying at Merton Priory, Walter drew up his last testament (*Fitznells Cart*, lxxv).

Two of the three documented interments in the conventual church, those of John Haun`sard and his wife Gundreda, belong to this period. They were buried during the prioracy of Eustace (1249–65) who granted them the right to choose their place of burial before the altar at which two canons would be assigned to pray for their souls, while their names were to be entered in the martyrology (ie list of the martyrs, read during the office of Prime) of the house and their anniversary was to be kept (Manning and Bray 1804, 258; VCH 1905, 96).

Archaeological evidence

Introduction

The collapse of the church tower in 1222 led to the rebuilding of much of the church, enlarging and extending it to the east, north and south (Fig 34). The original (period M1) presbytery was incorporated into the new church. The first identified in situ claustral complex was built to the south of the church comprising: the cloister walks (B3a) and garth (OA10), the chapter house (B3b), the east range to the south of the chapter house (B3c and 3d), the south range (B3e) and the slype (covered way or passage) (B3f) lying between the chapter house and the south transept (Fig 34). Unusually, a space (OA4) was left between the south nave wall and the north (free standing) wall of the cloister, as a probable lane between the two. A drain (S6) was constructed in the garth, draining from the north-east corner of the cloister walk.

The infirmary hall (B4a), infirmary chapel (B4b), the reredorter (B5) (Fig 57) and the infirmary kitchen (B6) were also constructed to the south and east. The reredorter/infirmary annexe (B7) was probably constructed shortly after these and included a drain (S4a and S4b) serving the kitchen and reredorter. The former garden or orchard (OA5) now formed the infirmary cloister garth between the monastic east range and the infirmary. Further buildings were constructed to the south and south-west of the infirmary complex: a ?storage building (B10) with associated south passage (S7), and an aisled hall (B11) and mill (B9) west of Open Area 8. Directly to the south of Building 10 was a chalk-paved fishpond (S9).

Parts of both cemetery areas (OA3 and OA6) were lost to the extended church but both areas continued to receive numerous interments. The path (R1) continued in use and a further path or trackway (R2) at the north edge of Open Area 6 may have been used to bring construction material to the new church. The stone precinct wall (S5; seen in trial trenches AH and AL, Fig 3) may have been completed during this period. Open Areas 7 and 9 were established to the south and east of the infirmary.

The later 13th-century church (B1)

The church crossing was not excavated and there is no archaeological evidence, such as in situ debris, for the documented collapse of the tower, presumably a central crossing tower. It is probable that any debris was removed to re-establish access to the (period M1) presbytery. The remaining, western three-quarters of the existing church were demolished and the materials reused. A terminus post quem of c 1230 is provided by Kingston-type ware (KING) pottery in backfill [5628] over one of the robbed foundations and construction debris and levelling in the north nave. A line of stakeholes, c 2m inside the new south wall, indicated scaffolding used during the reconstruction. Other stakeholes, postholes and small pits lay inside and outside the church, filled with mortar and crushed Reigate stone. These materials also occurred in layers across the church interior. The new foundations were generally c 1.5–2m wide and up to 1.6m deep, constructed from flint and Reigate stone bonded with a

sandy mortar. The west front was moved a few metres east and the internal length of the church shortened to c 62m (Fig 34).

The original (period M1) east wall of the north transept was incorporated into the west wall of the new north transept and it is suggested that this was also the case for the south transept. This moved the transepts to the east, greatly shortening the existing retained presbytery in relation to them (cf Fig 10). The interior width north–south across the transepts was c 42.5m. The presbytery had presumably escaped damage during the fall of the tower and remained largely unchanged, although part of its north wall was rebuilt. Excavation, mainly by Bidder, established that there were no foundations (except for the later Lady chapel) extending the presbytery to the east at this date, leaving the church with a much-shortened east end. The new transepts (Fig 35) were c 9m further east than their predecessors, reducing the external length of the presbytery so that it projected only c 6m. However, internally, the west end of the presbytery would have been determined by the east side of the crossing; this was not excavated but can be assumed to have shared the same median line as the west (arcaded) wall of the north transept chapels. This would have created a short square presbytery, a familiar feature in Cistercian churches (Chapters 4.2, 4.3; Fig 142; Fig 143). This is admittedly unusual at this date, but Bidder's plans and descriptions are clear (Fig 2) (Bidder and Westlake 1930, 60, and fig 5). Economy may have dictated the temporary retention of the earlier (period M1) east end.

The foundations give internal dimensions for the north transept of north–south c 12m, and east–west c 7.5m but c 12m including the chapels, making it approximately 12m square. In practice, the north transept would have commenced at the north side of the crossing (not seen); this would make it c 15.5m long. It was divided on its eastern side by arcading into four compartments or potential chapels, each c 3–4m². Altar foundations, later robbed out, but up to 2.5m by 1.5m in size, occupied the eastern end of each of the three northern chapels; these three were separated by stone screens probably as each altar was dedicated. At the base of the cut for the central chapel's altar base were slots, 0.10m wide and up to 0.95m long, and stakeholes possibly associated with the altar's construction. The southernmost chapel skirted the north-east crossing pier and was probably left clear to ease circulation (Fig 34). The heavy external buttressing of the east and west walls of the transepts suggests that they were high and completely vaulted.

The south transept, measured north–south between the crossing and the slype, was c 2.4m shorter than its northern counterpart. The south transept was heavily robbed and not fully excavated, but the surviving eastern buttresses indicated that the transept bays were 'compressed' from north to south compared to the north transept, reducing the width of each. The south transept does not appear to have been partitioned into eastern chapels like the north transept, although five burials (see below) were found in the south-east corner, which may have functioned as a chapel. The interpretation of several internal features can only be tentative. A large, partly robbed, masonry feature, 1.4m east–west by 2.8m north–south and 1.0m deep, lay to the west of the burials. This may be the remains of an altar foundation comparable

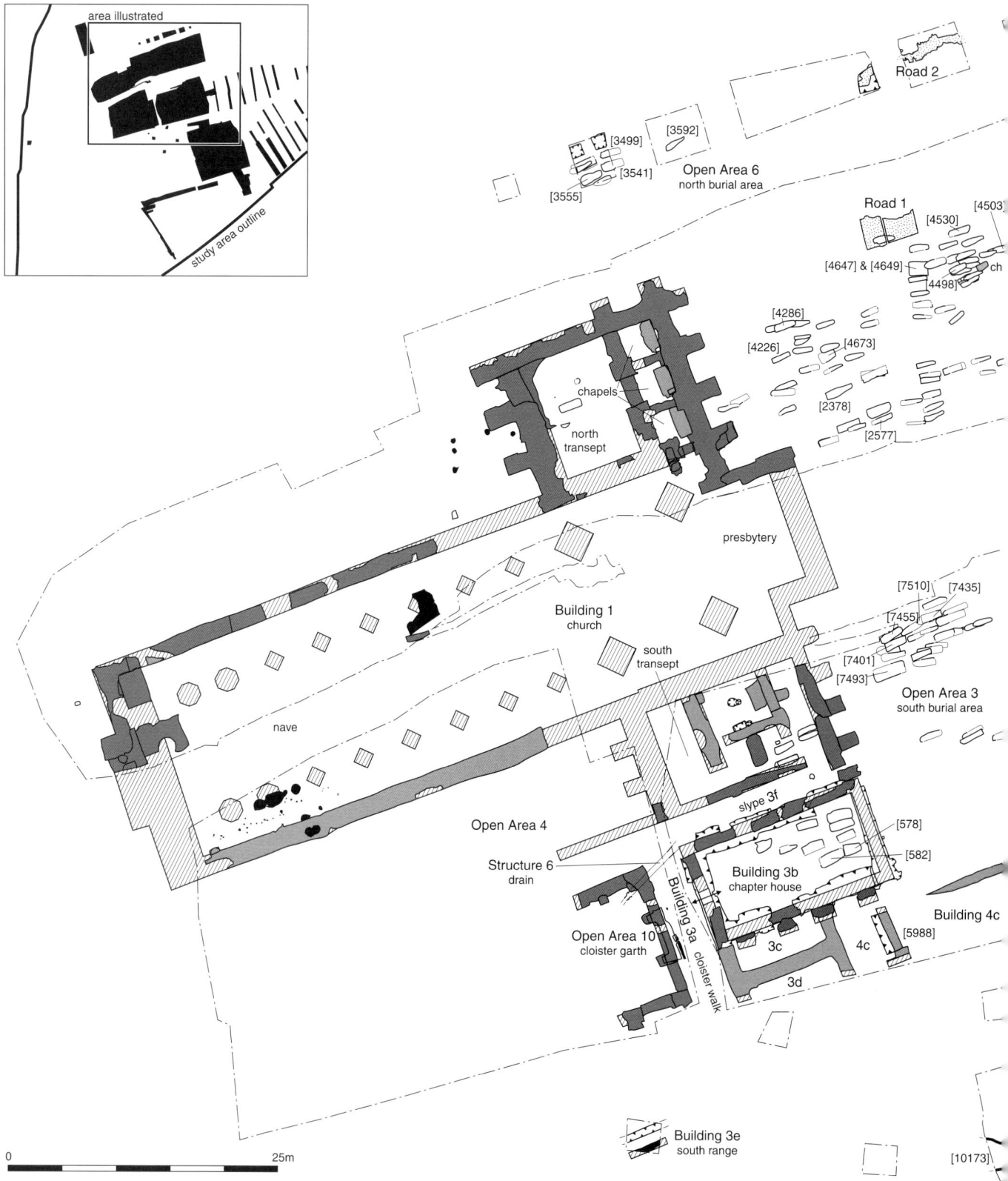

Fig 34 Plan of principal archaeological features in the north part of the precinct, 1222 to c 1300 (period M2) (scale 1:500)

to those found in the north transept. The remaining stonework included worked Reigate stone pieces, some of considerable size, and half a ?Purbeck marble coffin lid from [5647], inscribed with a cross, which presumably originated from the period M1 church or cemeteries. In addition, the south transept was possibly much altered over time. A small central chapel may have

been created to the north of the possible altar foundation: robber trenches defined a space c 6m by 5m, with a second possible altar foundation, c 1m by 2m, against the east wall/side. Unfortunately, evidence for this structure survived only as post-Dissolution robber trenches, indicating that it still stood at the Dissolution, but making it impossible to otherwise phase. The

N

[4658]

[4655]

[7403]
[7512]

stalls

Building 4b
infirmary chapel

stalls

[5794]
[5793]

[5903]

Building 4a
infirmary hall

Building 6
infirmary kitchen

m

[1105]

h

h

[1102]

m

yard

Building 4c

[1093]

Building 8

Open Area 5
infirmary cloister garth

water pipe
trench

area of
burning

Open Area 9

path

[10187]

[10173]

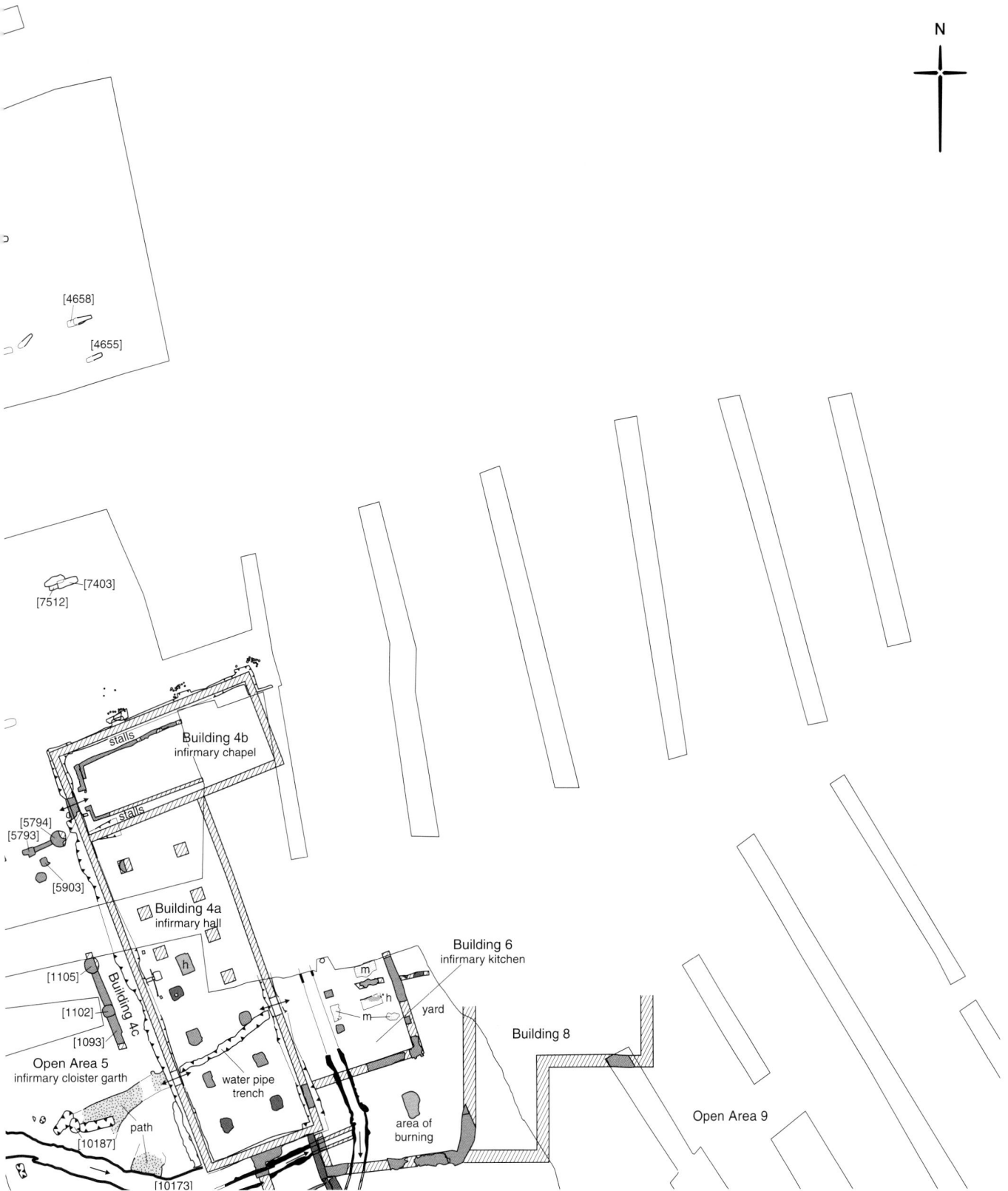

robber trench on this structure's west side was wider than those to the south and east – which might have supported timber or metal screens – and the west footing may have been for a set of night stairs against which the chapel was constructed. The robbing of the east and west foundations extended south of the south foundation, suggesting either buttresses/piers or overzealous robbing; the latter might also account for an apparent small buttress/pier on the east side of the east wall.

The new nave, measuring 43.4m by 18.6m internally, composed a far greater proportion of the length of the church than its predecessor. It accommodated two aisles, which on the basis of the *ex situ* moulded stone recovered were divided from

Fig 35 *The north transept (centre) and nave (top left) under excavation, looking west (the foundations in the left foreground belong to the period M3 presbytery)*

the nave by arcades. No *in situ* evidence was obtained because the central area of the church was not excavated. Part of the footing and base course of Reigate stone blocks of a possible rood screen or pulpitum [5463], measuring *c* 4.0m north–south by 3.3m east–west, and 1.3m high, was exposed on the north side of the nave. Set *c* 28m from the west end, it may have spanned the whole width of the nave.

Ex *situ* moulded stone thought to derive from this church included pieces of vaulting, shafts, arcades, parapets and finials, windows, doors, string courses, base courses and stair turrets.

The vaulting is well represented by several surviving rib voussoirs and is the best evidence that the nave aisles were not built until the 13th century. Two main forms are represented. In both the beaked roll, employed in the main arcades at Salisbury Cathedral (Wiltshire) after *c* 1220 (Morris 1992, 4), is distinctive. A skilfully executed rib moulding (<A63>, Fig 181) is derived from a substantial vault. The best-understood vault may have derived from an aisle of the rebuilt nave and forms important evidence of the nave's stylistic affinities (<A56> and <A57>, Fig 36). The springer block <A57> probably derives from the end of a vault compartment and incorporates the diagonal rib of a quadripartite vault. A voussoir (<A55>, Fig 181) may be a transverse rib from the aisle vaulting, but could be the minor order of an arcade or crossing arch.

An angle-roll voussoir <A59> (Fig 181) is likely to derive from the arcading of this church; it can be identified as the

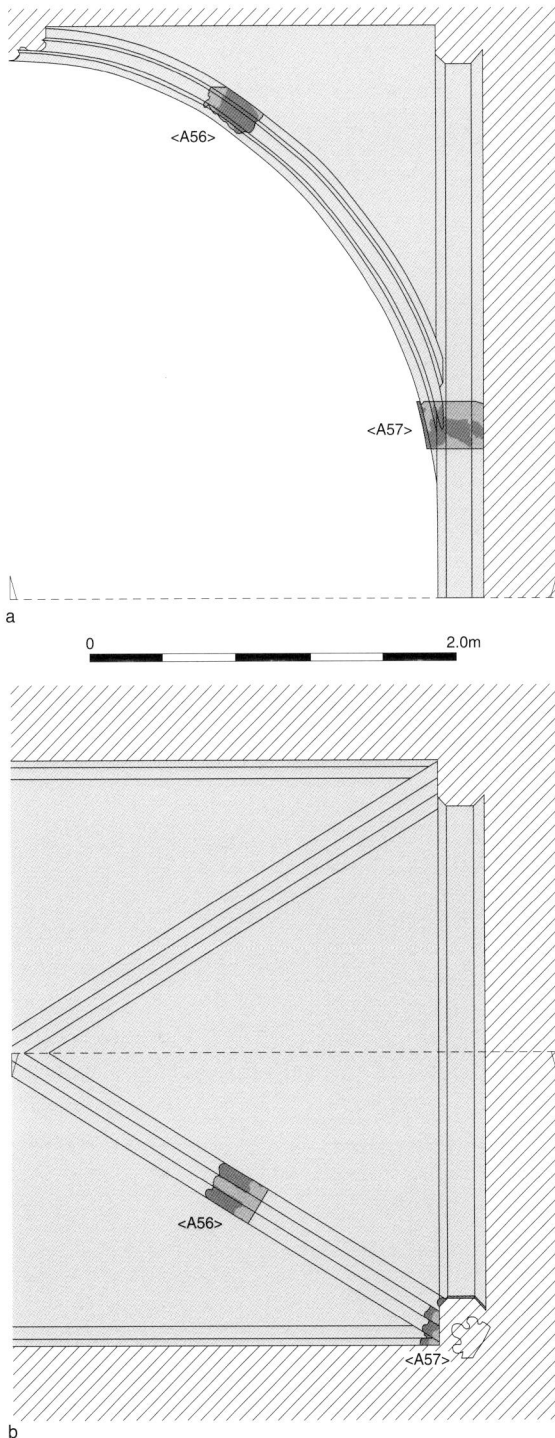

Fig 36 *A reconstructed aisle vaulting compartment (period M2): a – longitudinal section; b – inverted plan <A56> and <A57> (scale 1:40)*

major order of the arch. Another fragment of voussoir <5467> shows that this arch was pointed. Purbeck marble shafting (eg <2185>) would have had decorative capitals. Fragments of these shafts demonstrate the high standard of ornament that may have been present in the church.

Grouped lancets are represented by a Nonsuch fragment and other excavated stone (<A58>, Fig 181). Thin shafts divided a row of sharply splayed embrasures. This window, perhaps in the transept, may have resembled the east window of the Augustinian priory at Chetwode, Buckinghamshire (RCHM 1913, 85).

There was no evidence for any doorway comparable to the west portal of the earlier (period M1) church. However, stone from a roughly finished, narrow (under c 640mm wide) doorway was recorded (<2423>). The simply chamfered door arch was apparently internal and the embrasure was rectilinear in plan. The door was demolished and its fragments reused elsewhere prior to the Dissolution.

Four surviving examples of a string course suggest it was extensively employed in the church interior; the bold, simple mould is apparently unusual (<A54>, Fig 181). A solitary coping stone <4729>, from a two-course parapet coping with sharply pitched weatherings (the sloping horizontal surfaces on exterior elements which throw off water), was found reused in the infirmary kitchen (B6, period M3) and probably derived from the church. Parallels at Whitby Abbey (Yorkshire North Riding) suggest a date c 1220 (Webb 1956, 102).

A curved ashlar <2180> is likely to come from the newel of a stairwell. The piece indicates that the width of the stairwell was 1.4m (4ft 9in). Two other stairwell ashlars were found in the foundation of a reinforced buttress [4379] and this suggests that a stair turret was demolished when repairs were carried out to the later eastern extension (period M3). An external superstructure <A60>–<A62> (Fig 182) may derive from part of the ?tower.

There is evidence that this church stood on an elaborate and massive sloping base course typical of the great church architecture of this period. The entire base course was probably six to eight courses high, but only an intermediate part of the profile is represented (<2151>, <2155>, <2317>). The weathering was formed from blocks nearly a metre long. The weathering was interrupted by an overhanging step while a drip mould formed the lower margin.

Consolidated spreads of mortar in the transepts and along the north edge of the crossing were overlain in places by crushed Reigate stone and fragments of Reigate stone slabs, suggesting that some areas, at least, were floored with Reigate paviors. Elsewhere, the mortar was probably bedding for ceramic tiles. Some areas were probably paved in small plain-glazed mosaic tiles made from similar clay to later 'Westminster' tiles, probably made close to London (Chapter 7.3, '"Westminster" tile'). Seven mosaic shapes were identified, undoubtedly used together to form decorative mosaic patterns in prominent areas of the church. The rectangular tiles were probably all yellow but the lozenge shapes almost certainly alternated in colour between yellow and brown or dark green (<T71>–<T78>, Fig 198). It is possible to tentatively reconstruct how they fitted together in the floor (Fig 37).

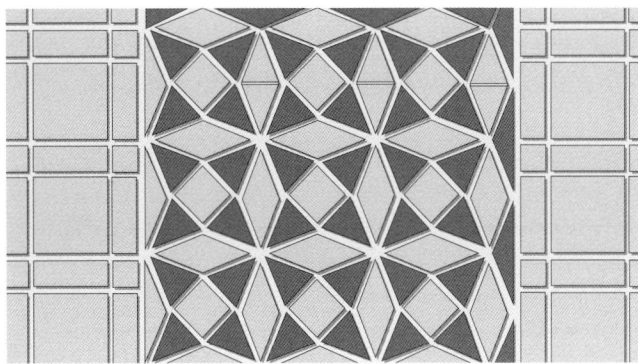

Fig 37 *A suggested reconstruction of a mosaic floor of plain-glazed tiles from St Mary Merton (not to scale)*

Some tiles appear to be discards. A square tile <T78> has been deeply scored to make smaller square mosaic tiles similar to <T75>, although this was never carried out. Similarly, two examples of a diamond-shaped tile have been scored to make smaller mosaic shapes but not broken so: <T71ii> to make <T72>, and <T71iii> to make <T73> or halved again. This suggests mosaics were purchased in complete patterns and the original pattern was altered, or installed to fit the floor area; tiles were cut to fit as necessary, leaving surplus tiles.

London-made 'Westminster' tiles, of c 1250–c 1300 date, were used reasonably extensively in the church. Many came from later burials within the north transept and originally formed the transept floor. The tiles have either a plain yellow or green glaze or are decorated (<T55>, <T57>, <T61>, <T68> and <T69>, Fig 197; see Table 30 for concordance with Betts 2000). There are also tiles from the keyed, white slip group (<T39>, <T44>–<T46>, Fig 195) and from the pink slip group (<T51>, <T54>, Fig 196), which are probably similar in date. Certain tiles (<T39>, Fig 195) have been scored and cut into four smaller tiles.

Ceramic peg tiles found in small patches may have been used as flooring in the south nave [5294] and the north transept [2943]. In the latter area a small number of half-complete tiles, measuring 157–161mm wide x 17–18mm thick, were recorded.

Various fragments of Coggeshall-type bricks came from the rebuilt church whilst further bricks were found in construction levels. These would have been used around window and door openings and possibly as cornices. Such bricks are dated to c 1220 at their type-site (Gardner 1955, pl XIII; Lloyd 1983, 104–5) and are most likely to have been used at Merton in the reconstruction of the priory church after 1222. The Coggeshall-type bricks at Merton were rectangular with a quadrant missing from one corner (<T111> and <T112>, [2799] and [5725]) and bricks of at least two sizes were used. These are the first examples of their type to have been found outside Essex; they are in a different fabric to the Coggeshall examples and were probably made locally to Merton.

Two examples of a second type of thin brick or tile came from the reconstruction of the church after 1222. Many have either a splash or more uniform covering of glaze. All, however, are straight sided (rather than bevelled which is characteristic of floor tiles) suggesting use as walling rather than flooring. Glazed bricks of similar appearance decorated the walls at Westminster Abbey during the 11th century (Betts 1996, 19) and may have been similarly used at Merton, although the Merton bricks are clearly later and the one brick with a surviving length is smaller than all the Westminster examples.

A Purbeck marble grave slab (<A64>, Fig 38), broken up and reused in the later (period M3) eastern extension of the church, probably came from this (period M2) church. The absence of weathering suggests that it was internal and Purbeck monuments of this date were generally high status. The stylised staff and 'pill box' design, with a cross formed from four circles, was a common one in the 13th century; it is unlikely to be of 14th-century date.

Seven burials were identified within the church, two from the north transept and five at the south end of the south transept, in what may have been a chapel (see above). The burials were plain and only their position within the church distinguishes them from the majority of contemporary external burials. Those from the north transept were available for analysis, but the age and sex of only one, a young adult male, could be determined. Skeletal analysis was undertaken on three of the burials from the south transept: a child of approximately 7–12 years, a mature adult male and an older adult male. This does not constitute an obvious family group and none of the three exhibit any non-metric traits that perhaps might suggest relationship.

There is no osteological evidence from the subsamples from the north and south transepts that different parts of the church building were allocated to specific groups of people for use for

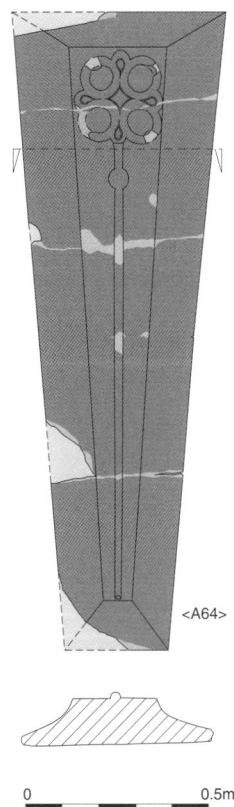

Fig 38 *Purbeck marble grave slab <A64> (scale 1:20)*

burial. Both subsamples are very small; two and three individuals respectively, so any interpretation has to be made with caution, but there was no evidence of any significant differences between them (Chapter 7.11, 'Methods', '1222–c 1300 (period M2)', 'The church (B1)'). The only notable difference between the two groups was the high rate of alveolar resorption and periodontal disease in those in the south transept compared to all other subsamples, and an absence of the two conditions in those from the north transept. However, this is most likely simply a product of the very small sample size and the presence of the older individual in the south transept as both can be age-related conditions.

A slype (B3f)

A 2m-wide passage or 'slype', 14m long, occupied the position that would have been taken up by the south bay of the south transept if the north and south transepts had been symmetrical (Fig 34). The slype was perhaps structurally part of the south transept. The slype north wall foundation, 1.0m thick by 0.7m deep and constructed from flint and occasional Reigate stone [707], was narrower than the east wall of the transept, and than the walls of the north transept. Nor did the north wall reach the east transept wall, suggesting access to the south-east corner of the transept there. Presumably there was also access to the cemetery to the east; to the west there would have been access to the cloister. The area could have been used as the sacristy and/or vestry. Its original floor levels (mortar [706], [713], [723]) became very worn and uneven and were relevelled with crushed Reigate stone [711]. Further refloorings in clay raised the floor level by c 0.2m. These levelling layers contained Kingston-type ware (KING) pottery post-dating c 1230. A further 20mm thick layer of mortar [609] formed the last floor surface or bedding layer during this period.

A lane/yard to the south of the nave (OA4)

To the south of the nave the cloister was not attached to the church; instead a lane or yard (OA4 in reduced form) apparently lay between the nave and the cloister (B3a/e) (Fig 34). There was no surviving evidence for a floored stone north alley to the cloisters or timber pentice here. Open Area 4 was presumably extended to the east over the demolished earlier (period M1) south transept.

The cloister (B3a/e)

Only the north-eastern corner, parts of the north and east garth walls of the cloister (B3a) and possible fragments of the south garth wall (B3e) were within the excavated area (Fig 34). The north wall of the north walk may have reused the earlier (period M1) south transept wall or its line, but this was completely robbed at the Dissolution or earlier and no in situ trace of such a wall was found. The north and east garth walls had also been heavily robbed but lengths of mortared flint and Reigate stone footings, 1.0–1.4m wide and bedded in orange

sand, remained. The north and east garth walls had c 1m-square buttresses at intervals of c 2–3m on the garth facade (OA10). The east cloister walk was c 3.5m wide and at least 18m north–south; the southern limit was beyond the excavation area. Its primary floor surface was of yellow mortar, with flint and chalk, bedded on sand.

A robbed flint foundation, 2.7+m long by 0.8m wide and approximately 0.5m deep (B3e), parallel to the north cloister walk may be the south garth wall, although it was considerably less substantial in the short length excavated than its northern counterparts. This may suggest that it was a later addition, or rather that it was part of a lavatorium or washing place within the garth or an internal wall in the south range, possibly the refectory. To the north of this was a parallel shallow (0.14m deep) gully.

An east–west footing composed of mortared flint rubble abutted the southernmost excavated buttress of the east cloister garth wall, giving the wall, buttress included, a length of 5.4m. The footing was 1.25m wide and there was evidence for a southern return at the west end. This return could only be traced for 0.5m before it reached the limit of excavation. These footings may be for a small building in the garth or to support a building over the south-east corner of the cloister. It is also possible that this wall formed the south garth wall of a much smaller cloister, but if this is the case it was a later addition with no buttresses on the garth facade.

THE CLOISTER GARTH (OA10)

If the walls noted above under Building 3a/e defined the garth, it measured excluding the garth walls, at least c 10m north–south (c 22m if B3e represents the south garth wall), and exceeded 7m east–west. Pottery dating to c 1230–c 1400 (KING) and a base fragment of a glass urinal (<7064>, <S279>) came from the mixed deposits within the garth.

A DRAIN IN THE CLOISTER (S6)

A small tile drain crossed the east cloister walk (B3a) and the north-east corner of the garth (OA10). It was built from horizontally laid, ceramic roof tiles, up to eight courses deep on the sides and three to four deep along the base, bonded in a white mortar. As only a c 1m length was exposed, its full course is unknown.

The chapter house (B3b)

The chapter house lay immediately to the south of the slype (B3f) (Fig 34). It was rectangular and 15.18m by 7.56m internally. This corresponds closely to a 'double square' plan of 25ft x 50ft. The stone footings were set on yellow sand and gravel within a 1.8m-wide foundation trench. Construction rubble and black clay had been dumped into the trench before the overlying wall footings were constructed. These footings formed a 'cap' on the c 1.0m-thick construction rubble of flint and chalk bonded with a lime mortar. An earlier small clay-filled channel [797] (period M1; not illustrated) lay beneath the north wall and unstable ground in this location may have

41

been a reason for the wide chapter house foundations and a factor in the subsidence of the chapter house walls which is evident subsequently. Four small shallow external buttresses were constructed along the south wall. The base of the eastern portion of the north wall had slipped to the south, while the base of the western wall had slipped east. Construction debris around the walls contained Kingston-type ware (KING) pottery ([849]; [858]) dating the construction to after *c* 1230.

The internal decoration is hinted at by fragments of pinkish-white painted wall plaster from a robbed grave, while fragments of coloured and painted window glass, including <S80> and <S82> (Fig 39) from the fills of a later (period M3) grave adjacent to the chapter house, may derive from windows that illuminated the east end of the chapter house during this period. Both illustrated pieces have complex outlines; <S80> is painted with the knee and lower leg of a human figure, possibly clothed.

No *in situ* floor layers were identified, but a large number of floor tiles were found within the trench that robbed the chapter house north wall at the Dissolution (period P1). The tiles include decorated (<T1>–<T24>, Fig 40) and plain (<T25>–<T34>, Fig 41) glazed mosaic floor tiles. The decorative designs are highly elaborate with detailed

representations of humans and animals, including a magnificent circular frieze showing a continuous line of robed figures. The decorated tiles probably formed the central part of the floor in the mid 13th century; they were badly worn and presumably in a prominent position. Few mosaic tile shapes remain to

Fig 39 Painted window glass <S80> and <S82> (scale c 1:1)

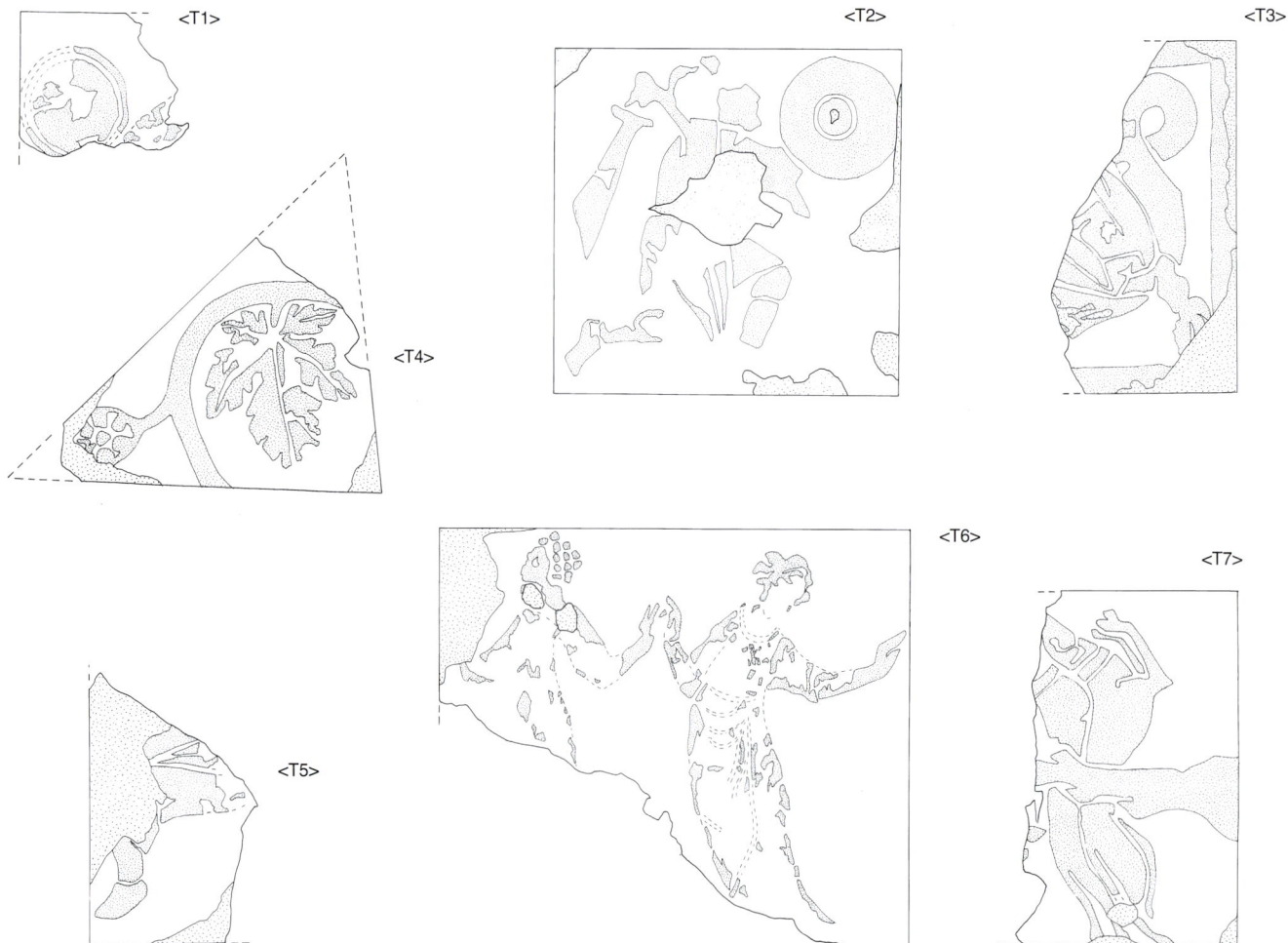

Fig 40 Decorated mosaic floor tiles <T1>–<T24> (scale 1:3)

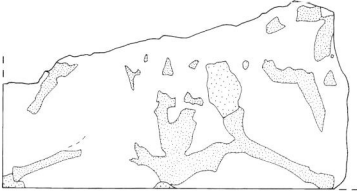

<T8>

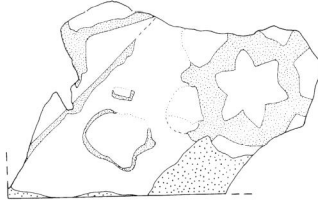

<T9>

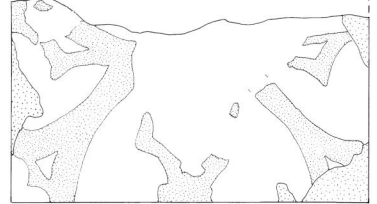

<T10>

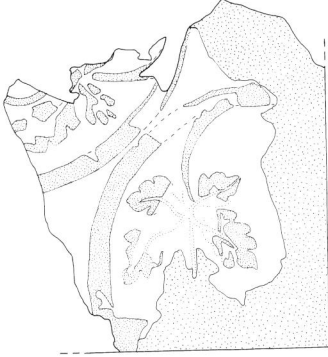

<T11>

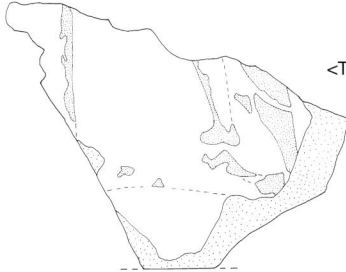

<T12>

<T13>

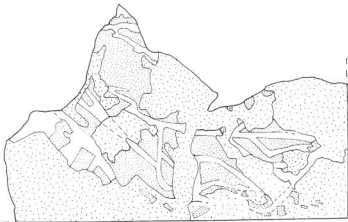

<T14>

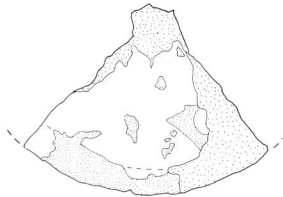

<T15>

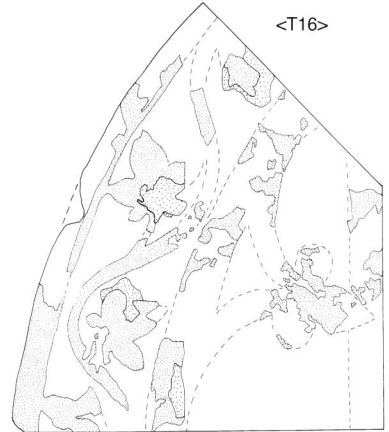

<T16>

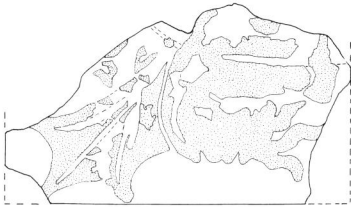

<T17>

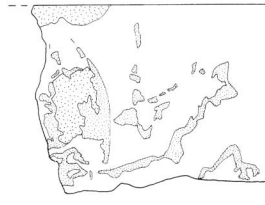

<T18>

<T19>

<T20>

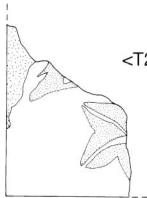

<T21>

<T22>

<T23>

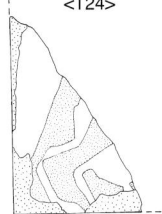

<T24>

decorative slip

lost/damaged surface

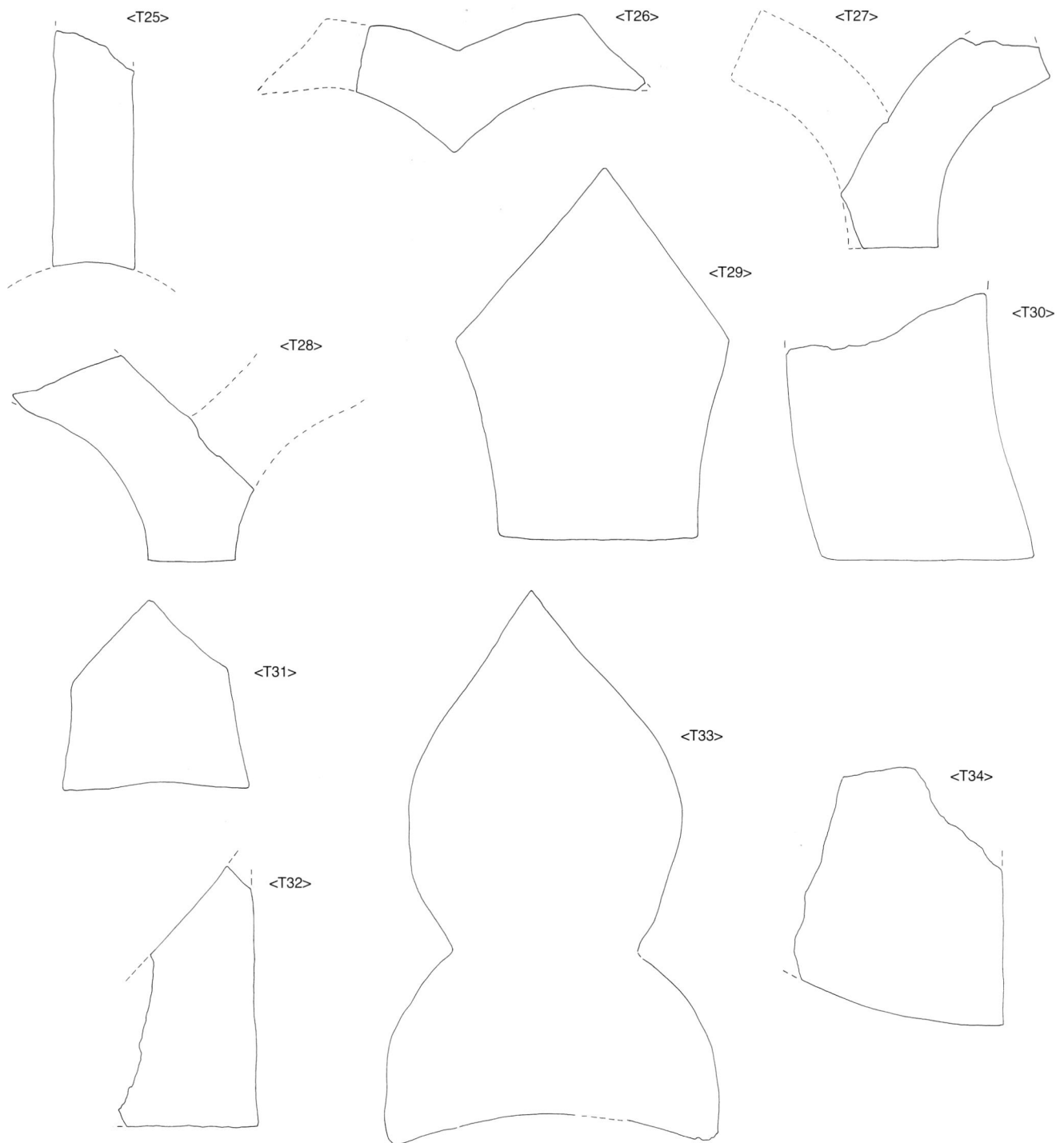

Fig 41 Plain-glazed mosaic tiles <T25>–<T34> (scale 1:3)

complete the floor pattern, but at least two plain forms <T26> and <T33> can be placed together (<T35>, Fig 193). Building debris associated with later, period M3, modifications to the chapter house included plain and decorated, 'Westminster' floor tiles (<T60>; Betts 2002, type W53) of 13th-century date. These are also likely to have derived from this floor.

Nine burials were interred within the eastern and northern parts of the chapter house. Three burial types were evident: cist burials, burials within wooden coffins and graves with no lining. The sequence suggests that those graves to the north were earliest, followed by a row from north to south, along the

east wall. When the east end was full, the next grave [582] was placed further west but in line with grave [578] at the east end. These graves were generally disturbed or truncated by later building activity. Grave [582] contained the disarticulated bones of a male adult [677] piled up within the eastern end of the grave. The skeletons from the other graves may have been removed during building work in the 14th century (period M3) and placed within a charnel pit located to the east of the chapter house in Open Area 3. Only three complete or near-complete skeletons, all male, survived for analysis: one was a mature adult and the others were older adults.

Fig 42 *Reigate cist burial [7493] (OA3, period M2), with lid in place; south is to the top (0.5m scale)*

The positioning of the southernmost graves, about 1m from the south wall, suggests a bench along the wall.

The east range (B3c–d)

The east range was subsequently extended southwards from the chapter house. Only partially robbed footings, c 1m wide and of flint bonded with orange sand, survived (Fig 34). The range is likely to have extended as far south as the reredorter (B5; Fig 57) and to have been c 50–60m long. However, only the northernmost 6m lay within the excavation. Here the ground floor was divided into two rooms, with the western walk of the infirmary cloister (B4c) on its eastern side. The northernmost room (B3c), only c 3.0m wide, was possibly a parlour or a slype leading to the infirmary cloister; the southern room (B3d) may have been the canons' day room or a warming room (originally the only room in a monastery, other than the infirmary and kitchen, where a fire was permitted).

The monastic cemetery

SOUTH BURIAL AREA (OA3)

The western part of the area was now covered by the south transept and chapter house and delimited to the south by the infirmary complex (see below), but the eastern boundary remains unknown, as does any northern boundary if the area was physically separated from Open Area 6 (Fig 34).

The area was covered by a general deposit of brown clayey silt [666], [7425], [7757], interspersed or overlain by construction debris [7740], [7698], which included Kingston-type ware (KING) pottery post-dating c 1230. A total of 29 burials cut these deposits and 22 were available for osteological analysis. Eighteen were male, of whom nine were mature adults and nine older adults. The sex of four, aged as adult, could not be determined.

Individuals were laid supine with their heads to the west. No clear rows were identified; the burials were mainly clustered

immediately south-east of the presbytery. Four were interred in cist graves, including burial [7493] (an older adult male) within a cist made of 19 Reigate stone blocks, tooled on the inner face, with a lid constructed from large Reigate stone blocks (Fig 42; Fig 43). Burial [7455] (an older adult male)

Fig 43 *Reigate cist burial [7493] (OA3, period M2), with lid removed, looking west (0.5m scale)*

was interred in a ?sandstone cist built from 16 blocks including one block shaped to fit around the individual's head. Burial [7510] (a mature adult male) was also interred in a cist of ?sandstone blocks. Two empty cist graves were also noted. Cist [7403] consisted of a number of disturbed Reigate stone blocks, while, although truncated, the extant portion of [7435], constructed from seven chamfered blocks, six of sandstone and one of Reigate stone, was fairly intact. Burial [7512] (an older adult male) was interred in the partial remains of a wooden coffin and another older adult male [7401] lay within a monolithic stone coffin [7400], 2.2m long, and thought to be carved from sandstone (Fig 44). It had a central elliptical drainage hole in the base and walls 50–90mm thick.

NORTH BURIAL AREA (OA6)

The repositioning of the north transept meant that part of the original (period M1) area was lost beneath the church (Fig

Fig 44 Burial [7401] in a ?sandstone coffin (OA3, period M2), looking west (1.0m scale)

34). The boundaries of the cemetery, other than the church walls, were not defined. The northern limit was ambiguous: nine burials were found c 12m north of the transept but no interments that far north were encountered further east. On the contrary, Road 2 may have marked or lain beyond the northern edge here. Nor were other burials located between the transept and this group, which may suggest a separate burial area. The burials within this apparently discrete group were supine, with their heads to the west; they appeared to be shroud burials although a mature adult male [3499] may have been interred in a coffin. Graves [3541], an older male, and [3555], a mature male were buried relatively deeply. The grave bases in the rest of Open Area 6 were at 11.73–12.07m OD compared to 11.72–12.26m OD in this area. The pottery recovered from grave fills dated to c 1230–c 1400, but may all have been redeposited.

Deposits of crushed Reigate stone, sand and mortar to the north of the transept and east of the presbytery were possible residues from the rebuilding of the church. Other layers [3468], [3528], [3469] and [3550] to the north are possibly evidence of demolition although well away from the church; they may also represent stone dressing. These dated to c 1230–c 1400 and pre-dated one section of Road 2. The pottery recovered from graves and cemetery soils, such as [2318], again dated to c 1230–c 1400 (KING). A copper-alloy buckle (<S215>, Fig 45) was recovered from this deposit [2318], while layer [4269] to the north of the church contained a strapend (<S242>, Fig 45).

Eighty-nine burials, including one small charnel pit, cut these deposits. Twenty-nine to the east were cut or overlain by the later (period M3) church. Others were cut or sealed by later interments or deposits. With the exception of the group of nine burials mentioned above, interments were concentrated to the east of the transept where 80 graves were recorded. Some rough rows were evident and most graves were parallel to the west–east axis of the church, although a slight rotation to the north-west and occasionally to the south-west did occur. Two graves were empty. One burial to the north-east, a mature adult male [4503], was prone (Fig 46). The body had been laid with its arms crossed under the chest. The feet, at 0.3m apart, were a little splayed, suggesting the body was not interred in a shroud. No evidence of a coffin survived. The remaining 77 burials were supine, with their heads to the west. The arms were

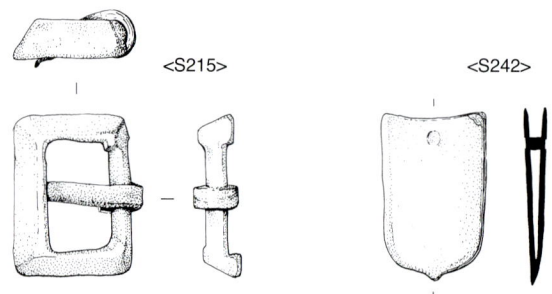

Fig 45 Copper-alloy buckle <S215> and strapend <S242> (OA6, period M2) (scale 1:1)

Fig 46 Prone burial [4503] (OA6, period M2), looking west (1.0m scale)

generally by the side but occasionally placed over the body with the hands resting on the pelvis and at times crossed.

Seven graves contained traces of wooden coffins in the form of cover planks or cover and container. A double burial contained an older adult male [4647] and probable mature adult male [4649], beneath one or more planks or a plank structure (Fig 47). Burials [4655] and [4658], both mature males, were also covered by planks, as were [4286] (older adult male) and [4498] (adult female). An oak plank, dendrochronologically dated to after 1107 (Table 71), also covered mature adult male burial [4530] and three Reigate stone blocks surrounded the head area (Fig 48). The 'coffin' of [4673] (unsexed adult) was unusually wide (0.8m) in relation to the body and yet too short (Fig 49). The body was placed in a wooden container and overlaid by four overlapping wooden planks laid lengthwise, supported by a thin crosspiece and, at the eastern end, by a plank secured over (Chapter 4.10, 'Burial practice', 'Wooden coffins').

There were three cist burials. A mature adult male [4226] was in a cist of chalk blocks tooled on the faces lining the burial but otherwise unworked suggesting they were cut for the burial (Fig 50). Burial [2378], an adult, was in a cist of flint nodules set in clay roughly shaped around the head and possibly sealed by a lid. A young adult male [2577] was interred in a grave lined with small fragments of chalk set in mortar.

Eighty-three individuals were available for analysis. These included two children, aged 1–6 years and 7–12 years. Males made up 68.7% of the subsample. Of these 57 individuals, 4 were young adults, 30 were mature adults, 19 were older adults and 4 could not be aged any more precisely than adult. Twelve

Fig 47 Double burial [4647] and [4649] beneath wooden planks (OA6, period M2), looking west (1.0m scale)

females were present: 6 mature adults, 5 older adults and 1 could not be aged. There were also 12 individuals of indeterminate sex. One of these could be aged as a young adult, eight as adult, one as immature. It was not possible to assign any age estimate to two individuals.

A small (c 1.0m x 0.5m), roughly rectangular charnel pit [4465] lay north of the presbytery and contained pottery dated to c 1230–c 1400 (KING). The disarticulated human bone probably came from this cemetery.

Small-scale, copper alloy casting waste was found in the form of residues varying in weight between 4.5g and 478g ([2318]; [3510]; [3511]; [3741]), the largest fragment in a pit to the north (<S302> [3510]). Iron-working slag occurred, redeposited, in two graves, [2560] and [3526]. Burial [2309] contained three pieces of slag <S313>, with a total weight of c 1kg. These suggest small-scale metalworking around the church, possibly on the periphery of the cemetery.

POSSIBLE CEMETERY PATHS (R1, R2) IN THE NORTH BURIAL AREA (OA6)
The east–west path across Open Area 6 was partially covered by construction debris and tread (the latter, [4012], containing pottery dating to c 1230–c 1400, KING), and then remetalled (R1; Fig 34).

The construction debris in Open Area 6 was sealed by a thick east–west deposit of chalk with probable wheel ruts along the length. This deposit contained pottery dating to c 1230–c 1400 (KING), and may have been used for the construction of the church, but could be later. Evidence of copper alloy casting in the form of a small (14g) piece of copper alloy <S305> was recovered from the path (R2).

Fig 48 Burial [4530] with covering plank and Reigate stone blocks around the head (OA6, period M2), looking west (1.0m scale)

Fig 49 The large wooden container of burial [4673] (OA6, period M2), looking west (0.5m scale)

The infirmary hall (B4a)

The flint foundations of the infirmary hall defined a rectangular, north–south building with internal dimensions of *c* 30m by 9.5m (Fig 34; Fig 51; Fig 57). This was on the east side of the infirmary cloister (B4c). Two rows of seven, 1m deep, square flint and mortar bases were found within the building. At ground level, square recesses lined with blocks of Reigate stone were set into each base surface to hold vertical timber posts 0.21–0.30m square. The posts divided the building into eight north–south bays; the six central bays being *c* 4m wide and the end two *c* 3m wide. The width of the building was divided into two narrower aisles flanking a wider central area. The doorway to the infirmary cloister was in the third bay from the south.

Construction debris and make-up contained pottery post-dating *c* 1230 (KING). The earliest floor surfaces were represented by patchy areas of white mortar, chalk and crushed Reigate stone; these would probably have been covered with rushes and/or sedges, whose seeds were recovered in samples in the infirmary area from several periods (including the infirmary cloister garth in period M2 and the infirmary hall in period M3) (Chapter 7.6). A fragment of a copper-alloy sacring bell (<S50>, Fig 52), a bell rung when the host was elevated at Mass, came from a floor surface [1081] (cf Biddle and Hinton 1990, 725–7).

Fig 50 *Burial [4226] in a cist of chalk blocks (OA6, period M2), looking west (0.5m scale)*

Fig 51 *The infirmary hall (B4a) after excavation, looking south (2.0m scales)*

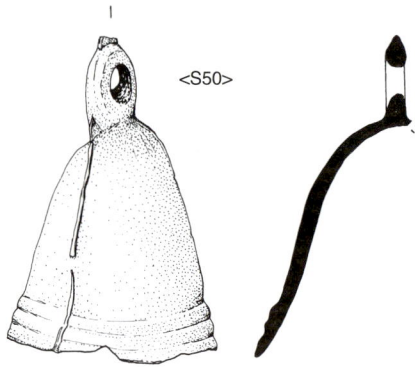

Fig 52 *A copper-alloy sacring bell fragment <S50>, from the infirmary hall (B4a) (scale 1:1)*

A hearth [1047], 1.84m north–south by 1.22m east–west by 0.28m high, built from roof tiles set pitched at 45° in clay packing (Fig 53) was positioned roughly central, in the fourth bay from the north. The hearth produced an archaeomagnetic date of AD 1220 ± 20 (Clark and Simmonds nd). A line of four Reigate stone blocks [1107], [1096], [1097] and [1100], close to the hearth, may represent foundations for a cupboard against the west wall. The blocks, of average size 250mm by 200mm by 70mm thick, were at c 2m intervals, c 1m from the wall. A nearby north–south slot, 2.5m long by 60mm wide by 50mm deep and filled with crushed chalk, may represent the position of a timber screen.

A short length of in situ lead pipe, set in clay, crossed the infirmary hall west to east from the infirmary cloister doorway to the infirmary kitchen (B6). The direction of flow was eastwards and this water pipe was almost certainly a continuation of a robbed pipe found in the infirmary cloister garth (OA5), and related to a robbed feature there, possibly a storage cistern or a laver (below, 'The infirmary cloister garth (OA5)').

Evidence for the superstructure of the infirmary hall is slight. Fragments of window glazing and lead, recovered from debris created by the repair and partitioning of the infirmary hall in the 14th century (period M3), possibly come from the windows of the 13th-century infirmary hall (and see below, 'The infirmary chapel (B4b)'). The glass included plain green, and painted geometric (perhaps border) and foliate designs (<S160>–<S162>, <S164> Fig 54, <S165>). One blue fragment (with similarities to <S80> and <S82>, Fig 39) was a complex shape with traces of painted ?wing (<S163>, Fig 54).

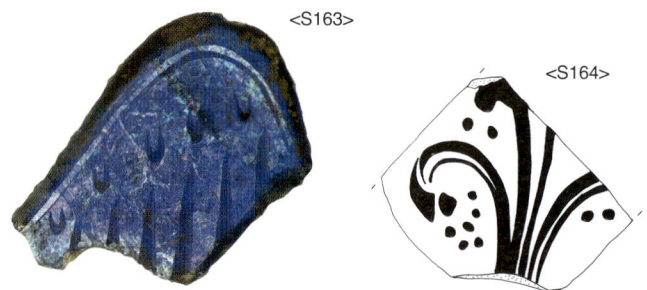

Fig 54 *Painted window glass <S163> (scale c 1:1) and <S164> (scale 1:2)*

Fig 53 *The pitched tile hearth (right) within the infirmary hall (B4a), with the infirmary cloister eastern walk (B4c) to the left (period M2), looking north (2.0m scale)*

Fig 55 *The west end of the infirmary chapel (B4b, period M2), looking south (1.0m scale)*

The infirmary chapel (B4b)

At the northern end of the infirmary hall lay its chapel (Fig 34; Fig 55), aligned east–west at right angles to the hall, 17.85m long by 6.75m wide internally. The flint and chalk foundations of the north wall were buttressed externally. The buttress spacing suggests the north facade was split into three equal bays. Postholes, probably for scaffolding, were found around the buttresses (Fig 56). The chapel entrance was at the west end.

Within the chapel, a silt layer [5787] was laid sloping down from the west door by 0.15m, forming a ramp. Above this a 10mm thick mortar layer [5776] was cut by flint and chalk foundation walls for stalls, set c 1m within the main foundations; further make-up of chalk, mortar and crushed Reigate stone was then laid. The nature of the floor above is unknown. The stalls, 0.35m wide by 0.25m deep and at least c 10m east–west, extended around (with the exception of the west door) the excavated western two-thirds of the interior but were apparently absent within the excavated north-east corner.

A fragment of window glass painted with a geometric design <S172>, from a later deposit (period M3) in the infirmary cloister walk (B4c) close to the chapel (B4b), may have formed part of the glazing of either the chapel or the infirmary hall (above) during this period.

The infirmary cloister (B4c)

The western infirmary cloister walk was formed by a passage, up to 4m wide, immediately east of the east range (B3c–d) (Fig

Fig 56 *The north wall of the infirmary chapel (B4b, period M2), showing the postholes for ?scaffolding, looking east (1.0m scale)*

51

34). A robbed foundation and wall [5988] formed the garth wall here and adjoining this, at the southern limit of excavation, was a base, possibly for an arch or a porch. This walk was partly floored with roof tiles [5961], which survived along the eastern edge. A trampled silt [5960] and a flint and mortar metalled floor [5945] both contained pottery sherds of London-type ware (LOND), with a date range of c 1080–c 1350. An east–west wall trench, between the chapter house and the infirmary chapel, may be the garth wall of the north walk but was obscured by the cloister wall built later (period M3) making interpretation difficult. Further east, close to the infirmary chapel was a pit [5793] filled with flint and Reigate stone, as well as two further pits [5794] and [5903], both filled with flints in a clayey silt. These may represent the robbing of foundations associated with the north-east corner of the garth walls. The east garth wall survived as two further robbing pits [1105], [1102] and a wall trench [1093]. No trace of a south walk was found. The walks on the east and north sides were c 2.5m wide. Within the walks the floor surfaces were largely of patchy mortar on sand and crushed Reigate stone. The lower make-up deposits for these contained vertebrate faunal remains discarded as food waste, mainly the major domesticates with a substantial component of chicken and some goose (Table 5). There were occasional bones of passerine birds, fallow deer and rabbit, and fish (gadids, and clupeids with one thornback ray). This suggests a varied, good quality diet with occasional higher-status consumption. Much of this assemblage was recovered from outside the infirmary hall entrance and may represent general waste clearance into the walk.

Table 5 *Recovery of hand-collected vertebrate fauna from the infirmary cloister walk (B4c, period M2), by fragment count*

Common name	Latin name	No. of frags	%
Fish			
Fish unidentified		2	0.4
Thornback ray	*Raja clavata*	I	0.2
Cod family	Gadidae	2	0.4
Cod-sized		2	0.4
Birds			
Bird unidentified		I	0.2
Chicken	*Gallus gallus*	I5	3.4
Chicken-sized		I	0.2
Goose	*Anser anser*	5	I.I
Thrush unidentified	*Turdidae*	I	0.2
Mammals			
Mammal unidentified		I90	42.7
Cattle	*Bos taurus*	8	I.8
Cattle-sized		30	6.7
Sheep/goat	*Ovis aries/Capra hircus*	38	8.5
Sheep-sized		I00	22.5
Pig	*Sus scrofa*	46	I0.3
Fallow deer	*Dama dama*	I	0.2
Deer unidentified	Cervidae	I	0.2
Rabbit	*Oryctolagus cuniculus*	I	0.2
Total		**445**	

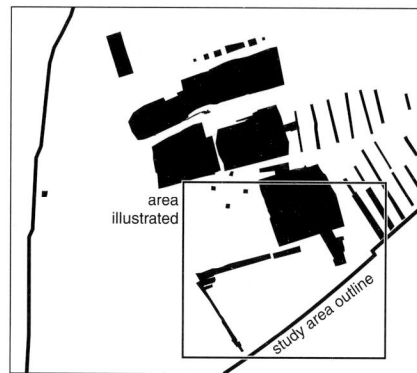

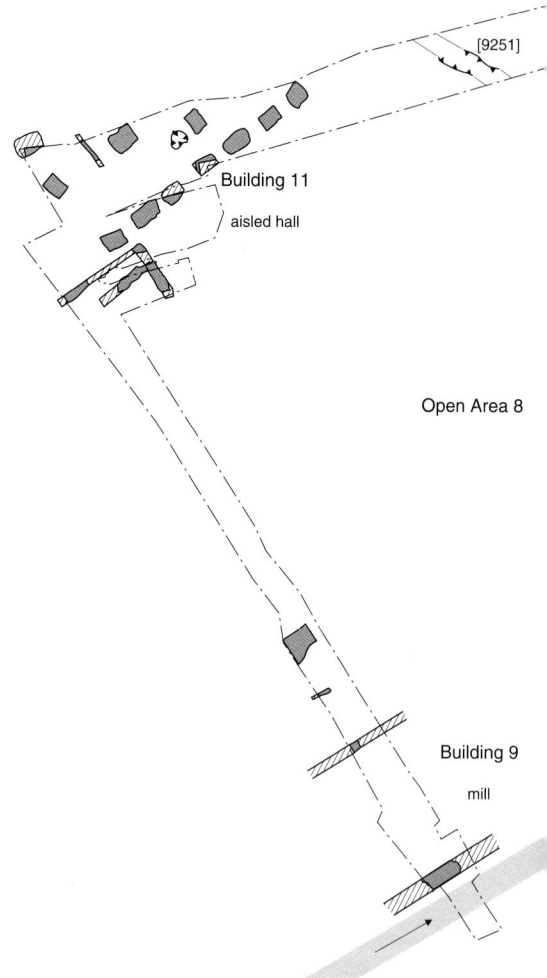

The infirmary cloister garth (OA5)

The infirmary cloister garth, a reduced Open Area 5, formed an area c 32m north–south by 15+m east–west (Fig 34; Fig 57). Within the garth were clay and silt deposits containing a

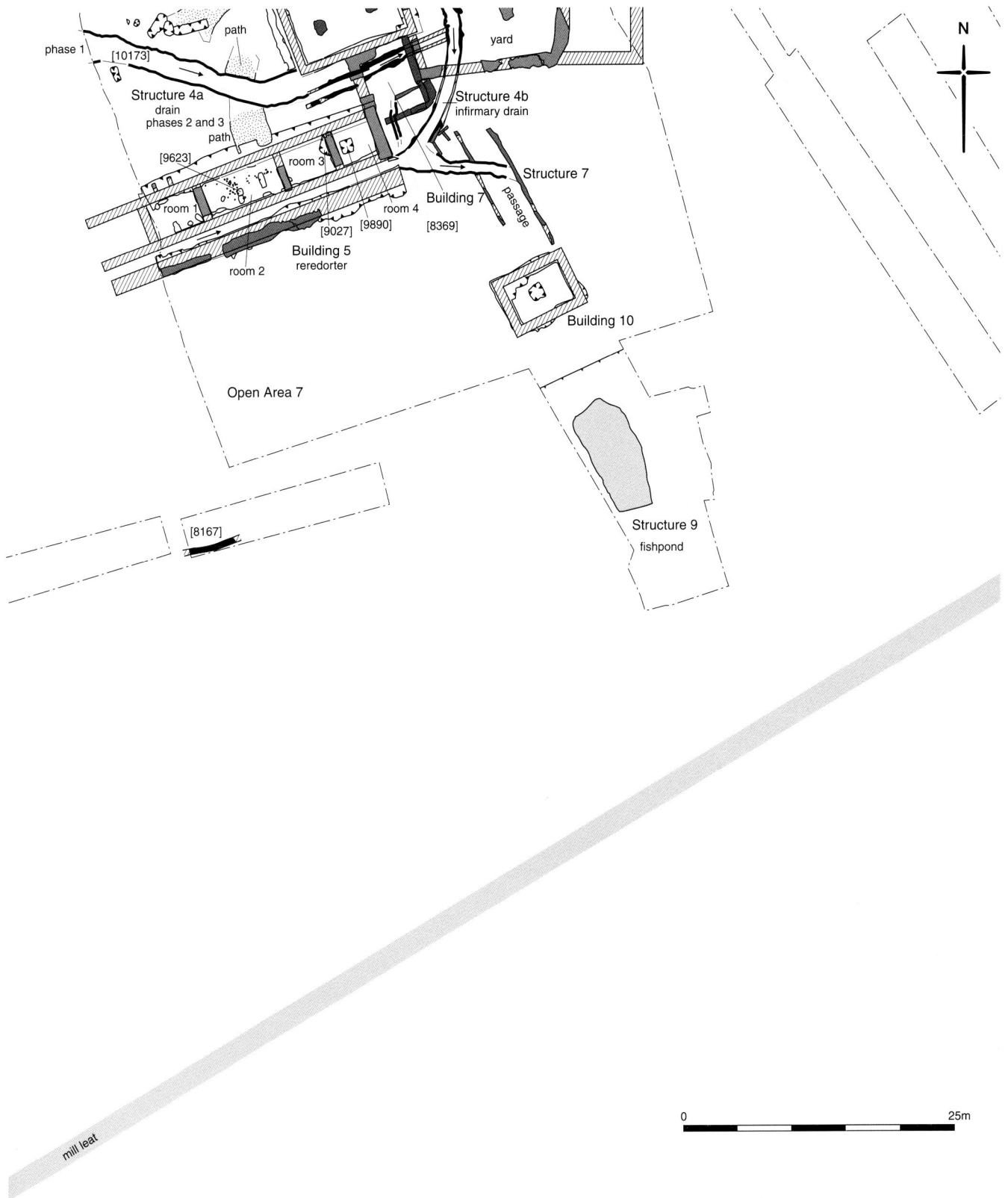

N

phase 1
[10173]

Structure 4a
drain
phases 2 and 3
path

[9623]

room 3

room 1

[9027] [9890]
room 4
Building 5
reredorter
room 2

yard

Structure 4b
infirmary drain

Building 7

[8369]

passage

Structure 7

Building 10

Open Area 7

[8167]

Structure 9
fishpond

0   25m

mill leat

Fig 57 Plan of principal archaeological features in the south part of the precinct, 1222 to c 1300 (period M2) (scale 1:500)

distinctive Earlswood-type ware (EARL) jug handle <P1> (Fig 58) and a shank of an iron ?casket key <S196>; these were sealed by a possible cobbled floor surface and further layers of clay and silt, dated by Kingston-type ware (KING) pottery to c 1230–c 1400.

A path crossed the garth from the west doorway of the infirmary hall. This sealed deposits of burnt clay and charcoal overlain by silt containing pottery dated to c 1230–c 1400

53

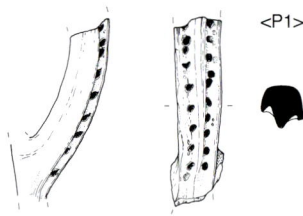

Fig 58 *Stabbed and moulded Earlswood-type ware jug handle <P1> (from OA5)* *(scale 1:4)*

(KING), a large quantity of oyster shells, a pair of copper-alloy tweezers <S255>, and a concentration of animal bone outside the infirmary hall entrance. These deposits represent rubbish disposal from the infirmary hall into the cloister. The path make-up above was of clay (with pottery dated to c 1230– c 1400: KING), sand, silt and gravel. The surface was of crushed Reigate stone, mortar and pebbles. Cutting the path was an east–west trench [10187] containing clay packing around a 50mm wide round void, suggesting a robbed lead pipe, a continuation of that found in the infirmary hall. At the western end of the path were two pits. These may represent the robbed remains of a laver (or washing place or basin), or of another feature related to water supply or disposal, such as a storage cistern or dipping-tank (Bond 2001, 96–9). A second path, of compacted brown silt overlain by clayey gravel [10403], led into the garth from room 2 of the reredorter (B5). The drainage ditch which ran south-east across the infirmary cloister garth, before turning east to pass between the reredorter and the infirmary hall, is discussed separately (below, S4a).

An abundance of vertebrate fauna (1416 fragments) recovered from the garth forms a diverse assemblage (Table 6), comparable to that from the infirmary kitchen (B6) (see below). Although unidentifiable mammal and 'sheep-sized' mammal fragments provided the main component of the fragment count, the identifiable material was dominated by pig with smaller counts of sheep/goat and then cattle. There were substantial components of chicken and, to a lesser extent, goose, with occasional common partridge, roe deer, brown hare and rabbit; the only fish recovered in this hand-collected assemblage was cod.

A drainage ditch (S4a) flowing east from the infirmary garth (OA5)

A drainage ditch ran south-east across the infirmary cloister garth before turning east to pass between the reredorter and the infirmary hall; the flow was eastwards (Fig 34; Fig 57). There appeared to be three phases.

PHASE 1
Its earliest phase [10173], a ditch 17.88+m in length and 1.5–2.0m wide by 0.4–0.7m in depth, was severely truncated but appeared to pre-date the south wall of the infirmary hall (B4a). Its lower fills contained a buzz bone (<S31>, Fig 59) carved from a pig metapodial – buzz bones were put on a

Table 6 *Recovery of hand-collected vertebrate fauna from the infirmary cloister garth (OA5, period M2), by fragment count*

Common name	Latin name	No. of frags	%
Fish			
Cod family	Gadidae	2	0.1
Amphibian			
Frog/toad	Ranidae	1	<0.1
Birds			
Chicken	*Gallus gallus*	53	3.7
Chicken-sized		1	<0.1
Goose	*Anser anser*	29	2.0
Goose-sized		2	0.1
Partridge, grey	*Perdix perdix*	1	<0.1
Mammals			
Mammal unidentified		368	26.0
Cattle	*Bos taurus*	98	6.9
Cattle-sized		106	7.7
Sheep/goat	*Ovis aries/Capra hircus*	182	12.9
Sheep	*Ovis aries*	8	0.6
Goat	*Capra hircus*	3	0.2
Sheep-sized		305	21.5
Pig	*Sus scrofa*	247	17.4
Dog	*Canis familiaris*	1	<0.1
Cat	*Felis catus*	1	<0.1
Deer, roe	*Capreolus capreolus*	1	<0.1
Hare, brown	*Lepus europaeus*	6	0.4
Rabbit	*Oryctolagus cuniculus*	1	<0.1
Total		1416	

length of string that was twisted by hand to produce a whirring noise – in addition to 12th-century pottery which included sherds from an imported blue-grey ware (BLGR) ladle (<P2>, Fig 60). The freshwater molluscs present indicate that the water within the ditch was slow flowing ([10255], Table 49) and it appears to have functioned as an open surface drain. A large dump of oyster shells ([10176], Table 49) was possibly kitchen waste. Pottery recovered from this dump dates to c 1150–c 1300 (calcareous London-type ware (LCALC), coarse London-type ware (LCOAR), London-type ware (LOND),

Fig 59 *Buzz bone <S31> (from S4a, phase 1) (scale c 1:1)*

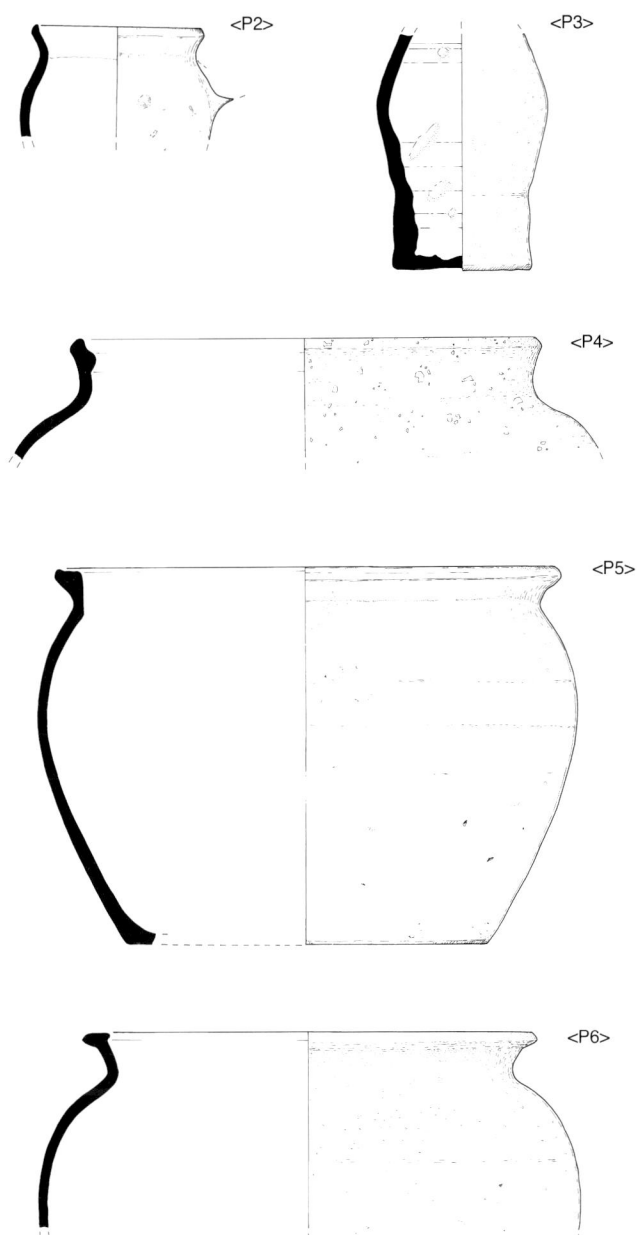

Fig 60 *Pottery from the drainage ditch (S4a): phase 1 — a blue-grey ware ladle <P2>; phase 2 — a coarse London-type ware jug <P3>, and cooking pots in early medieval shell-tempered ware <P4>, Limpsfield-type ware <P5> and coarse Limpsfield-type ware <P6> (scale 1:4)*

south Hertfordshire-type greyware (SHER), shelly-sandy ware (SSW)). A second sacring bell <S51> was recovered from this ditch. The first phase may, therefore, belong more correctly to period M1.

PHASE 2

The eastern part of the ditch, between the infirmary and the reredorter, was recut [9975], being 16.77m long by 1.60m wide as found. The western part contained timber stakes driven at approximately 35° to form a V-shaped revetted drain, *c* 0.8m wide at its base. Further east the sides became vertical and the base dropped gently eastwards. The fills [10016], [9998] and [9974] contained animal bones, including chicken, ox,

sheep/goat, pig and occasional finds of rabbit and horse, and 12th- to 13th-century pottery (including in [9998] Kingston-type ware, KING), principally fragments from cooking vessels, including further blue-grey ware (BLGR) ladle fragments from at least four vessels, a coarse London-type ware (LCOAR) jug <P3> and cooking pots in early medieval shell-tempered ware (EMSH) <P4>, Limpsfield-type ware (LIMP) <P5> and coarse Limpsfield-type ware (LIMP COAR) <P6> (Fig 60). This assemblage would date the fill to *c* 1200–30. A sliver from a Norwegian stone hone <S271> was also recovered.

The base of the eastern end lay below the stone base of the infirmary drain (S4b) indicating this second phase pre-dated the infirmary drain, and again possibly dated to period M1. The eastward extent of the drain is unknown.

PHASE 3

The drain was again recut and lined with Reigate stone blocks [9981] packed with flint behind to form a channel 0.7m wide (Fig 61). The eastern end was now jointed into the infirmary drain, into which it drained, and the two were clearly contemporary. When the ? latrine/wash house (B7) was built, or later, a secondary wall was inserted along the west side of the infirmary drain to block the outflow of this drain into it.

Fig 61 *The flint backing of the drainage ditch (S4a phase 3, period M2) flowing east from the infirmary garth, looking west (2.0m scale)*

The infirmary kitchen (B6)

The infirmary kitchen (Fig 34; Fig 62) abutted the east wall of the infirmary hall (B4a). Only the southern part was excavated. It measured c 10m east–west by at least 9m north–south. The wall construction trenches were filled with orange sand with occasional flint and chalk. Two flint and chalk column bases, 0.6m², were set 3.2m apart and aligned north–south. The alignment was slightly to the west of the kitchen's centre line. Water was supplied to the kitchen by the lead water pipe crossing the infirmary hall. Other functions for this building may be suggested, such as the infirmarer's lodging or a bloodletting house, but it is identified here as the infirmary kitchen.

Floor levels with silty surfaces [10358], [10955], [10957], produced pottery post-dating c 1230 (KING). Part of a carved lion's head label stop (<A9>, Fig 63) was found within these floors and dated stylistically to c 1120–c 1250. Fresh and unabraded, with the top cut as if to take a stone dressing, it may have decorated the interior of the kitchen. Food waste from the floors was largely fragmented and unidentifiable bird and mammal bones (Table 7; Table 8). The identifiable material

Fig 62 Pitched tile hearth in the infirmary kitchen with (centre) the infirmary drain, looking west; the infirmary hall lies beyond

<A9>

Fig 63 Sculpted label stop <A9>, carved in the shape of a lion's head (scale c 1:2)

was dominated by ox, sheep/goat and pig, with a smaller component of chicken and goose and occasional recovery of game species, wild duck and brown hare. The fish were mainly clupeids and smelt, with fewer gadids and occasional gurnard, plaice/flounder, mackerel, conger eel, salmon and cyprinids.

The columns were subsequently removed and the roof or upper floor presumably modified accordingly. The label stop may have been discarded at this point. New floor levels, generally successive layers of crushed Reigate stone, sand, chalk and mortar, were laid, but a surface of flint cobbles [10409] was inserted to the north. This floor was heavily smeared with charcoal [10277], possibly burnt fuel raked out of hearths; a few charred cereal grains were also found (Chapter 7.6; [10277], Table 42). A varied assemblage of roughly equal counts of clupeids, gadids, smelt, plaice/flounder, eel, gurnard and a single salmonid was recovered from these surfaces; this assemblage probably represents the refuse deposited during the resurfacing of the kitchen.

The kitchen was again resurfaced with mortar and this time with roof tiles, and then again by mortar, chalk and crushed Reigate stone. The peg roof tiles all roughly measure 186–195mm in breadth by 11–17mm in thickness. These are all of standard two round nail hole type, with splash glaze present on the bottom third of many examples. There are no tiles with a complete length, but other priory tiles of this breadth are 293–302mm in length.

The latest trampled floor was a fine silt with charcoal. A large number of black mustard (Brassica nigra) seeds recovered from this floor ([9636], Table 42) may have been used as a spice or for medicinal purposes (Chapter 7.6). Further food waste included animal and fish bones dominated by clupeids (including herring), with some chicken, eel, cyprinids and smelt, and gadid bones.

The eastern part of the kitchen was partitioned by a short (1.5m long) east–west aligned wall footing constructed from flint, Reigate stone and tile ([10352]; Fig 34). To the south of the partition was a tiled hearth constructed from vertically set roof tiles.

Table 7 Recovery of hand-collected vertebrate fauna from the infirmary kitchen (B6, period M2), by fragment count

Common name	Latin name	No. of frags	%
Birds			
Bird unidentified		4	1.7
Chicken	Gallus gallus	14	6.1
Goose, domestic	Anser anser	2	0.9
Duck unidentified	Anatidae	1	0.4
Mammals			
Mammal unidentified		28	12.2
Cattle	Bos taurus	7	3.0
Cattle-sized		25	10.9
Sheep/goat	Ovis aries/Capra hircus	25	10.9
Sheep	Ovis aries	1	0.4
Sheep-sized		98	42.6
Pig	Sus scrofa	21	9.1
Horse	Equus caballus	1	0.4
Dog	Canis familiaris	1	0.4
Hare, brown	Lepus europaeus	1	0.4
Rat unidentified	Rattus sp	1	0.4
Total		230	

Table 8 Recovery of wet-sieved vertebrate fauna from the infirmary kitchen (B6, period M2), by fragment count

Common name	Latin name	No. of frags	%
Fish			
Fish unidentified		1	0.4
Herring family	Clupeidae	73	26.9
Herring	Clupea harengus	3	1.1
Salmon family	Salmonidae	1	0.4
Smelt	Osmerus eperlanus	51	18.8
Carp family	Cyprinidae	2	0.7
Cod family	Gadidae	6	2.2
Gurnard	Triglidae	2	0.7
Plaice/flounder	Pleuronectidae	2	0.7
Conger eel	Conger conger	1	0.4
Eel	Anguilla anguilla	6	2.2
Mackerel	Scomber scombrus	1	0.4
Amphibian			
Frog/toad	Ranidae	2	0.7
Birds			
Bird unidentified		17	6.3
Chicken	Gallus gallus	4	1.5
Chicken-sized		13	4.8
Goose, domestic	Anser anser	1	0.4
Passerine		3	1.1
Passerine, large		1	0.4
Woodcock	Scolopax rusticola	1	0.4
Mammals			
Mammal unidentified		55	20.3
Cattle-sized		1	0.4
Sheep/goat	Ovis aries/Capra hircus	1	0.4
Sheep-sized		16	5.9
Pig	Sus scrofa	3	1.1
Rabbit	Oryctolagus cuniculus	3	1.1
Mammal, small		1	0.4
Total		271	

Abutting the east wall were mortar floor surfaces and the remains of a narrow east–west Reigate stone wall footing, possibly for an extension to the kitchen to the north, perhaps a food preparation area, or delimiting the yard to the south (Fig 34). To the south of this, abutting the south-western corner of the infirmarer's ? lodging/kitchen (B8) and adjoining the ? latrine/wash house (B7, Fig 57), was an east–west flint wall constructed within a shallow foundation, 30–300mm deep, and probably a 'garden' wall rather than part of a building. To the north of this was a flint-pebbled surface. A number of burnt roof tiles, Reigate stone and flint [9356] in the middle may represent a hearth, dated to after c 1230 by Kingston-type ware (KING) pottery.

The infirmary drain (S4b)

The infirmary drain (Fig 64) flowed beneath the infirmary kitchen and yard, parallel with the infirmary hall. The base was made of Reigate stone slabs, each c 0.3m square, bedded in mortar. The sides, two courses of Reigate stone blocks overlain by flint and chalk, sat over the edge of the base slabs. The channel had an internal width of 0.8m and sloped gently southwards. A c 25m length of the drain was traced; south of the infirmary kitchen it turned south-westwards to join the outflow from the reredorter drain (B5).

The reredorter (B5)

Flint and mortar wall footings defined an east–west building on the south side of the infirmary cloister (Fig 57; Fig 65; Fig 66).

Fig 64 *An excavated length of the infirmary drain (S4b, period M2), looking north (1.0m scale)*

Fig 65 *The reredorter (B5, period M2) in the foreground, with the infirmary hall (B4a) behind (upper left), looking north (2.0m scales)*

Fig 66 *The reredorter (B5, period M2) and (lower right) the southern end of the infirmary hall (B4a), looking south-west*

The east end lay south of the infirmary hall and the west is likely to have abutted the southern end of the east range, that is the canons' dormitory. Thus the reredorter was probably c 27.8m long, although only the eastern 23m were excavated. This building would have had two floors, the ground floor being an undercroft divided into smaller rooms, with latrines above on the first floor. The building was 8m wide externally; the north wall was 0.8m thick but the south was 1.5m thick. Half the width of the ground floor, to the south, was occupied by the latrines' drop to the reredorter drain, while the northern half was occupied by rooms. Four ground floor rooms, numbered 1–4 from the west, were recorded. Room 2 was the largest, c 7m by 3m internally, at the centre of the building's conjectured length. A path across the infirmary cloister garth led towards this room suggesting a doorway into the reredorter here. Smaller rooms, room 3 (c 4m by 3m) and room 4 (c 3m square), were to the east. It is likely that a similar arrangement existed to the west but here only room 1 (c 4m by 3m) lay within the excavated area.

Masonry reused in buttress foundations when the reredorter was rebuilt (eg <5264>, <5272>, [8361]; period M3) is presumed to be from this reredorter. The Reigate stone undercroft would have had a barrel vault supported by heavy transverse ribs 242mm wide, chamfered for functional reasons and rather roughly executed (not illustrated). Two types of springer were recognised: one was angled to support a

segmental vault while the other supported a semicircular vault. In both cases, the ribs die into the wall face without ornament. The ribs were keyed into the vault web by a slight 'spine' on the reverse. A 1.18m-square column base [9890] was set in the western part of room 4, but the relationship with the presumed barrel vault remains obscure. Reigate stone lancet window fragments indicate at least four window heads and permit the reconstruction of a lancet opening (<A66>–<A68>, Fig 67). The tooling is unusually rough and can be broadly dated c 1200–75. The head was cut from a single block, apparently by eye. The wall was only 0.34m thick and the lancets were probably set within larger embrasures; the internal splays were whitewashed. The windows were presumably closed by timber shutters set into the external rebates. A piece of very corroded decorated glass <S184> (Fig 216) was recovered from floor surfaces in room 4. The windows presumably provided light and air to the first floor of the reredorter.

The extant floors within the four rooms were generally patches of mortar bedding layers. The presence of two decorated floor tiles – a 'Westminster' tile with design W136 (<T56>, Fig 197) and a keyed white slip group tile (design 4, <T43>, Fig 195) – along with a number of fragments of roof tile, suggests that at least one of these rooms was tiled. Equally, fairly large numbers of seeds of rush (Juncus spp) (in room 1) and sedge (Carex spp) (room 2) may represent the residues of flooring materials (Table 42). In room 1, a sherd of early Surrey

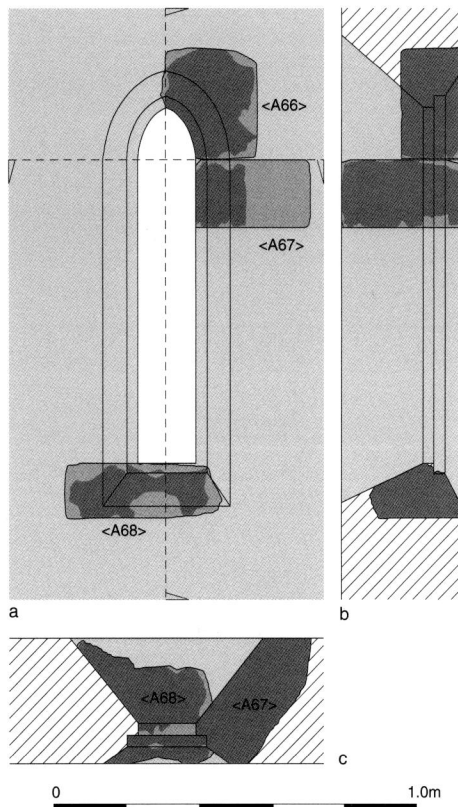

Fig 67 *A reconstruction of a lancet window <A66>–<A68> (period M2): a – elevation; b – transverse section; c – plan at the springing line (scale 1:20)*

ware crucible might suggest industrial activity either within the room or close by. A fragment from a glass urinal <S286> was also recovered in room 1. Room 2 contained a small pit [9623] which produced an oyster shell palette <S34> on which traces of purplish-red pigment, probably red lead, were extant. In room 3, the mortar floors contained patches of burnt silt and charcoal [9106], probably from a hearth. Another small pit, containing hearth rake-out, was in the north-east corner.

Food waste from the floors of rooms 1 and 2 included a few charred cereal grains, a few fruit seeds and stones (Table 42), and mammal, fish and bird bones (Table 9; Table 10) and oyster shell (Table 49). The animal bone assemblage is dominated by the major mammalian domesticates, with major

Table 9 *Recovery of hand-collected vertebrate fauna from the reredorter (B5, period M2), by fragment count*

Common name	Latin name	No. of frags	%
Fish			
Fish unidentified		6	0.4
Conger eel	*Conger conger*	3	0.2
Cod-sized		6	0.4
Cod family	Gadidae	5	0.3
Haddock	*Melanogrammus aeglefinus*	4	0.3
Birds			
Bird unidentified		111	7.1
Chicken	*Gallus gallus*	228	14.7
Chicken-sized		3	0.2
Goose, domestic	*Anser anser*	37	2.4
Goose-sized		13	0.8
Mallard/domestic duck	*Anas platyrhynchos*	2	0.1
Partridge, grey	*Perdix perdix*	2	0.1
Duck unidentified	Anatidae	1	0.1
Mammals			
Mammal unidentified		237	15.2
Cattle	*Bos taurus*	33	2.1
Cattle-sized		60	3.9
Sheep/goat	*Ovis aries/Capra hircus*	96	6.2
Sheep-sized		470	30.2
Pig	*Sus scrofa*	226	14.5
Horse	*Equus caballus*	1	0.1
Cat	*Felis catus*	1	0.1
Hare, brown	*Lepus europaeus*	5	0.3
Rabbit	*Oryctolagus cuniculus*	5	0.3
Total		**1555**	

Table 10 *Recovery of wet-sieved vertebrate fauna from the reredorter (B5, period M2), by fragment count*

Common name	Latin name	No. of frags	%
Fish			
Fish unidentified		2	0.2
Thornback ray	*Raja clavata*	4	0.4
Sturgeon	*Acipenser sturio*	1	0.1
Salmon family	Salmonidae	1	0.1
Smelt	*Osmerus eperlanus*	125	11.0
Herring family	Clupeidae	255	19.9
Herring	*Clupea harengus*	15	1.3
Carp family	Cyprinidae	16	1.4
Cod family	Gadidae	148	13.1
Haddock	*Melanogrammus aeglefinus*	1	0.1
Conger eel	*Conger conger*	6	0.5
Plaice/flounder	Pleuronectidae	30	2.6
Plaice	*Pleuronectes platessa*	1	0.1
Eel	*Anguilla anguilla*	60	5.3
Gurnard	Triglidae	16	1.4
Amphibian			
Frog/toad	Ranidae	3	0.3
Birds			
Bird unidentified		58	5.1
Chicken	*Gallus gallus*	34	3.0
Chicken-sized		67	5.9
Goose	*Anser anser*	2	0.2
Goose-sized		1	0.1
Partridge, grey	*Perdix perdix*	1	0.1
Passerine		53	4.7
Thrush, large	Turdidae	4	0.4
Thrush, small	Turdidae	12	1.1
Mammals			
Mammal unidentified		77	6.8
Cattle-sized		2	0.2
Sheep/goat	*Ovis aries/Capra hircus*	16	1.4
Sheep-sized		89	7.9
Pig	*Sus scrofa*	14	1.2
Small mammal		11	1.0
Shrew, common	*Sorex araneus*	1	0.1
Hare, brown	*Lepus europaeus*	1	0.1
Mouse/vole	Muridae	2	0.2
Rabbit	*Oryctolagus cuniculus*	2	0.2
Rat unidentified	*Rattus sp*	1	0.1
Vole	Muridae	1	0.1
Total		**1133**	

contributions, each more than 14% of the fragment count, from both chicken and pig. There were occasional finds of other poultry, goose and mallard/domestic duck; with small contributions of game; wild duck, hare and rabbit. The fish fauna are abundant and diverse; dominated by clupeids (including herring), smelt and gadids (including haddock); with smaller contributions of salmonid, cyprinid, eel, gurnard, conger eel and plaice/flounder. Two wild plants, henbane (*Hyoscyamus niger*) and hemlock (*Conium maculatum*), were fairly well represented in room 2 and may have been used for their medicinal properties (Table 42).

The reredorter drain did not survive later robbing but the depth of the robbing trench suggests the drain base was c 0.4m below the ground floor surface within the reredorter. It was probably lined originally with Reigate stone blocks, and may also have had a Reigate stone or tile lid. At its eastern end the drain emptied into a north-west–south-east aligned ditch [8368], which dropped to the south-east and flowed in the direction of where the fishponds were located (Saxby 2005b).

A ? latrine/wash house (B7)

A small building was inserted in the angle formed by the east wall of the reredorter and the south wall of the infirmary hall (Fig 57). The mortared flint and chalk footings define a building c 6m north–south by c 4m east–west internally. The south-east corner avoided crossing the infirmary drain but the

south wall was reinforced there by a supporting square pile, 0.23m deep, of unmortared flint nodules [11260]. A north–south drain [8369], 0.5m wide and made from roofing tile, flowed through the south wall to the reredorter drain (Fig 68). Since this building (B7) also overlay the drain from the infirmary garth (S4a), the routeing of the tile drain to the south may perhaps suggest that the drain from the infirmary garth was already out of use (above, 'A drainage ditch (S4a) flowing east from the infirmary garth (OA5)', 'Phase 3').

An east–west interior partition was marked by a mortared flint wall footing. The floor surface of trampled gravelly clay ([9987]; [9797]; [10127]) contained a solitary sherd of Saintonge ware with even green glaze (SAIG) pottery post-dating c 1280 (Pearce et al 1985, 18). A series of metalled floor surfaces [8498] to the north contained part of a rim from a copper-alloy vessel <S275>. Another, small east–west partition wall was defined by five stakeholes; it was removed and further clay, silt and crushed Reigate floor surfaces laid.

The presence of large dumps of oyster shell, together with the drains and their fills which contained numerous sherds of pottery associated with food production and serving, may suggest that Building 7 acted as a food preparation area. However, the absence of a hearth suggests no cooking took place, and the waste may derive from other parts of the infirmary. The building possibly functioned as a latrine or wash house, a suggestion reinforced by the presence of an internal drain.

Fig 68 *The tile drain leading southwards from a ? latrine/wash house (B7, period M2) to the reredorter drain, looking east (1.0m scale)*

61

An infirmarer's ? lodging/kitchen (B8)

To the east of the infirmary was a north–south wall forming the west side of Building 8, the easternmost building excavated and that only partially (Fig 34). The surviving fragmentary flint, chalk and Reigate stone, wall foundations of the southern and eastern parts of the building allow only a tentative conjecture of the size and shape. It may have been 'T' shaped and measured c 28m north–south by c 18m east–west. Possible floor surfaces, of flint pebbles and crushed chalk, were found within the eastern part and can be dated by a keyed white slip floor tile to the 13th century (Chapter 7.3). Further floor tiles, including 'Westminster' floor tiles of c 1250–c 1300, were recovered from demolition deposits and later ditches close by. These were probably used to floor this building during the 13th century. It was probably, from its position, ancillary to the infirmary and thus perhaps the infirmarer's lodging or kitchen.

A ? passage/pentice to the infirmary (S7)

A 3m-wide passage or pentice, defined by two parallel north–south walls, ran between Building 10 and the infirmary hall (B4a) (Fig 57). A 9.5m length of the western wall [8714] was traced. This flint and Reigate stone wall was founded on a bed of tiles. Kingston-type ware (KING) pottery, dated to after c 1230, was recovered from the foundations. The eastern wall [8701], of which a 12m length was recorded, was also built from flint and Reigate stone but lacked the tile course and appeared to be unbonded. A piece of a Reigate stone mortar <S295> (Fig 161) was incorporated within the foundations.

A ? storehouse/cold larder/wash house for the infirmary (B10)

Building 10 was to the south of the reredorter in an area of damp, low-lying ground, possibly prone to flooding (Fig 57). The thick (0.95m), flint and Reigate stone foundations [11219] indicated a rectangular, east–west building, c 5m long by 3.5m wide internally. The entrance presumably lay in the east section of the north wall, at the south end of the passage/pentice (S7). A thick (0.35m) floor deposit of crushed Reigate stone and sand, sealed by a second surface of flints set in silt, lay within. Towards the centre a pit had been lined with mortared courses of roofing tiles laid on bed and then rendered to form a recess 1.3m square by 0.41m deep (Fig 69). This may represent a tank. The building's thick walls may have kept the inside cool.

A watermill (B9) in the ? outer court (OA8)

Mortared chalk walls in the southern part of the monastic complex formed a building c 25m in length by c 11m wide (Fig 57). Archaeological excavation (in 2001 and 2003) of this building and an associated pond identified it as a watermill (Saxby 2005a). The entrance was in the north wall. Pottery dating to c 1080–c 1200 from the construction deposits suggest that it was built in the late 12th or early 13th century (ibid, 22–3).

The mill leat was to the south. A millpond lay to the west supplying the mill with water from west to east. The main fill of the millpond produced sherds of 13th-century pottery along with a concentration of cattle and sheep metapodials, the great majority of which were burnt. Evidence of ironworking in the form of hammerscale (flake and spheres) and cinder was also found (ibid, 23–4).

Fig 69 The lined and rendered pit within Building 10, a ? storehouse/cold larder/wash house for the infirmary (period M2), looking west (0.2m vertical scale)

An aisled hall (B11) in the ? outer court (OA8)

Chalk and Reigate stone walls, one containing a relieving arch, and pier base foundations formed the evidence for a large aisled hall to the south of the south range (Fig 57). This building was not fully excavated; the external walls in particular lay beyond the limits of the excavation, and the full size and function remain unclear. Seven pier base foundations, c 1m by 1.7m, and 0.6–1.0m deep and 2.5–2.8m apart, were aligned north-east–south-west and formed parallel aisles. A single pier base was located c 5.5m to the north of this alignment.

The earliest floor was of trampled clay [9240] and crushed Reigate stone [9244]. A metalled cobbled surface replaced this flooring; burning on this floor to the north [9595] and west [9481] suggested the location of hearths. Cooking may have taken place to the north where food debris, including charred cereal grains, wild fruit remains, fish and bird bones and molluscs including oyster shell, was found. Later floors metalled with crushed Reigate stone ([9391]; [9501]) contained Kingston-type ware (KING) pottery post-dating c 1230, as did small rubbish pits dug through the floors.

The precinct wall (S5)

Part of the foundations of the precinct wall was found on the south-eastern site boundary (trial trenches AH and AL, Fig 3). It was constructed from mortared flint with occasional Reigate stone blocks at the base. Further to the north, along the banks of the River Pickle, part of the east precinct wall still stands c 2.4m high (Fig 150).

A stone-paved fishpond (S9)

A stone-paved fishpond (Fig 70) was found to the south of Building 10 (Fig 57). The irregular chalk paving covered an area 19m north–south by 5m east–west at the base of the pond. Recent excavations have revealed further (unpaved) fishponds located to the east (Saxby 2005b, 11–25). The surviving primary (?medieval) silt [10319] (such a structure may have been regularly cleaned out) contained a timber which was sampled for dendrochronological analysis (Table 71).

A wall in the ? outer court (OA7)

A c 5m length of an east–west flint wall [8167] to the south of the reredorter (OA7) may have formed part of a building or other structure (Fig 57). The wall continued beyond the limits of excavation.

South of the cloister/claustral area in the ? outer court (OA8)

The wattle-lined north-west–south-east ditch [9237]/[9264] (period M1) may have remained open during this period, draining water from Building 11 to the river channel to the

Fig 70 The chalk paving at the base of the fishpond (S9, period M2), looking north (2.0m scale)

south (Fig 57). The botanical remains from the upper ditch fill/alluvial deposit [9251] included evidence for several aquatic and bankside/marshland species while there were seeds from a small number of plants of disturbed ground and waste places, presumably growing close by (Table 42).

A marshy area in the outer court (OA9)

Open Area 9 extended east of the infirmary to the River Wandle and excavation in the south part extended into the medieval river channel itself (Fig 3; Fig 5; Fig 34). Deposits containing pottery dating to c 1230–c 1400 were recorded, including a fragment from a Kingston-type ware (KING) alembic <P7> (Fig 159). A small area of organic silt, 0.5m in diameter, produced thousands of black mustard seeds. These may have been imported on to the site either as food or for medicinal purposes and were probably accidentally spilled. There was also a wide range of aquatic and bankside/marshland species represented in two samples from the organic silts and clays, particularly freshwater algae, stoneworts (Characeae) and the aquatic plant, horned pondweed (*Zannichellia palustris*). Collectively, the botanical and insect remains ([7921], [7924], Table 42; [7921], Table 52) combined with the low-lying nature of this area suggest the slow-flowing margins of the River Wandle, reed swamp or marshland.

Discussion 1222–c 1300 (period M2)

The lengthy programme of rebuilding and expansion initiated in the early 13th century probably began as a response to the damage caused by the collapse of a tower, probably that over the church crossing, in 1222 (*Ann Monast*, iii, 76), and by the desire to replace wooden conventual structures in stone. The new church retained the original eastern end, possibly for worship during the construction of the remainder.

The earlier nave foundations may have been retained as footings for the new nave arcade pier bases. The heavy buttressing of the transepts indicates that they were high and completely vaulted. Similarly, the absence of external nave buttressing suggests a timber ceiling in the central vessel rather than a vault. The aisle vault compartment at Merton was c 2.8m wide (measured from the internal wall faces) and the rectilinear proportions of the compartment can be reconstructed as 1:1.6. The excavated north aisle was c 2.8m wide between foundations. In the 1920s no direct evidence was found for the bay interval of the nave (Bidder and Westlake 1930, 57), but buttress foundations were excavated more recently on the south side of the nave. These appear to respect a bay interval of c 4.3m, except towards the west end where they are more 'bunched'. The observed interval seems rather slight for a nave of this period. The nave of Augustinian St Bartholemew West Smithfield retains evidence for an interval of 4.34m (Webb 1913, pl 8) but this building is about 80 years older than the Merton nave. The width of the nave at Merton was determined by that of the presbytery. In so far as it is possible to measure the excavated foundations, the Merton dimension follows practice at other

Augustinian priories where a width of 9.0–9.4m was widely respected (Chapter 4.3).

Whereas the north transept was clearly divided into chapels to the east, the south transept was built as one with the cloister and chapter house, or possibly slightly after the chapter house, and is more difficult to interpret. The slype or sacristy/vestry (B3f) was either structurally within the transept or the south transept arm was more 'compressed' than the north with Building 3f in the east range. The slype or sacristy/vestry area was screened from the main body of the south transept by a wall and it would have afforded access to the cloister. The transept was not split into three or four eastern chapels. Elsewhere in the transept, the evidence, consisting of foundations, burials and robber trenches, may suggest at least one chapel in the south-east corner, and a second chapel, possibly later, in the central space. The possible construction of the chapter house before the south transept may explain the need to shorten that transept in comparison with its northern counterpart, given the reuse of the nave foundations and the presbytery of the earlier church. The atypical inclusion of a space (OA4) to the south of the nave suggests no access to the nave from the cloister for the canons (Chapter 4.2). The buttresses on the south side of the chapter house suggest it may also pre-date the construction of the dormitory, which may have existed elsewhere early in this period or still have been in timber to the south. But the buttresses were small and shallow, and need not necessarily preclude the construction of a stone dormitory in a single building programme from north to south.

The chapter house was a simple rectangular square-ended building that did not project significantly east of the east range. The decoration found on the chapter house floor tiles is not known from elsewhere, so these and the plain-glazed examples can be presumed to be of local manufacture. Such tiles were time consuming to make and correspondingly expensive. They were probably made to order, perhaps in the priory's own tilery. Precedents for this exist, for example, at Meaux Abbey (Yorkshire East Riding), where the lay brothers made the tiles to pave the church between 1249 and 1269 (Eames 1992, 15). It is difficult to date the plain and decorated floor tiles from Merton, but comparison with mosaic pavements elsewhere would suggest the mid 13th century. The running dog design with a tree behind (<T7>, Fig 40) and some of the figures are very reminiscent of the decorative style used on certain tiles found in Westminster Abbey chapter house paved by 1258 (Eames 1992, 42).

The size of the cloister is uncertain. The north and east walks were well defined in the north-east corner, except for the north wall of the north walk. It is likely that the wall of Building 3e represents the south garth wall or, more probably, a lavatorium or washing place close to the refectory; it is not substantial enough to be the north external wall of the refectory, but is also not as substantial as the northern garth walls, and must be of a different build if it is a garth wall. This, if the cloister is taken to be square, would make the garth c 530m² and allow the north-west corner to coincide with the west corner of Building 13 (period M4) (Fig 129). This would place the east–west wall abutting the southernmost buttress of the east garth wall nearly central on the east side of the cloister, possibly as part of a small square porch or the foundations for stairs (as at Westminster: Westlake 1923, unnumbered plan at the end of vol 2), or as the northern foundation support for a larger building over the south-east corner of the cloister. However, it is conceivable that this east–west wall was the south garth wall, making any square garth *c* 100m², and a rectangular one, to fit with Building 13, 230m² and making Building 3e probably internal to the refectory. The two latter cloister options appear small and unusual, although it is possible that healthy priory inhabitants as well as the infirm also used the large infirmary cloister.

The expansion of the priory involved the provision of a large and imposing infirmary complex to the east with a rectangular cloister garth approximately 450m². The infirmary hall is dated to after *c* 1230 by pottery in its make-up layers but the sculpted label stop of *c* 1120–*c* 1250, which may have come from the infirmary kitchen, could suggest that significant parts of the complex were complete by the mid 13th century. The identification of a number of the buildings is a matter of conjecture. While the hall, cloister and chapel seem reasonably secure, the building identified here as the infirmary kitchen may in fact be the infirmarer's lodging or a building more purely ancillary to the infirmary such as a bloodletting house, while Building 7 is perhaps a kitchen or a garderobe or wash/bath house, and the fragmentary Building 8 another candidate for either a kitchen or the infirmarer's lodging. The provision of a passage/pentice, Structure 7, also suggests a link between the infirmary complex and Building 10 and that the latter too may have been one of the buildings identified above.

The reredorter occupied the south side of the infirmary cloister and, if monastic parallels elsewhere are followed, would have communicated, at first-floor level, with the canons' dormitory in the southern end of the east range of the main cloister (Robinson 1998, gazetteer eg 68, 86, 112, 161–2).

The aisled hall (B11) may indicate the location of the prior's lodging or, since it is well away from the main complex, extensive guest quarters or a *hospitium* (guest house). The repairs noted in 1257 to the king's chamber and that of the king's chancellor suggest extensive separate provision for important guests over and above the usual guest lodgings.

The topography of the precinct was unchanged. The soils in the north burial area lay at a maximum of 12.9m OD, although the relaid Road 1 was at *c* 12.5m OD. Within the church mortar spreads lay at 12.72–12.95m OD. The variation in levels possibly resulted from subsidence as there was evidence of patching and levelling but the floor may not ever have been entirely level. Further south, the floor of the infirmary kitchen was at 12.49m OD, with the infirmary cloister garth at almost the same level. To the south-west, the primary floor of the aisled hall (B11) lay at 12.68m OD. To the south and east the ground sloped down to a maximum of 12m OD in Open Area 9, with the base of the marshland at *c* 10m OD.

The south transept burials included a child of 7–12 years, a mature male and an older male, but there was no evidence of familial connections. Both the bodies from the north transept and three from the south were available for osteological analysis, but these samples are too small for firm conclusions to be drawn.

In the cemetery, differentiation between the north and south areas perhaps existed. The four, possibly six, cist burials to the south (20% of the total) compared to three cist burials to the north (3% of the total) may be the result of archaeological survival, but could suggest a higher or differing status for those buried to the south. Perhaps the increased wealth of the house allowed more opulent burials within the community. The chapter house also produced burials for this period. In common with the church and Open Area 3, those that could be sexed were male. This is probably in accordance with the practice of reserving the chapter house for burial of priors and higher monastic personnel.

3.3 The priory in the 14th century, *c* 1300–*c* 1390 (period M3)

Documentary evidence

The documentary sources for the priory during this period are mainly concerned with everyday activities such as corrodies, the election of priors and the priory's relationship with the Bishop of Winchester. There is only limited description of the fabric and little reference to building work. Not until the end of the 14th century do we find an indication as to the state of the priory.

Some of the buildings are mentioned in a number of corrodies granted during the early part of the 14th century. One, in 1301, refers to a mansion within the close with a competent dwelling, formerly held by William de Oulton, with a garden and easement pertaining (Heales 1898, 188–9 and appendix XCIV). The corrody of Richard de Pennark, clerk, granted in 1312, granted him a place *infra mansum curie nostre* to dwell in and laid down that provisions were to be received in the great gate (*hostium*) of the kitchen (Heales 1898, 211–12). The corrody granted to Henry Hoclegh in 1310 included the custody of the great gate, with residence in the chambers annexed (ibid, 204), probably in connection with Edward III's instruction of 1339 to the escheator this side of the Trent not to meddle with the custody of the priory following the death of Prior Kent, but to restore its issues to the subprior and depute a man to the custody of the great gate of the priory 'in the name of the king's lordship' during the ensuing vacancy, as was customary (*Cal Close* R, 1339–41, 195). A similar arrangement was made in 1361 following the death of Prior Freston when the escheator was ordered to keep the outer gate of the priory, called the great gate, in the name of the king's lordship (ibid, 1360–4, 196).

A key feature in the life of any religious house was its

relations with the local bishop, and perhaps the most significant contact between Merton Priory and the bishop of Winchester during this period occurred at the very beginning with the replacement of Prior Edmund Herierde. This episode is almost exclusively documented in the registers of Bishop Henry Woodlock and fully illustrates the extent and limitations of episcopal authority.

At the turn of the century, on 4 May 1301, Prior Herierde was already under threat of excommunication from the bishop for having made a subsidy to the king 'from fear of loss of temporal goods', his absolution depending on the performance of a penance prescribed by the Holy See (Heales 1898, 188 and appendix XCVI), and a similar penalty was shortly imposed upon him in consequence of a visitation by the archbishop of Canterbury, carried out late in 1304 while the see of Winchester was vacant following the death of Bishop Pontissara. In the light of this a number of unspecified irregularities were alleged against the prior, with drastic consequences. On 22 March 1305 the new Bishop of Winchester, Henry Woodlock, moved to have the prior of Merton absolved from any sentence of excommunication already passed upon him by the archbishop (Reg Woodlock, 4). Edmund was not summoned before his bishop until 11 August 1305 (Heales 1898, 192–5, appendices XCVII–XCVIII), and as the prior vehemently protested his innocence the proceedings were protracted, and it was not until 25 September that he was prevailed upon to resign. Even then Edmund managed to wring the concession that he should enjoy the use of the chamber within the bounds of the priory built by Prior Gilbert (1252–92) iuxta Beaulieu, together with a companion and a servant of his choice from the convent (ibid, 193–4 and appendix XCVII) which might suggest that political considerations as much as moral shortcomings underlay his removal from office.

At the meeting with the Merton chapter at which Edmund resigned, the bishop proposed holding a visitation of his own to correct the shortcomings detected at the archbishop's visitation (Reg Woodlock, 46). In the meantime and pending the equally pressing matter of electing a new prior, the bishop, like the king, dealt with the subprior, as on 13 November when he issued a mandate to Brother Henry, the subprior, to restrain the canons from wandering outside the 'monastery' without leave (ibid, 65). An enquiry held at Merton by the king's command resulted in the two rival candidates, William de Brokesburn and Edmund Herierde, agreeing to submit to the bishop's ruling, but that expedient fell through. The king now lost patience and on 27 December ordered the bishop to find and appoint a new prior (Cal Pat R, 1301–7, 411), although even then it was not until 6 March 1306 that Geoffrey of Alkmundbury (?Alconbury) was finally provided (Reg Woodlock, 768; Heales 1898, 196). Documents transcribed in the bishop's register include a letter of 30 December 1305 from the subprior and convent begging the bishop to intervene, since they feared injury to their house from a prolonged vacancy and especially the king's anger; the bishop's provision of Geoffrey of Alkmundbury as the new prior; and a letter of 6 March 1306

from the bishop to the king informing him of Geoffrey's appointment and asking the king to restore the temporalities to the priory (Heales 1898, 91–108). No other elections seem to have proved as problematic as this one, although some were undoubtedly disputed. On 1 April 1335 Bishop Orleton made himself available to hear objections to the election of Thomas of Kent as successor to William de Brokesburn, and subsequently confirmed his election on 24–25 April 1335, having heard a further objection (Heales 1898, 233–4 and appendices CXVII–CXVIII).

Further visitations are recorded in July 1314 (Heales 1898, 214 and appendix CVII), and in July 1316 Merton was exempted from visitation during the vacancy of the see of Winchester (ibid, 217). Corrections were required following a visitation in March 1335 (ibid, 233 and appendix CXVI), and it was perhaps in connection with another visitation that Bishop Orleton informed the priory on 13 January 1341 of the unseemly state into which it had fallen (ibid, 245). Later visitations included those held by Bishop Wykeham in 1387 and 1392, both of them followed by letters of protest to the bishop from the canons (Bodleian, Laud MS 723, fos 77, 78v; Heales 1898, 265, 277–9 and appendices CXXXIX and CXL). One prominent matter to which these later visitations drew attention was the priory's poor record of maintenance of the parish churches in its possession, notably Kingston (Surrey) and Effingham (Surrey). The later visitations drew particular attention to the fabric of both churches and dependent chapelries.

One of a bishop's routine duties was to officiate in inductions to livings, and in 1306 Bishop Woodlock inducted William de Hovyngham, presented by Merton, to the benefice of Carshalton (Reg Woodlock, 721), and in 1326 Bishop Assier admitted Roger de Kingeston to the vicarage of Kingston (Heales 1898, 226). Almost as often the bishop would intercede with a head of house on behalf of individual clerics. In 1314 Archbishop Reynolds requested Merton to find a place for Thomas Gydy (ibid, 214 and appendix CVIII), and in 1330 Bishop Stratford made a similar request on behalf of a poor clerk from London (ibid, 229). Diocesans were also involved in less routine aspects of the regular life, such as the annulment in 1331 of the profession as a canon of one of the Merton brothers because of a previous marriage contract (ibid, 231 and appendix CXIII), the reconciliation in 1335 of one of the canons who had fled the house (ibid, 232 and appendix CXV), the absolution by the prior of another errant canon, John Paynel, from sentence of excommunication, in 1347 (ibid, 249 and appendix CXXX) or the transfer to Merton of John Cherteseye, canon of the Augustinian house at Newstead (Nottinghamshire) and a perpetrator of 'illicit and monstrous acts', noted in 1387 (Heales 1898, 274 and appendix CXXXV).

Diocesans also mediated between religious houses and the papacy, most often in the matter of taxation. On 27 June 1306 Bishop Woodlock responded to a request from William Testa and William Geraldi, papal nuncios and collectors of first fruits, for a listing of benefices that had been vacant in the three years preceding 1 February last, by affirming that, while Merton

Priory was indeed vacant on that date, he was ignorant of the total value as its property (like that of other religious houses) was in various dioceses (*Reg Woodlock*, 132–3), repeating this on 19 June but undertaking to forward a return in due course, 'if desired' (ibid, 204–5). Three years later, on 2 February 1309, the bishop was still professing ignorance of Merton's finances (ibid, 337). In 1316 the priory was acquitted from papal procurations (or visitations fees; Heales 1898, 217), although in 1317 the prior received a request from the bishop to give a further account of his collection of procurations in the diocese (ibid, 219), possibly because this time it was a question of diocesan visitations.

In 1344 Merton was selected to provide 'a suitable and strong house' (*domum congruam et fortem*) with free access for the use of the collectors for the Surrey part of the tenth and fifteenth granted by parliament (*Rot Parlt*, ii, 451a, no. 114). This was probably a repeat of the arrangements in 1235, when the priory was the collection point for the royal aid. In 1347 the prior of Merton was 'invited' to contribute an aid for the war with France (*Cal Close R*, 1346–9, 265) which had just broken out. At the end of the century, in 1397, the king acknowledged his obligation to repay to the prior of Merton, among many other such creditors, a loan of £40 (*Cal Pat R*, 1396–9, 182).

Between 1346 and 1349 royal sports were held at St Mary Merton on the feast of Epiphany, presumably for the amusement of Edward III. The accounts of the Great Wardrobe of King Edward III show that supplied were 13 visers (vizards or masks) with heads of dragons, and 13 with heads of men and 10 courtepies (short cloaks) of black bokeram and 12 yards of English canvas of flax (Heales 1898, 248).

During the 14th century corrodies continued to be the most regular and perhaps the most burdensome service provided by the priory for the Crown. Other large religious houses in the vicinity of London, notably Bermondsey (Steele in prep), were similarly burdened, and if the king made any financial contribution towards the support of his former retainers' arrangements his letters all signally fail to mention the fact. It is hardly surprising that in his injunctions of 1387, following a visitation, the bishop of Winchester observed that much loss had occurred through the injudicious grant of corrodies to the injury of resources left for the increase of divine worship and bestowed by the pious devotion of the faithful for the upkeep of the poor and infirm, and therefore forbade under pain of the greater excommunication the grant or sale of corrodies to any person whatsoever, without episcopal consent and special licence (Heales 1898, 270). This does not appear to have had any effect at all. On the contrary a spate of royal corrodies followed in the 1390s: not only John Maudelyn, yeoman of the king's robes, but his wife Alice too were sent on 8 March 1391 (*Cal Close R*, 1389–92, 315). After John's death the priory petitioned the king for the relaxation of Alice's corrody (Bodleian, Laud MS 723, fo 65v), which they must have regarded as a highly undesirable precedent. John's own place was promptly taken by John Fr’anceys on 16 February 1400 (*Cal Close R*, 1399–1402, 117; Heales 1898, 293–4).

Documentary sources relating to the conventual church exist from the latter part of the 14th century. On 9 June 1382 Bishop Wykeham permitted the prior and convent to have three altars consecrated or dedicated within their church by Bishop William of Nantes, together with two portative altars or altar tops (Heales 1898, 264 and appendix CXXXIII). A set of injunctions made by the bishop on 27 September 1387, following a visitation, noted that 'in your priory and church, and in some dwellings, the walls and enclosures of your church and manors, which your predecessors constructed with industry and expense are in part in extreme disrepair, whence the condition of the priory is disfigured and many inconveniences follow; all were to be made good within six months from the present notice, under pain of suspension' (ibid, 269–70). The injunctions also required that the doors of the church and monastery were to be kept closed at due times, on account of 'suspected and dishonest persons frequently walking about the church and monastery in dark and shady places', the doors being closed and fastenings kept by fit persons at accustomed times. In particular, the doors between the nave and choir were to be closed, while secular persons were to leave the monastery 'from morning until prime begins in choir, and at time of meals, and in the evening after collation begins', the doors being opened only for reasons approved by the prior or subprior (Heales 1898, 267, citing Bodleian, Laud MS 723, fos 52 et seq).

A further shortcoming observed during the visitation of 1387 was that a third or a half of the inmates did not eat in the refectory as provided in the Constitutions, and this was to be remedied; 'henceforth a third, or at least half', were to eat every day at meal-time in the refectory, none being permitted to eat in private houses or places with their guests, whether regular or secular, or their confraters, except in the guest room and in recreation time, and only in the hall (*aula*) (Heales 1898, 271, citing Bodleian, Laud MS 723, fos 52 et seq). The 'hall' presumably refers to the hall of the guest room (or guest house) and not the main refectory. Heales notes that copies of the bishop's injunctions found their way to New College, Oxford, which Wykeham founded, and Selbourne Priory (Hampshire), also in the diocese of Winchester (1898, 273). Was it, as Heales speculated, a general set of rules not framed with any particular house in mind, or a set specifically arising from a visitation of Merton and found to be more widely applicable without further alteration?

Archaeological evidence

Introduction

The presbytery was considerably enlarged and a Lady chapel added to the church, resulting in a further loss of space within the cemetery and a clearer division between the burial areas to the north and south of the church (Fig 71). Worked stone retrieved from and near the site suggests the cloister was rebuilt in this period. The chapter house (B3b) was converted from a rectangular to an apsidal building. The infirmary hall (B4a) was partitioned replacing the earlier open hall with smaller individual rooms. The reredorter (B5) was rebuilt on the existing foundations (Fig 121). The infirmary kitchen was replaced by a much smaller building (B12) also attached to the eastern wall of the infirmary hall. The infirmary cloister was rebuilt and floored with roofing tiles, replacing the earlier metalled pebble floor surfaces. The aisled hall (B11) was enlarged and strengthened with the addition of much larger column bases.

The 14th-century church (B1)

A larger presbytery and a Lady chapel were constructed in one operation (Fig 71). Preparatory levelling and some extensive scatters of building debris contained a broken hone-stone, in Norwegian schist (<S268>, Fig 72) possibly discarded during building work. An east–west alignment of pits and postholes, some containing stone packing, c 1–2m from the interior face of the north wall of the Lady chapel, suggest scaffolding.

The foundations, up to 1.80m wide (Fig 73), consisted of large flint nodules with occasional blocks of Reigate stone (probably reused), peg tiles and fragments of Coggeshall-type bricks set in a sandy mortar. External buttresses, c 1–2m square, were provided around the presbytery and Lady chapel at intervals of 5.93m and 5.30m respectively.

The new presbytery (Fig 74) extended the earlier presbytery eastwards using the existing presbytery foundations to support the two westernmost bays of the new arcade, with an aisle or ambulatory around the arcade. Internally, the presbytery was 27.36m long and the aisles increased its width to 20.25m. The Lady chapel was 9.14m wide internally and extended a further 10.67m to the east of the ambulatory. The church now had an internal length of c 90m (Fig 75).

Some evidence that the eastern extension was constructed around the existing presbytery, to minimise the disruption of daily worship, is provided by a c 4–5m length of wall built on to the southernmost buttress of the north transept. This wall, of flint and some peg tile bonded in a yellow mortar, was a different build to the remainder of the new north presbytery wall and on a slightly different alignment. The wall could represent the first stage of reconstruction, or even an aborted earlier phase, but is more likely, given the odd alignment, to have been built last to close an access maintained for construction work.

Moulded stone belonging to this period of building was recovered from the later (period M4) buttress extensions at the east end of the church, and from further afield at Clattern Bridge in Kingston (Surrey) (A Skelton, pers comm; Chapter 7.2, 'Construction phase 5 (the eastern extension of the church) …'). It included fragments of major and minor piers and arcades, vaulting, buttresses, gables, windows and a piscina (a hand basin with a drain, usually set against or into the wall).

Remnants of two window types, both in Reigate stone, which were probably originally set in the extension, were designed on different scales (Fig 76; Fig 79). The larger had a strong mullion 0.67m in wall depth (on its long axis), probably for an aisle window or the great east window (<A83>–<A86>,

Figs 76–8). The smaller window's strong mullion was probably 0.61m in wall depth (<A78>, Fig 79; Fig 80; Fig 187). This was stylistically linked to vault ribs (see below) and probably formed the clerestory window form. The moulding is of the Decorated style and resembles existing windows in the nave aisles at York Minster enough to suggest a similar date. The York work is thought to date shortly after 1291 (Morris 1979, fig 11 p). The smaller window shows affinities with major court work of the 1300s (see below). The stylistic resemblances of the window moulding to the arcade (see below) suggests both are part of the same campaign of construction. The major order was twice the width of the minor. Consequently the latter can be reconstructed. Large round openings (oculi) probably formed the central feature of the tracery scheme in both cases (Fig 78; Fig 80). These were dressed to hold timber frames. It may be that these held round pivoting windows for ventilation. Both oculus fragments were reused in the same area of the eastern extension. A traceried window, apparently contemporary, survived as part of the ?abbot's chapel until the 19th century (Fig 149). This too shows a large central oculus, however, not the opening kind but provided with cusps. Fragments of traceried window from a Dissolution layer to the east of the Lady chapel may have originated there (<A76>, Fig 184). The mould was simple with a highly complex tracery scheme and the presence of open cusps indicates that the window was of the Decorated period. However, the small scale and weakness of execution suggests that it more probably derived from, for example, the infirmary chapel than the church.

The piers and arcade arches were built from pale blue/grey Purbeck marble superficially similar to the stone used in the piers of Exeter Cathedral (Devon) (see eg Cherry and Pevsner 1991, 366–7). The minor (<A70>–<A72>, Fig 81) and major (<A74>, Fig 82) pier mouldings confirm the use of the 'rotated-square' method of pier design. The method of designing by the rotated square was certainly employed in the late 15th century when the German mason Mathes Roriczer wrote his booklet on pinnacle design (Coldstream 1991, 34) and this clear-cut example confirms its use in late 13th-century England. Its use in Augustinian priories has been argued for the layout of cloisters in late 12th-century Scottish foundations (Gallagher 1994) and while the examples given are not entirely convincing, this Merton example lends weight to the antiquity of the method. The wholly graphic method employed allowed the square root of two (1:1.414) to be quickly determined without the need for calculation. Both have two-way symmetry and are adorned by axial triple-rolls-in-echelon separated by hollows. The natural bedding of the stone was kept horizontal. AutoCAD reconstructions of the minor and major pier shafts are shown in Fig 83 and Fig 84, respectively. The major pier's elaborate moulding can be appreciated in the AutoCAD reconstruction of the detail of the shafting (Fig 85).

Part of a pier from Kingston Library was found during work on Clattern Bridge, Kingston (Finny 1929, 104). Despite being in poor condition, this pier is the only evidence for the minor pier base (Fig 86). An AutoCAD perspective view of the base is shown in Fig 87. The capital of the Kingston pier (Fig 88) was

area illustrated

study area outline

Structure

mortar ar
crushed Reiga

mortar-mixing pit ⬭ch

Open Area 6
north burial area

[2352] & [2353]

north [2402]
transept
[2114]   [3379]

chapel

[4039]

[4081]

[2381]

[2858]   ch
[2701]

[2844]

[2712] & [2856] & [2855]

[2651]
[2934]
[3172]

[2951]

[2595]

[2531]   [2905]

Building 1
church

[5758]

[5250]

[5247]

nave

south
transept

slype 3f

Building 3b
chapter house

[716]

Open Area 4

Building 3c

3d

Open Area 10
cloister garth

burials post c 1350

0   25m

Building 3e
south range

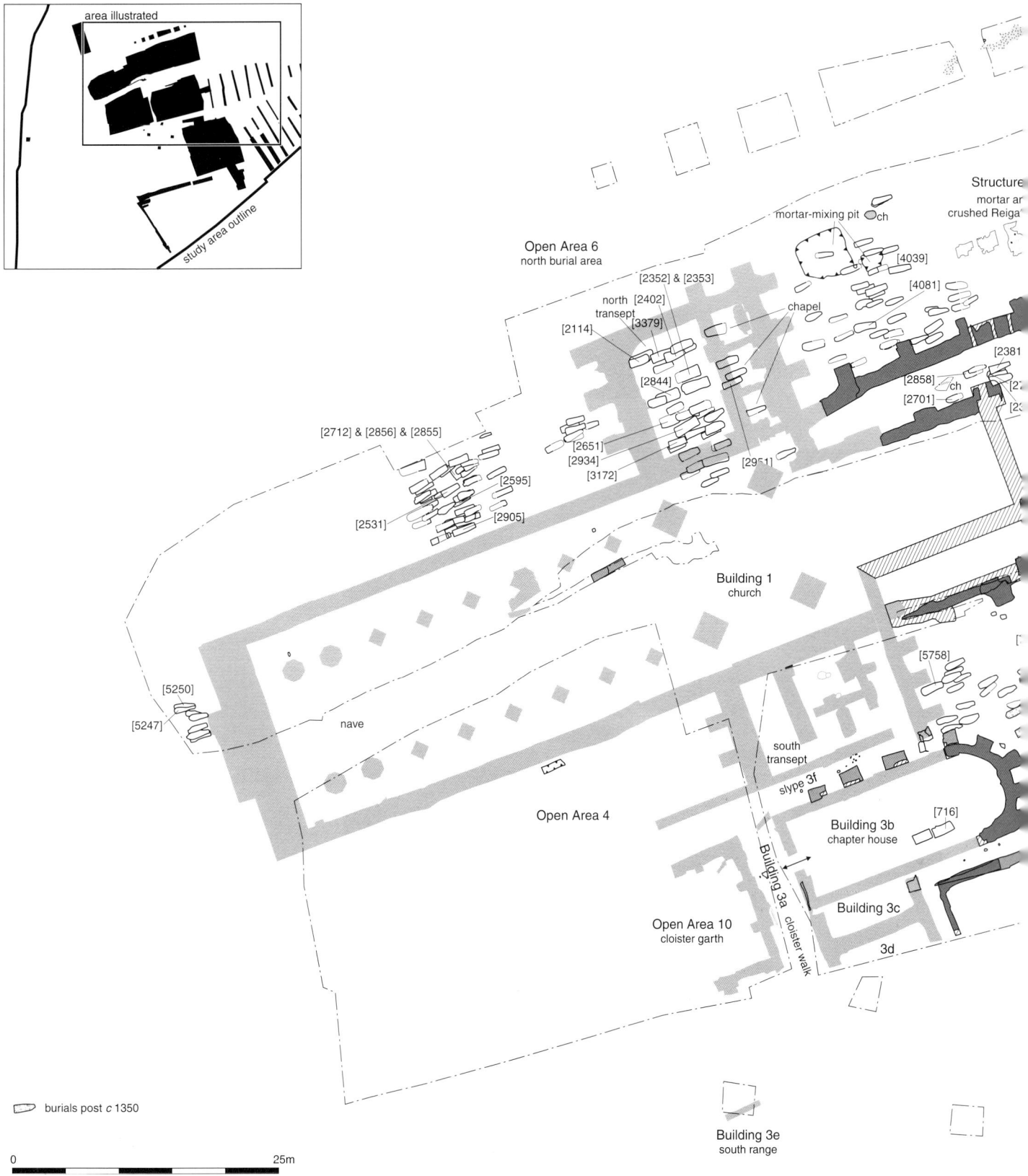

Fig 71 Plan of the principal archaeological features in the north part of the precinct, c 1300 to c 1390 (period M3) (scale 1:500)

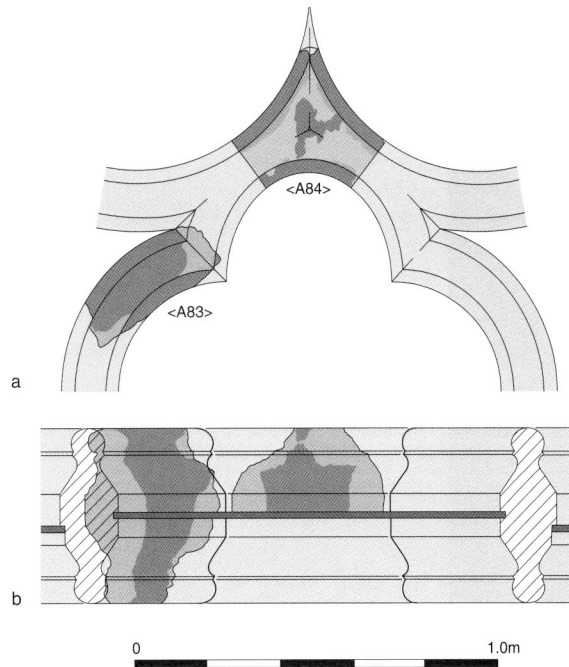

Fig 77 Openwork trefoil and archlet detail <A83> and <A84>, of the ? aisle/east window (period M3): a – elevation; b – inverted plan at archlet springing line (scale 1:20)

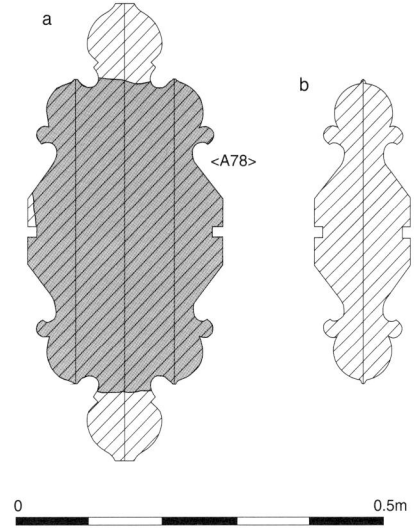

Fig 79 ?Clerestory window <A78> (period M3): a – major order; b – minor order (scale 1:10)

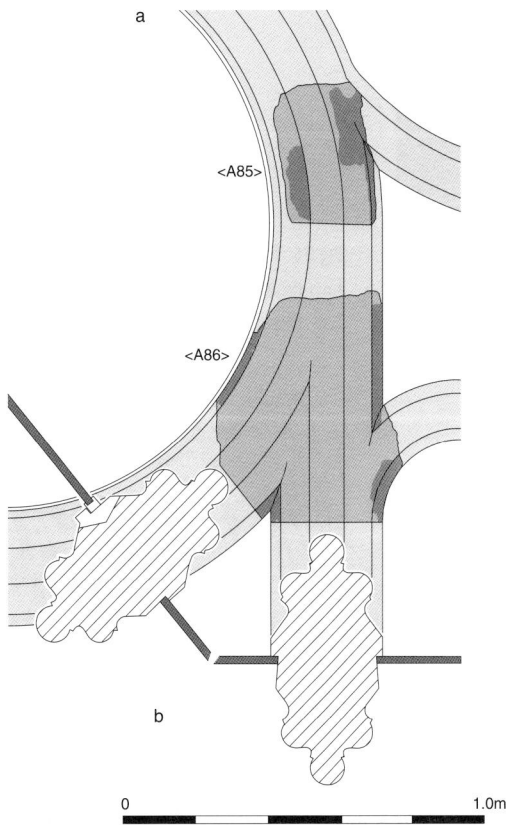

Fig 78 Hinged oculus detail <A85> and <A86>, of the ? aisle/east window (period M3): a – elevation; b – mouldings, modification of glazing rebate (scale 1:20)

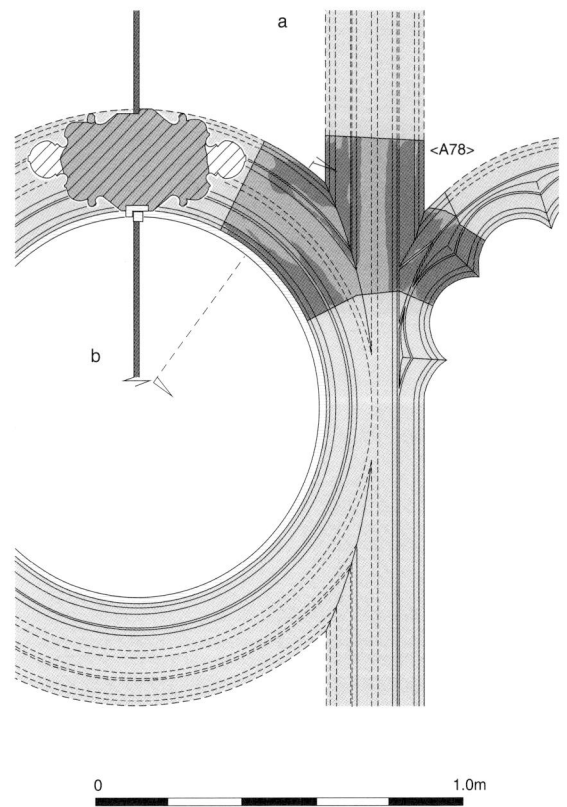

Fig 80 Hinged oculus detail <A78> from the ?clerestory window (period M3): a – elevation; b – moulding, modification of glazing rebate (scale 1:20)

N

area illustrated

study area outline

Open Area 6
north burial area

Structure 8
mortar and
crushed Reigate stone

mortar-mixing pit ch

[4039]

[4081]

[4768]

[2352] & [2353]

north [2402]
transept

chapel

[2114] [3379]

[2381]

ch

[2844]

[2858] ch [2703]

[2701] [2387]

Lady chapel

[2712] & [2856] & [2855]

[2651]
[2934]
[3172]

[2951]

[2595]

[2531] [2905]

Building 1
church

Open Area 3
south burial area

[5077] [5005] [5080]
[5056] [7060] [7235]

[7061]

[7634]

[5758]

ch

[5250]

[7098] [7163]

[5247]

nave

ch

[839] [5023]

[5060] [5002]

Building 4b
infirmary chapel

Open Area 4

south
transept

slype 3f

Building 3b
chapter house

[716]

4c

room 1

Building 3a

Building 4a
infirmary hall

room 6

room 2

cloister walk

Building 3c

room 3

t [1016]

t

room 7

Open Area 10
cloister garth

3d

cloister walk 4c

room 4

Building 12

Building 8

Open Area 9

[8096]

room 5

yard

path

burials post c 1350

Open Area 5
infirmary cloister garth

path

Building 3e
south range

Structure 4b
infirmary drain

0 25m

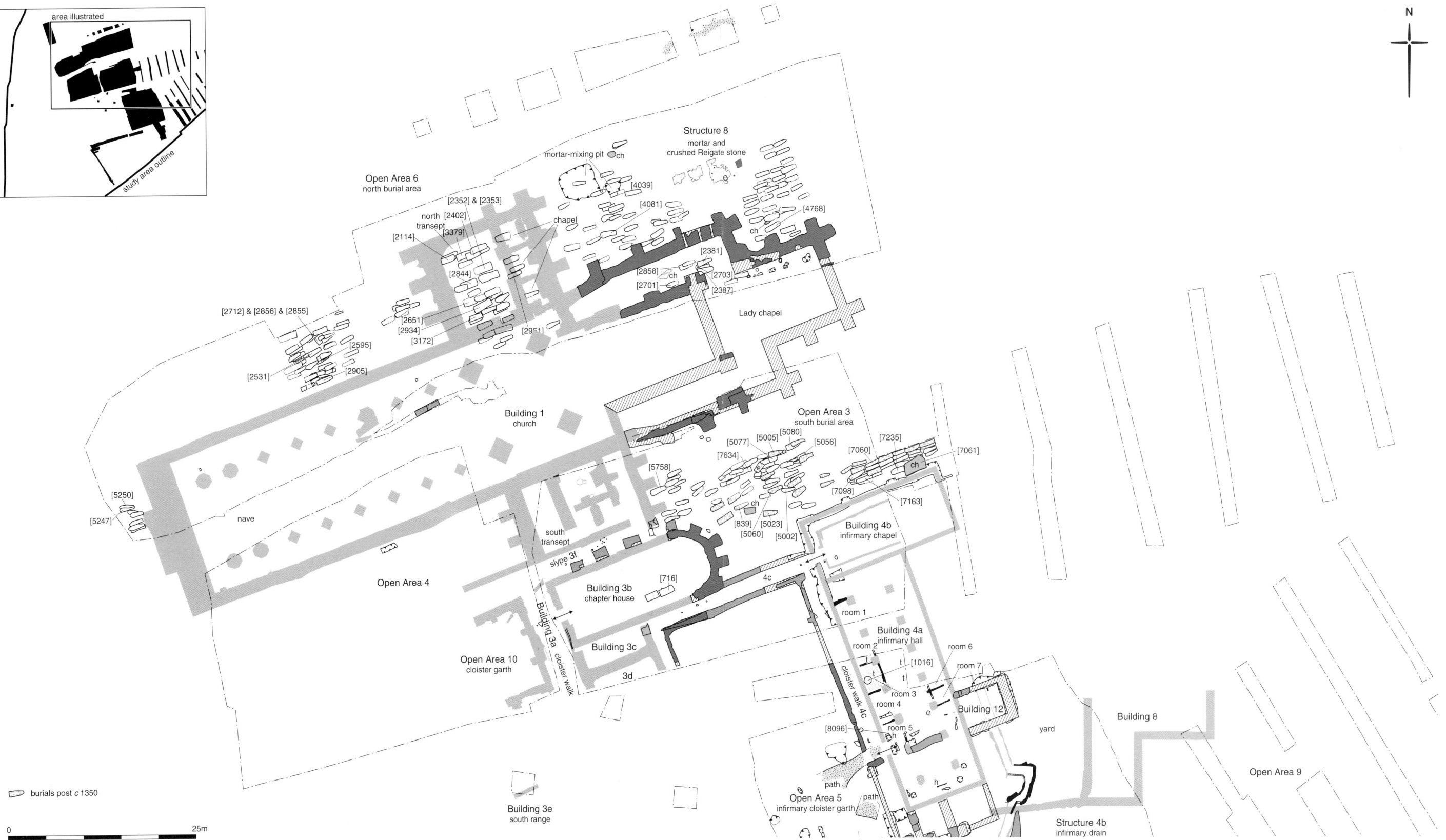

Fig 71 Plan of the principal archaeological features in the north part of the precinct, c 1300 to c 1390 (period M3) (scale 1:500)

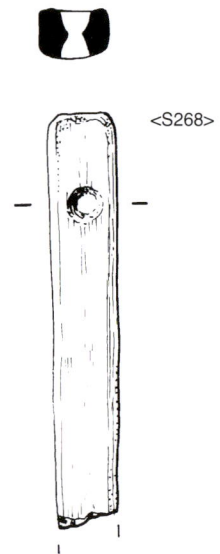

Fig 72 Broken stone hone <S268>
(scale 1:1)

Fig 73 The interior of the east end of
the church (B1) under excavation,
showing the flint foundations (period
M3), looking north-west

Fig 74 The east end of the church (B1, period M3),
with the north aisle/ambulatory (centre) and north side
of the presbytery (right), looking east towards the Lady
chapel (2.0m scale)

Fig 75 The north side of the church, looking east from the west front (foreground) to the east end and Lady chapel

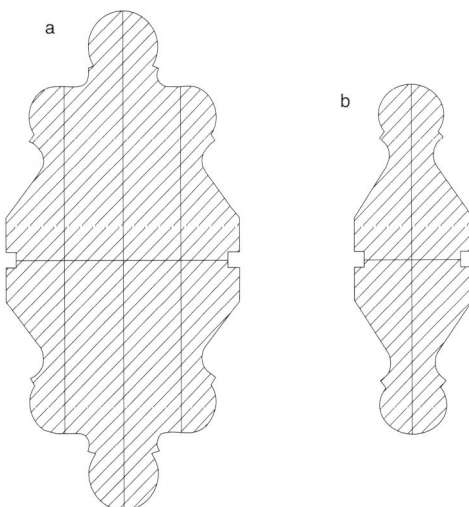

Fig 76 *? Aisle/east window moulding (period M3): a — major order; b — minor order (scale 1:10)*

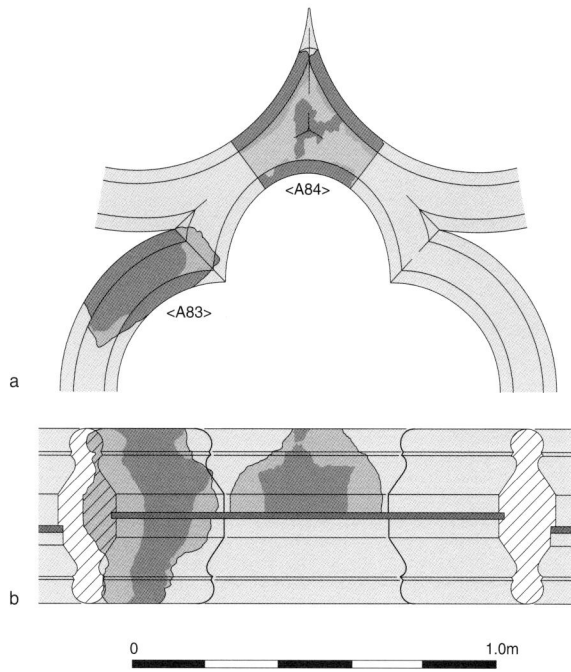

Fig 77 Openwork trefoil and archlet detail <A83> and <A84>, of the ? aisle/east window (period M3): a – elevation; b – inverted plan at archlet springing line (scale 1:20)

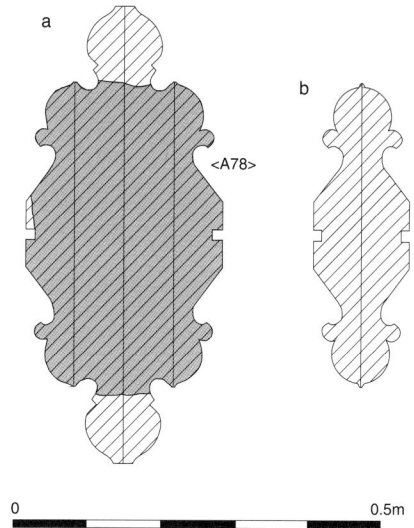

Fig 79 ?Clerestory window <A78> (period M3): a – major order; b – minor order (scale 1:10)

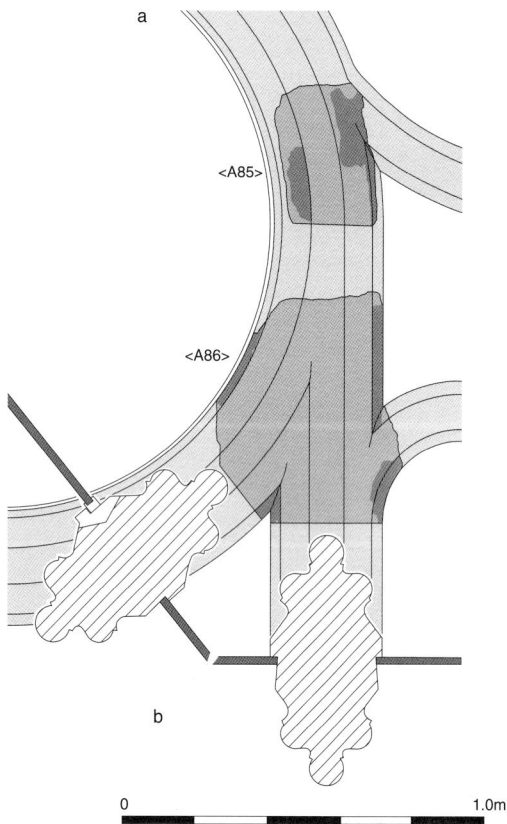

Fig 78 Hinged oculus detail <A85> and <A86>, of the ? aisle/east window (period M3): a – elevation; b – mouldings, modification of glazing rebate (scale 1:20)

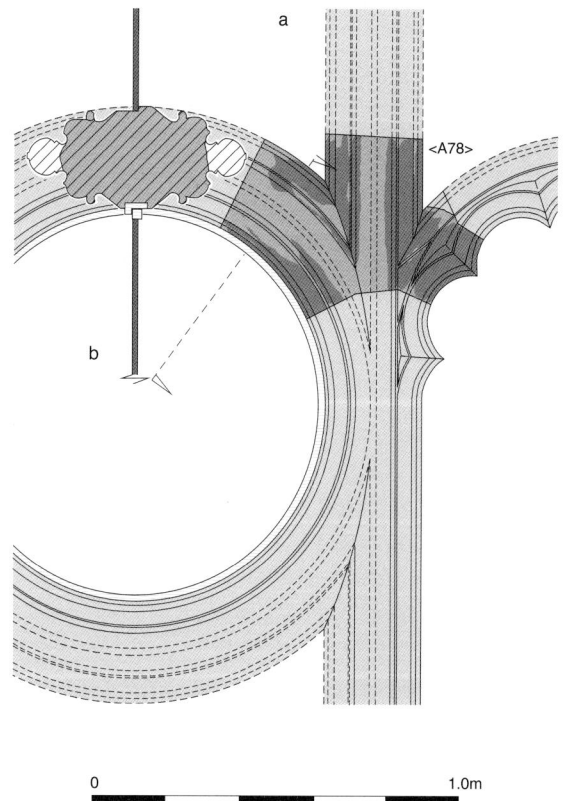

Fig 80 Hinged oculus detail <A78> from the ?clerestory window (period M3): a – elevation; b – moulding, modification of glazing rebate (scale 1:20)

a

b

<A70>

c

<A71>

<A70>

<A72>

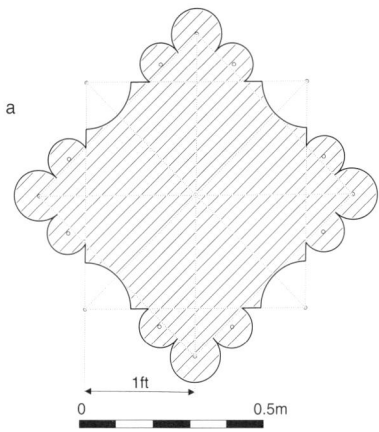

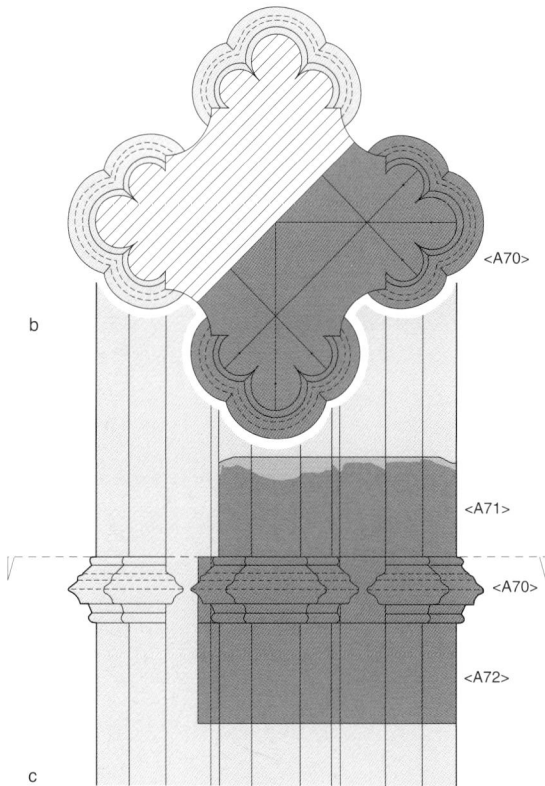

Fig 81 Minor pier shaft (period M3): a — designing the moulding using a 2 x 2 foot rotated square; b — the moulding at annulet level showing compass points and setting-out lines; c — elevation of the shaft with annulets <A70>–<A72> (scale 1:20)

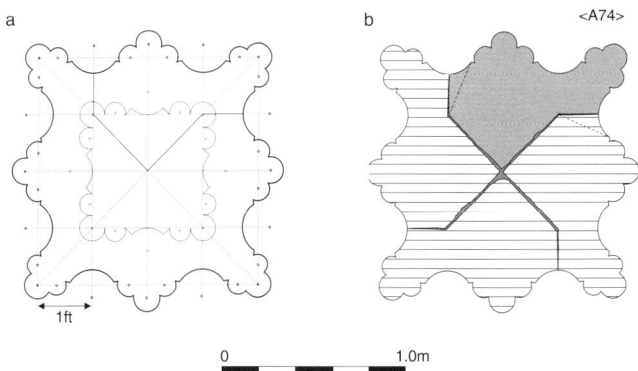

a

b

<A74>

Fig 82 Major pier shaft <A74> (period M3): a — the use of a 4 x 4 foot square as a geometric basis of the moulding; b — the method of cutting and fitting blocks using the module (tone shows module) (scale 1:40)

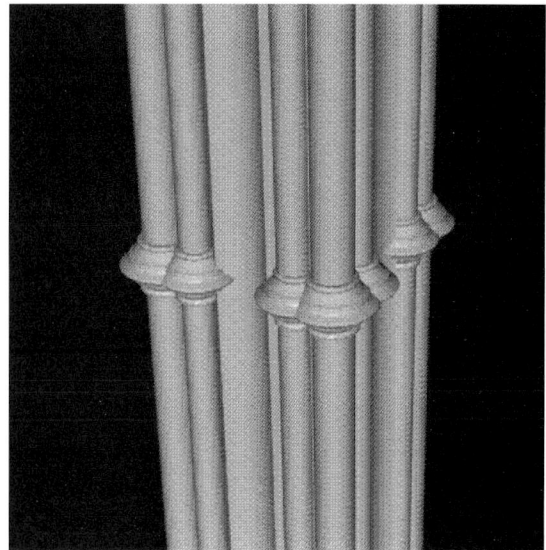

Fig 83 Minor pier shaft (period M3): *perspective view of shaft with annulets from above*

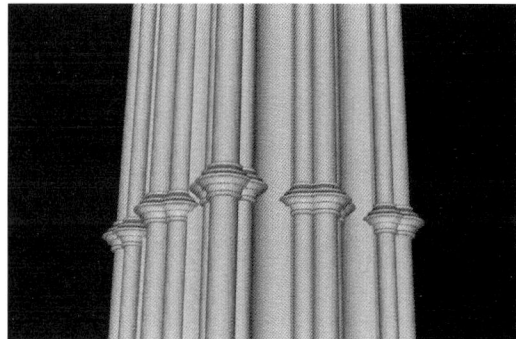

Fig 84 Major pier shaft (period M3): *perspective view showing probable arrangement of annulets*

Fig 85 Major pier (period M3): *perspective detailed view of the clustered shafts*

73

apparently a three-unit form with a plain bell and 1ft high (allowing for the deterioration of the impost). Weathering has removed all fine detail but the original can be inferred (Fig 89); the capital probably resembled the corbel used on the contemporary Purbeck marble piscina (<A75>, Fig 98; Fig 185). The only evidence of the arcade arch moulding is a flawed arcade voussoir (<A73>, Fig 90). This confirms that the Purbeck marble was cut on site. Bidder records that the flint concrete foundations of the eastern pair of arcade bases were diagonally set, being 'diamond shaped at ground level' (Bidder and Westlake 1930, 63). The arcade mould follows the overall form of the minor pier. The continuous foundation around the inner presbytery suggests the reredos (decorative screen behind the altar) and side screens were built as a single entity with the pier bases abutted by the screens; the excavated fragments and those at Kingston Library presumably derived from the free-standing piers further west (bays 5 and 6). It is probable that the top of the reredos and screens terminated at annulet level. There is no evidence that the major pier employed annulets although this seems likely (Fig 84). This evidence allows an alternating scheme to be constructed. The arcade arches (Fig 90; Fig 91) were no wider than the minor piers and the diagonal shafts of the major piers apparently continued upwards into triforium and clerestory level as moulded responds or 'masts' to support the vault.

Fragments of rib mouldings excavated in demolition deposits have allowed a massive boss (<A89>, Fig 92) found at Nonsuch (and now in the Museum of London gallery) to be identified as part of the vault of the presbytery/Lady chapel. It allows a much more detailed understanding of the vault than would otherwise be possible. The ornament of grapevines is a common symbol of the Eucharist (Hall 1979, 322). The boss demonstrates how the heavier ribs <A87>, <A88> served as the diagonal ribs, while lighter ribs formed level ridge ribs (Fig 93). The boss indicates a conventional quadripartite vault. The convergence angles of the ribs allow the proportion of the vaulting compartment to be determined by $\tan 28.375$ (1:1.85). The proportion is compatible with the known proportion of the presbytery bays (1:1.80) although there are difficulties and these may never be fully resolved.

The foundations excavated by Bidder indicate an alternating scheme of 'minor' and 'major' piers (Fig 188). The 'median' triple rolls on the major pier probably rose as wall shafts to the springing of the vault, which was marked by capitals as at St Augustine's Bristol (Gloucestershire) (now Bristol Cathedral) with whose eastern extension Merton's displays striking similarities (Chapter 4.3). The Merton 'minor' piers did not apparently support wall shafts and the vault springing must have been supported at these points by corbels at a greater height. It seems likely the 'major' divisions were emphasised by large transverse arches rather than ribs. It is also not clear if this scheme was carried into the Lady chapel without change, as is likely. The retention of the earlier crossing would have caused grave problems, which the vault design had to accommodate as best it could. Overall, the scheme was more conventional than at Bristol, lacking lierne (ie a tertiary rib, one which does not

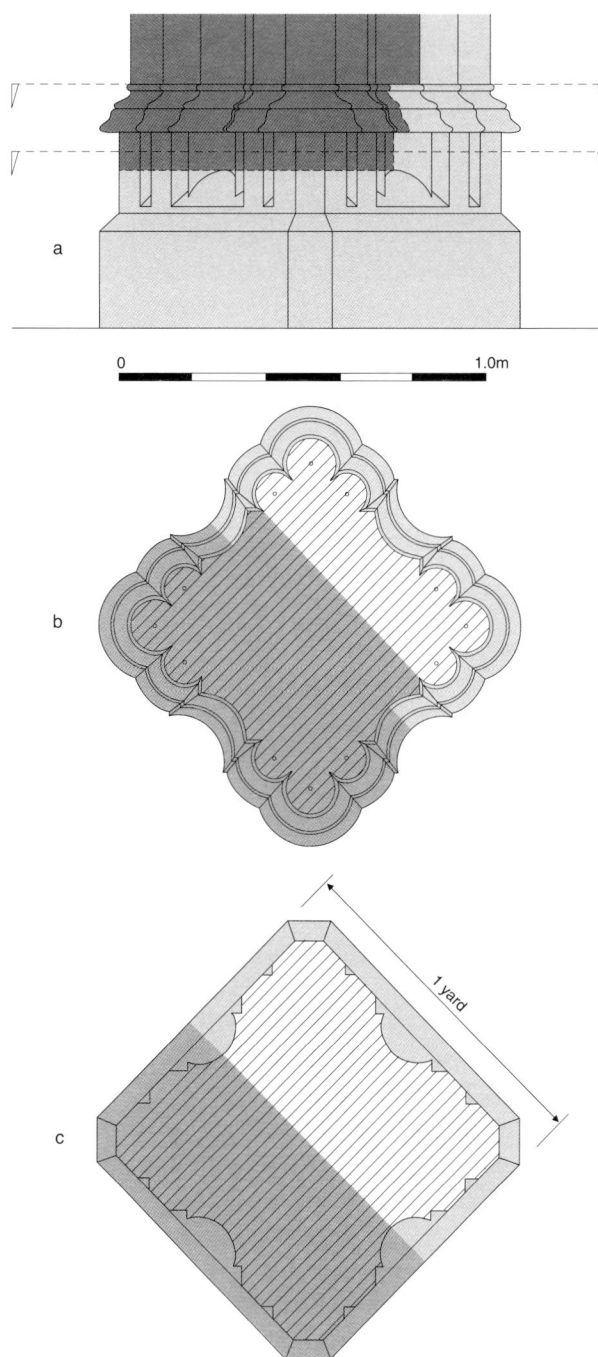

Fig 86 *Minor pier base (period M3) from Kingston Library: a – elevation; b – plan at base of shaft; c – plan above plinth (scale 1:20)*

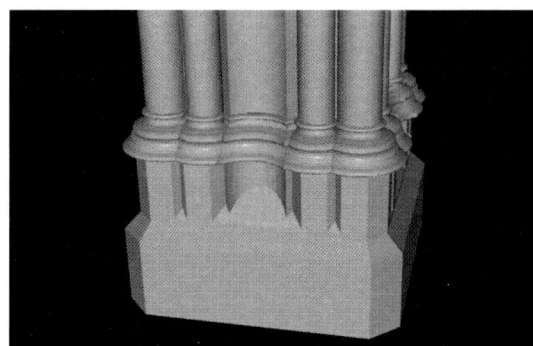

Fig 87 *Minor pier base (period M3): perspective view*

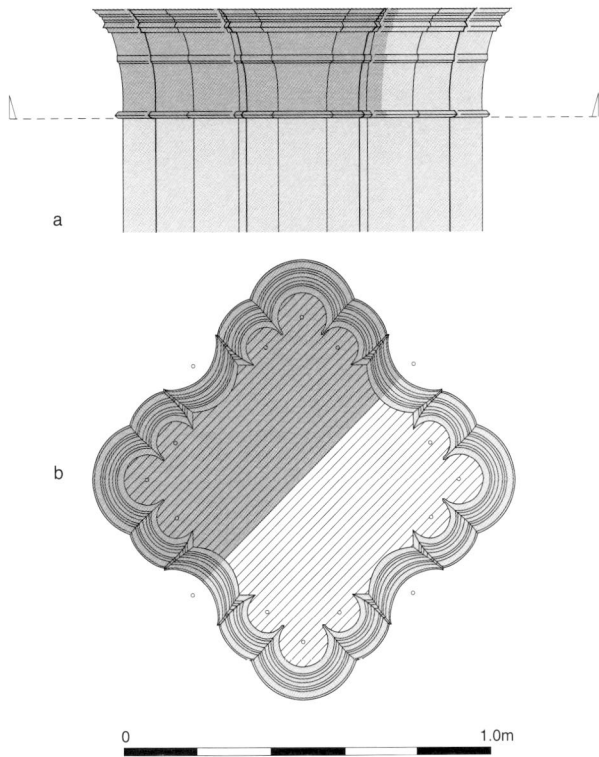

Fig 88 *Minor pier capital (period M3) from Kingston Library: a – elevation; b – inverted plan (scale 1:20)*

Fig 89 *Minor pier capital (period M3): perspective view*

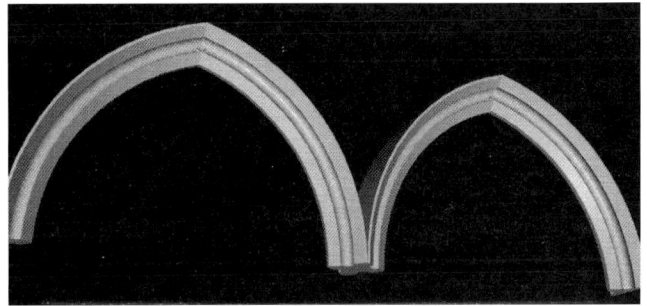

Fig 91 *Perspective view of paired arcade arches (period M3)*

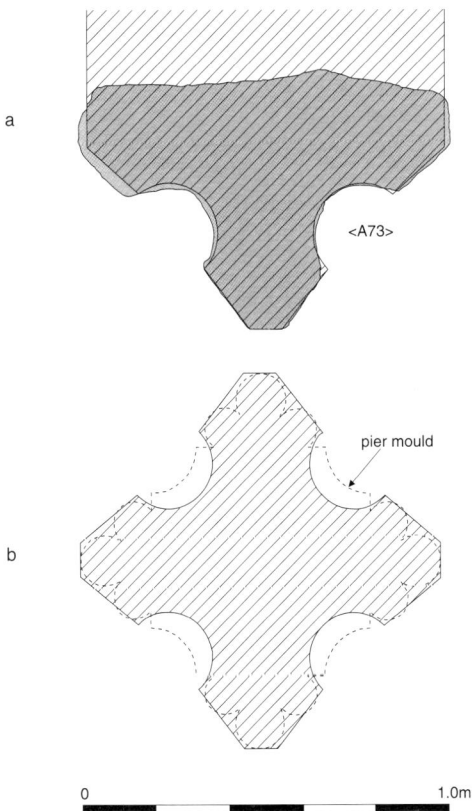

Fig 90 *Arcade arch (period M3): a – unfinished voussoir <A73> as found, hatching indicates intended moulding; b – conjectural reconstruction of arcade arch moulding at spring line (scale 1:20)*

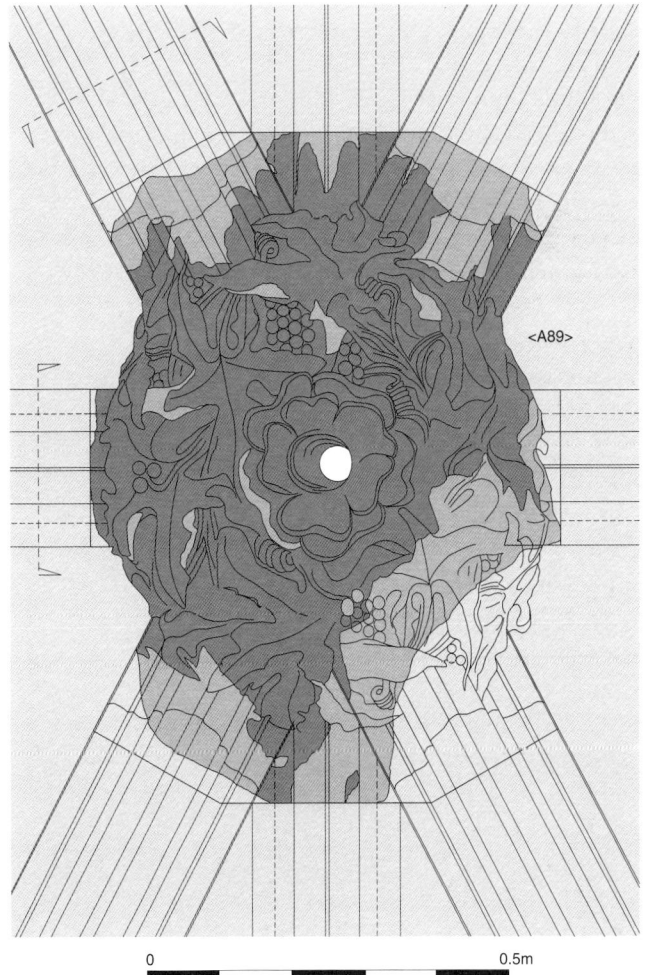

Fig 92 *Vault boss <A89> from Nonsuch (see Fig 93 for rib mouldings) (scale 1:10)*

spring from either one of the main springers or the central
boss) or tierceron (ie a secondary rib which does spring from
one of the main springers or central boss) ribs, but employing
ridge ribs absent there.

Details of the boss bear witness to the structural problems
recorded in this period. The boss bears signs of having been
removed and roughly reset, probably in the 1390s when large
parts of the vault were probably rebuilt (below, 3.4,
'Archaeological evidence'). The suspension hole, worn with
use, probably suspended a corona (circular chandelier) or pyx
(container storing the consecrated bread) over the high altar. As
is usual, the reverse (top) of the boss is flat, with radiating
setting-out lines, to ease manufacture and assembly of the vault.
Traces of paint on the boss (revealed by cleaning prior to
display) show it was brightly painted.

Evidence for the external appearance of the eastern extension
is provided by various *ex situ* mouldings. Two pieces of Kentish
ragstone, found in a later pit, appear to represent the original
buttress weatherings and it is likely the simpler element <A81>
capped the ground table while the 'notched' element <A82> was
an unknown height above it (Fig 94). This implies that the base
course had two offsets, marked by weatherings running without
interruption along buttresses and walls. Fig 94 and Fig 95 show
an elevation, profiles and a reconstruction of this ground table,
employing the dimensions of the excavated foundations. A
solitary abutment (<A79>, Fig 96) of a flying buttress arch
survives, while curved flying buttresses are apparently
represented by curved coping stones <2270>, <2273>; these
are matched by coping fragments from the gable of the
presbytery (below, <A80>, Fig 97). These badly weathered
Reigate stone fragments can be assumed to derive from the very
end of the construction of the eastern extension.

The church's main parapet coping (of which many fragments
were preserved in the later buttress extensions, eg <2179>,
<2731>; CP5.15; not illustrated) was apparently uncrenellated
and its moulding approaches the standard form of the 15th
century. It was different from the contemporary but more
decorative crenellation used on the gable. Here a uniform coping

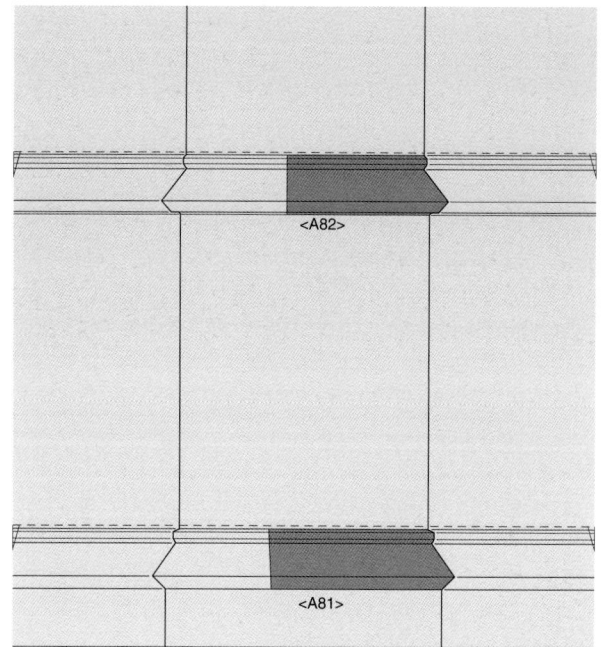

a

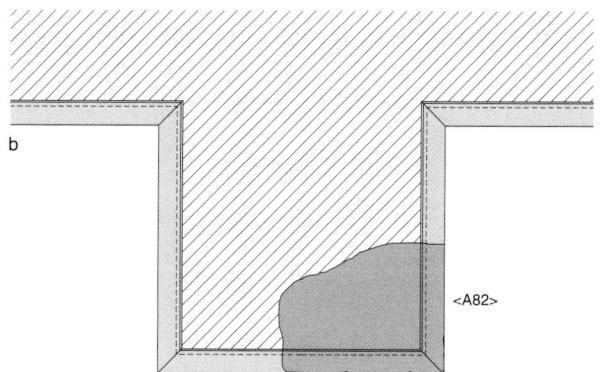

b

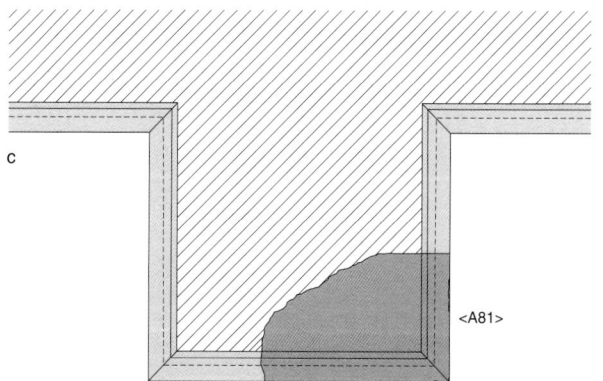

c

Fig 94 *A conjectured reconstruction of a north aisle buttress based on* ex situ
*mouldings <A81>, <A82> and the dimensions of the excavated foundations
(period M3): a – elevation; b – profile at raised weathering; c – profile at ground table
(scale 1:40)*

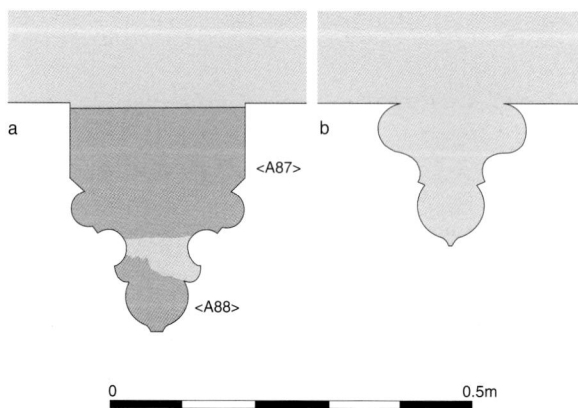

Fig 93 *Rib mouldings (period M3): a – diagonal rib <A87>, <A88>;
b – reconstruction of ridge rib (scale 1:10)*

Fig 95 Perspective view of two buttress feet (period M3)

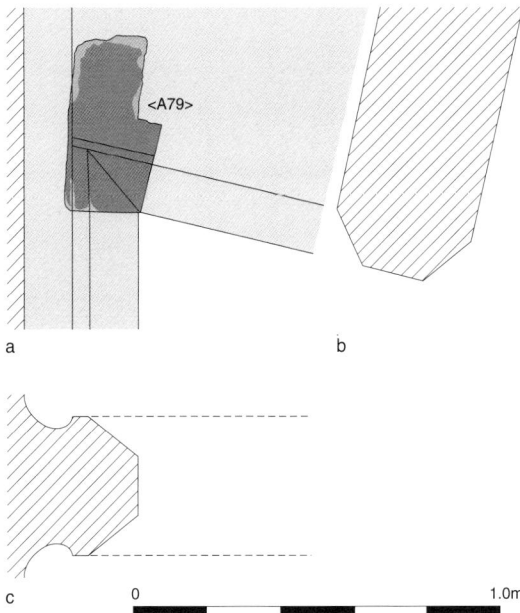

Fig 96 A possible flying buttress fragment <A79> (period M3): a – transverse elevation; b – profile of bridge; c – moulding of respond between ?window casement hollows (scale 1:20)

Fig 97 East gable crenellated parapet <A80> (period M3): a – moulding coping (restored); b – elevation (scale 1:20)

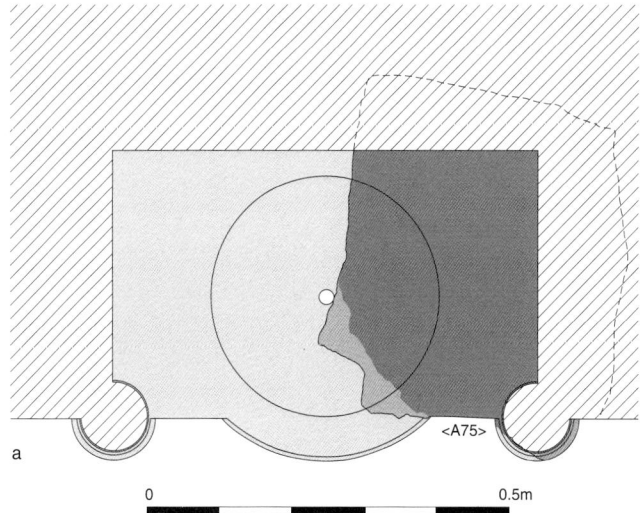

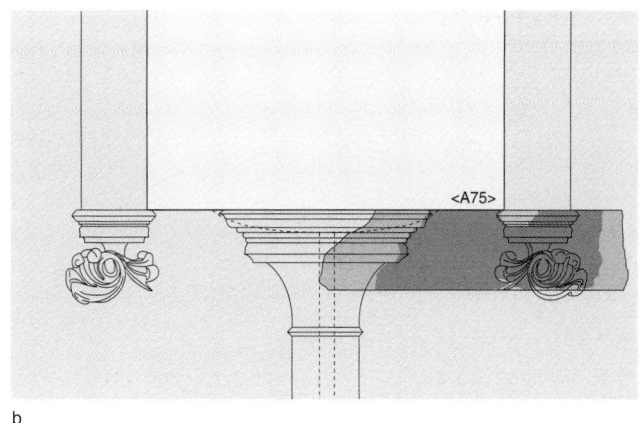

Fig 98 Piscina <A75> from the eastern part of the church (period M3): a – plan; b – elevation (scale 1:10)

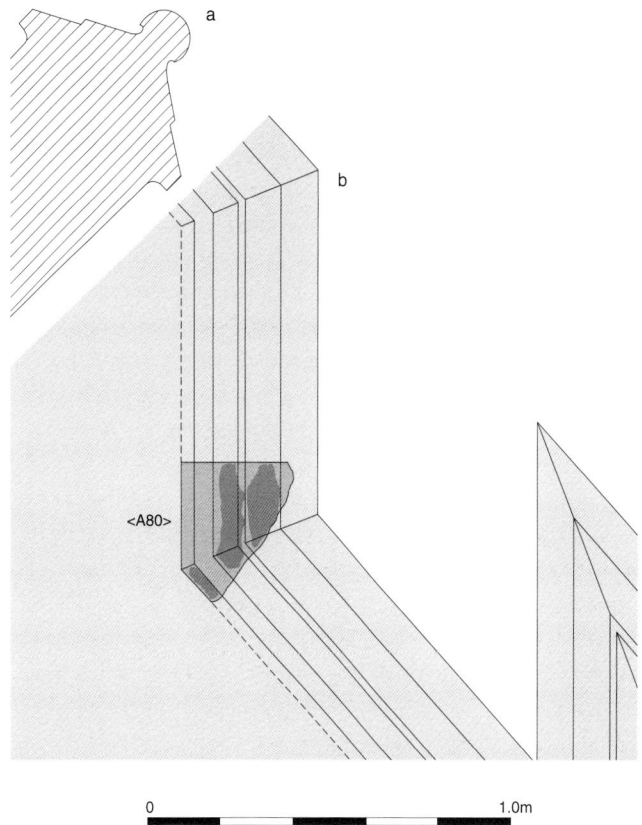

moulding with a central 'handrail' and stepped weatherings sloping at 30° probably formed part of a crenellated parapet cresting a gable steeply pitched at 42.6° (<A80>, Fig 97).

A probable stair tread from a newel (<2404> [3775]; CP5.4; not illustrated) was found in a destruction deposit near the east end; the mixed tooling suggests reuse from an earlier period. The east end most probably had stair turrets at the re entrants between the Lady chapel and ambulatory (Fig 148c).

Contemporary with the eastern extension of the church is a fine Purbeck marble piscina; this was probably sited close to an altar in the east arm, perhaps in a chapel in the aisle/ambulatory or in the south wall of the presbytery. The base can be reconstructed in its entirety (<A75>, Fig 98). The alcove was 2ft (0.61m) wide and contained a finely cut basin; a drain hole ran through the centre of the basin. The alcove was flanked by three-quarter shafts resting on delicately carved corbels with elegant foliated pendants. The basin's projecting lip was carved as a capital, apparently a three-unit form.

A decorated late 13th- to early 14th-century Eltham Palace/Lesnes Abbey (Kent) floor tile from a debris deposit in the Lady chapel (<T92>, Fig 201), and a number of plain and decorated floor tiles, including 14th-century Penn tiles (design E2027; Chapter 7.3; Table 33), from later burials within the new east end suggest areas of the Lady chapel and presbytery were paved in plain and decorated tiling.

There was no evidence for major alterations to the fabric of the rest of the church although internal refurbishments may have occurred. For example, the recutting of the two northern altar bases in the north transept suggests that these were rebuilt or modified. The altar in the central chapel was rebuilt as an irregular pentagon but the new base in the northern chapel retained a rectangular form. A diverse mixture of plain and decorated floor tiles ranging in date from early or mid 13th to mid 14th century were found in burials in the north transept and hint at successive tile floors (Fig 202, <T95>). However, crushed Reigate stone and mortar spreads in the north transept included some Reigate stone paving slabs and show that at least part of the transept had a stone floor.

At the east end of the nave, parts of two adjacent foundations, one of mortared flint and the other of mortared Reigate stone, were exposed (Fig 71). The foundations, running north–south,

may be the remains of a pulpitum replacing the earlier (period M2) screen structure, with two phases of construction or two separate construction methods on the same footing.

Seven burials within the north aisle/ambulatory of the presbytery and two in the Lady chapel could be securely attributed to this period because they either cut into the earlier presbytery foundations or were later than other deposits associated with the eastern extension. Other burials within the presbytery may be contemporary but could not be dated with confidence and are assigned to periods M1–M4 (below, 3.5). An adjacent charnel pit, which contained mainly long bones (and one skull), could be dated by pottery ([2894], coarse Surrey-Hampshire border ware, CBW) to c 1270–c 1500. It was probably for burials disturbed by construction. Three presbytery burials were interred in coffins. Burial [2381] (an older adult male) was interred in a carved monolithic stone coffin [2164], possibly sandstone, 2.09m long and tapering slightly towards the feet. The coffin walls were c 50–60mm thick and the interior shaped to accommodate the head. Burials [2703] and [2701], adult males, were in lead coffins (respectively, <S12> Fig 99; <S13> Fig 100), both also shaped around the head and tapered towards the feet. Small amounts of a white material (not analysed) found with [2703] suggested a possible shroud. Individual [2387] (adult male) was in a rough cist grave of mortared flint and Reigate stone fragments with part of the south side lined with peg tiles. Another burial [2858], an older

Fig 99 Lead coffin <S12> of burial [2703] in the presbytery (B1, period M3), looking west (1.0m scale)

Fig 100 Lead coffin <S13> of burial [2701] in the presbytery (B1, period M3), looking west (1.0m scale)

adult ?male, was most probably clothed: two buckles <S206>, <S207> were found in the upper thigh region (Fig 101). There were two burials at the western end of the Lady chapel. The northern burial was disturbed by an internal repair to the north presbytery wall thought to post-date the 1390s. Of the nine burials in the north aisle/ambulatory and Lady chapel, six skeletons were analysed. Five were male and the sex of one undetermined. Two were older adults, but the age estimates for the remaining four adults could not be refined.

There were 33 burials in the main body of the north transept and five within the chapels, three in the central chapel and one each in the north and south chapels. In contrast no burials were recorded in the south transept, although this may be a result of truncation. The north transept burials were generally aligned with the walls but with some intercutting. The burials in the main body were richer, with more grave goods, than those in other burial areas. Individual [3379], an older adult male, probably a priest, was interred with a lead/tin chalice <S23> and paten <S26>, while gold thread <S21> found around the head and on the left knee suggests vestments. It is possible the gold thread <S19> in burial [2402] also derived from ecclesiastical dress. Other burials suggested further interments in clothing rather than shrouds, such as the copper-alloy buckle <S208> on the left hip of burial [3172], a young adult male. Textile, possibly worsted and silk, came from burial [2651], an older adult male, and the presence of two leather soles <S18> near his feet indicate shoes. Small metal pieces, probably shoe buckles <S232>, were found around the feet of burial [2114], a mature adult male. Mature adult male [2934] was in a monolithic coffin [2933], 2.1m long, possibly of limestone, with a carved head recess and central base drainage hole; a chalk pillow was set beneath the head (Fig 102). A piece of material, over the right ribs, suggests he was either dressed or wrapped in a shroud. Tile and mortar bedding around the grave may indicate a tile capping but may alternatively be all that survives of a more general floor. Burials [2352] (a mature adult female) and [2353] (an older adult male) shared a dressed Reigate stone, cist grave. The bodies were on top of each other, rather than side-by-side and could be a married couple. Mature adult male [2844] was interred in a cist grave of chalk blocks

shaped around the body and head. Evidence for inscriptions or markers possibly associated with these burials was also found: a copper-alloy letter 'A' <S17> came from the backfill of a grave and a letter 'I' <S16> (Fig 103) from the bedding of one of the north transept floors. Thirty-six individuals from the north

Fig 102 Burial [2934] in a stone coffin [2933] with a chalk pillow, in the main body of the north transept (B1, period M3), looking west (1.0m scale)

<S16>

Fig 103 Copper-alloy tomb-inscription letter 'I' <S16>, from the north transept (B1, period M3) (scale c 1:1)

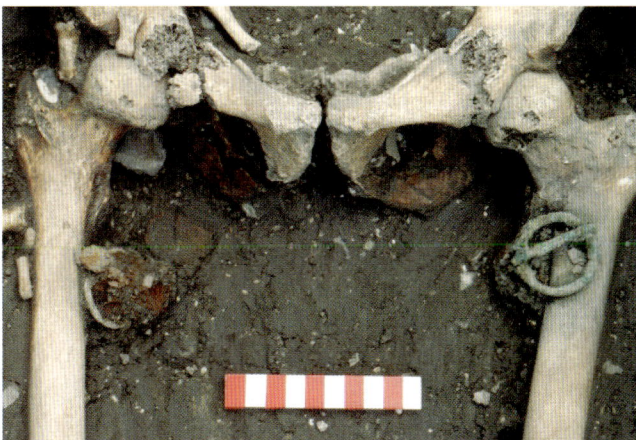

Fig 101 Buckles <S206> and <S207> on burial [2858] in the presbytery (B1, period M3) (0.1m scale)

transept were available for osteological analysis: 30 male, 5 female and 1 could not be sexed and all were adult. Of the males, 4 were young adults, 16 mature adults, 8 older adults, 2 could only be identified as adults; the females included 3 mature and 2 older adults.

The slype (B3f)

A series of mortar deposits were laid, as either successive surfaces in their own right or bedding for tiles or paviors. The structure was not otherwise rebuilt or repaired but the buttresses constructed on the north side of the chapter house (Fig 71 and below, this section) would have partially blocked it.

The lane/yard to the south of the nave (OA4)

A possible drainage ditch to the south of the nave at the east end of Open Area 4 measured approximately 2m east–west by 0.6m north–south and was filled with a stony silt (Fig 71). Overlying the ditch was a deposit containing coarse Surrey-Hampshire border ware (CBW) (c 1270–c 1500).

The cloister (B3a/e)

Evidence for a new cloister arcade dated to c 1375 is provided by ex situ mouldings from the archaeological excavations at Mill Road, Merton (MIS92), and at Nonsuch Place in Cheam (Surrey) (NON59) (<A99>, <A94>–<A98>, Fig 104a–c; Fig 105). This material is interpreted as deriving from a rebuilding of the main cloister, and not from the late 14th-century rebuild of the infirmary cloister (below). It was possible to reconstruct accurately the three orders of tracery. At least two similar types of window, differing in only minor details, were represented. The arched margin of the tracery met a deep casement hollow in the sides of the ?buttressed dividing piers. The mullion from Nonsuch (Morris's type 6: Fig 104d) does not fit easily with these pieces because the axial terminations would have had to plunge into the surrounding hollow casement in a clumsy way. It has therefore not been employed in the suggested reconstruction (<A94>–<A98>, Fig 105). The tracery scheme with four lights had cinquefoil heads, each probably 2ft wide (609mm). Four supermullions, each 8in (192mm) wide, rose from the apices of the cinquefoils and a fifth rose from the central springing. Reticulations between the two outer pairs of supermullions were sub-reticulated, each with round openings with trefoil cusping. The gaps were filled by small quatrefoil eyelets. The tracery was uniform apart from slight rearrangements in the sub-reticulations and their capping straight pieces. The window arch is a sharply four-centred form

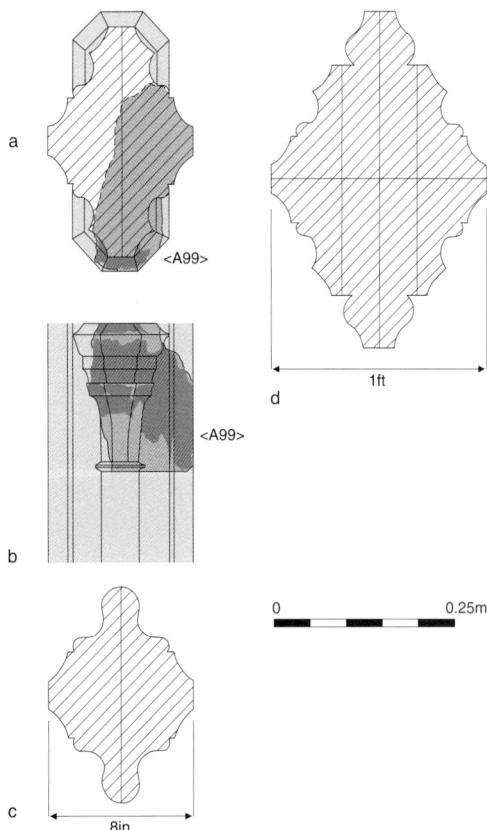

Fig 104 Cloister arcade mouldings (period M3): a – tracery based on minor mullion <A99> and Morris's Nonsuch type 11; b – elevation of the <A99> minor mullion capital; c – conjectured mullion; d – strong mullion based on Morris's Nonsuch type 6 (scale 1:10)

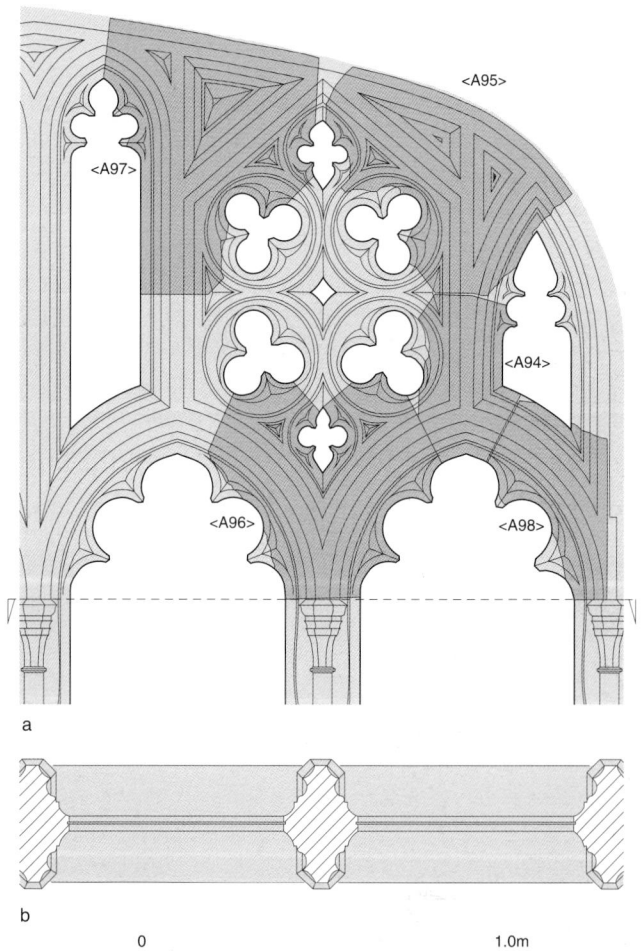

Fig 105 A reconstruction of cloister arcade tracery (period M3), based on fragments reused at Nonsuch Palace <A94>–<A98>: a – elevation detail; b – plan at the springing line (scale 1:20)

probably framed by a cloister vault. No vault fragments have been recognised however. The calculated width of the window bay, from reveal to reveal, is 3.05m (10ft) and compatible (if allowance is made for intervening piers) with the bay width of *c* 3.87m (*c* 12ft 9in) defined by the best-preserved part of the main cloister foundation near the chapter house (Fig 71). Glass seems to have been absent from the main lights but was used in the tracery, although this was probably subject to variation.

Decorated and plain floor tiles of various types were found *ex situ* in the cloister walk; their original, *in situ* location was uncertain. Certain decorated tiles, belonging to the Eltham Palace/Lesnes Abbey group (<T85>, Fig 201) and many of the plain-glazed Low Countries (also known as 'Flemish') tiles, date to this period and later (period M4).

The cloister garth (OA10)

A flint feature, dated by pottery to *c* 1080–*c* 1350 and set in the north-east corner of the garth, may be associated with the earlier tile drain (S6, period M2) although its function was uncertain. Fragments of glazed brick, possibly decorative walling, were found in the garth with pottery dated *c* 1080–*c* 1350 ([5725]).

The chapter house (B3b)

The east wall of the chapter house was removed and replaced by a buttressed apsidal eastern end (Fig 71; Fig 106) apparently solving earlier problems of subsidence. The eastern apse wall, 1.20m wide within a wall trench the same size, was solidly constructed from flint, chalk, Reigate stone, and Coggeshall-type brick fragments strongly bonded with mortar. The five external buttresses were integral with the wall. The curve of the apse meant that the building now had a maximum internal length of 20.18m. Buttresses were also added to the north wall, and the west wall was refaced. The regular spacing of these buttresses suggests (as is likely, on comparative evidence from the chapter house at St Augustine's Bristol) the original chapter house (period M2) was vaulted. This vaulting may have been removed or rebuilt when the apse was built. Floor surfaces survived beside the south wall and within the apse. These comprised yellow sand and mortar mixed with flint, overlying a 20mm-thick layer of plaster; which was possibly debris from limewashing or plastering rather than an earlier floor surface. A 0.12m thick layer of yellow-brown clay over this floor may be levelling.

Two burials were made in the south-east corner of the chapter house. One [575] was robbed but the other [716] contained an older adult male whose skeleton exhibited a number of pathological conditions, including diffuse idiopathic skeletal hyperostosis (DISH) and osteochondritis dissecans (Chapter 7.11, 'Characteristics of the skeletal material', '*c* 1300–*c* 1390 (period M3)', 'The chapter house (B3b)'). Within the grave were two iron nails perhaps suggesting a coffin but no wood traces were found.

The east range (B3c–d)

A small flint wall bonded with an orange mortar overlay the east wall foundation, joining the chapter house and the east range (Fig 71). This probably represented structural repairs. Within the slype/parlour (B3c) a series of mortars were laid

Fig 106 *The chapter house apse (period M3), looking south-east (2.0m scales)*

([5327]; [5484]; [5542]). These deposits were overlain by a brown silt [5269] containing a copper-alloy clasp <S246>.

The monastic cemetery

With the eastward extension of the church, the north (OA6) and south (OA3) excavated burial areas became better defined as distinct spatial entities.

THE SOUTH BURIAL AREA (OA3)

The western edge was formed by the south transept and chapter house, the north by the presbytery and Lady chapel, the south by the infirmary cloister and the infirmary chapel. Although few burials extended as far south as the infirmary cloister, a dense area of burials directly to the north of the infirmary chapel suggests an area opened up for new interments. The cemetery now covered an area of at least 20m north–south by 38m east–west or 760m^2.

The burials fall into two distinct stratigraphic groups. In the mid to late 14th century the area was covered by soil deposits, which contained debris likely to have come from the modifications to the church and chapter house. The latest pottery in these deposits dated to c 1350–c 1500 ([615] Cheam whiteware, CHEA). Of the 120 burials identified, 84 appear to pre-date this cemetery soil/levelling, but are stratigraphically later than the earlier (period M2) burials, and 36 post-date it. The later burials may have extended into period M4 and explain the lack of burials here attributable to that period; they are treated as a discrete group here. The two groups are distinguished on Fig 71, the stippled burials being those that post-date c 1350.

The burials were supine with their heads to the west unless otherwise stated. The majority were interred in shrouds but 22 (19 of the earlier burials and three of the later) were in wooden coffins preserved by deeper grave cuts and damper soil conditions. Burials [5060], [5080], [5077], [7163] and [7235] were plank burials. The plank over [7163] was beech but the timber, where identified, was otherwise oak. Dendrochronological samples from coffins [5293], [7121], [7635] produced dates of after 1131, after 1128 and after 1096, while the coffin [7099] of mature adult male [7098], a burial from the earlier phase, was dated to after 1076 (Table 71). None had the heartwood/sapwood boundary present, but the large time span between these dates and the date of burial could suggest that the wood was reused. Burial [7098] was distinctive because the body was prone, although this might simply be because the coffin was interred upside down. Of the 36 later burials two are also notable. Individual [5023] was interred in a monolithic Reigate stone coffin [5202]. The burial had been disturbed and the rectangular coffin was fragmentary but what remained measured 1.94m long by 0.72m wide and had a central drain hole. Burials [5002] and [5005] are both unsexed adolescents. Burial [7573] (an adult male) (not shown on period plan) was probably dressed as a copper-alloy buckle with associated mineralised textile was found in the pelvic region (<S214>, Fig 107). Burial [7606] (an older adult male)

<S214>

Fig 107 Copper-alloy buckle <S214> found with mineralised textile from the pelvic region of an adult male [7573], in the south burial area (OA3, period M3) (scale c 1:1)

(not shown on period plan) was also dressed, as on the right side of the pelvis (also near the right hand) was a copper-alloy buckle <S216> and two copper-alloy strapends <S244> and <S245>.

The dense group of burials directly to the north of the infirmary chapel spanned both phases. They were dug parallel with the north chapel wall in well-defined rows with virtually no gap between rows or graves. This density and order is unusual. A relationship with the infirmary chapel seems very probable, that is that this small area served as the burial ground for the deceased from the infirmary. Most were either in shrouds or wooden coffins but one, from the earlier phase, was in a lead coffin ([7060]; <S14>, Fig 108).

The graves in the remainder of Open Area 3, in contrast, were in less well-defined rows, although some rows were evident to the west. Burial alignments were reasonably regular but some were oriented slightly either to the south-west or north-west. Burial [839], near the chapter house, was on a bed of grey ash and charcoal approximately 50mm thick laid in the eastern two-thirds of the grave. The base of the cut was not level and the feet lay in a depression.

Of the 120 burials, 109 individuals were available for analysis. They were divided into two subsamples to reflect the apparent distinction between the western part of the cemetery and the area to the north of the infirmary chapel. The 78 individuals within the first group included 66 males, 2 females ([5758]; [7766] not shown on period plan) and 10 whose sex could not be determined. There were no children, and of the 66 males 3 were young adults, 34 were mature, 25 classified as older adults, 3 were only identifiable as adult and 1 could not be aged. The two females comprised one young and one mature adult. The 10 of indeterminate sex consisted of 3 mature adults, 1 older adult and 6 aged only as adult. The young adult woman [5758], from the pre-c 1350 phase, was interred next to a buttress of the south transept in a Reigate stone cist grave. The grave had been capped with a carved Reigate stone gravestone of which the eastern part remained in situ. The carving may have represented a cross (Fig 109).

The 31 individuals to the north of the infirmary chapel included two immature individuals aged between 13 and 16 years. This group were all male where sex could be determined, 26 individuals, of whom 2 were young adults, 12 mature and 12 older adults. Three adults could not be sexed and these

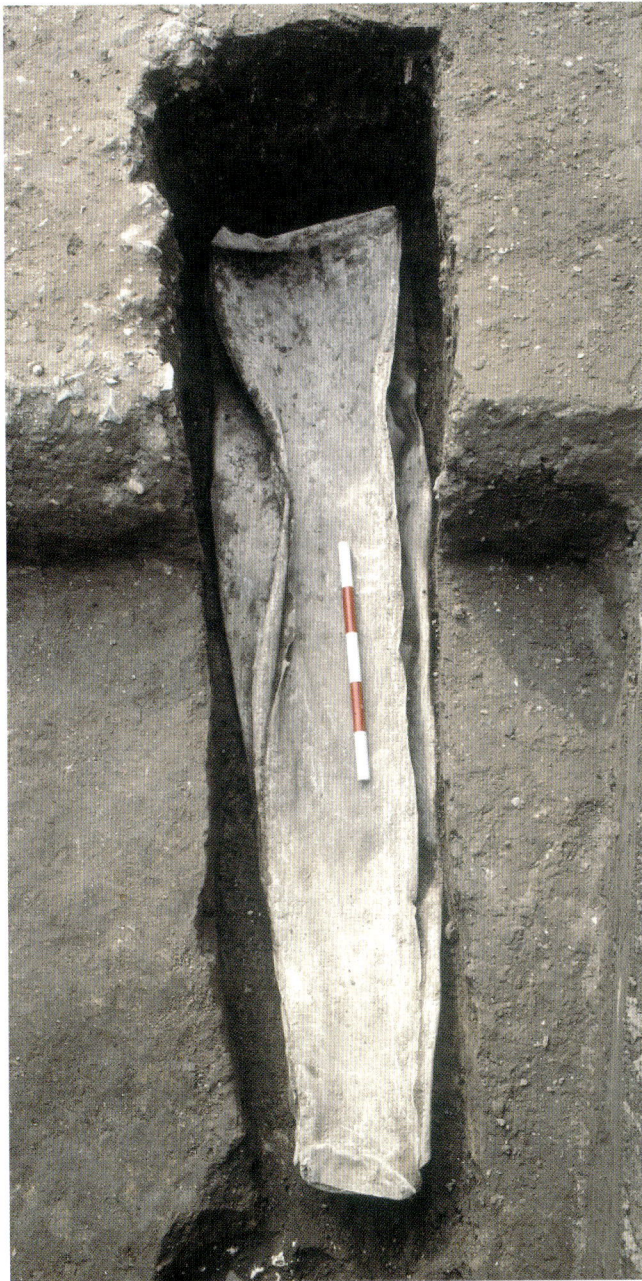

Fig 108 *Lead coffin <S14>, north of the infirmary chapel (OA3, period M3), looking west (0.5m scale)*

Fig 109 *The Reigate stone lid capping the cist grave of a young adult woman [5758] in the south burial area (OA3, period M3), looking west (1.0m scale)*

included one older adult.

Four charnel pits were also recorded in the cemetery. Three were relatively small. The largest [7061], approximately 3m by 2m and 0.5m deep, contained the bones of many individuals.

THE NORTH BURIAL AREA (OA6)

A horizon of construction debris [3807], particularly to the north-east of the presbytery, contained coarse Surrey-Hampshire border ware (CBW) pottery post-dating *c* 1270 and formed a diagnostic horizon through which the graves were cut. Some burials also cut diagnostic cemetery deposits, including debris pre-dating later repairs and buttressing (period M4). A mortar-mixing pit ([3222]; Fig 71), 4.5m by 3.5m and approximately 0.8m deep, to the north-east of the church, which contained

pottery dating *c* 1140–*c* 1350 (LOND, SSW) and a copper-alloy needle (<S297>, Fig 219), was also probably contemporary with the rebuilding. A small cut to one side of the main pit may be for the lifting gear. A second smaller mortar mixing pit, 2.0m east–west by 1.5m north–south and 0.29m deep, was found a metre away. Deposits over Road 1 suggest that it was no longer in use by this period.

The cemetery's boundaries, other than the church, were once again not identified, but burial appears to have expanded westwards into previously untouched areas. One hundred-and-forty-three burials were found: 74 of which lay to the east of the north transept with 62 burials to the west of it. A further seven burials at the west front also appear to date to this period. Burial in north–south rows becomes more apparent in this period, particularly north of the Lady chapel where at least five can be identified. The other burials to the east of the transept appear to be random but to the west another four, rough rows can be discerned, which appear to be the earliest burials there.

With the exception of a multiple burial of three (below), the inhumations were supine with their heads to the west. Most interments appeared to be simple shroud burials but four were probably within wooden coffins and two, a young adult woman [4039] and a probable mature adult female [4081], were buried in stone cist graves.

The 129 individuals available for osteological analysis constituted the largest subsample from the site. Almost all age groups were represented, amongst them 8 children of whom 3 (13- to 16-year-olds) were identified as male, 12 female adults, 93 male adults, 13 adults of indeterminate sex and 1 individual of indeterminate age and sex. Three of the children were aged 7–12 years and five were aged 13–16. The females included 2 young adults, 8 mature adults, 1 older adult and 1 that could be aged no more precisely than adult. The male age range included 3 aged 13–16 years, 9 young adults, 50 mature adults, 30 older adults and 4 defined only as adult. The 14 individuals of indeterminate sex included 1 young adult, 2 mature adults, 10 defined only as adult and a single individual who could not be aged.

The triple burial, to the west of the transept and stratigraphically early, contained two older adult males, [2712], [2856], and a child aged 7–12 [2855] (Fig 110). There was no evidence of a coffin and the splayed posture suggests the bodies were not in shrouds or coffins, but were casually disposed of,

possibly thrown in. Individual [2856], in the centre, was probably the first to be placed, and was face down. A small iron buckle, a shoe fastener, <S235> was found on the left hand, presumably redeposited. Burial [2712] was supine with the right arm splayed over [2856]'s leg and the left hand against his own throat. The child lay on its right side.

Burial [2905] (an older adult male) was to the north of the nave in a wooden coffin with a chalice and paten <S22> over his left hip, with his right hand near to his right shoulder (Fig 111; Fig 112). A stone slab bedded in mortar was set above the western end of the grave. At least two other wooden coffins were identified, while mature adult male [4768] (north of the Lady chapel) had two planks over the body. Burial [2595] (a mature adult male) was interred with five metal objects, but only a harness mount (<S358>, Fig 113) could be positively identified. Another copper-alloy object, c 40mm square, recorded as at an angle on the inside of the left tibia just below the knee, may be a medical support plate (not catalogued). A pattern on the metal suggests a fabric cover. The individual was

Fig 110 The multiple grave west of the north transept (OA6), containing (left to right) child [2855] and two older adult males, [2712] supine and [2856] (period M3), looking west (1.0m scale)

Fig 111 Burial north of the nave (OA6) of older adult male [2905] with a chalice and paten <S22> over his left hip (period M3), looking south (0.5m scale)

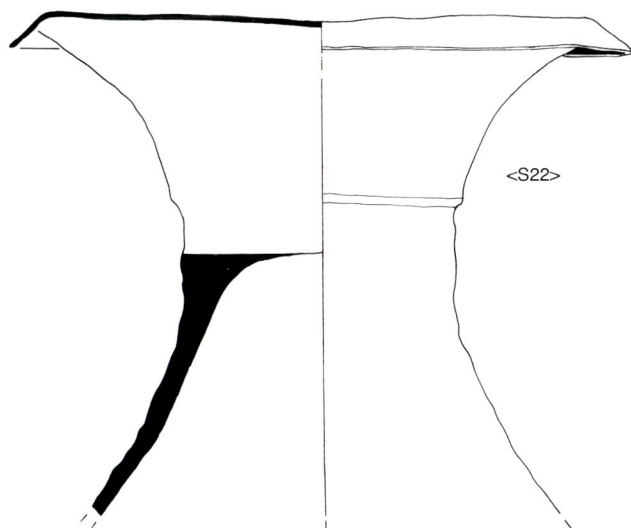

Fig 113 Copper-alloy mount <S257> from the ditch north of the nave and harness mount <S358> from burial [2595] (a mature adult male) (OA6, period M3) (scale 1:1)

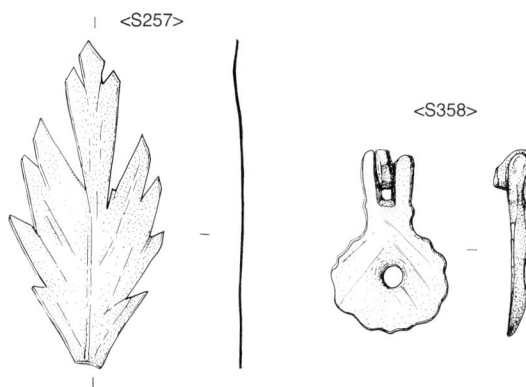

Fig 112 The lead/tin chalice <S22> from burial [2905] (period M3) (scale 1:2)

suffering from osteochondritis dissecans in the same region, a condition that could have resulted in inflamation of the knee area. Similar objects have been recorded at other monastic sites including in York at St Andrew's Gilbertine priory, Fishergate (Knüsel et al 1995), and in London at St Mary Stratford Langthorne and St Mary Spital (Barber et al 2004, 49; C Thomas, pers comm). Older adult male [2531] was presumably dressed when interred, as a copper-alloy buckle was found at the top of each leg (<S204>, <S205>).

The seven graves at the west front were all relatively plain and distinguished from the rest by nothing other than their location. Mature adult males [5247] and [5250] suggest a grave (that of [5250]) reopened to accommodate another individual [5247]. There was little disturbance to [5250] except for a slight dislodging of his right radius.

To the north of the nave, a 3m length of a wide east–west ditch (not illustrated) produced several objects, including a copper-alloy mount (<S257>, Fig 113), possibly from a religious furnishing, and a wooden bowl (<S294>, Fig 162). The pottery from the ditch fills dates to c 1080–c 1350 ([8518] LOND) and c 1230–c 1400 ([8519] KING) and the ditch may have silted up slowly. Deposits nearby produced other finds including an iron key <S198> and a decorated leather scabbard (<S265>, Fig 114).

A ?WORKSHOP (S8)

Within Open Area 6, about 5m north of the presbytery, mortar and crushed Reigate stone surfaces were found, with a 0.7m square flint and mortar foundation to the east and a smaller tile and flint foundation to the south, one posthole to the south and two stake holes to the west (Fig 71). These define a structure, possibly temporary and ad hoc, only partially revealed. To the west, cream mortar had been scorched to a deep rose colour. The deposits contained small vertebrate bones, the

85

<S265>

Fig 114 *Both sides of a decorated leather scabbard <S265>, found north of the nave (OA6, period M3) (scale c 1:1)*

most identifiable being fish, and pottery dated to the second half of the 13th and 14th century ([3360] LOND; [3365] KING).

To the west of this, evidence of lead recycling was identified. Silt deposits contained fragments of lead, including cames, and of window glass, and possibly window tracery, and inclusions of charcoal and chalk. These suggest the reuse of lead from the windows of the original east end of the church in the new presbytery and Lady chapel. Structure 8 may have been a temporary workshop built to undertake this work. The rose-coloured scorching on the floors may be from fires to melt the lead, the crushed Reigate stone the result of breaking up stonework. The vertebrate bones suggest food eaten in a potentially sheltered (and warm) workshop.

The infirmary hall (B4a)

Occupation deposits and mortar floor surfaces in the hall are dated to the first half of the 14th century by pottery with a date range of c 1140–c 1350 (LOND, SHER); a fragment of a coin

<S344>, issued 1351–82, from these surfaces may be intrusive. A pitched tile hearth [9250], built from roof tiles, was set against the south wall (Fig 71).

During the second half of the 14th century, however, the hall underwent major structural alterations. The earlier open hall was partitioned with timber and stone walls abutting the column bases to form rooms in the aisles (rooms 1–5 on the west side, rooms 6 and 7 on the east), although the central vessel remained open. The foundations for the partitions were slight (0.2–0.3m wide and 0.3m deep) and included reused Reigate stone and floor tiles. The superstructure may have been timber. A 1m-thick masonry relieving arch foundation was inserted west–east between two column bases to strengthen the structure (Fig 115). The arch was set 0.88m deep. The partitioning may have necessitated alterations to the existing windows: numerous pieces of glass and lead, recovered from pits and debris layers, probably came from the original 13th-century glazing. The presence in these deposits of pottery post-dating c 1350 (CHEA; Chapter 7.4) and a coin of Aquitaine of Edward the Black Prince c 1362–76 (<S343>, Fig 116) dates the work to the 1360s or later.

Rooms 1 and 2 were floored with roof tiles (eg <T103> [1022]) bedded in mortar and aligned east–west. Room 2 may also have had a tile hearth at its southern end (not illustrated).

Room 3 was the only complete room to be excavated and its dimensions could be established as 3.7m north–south by 2.4m east–west. It too was floored with roof tiles ([1018]; eg <T102>, Fig 205), mainly aligned east–west but with an area against the southern partition aligned north–south (Fig 117). A Reigate stone column base measuring 0.22m in diameter [1016] was located close to the west wall. A line of glazed floor tiles bordered the entrance, including 'Westminster' tiles (<T63>, Fig 197).

Room 4 was c 4.0m north–south by 2.4m east–west. The roof tile floor ([1035] eg <T101>, Fig 205) was more truncated than that in rooms 1–3.

Room 5 measured c 3.5m north–south by 2.4m east–west. Within it lay a crushed Reigate stone levelling layer overlain by a sequence of crushed chalk, silt and clay floor surfaces. The room was heated by a pitched tile hearth [8096] in the western wall. Fragments of roof tile bedded on burnt mortar [8824] may represent a floor or secondary hearth area.

Rooms 6 and 7 lay on the eastern side of the hall. They were smaller than the rooms to the west both being squeezed into one bay. Room 6 is conjectured at c 2.4m east–west by 2.0m north–south. Reused pieces of Reigate stone incorporated into the partition foundation between the rooms included part of a string course with Romanesque-style palmette ornament (<4482> [8722]; CP1.7) and a cut-down ashlar with a stylised nine-petalled daisy cut into the face (<A65>, Fig 183); the latter may have been a processional marker and perhaps derived from the infirmary chapel (Chapter 7.2). Room 7 would have measured c 2.4m east–west by 2.0m north–south. Within were floor and occupation surfaces of silt, sand and occasional mortar [9416]. These produced a bone die (<S32>, Fig 118).

The central vessel of the hall was surfaced with Low

Fig 115 *Relieving arch built between two column bases within the infirmary hall (B4a, period M3), looking north (0.5m and 2.0m scales)*

Countries-type floor tiles each 112–121mm square [1008] with either a yellow, dark green or brown glaze, bedded in yellow mortar. Alongside room 3 the tiles were arranged north–south to form a border between the central aisle and the room but in the middle of the hall the tiles were aligned at 45° to the walls. A silt layer [9861] produced a copper-alloy pentagonal strap loop <S240> and was overlain by the mortar bedding for a heavily truncated floor of glazed floor tiles ([9744]; [9725]). The broken end from a lead stylus <S44> and a turned bone bead (<S49>, Fig 118) were recovered from sand and gravel make-up to the south.

Food waste from the floors and associated pits and

Fig 116 *Aquitaine coin of Edward the Black Prince <S343>, c 1362–76 (scale c 2:1)*

Fig 117 *Glazed and peg roof tile floor within room 3 in the infirmary hall (B4a, period M3), with the earlier (period M2) pitched tile hearth in the foreground, looking west (2.0m scale)*

87

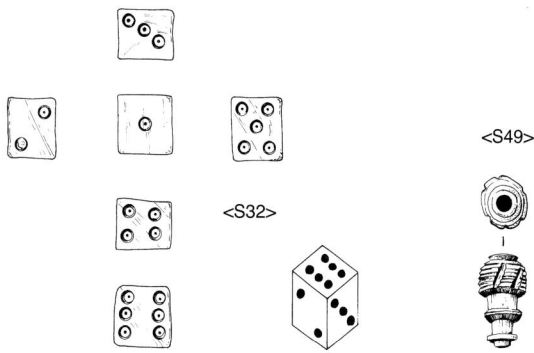

Fig 118 Bone die <S32> and bone bead <S49> from the infirmary hall (B4a, period M3) (scale 1:1)

postholes constituted the largest and most diverse animal bone group recovered from this period. The assemblage, when the large dominant component of unidentified and 'sheep-sized' mammal is ignored, consists mainly of cattle, sheep/goat and pig with an equally substantial component of chicken. There were a few fragments each of domestic goose, and mallard/ domestic duck. Game species were represented, in each case by a few fragments, by pigeon, partridge, passerine birds, brown hare and rabbit. The fish fauna was very substantial and diverse.

Table 11 Recovery of hand-collected vertebrate fauna from the infirmary hall (B4a, period M3), by fragment count

Common name	Latin name	No. of frags	%
Fish			
Fish unidentified		9	1.2
Cod family	Gadidae	4	0.5
Cod-sized		1	0.1
Conger eel	Conger conger	1	0.1
Amphibian			
Frog/toad	Ranidae	1	0.1
Birds			
Bird unidentified		18	2.4
Chicken	Gallus gallus	55	7.4
Chicken-sized		6	0.8
Goose	Anser anser	13	1.8
Goose-sized		2	0.3
Mallard/domestic duck	Anas platyrhynchos	2	0.3
Crow unidentified	Corvidae	2	0.3
Partridge, grey	Perdix perdix	2	0.3
Mammals			
Mammal unidentified		218	29.5
Cattle	Bos taurus	54	7.3
Cattle-sized		63	8.5
Sheep/goat	Ovis aries/Capra hircus	50	6.8
Sheep-sized		159	21.5
Pig	Sus scrofa	63	8.5
Horse	Equus caballus	1	0.1
Dog	Canis familiaris	1	0.1
Cat	Felis catus	2	0.3
Hare, brown	Lepus europaeus	4	0.5
Rabbit	Oryctolagus cuniculus	8	1.1
Total		**739**	

Clupeids (including herring) dominated, although smelt, gadids (including cod and haddock), eel and cyprinids each provided major components. There were occasional thornback ray, salmonid and plaice/flounder (Table 11; Table 12).

Table 12 Recovery of wet-sieved vertebrate fauna from the infirmary hall (B4a, period M3), by fragment count

Common name	Latin name	No. of frags	%
Fish			
Fish unidentified		2	0.1
Ray/shark		1	0.1
Thornback ray	Raja clavata	1	0.1
Salmon family	Salmonidae	2	0.1
Smelt	Osmerus eperlanus	95	6.6
Herring family	Clupeidae	363	25.1
Bream, common	Abramis brama	1	0.1
Carp family	Cyprinidae	115	7.9
Eel	Anguilla anguilla	73	5.0
Herring	Clupea harengus	33	2.3
Cod	Gadus morhua	2	0.1
Haddock	Melanogrammus aeglefinus	1	0.1
Cod family	Gadidae	79	5.5
Mackerel	Scomber scombrus	5	0.3
Conger eel	Conger conger	4	0.3
Plaice/flounder	Pleuronectidae	10	0.7
Amphibian			
Frog/toad	Ranidae	10	0.7
Birds			
Bird unidentified		107	7.4
Chicken	Gallus gallus	45	3.1
Chicken-sized		99	6.8
Goose	Anser anser	1	0.1
Goose-sized		3	0.2
Duck unidentified	Anatidae	2	0.1
Partridge, grey	Perdix perdix	1	0.1
Wood pigeon	Columba palumbus	1	0.1
Passerine		11	0.8
Crow unidentified	Corvidae	1	0.1
Dove	Columba livia/C oenas	3	0.2
Thrush, large	Turdidae	4	0.3
Thrush, small	Turdidae	3	0.2
Thrush unidentified	Turdidae	2	0.1
Mammals			
Mammal unidentified		102	7.0
Cattle	Bos taurus	1	0.1
Cattle-sized		7	0.5
Sheep/goat	Ovis aries/Capra hircus	20	1.4
Sheep	Ovis aries	2	0.1
Sheep-sized		139	9.6
Pig	Sus scrofa	34	2.3
Cat	Felis catus	4	0.3
Hare, brown	Lepus europaeus	7	0.5
Rabbit	Oryctolagus cuniculus	1	0.1
House mouse	Mus domesticus	2	0.1
Field vole	Microtus agrestis	1	0.1
Mouse unidentified		6	0.4
Mouse/vole	Muridae	3	0.2
Rat unidentified	Rattus sp	1	0.1
Small mammal		23	1.6
Shrew, common	Sorex araneus	3	0.2
Rodent, small		8	0.6
Vole	Muridae	5	0.3
Total		**1449**	

The infirmary chapel (B4b)

It is unknown whether the chapel was also repaired or rebuilt during the 14th century (Fig 71). A fragment of glass recovered from outside the chapel may suggest that new windows were made but is just as likely to relate to the rearrangement of the infirmary hall or be the result of an accident. Further tenuous evidence for 14th-century windows here may be the fragments of traceried window from a Dissolution layer to the east of the Lady chapel (<A76>, Fig 184), which may have been part of a smaller structure such as the chapel rather than the eastern extension of the church (above, 'The 14th-century church (B1)').

The infirmary cloister (B4c)

The cloister walk (Fig 71; Fig 119) was regularly resurfaced with gravels and crushed Reigate stone (such as [9592], [9429]) during the early 14th century and trampled silts accumulated upon the floors. A copper-alloy buckle frame <S224> came from these surfaces. A spread of tiles [9262] may indicate the last floor within this phase.

During the latter part of the 14th century the cloister was demolished and rebuilt to the earlier ground plan. The dating is derived from pottery within make-up layers ([492] TUDG; [5386] CHEA) associated with the reconstruction. The new cloister garth walls, constructed from flint overlain by Reigate stone blocks, formed a passage c 2.2m wide around the west,

north and east sides of the garth. However, there was again no evidence for a south walk along the north side of the reredorter, probably because buttresses were added to the north reredorter wall during this period (below, 'The reredorter (B5)'). Immediately south of the infirmary hall doorway (period M2), an east–west flint wall across the eastern walk may have partitioned off the southern part of the walk. Layers of mortar, crushed Reigate stone and sand were laid throughout the cloister walks. In the eastern walk compacted mortar [5349] formed a surface in its own right. Elsewhere these materials were probably bedding. The surfaces produced a number of small items including a gilded copper-alloy rivet from an ornate casket or chasse (<S256>, Fig 120) and an oval copper-alloy buckle (<S212>, Fig 120). Small fragments of copper and lead were also recovered. A worn and clipped silver Canterbury penny <S333> of Edward I or II and issued c 1302–10 came from the sequence in the north walk.

The infirmary cloister garth (OA5)

Occupation debris deposits accumulated in the garth; one contained a possible lead stylus <S45>. Pits and small ditches were also here (Fig 71; Fig 121). One ditch included an extremely rare fragment, over 200mm long, of a probable drain or gutter tile with a brown glaze on the curved inside ([10164] <T110>, Fig 122). This may have come from a drain within the infirmary cloister, or perhaps the reredorter or infirmary

Fig 119 The north-east corner of the infirmary cloister walk (B4c, period M3), looking east (2.0m scale)

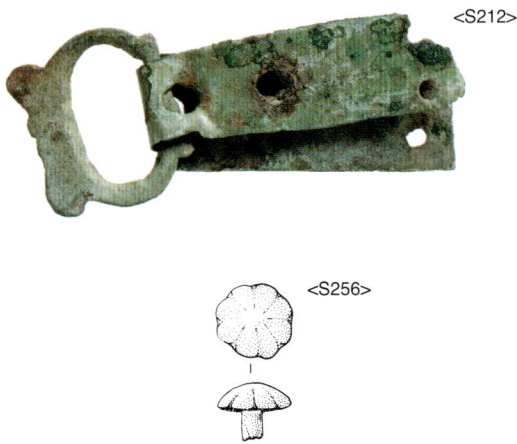

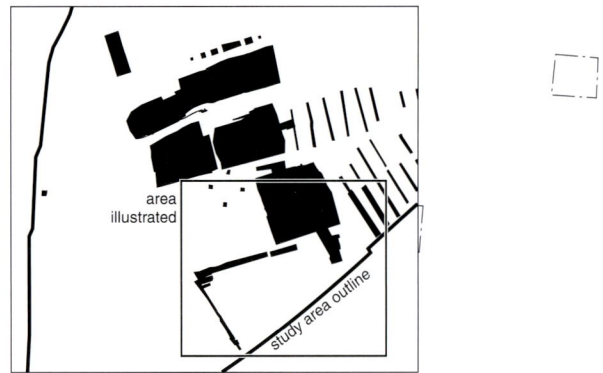

Fig 120 *Copper-alloy buckle <S212> and mount <S256> from the infirmary cloister (B4c, period M3) (scale 1:1)*

hall. The path from the infirmary hall into the garth was resurfaced a number of times during this period with deposits of gravel.

Food waste included roughly equal counts of cattle, sheep/goat and pig, with substantial amounts of chicken and rabbit bones. The fish fauna, however, was very sparse and consisted only of a few scattered clupeid, gadid and smelt vertebrae.

A drainage ditch (S4a) from the infirmary garth (OA5) eastwards

It is likely that the cloister drain became disused (below, 'The infirmary drain (S4b)').

The infirmary kitchen (B6)

The hearth (period M2) in the eastern part of the kitchen (not illustrated) fell out of use and was covered by a series of floor surfaces and other deposits, [10095] and [9952]. In the northern part, a possible floor of flint and gravel [9933] was laid down. Three plain-glazed Low Countries floor tiles found nearby almost certainly paved the kitchen. Food waste deposited here included higher counts of chicken, cattle, sheep/goat and pig, with a lesser retrieval of goose, hare and rabbit, and a single fragment of swan, an indicator of high-status consumption (Table 13).

A small wall was attached to the eastern wall of the infirmary kitchen before it was demolished, built from a line of reused Reigate stone blocks placed c 1m apart [10988]. One block was a reused parapet coping stone <4729>. Adjacent tile [10921] and mortar [10920] floor surfaces produced a sliver from a stone hone of Norwegian schist <S272>.

The food waste in the kitchen yard included a vertebrate assemblage that was dominated equally by clupeids (including herring), smelt and gadids, with smaller components of sheep/goat, pig, chicken, goose, rabbit, eel and plaice/flounder.

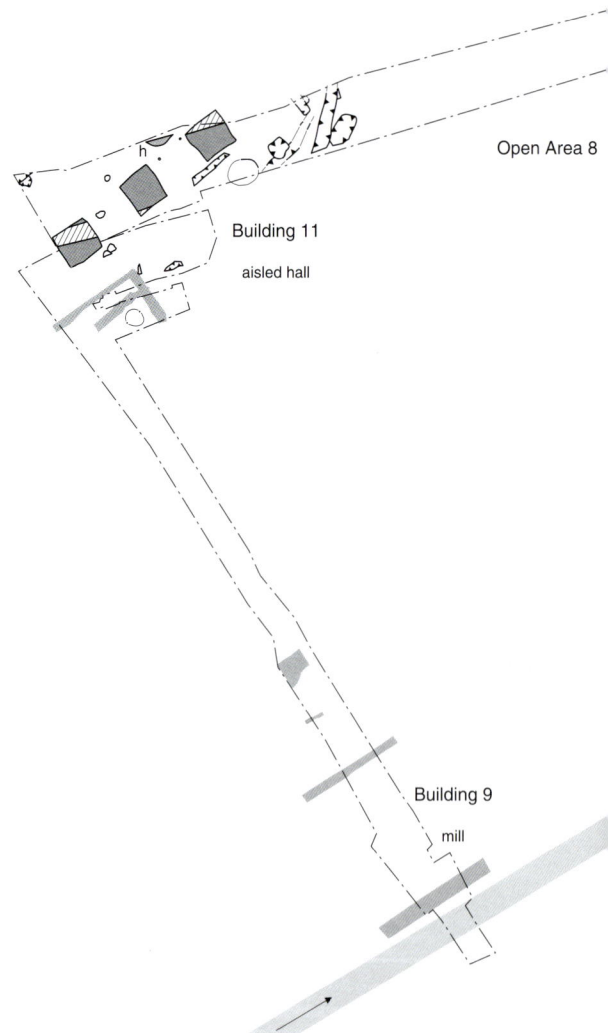

Fig 121 *Plan of the principal archaeological features in the south part of the precinct, c 1300 to c 1390 (period M3) (scale 1:500)*

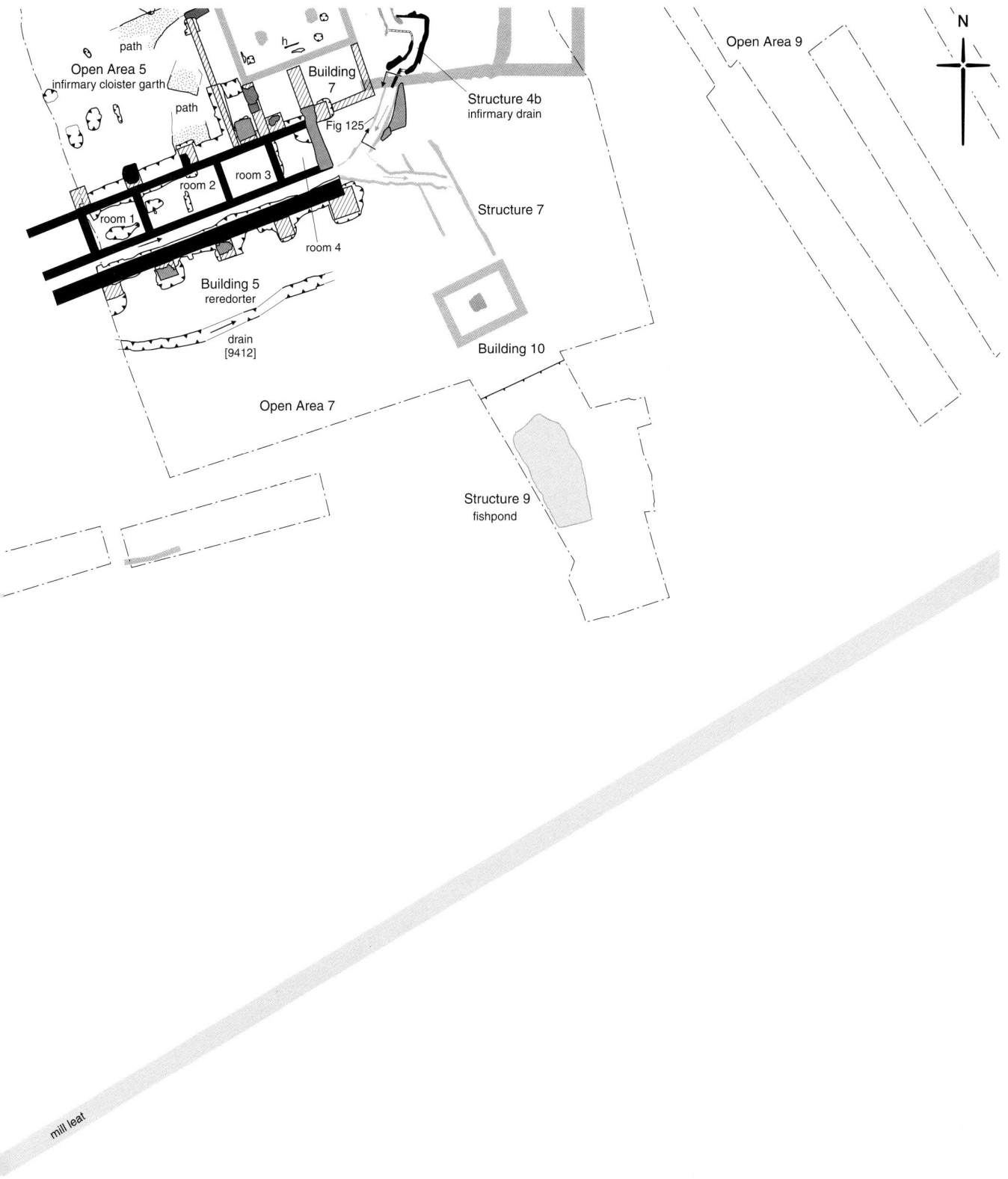

N

Open Area 9

Open Area 5
infirmary cloister garth

path

path

Building 7

Fig 125

Structure 4b
infirmary drain

room 1

room 2

room 3

room 4

Building 5
reredorter

drain
[9412]

Structure 7

Building 10

Open Area 7

Structure 9
fishpond

mill leat

0   25m

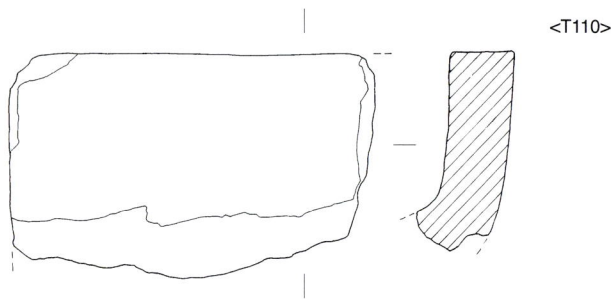

<T110>

Fig 122 Drain or gutter tile <T110>, glazed internally, from the infirmary cloister garth (OA5, period M3) (scale 1:4)

A kitchen or washroom/bloodletting house (B12)

The infirmary kitchen was probably demolished during the latter part of the 14th century, and replaced by Building 12, a kitchen or possibly washroom/bloodletting house (Fig 71; Fig 123). Like its predecessor, this was an addition to the east side of the infirmary hall, which formed the west wall, and the old doorway between hall and kitchen was retained. Building 12 was however, at 5.4m east–west by 4.0m north–south internally, much smaller than the earlier kitchen. A small area of tiles may represent the remains of a floor. Three decorated floor tiles, a 'Westminster' tile (<T56>, Fig 197) and two white slip group tiles (designs 4 and 10, <T43>, <T48>, Fig 195), found nearby in a later ditch and the infirmary drain may be from the floor of the demolished kitchen (B6), the new Building 12, or the infirmary hall.

The floors contained only a few fragments each of chicken, goose, cattle, sheep/goat and pig.

Table 13 Recovery of hand-collected vertebrate fauna from the infirmary kitchen (B6, period M3), by fragment count

Common name	Latin name	No. of frags	%
Birds			
Chicken	Gallus gallus	27	5.8
Chicken-sized		1	0.2
Goose	Anser anser	16	3.5
Swan	Cygnus sp	1	0.2
Mammals			
Mammal unidentified		87	18.8
Cattle	Bos taurus	27	5.8
Cattle-sized		46	9.9
Sheep/goat	Ovis aries/Capra hircus	48	10.4
Sheep	Ovis aries	1	0.2
Sheep-sized		134	28.9
Pig	Sus scrofa	66	14.3
Horse	Equus caballus	1	0.2
Cat	Felis catus	1	0.2
Hare, brown	Lepus europaeus	2	0.4
Rabbit	Oryctolagus cuniculus	5	1.1
Total		463	

The infirmary drain (S4b)

The drainage ditch, Structure 4a, flowing east from the infirmary garth (OA5) was blocked off and the infirmary drain (S4b) was detoured c 3m eastwards around what had been (period M2) their junction (Fig 71; Fig 121; Fig 124). The Reigate stone blocks of the walls and part of the base of the redundant section of the earlier infirmary drain were removed

Fig 123 The robbed walls of Building 12 (period M3), looking west, with the infirmary hall (B4a) in the background (2.0m scales)

Fig 124   The infirmary drain (S4b, period M3), looking north (2.0m scale)

and apparently reused in the detour. At its southern end, the new alignment was fed back into the earlier drain by two small walls on the base. Pottery dated c 1230–c 1400 was recovered from the construction fills, one, [10079], contained a London-type ware (LOND) drinking jug fragment. Where the north wall of Building 12 crossed it, the drain was arched with roof tiles bonded with a white mortar. The drain had an internal height of c 0.65m at this point. Elsewhere the drain top was truncated (Fig 125) and it is possible that the whole was arched thus. However, it is more likely that it was covered by Reigate stone slabs to ease access, and that the arches reinforced the drain beneath walls, as reconstructed in Fig 126.

The reredorter (B5)

The north wall of the reredorter drain was rebuilt [8145] a little further north than its predecessor, over the central partition wall [11254] of the 13th-century (period M2) undercroft, suggesting that the reredorter superstructure was extensively rebuilt and the drain widened. A ?undercroft vault corbel <5492> may come from this rebuilding. The division of the ground floor into rooms was, however, apparently unaffected (Fig 121).

External buttresses, set on 2m² mortared flint foundations, were added to the north and south walls – five pairs to the north and south – with a single buttress at the north-east corner. The foundations contained moulded stone from the earlier (period M2) reredorter. Similarly, evidence for the appearance of the new building was recovered from the buttresses as rebuilt later (period M4) and these pieces included four fragments of the

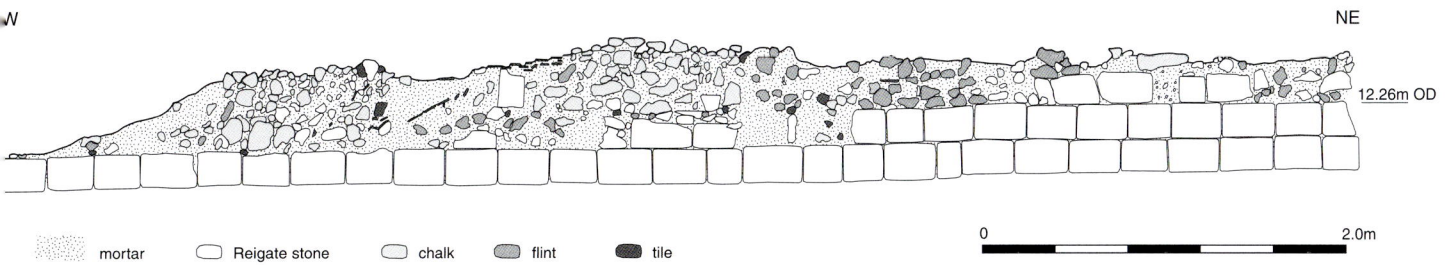

mortar · Reigate stone · chalk · flint · tile

Fig 125   South-east facing elevation along a stretch of the infirmary drain (S4b, period M3) (scale 1:40)

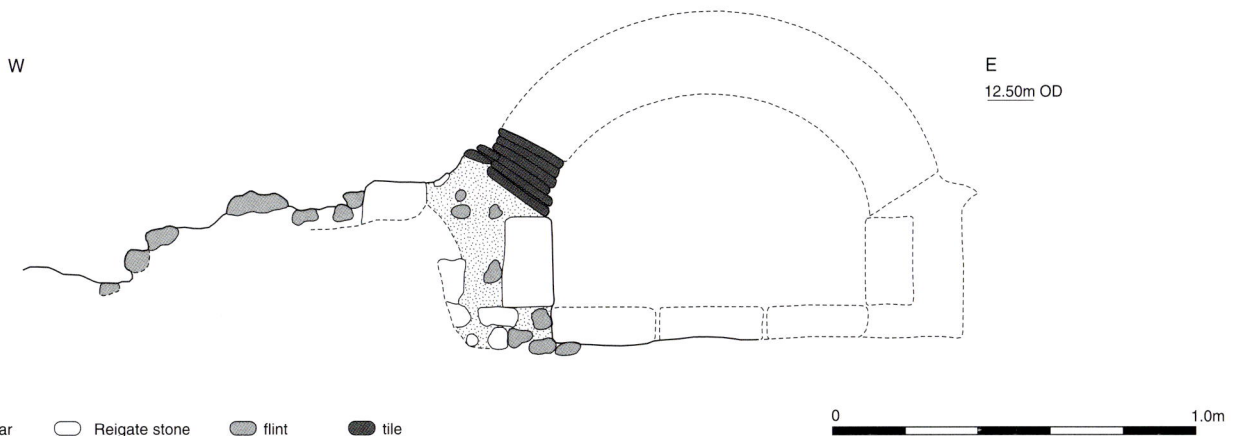

mortar · Reigate stone · flint · tile

Fig 126   A reconstructed elevation of the arch of the infirmary drain (S4b, period M3) at the point where the walls of Building 12 cross the drain (scale 1:20)

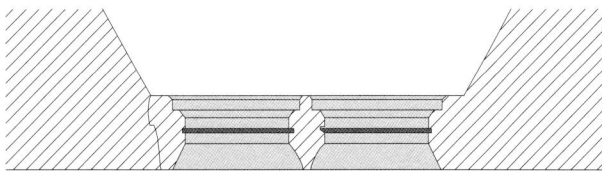

a

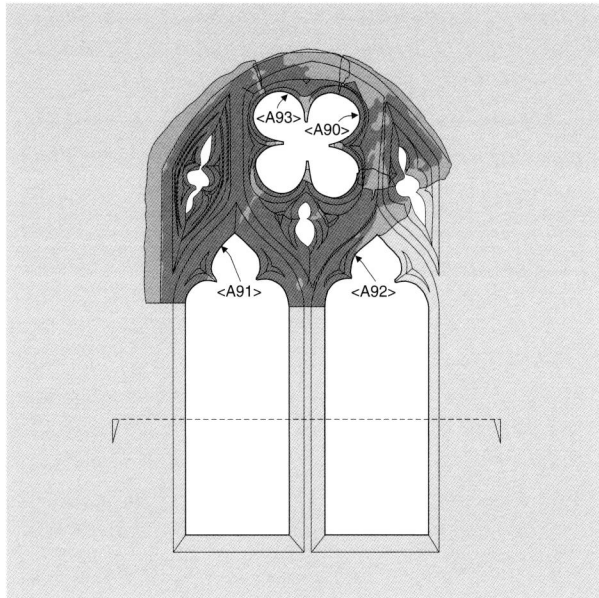

b

0   1.0m

Fig 127 A reconstruction of the two-light window <A90>–<A93> from the reredorter (B5, period M3): a – inverted plan; b – elevation (scale 1:20)

head of a two-light window (<A90>–<A93>, Fig 127). It was apparently badly cut from a single block causing problems for the glazier. Conventionally assembled tracery would have been provided with glazing grooves in even the smallest openings, but these were impossible to carve in this case. The main lights had conventional glazing grooves, but the tracery reveals were too inaccessible and dowel holes were instead drilled. Detachable glazing panels were held in place by the dowels. This arrangement may have leaked and additional glazing panels were attached to the tracery exterior with grooves and 'L'-shaped nails. The style is late Decorated but incipiently Perpendicular. The absence of weathering shows it was nearly new when destroyed and it is suggested that it was built c 1315–50.

The floors were relaid within the ground floor rooms of the reredorter. A dark brown clay [8341] in room 3 produced animal bone derived from roughly equal counts of chicken, goose, cattle, sheep/goat, and pig with occasional horse and cat. The fish fauna was dominated by clupeids (including herring) with smaller components of gadids (including cod) and smelt with one find of thornback ray.

A ? latrine/wash house (B7)

This building is likely to have continued in use early in the period but to have been demolished during the works on the reredorter later in the 14th century (Fig 71; Fig 121).

An infirmarer's ? lodging/kitchen (B8)

To the east of the infirmary, this building was apparently retained and continued in use (Fig 71; Fig 121).

A ? passage/pentice to the infirmary (S7)

This was resurfaced several times (Fig 121). A gilded copper-alloy harness mount in the shape of a cross, with lobed arms, came from one surface (<S359>, Fig 128). A substantial (225 fragments [9630]) animal bone assemblage (Table 45; Table 46) was mostly unidentified mammal or 'sheep-sized' mammal fragments. The identifiable material consisted of small numbers of chicken, cattle, sheep/goat and pig with occasional recovery of mallard/domestic duck and rabbit. Game species were represented by dove, partridge and two fragments of swan – a definite indicator of high-status consumption. The fish fauna was confined to two fragments each of sturgeon and cod.

<S359>

Fig 128 A copper-alloy harness mount <S359>, from the ? passage/pentice to the infirmary (S7, period M3) (scale c 1:1)

A ? storehouse/cold larder/wash house for the infirmary (B10)

Little evidence exists for any structural alterations to this building (Fig 121). A layer outside the presumed entrance, containing many iron nails, was sealed by roof tiles and possibly represented a floor here.

A watermill (B9) in the outer court (OA8)

During the 13th or 14th centuries the western end of the mill building was extended with a new room 11.00m north–south by 5.50m east–west (Saxby 2005a, 25–8). The eastern wall was heavily robbed, but the cut suggests the walls measured 800mm wide by 600mm deep. The surviving portion of the wall was of flint bonded with an orange sand mortar. Opposite the south-east corner was a flint abutment which formed the south side of the head-race to the mill producing a leat c 3m wide.

An aisled hall (B11) in the ? outer court (OA8)

Several pits were dug in the interior before the building was largely rebuilt (Fig 121). Much larger column bases, 2.5m² by 0.95m deep, replaced the earlier bases. The new flint, gravel and masonry bases were constructed slightly to the north-west of their predecessors with centres 6m apart. A series of pits were dug, dated by the presence of coarse Surrey-Hampshire border ware (CBW) to *c* 1270–*c* 1500.

The northern part of the building was floored with a compact gravel metalling [9519] dated to after *c* 1230 by Kingston-type ware (KING). A pitched roof tile hearth [9153] was surrounded by burnt clay and charcoal rake-out. Other floors, laid in the eastern end, consisted of clay, silt and further compacted metalled gravel; coarse Surrey-Hampshire border ware (CBW) pottery in [9415] dated this to *c* 1270–*c* 1500. Of note was a sherd from a KING dripping dish: an elongated vessel with rounded ends used to collect dripping from roasting meat.

Food waste recovered from the floors included a small assemblage (Table 14; Table 15) of animal bone deriving from predominantly sheep/goat (including sheep), cattle and pig, with a small component of chicken and goose. Game species were confined to single bones of brown hare and rabbit. The fish fauna was dominated by clupeids (including herring) with a smaller component of smelt. There were occasional salmonid, eel, cyprinids and gadids.

A garden in the ? outer court (OA7)

A 7.6+m length of an eastward flowing drain, 1.0m wide north–south by 0.8m deep, was recorded; it was constructed with a base lined with roof tiles and occasional floor tiles [9412] (Fig 121). Pottery recovered from the fill dates to *c* 1350–*c* 1450. Also recovered from the fills were two, very corroded, glass urinal fragments <S287> and <S288>.

The drain went out of use and was overlain by dark brown

silt deposits, which characterised much of the area and are interpreted as cultivated or garden soils. These layers, found particularly to the south of the reredorter, produced pottery dating to *c* 1350–*c* 1400, a turned bone bead (<S48>, Fig 215) and a copper-alloy stamped thimble <S298>, the corroded neck from a glass bottle <S277> and a lead weight or ingot <S331>. Fish and small mammal bones were also present in moderate quantities but included a near complete pig skeleton and the skeleton of a rabbit (Table 16).

A marshy area in the outer court (OA9)

To the east of the fishpond (S9), part of a north–south drainage ditch was recorded (not illustrated). The fills and overlying alluvial deposits [8315], [8326], [8385] produced pottery post-dating *c* 1230 and seeds mainly from a range of well-represented aquatic and bankside/marshland plants and disturbed and waste ground weeds. The latter included large numbers of seeds of corn spurrey (*Spergula arvensis*), which can also be grown as an oil crop, while some of the wild plants represented in these samples may be food remains, together with the large number of black mustard seeds. The presence of water flea eggs (*Cladoceran ephippia*) suggests that the ditch was at least periodically submerged.

Discussion *c* 1300–*c* 1390 (period M3)

During this period extensive building campaigns and repairs to existing buildings were initiated for which there is scant

Table 14 Recovery of hand-collected vertebrate fauna from the aisled hall (B11, period M3), by fragment count

Common name	Latin name	No. of frags	%
Fish			
Salmon family	Salmonidae	1	0.3
Cod-sized		1	0.3
Birds			
Bird unidentified		1	0.3
Chicken	*Gallus gallus*	13	3.4
Goose	*Anser anser*	6	1.6
Goose-sized		1	0.3
Rock/stock dove	*Columba livia/C oenas*	2	0.5
Mammals			
Mammal unidentified		98	25.9
Cattle	*Bos taurus*	29	7.7
Cattle-sized		43	11.4
Sheep/goat	*Ovis aries/Capra hircus*	36	9.5
Sheep	*Ovis aries*	2	0.5
Sheep-sized		93	24.6
Pig	*Sus scrofa*	45	11.9
Horse	*Equus caballus*	1	0.3
Dog	*Canis familiaris*	1	0.3
Cat	*Felis catus*	3	0.8
Hare, brown	*Lepus europaeus*	1	0.3
Rabbit	*Oryctolagus cuniculus*	1	0.3
Total		378	

Table 15 Recovery of wet-sieved vertebrate fauna from the aisled hall (B11, period M3), by fragment count

Common name	Latin name	No. of frags	%
Fish			
Smelt	*Osmerus eperlanus*	21	11.4
Herring	*Clupea harengus*	1	0.5
Herring family	Clupeidae	70	38.0
Cod family	Gadidae	8	4.3
Eel	*Anguilla anguilla*	1	0.5
Carp family	Cyprinidae	2	1.1
Amphibian			
Frog/toad	Ranidae	2	1.1
Birds			
Bird unidentified		31	16.8
Chicken	*Gallus gallus*	2	1.1
Chicken-sized		2	1.1
Passerine		1	0.5
Mammals			
Mammal unidentified		28	15.2
Sheep/goat	*Ovis aries/Capra hircus*	1	0.5
Sheep-sized		11	6.0
Pig	*Sus scrofa*	1	0.5
Cat	*Felis catus*	1	0.5
Rat unidentified	*Rattus sp*	1	0.5
Total		184	

Table 16 Recovery of hand-collected vertebrate fauna from Open Area 7 (period M3), by fragment count

Common name	Latin name	No. of frags	%
Fish			
Fish unidentified		1	<0.1
Thornback ray	*Raja clavata*	1	<0.1
Cod	*Gadus morhua*	3	0.2
Cod family	Gadidae	3	0.2
Cod-sized		3	0.2
Birds			
Bird unidentified		8	0.5
Chicken	*Gallus gallus*	46	3.0
Chicken-sized		28	1.8
Goose	*Anser anser*	15	1.0
Goose-sized		2	0.1
Mallard/domestic duck	*Anas platyrhynchos*	5	0.3
Duck unidentified	Anatidae	2	0.1
Rock/stock dove	*Columba livia/C. oenas*	1	0.1
Partridge, grey	*Perdix perdix*	2	<0.1
Thrush unidentified	Turdidae	1	<0.1
Buzzard	*Buteo buteo*	1	<0.1
Mammals			
Mammal unidentified		439	28.9
Cattle	*Bos taurus*	158	10.4
Cattle-sized		162	10.7
Sheep/goat	*Ovis aries/Capra hircus*	71	4.7
Sheep	*Ovis aries*	8	0.5
Sheep-sized		415	27.3
Pig	*Sus scrofa*	117	7.7
Dog	*Canis familiaris*	2	0.1
Cat	*Felis catus*	7	0.5
Hare, brown	*Lepus europaeus*	1	<0.1
Rabbit	*Oryctolagus cuniculus*	19	1.3
Total		**1521**	

documentary evidence. Only references to the disrepair of the church and other buildings, and the dedication of new altars in 1382 by Bishop William of Nantes may imply such work (Heales 1898, 264 and appendix CXXXIII; above, 'Documentary evidence'). The majority of the stonework retrieved suggests the main work on the eastern extension of the presbytery and the construction of a Lady chapel took place *c* 1310–*c* 1340, but the main parapet coping suggests that the completion of some of the detailing may not have occurred until the 15th century (CP5; Chapter 7.2).

It is probable that the new east end was initially built around the earlier presbytery. The Lady chapel, aisles, and easternmost bays of the presbytery could have been vaulted before the old presbytery was demolished and the foundations used to support the arcade of the two western bays of the new presbytery. They seem to have been unequal to the task and this arcade, among other parts of the church, is probably what was being referred to as in 'extreme disrepair' in 1387 (Heales 1898, 269–70). It had to be demolished *c* 1390, the masonry being reused in later repairs (period M4). The eastern extension, therefore, survived in its original form for at most 80 years.

The *ex situ* moulded stone assemblage also suggests that the main cloister was remodelled *c* 1375, although stratigraphic evidence is lacking. Nor is it known whether the cloister was moved. It certainly was not reconstructed to adjoin the nave and the lane/yard (OA4) continued to exist. The foundations exposed to the west of the the excavated cloister, Building 13 (period M4, Fig 129), suggest that the walks and garth remained in their original position.

The chapter house was extended eastwards by *c* 5m (internally) with the addition of an apsidal end and reinforced to the north and east with large buttresses. The buttressing, which must have blocked or partially blocked the slype, perhaps suggesting disuse, also suggests structural problems with the chapter house. The construction of an apsidal end to a chapter house was, in the 14th century, archaic and unusual and is fully discussed in Chapter 4.3.

The reredorter must also have been effectively rebuilt, since it was provided with a new vaulted undercroft. Although the rebuild reused the earlier foundations it was now supported with buttresses along the north and south walls. New windows were probably added to the building.

In the infirmary hall, the partitioning of the aisle bays into rooms in the mid to later 14th century is indicative of the relaxation of monastic rule in that century. The infirmary kitchen (B6) was replaced with a smaller building (B12), either another kitchen or possibly a washroom or bloodletting house located over the infirmary drain (S4b). The infirmary cloister was also rebuilt during this period but the abandonment of the drain (S4a) within it suggests remodelling or possibly closure of buildings in the east range of the main cloister – from whence the drain probably originated – perhaps the dormitory. This may be a further hint of relaxation and the adaptation of the formal monastic plan.

South of the main cloister, the aisled hall (B11) was rebuilt, in a substantially strengthened and possibly heightened form. Interpreted as lodgings for the prior or guests, this may suggest Merton continued to provide extensive accommodation for important guests.

The topography of the precinct was unchanged, although small increases in the prevailing ground level were apparent. The levels of grave slabs suggest that the north burial area (OA6) lay at *c* 13m OD and the south burial area (OA3) at *c* 12.9m OD. Where floor levels could be defined, in the Lady chapel, these lay at 13.07m OD. To the south of the reredorter (OA7) ground level lay at *c* 12.25m OD and to the east of the infirmary in the marshy area in the outer court (OA9) at 10.20m OD.

This period showed an apparent increase in burial numbers in the cemetery and in the church, although the whole extent of neither was available for excavation and 122 burials were unphased (below, 3.5).

The burial rows immediately to the north of the infirmary chapel (OA3) were apparently marked out with the intention of saving as much space as possible. Such close, yet not intercutting, burials are most easily made when burials occur within a short space of time. These interments may be a response to a sudden rise in mortality such as an epidemic, natural or man-made disaster (including eg plague and war) but there was no specific documentary or pathological evidence to indicate this. The density may more likely indicate a popular and well-ordered but limited burial plot adjacent to the infirmary chapel.

There were 120 interments in the south burial area (OA3), although it should be noted that the later, post-*c* 1350, phase may be later still (period M4). Eighty-four would appear to have died before *c* 1350 and 36 after. Even if the later group of 36 is discounted, the increase in burial numbers compared to previous periods is marked. Thirteen burials in the 12th and early 13th century rise to 29 in the later 13th century and then to at least 84 here. At the very least the 14th-century burials represent an increase of almost 190% compared to earlier (period M2).

Similarly, there is a rise (*c* 63%) in interments in the north burial area (OA6) during this period. There were 84 and 88 burials – excluding the charnel pit – attributable to the earlier periods (M1 and M2 respectively), while here there were at least 143 in an area extended to the west, and better defined from the south burial area (OA3) by the extended presbytery and the Lady chapel. The majority of the north area was not excavated and the extent is unknown, but an empty coffin [5518] found next to the western end of the exterior north aisle wall, although undated (below, 3.5; Fig 141), shows that burial occurred at least this far west. The burials included a priest [2905] buried with chalice and paten, close to the nave aisle wall, and the multiple burial of three individuals [2712], [2855], [2856] more convincingly suggesting victims of a local episode of infectious disease or an accident but again without further pathological data to support this. The expansion of the burial area to the west may in part be compensation for space lost to the east – beneath the presbytery and Lady chapel – but, taken with the apparent increase in numbers buried, may suggest a change in the size or type of catchment for the north burial area (OA6).

The burials at the west front may indicate individuals trying to 'enter the church' or liminal between exterior and interior, equating 'with the soul crossing the boundary from earth to the afterlife' (Daniell 1997, 100). Threshold burials have been interpreted as penitential, and porch burials or burials close to the porch as a gesture of humility (Gilmour and Stocker 1986, 29). However, those buried here were not quite on the threshold, and as burial in the church interior was preferable to the exterior, it may simply be a case of getting as close as was possible, that is it was the best they could afford. The imposition of new rows north of the Lady chapel, aligned to the new chapel, in an area earlier used for interments, demonstrates reorganisation of this part of the cemetery, possibly as another popular, well-organised but limited burial area that might usefully be compared to that north of the infirmary chapel in the south burial area (OA3).

It is within the church that the rise in burial numbers is most dramatic. Seven burials earlier (period M2) rises to 47 here. Increased mortality rates may again be a factor but it is more likely to reflect an increase in the size, or a change in the type, of the catchment for burial in this period, either because

restrictions on non-canon burials were further relaxed or, perhaps, because more people could afford, and desired, burial within the church.

The single individual from the chapter house analysed was, like the majority of the earlier (period M2) interments; an adult male; he suffered from DISH as did one of the earlier individuals.

3.4 The priory in the 15th and early 16th centuries, *c* 1390–1538 (period M4)

Documentary evidence

The documentary evidence hints that the church was in disrepair by 1387 (above, 3.3, 'Documentary evidence'). In April 1393, a certificate sent to the Bishop of Winchester by the prior stated that the chapel of the Blessed Mary was 'in a truly decayed and ruinous state' and, in the opinion of the masons and carpenters, would cost 240 marks (£160) to repair (Heales 1898, 284, citing Bodleian, MS Laud 723, fo 81), whilst the dilapidated nave would require 2000 marks (£1333 13s 4d).

In common with other religious houses in the London area, St Mary Merton is much less well documented during the 15th century than in the 14th. Most marked, perhaps, is the diminution in the number of royal Letters Patent and Close Rolls concerning matters other than vacancies, elections, confirmations and corrodies.

On 24 November 1406 the king pardoned the papal grant to Richard de Bowdon, chaplain and warden of the chantry of St Mary Magdalen Kingston (Surrey), of a benefice at the disposal of the prior and convent of Merton, and licensed the execution of the papal bull as far as future vacant benefices were concerned (*Cal Pat R*, 1405–8, 273). The background to this papal intervention and royal reproof is not known; the prioracy was not vacant in 1406 but the appointment may have dated to the interregnum between Priors Robert de Wyndesore (Windsor) and Michael Kympton in 1403. In 1420 Henry V appointed a commission to arrest Walter Somerton and William West, 'canons of Merton of the Order of St Augustine and professed in the Order' who had broken their vows and were wandering about, to deliver them to the prior or his attorney for chastisement (ibid, 1416–22, 321). Both these incidents would imply a loss of control over its affairs on the part of the priory.

An account of the election of a successor to Prior John Kingston who died on 2 January 1485 refers to several priory officers, the chapel of Blessed Mary, the infirmary which one of the canons was too sick to leave, and also to several chambers involved in various consultations preceding the election: 'a small low chamber' (*quadam parva bassa camera*) forming part of the dormitory; an upper chamber close to the dormitory long occupied by the cellarer; and a further apparently distinct 'lower chamber' of uncertain relation to the other two also described as the serving or refectory for one (*pro communi solatio sive refectione canonicorum*) (Heales 1898, 303–6).

In the visitation of 30 April 1501 Robert Doo precentor and master of the chapel of the Blessed Virgin was one of those who testified (*VCH* 1905, 101). The chapel seems to have been located away from the precinct, close to a tenement called Salyngs, rent for the lease of which by John Clerk in 1536 was payable to the keeper (*custos*) of the chapel (TNA: PRO, SC6/Henry VIII/3463 m 5).

On 31 March 1520 Bishop Fox had a decree placed in the chapter house and church, and affixed to the church door towards the cloister, requiring all persons opposed to the confirmation of John Lacy as next prior to appear in the conventual church at Merton (Heales 1898, 326–7). On Lacy's election a canon, prevented by infirmity from appearing personally in chapter and placed in a certain lower chamber or cell of the infirmary, appointed other canons to act in his place (ibid, 331). References to an inner chamber in the infirmary, commonly called 'the priors chambre', and to George Albyne master of St Mary's chapel occur in accounts of John Ramsey's election, in January and February 1530 (*RegWolsey*, 73–99; Heales 1898, 332).

In his will of 1428, Roger Tye of Merton requested burial in the church before the image of St Michael at the altar of Holy Trinity (TNA: PRO, PROB11/3, fo 95) and in 1433 Beatrice Hayton of Merton, specified as her burial place the priory church against the same altar where Thomas Hayton her late husband rests. Her will of December 1433 also bequeathed to the priory 10 marks (£6 13s 4d), and 10s to the fabric of the church (ibid, fo 143). In his will of 1517 Thomas Salyng, woodmonger, requested burial in the church before the altar of St Frideswide, near to where his brother, the prior, was to be interred (TNA: PRO, PROB11/18, fo 263v). His brother was most probably William Salyng, elected prior in 1502 (*Cal Pat R*, 1495–1509, 262). At William's death on 14 March 1520 he was buried 'as was becoming and according to custom within the precincts of the conventual church' (Heales 1898, 324). The locations of the altars mentioned are unknown and it is uncertain if any but William Salyng's request were met; however, these named individuals could conceivably be among the burials found and attributed to this period.

A reference to 'new work' at the priory occurs in the will of William Clopton, dated 29 May 1521 and proved on 28 June following, bequeathing £6 13s 4d for the purpose (TNA: PRO, PROB11/20, fo 86).

The *Valor* of 1536, which surveyed the possessions of religious houses before their dissolution, described the priory in conventional terms, comprising courtyards, gardens, orchards and ponds, with diverse other houses within the precinct (*Val Eccl*, ii, 48).

Archaeological evidence

Introduction

Repair work to the fabric of the church was undertaken including the nave, presbytery and Lady chapel, probably after 1393 when the prior pleaded for money for important repairs (above, 'Documentary evidence'). Some refurbishment also took place within the church and the latest floor identified was probably laid. The slype and infirmary cloister were modified, perhaps to subdivide them into smaller rooms. Burial continued in the church, chapter house and exterior areas. The reredorter was strengthened with the rebuilding of some of the earlier buttresses along the north wall (Fig 129; Fig 139).

The 15th- and 16th-century church (B1)

Five of the eight buttresses on the north side of the presbytery and Lady chapel, the two westernmost buttresses on the south side of the presbytery and the two northern buttresses on the east side of the south transept were reinforced and extended (Fig 129). Scaffolding postholes and pits associated with these repairs were found around the buttresses. Two large pits to the north of the presbytery also seem to be associated with this work. These new foundations, of reused Reigate stone, flint and occasionally ragstone in a lime mortar, were distinct from the buttress or wall to which they were attached. The northern, internal, junction between the Lady chapel and presbytery was also reinforced. The dimensions of the new foundations varied; each support was probably built to solve specific structural problems.

Substantial repairs were made to the north side of the nave: the wall was thickened, by 1.5m, over a length of 14.5m, corresponding to bays 6–8 (from the west) and the bay divisions reinforced by buttresses (Fig 130). The eastern, largest buttress was *c* 6m long and 3.5m wide but the western, smallest, only 1.65m long by 1.15m wide. The variation in size again suggests a tailored response to a specific problem with the north-west corner of the crossing. Seven buttresses, reinforcing the bay divisions of bays 2–7, were added to the south wall of the nave (Fig 131) and are probably also attributable to this repair campaign. Again, the dimensions of the buttress foundations varied, but the buttress superstructures were almost certainly uniform.

The nave and transept floors were relaid with Reigate paviors 200–280mm square and, although difficult to date, this final floor was probably laid during this period. In the central part of the nave the slabs were at *c* 45° to the west–east axis of the church (Fig 132). In the aisles, however, they were parallel to the walls (Fig 133). Areas of both plain and glazed tiles, many Low Countries, were also laid in the nave and north transept. In the transept, a small area of yellow- or green-glazed tiles remained extant, laid in a chequerboard pattern. In the nave, plain tiles were used as repairs to the stone paving. Bidder recorded tiles in the nave, in association with the Reigate paving and within the north aisle. The tiles were 210–230mm square by 28–31mm thick and their size suggests a late 15th- or 16th-century date. Further plain and decorated floor tiles were also present in Dissolution rubble (<T37>, Fig 194; <T49>, Fig 195; <T53>, Fig 196; <T81>, Fig 200; <T94>, <T96>, Fig 202).

Post-Dissolution demolition layers also contained fragments of Coggeshall-type-shaped brick, medieval yellow brick, late

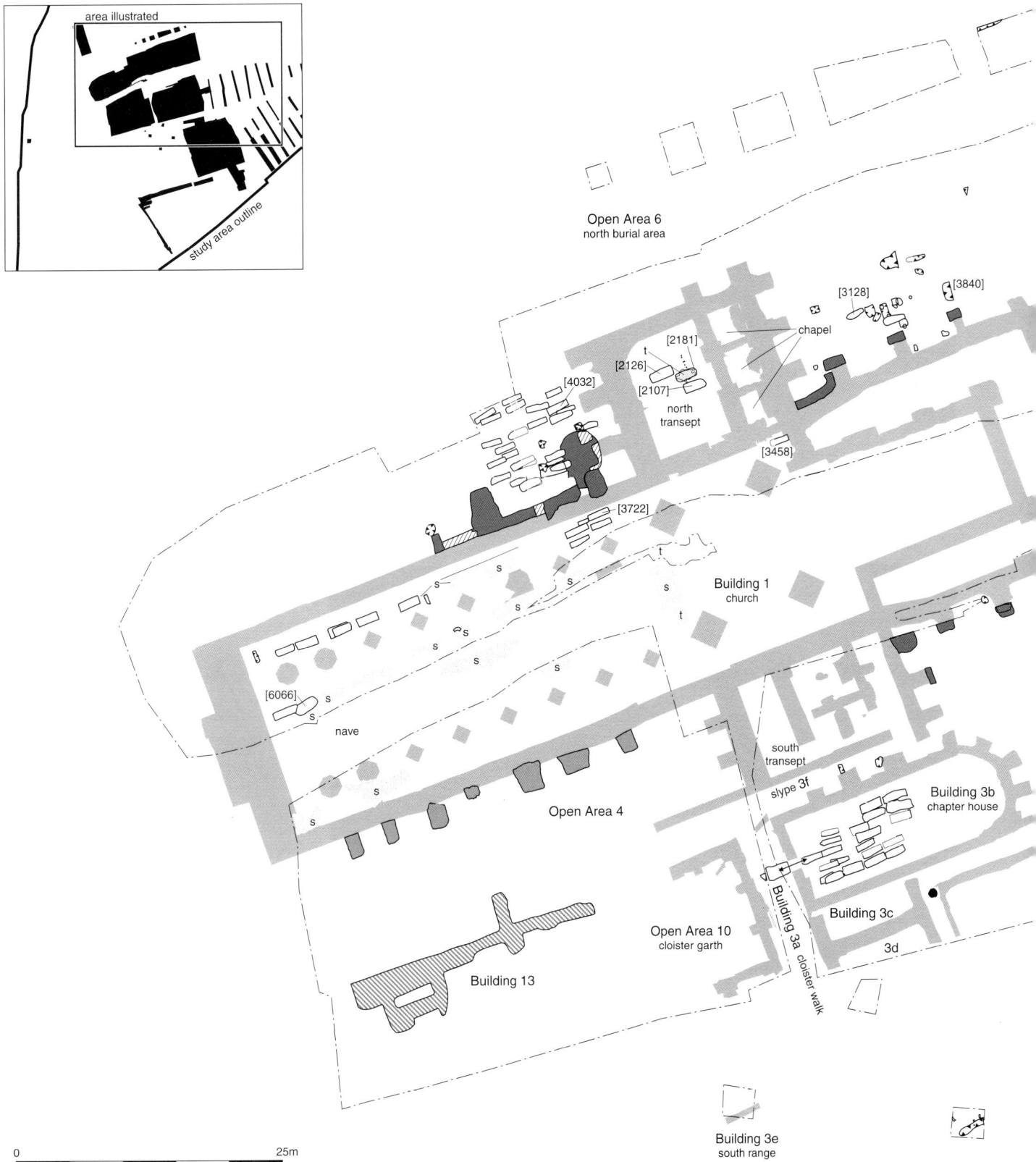

Fig 129 Plan of the principal archaeological features in the north part of the precinct, c 1390–1538 (period M4) (scale 1:500)

15th or early 16th-century red brick, sandstone roofing and two fragments of glazed brick, possibly wall decoration. A particularly unusual item was a probable roof tile, unusually thick (18–19mm), with yellow and light green lead glaze covering the upper surface, which was possibly made for a prominent roof, such as a porch, where the glazed colour could be readily admired.

Seventeen burials, 13 in the north aisle and north side of the nave, 3 in the north transept and 1 in the north-east corner of the aisle crossing, were found. The burials within the aisle

99

N

Lady chapel

Open Area 3
south burial area

Building 4b
infirmary chapel

4c

room 1

Building 4a
infirmary hall

room 2

room 6

room 3

room 7

[10990]

cloister walk 4c

room 4

room 5

Building 12

Building 8

Structure 4b
infirmary drain

Open Area 9

Open Area 5
infirmary cloister garth

area illustrated

study area outline

N

Open Area 6
north burial area

[3128]

[3840]

chapel

[2181]

[2126]

[4032]

[2107]

north
transept

Lady chapel

[3458]

[3722]

Building 1
church

Open Area 3
south burial area

south
transept

slype 3f

Building 4b
infirmary chapel

Building 3b
chapter house

4c

Open Area 4

room 1

Building 4a
infirmary hall

[6066]

room 2

room 6

Building 3c

nave

room 3

room 7

3d

cloister walk 4C

[10990]

Open Area 10
cloister garth

3d

room 4

Building 12

Building 8

Building 13

Building 3a cloister walk

room 5

Structure 4b
infirmary drain

Open Area 9

Open Area 5
infirmary cloister garth

Building 3e
south range

0   25m

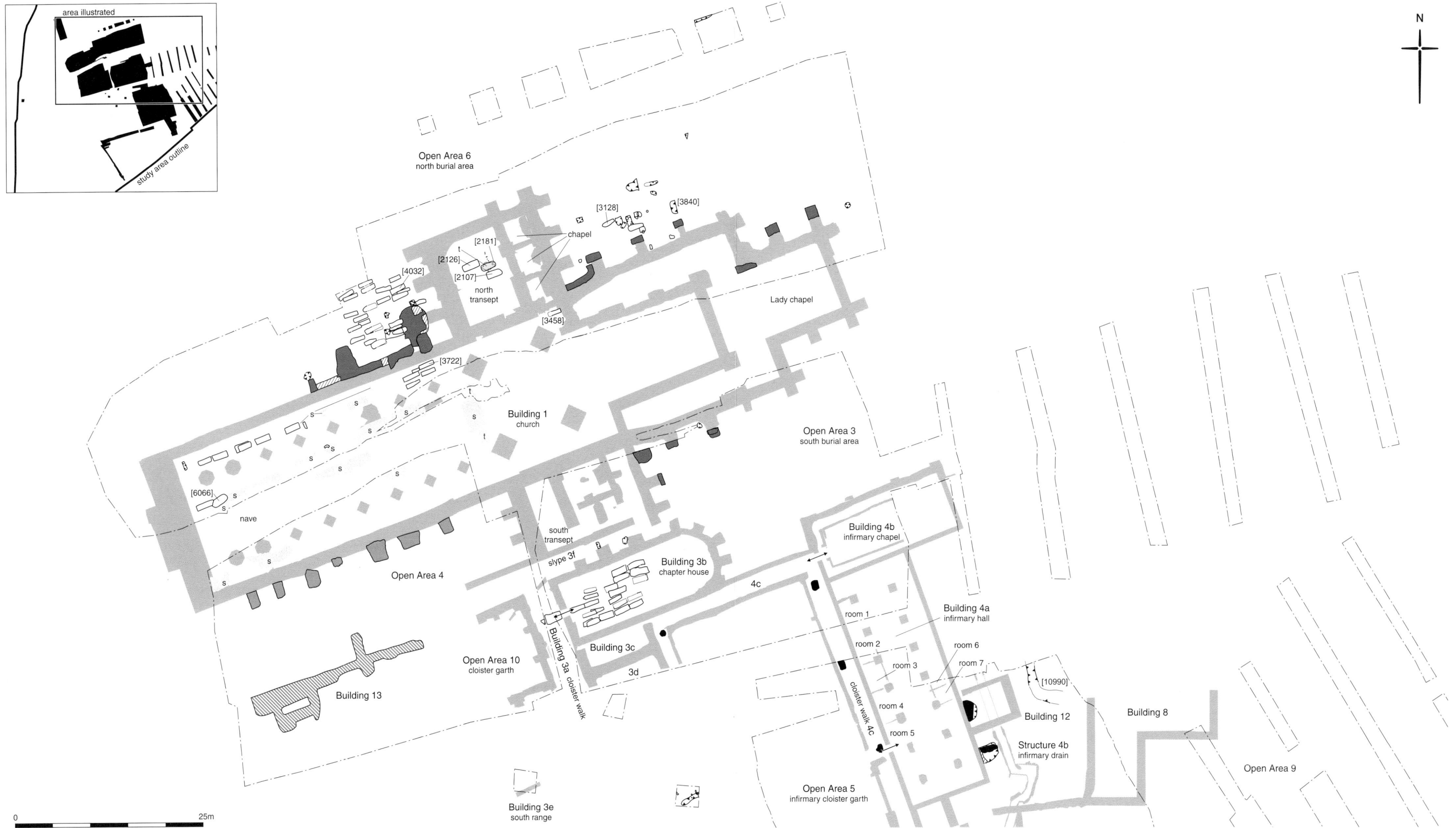

Fig 129 Plan of the principal archaeological features in the north part of the precinct, c 1390–1538 (period M4) (scale 1:500)

15th or early 16th-century red brick, sandstone roofing and two fragments of glazed brick, possibly wall decoration. A particularly unusual item was a probable roof tile, unusually thick (18–19mm), with yellow and light green lead glaze covering the upper surface, which was possibly made for a

prominent roof, such as a porch, where the glazed colour could be readily admired.

Seventeen burials, 13 in the north aisle and north side of the nave, 3 in the north transept and 1 in the north-east corner of the aisle crossing, were found. The burials within the aisle

Fig 130 *Earlier masonry reused in the buttressing of the north side of the church nave (B1, period M4), looking east (1.0m scale)*

Fig 131 *The robbed-out south nave wall and buttresses (B1, period M4), looking west (2.0m scale)*

Fig 132 *Stone floor in the central part of the nave (B1, period M4), looking west (1.0m scale)*

Fig 133 *Stone paving surviving next to a grave in the north nave aisle (B1, period M4), looking west (0.5m scale)*

and nave were stratigraphically late. The nave was not fully excavated; earlier burials probably existed there. Some of the unphased burials in the presbytery and Lady chapel were possibly contemporary (below, 3.5). Although no traces of wood survived, the shape of most grave cuts suggested coffins.

The three burials found in the transept, the last in this part of the church, post-date c 1350. The buckles with burials [2181] and [2126], mature adults, the former male, the latter probably male, suggest they were dressed when interred. A grave lined with chalk rubble and mortar contained a probable mature adult male [2107]; around his pelvis lay organic materials (a strap?) overlying an iron sheet, possibly a hernia belt (<S254>, Fig 134; Fig 156; Chapters 4.6, 7.5). Both hands appeared to be clutching the strap with some of the digits overlying it and some behind. The grave fill also contained a (redeposited) base from a pendent glass lamp <S259> (Fig

218). The skeletal and dental pathology of these three adult males or probable males was possibly interesting – very high rates of ante-mortem tooth loss and dental caries, yet very low rates of calculus, alveolar resorption and periodontal disease – but the sample was very small (Chapter 7.11, 'Characteristics of the skeletal material', 'c 1390–1538 (period M4)', 'The church (B1)').

One further burial in the vicinity of the transept was [3458], an older adult male placed in the north-east corner of the aisle crossing. He was presumably interred clothed as he was found with a belt and a number of copper-alloy dress accessories (<S226>, Fig 217) – a buckle, mounts, a strap loop and a strapend. This individual exhibited the classic characteristics of DISH, and had periosteal new bone affecting his tibiae, possibly as a reaction to an infection of the overlying soft tissue.

Of the burials within the nave, two were in the central nave and the remainder in the north aisle. No grave markers remained but it was obvious that these had been removed, leaving voids in the paving. Of the 12 individuals available for analysis, 11 were males and one a mature adult female. The males comprised 1 immature individual aged 13–16 years, 5 mature adults, 4 older adults, and 1 adult.

101

Fig 134 The possible hernia belt <S254> in situ on ?mature adult male [2107] buried in the north transept (B1, period M4), looking south (1.0m scale)

The slype (B3f)

A flint wall footing divided the passage, extending the central chapter house buttress (period M3) north to form two small rooms, each measuring c 7m by 2m (Fig 129). Within the western part of the eastern room, burnt floor surfaces and charcoal patches suggested a hearth. A number of plain-glazed 13th-century 'Westminster' floor tiles recovered from a clay floor layer were possibly evidence for tile paving here.

The lane/yard to the south of the nave (OA4)

The construction of the external buttresses to the south of the nave indicates that this area (OA4) remained open between the church and cloister (Fig 129). Deposits here [5476] contained pottery dated c 1270–c 1500 (CBW) and may be associated with the construction of the buttresses.

A ? west range and cloister (B13)

East–west and north–south, mortar, flint and Reigate stone filled robber trenches were found approximately 13.0m to the south of the nave, to the west of the excavated cloister (B3a) (Fig 129). The extent of the east–west footing was approximately 23.0m by up to 2.5m. To the west the foundation had a rectangular projection, c 5.0m east–west by 2.5m north–south. To the east of this a north–south foundation crossed the east–west. These foundations probably related to the west range and the west and north cloister alleys, although they did not join the cloister walls excavated to the east. As they were not excavated but only exposed, any construction or robbing date is uncertain, and they have been

assigned a separate building number to the cloister and phased here.

The cloister (B3a/e)

A single grave, a Reigate stone cist containing the disarticulated bones of at least four individuals, was dug in the cloister walk immediately outside what is presumed to have been the chapter house door (Fig 129). The bones may represent charnel from the chapter house, the cist grave a burial, possibly one that could not be fitted into the chapter house, reused for this.

The chapter house (B3b)

The chapter house floor was probably relaid or resurfaced several times (Fig 129). Plain and decorated 13th-century 'Westminster' floor tiles were found within a clay bedding layer in the apse and may come from the chapter house floor. The decorated tiles comprise three designs (<T59>, <T69>, <T70>, Fig 197). Two further tiles recovered from a grave fill and from building debris within the apse may result from rebuilding or repairs to the walls and floors (<T58>, <T66>, Fig 197). Many of the plain tiles, yellow, green and brown, have been cut triangularly. Post-Dissolution layers around the chapter house contained floor tiles including four, keyed white slip tile designs (<T38>, <T40>–<T42>, Fig 195) and two, pink slip floor tiles (<T50>, <T52>, Fig 196), which possibly also formed elements of the chapter house.

Also present in post-Dissolution layers were pieces of window glass including two durable-blue roundels <S71>, <S74>, and three fragments of two different greens <S77>; a further piece <S91> was a flash-ruby, sub-lozenge-shaped

<S71>

<S74>

<S77>

<S91>

<S15>

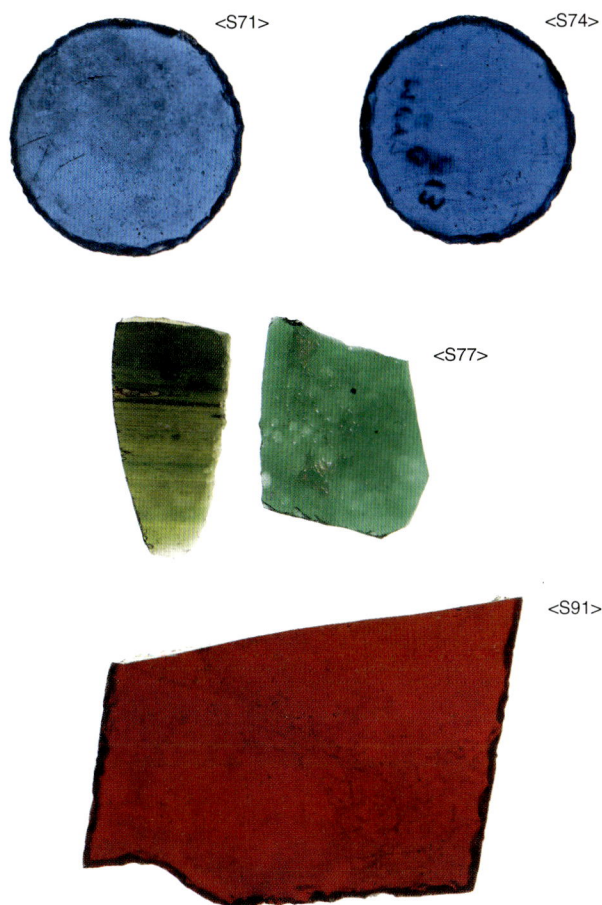

Fig 135 *Coloured window glass fragments <S71>, <S74>, <S77> and <S91> (scale c 1:1)*

Fig 136 *Copper-alloy monumental inscription <S15>, possibly for Prior Michael Kympton (scale c 1:1)*

engraving suggests this was on a floor, perhaps the chapter house: it was reused and incomplete but a partial legend – […] /…[?m, n or u]pton qu…/…*puletur*… – remained and may refer to the burial ([*se*]*puletur*) of the prior Michael Kympton who died in 1413.

The east range (B3c–d)

There is limited evidence for activity in the east range. The remains were recorded of a bedding layer of sand overlain by a mortar floor surface in this area.

The monastic cemetery

THE SOUTH BURIAL AREA (OA3)

No burials here were attributed to this period, but some of the 36 burials grouped earlier (period M3) may post-date *c* 1390.

THE NORTH BURIAL AREA (OA6)

Twenty-eight burials are thought to date from this period. Twenty-six were to the west of the north transept and two to the east (Fig 129). The burials were supine with their heads to the west.

Four approximate rows were recorded to the west of the transept, although intercutting suggests these were not well defined. Most burials were probably in shrouds and unremarkable. The only exception was individual [4032], whose head and shoulders were set within a Reigate stone and chalk surround. Three burials cut into the large buttress repair to the west of the transept. All of the 26 individuals to the west were available for skeletal analysis. Twenty-two were male, two were adults of indeterminate sex and two were children aged 7–12 years. The adults included 2 young adults, 12 mature, 6 older, and 4 who were aged as adult.

To the east of the transept only two burials could be confidently assigned to this period. The fall in burial numbers here may suggest it was becoming overcrowded. Both individuals were available for skeletal analysis. They were male,

quarry (Fig 135). These may perhaps have come from the chapter house windows; <S73>, <S74> and <S77> were recovered from demolition deposits east of the chapter house (period P2).

The 21 burials found and attributed to this period form the largest group from the chapter house. Previous burials were concentrated in the northern and eastern parts of the chapter house whereas here they concentrated in the western two-thirds of the building, initially in the centre and subsequently along the south wall. Any bench seating (cf Fig 34) was either removed or the burials inserted beneath. The apse remained unused for burials. One grave was dated by two silver coins of Edward IV, with a *terminus post quem* of 1473–76 (<S334>, <S335>). The majority of the interments were in stone cist graves but the latest three burials, placed close to the western entrance, were in wooden coffins.

Nineteen individuals were available for analysis, of whom 1 was an adult of indeterminate sex and the remaining 18 were male, comprising 1 young adult, 5 mature, 10 older adults and 2 that could not be aged other than as adult. The most common skeletal pathology excluding general degenerative conditions was DISH, with two of the 19 individuals definitely or possibly affected (Chapter 7.11; Table 69).

A post-medieval deposit overlying the chapter house contained a copper-alloy tomb inscription (<S15>, Fig 136). The deep

a young adult and a mature adult. One burial post-dated pit [3840] probably associated with the reconstruction of the northern presbytery buttresses. The other burial [3128] appeared to cut a demolition deposit, which, as the burial was undisturbed, could suggest it was dug after the start of the demolition of the church, thus at the Dissolution. This is unproven; the burial is considered very late monastic.

The infirmary hall (B4a)

The eastern wall was strengthened with two buttresses, possibly for the addition of a second floor (Fig 129). Few later floors remained extant but pottery within a sandy layer [5540] in room 1 post-dated c 1350 (TUDG) and was sealed by surfaces of silt and crushed Reigate stone which contained pottery post-dating c 1480 (PMRE).

Tiles recovered from demolition deposits in this area included two 'Westminster' tiles (<T62>, <T64>, Fig 197), and possibly formed part of the floor here. A 15th-century gold finger ring (<S252>, Fig 153) engraved with [Je] ne weil [= ?veille] aymer autre que vous ('I am not seeking to love anyone but you') was found in a post-Dissolution demolition deposit at the southern end of the hall, together with an engraved composite buckle (<S223>, Fig 165) while a robber trench there produced a tuning peg (<S29>, Fig 154).

A curving ditch [10990], c 4.0m north–south by 1.0m east–west, by 0.39m deep, truncated the walls of Building 8 to the east of the infirmary. The ditch fill ([10790]; [10796]) included pottery post-dating c 1480. Animal bone recovered included a small assemblage of pig with gadids (including haddock), chicken, goose, ox, sheep/goat and rabbit.

The infirmary cloister (B4c)

Several large pits may suggest the partitioning of the cloister walks into rooms each measuring c 9m by 2m; equally the pits may suggest attempts, possibly temporary, to support the roof or scaffolding for the infirmary hall. Associated with a possible blocking wall within the northern walk were a few peg roofing tiles and plain and decorated floor tiles. These include two plain-glazed Low Countries tiles and a decorated Penn tile of uncertain design (possibly E1455; Table 33) dating to the 14th century. A demolition layer contained a white slip floor tile (<T47>, Fig 195), possibly used within this cloister. Also present was a peg tile in a rare (ie non-London area) fabric (type 3201; Chapter 7.3, 'Peg roofing tile').

Fragments of window glass were found in the infirmary cloister garth (OA5); much was durable blue quarries (eg <S153>, <S155>, <S156>, not published) and some were painted (eg <S153>, Fig 137, possibly a border quarry). Frequent fragments were also recovered from Dissolution and later demolition deposits (periods P1–P3) within and around the infirmary hall and cloister, including part of an amethyst quarry of a complex shape (<S113>, Fig 137) and a green

Fig 137 Plain <S113>, <S141> and painted <S130>, <S147>, <S153> window glass (scale c 1:1)

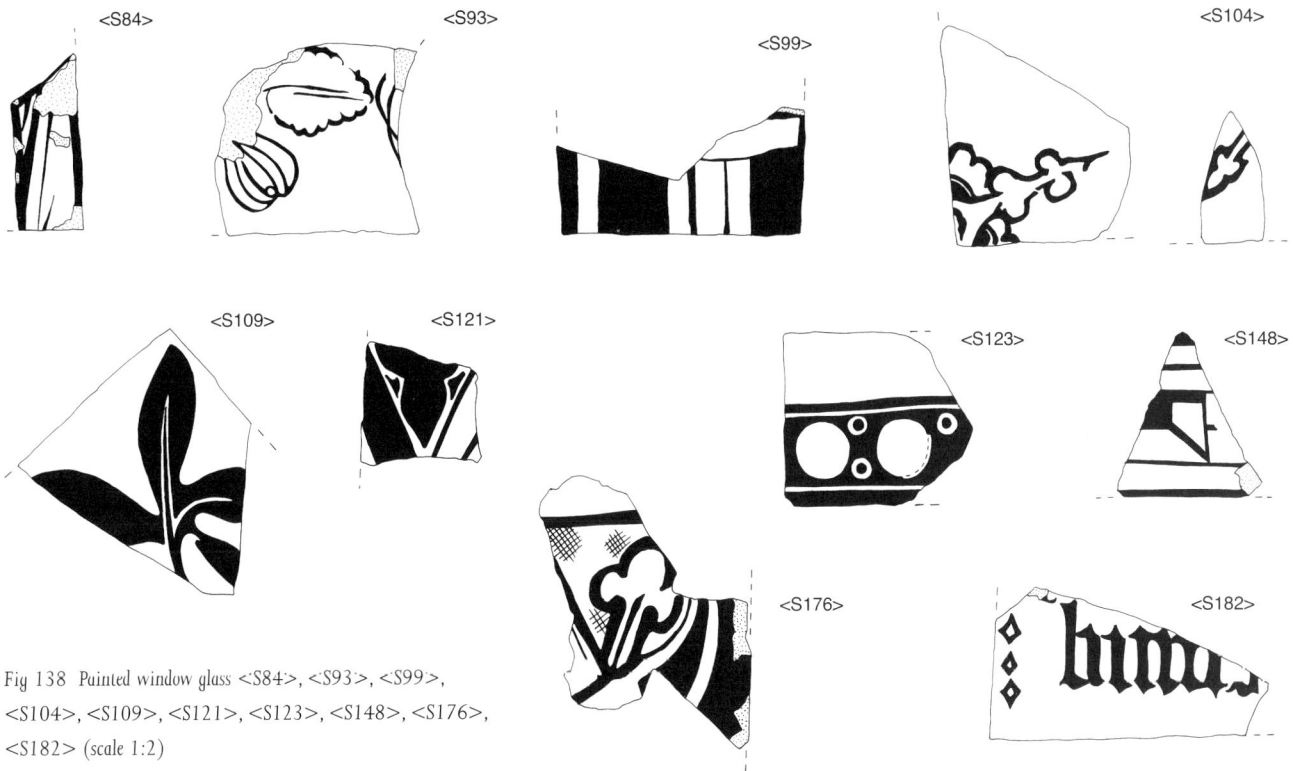

<S84> <S93> <S99> <S104>

<S109> <S121> <S123> <S148>

<S176> <S182>

Fig 138 Painted window glass <S84>, <S93>, <S99>, <S104>, <S109>, <S121>, <S123>, <S148>, <S176>, <S182> (scale 1:2)

quarry (<S141>, Fig 137), as well as painted designs (<S130> and <S147>, Fig 137; cf Fig 138). This glass may have glazed the infirmary hall and/or cloister.

The infirmary drain (S4b)

The drain was presumably regularly cleaned out prior to the Dissolution. The surviving monastic primary fill [9493] produced freshwater snails characteristic of still or slow-flowing weedy water. Food waste included abundant numbers of common whelk shells and low numbers of oyster shells. A rim fragment of a cast copper-alloy cauldron <S274>, possibly from the infirmary kitchen, was also present. A fragment of ornate bone spectacles (<S253>, Fig 157) also recovered from the drain may come from a post-Dissolution demolition layer.

The reredorter (B5)

At least one of the north wall buttresses was modified or rebuilt (Fig 139). The flint and reused Reigate stone foundations included the four fragments of the single shattered window head from the earlier (period M3) reredorter (<A90>–<A93>, Fig 127). The window fragments were unweathered and likely nearly new when replaced suggesting that the new buttress was not later than c 1450.

Ditch [8368], probably first cut in the 13th century and subsequently periodically cleaned out, flowed south-east from the eastern end of the reredorter. At its north-western end, the lowest surviving fill [8794] included a base fragment from a glass urinal <S283>. Overlying silt deposits contained a fragment of stone roofing tile complete with a 11mm diameter nail hole; only a few small fragments of laminated sandstone

suitable for use as roofing have been found at Merton suggesting it was used infrequently. A possible lead/tin brooch frame fragment (<S249>, Fig 140) and pottery, including Cheam redware (CHEAR) dating to c 1480–c 1550, were also recovered from the fill.

A watermill in the outer court (B9)

During the later medieval period a large stone-lined tank was constructed inside the mill building. Recent excavations of the mill have revealed the tank's full size: 12m east–west by 5m north–south, by 830mm deep (Saxby 2005a, 30–2). It had been constructed from reused Reigate stone ashlar blocks, each around 300–400mm wide and bonded with an orange sand mortar. A water inlet for the tank was near the western end of the south wall.

A ? passage/pentice to the infirmary (S7)

The passage was resurfaced with a small patch of crushed Reigate stone [9365] and yellow/brown clay [9188]. Pottery from the clay surface included Raeren stoneware (RAER) dating to c 1480–c 1550.

Discussion c 1390–1538 (period M4)

A great deal of effort was expended on repairs to the church and surrounding buildings. This appears to have occurred in the years following the certificate of 1393 from the prior to the bishop of Winchester concerning the dilapidated state of the house. The repairs to the north and south sides of the church mainly involved the addition of extra buttresses (or buttress supports) but a supporting wall also reinforced the north nave wall. A number of factors may have contributed to the structural problems. The reuse of the foundations of the earlier presbytery for the western arcade of the new choir may have been unwise. The foundations in general may not have been sufficiently deep to compensate for the soft alluvial silts and peats upon which the church was built and subsidence may have resulted. The presence of the Roman road below the north transept may also have caused differential subsidence, with the area to the south sinking more sharply because it was not supported on the *agger* (Fig 5; Chapter 2.3). The massive external buttressing at the junction between the nave and north transept indicating reinforcing of the north-west corner of the crossing suggests the crossing weight created particular structural problems. These may have worsened gradually from the 13th century onwards, or been the result of, or exacerbated by, work carried out in the 14th century. They may suggest ill-thought-out building programmes and/or poor construction techniques, and possibly changes in the local water table.

The robbed foundations noted collectively as Building 13 could be wholly or in part derived from an earlier period. In particular the east–west and north–south foundations to the east appear to show the north-west corner of the cloister garth walls, with possible sleeper walls across the existing north and west alleys. Indeed, if the wall of Building 3e (period M2) is taken as a lavatorium or the south garth wall, the eastern parts of Building 13 confirm a larger square garth c 530m^2. The western extent of Building 13 suggests unidentified (and unphaseable) buildings in the west range.

The chapter house, infirmary hall, infirmary chapel and reredorter changed very little but two buttresses added to the eastern wall of the infirmary hall and the rebuilding of buttresses along the north wall of the reredorter indicate that structural problems also beset these buildings. The infirmary cloister walk may have been divided into smaller rooms perhaps used by corrodians or canons who wanted more private space, but the pits found may suggest further structural problems – perhaps scaffolding for repairs to the infirmary hall or temporary columns to support the roof during repairs, or columns inserted to do the same on a permanent basis.

Within the church, burials were made in the north transept and in the north side of the nave and north aisle. The 14th-century burials in the north transept may have effectively filled the transept and meant that the nave was now also used, but the limited excavation in the nave makes this impossible to prove – there may be a great many earlier burials there. However, the north nave burials were well spaced and none were found to the south. The nave does not therefore appear to have been as popular as the north transept. One explanation for this could be that there were fewer altars within the nave and aisles. It was not uncommon for wills to request a burial near an altar (Daniell 1997, 98). The most desirable locations, like the high altar, were most probably restricted to senior members of the priory, wealthy benefactors or people with political power. There are few actual references to either priory officials or laity being buried within the church, although the case of William

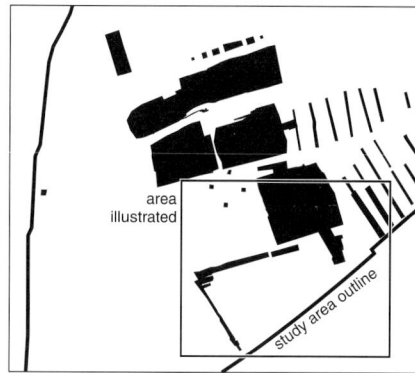

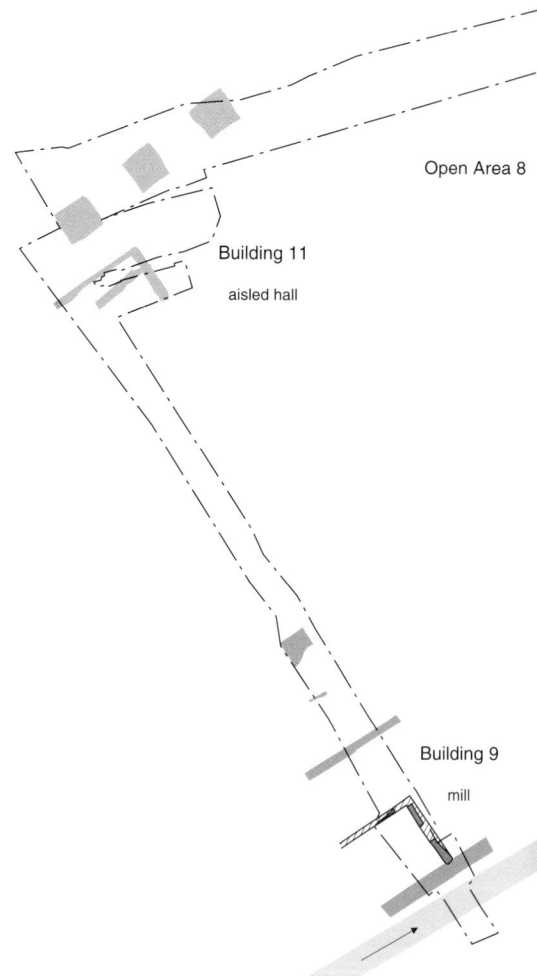

Salyng suggests that it was customary for priors to be buried within the 'precincts of the conventual church'.

Comparison of the individuals buried in the north transept and in the nave and aisle is hampered by the small size of the

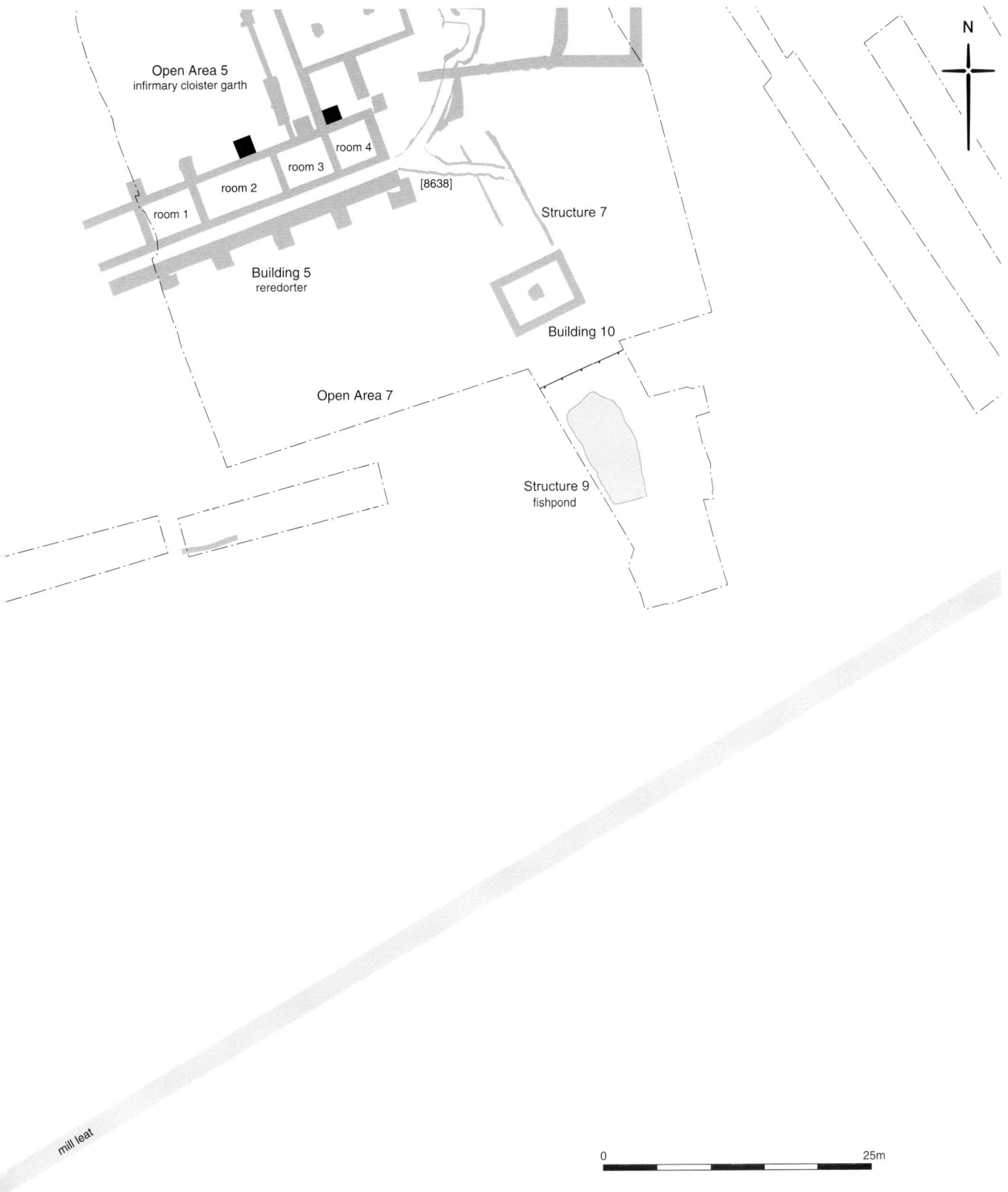

Open Area 5
infirmary cloister garth

room 4

room 3

room 2

room 1

[8638]

Structure 7

Building 5
reredorter

Building 10

Open Area 7

Structure 9
fishpond

N

0   25m

mill leat

Fig 139 Plan of the principal archaeological features in the south part of the precinct, c 1390–1538 (period M4) (scale 1:500)

skeletal subsamples (numbering 3 and 12, respectively). Apart from the inclusion of a single female in the north nave, the subsamples were extremely similar. While it is likely that diffuse idiopathic skeletal hyperostosis is an indicator of relative affluence, the high rate (16.7%) in the north nave and aisle subsample may be a result of small sample size (Table 58).

Within the chapter house the 19 burials followed the pattern established in previous periods, that is, use by adult, mature to older males exclusively (apart from a single young adult). The high prevalence of DISH amongst individuals buried here continued. This condition was also noted in the north aisle of the nave. The latest three chapter house burials were within wooden coffins rather than the stone cist graves common earlier. This may suggest a change of custom or a lack of status or money during the late 15th/16th century.

All bar two of the 28 burials in Open Area 6 lay west of the north transept but this apparent topographical shift and the seemingly dramatic decline from the previous period may be misleading and offset by the large number of unphased burials (M1–M4) to the east of the transept (below, 3.5).

There was no definable modification to the topography of the site. The final church floor lay at a maximum of 13.04m OD. The height of the floor varies considerably and may reflect the subsidence that was probably the root of the priory's structural problems.

3.5 Burials 1117–1538 (periods M1–M4)

A total of 122 graves could not be assigned to a period, including ten unphased charnel pits (Fig 141). The burials were located in either Open Area 6 or possibly the presbytery; 113 individuals were analysed (Chapter 7.11, 'Unphased medieval burials (periods M1–M4)').

The group also includes an empty monolithic stone coffin probably found by Bidder (Bidder and Westlake 1930, 66). The coffin [5518] was adjacent to the north nave wall and measures 1.94m by 0.57m with a central drainage hole. During the excavations in the 1980s this coffin was re-excavated and discovered to be empty. Bidder described the grave as 'containing the skeleton of a very large man, whose body had been crammed into the coffin with greatest difficulty'. To the east in either Open Area 6 or the later presbytery were seven burials also excavated by Bidder (Bidder and Westlake 1930, 66). Six were recorded as cist burials and one, described as lying '30 feet to the south of the north transept', was covered by a slab with a moulded edge. Bidder apparently did not excavate this burial and it has not been excavated since.

There was also a single isolated burial of an older adult male [11203] found to the east of the infirmary hall, well to the south of Open Area 3.

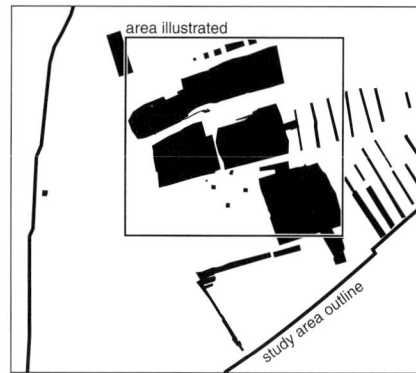

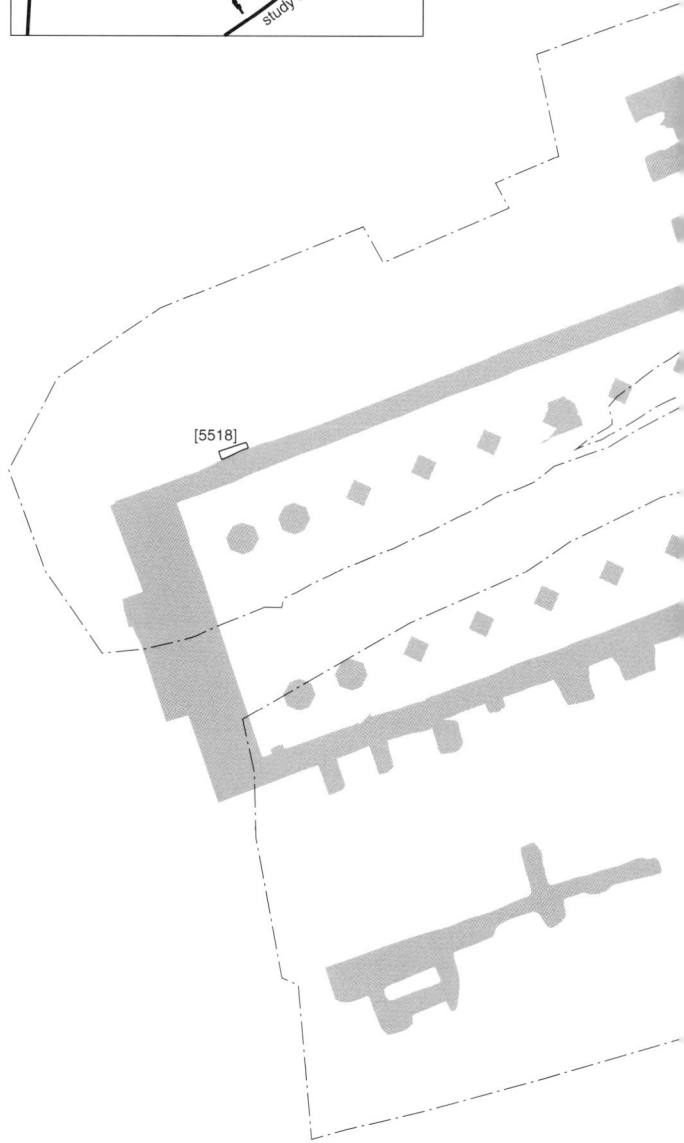

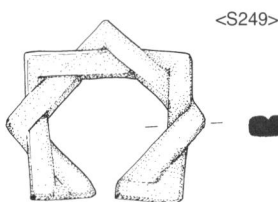

Fig 140 'Star'-like lead/tin brooch frame <S249> (scale 1:1)

Fig 141 Plan of unphased medieval burials, c 1117–1538 (periods M1–M4) (scale 1:500)

N

Open Area 6
north burial area

[4567]

ch

[4707]

ch

ch

ch

ch

burials excavated by
Colonel Bidder

[11203]

4

Aspects of the priory

4.1 The foundation of the priory

The foundation story of St Mary Merton contains elements common to many monastic foundations: the lack of a precise date for the foundation; the removal to a second more suitable site; the construction of early buildings in timber; and the period required to ensure the survival of the house, in other words to achieve stability and construction in stone.

With respect to the date of foundation, St Mary Merton's is perhaps more precise than some, but there is still some confusion in the sources. The founding of any monastic house was a complex business. Unlike the Cistercians, the Augustinians lacked constitutional documents and central authority. Whereas the white monks had set rules and formal stages governing foundations, the canons simply acquiesced to the wishes of the founder. The date of foundation for Merton could be taken as any point between 1114, the year Gilbert acquired the vill, and 3 May 1117, the foundation date recorded in the Waverley Annals and Matthew Paris (Chapter 3.1, 'Documentary evidence'). Gilbert's invitation to settle to Robert Bayle must have occurred in 1114 or very shortly thereafter. The construction of some buildings on the original site had occurred before 1117 and also on the new site before the transfer, when the canons resident already numbered 17. Thus, although the date of foundation is generally taken as the date the second site was formally occupied (ie 3 May 1117), it probably occurred c 1115, the suggested date of Prior Robert's appointment. Such uncertainty over the foundation date is not uncommon for early Augustinian houses in Britain, and compares with Guisborough Priory (Yorkshire North Riding) 1119–24 and Drax Priory (Yorkshire West Riding) 1130–9, and is rather better than for Arbury (Cambridgeshire), Elsham (Lincolnshire) and Penmon (Anglesey). The dating also places Merton very much in the first wave of British Augustinian foundations in 1100–35, when the Order was concentrated in, but already expanding from, south-east England (Robinson 1980, 22–7).

Many monastic houses found it necessary to relocate for a variety of reasons, some no longer known. Twenty Augustinian houses moved once or more from their original site, and at least 30 Cistercian houses did so, many within a year or so of their foundation (Burton 1994, 133). Merton's canons appear to have done so for the most usual reasons given: the unsuitability of the first site chosen or the greater suitability of the new site suggested. Different orders might have slightly different requirements for a suitable site, but all had two basic needs: sufficient room to construct a church and necessary buildings, and a good supply of water. Merton's first site, unknown, was chosen by the founder, who appears to have started construction prior to inviting the Augustinians to settle, and may therefore have had a poor understanding of their requirements; the second was apparently chosen by the first prior, who should have had a far better understanding. That the transfer was effected rapidly, soon after Robert's arrival, may suggest that the first site was very clearly unsuitable, although the text implies only that the second was more suitable – which may indicate that Prior Robert would not accept 'adequate' if he could get 'excellent'. There is no suggestion in the sources that the first site was only intended to be temporary while a more suitable location was found as may have occurred elsewhere, although the quick transfer makes this a possibility. If the former site was located close to the parish church, it lay some distance from any water source. The new site had a more diverse environment, suitable topography, and an excellent water supply – from the Wandle – to make it seem ideal. The main priory church could be, and was, constructed upon the higher ground, the claustral complex to the south, but generally still on drier ground, with the reredorter in the lower margins where the drain utilised the natural slope to feed from the west and empty to the east. Botanical and molluscan evidence recovered confirm the overall impression of the environment suggested by the topography, but they also suggest what may not have been immediately apparent, or not considered a major problem at the time: the river margins were prone to flood and much of the underlying riverine deposits were unsuitable for the construction of large stone buildings. These problems are apparent in the later buttressing and repairs, but did not result in the further removal of the monastery to another site after the elapse of a significant number of years as sometimes occurred, for example at Stanlow (Cheshire) on the Mersey estuary where the Cistercian monks endured 124 years of intermittent flooding before transfer to Whalley in Lancashire (Burton 1994, 134).

There is some evidence for the temporary timber buildings constructed to house the canons while the priory became sufficiently endowed to ensure survival. Stability could take many years to achieve, and the 'temporary' nature of timber constructions sometimes seems questionable. This may be the case with Merton, although there is no suggestion that the priory lacked the funds to build in stone from an early date. Work on a stone church may have begun in 1125 and was under way in the 1130s. But beyond that church, a possible partial or intended stone cloister, and a possible chapel or guest house in stone by c 1170, much else may have been in timber. The earliest in situ archaeological evidence for extensive stone claustral buildings does not occur until the early to mid 13th century, which may suggest timber buildings, pre-dating or contemporary with the (?)second church built c 1170 (period M1), and used for a long period, have been lost. A timber and daub building (S1, Fig 9), apparently destroyed by fire in the early 13th century, was conceivably part of the early domestic accommodation for the canons, still extant over a hundred years after foundation, although probably not still used as such. Further tantalising evidence for early timber structures comes from the dendrochronological dates obtained for particular coffins and plank burials within the cemetery from the 12th century onwards (below, 4.10, 'Burial practice', 'Wooden coffins' and 'Plank burials').

In this slight archaeological evidence for early timber structures, Merton has much in common with other sites. Such buildings have been identified rarely: for example at Cistercian Fountains Abbey (Yorkshire West Riding), Augustinian Norton Priory (Cheshire) and more recently in London for the

Augustinian nunnery at St Mary Clerkenwell (Gilyard-Beer and Coppack 1986; Greene 1989, 73; Sloane in prep). This undoubtedly reflects the lack of archaeological survival and detection rather than an original absence of the buildings themselves. The timber buildings, conceived as temporary, were not required to be laid out according to the standard monastic plan, and may have been elsewhere, in areas unexcavated, to avoid interference with the construction of later stone replacements. The lack of extensive evidence for a full stone claustral complex prior to c 1230 might conceivably suggest that Merton did not achieve financial stability as a community until the time of Henry III's lavish patronage (Chapter 3.2, 'Documentary evidence'), a period of more than a hundred years, although this seems excessive and earlier stone buildings may have been obliterated in the 13th century.

4.2 The general layout of the priory

St Mary Merton started as a small monastic house and probably had little initial impact on the locality. From c 1125 the priory expanded, which must have caused some disruption: the construction of the church on the main thoroughfare through Merton caused a re-routing of the road to the north (Fig 1). The precinct wall followed the present High Street forming the northern perimeter of the precinct and the manor of Merton as mentioned in the Saxon charter, before turning southwards along the Abbey Road. Traffic now travelling along 'Stane Street' from the north would have been diverted westwards around the precinct.

Within the precinct few details of the monastic layout have been recovered with certainty before c 1230 with the exception of the church. Initial construction, after any temporary timber accommodation, would have centred on the church. Ex situ moulded stone suggests the presence of a mid 12th-century church which may equate to the documented building work carried out from c 1125 onwards, but with the fragmentary exception of a possible earlier church (B2), close and to the north-east of the church commenced c 1170 (B1), there is no conclusive evidence for the location of this. However, in all probability, it would have been on the higher, drier ground subsequently occupied by the later church, so Building 2 must be considered a reasonable candidate for part of the earlier, possibly incomplete, church (Fig 9).

With the construction of the late 12th-/early 13th-century church (B1) comes the first real evidence for the intended future layout of the complex, but few details beyond the church have been recovered. A possible guest house or chapel was constructed c 1170 well to the west of the church, which may imply extensive construction in stone in the main claustral complex prior to this. If so, the latter has not survived. There were no apparent constraints preventing construction on the south side of the church, but little evidence for a completed stone cloister there at this date, although some evidence both in situ and ex situ of the intention to do so. It is uncertain if a wooden cloister existed. There was no evidence for other formally laid out conventual buildings, and the only evidence for domestic buildings during the 12th century occurred well to the south of the church which was orientated more south-west to north-east than strictly west to east. The monastic cemetery appears to have been established by the late 12th century.

During the 13th century the monastic buildings were rebuilt, expanded or refurbished. The initial impetus at Merton was probably damage to the church with the fall of the tower in 1222, but as with monasteries elsewhere other factors, such as an increase in patronage, here from Henry III and his court, and the need to replace timber structures in stone, may have underpinned the work. At Norton Priory a fire in 1236 necessitated amongst other repairs the reconstruction of part of the cloister (Greene 1992, 17). At Cistercian Tintern Abbey (Monmouthshire) the domestic range was enlarged from c 1220 (ibid, 87). Building work was also carried out at Cistercian Rievaulx Abbey (Yorkshire North Riding) from c 1230 on the presbytery, tower and transepts (Peers 1986). At Lewes Priory, wealth obtained during the 12th century funded a large rebuilding programme: in 1180–1200 a new reredorter was constructed and in 1218–19 work was carried out on the infirmary (Lyne 1997, 11). While such work could result in

extensive debt, as at Lewes (ibid, 12–13) and Rievaulx (Peers 1986), Merton appears to have had sufficient funds both to pay for the work and to lend to the Crown. On 25 April 1286 the Crown acknowledged the 'loan' from Merton of £300 in relation to the tenth due from the clergy in respect of the Holy Land (Cal Pat R, 1281–92, 232), and a further sum of £500 was recorded the following month (ibid, 244).

The ambitious building programme, dated archaeologically to c 1230–50, included a new church, cloister, chapter house, dormitory, infirmary complex, reredorter, and the aisled hall to the south-west (Fig 142). The slype may have led to the monastic cemetery, as at Haughmond (Shropshire) and Llanthony (Monmouthshire), both Augustinian foundations; alternatively it may have served as a sacristy and/or vestry and may have only given access to the transept, as at Strata Florida (Cardiganshire) where the book store/vestry could be entered from the cloister and south transept. Conceivably it may also have been the canons' only access from the cloister to the church, and if the dormitory was not built, at least at first, in the usual position over the chapter house, there may also initially have been no night stairs. At Llanthony the dormitory was located in the west range (Butler and Given-Wilson 1979, 289). Nevertheless, the positioning of the reredorter to the south of the east range implies that a dormitory existed in the

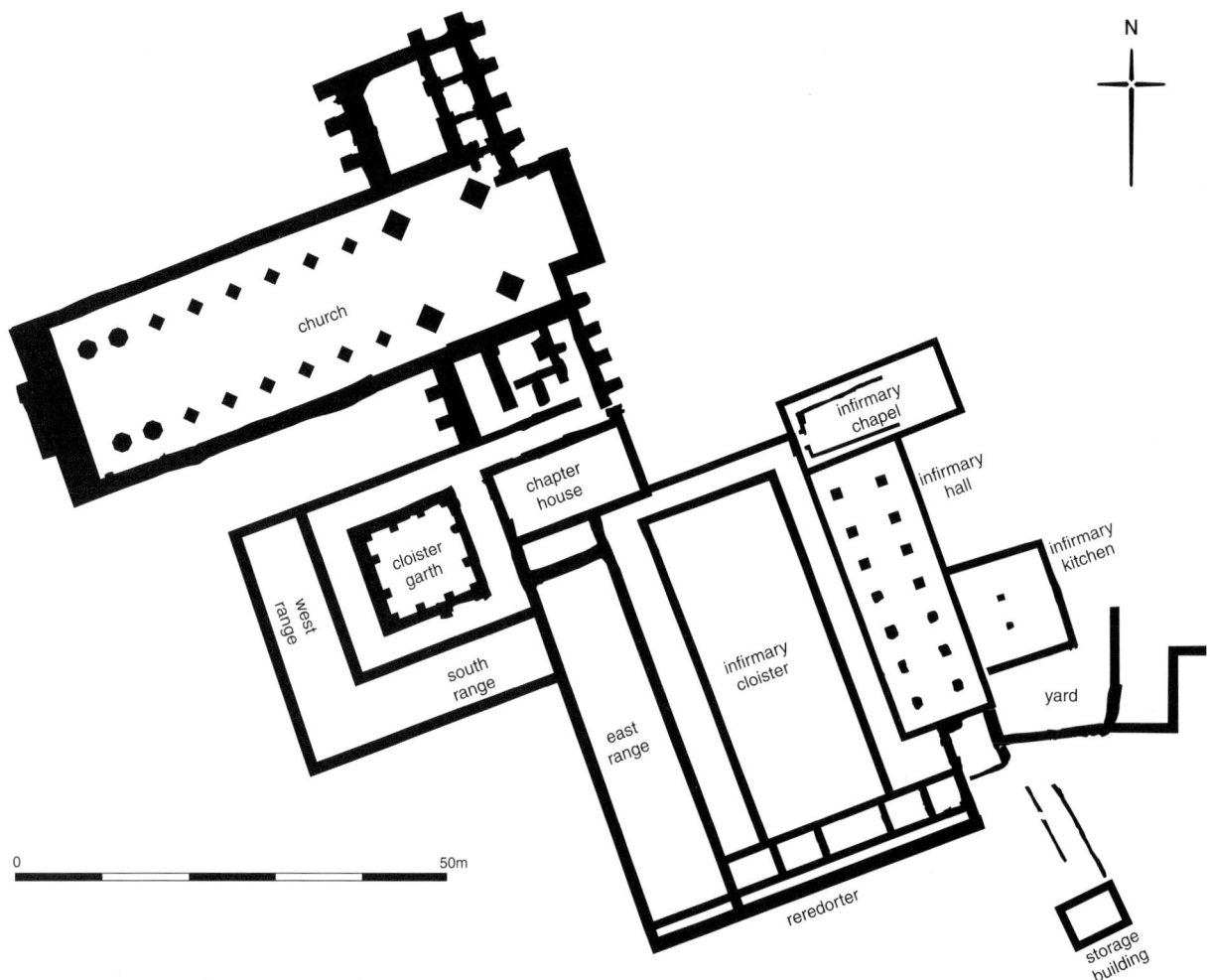

Fig 142 Conjectural reconstruction of the layout of the priory in the mid to later 13th century (period M2) (scale 1:800)

standard position by the end of the 13th century.

The main body of the eastern extension of the church was probably started in c 1310 and finished by c 1340. This included provision for a lady chapel, a popular choice for many monastic establishments of the day. The identification of the Lady chapel rests on its excavated remains and the mention of a chapel of the Blessed Mary in 1393 (Heales 1898, 284, citing Bodleian, Laud MS 723, fo 81). A chapel of St Mary had existed in or from the mid 13th century but this may have been elsewhere – possibly the infirmary chapel (Heales 1898, 139, appendix LXXVII; Chapter 3.2, 'Documentary evidence'). The chapel may have had another designation, or simply been the new presbytery with the choir now moved east to the bays above the old presbytery, but the position and size are typical of a Lady chapel as, for example, at Thornton Abbey (Lincolnshire), Winchester and Chester (Cheshire) Cathedrals.

The mention above of access to the church from the cloister brings us to the most obvious problem of the layout: the atypical cloister in a house that otherwise largely conformed to the standard plan. The 13th-century cloister, to the south of the church, was apparently separated from the nave by a space (OA4) and there may have been no access from it to the nave. This seems distinctly odd given no apparent constraints preventing the usual arrangement being implemented, and unparalleled in an Augustinian house. Faversham Priory (Cluniac) in Kent had a cloister in a similar position, possibly the result of incomplete rebuilding schemes (Philp 1968), and a similar space exists at Salisbury Cathedral, the Plummery – suggesting a lead-working area – while friary complexes also frequently had an open court or lane between the cloister walk and nave, as for example at Walsingham Friary in Norfolk (Gilyard-Beer 1972, plan, fig 20; Greene 1992, 161). It is possible at Merton that retained pre-existing buildings not identified (eg the 12th-century south transept) hindered construction of a cloister directly to the south of the church and, after their removal, created wasted space not subsequently filled, or that some intended southward extension of the nave was never carried out. This seems unlikely: the space was maintained until the Dissolution despite an apparent rebuild of the cloister in the 14th century (Chapter 3.3). The relatively sterile deposits found here suggest the area was not used for any industrial function; evidence for metalworking at Merton appeared to be more prolific on the north rather than the south side of the church and was not found in this area. In contrast to the Augustinian canons, the friars were preachers and encouraged the laity to use their naves, necessitating the construction of lanes to minimise disturbance to their cloister. The Dominicans and Franciscans colonised Britain from c 1220 onwards, and were increasingly popular. That this coincided with Henry III's favouring of Merton, to the extent that he and members of his court had chambers built there, and with a period when Merton was more generally known for its hospitality to pilgrims and travellers, may well indicate a similar response to regular use of the nave by laypersons, although a separate chapel is thought to have existed (extant until at least 1680 – see below, 4.4) that may have provided for the laity. This

does not suggest the church had a general 'parochial' function; a parish church existed in Merton from at least the later 11th century, as recorded in Domesday. Nor does this imply that the space was actually a 'lane' per se: there was little evidence for surfacing, and it may not have given access to the nave, the south transept or the cloister. The laity could easily have used the west door.

The size of the cloister is uncertain (Chapter 3.2). If square, and with an internal garth, excluding the garth walls, of 100m^2 (1076ft^2) or including the eastern cloister walk and a postulated western walk, of c 380m^2 (4090ft^2), it would be comparable to the smaller cloisters of the Augustinian Order (Robinson 1980, appendix 19, 398). Only five houses, Penmon, Portchester (Hampshire), Selbourne, Shulbred (Sussex) and Weybourne (Norfolk), present smaller postulated cloister areas. This is comparable however to the earlier 12th-century garth at Norton Priory (Greene 1989, 80, fig 36) to which other comparisons can be ascribed (such as similarities between the 12th-century churches at both houses: below, 4.3). Perhaps this small size reflected modest numbers present in the house. In c 1130 the priory had 36 canons, but by the beginning of the 16th century this had fallen to 20 (Robinson 1980, appendix 20, 401). In the 13th century the number may have been somewhere between these figures, but, given the status and apparent wealth of the house, might have been around 40. This was relatively high for an Augustinian house (most houses supported 13 or less) but not comparable to some orders; Benedictine or Cistercian houses sometimes supported far larger numbers in extensive claustral ranges. However, even a community of up to 36 canons would suggest a larger cloister, and what evidence exists for the surrounding ranges suggests that at 380m^2 (4090ft^2) the cloister would be small in comparison. Sufficient archaeological evidence exists for a larger 530m^2 square garth, or c 900m^2 (9688ft^2) including the cloister walks, with a small building in it adjacent to the east walk. This would make Merton's overall cloister of a more comparable size to the larger houses recorded by Robinson and more usual for this size of house, although not the 7820ft^2 (726m^2) given for Merton by Robinson (1980, appendix 19, 398). The slype or parlour to the south of the chapter house would give the canons and novices access to both the main cloister and the infirmary cloister, and the large infirmary cloister was perhaps also used by healthy priory inhabitants, as well as the infirm.

The extensive infirmary complex was in the usual position, that is to the south-east of the church, away from the bustle of the main complex with a view of the cemetery, and, given the less formal layouts for infirmaries compared to the main claustral range, not unusual in layout (Byard 2001, 83). The principal components of a hall, chapel and cloister are readily identifiable and of the standard design: the hall for instance was a large undivided building, with two aisles for the beds, and a central walking space that was subdivided into individual rooms for greater privacy in the 1360s–70s following a recognised common pattern (Coppack 1993, 76–8; Burton 1994, 145–6). The precise identification of the other buildings and structures, however, is problematic. A number of suggestions have been made in the period discussions – infirmary kitchen, bleeding room, meat kitchen, washhouse, latrine, infirmarer's lodging, but given the lack of, or equivocal, evidence, none of these can be regarded as secure; they are discussed in detail below (4.5).

The building work of the 14th century does not appear to have greatly affected the overall layout of the priory, although the church was extended – thus perhaps finally dividing the monastic cemetery properly into two – as was the chapter house, and many conventual buildings were apparently rebuilt, for example the reredorter and the infirmary hall and cloister. A composite plan of all known phases of the church, chapter house, cloister, infirmary and infirmary cloister (with conjectured cloister and east range of the infirmary cloister) is shown on Fig 143.

The positioning of the aisled hall (B11), well to the south-west of the main complex but presumably close to the main kitchen (not excavated but assumed to be located in or adjacent to the south range), strongly suggests well-set-up guest accommodation for high-status lay folk such as Henry III or members of his court. However, the possibility that this was the prior's dwelling should not be discounted. In either case the position of the building would not be unusual.

Water management

The flow and position of the River Wandle was a powerful influence on the topography of, and development within, the precinct. The extant reredorter was not built until the 13th century, after the second extant church and the chapter house and possibly other conventual buildings. However, given the importance of water to the communal life, the position of the reredorter was an important consideration in the planning of the monastic complex, so it is likely, given St Mary Merton's largely conventional layout, that a reredorter was always intended for that position if not actually built at an early stage.

Water was required to flush the reredorter drain and would have been channelled to the south of or through the south and east ranges to the reredorter and any latrines south of the infirmary hall; this sewer finally exited east, enriching fishponds identified here (Saxby 2005b, 11–25) and finally emptying into the Wandle in its former course to the south-east (Fig 5; Fig 144). A sluice was probably used to control the flow

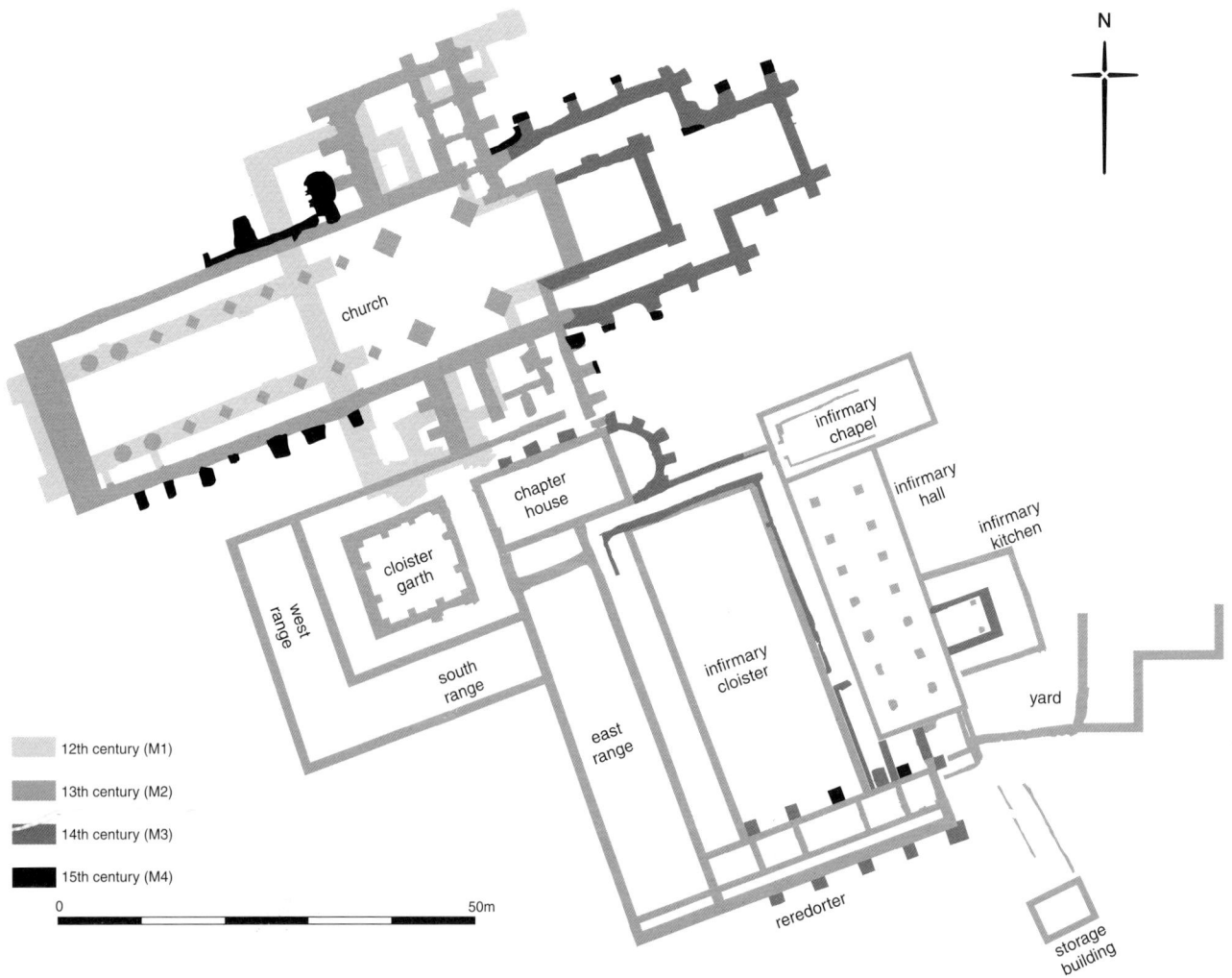

Fig 143 *The conjectural development of the church, chapter house, infirmary and infirmary cloister from the 12th to the 15th century (scale 1:800)*

N

precinct wall

supposed site of 'Amery mills'

ancient course of River Wandle

The Pickle

supermarket

church

chapter house

infirmary chapel

infirmary hall

Merantun Way

marsh

infirmary kitchen

west range

south range

east range

kitchen area

reredorter

fishponds

site of Abbey House

Structure 10

River Wandle

Merton Abbey Mills

aisled hall

medieval trackway

mill leat

Bennett's Ditch

mill

precinct wall

mill pond

path

	original river
	medieval watercourses
	supposed watercourse to feed 'Amery mills'
	later river and watercourses
	high ground
	intermediate ground

0   100m

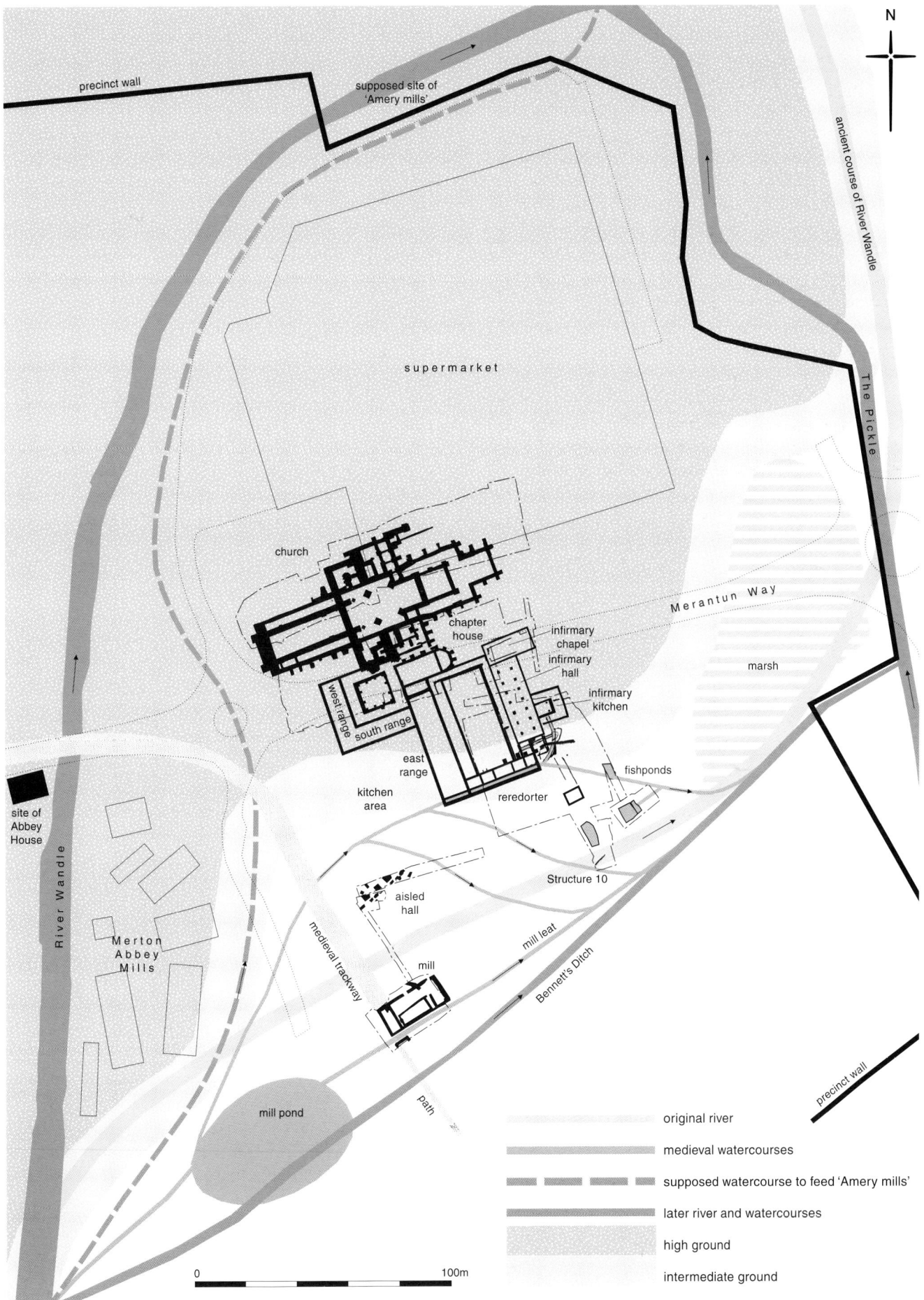

Fig 144 *Water management at the priory, incorporating evidence for the priory mill and fishponds from excavations in 2001 and 2003 and showing all building-related features (including conjecture) (scale 1:2000)*

of water (although not found). A drain (S4a) probably took waste water away from the refectory kitchen and/or a lavatorium or washing place in the south range of the church cloister, as well as the east range. The closure of this drain (period M3) may imply the closure of such a kitchen or refectory late in the monastic period. Another drain (S4b) clearly served the infirmary, for a kitchen, bloodletting, or washing, and buildings to the north. The infirmary was supplied with water from a lead pipe, with a possible laver or storage cistern in the infirmary cloister garth (Bond 2001, 95–9). Smaller drains in the church cloister garth (eg S6) may have dealt with rain-water run-off. These may have ultimately been linked via the south range, and Structure 4a, to the reredorter sewer. Rain-water run-off in the cloister may have been collected to feed the lavatorium in or near the south cloister walk close to the refectory (cf ibid, 103–4). To the south of the reredorter and east of the aisled hall (B11), a series of drainage channels probably served to take waste water away from this building and any kitchens associated with it. This piecemeal evidence may be compared with the detailed documented course and construction in 1220–2 of a 5km conduit and its cisterns, bringing water to the lavatorium and kitchen, at Augustinian Waltham Abbey (Essex) (ibid, 127). In the south-west part of the site was a mill and millpond excavated in 2001 and 2003 (Saxby 2005a) (Fig 144).

The widespread occurrence but low abundance of whelk and oyster suggests no obvious large-scale dump or rubbish pit deposits and it is open to speculation as to where rubbish was disposed of in quantity. The relative sparsity of material may imply that the retrieved freshwater molluscan assemblage is accidentally dropped material rather than deliberate waste deposition. Analysis of these species from the various channels and associated bankside and emergent vegetation suggests a diverse fauna mainly associated with slow-flowing or still, well-oxygenated and well-vegetated waters with very scant recovery of species able to tolerate even mild pollution. This does not suggest routine disposal of organic waste material into water to any significant degree. Similarly, the presence of a diverse terrestrial and freshwater/marginal fauna throughout the site and from all periods does not indicate any focal points for organic pollution such as would occur through sustained dumping of post-consumption faunal waste.

4.3 Architectural aspects of the priory church and chapter house

A mid 12th-century priory church

If the early stonework (Chapter 3.1; CP1) found relates to the church Gilbert started in 1125 this may still have been under construction in the mid 12th century and possibly later. The decorative motifs and mouldings were widespread in south-eastern English church architecture. The probable internal

appearance of such a building is conveyed by structures like the presbytery of St Lawrence Upton (Buckinghamshire). Similar work has been recorded at Selby Abbey, Chichester Cathedral, Peterborough Cathedral, and closer to hand in London at St John Clerkenwell and St Saviour Bermondsey. The vaulting and scalloped pilaster capitals may have come from the presbytery, the commonest use of vaulting in parish churches during this period (Hoey 1997, 145). The short-lived daughter house founded in Dover, St Martin's (1131), was provided with a rectilinear presbytery with an internal width of c 9.4m (Plumptre 1861, pl III); this square east end was of exceptionally early date and may reflect an early attempt to take Augustinian liturgical requirements into consideration (see below).

The priory church (B1)

c 1170s–1222 (period M1)

The worked stone suggests that this church was started c 1170 but was not a single-phase build; stylistic changes occurred during its construction. The end of the 12th century was a period of great stylistic complexity and there is difficulty in attributing fragments that date around the cut-off point in 1222.

The plan is best compared with other late 12th-century Augustinian aisleless churches with projecting square-ended presbyteries and flanking rectilinear chapels such as Lilleshall, Norton and Newark (Fig 145; Fig 146). It closely resembled the existing ruin at Lilleshall (1148+) in overall size, although later in its details, but Newark, 25km south-west of Merton, is closer in time and space. It was founded in the reign of Richard I (*VCH* 1911, 103) suggesting construction began about the time the first Merton church was completed. It is likely that the architect of Newark was aware of the important new church to the north-east. Both were new foundations that allowed an exact expression of Augustinian liturgical requirements. It is probable that the late 12th-/early 13th-century (period M1) Merton church was, like Newark, symmetrical. The nearness of these two Augustinian houses suggests institutional links hinted at in surviving records; the prior of Merton carried out at least one visitation of Newark in 1387 (*VCH* 1911, 104). The Newark plan, little studied, appears to have been originally aisleless (Pearce 1932, 8), again a point in common.

The dimensions of the presbytery were, liturgically, the most important in the church and it is here that stereotyping of dimensions might be expected. The internal width of the earliest presbytery was c 9.0m, comparing well with Lilleshall (c 9.25m) (M Samuel, pers observation; see eg Ferris 2000, 17), Lesnes (8.99m) (Clapham 1915, 44) and St Martin's Dover (c 9.4m). A standard dimension of 30 feet (9.14m) seems to have been used. This places the presbytery in the largest of three standard classes defined for Augustinian churches (Gallagher 1994, 169). The two side chapels paired in echelon off each transept provided additional space for private Masses and closely parallel Newark and Lilleshall. Newark was significantly smaller than Merton but the innermost pair of chapels were

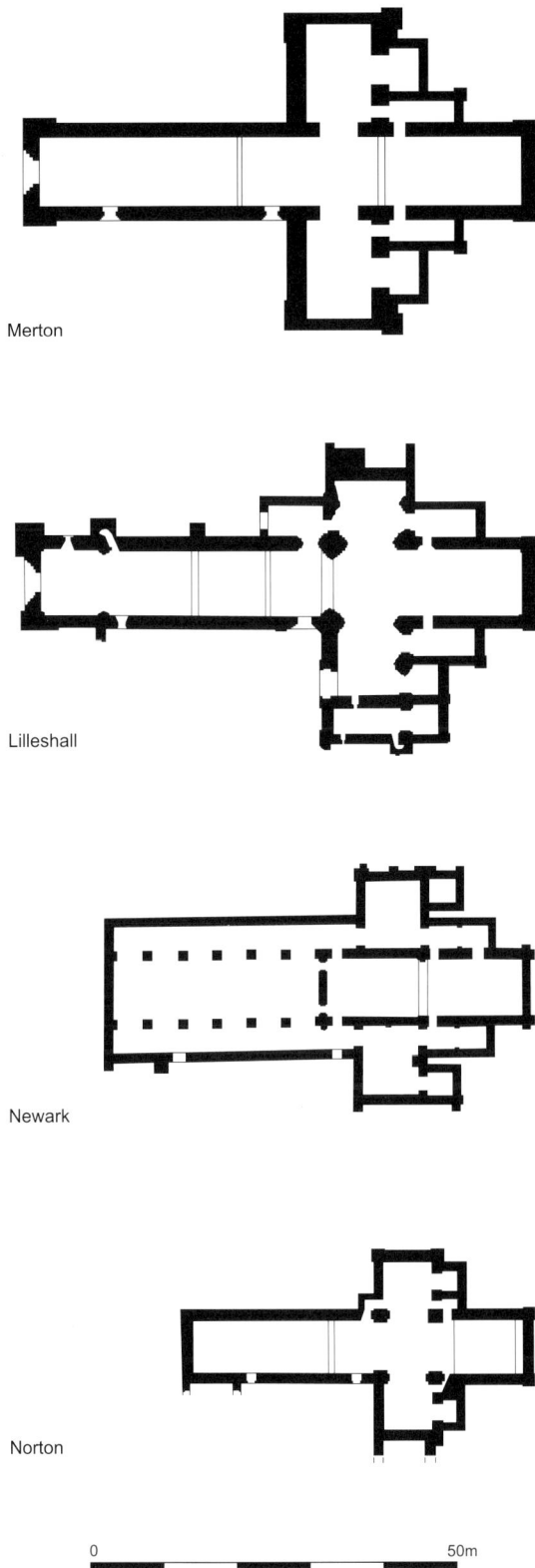

Merton

Lilleshall

Newark

Norton

0   50m

Fig 145 *Comparative simplified plans of (from top) the late 12th-/early 13th-century (period M1) church at Merton (conjectured) and Lilleshall, Newark (with aisles added) and Norton (scale 1:1000)*

similar in size while the outer chapels at Merton were larger. A narrow gap separates the chapels at Newark whereas at Merton they were joined. At Newark the chapels were apparently built against completed transepts. Solid walls pierced by small doors

separate the inner chapels from the presbytery at Newark and Lilleshall, and Merton is reconstructed similarly in Fig 145. Parallels can also be drawn with the north transept of the 12th-century church at Norton (Greene 1989, 80, fig 36). Haughmond (Shropshire) had a similar arrangement of transepts, but its surviving remains are very fragmentary (St John Hope and Brakspear 1909, 288).

The west end of the church is difficult to define but the internal length was probably about 63m, similar to Lilleshall (67.87m) and Repton (Derbyshire) (59.74m) (St John Hope 1884, 358) but smaller than Lesnes (71.32m) (Clapham 1915, 49), suggesting that overall the church was of intermediate size. Yet, by 1200–16 the priory was large enough to be used as an alternative 'court' (Green 1977, 97), so the relatively small scale and simplicity of the church suggests a chequered history up to *c* 1200 with 'stop-go' funding that made it difficult to alter the relatively modest design even in the early years of Henry III – prior to 1222.

Cistercian influence may be observed to some extent in the architecture of the earliest church. The austere building was apparently devoid of figurative ornament, lancets were widely used, and the absence of nave arcades and triforia greatly reduced the scope for internal ornament, but to what extent this was an intentional emulation of Cistercian practice is hard to determine. There is tenuous evidence that in its final form the church may have had some ornately undercut mouldings. These were made feasible by the comprehensive use of Reigate stone. A beak-moulded arch order is present of the sort seen in the highly ornate West Walton church (Norfolk), an exemplar of the 'Early English' style. The overall plan resembles the 'first generation' of Cistercian churches in England, such as Waverley Abbey (Surrey) but should probably be regarded as a standard 'minimalist' church design for about 13 brethren (Greene 1989, 85). The canons' churches are now thought to follow 'guidelines' (Gallagher 1994, 169), although the Cistercians probably exerted greater central control over the form of their monasteries. The high social level of patronage of Augustinian foundations suggests that regional influence was less important than these distant institutional connections (Cambridge 1977, 286). Yet the early Augustinian churches were subject to great variability and it is dangerous to assume that a daughter house would resemble the parent; the plans of Holy Trinity Priory, Aldgate, and its daughter house Lesnes Abbey (Clapham 1915, 43) have little in common. Lesnes, Merton and Newark can be regarded as 'second wave' Augustinian foundations analogous to the second wave of Cistercian foundations.

The builders used 'Reigate stone' from the Upper Greensand of Surrey and a straw-coloured oolitic limestone, probably 'Taynton stone', interchangeably (Chapter 7.2, 'Methodology'). In the medieval period extraction of Reigate stone was concentrated in the parishes between Brockham in the west and Godstone in the east, where it was mined in galleries (adits) (Lockwood 1993, 18). Henry II gave Merton Priory the manors of Kingswood and Shelwood in 1156 (Heales 1898, 20), although no mention is made of a quarry. Earl William de Warenne granted a quarry to the canons of Waltham at Reigate in 1218 and the king's grant was perhaps a similar pious act. Kingswood Manor is to the north of the Upper Greensand belt below the Mertsham scarp. Stone for Windsor Castle was carried across land to a stone quay at Kingston and then carried up the Thames on barges in 1351–65 (VCH 1905, 277), but it is possible that the River Mole was also exploited for transport (Samuel 2004a, 133). The Taynton stone formation covers a wide area and medieval quarrying was principally carried out at Taynton (Oxfordshire), the largest quarry, and also at Burford (Oxfordshire), Barrington, Sherborne and Windrush (all in Gloucestershire) (Arkell 1947, 54–78 and fig 27; D Williams, pers comm).

The masons seem to have used whatever stone was available from day to day. The statute inch and foot (12in) was established by this date and round measurements of inches are common (Fernie 1985, 252). Some architectural features were dressed only with Reigate stone, others with oolitic limestone or a mixture of stones. The oolitic limestone resists weathering, but there is no evidence this characteristic was deliberately exploited (Chapter 7.2). Both types of stone were used in the string course (CP2.38). One type of window was cut from these two building stones as well as from a fine-grained yellow limestone which was probably quarried near Caen (Normandy, France) (CP2.35). The latter stone was also used in a substantial string (CP2.57) and an abacus (CP2.11). Its sparing use may reflect its cost. Faint traces of plaster and whitewash suggest that bare stone was never visible in the interior of the church.

c 1222–c 1300 (period M2)

The overall plan of the 13th-century church as modified (Fig 146) resembles that of the priory church of Lesnes of c 1187. Lesnes was influenced by Cistercian practice (Clapham 1915, 43) and this type of plan – a plain short square- (or flat-) ended presbytery, with rectangular or square deep transepts with eastern chapels ending in a continuous flat wall, and aisles – was belatedly introduced at Merton. The rebuilding of the transepts and the creation of nave aisles, while retaining the original central vessel, heighten this similarity. The rebuilt nave was apparently slightly longer than at Lesnes but narrower (Merton c 43.3m; Lesnes 40.46m). The lack of external buttresses suggests the nave had a timber roof, but stone vaulting may have been used in the aisles; the transepts appear to have been fully vaulted. Novel vaulting techniques were used with variants of the tas-de-charge (a series of horizontal through-stones that form the lowest courses of a vault springer, locking the converging vault ribs into the wall). The bay interval of the nave at Lesnes was c 5.12m compared to 4.3–4.7m at Merton; the contemporary choir of Waltham Abbey (c 5.1m) and the choir of St Andrews Cathedral (Fife) (c 4.7m) also show such a spacing to be acceptable. The lengthening of the nave was at the expense of the presbytery, which was made shorter than its counterpart at Lesnes. There is no evidence this was a temporary state of affairs. Such short square presbyteries are encountered in Cistercian churches, such as Buildwas (Shropshire); the transept with three chapels and a square-ended presbytery are

reminiscent of Strata Florida and Kirkstall (Yorkshire West Riding).

The new north transept shared the east–west external dimensions of its Lesnes counterpart, but was longer permitting the construction of an additional chapel. The relative shortness of the south transept is intriguing. The transept appears to have been 'compressed' between the crossing and the slype (B3f); the slype may have been a low screened passage structurally within the transept. It is therefore possible that the chapter house had been constructed in advance of at least part of the new church. The absence of such constraints on the north side allowed a long north transept, at the cost of symmetry.

The church was built probably of Kentish rag or chalk rubble, faced either with coursed rag rubble as at Lesnes or flint as at Newark. All the dressings were of Reigate stone, presumably deriving from the same unknown quarries in the North Downs as for the late 12th-/early 13th-century church. Taynton stone apparently was not used; although it is hard

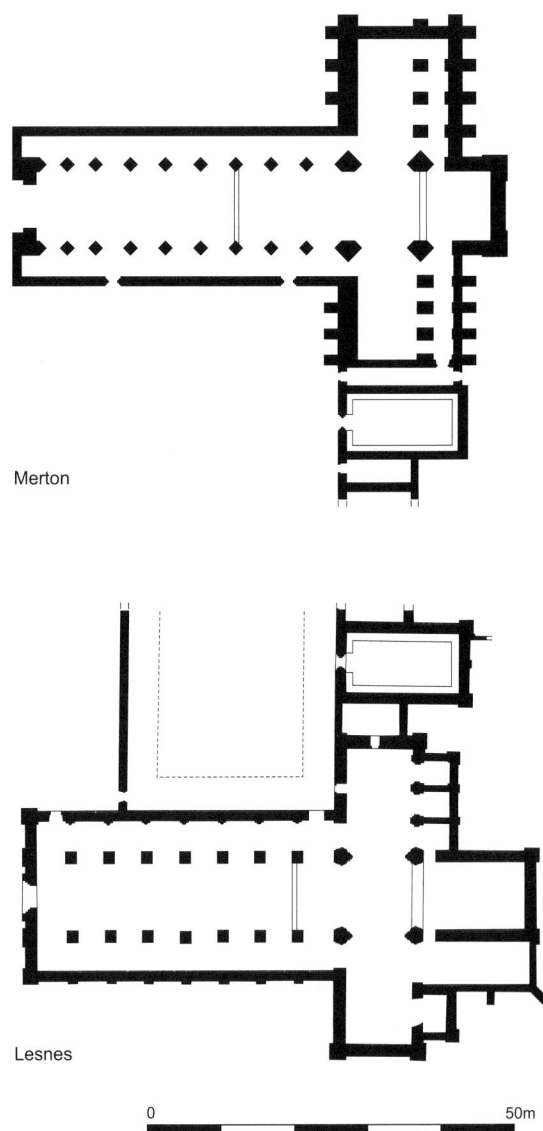

Fig 146 Comparative simplified plans of the mid 13th-century (period M2) church at Merton and Lesnes (with Lady chapel added) (scale 1:1000)

wearing, it does not readily take fine modelling, whereas Reigate stone excels in this respect. The only other stone that occurred in significant quantities was polished Purbeck marble. This seems to have been used as decorative shafting in the 13th-century church and probably its claustral structures. When complete, the new nave must have closely resembled the smaller but directly contemporary presbytery at Benedictine Boxgrove Priory (Sussex), where Purbeck marble was used for shafting with growing confidence.

Fragments of reddish-brown Coggeshall-type bricks were associated with the 13th-century church; used around window and door openings, and possibly as cornices, they would have contrasted with grey-coloured flint rubble walls on the church exterior. A second type of thin brick or tile with either a splash or more uniform covering of glaze was also used. Similar in appearance to decorative bricks used at Westminster Abbey during the 11th century (Betts 1996, 19), the Merton examples are clearly later in date but may have been set as decoration in the walls in association with moulded stone or flintwork.

The mosaic tile floors, made from a clay similar to later 'Westminster' tiles, were probably installed in the 1230s or 1240s, making them contemporary with the earliest mosaic tiling found in many other parts of England. The earliest mosaic pavements accurately dated are those at Fountains Abbey (Yorkshire West Riding), laid 1220–47 (Eames 1992, 30), whilst at Salisbury Cathedral the earliest mosaic tiling has been dated to between 1225 and c 1240 (Norton 1996, 91). The only earlier tiles are those at Canterbury Cathedral laid 1213–20 (Eames 1980, 34). The ornate patterns have parallels with mosaics found at Fountains and Byland (Yorkshire North Riding), and at Guisborough Priory (Yorkshire North Riding).

The Merton seal matrix possibly provides evidence for the appearance of the reconstructed church (Fig 147). A canopy over the Virgin is created by a stylised architectural drawing of a church. This cannot be thought to be a literal depiction of Merton but is stylistically compatible with the date of the seal.

Fig 147 *The Merton seal (replica, 85mm x 52mm, of an impression of the obverse of British Library seal xxi.25)*

The seal was renewed in silver between January 1239 and 11 December 1241 when it was received (Bruce and Mason 1993, 1). The central structure employs elements suggestive of a church west front: a gable is flanked by spired turrets comparable to those on the east front of Whitby Abbey (c 1220) but the central quatrefoil window resembles the blind quatrefoil openings of the ground-stage of the west front of Wells Cathedral (Somerset) (c 1230–40). Both this gable and the gables of the flanking ?transepts (shown in three-quarter view) apparently have single trefoil openings while grouped lancets of equal height light the ?transepts. The roof is leaded with diamond-shaped sheets. A similar west front gable window existed at St-Nicaise Reims (Marne, France) (Wilson 1990, fig 94), begun c 1240. The two lowest sharply pitched minor gables could represent a galilee (chapel or vestibule, usually enclosing the porch at the west end of the church) as at St-Nicaise. This plausibly depicted, French-influenced structure may be entirely imaginary but suggests the recutting of the seal marked the completion of Merton's own reconstruction. The seal-cutter was very aware of fashionable architectural motifs and it seems likely that some, if not all of these, were used in the 13th-century church at Merton.

c 1300–c 1390 (period M3)

The eastern extension of the church (Fig 148) was described by Bidder as 'almost identical' with the extension eastwards of St Augustine's Bristol (now Bristol Cathedral). So close is it, that it is impossible not to believe that the builders of Bristol had Merton in their minds (Bidder and Westlake 1930, 63). Merton should be considered in the architectural context of the first quarter of the 14th century, and as a major lost work of the Decorated period in south-east England. Bristol Cathedral and Merton Priory were both built under Augustinian Rule. Various key dimensions of the two eastern extensions can be compared (Table 17). Bidder's dimensions for Merton are given except for the last (the total internal width), which is measured from the excavated evidence; for Bristol a published plan is used (Paul 1913, pl xxxiv).

The plans are similar, but not identical as Bidder would have it (Chapter 7.2, 'Construction phase 5 (the eastern extension of the church) equates approximately to period M3'; Fig 188). The lengths of the extensions differed because both churches had to be adapted to pre-existing crossings and east arms. There is little in common in the form of the mouldings, and the Bristol arcade lacks the alternations used at Merton. Despite these differences, it seems reasonable to use the known dimensions at Bristol to illustrate what is otherwise unknown at Merton. The heights of the piers at Bristol measured from Britton (1836, pls vi, vii) indicate that the piers were c 8.65m high; annulets in the Lady chapel responds are c 4.92m above the ground (upper bed). Bristol was the earliest example of a 'hall church' in England (Pevsner and Metcalf 1985, 38) with aisle and central vessel at the same height. Merton was not a hall church and had a more conventional layout, although executed with considerable ingenuity.

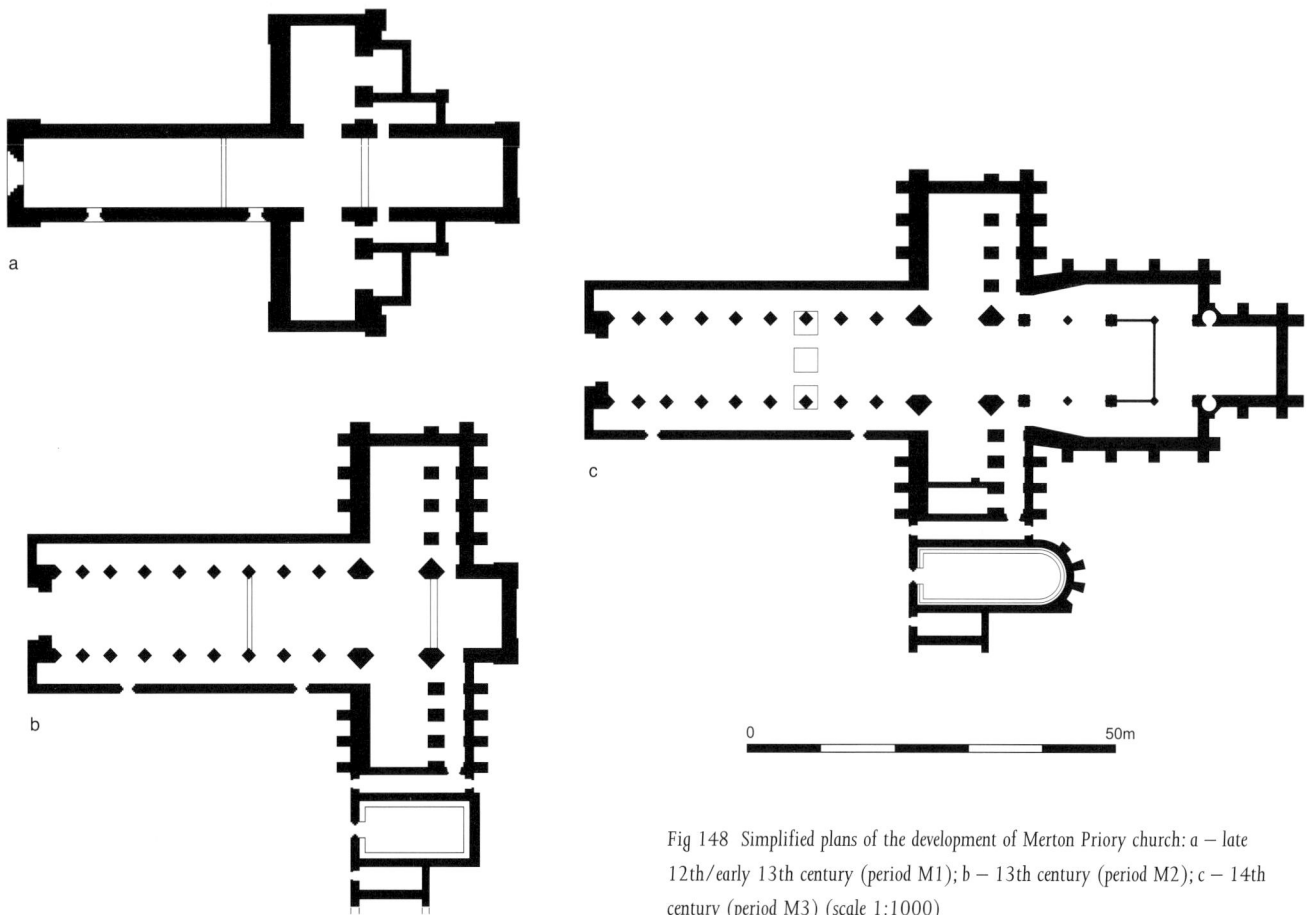

Fig 148 Simplified plans of the development of Merton Priory church: a – late 12th/early 13th century (period M1); b – 13th century (period M2); c – 14th century (period M3) (scale 1:1000)

Table 17 A comparison between the eastern extensions of Merton Priory and St Augustine's Bristol

| | Merton Priory | | St Augustine's Bristol | |
	Width (m)	Width (ft) (decimal)	Width (m)	Width (ft) (decimal)
Lady chapel	9.14	30.00	c 9.27	c 30.40
Bay	5.94	19.50	c 5.90	c 19.35
Total internal	20.25	66.44	c 20.33	c 66.70

The Bristol east arm was commenced in 1298 and thought to have been completed about 40 years later (Paul 1913, 240–2). Statistical study of the moulding date-spans indicates a building campaign c 1300–30 at Merton. Bristol and Merton were therefore contemporary. This suggests that one of the architects from St Stephen's chapel Westminster (Michael of Canterbury, his son Thomas and William Ramsey I) or a trainee may have overseen both projects. The lower storey at St Stephen's was begun in 1292 and completed by 1297 (Wilson et al 1986, 337). The presence of relatively unusual window moulding details in the crypt of St Stephen's and in the ?clerestory of Merton possibly pushes the commencement of the Merton eastern extension back to the 1290s.

If influences can be traced at all, they are more probably those of London than the West Country. Technical as well as moulding dissimilarities in the two window types of the eastern extension (Chapters 3.3, 7.2, CP5.9, CP5.12) suggest distinct building campaigns. The axial terminations of the larger window compare to mouldings used in the 1330s at Gloucester Cathedral (Gloucestershire) (Harvey 1978, fig 2). Neither tracery scheme can be entirely reconstructed, but the ?aisle window used large skeletal cusps and trefoils in a manner reminiscent of St-Urbain Troyes (Marne, France), dated to c 1270 (Wilson 1990, fig 85) and St Ethelreda's, Ely Place London, begun 1284 (Coldstream 1987, 94). The Merton eastern extension is therefore of an international style, marking the point at which national styles went their separate ways.

The Merton pier mouldings are apparently unique, and thought to date between c 1290 and c 1325 (R K Morris, pers comm). Piers at Exeter Cathedral have only a slight similarity in moulding despite technical similarities; the Exeter hollows are feeble and quirks are absent. Despite their peculiarities the Merton major piers (Chapters 3.3, 7.2, CP5.3) are an early occurrence of widespread and broadly similar Perpendicular effects employed in, for example, the south arcade at Worcester Cathedral (Worcestershire) (1357–86) (Harvey 1978, fig 25). The type also occurs in a blind tracery fragment from St Paul's, London (reference collection of moulding records, History of Art Department, Warwick University, no. LSP 1017). The boldness, regularity and clarity of the Merton design are unparalleled and hint at equally bold structural solutions in the articulation of the east end. The innovative double-bell minor pier base form (known from the surviving pier at Kingston Library) is first recorded in the presbytery north arcade at Ely Cathedral (Cambridgeshire) (Morris 1979, 29, fig 17 q) after 1322. The annulet in the responds of the Lady chapel and choir aisles at Bristol occurs in a taller more massive form (Britton 1836, pl vi) but is otherwise similar.

Like the clerestory window, the ribs (Chapter 7.2, CP5.13) employed rounded axial terminations and flanking beaks. The mouldings of the major and minor ribs can be closely paralleled, the former in the cloisters of Norwich Cathedral (Norfolk) (from 1279: Morris 1979, fig 15 e) while the latter is very similar to those used in the cloister at Lincoln Cathedral (Lincolnshire) (from 1295: Morris 1979, fig 14 d). A simple hollow chamfered rib only known from the Nonsuch assemblage may derive from the aisle vaults. The unusual design of the east arm, with its lavish use of Purbeck marble in a structural role, suggests a prosperous community, but its incompleteness may mark a change of fortunes.

c 1390–1538 (period M4)

Work during this period appears to have been limited to the repair and refurbishment of the existing church building. The apparent instability of the earlier eastern extension and perhaps long-standing faults in the foundation of the 13th-century work were taking their toll.

The chapter house (B3b)

Originally the chapter house was rectangular and incorporated entirely within the main body of the east range, that is it did not project east of the transept. It was a double square in plan, probably 25 x 50 statute feet internally, with four vault compartments covered by a quadripartite vault. There were no internal subdivisions or columns. The buttressing to the south (Fig 34) suggests a vault height only slightly less than the transept. This may suggest the lack of a 'dormitory-over' arrangement. At Holy Trinity Aldgate the chapter house rose through two storeys and the dormitory range did not cross over at first-floor level (Schofield and Lea 2005, 124). At Merton a lower western vestibule for access above to the transept remains a possibility. The positioning of graves within the chapter house indicates space was allowed for only a single bench around the walls rather than the double bench seen at, for example, Lesnes. The similarity in width to the chapter house at Bristol Cathedral was commented on by Bidder (Bidder and Westlake 1930, 62). Stereotyping in size can be detected in 12th-century Augustinian churches, but can similar patterns be detected in chapter houses? A selective review of simple rectilinear 12th-century chapter houses, mostly in south-east England, shows that the size of the chapter house relates rather well to the known size of the priory and its relative importance, but classification into set sizes is not apparent. Newark has a small chapter house, while the great royal foundation at Waltham was not surprisingly lavish in its chapter house dimensions, being even slightly greater than Merton. Proportions seem to have

been irregular, apart from a probable 1:2 relationship at Merton and Lesnes. The lost apsidal chapter house of St Martin's Dover (Plumptre 1861, pl 3) apparently shared a 25-foot width with Merton that may reflect the connection between the two priories. The relationship between size and importance supports the impression that care was usually taken to provide for an optimum number of canons. The study of such 'elite' structures is vital to social and spatial analysis of monastic excavations.

The early chapter house falls into a group of approximately double-square undivided chapter houses built earlier, in the 12th century. Columnar chapter houses were more typically built in the 13th century, appearing as early as c 1150–75, and Merton's undivided form is therefore archaic for the time of construction. However, the chapter house, like the church, is similar in approach to that at Lesnes, set out 40 years earlier, but it would be inadvisable to see any one chapter house as a prototype. Nor is this the only example of the archaic form in the 13th century, suggesting a more comprehensive study is needed: the chapter house at Augustinian Hardham Priory (Sussex) is very similar to Merton being rectangular, a double-square 14m by 7m internally, and dating to c 1250 (Hills 1866, 54–9). This form was also used in later friaries, like Walsingham Greyfriars (Norfolk), and in London at Cistercian St Mary Graces where the simple undivided chapter house measured 12.75m by 6m internally, being built c 1360–75 and coincidentally employing similar foundation construction techniques (Grainger and Phillpotts in prep a).

The change in the 14th century at Merton to an apsidal chapter house that projected eastwards is unusual in monastic architecture. Eastern apsidal projections were added to a few rectangular chapter houses, such as at Gloucester and the first Llanthony (Little 1979, 33), but more usually apsidal chapter houses were replaced by c 1200 by rectangular examples. It is possible the extension at Merton was a response to a growing number of canons and to structural problems caused by subsidence to the north; the apsidal end perhaps provided stronger support. The rebuild was presumably successful: the chapter house continued until the Dissolution in 1538 without any obvious further changes. Equally, the extensive buttressing on the east and north sides (Fig 71) may suggest a rather grander building than its predecessor, with no provision for a vestibule and access to the dormitory from the transept.

4.4 A chapel and a ? guest house in the outer court

A few structures to the west, within what must presumably have been the outer court, survived after the Dissolution – notably it appears the chapel of the Blessed Virgin Mary and the tenement and mansion referred to as Salyngs in the early 16th century (Chapters 5.2, 7.1, 'The land called Salyngs'). The 16th-century and later 'Abbey House' apparently incorporated earlier remains, recorded in 1914 by the Ministry of Works, including an elaborate 12th-century arch discovered in the north front wall of the house (Fig 33) (TNA: PRO, WORK 14/740; S Brindle, pers comm). The arch was purchased by Gilliat E. Hatfield of Morden for £100 (ibid, 11 July 1914); reconstructed, it now forms the entrance to the churchyard of Merton parish church (cover illustration). Salyngs and/or Abbey House may have occupied the site of what was previously perhaps the guest house or *hospitium*.

The arch has a number of parallels that suggest interpretations for its use. It resembles the outer three orders of the church doorway to the cloisters at Lilleshall, both being carved with a very rich, interrupted and enriched chevron moulding. The doorway also resembles the suggested entrance to the nave from the western cloister walk at Norton Priory (Greene 1992, 103). The Merton example (which survives in a mutilated state) was even more elaborate than at Norton, the lozenges being filled with foliage and flowers. Its ornament also parallels the frater doorway at Lilleshall. Other examples of this ornament can be found in the Augustinian Cartmel Priory (Lancashire), St Werburgh's Abbey Chester (ibid), and Surrey parish churches, such as Shere (Johnston 1914, 138). Because of its location (Fig 150), this elaborate doorway has been interpreted as the entrance to the guest house (ibid), but may have originated elsewhere in the priory.

A chapel was mentioned in 1680 when Merton Abbey was advertised to be let and described as containing several large rooms and a very fine chapel (*Domestic Intelligencer*, 5 March 1680). John Aubrey describes the 'Abbey' as having walls of flint 8ft (2.44m) high and enclosing 65 acres (26.30 hectares); a 'fine clear stream runs through here, wherein are excellent trouts; it passes by the kitchen and drives a mill' (Aubrey 1718, 226). There was also a chapel with an 'old pulpit and two old gates' (Jowett 1951, 81). In 1725 the site was visited by Bishop Willis, who reported that the chapel still existed but was not used for services (ibid, 90). In 1730 George Vertue described the chapel as being entire and resembling a 'Saxon building' (Thorne 1876, 427). In 1792 Lysons said that 'Devine Service had been performed in the chapel and persons christened there' (Lysons 1792, 345). In 1804 Manning declared 'at the present stage there is no other vestige of the building than the east window of a chapel of crumbling stone which seems from its style of architecture, to have been built in the 15th century' (Manning and Bray 1804, 258). This chapel window was illustrated in an accompanying engraving by J P Malcolm (MLHS; Fig 149). The geometric tracery is closely paralleled by the (heavily restored) windows of the Maison Dieu Hall, Dover (Kent), in the use of a cusped central oculus with flanking daggers (M Samuel, pers observation). To what extent these windows are exact reconstructions is unknown, but their appearance is consonant with the documented construction date of the hall in 1253. The Merton chapel can therefore be seen as a by-product of the same late 13th-century prosperity that culminated in the construction of the new eastern extension of the church (below, 4.9).

The two old gates Aubrey referred to must have been those opposite the entrance to 'Abbey House' (the former ? guest

Fig 149 J P Malcolm's engraving, c 1800, of the remains of a chapel to the west of the priory site (courtesy of Merton Library and Heritage Service)

house; for location see Fig 150). The small gateway (Fig 151; marked as 'Gateway' on the 1894 Ordnance Survey map, Fig 150), with a round-headed ?medieval arch, survived in a wall of the outer court until the 1980s, when it was replaced with a replica; it formed the entrance to the 'Abbey House' property. Part of a boundary wall stretches westwards from this gate and stands today, constructed from flint. Three pointed arches were incorporated in this wall, possibly formed with reused Roman tiles and originally perhaps part of an arcade in a cloister or ambulatory (Walford 1895, 519). The larger gate or 'Highgate' lies just to the north of the earlier gate and represents the rear entrance to the post-medieval property known as 'Abbey Gate House' or 'Gatehouse' (south of the property named as Abbey House in 1894, Fig 150).

The only parts of the priory extant now are stretches of the boundary walls, most notably of the precinct wall to the east of the main priory buildings.

4.5 The infirmary

A monastic infirmary, being part of a religious house, was not technically a hospital – a distinct institution with medical and caring functions for all – in the modern sense, but this distinction was blurred to the medieval mind. Medieval hospitals, particularly those of the Augustinian Order, like St Mary Spital, regarded themselves principally as religious houses, and shared many of the buildings, such as church/chapel,

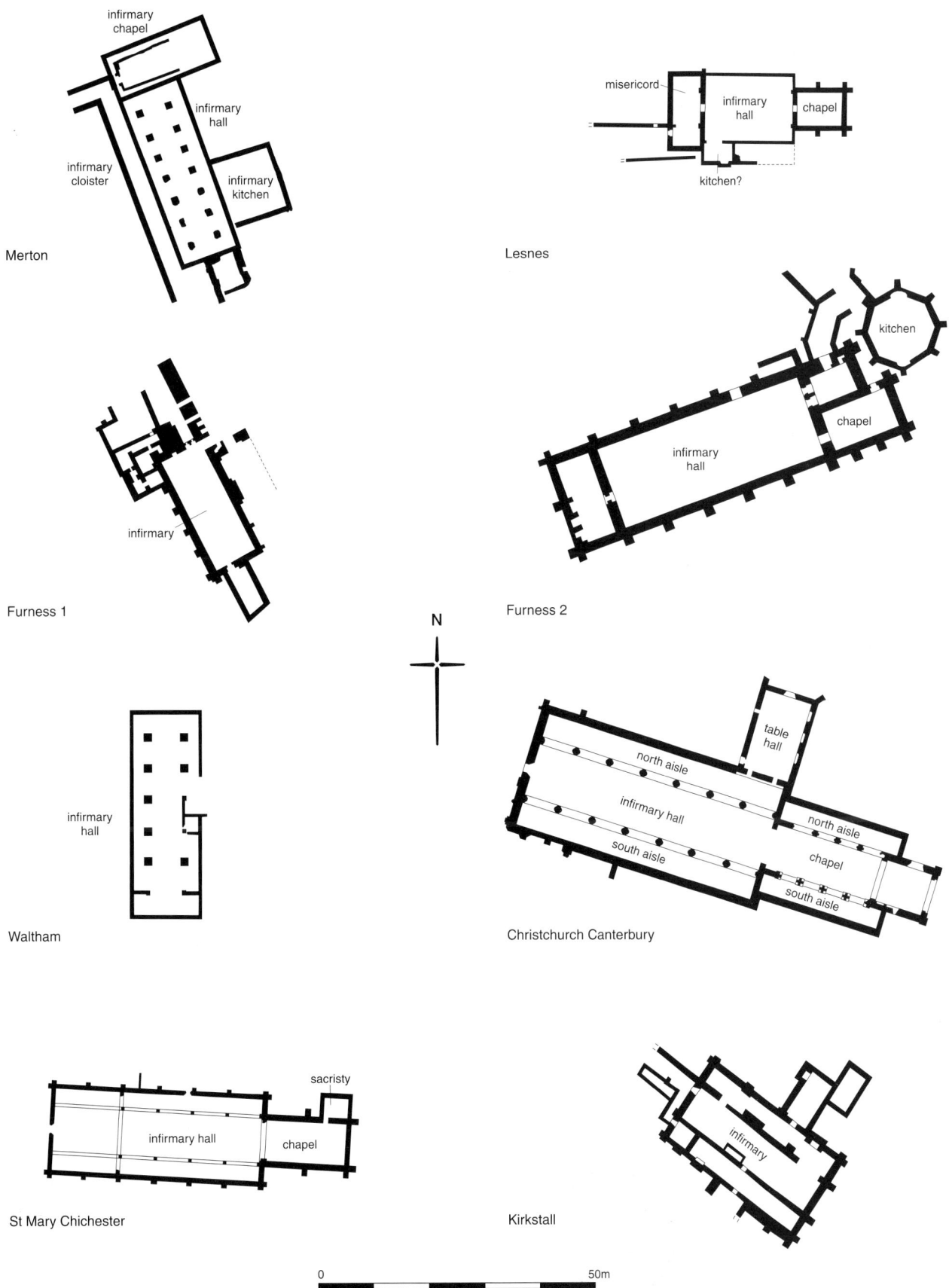

Merton

Lesnes

Furness 1

Furness 2

Waltham

Christchurch Canterbury

St Mary Chichester

Kirkstall

Fig 152 Simplified comparative plans of infirmary halls and related buildings: Merton, Lesnes, Furness 1 and 2, Waltham, Christchurch Canterbury, St Mary Chichester and Kirkstall (scale 1:1000)

During the 14th century there was a shift from communal living to private accommodation within infirmaries and hospitals (Orme and Webster 1995, 90–1). Private dwellings were provided there for the abbot and master or warden (Prescott 1992, 38). References to 'the priors chambre' in the infirmary occur in 1530 at Merton (*Reg Wolsey*, 73–99; Heales 1898, 332). This lapse in the original foundation statutes eventually encompassed the brethren. Open infirmary halls were divided into smaller individual cells or rooms. This became commonplace after *c* 1350 (Prescott 1992, 41). At St Mary's Canterbury, excavations revealed postholes for partitions dating to *c* 1370 and also this occurred within the small hospital of the New Work of St Mary of Strood by Rochester (Kent) (ibid, 43). At Waltham Abbey excavation also revealed divisions within the hall, with one room measuring 2.60m² and containing a hearth and a bed space (Musty 1978, 133; P Huggins, pers comm).

At Merton, during the 1360s–70s, the infirmary hall side aisles on the ground floor were divided into single rooms for about 14 inmates (or 28 if subdivided as with rooms 6 and 7), assuming the central aisle remained an open space (Fig 71). This layout was similar to that of Fountains Abbey and St Mary's Hospital Chichester (Godfrey 1959, 135). These rooms and the central space were better floored – with either roof tiles or Low Countries floor tiles – than the earlier open plan hall. The floor tiles in the central space showed considerable signs of wear, paralleling the infirmary hall at St Mary Spital (Thomas et al 1997, 32). Further evidence of comfort comes from the possible hearth in room 2. The Reigate stone column or pedestal bases found in rooms 3 and 4 divided each room into two areas of 1.0m wide and 2.0m wide but do not appear to be for partitions. A reference in 1520 to a lower chamber or cell of the infirmary (Heales 1898, 331) suggests more than one floor in the hall or at least part of it and the columns may have supported an upper level. The buttressing along the eastern wall, possibly 15th century, may suggest the addition of an upper floor (Fig 129). At Furness 1, the infirmary hall was converted into the abbot's house in the 15th century, with the addition of buttressing along the eastern wall suggesting a second storey was added (Byard 2001, 136). The division of the hall into two floors also occurred at Fountains (Coppack 1990, 78).

The amatory inscription on the gold finger ring <S252> (Fig 153) found in a demolition context within the former hall

area (OA12, period P2) may suggest that male corrodians or guests were now resident in the hall. Greene suggests that elderly laypersons were accommodated within the infirmary (1992, 158), while at Fountains a corrody was granted to a priest, Thomas Wells, with living quarters in the infirmary, and at Westminster Abbey only two of the six or seven chambers were actually used by the sick (Harvey 1993, 87). Monastic infirmaries also occasionally received sick men who wished to end their days as monks (Byard 2001, 48). In 1190 Alan, son of the priest of Clapham, gave two bovates of land to Furness Abbey in case he was overtaken by sickness or old age (ibid, 91). The sacring bells <S50> (Fig 52) and <S51> (period M2), bone die <S32> (Fig 118) (period M3), and from demolition contexts (OA12, period P2) the tuning peg <S29> (Fig 154), and buckle <S223> (Fig 165), engraved with the Lamb of God, have more religious associations. The bone die may have been used to draw divine guidance to select an appropriate course of action (Biddle 1990, 698), while the bell was rung when the host was elevated at Mass (Biddle and Hinton 1990, 725–7). Tuning pegs from stringed instruments have been found at Battle Abbey (Sussex), at St Augustine's Abbey, Canterbury and more locally at St Saviour Bermondsey (Steele in prep). Lead styli <S43> and <S44> were also recovered.

The evidence for the subdivision of the infirmary cloister walks into separate rooms 10.00m by 2.00m at Merton during the late 14th to early 15th century is questionable, but the walks probably were at least glazed for greater comfort. Senior members of monastic communities did set up extensive private residences within the infirmary: at Waverley the abbot moved his quarters there, using the misericord (the infirmary refectory or dining hall where meat was prepared for the sick and other members of the community) as his hall and having his meals prepared in the infirmary kitchen (Coppack 1993, 78), while at Westminster the rebuilt infirmary cloister garth offered wealthy guests accommodation (Byard 2001, 162).

As noted above (4.2), the identification of the other buildings of the infirmary beyond the hall, chapel and cloister is uncertain. The 9th-century St Gall plan shows an idealised monastery compound where the bath house (or houses) is adjacent to a kitchen to facilitate the provision of hot water (Horn and Born 1979). At Merton, if Building 6 (periods M2, M3; Fig 152) is the infirmary kitchen and not a wash or bath house, there may have been a bath house to the north. The

<S252>

<S29>

Fig 153 *The gold finger ring <S252> recovered from a demolition deposit in the former infirmary hall and inscribed with [Je] ne weil [= ?veille] aymer autre que vous ('I am not seeking to love anyone but you') (scale 1:1, inscription 2:1, photo c 4:1)*

Fig 154 *The bone tuning peg <S29> recovered from post-Dissolution robbing of the infirmary hall (scale c 1:1)*

north end of the hall, closest to the chapel at Merton, is traditionally thought to have held the sickest or eldest monks, convenient following death for the corpse to be washed before burial (Byard 2001, 197). But a bath house may have been south of the infirmary hall, in Building 7 (periods M2, M3). A bloodletting house was also not positively identified at Merton. The St Gall plan depicts a building to the north-east of the infirmary, quadrangular with a single entrance to the south (near the bath house); it was to have six benches, six long tables and a stove in each corner (Byard 2001, 187). A bloodletting house is another possibility for Building 6 or, more likely, its replacement Building 12 (period M3), or for Building 7 or the building (B10; periods M2, M3) to the south reached by a passage/pentice; or, again, bloodletting could have taken place in a room on the ground floor of the reredorter as at Evesham (Worcestershire) (Bottomley 1995, 42).

Other buildings possibly present, but unidentified, include a dining hall or 'table hall' where those who had undergone bloodletting were allowed to eat meat, later generally used by all the inmates of the infirmary. At Christchurch Canterbury this was off the north aisle of the infirmary (Fig 152) and at St Augustine's Canterbury to the north-east of the infirmary (Byard 2001, 126). Again, at Merton a room on the ground floor of the reredorter could have acted as a dining hall. Animal and fish bones recovered from the floors there indicate a diet similar to that supplied by the infirmary kitchen (Chapter 3.2).

The infirmary cloister was large (c 32m x 15+m), although not as large in area as that of Rievaulx (c 25m square) (Peers 1986, plan), and more formally laid out as a cloister (with, at least three, covered alleys) than most such areas. In Cistercian houses the ground floor chambers of the reredorter are usually identified as the novices' dormitory or infirmary; this arrangement is illustrated at the Cistercian abbeys of Netley (Hampshire), Rievaulx and Jervaulx and probably at the Benedictine priory of Worcester (Byard 2001, 183). An account by Didron describes large ground-level halls near the 'great infirmary of the religious' including the novices' study room, their dormitory and their infirmary (Didron 1845, 23; Byard 2001, 182). At Cluny (Saône and Loire, France) the novices' quarters were close to the infirmary (Stratford 1992, 397; Byard 2001, 182). If Merton, as suggested by the layout of the reredorter, had a large dormitory bordering the infirmary cloister this may suggest a relatively large number of canons. As suggested above (4.2), healthy and sick clerics may have shared the extensive and potentially segregated infirmary complex. Novices may have been included: they could be supervised well away from the church and lay access to the west, stopping them straying from religious observance (Byard 2001, 194).

4.6 Medical care and treatment

The monastic infirmarer was not only there for the care of the sick but also for the care of the soul. The Barnwell Observances outline three kinds of sick persons allowed within the infirmary: those suffering exhaustion and weakness from overwork or overindulgence; those suffering fevers, bodily pains or spasms; and those struck with sudden illness – possibly strokes and heart attacks. The first were to be allowed only to rest for a short period in the infirmary; the second needed a physician, baths and medicine; for the third, only care for the departing soul was deemed effective (Clark 1897). The archaeological evidence for the care of the sick, over and above the buildings discussed above (4.5), comes in three forms: evidence of medical problems and intervention from the skeletal assemblage; objects and vessels associated with medicines and medical care; and potential medicines from plant remains.

The most conspicuous evidence for medical intervention is often the treatment of fractures. An abundance of well-aligned, healed fractures with no sign of infection argues for treatment, whereas malformation argues against reduction being performed. There was strong evidence that many of the Merton burials had received treatment. Within the skeletal assemblage, 13% of individuals recorded had suffered a fracture (Table 64). The majority were well healed (Table 65) and more were aligned than misaligned, although a fracture evident in an individual in the north burial area (OA6) appears to have gone partially untreated (Fig 155). Relatively few had evidence of infection. However, broken bones are not one of the conditions listed as treated in the infirmary in the Barnwell Observances and the occurrence of a well-healed fracture in the monastic cemetery does not necessarily imply the intervention of the infirmary.

The burials also provide limited evidence for medical care in the form of objects buried with them – the possible hernia belt <S254>(Fig 156) (B1, period M4) and the copper-alloy possible medical support plate on burial [2595] (OA6, period M3). Both were associated with mature adult males, possibly treated in the infirmary, but both surgical objects were probably sourced from elsewhere. The identification of the medication plate may not be secure but the individual suffered from osteochondritis dissecans resulting in inflammation of the knee where the object was found and the sheet was possibly used in the curative manner copper bracelets are today. Similarly, it is unlikely that the ornate spectacles <S253> (Fig 157) were either made or supplied by the infirmary. However this fragment, of the bridge side of the frame for one of the lenses, from the most ornate spectacle frames so far indentified from the medieval period suggests eye conditions were being treated. The quality of the carving, with motifs reminiscent of ecclesiastical tracery, is very fine. Other, less ornate, examples are known from ecclesiastical sites including Battle Abbey, the Dominican friary at Chester, Wells Cathedral (Somerset) and the Brigittine monastery at Syon (Middlesex) (Egan 1998, 277a; Rodwell 2001, 530, fig 521 no. 5, 531; Foyle 2004, 555); the openwork on the example from Wells is so similar that they may be from the same workshop.

No positively identified surgical or medical implements were recovered from the excavations. However, a pair of copper-alloy tweezers <S255> was possibly used for medical purposes. Sherds found in the north burial area (OA6) from Spanish tin-glazed ware (STGW), probably an albarello (a type of drug jar),

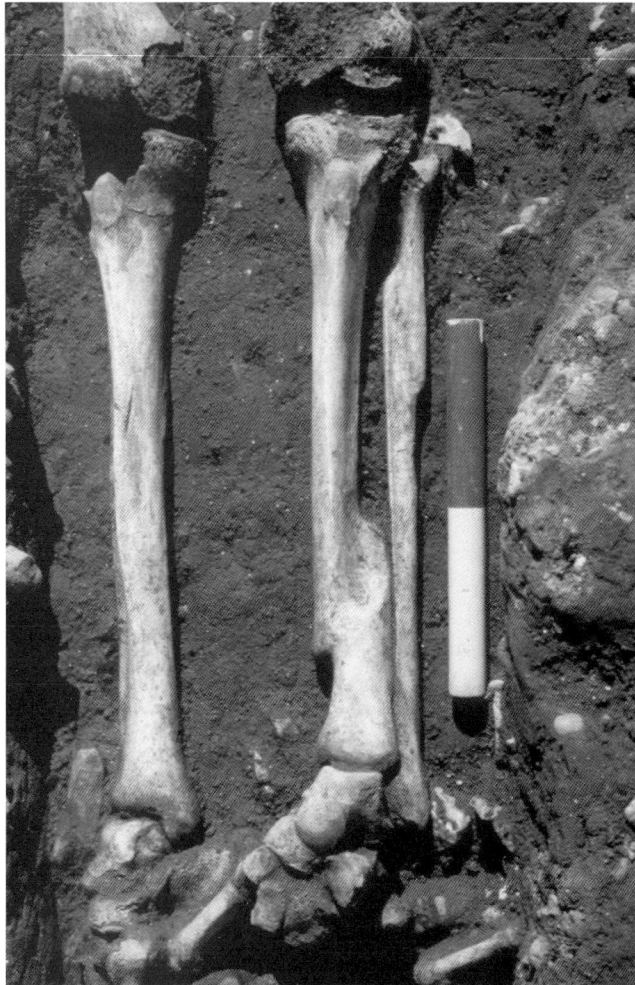

Fig 155 *A non-aligned healed fracture on the left leg of individual [2817] (periods M1–M4, OA6) (0.2m scale)*

may tentatively suggest the use of imported pharmaceutical jars in the infirmary. Glass urinal fragments from the infirmary drain and the reredorter (Fig 158) indicate the diagnostic inspection of urine in the vicinity. Uroscopy was widely practised throughout the medieval period and formed one of the most important medical skills within the infirmary.

The pottery recovered from around the infirmary hall suggests that no specific vessels beyond cooking pots and jugs (eg <P3>–<P6>, Fig 60) were used there, paralleling St Mary Spital (Thomas et al 1997, 59). A possible exception are blue-grey ware (BLGR) ladles, fragments of which were found in the drain (S4a, phases 1, 2) crossing the infirmary garth at Merton (<P2>, Fig 60), and identified among the pottery assemblage at St Mary Spital as for heating and consuming individual portions or serving (ibid). One ladle <P2> was subjected to subsurface residue analysis, which indicated the presence of fats/oil, and cereal (?wheat) (Chapter 7.4, 'Pottery residue analysis'). Other vessels worthy of mention are fragments from two alembics, a Kingston-type ware (KING) vessel <P7> (OA9, period M2) and a London-area early post-medieval redware (PMRE) example <P8> (OA11, from period P1 demolition deposits in the infirmary drain S4b) and an alembic stillhead <P9> also in PMRE, suggesting distillation (Fig 159). The stillhead <P9> (OA12, period P2) was subjected to subsurface residue analysis (Chapter 7.4, 'Pottery residue analysis'), and indicated the distillation of a fermented product, possibly beer; although conceivably this may have been part of the preparation of herbal remedies. A London-type ware (LOND) drinking jug fragment <P10> (Fig 159) is also an indicator of consumption.

The potential medicinal plants recovered included exceptionally large numbers of black mustard seeds in several samples from the area east of the infirmary (OA9) and, to a lesser extent, the infirmary kitchen (Chapter 7.6). Although also used for food, the range of medicinal uses for this plant are listed by the 17th-century herbalist, Nicholas Culpeper: for example, in wine as an antidote for poison; in honey for treating coughs; it

Fig 156 *The possible hernia belt <S254> during conservation, on its soil block*

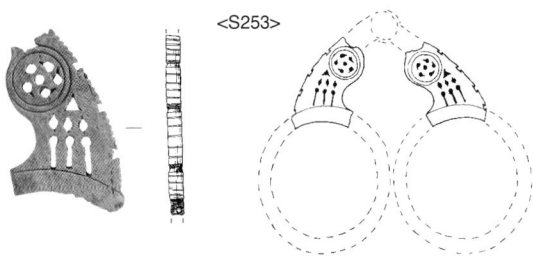

Fig 157 *The bone spectacles <S253> (scale 1:1; reconstruction 1:2)*

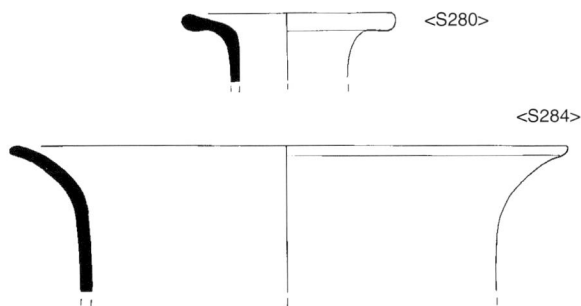

Fig 158 *Glass urinals <S280> and <S284> (scale 1:2)*

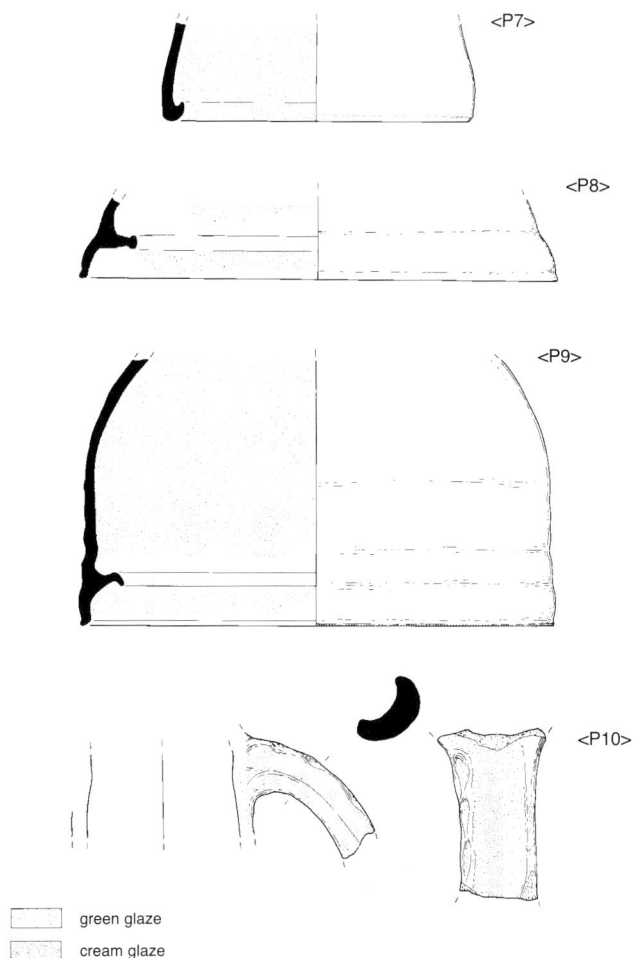

green glaze

cream glaze

Fig 159 *Pottery alembics <P7> (in Kingston-type ware), <P8> and <P9> (both in London-area early post-medieval redware); and a London-type ware jug <P10> (scale 1:4)*

was chewed for toothache; and, externally, used for throat swellings, clearing up skin lesions and even leprosy and hair loss (Culpeper 1653). Other weeds represented in the samples may have been exploited in the infirmary: henbane, black nightshade (*Solanum nigrum*) and hemlock, all of which were used for treating inflammations and swellings (ibid). These plants, however, were mainly represented by small numbers of seeds and in mixed plant assemblages and therefore may simply represent the residues of weeds, although moderate numbers of henbane and hemlock seeds were recovered from room 2 of the reredorter (B5, period M2) while a large number of seeds of greater celandine (*Chelidonium majus*), a plant formerly cultivated and used by herbalists for warts and eye trouble (ibid; Gerard 1994), were found in the sample from the infirmary cloister garth drain ([10255], S4a in OA5, period M2).

4.7 The inhabitants of the priory

Priors and other office holders

Known priors are listed in Table 18, but there are few biographical details beyond those already presented in other sections of this volume. The list is not quite complete: while the 12th-, early 13th- and 14th- to 16th-century sources suggest that some confidence can be placed in the completeness of those parts of the list, sources for the middle years of the 13th century suggest a number of missing priors, although perhaps not many. Thus, with provisos, the list can usefully be compared to other evidence. Of the 34 known priors, 20 appear to have died in office, 3 to have resigned, with 1, Walter, leaving to join the then popular Carthusians in 1218, while 2 were deposed – Robert de Heyham by papal cleric in 1244–9, and John de Littlington in 1345. The chapter house was, like the church, traditionally reserved for the burial of priors, but of 32 burials recorded there for all periods, the majority (21) were interred in the 15th and 16th centuries (period M4), during which only ten priors are known to have served, seven of whom died in office, while John Lacy probably also did, Thomas Shirfield (Shirfeld) resigned, and John Ramsey (alias Bowle) survived the Dissolution. One prior, Michael Kympton 1403–13 may have been buried in the chapter house (<S15>, Fig 136). Given the relatively complete excavation of the chapter house, it is clear from the above that not all those buried there later could have been priors; other senior monastic personnel and higher status laity must also have been interred. Conversely, it is probable for the earlier periods (after making allowance for the removal of earlier burials and charnel) that not all the priors could have been buried there, given that 24 served before 1368 (when Robert de Wyndesore took office, living until 1403) of whom 12 are known to have died in office and a further 5 may have done so, against 11 recorded burials.

Comparison of Table 18 with a list of known obedientiaries, that is officeholders under the prior (Table 19), and reference to

Table 18 Priors of St Mary Merton

Prior	Dates	Notes	References
Robert Bayle	c 1115–50		
Robert II	1150–67	died 9 April 1167	Heales 1898, 24, citing [Parker Library] Corpus Christi College MS 59
William	1167–78	died 24 February 1178	Heales 1898, 24, citing [Parker Library] Corpus Christi College MS 59
Stephen	1178	died 6 October in the same year	Heales 1898, 24, citing [Parker Library] Corpus Christi College MS 59
Robert III	1178–86	died 1180 according to [Parker Library] Corpus Christi College MS 59: Heales 1898, 39	Heales 1898, 39, citing Lambeth Palace Library MS 585, fo 105
Richard	?1186–98	died 1 April 1198	Heales 1898, 24, citing [Parker Library] Corpus Christi College MS 59, and Lambeth Palace Library MS 585, fo 105
Walter	1198–1218	elected 17 May 1198; left to join Carthusians	*VCH* 1905, 102
Thomas (? de Wllst)	1218–22	former cellarer; died autumn 1222	*VCH* 1905, 102
Giles de Bourne	1222–31	installed 24 November 1222; resigned	*VCH* 1905, 102
Henry of Basinges	1231–8	canon elected November 1231; died 1238	*VCH* 1905, 102
Robert de Heyham	1239–44/?9	installed 6 January 1239; deposed by papal cleric	*VCH* 1905, 102
?William de Axemuth'	?1249	prior of Merton to be guarded as long as king wishes, 12 October 1249	*Cal Close R*, 1247–51, 207; not listed in *VCH* 1905, 102
Eustace	1249–52+	canon, elected 1249; in office May 1252	*VCH* 1905, 102
?Nicholas de Brichill'	1254–?	prior of Merton, referred to 16 June 1254	*Cal Close R*, 1253–4, 144
?Prior Walter	1256–?7	referred to in 1256–7	*Chron Majora*, vi, 326–7, 340
Gilbert de Asshe	?1265–92	referred to 1265, 'Prior G' 1269, 1286; died 21 March 1292	*VCH* 1905, 102
Nicholas Tregony	1292–6	subprior elected May 1292; died 26 September 1296	*VCH* 1905, 102
Edmund de Herierde	1296–1305	elected November 1296; resigned 25 September 1305	*Reg Woodlock*, 44
Geoffrey of Alkmundbury	1306–7	installed as prior 25 March 1306; died 15 March 1307	Heales 1898, 196, 198, citing Bodleian, Laud MS E.54
William de Brokesburn	1307–34/5	letters for election issued 26 March 1307; royal assent to election of, granted 3 May	*Cal Pat R*, 1301–7, 511; ibid, 524; *VCH* 1905, 102
Thomas de Kent	1335–9	canon, royal assent to election of, 24 March 1335; dead by 24 September 1339	*Cal Pat R*, 1331–8, 87; ibid, 1338–40, 316
John de Littlington	1339–45	canon, royal assent to election of, granted 13 October 1339; elected on 6 November; king informed of deposition on 14 August 1345	*Cal Pat R*, 1338–40, 322; Heales 1898, 243; *Cal Pat R*, 1343–5, 537
William de Freston	1345–61	canon, royal assent to election of, granted 24 August 1345; dead by 20 August 1361	*Cal Pat R*, 1343–5, 536; ibid, 1360–4, 196
Geoffrey de Chaddeslee	1361–8	canon, licence to elect issued 22 August 1361; royal assent to election of, granted 31 August; died c September 1368	*Cal Pat R*, 1361–4, 53; ibid, 56; Heales 1898, 258
Robert de Wyndesore	1368–1403	canon, licence for election of prior, 7 October 1368; elected by 27 October; dead by 11 May 1403	*Cal Pat R*, 1367–70, 151; Heales 1898, 259; *Cal Pat R*, 1401–5, 226
Michael Kympton	1403–13	elected by 26 May 1403; dead by 27 March 1413	*Cal Pat R*, 1401–5, 227; ibid, 1414–16, 14
John Romeney	1413–32	elected by 28 April 1413; dead by 31 August 1432	*Cal Pat R*, 1414–16, 16; ibid, 1429–36, 214
Thomas Shirfield	1432+	elected by 23 September 1432; resigned 1432	*Cal Pat R*, 1429–36, 222; *VCH* 1905, 102
William Kent	1439–42	elected by 24 March 1439; dead by 17 November 1442	*Cal Pat R*, 1436–41, 248; ibid, 1441–6, 173; *VCH* 1905, 102
John Kingston	1443–85	elected by 28 November 1443; died on 2 January 1485	*Cal Pat R*, 1441–6, 138; Heales 1898, 304
John Gisborne	1485–1502	elected by 18 January 1485; dead by 14 March 1502	*Cal Pat R*, 1476–85, 535; Heales 1898, 310
William Salying	1502–20	elected 16 March 1502; died 14 March 1520	Heales 1898, 310; ibid, 324
John Lacy	1520–	elected 26 March 1520	Heales 1898, 324
John Ramsey (alias Bowle)	1530–8	elected 2 February 1530; in office until surrender and Dissolution on 16 April 1538	Heales 1898, 330–2

Table 19 Obedentiaries at St Mary Merton

Office	Name	Dates	References
Subpriors	Robert	1145	*Early Charters St Paul*, no. 154
	Teoldus	1173	Heales 1898, 26
	Nicholas	1174–86	Heales 1898, appendix XVIII
	W *supprior de Merton*	3 June 1258	Heales 1898, appendix LXXIII
	Nicholas Tregony	elected prior May 1292	

Table 19 (cont)

Office	Name	Dates	References
	Brother Henry	13 November 1305	*Reg Woodlock*, 65
	John de Peverwiche	6 November 1339	Heales 1898, 243
	John Schaldbone	8 November 1398	Heales 1898, 291
	William Sandwiche	15 November 1492; March 1502	Heales 1898, 309; ibid, 311
	Sir John Lacy	23 March 1520	Heales 1898, 324
	John Ramsey	31 January 1530	Heales 1898, 331
	John Debnam (Debenham)	in office 16 April 1538	Heales 1898, 349
Almoners	unnamed	early 13th century	*Cat Anc Deeds*, iii, A 4014
	A *elemosinar*	3 June 1258	Heales 1898, appendix CXXIII
	Robert Doo	March 1502 doubling with precentor, infirmarer and master of the order	Heales 1898, 311
	Walter Burton	23 March 1520	Heales 1898, 324
Cellarers	C *cellerar*	3 June 1258	Heales 1898, appendix CXXIII
	William Odiham	April 1399	Heales 1898, 292–3
	John Gisborne	2 January 1485	Heales 1898, 303–6
Subcellarers	Henry subcellarer	early 13th century	*Ann Monast*, ii, 310, 319; iii, 128, 148
	Office noted	2 January 1485	Heales 1898, 303–6
	John Labrum	March 1502 doubling as cook	Heales 1898, 311
Chamberlains	Philip	1177–88	Heales 1898, appendix XVI
	H camerar	3 June 1258	Heales 1898, appendix CXXIII
	camerarius	1307	Heales 1898, 199, appendix XCIX
	Thomas	8 November 1398	Heales 1898, 291
Subchamberlain	Thomas Schirfeld	April 1399	Heales 1898, 292–3
Excorcist	John Huntyngdon,	March 1502	Heales 1898, 311
	William Farely	23 March 1520	Heales 1898, 324
Hosteler	H *hostilar*	3 June 1258	Heales 1898, appendix CXXIII
	William Salying	March 1502 doubling with *sectator*	Heales 1898, 311
Infirmarer	Robert Doo	March 1502 doubling with precentor, master of the order and almoner	Heales 1898, 311
	John Debnam	31 January 1530	Heales 1898, 331
Inspector		office noted 2 January 1485	Heales 1898, 303–6
Kitcheners	Humphrey	1150–67	Heales 1898, 16, appendix IV
	Ralph	1177–88	Heales 1898, appendix XVI
	John Labrum	March 1502 doubling as subcellarer	Heales 1898, 311
	John Sandwyche	23 March 1520	Heales 1898, 324
	Thomas Wansworth	31 January 1530	Heales 1898, 331
Master of novices	John Bardy	March 1502 doubling as refectorer	Heales 1898, 311
Master of the order	Robert Doo	March 1502 doubling with precentor, infirmarer and almoner	Heales 1898, 311
Precentors		office noted 2 January 1485	Heales 1898, 303–6
	Robert Doo	March 1502 doubling with master of the order, infirmarer and almoner	Heales 1898, 311
	Andrew Pannell	23 March 1520	Heales 1898, 324
	Richard Wyndesore	31 January 1530	Heales 1898, 331
Refectorers	Office noted 2	January 1485	Heales 1898, 303–6
	John Bardy	March 1502 doubling with master of the novices	Heales 1898, 311
	Thomas Godmanchestre	23 March 1520	Heales 1898, 324
Sacrist	John atte Waterer	1399 April	Heales 1898, 292–3
		office noted 2 January 1485	Heales 1898, 303–6
	William Russell	March 1502	Heales 1898, 311
	Ambrose Tawnton	23 March 1520	Heales 1898, 324
	John Codyngton	31 January 1530	Heales 1898, 331
Suitor	William Salying	March 1502 doubling with hosteler	Heales 1898, 311
Seneschal	R *senescallo de Merton*	3 June 1258	Heales 1898, appendix CXXIII
Succentor		office noted 2 January 1485	Heales 1898, 303–6
	Godfrey Westmynster	March 1502	Heales 1898, 311
	Richard Bevys	31 January 1530	Heales 1898, 331
Treasurer	Richard Wakefield	1393–4	Bodleian, Laud MS 723, fo 47r
	Thomas Aston	1399 April	Heales 1898, 292–3
Keeper/master of the chapel of the Blessed Mary		office noted 2 January 1485	Heales 1898, 303–6
	Arnold Bynchester	March 1502	Heales 1898, 311
	George Albyne	31 January 1530 master of the chapel of Blessed Mary in the conventual church	Heales 1898, 331

other documentary sources, shows that a large number of priors were elected to that post from within the conventual establishment, whether obedientiaries or canons. Robert II, second prior 1150–67, was probably Robert the subprior noted in 1145. Two later subpriors, Nicholas Tregony and John Ramsey, became priors, while Sir John Lacy, who became subprior on 23 March 1520, appears to have been elected prior on 26 March of the same year, the previous incumbent William Salying also dying in that month. Two cellarers were elected prior, Thomas (? de Wllist/Wllst) in 1218, and John Gisborne in 1485, while prior Thomas Shirfield elected in 1432 and resigning that year was probably the subchamberlain Thomas Schirfeld noted in 1399, and William Salying had been both suitor and hosteler. A number of Merton canons, apparently without previous office, were also elected prior, while some of the office holders, like William Salying, held several offices simultaneously.

It is also hard not to have some sympathy for Giles de Bourne: installed as prior on 24 November 1222, the church tower collapsed the next month; Giles resigned in 1231.

Canons

The actual number of canons at the priory is only known in the early 12th century and the late 15th and first half of the 16th century. No attempt has been made at a comprehensive collection of names of canons, whose completeness would in any case vary widely from period to period, but several lists survive from the election of priors during the final phase of the priory's existence from 1492.

In c 1130 the priory community had 35 canons (excluding the prior) (Colker 1970, 245); in 1492 there were thought to be 23 and in the early 16th century this fell to 19–20, and then 13 at the Dissolution. A list of the canons from 1492, 1502, 1520, 1530 and 1538 is in Table 20. Canons could be elected or appointed to various posts within the priory. Below the priors specific posts were held by obedientiaries including a subprior, almoner, cellarer and subcellerar, chamberlain and subchamberlain, infirmarer, precentor, sacrist, refectorer, kitcheners and others.

The canons' daily life was structured by several services of communal worship throughout the day and night, with the remainder probably spent on practical activities. Robert, a canon of Bridlington Priory, lists the suitable occupations for a canon when he was not in church: reading, explaining and preaching the word of God; practising for divine worship; preparing parchment, writing, illuminating and correcting books; making and repairing clothes; making implements such as wooden spoons and candlesticks, and weaving mats; and working in the gardens and fields (Burton 1994, 65).

At the election of John Lacy in March 1520 biographical notes of certain of the canons were recorded (Heales 1898, 327–8):

Pannell (Panell), 'third prior', aged 58, at priory 40 years, known Lacy 10.
Marshall, canon, aged 53, at priory for 37, known Lacy 20 years.

Sandwich (Sandwyche), canon, aged 35, at priory for 27 years, known Lacy 20 years.
John London, canon, aged 30, at priory 17 years, knew Lacy since entering religion.

Some discrepancies are apparent here: Pannell claims to have known Lacy for only 10 years, when Marshall and Sandwich had been acquainted with him for 20 and London at least 17; Lacy must have arrived at the priory very shortly after the 1502 listing. John Sandwich had, on this reckoning, been at the priory since 1493 when he would have been only about 8 years old (a William Sandwich was subprior then, and was perhaps related?). John, however, does not appear on the 1502 list, and this again throws some doubt on the reliability of such lists.

Novices

The priory also housed novices, those who were seeking admission to the monastery, both as adults and, in the earlier years, children placed in the priory as oblates (Burton 1994, 174). The class of oblate was officially abolished at the 4th Lateran Council in 1215 (ibid) and the practice eventually died out. After this postulants were usually admitted at 17 to 19. It is uncertain how many novices were admitted each year to the priory. Burton suggests limited resources could mean only two to three vacancies were available each year at an abbey (1994, 175). The novices admitted would thus be dependent on the wealth of the house and the existing number of canons in the priory.

Lay brethren, servants and lay people

The priory was not exclusively home to canons but also to a relatively large group of servants and possibly lay brethren. Lay brethren were not canons but were under vows and provided an additional labour force within the priory. While it is probable that Merton had some lay brothers, there is no proof of this. Dickinson indicates that 'The Augustinian and Benedictine orders had only very small numbers of lay brethren and it is not clear where they lodged' (1961, 38), while Burton suggests, with the exception of Cistercian houses, that there were probably twice as many servants as monks, canons or nuns in monastic houses (1994, 178). Considerable numbers of servants were required to carry out the menial tasks within a monastery, but here the records seldom refer to servants. There are occasional mentions with regard to their posts or their daily allowances. In 1178 'the Sacristan ought to have two servants and one boy. The servants shall have such allowance as they are used to have: the boy, ten loaves of the boys' bread' (Heales 1898, 33). Although some servants probably resided in the priory some may have lived nearby. Equally, any lay brethren may also not have been housed at the priory but lived on outlying granges supplying food and commodities.

It is unlikely that the priory's inhabitants were exclusively male; some female servants and corrodians (below, 'Corrodians') and the relatives of such, would probably have

Table 20 Canons at St Mary Merton (priors and subpriors are omitted)

14 November 1492	7 March 1502	23 March 1520	31 January 1530	16 April 1538
William Ball				
John Byrde				
Robert Doo	Robert Doo			
John Moore	John More			
John Richmond				
John Berde	John Bardy			
William London				
Godfrey Westminster	Godfrey Westminster			
Robert Stone				
Thomas Bell				
William Iche				
John Satt				
William Salying				
Andrew Pannell	Andrew Panelle	Andrew Pannell		
William Russell	William Russell			
John Mershall	John Marshall	John Marshall		
William Durnford	William Derneford			
Clement Saunderson				
John Laborne	John Labrun			
James Newlond				
Arnold Binchester	Arnold Bynchester			
Robert Sturgeon	Robert Sturgeon			
Walter Burton	Walter Burton	Walter Burton	Walter Burton	
	Thomas Gunchester *d*	Thomas Godmanchester	Thomas Godmanchestre	Thomas Godme'chester
	John Wynborn *d*			
	William Smith *d*			
	Richard Eland *d*			
	John Huntyngdon			
	William Dunstyw *a*			
	Thomas Wandesworth		Thomas Wansworth	
		John Sandwyche		
		John London		
		John Goldsmith		
		John Cuddyngton	John Codyngton	John Codyngton
		John Ramsey		
		Ambrose Tawnton		
		Richard Wyndsor	Richard Wyndesore	Richard Wyndesore
		Thomas Thwinge		
		William Egliston		
		Thomas Augustine *d*		
		George Abbyn *sd*	George Albyne	George Albyn
		John Debnam *sd*	John Debnam	
		Robert Guy *a*		
		John Bellamy *a*		
		Henry Hall *a*	Henry Hall	
		William Farely		
			Richard Bevys	Richard Benese (Beneys)
			John Salcoke	
			Thomas Mychell	Thomas Mychell
			John Page *d*	John Page
			Edmund Dowman *sd*	Edmund Dowman
			John Salyng *sd*	John Salyng
			John Martyn *sd*	John Martyn
			John Feysye *a*	
			Robert Knyght *a*	Robert Knyght
			Thomas Panell *a*	Thomas Paynell
			John London *a*	
				John/George Hayward
23	**19**	**20**	**19**	**13**

a: acolyte (ie novice)
d: deacon (ie cleric ranking immediately below a priest)
sd: subdeacon (ie assistant cleric to the deacon)

Source: Heales 1898, 309, 311, 324, 331, 349, appendix CLI, cxvii

been present in small numbers. This is suggested by the overall ratio of 11.2 males to 1 female in the burials, although a number of these may not represent the burial of those resident.

Children

In the 12th century, oblates were educated at priories and monasteries and after that date it is possible that children, not part of the religious community, continued to be educated within the priory. Two famous men were educated as children at the priory, St Thomas Becket in the late 1120s and Nicholas Breakspeare in c 1120, the only Englishman to become pope as Adrian IV (1154–9). As discussed above, children were also present as servants and a small number may have resided as the dependants of servants. Earlier juvenile burials may represent children acquiring an education at the priory but others may be external children granted burial at their parents' request.

Corrodians

The first known corrody at Merton occurs in 1216 and was, like all such early arrangements, a private agreement with the priory. For a lump sum (details of this part of the transaction are rare) a person, usually a clergyman or a prosperous citizen of London, could purchase what was in effect a retirement home within the priory precinct, receiving stipulated rations of food and drink from the kitchens, and other commodities such as clothing and candles. 'Private' corrodies persisted throughout the existence of the priory, but from the 1260s they were all but overtaken by a practice that caused severe problems for Merton and other religious houses in the London area: the obligatory imposition by the Crown of superannuated royal servants and their wives for life, apparently at the expense of the host monastery.

The corrody granted to Amicius in 1216 (Heales 1898, 71 and appendix XLIII) suggests this particular corrodian had already built at least two houses within the precinct. This was probably advantageous to Merton for on his death the property would revert to the priory. A fuller picture of the arrangement emerges from the case of Geoffrey de Mora, clerk, in the time of Prior Giles (1222–31). Geoffrey was granted by the priory for life the sum of 10 marks (£6 13s 4d) yearly 'unless he wished to become a canon', his accustomed house and garden, if he wished, and a suitable household, together with two miches (small loaves) and 3 gallons (13.64 litres) of convent beer a day from the cellarer, and from the kitchen the full daily ration of a canon. Provision of stabling and forage was to be available for his six horses, and his servants were each to receive a stipulated number of loaves, 2 gallons (9.09 litres) of ale from the cask (de tina) and a general ration (ferculum generale de aula) each day; all as long as he wished to live within the priory curia (ibid, 82 and appendix LI). The priory also granted to Robert de Bokland in 1231–8 the corrody of a canon while living within the (priory) fold (infra septa circitie nostre), or its value if he left; his wife was to receive a corrody weekly for life (ibid, 94 and appendix LIX). At the same period Michael the

merchant was to receive the same while living within the convent walls, together with the house which Warin the merchant had received during his life (ibid). In a court case of 1239–44 William and Theophilia de Southwark effectively exchanged their property in Southwark for an annual payment of 10 marks (£6 13s 4d) for life (as for Geoffrey de Mora, above) with a corrody of bread and beer and two loads of brushwood, together with a suitable residence in the curia (ibid, 113).

Subsequent grants follow the same basic pattern, although often varied widely in scope and detail. In 1286 Master Dionysius de Thorrok, clerk, received a corrody of the usual allowance of a canon while living at the priory, but also a measured site between the sacristy and the house of the chaplains and bounded by ditches, which he was to fence at his own expense and risk, and on which he had permission to build a house, to be maintained at his own expense (Heales 1898, 168). In 1301 Richard and Eline de Wolcherehaw were granted a corrody for life with a plot comprising a dwelling and a garden within the close, formerly held by William de Oulton; again Richard and Eline were to maintain the property, its buildings, walls, hedges and garden from waste and destruction, any damage to be made good by their executors (ibid, 188–9 and appendix XCIV). The corrody granted to Richard de Pennark, clerk, in 1312, was not to be sold, save to the prior, and provisions were to be received in the great *hostium* of the kitchen; a place within the curia was also granted where he might dwell at his own cost (ibid, 211–12). Henry Hoclegh's corrody granted in 1310 included the custody of the great gate of the priory with residence in the chambers annexed (ibid, 204 and appendix C, lxvi–lxvii).

In 1394 John Bradmore citizen and physician of London sought from the prior and convent a corrody with the following specification: two casks of convent ale worth 30s yearly; two *panes armigorum* (bread allowances of unknown character) worth 25s 2d; three *lag' servic'*, worth 45s 6d, two general convent rations worth £4 11s and the ration of a subprior or president as served in the refectory (*ferclum prout suppriori vel president' servit in refector'* worth 30s 4d, and a dwelling with a garden (Bodleian, Laud MS 723, fo 57v) – it is not clear whether he received this.

Another insight into the acquisition of corrodies is provided by the priory's grant to John Masham, clerk of London, in 1443, in exchange for a down payment of £300 paid beforehand: this entitled Masham to an annual 'rent' of 40 marks (£26 13s 4d) for life from the priory manor at Ewell and paid out at the rood at the north door of St Paul's, together with a further grant of a gown of the canons' own livery at 8s pa for life, a chamber within the close and precinct of the priory, suitable to his degree and to be maintained at the priory's cost, and a horse for his use every day (*Cal Close R*, 1441–7, 136–7). No food or drink is mentioned, apart from that provided for the horse. In a further grant of 14 January 1458 the priory granted Masham the tenement or dwelling within the priory with houses and garden attached and once occupied by John Chynnour, provided that he maintain and repair the premises (ibid, 1454–61, 270–1).

The first recorded Merton corrody granted to a Crown servant dates from 1262–72 when Hugh, the king's doorkeeper (*portarius*), and his servant were to be provided for life 'so long as he remained in their courts' (Heales 1898, 139). In 1297 Edward I informed the prior and convent that he was sending to them Nicholas Morel 'incapacitated from work by illness' with a request that they admit him to their house with groom and horse, and find him the necessaries according to the requirements of his estate (*Cal Close R*, 1296–1302, 81). This was simply a temporary arrangement, and was subject to Nicholas's courteous and honest behaviour. Perhaps this was also the case with similar requests made in 1303 in respect of Richard Jolif, the king's serjeant, and his groom (*Cal Close R*, 1302–7, 91), in March 1304 in respect of William de Kancia, previously sent to the abbot and convent of Colchester (ibid, 203), and in April 1304 in respect of Nicholas de Northwode (ibid, 210). However, such arrangements soon became permanent, if they were not already so. In 1313 Lambert Clays, who had long served the king and his father, was sent to Merton to receive the necessaries of life in food and clothing in that house for life (*Cal Close R*, 1307–13, 565). By 1318 the king was demanding that the prior issue letters patent under the conventual seal granting maintenance to Geoffrey de Thorpe whom he was sending to the priory, and requiring the prior to write back with an account of their proceedings in the matter (*Cal Close R*, 1318–23, 117). Soon the king was stipulating that his new candidates should receive the same hospitality and conditions as that enjoyed by previous and recently deceased corrodians. Thomas Holbode, *portitor* of the king's household, was required in 1331 to receive the allowance formerly received by John le Bul (*Cal Close R*, 1330–3, 308); on 12 April 1340 Bartholomew de Langele, who had long served the king, was to receive such maintenance in that house as Nicholas de la Garderobe, deceased, had enjoyed at the request of Edward I (*Cal Close R*, 1339–41, 466), and in 1343 the priory was called upon to grant John Marreys the facilities granted to John Nichol, deceased, at the king's order (*Cal Close R*, 1343–6, 107). Similar instructions were issued on behalf of Giles de la Cusyne in 1351 (*Cal Close R*, 1349–54, 362) and John Gregge in 1361 (*Cal Close R*, 1360–4, 290).

It seems hardly surprising that the Bishop of Winchester's visitation of 1387 should find that 'whereas much loss has happened through the injudicious grant of corrodies to the injury of the property left for the increase of divine worship and bestowed by the pious devotion of the faithful for the sustentation of the poor and infirm, we forbid under pain of the greater excommunication, the grant or sale of corrodies, liberations or pensions to any persons in perpetuity, to any person whatsoever, without our consent and special licence' (Heales 1898, 269–70). Unfortunately this had no immediate effect on the king who in 1391 notified the priory that John Maudelyn, yeoman of the king's robes, and his wife Alice were to be sent to take such maintenance for life in that house as Edmund Tettesworth deceased had in his lifetime by command of the king 'such as pertains to the king's gift' (*Cal Close R*,

1389–92, 315, 339). However, this demand was followed in 1392 by the concession from the king that although the priory was prepared to comply with his application on behalf of John Maudelyn, it should not be prejudiced or charged in respect of any other such grant of maintenance, unless at the will and upon the resignation of John or Alice (*Cal Pat R*, 1391–6, 51).

Thereafter the number of applications fell away sharply. Merton was directed in 1400 to maintain John Fraunceys (Heales 1898, 293–4) without reference to any existing corrody, and in 1402 sanctioned the amendment of the terms of Alice Bromhole's current corrody at her request in order to include her husband John in the arrangement (*Cal Close R*, 1399–1402, 594). A further request was made by Henry VI in 1441 for the accommodation of John Somerset and his wife Agnes (ibid, 1435–41, 479). Thereafter nothing is recorded until 1516 when the priory was instructed to award Launcelot Lisle a corrody on its vacation by Gilbert Mawdesey, serjeant at arms (*L and P Hen VIII*, ii(1), no. 1809). In 1521 orders were sent that Lisle and John Pate, groom of the wardrobe, hold in survivorship the corrody previously held by Lisle alone (ibid, iii(1), no. 1265.25), and finally in April 1538, within a fortnight of the Dissolution, the reversion of Lisle's corrody on his death or surrender was granted to William Throwgood (ibid, xiv(1), no. 905.7). The custom which had emerged in the mid 14th century, whereby a newly elected prior granted a pension to a clerk of the king's nomination pending the award of a benefice, continued with the forwarding of John Wetwode in 1520, after the election of John Lacy (ibid, iii(1), no. 716.30) and of Sir Bryan Case in 1530, after that of John Ramsey (ibid, iii(1), no. 6248.14). Both were described as 'ministers' of the Chapel Royal.

Visitors

Guests and travellers, whether poor, rich or sick, were transient inhabitants of the priory. The guest house or hospitium is thought to have been located to the west of the church (above, 4.4). Additional, possibly royal, accommodation was provided, possibly the excavated aisled hall (B11). The royal visits to Merton, together with the priory's proximity to the capital have been discussed above (Chapter 3.2, 'Documentary evidence'). Merton, unlike a number of houses, was not a centre of pilgrimage, but may have been a rest stop for some en-route to Canterbury.

Henry III's sojourns at Merton generated orders for the supply of wine there. In 1237 orders were given for the carriage of ten casks of wine for the king at Windsor, four to Guildford and four to Merton (*Cal Close R*, 1234–7, 428), and in 1240 the king's chamberlain in London was ordered to deliver to the sheriffs two casks of wine to be carried to Merton (ibid, 1237–42, 258). In 1253 the same official was ordered to allow the prior and convent of Merton one cask of the king's wine (ibid, 1251–3, 314), and in 1255 one more (ibid, 1254–6, 62), while in 1256 the chamberlain was to take 122 casks of wine and deliver one of them for the king's use at Merton (ibid, 261). The prior was to benefit in this way again in 1257 and 1258 (ibid, 1256–9, 21, 185). Two further casks were ordered to Merton from London in 1259 (ibid, 377). Most of these orders can be associated with known visits to the priory, although the one issued in 1240 must have been for a visit not otherwise recorded.

Merton underwent numerous visitations from the Bishop of Winchester dealing with official business and problems within the house. The priory was also selected as a venue for county business and in 1344 provided a suitable and strong house (*domum congruam et fortem*) with free access for the use of the collectors for Surrey of the tenth and fifteenth granted by parliament (*Rot Parlt*, ii, 451a, no. 114). This was presumably located within the precinct as it was probably a repeat of the arrangements in 1235 when Merton was made the collection point for the royal aid levied in Surrey (*Cal Close R*, 1234–7, 191).

From the last 13 years of the priory's existence there are records of its hospitality to two particularly exalted visitors. The accounts of the Duke of Richmond for the period 16 June to 31 December 1525 include the expenditure of £91 14s 7d for the Duke and his council for 25 days 'from Merton Abbey to York' (*L and P Hen VIII*, iii(2), no. 1852), while there is a reference on 31 July 1526 to the household of the Duke of Richmond and Somerset at London, '*abbathiam de Merton*, Colyweston, Ebor, and Sheriff Hutton' (ibid, no. 2359). Princess Mary's household accounts for the year ending 30 September 1533 show that on 17 October the princess travelled from Chertsey, where she had dined, to supper at Merton, where she stayed until dinner on the 19th before departing for supper at Oxford (ibid, vi, no. 1540).

Institutional, religious and personal activities

Little was found at Merton that testifies to the religious life of the priory. The Dissolution effectively removed most of the movable goods and most of the choir was not excavated so the liturgical organisation at the heart of the church can only be hinted at.

A tiny fraction of the number of objects that would have been used in daily worship have survived: two sacring bells <S50> (Fig 52) and <S51>, two possible rosary beads <S48> and <S49> (Fig 118; Fig 215), and three sets of chalice and paten, together with a fourth chalice <S22>–<S27> (Fig 24; Fig 111), used in life for drinking unconsecrated wine after communion (Daniell 1997, 170) but here buried with (presumably) priests. As noted above (4.5), a tuning peg <S29> (Fig 154) from a stringed musical instrument may have been for personal use rather than religious services. Equally, the bone die <S32> (Fig 118) also discussed above, was indistinguishable from those used for gaming but in the context of the religious house may take on a religious significance. A metal clasp <S247> (Fig 160), with a decorative motif that looks like a mitre, suggests a religious accessory.

The chanting of the *opus Dei* and the conventual Masses took place respectively in the largely unexcavated choir and presbytery. What excavation there was here indicated only passageways and

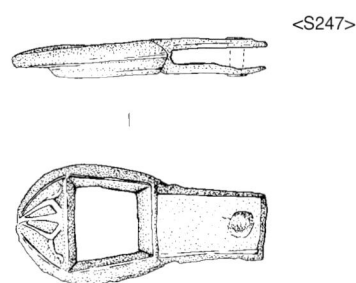

Fig 160 Lead/tin clasp <S247> (scale 1:1)

burial; no evidence was found for the choir stalls or the high altar. The chapels, identified and inferred, indicate the canons' need for additional altars to say private Masses for the souls of dead patrons. Of these only the three in the north transept, and possibly one or more in the south transept of the 13th-century church, indicate their liturgical layout. The addition of aisles to the nave in the 13th century may have been done to aid conventual processions or to provide better access to the choir and presbytery. The probable pulpitum or rood screen base in the 13th-century church (Fig 34) indicates the liturgical division between the choir and nave, probably dividing the areas of worship for the canons to the east and the servants, lay brothers, corrodians and visitors to the west.

Artefactual evidence for non-religious daily life includes part of a sizeable cast copper-alloy cauldron <S273> (Fig 161), a fragment of another and part of the rim of a sheet vessel (<S274> and <S275>). The first along with a Reigate stone mortar <S295> (Fig 161) are items of kitchen equipment appropriate for a large monastery, as are the various ceramic cooking pots found in the vicinity of the infirmary (eg <P4>–<P6>, Fig 60; <P11>, Fig 161) and a Kingston-type ware (KING) dripping dish. Six turned wooden table vessels <S289>–<S294> may be from the infirmary hall or the refectory. Three had marks of ownership either carved or burned on to the base (Fig 162). It is probable that this form of tableware was the most common used at the priory because of its durability. Bowls with their ownership marked were also found at St Mary Spital where it is suggested that inmates were supplied with personal cutlery, bowls and drinking vessels on admission to the hospital (Thomas et al 1997, 109). In London, wooden bowls have also been retrieved from Holy Trinity Priory, Aldgate (Schofield and Lea 2005, 250–1), while a large assemblage of bowls and platters, some marked and possibly from the nearby Greyfriars friary, were found in the backfilled city ditch (Keily in Lyon 2007, 88–90). Ceramic tableware, for example jugs, bowls and dishes, was also in use, with drinking and serving vessels the most commonly recorded. Knives <S262>–<S264> (<S262>, Fig 22) were also possibly for individual use, as may have been the hones found scattered across the site.

Nine styli – one of bone (broken) <S37> (Fig 163) and eight of lead <S38>–<S45> (Fig 163) testify to the production of written documents. Four shell palettes still holding paint <S33>–<S36> suggest the illustration of books and

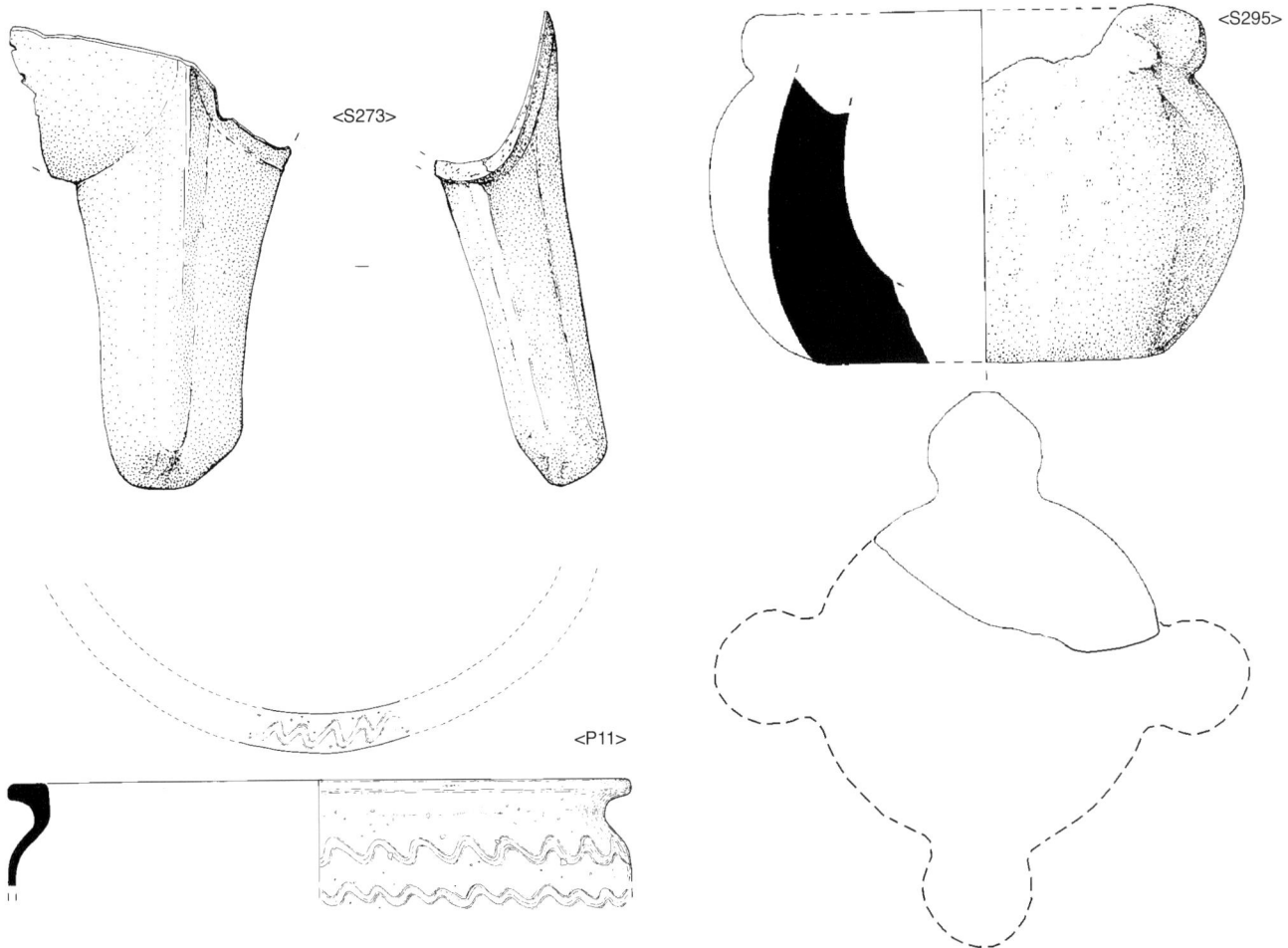

Fig 161 Kitchen equipment: copper-alloy cauldron foot <S273> (scale 1:2); a stone mortar <S295> and shelly-sandy ware cooking pot <P11> (scale 1:4)

manuscripts or mural painting. Two oyster shells <S34> and <S35> contained a red pigment, probably natural cinnibar or artificial vermilion, and a purplish-red pigment, probably red lead. Book mounts <S46> (Fig 163) and clasps <S47> are survivals from book covers.

Aside from the commonly encountered needles and thimbles indicating textile/leather working as in the making and repairing of clothes (one of Robert of Bridlington Priory's list of suitable occupations for a canon), evidence for the production or repair of metal items exists (Burton 1994, 165). The copper alloy casting could have given the institution its bells. The modest iron-working assemblage found is unusual for religious houses in the London area, but lead working is universally attested to at religious institutions. The sherd from a Kingston-type ware alembic <P7> (Fig 159) also indicates some industrial process in the 13th century. The glass urinals <S279>–<S288> (Fig 158) found may suggest the collection of urine for tanning. Working in the gardens and fields was another suitable occupation for canons; a Dissolution-period (P1) robber trench produced a London-type ware (LOND) sprinkling pot (<P12>, Fig 164), perhaps used to water the plants and trees within the gardens and orchards in the 12th to 13th centuries (below, 4.8).

General infrastructural needs like lighting and water management are indicated in the form of glass <S259> (Fig 218), <S260> and stone <S261> (Fig 218) lamps, lead piping <S190> and the network of drains (above, 4.2). Although a reredorter and possibly other toilets were provided, the glass urinals suggest that specifically designed vessels were in use for urine collection and/or disposal, as were possibly other vessels such as jugs (above, 4.6).

Private possessions were theoretically not allowed for the canons or lay brethren, given their vow of poverty, but others in the community were not under such a vow, and some personal items, mainly dress accessories, were present. There was a heavy emphasis on buckles in the assemblage, with 41 recorded. These were generally plain, circular and of copper alloy or iron, and functional enough not perhaps to conflict with any vow of poverty. Some found on burials in pairs, at the pelvis or feet, suggest clothing or footwear. A few decorative examples including a plate engraved with the Lamb of God <S223> and other forms <S219> and <S220>; the first of these suggests more ostentation (Fig 165). Clearly belts were worn, strapend <S241> with buckles <S218> and <S221> (Fig 165), and do not suggest undue display even if worn by a canon, but one burial [3458] had seven belt accessories <S226> (Fig 217), some of types previously unknown, again suggesting some ostentation.

Purse bars <S250> and <S251> and a purse hanger <S239> (Fig 166) indicate the carrying of valuables, usually

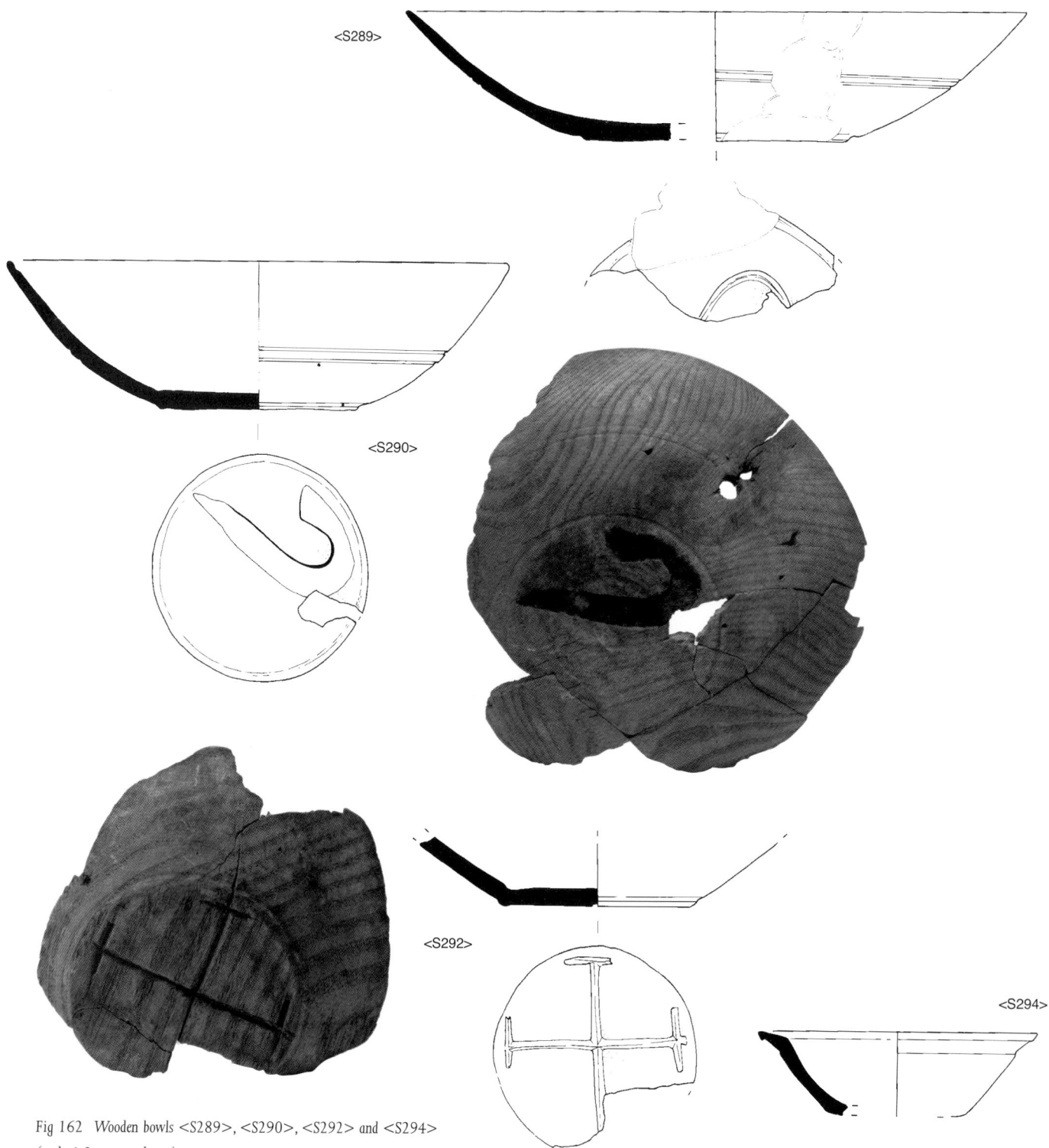

Fig 162 *Wooden bowls <S289>, <S290>, <S292> and <S294>*
(scale 1:2, except photos)

coins (Egan and Pritchard 1991, 342). Purses were worn by both men and women in the 13th and 14th century and probably belonged to laity, but obedientaries like the cellarer, almoner or sacristan may have needed one. Jettons, both English (eg <S348>, Fig 166) and Continental, could equally have belonged to both groups. The gold finger ring, <S252> (Fig 153) with its amatory legend, probably did belong to a layperson, as did lesser quality jewellery like a brooch of copper alloy <S248> (Fig 166) and one of lead/tin <S249> (Fig 140). Lockable caskets are suggested by copper-alloy <S256>

(Fig 120) and iron <S258> mounts. A bone panel is possibly part of an early small casket <S28> (Fig 166). A slide-key padlock <S191> and 11 rotary keys <S192>–<S202> further suggest security as a preoccupation. Visitations could involve the inspection of chests and carrels, including the breaking open of locks to ensure that no private processions were being kept (Burton 1994, 184–5). Further evidence of the playing of music is suggested by a Jew's harp <S30> (Fig 166) and a buzz bone <S31> (Fig 59), but it is uncertain whether these two were used at services or for personal entertainment by guests.

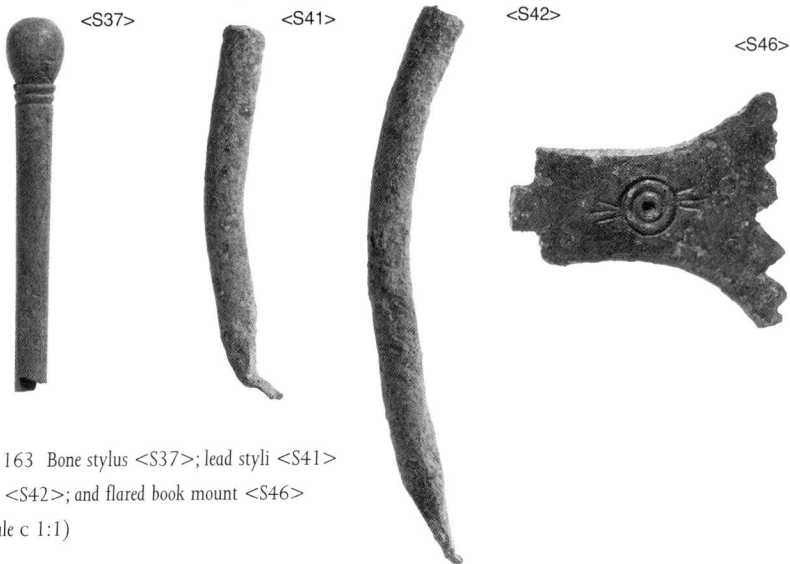

Fig 163 Bone stylus <S37>; lead styli <S41>
and <S42>; and flared book mount <S46>
(scale c 1:1)

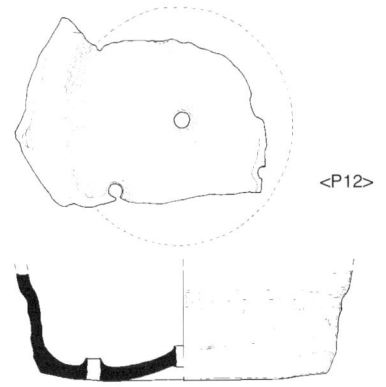

Fig 164 The base of a London-type ware
sprinkling pot <P12> (scale 1:4)

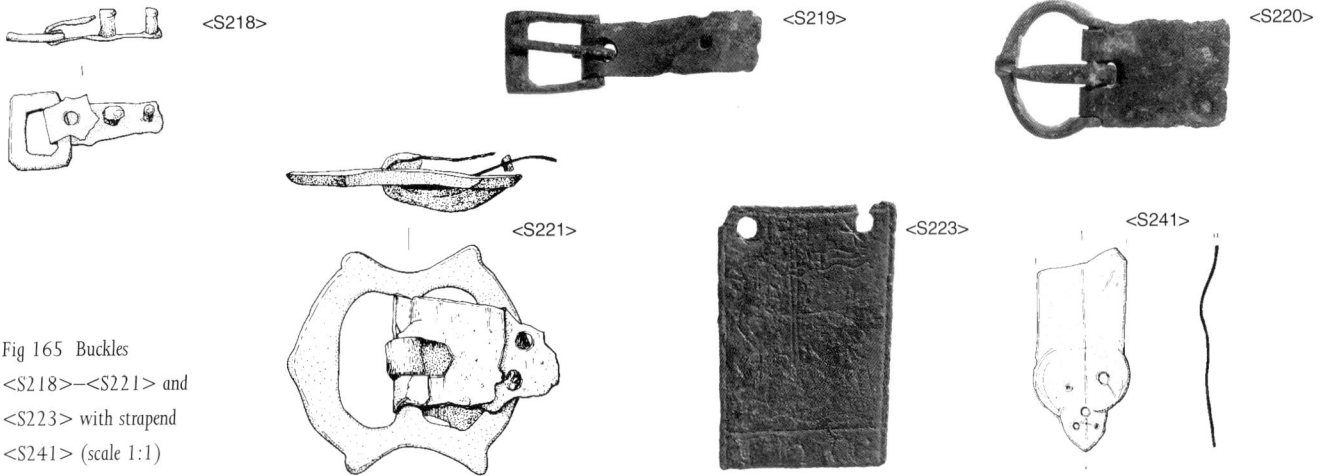

Fig 165 Buckles
<S218>–<S221> and
<S223> with strapend
<S241> (scale 1:1)

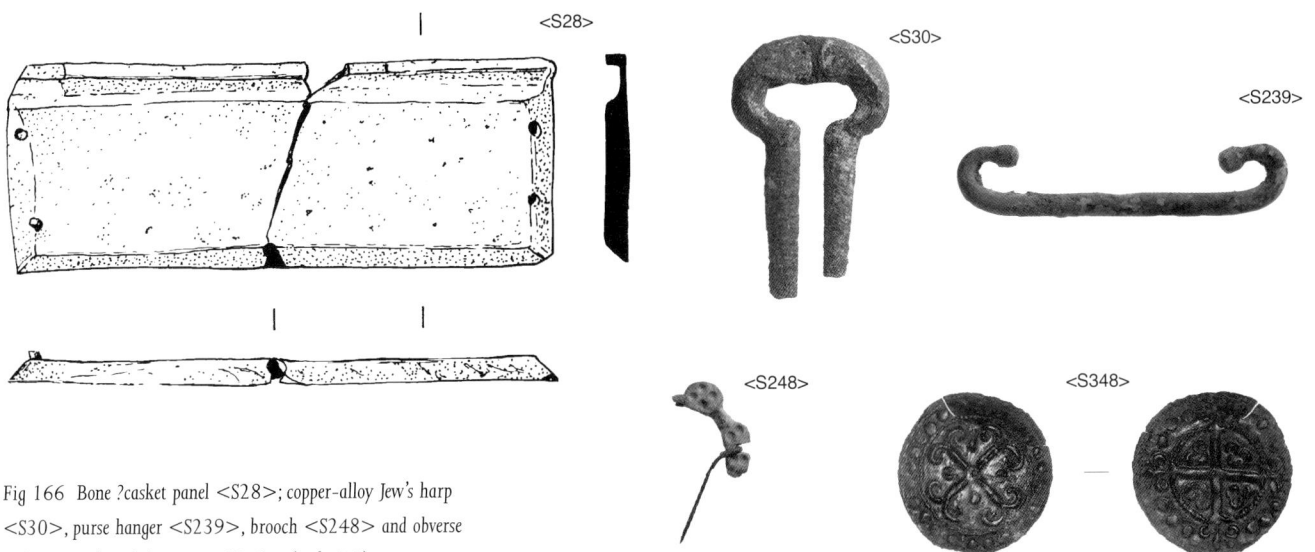

Fig 166 Bone ?casket panel <S28>; copper-alloy Jew's harp
<S30>, purse hanger <S239>, brooch <S248> and obverse
and reverse of English jetton <S348> (scale 1:1)

4.8 Food and diet

St Mary Merton was in an area ideally suited to a religious house: a constant supply of fresh running water from the Wandle, with water meadows along the river margins and hay meadow on the higher ground. This environment could produce an abundance of locally grown fruits and vegetables, cereals, and fresh fish. Leases after the Dissolution mention that the priory had gardens, orchards, stables, dovecotes, mills, waters, ponds, vineyards and fisheries all existing within the precinct of the priory (TNA: PRO, C66/1286 m 42). Monastic meals consisted largely of bread, cheese, vegetables, beans and cereals with pittances (extra dishes) of fish and eggs on special occasions (Burton 1994, 166). The seasons defined the number of meals a day but generally two were taken. At Westminster Abbey, records from 1495 to 1525 show that on an average day bread made up 35% of the total energy value of the monks' allowance of food and drink, with a basic ration of 8 pints (4.55 litres) of ale (Harvey 1993, 58–9). Together, bread and ale made up 60% of the daily consumption of foods, which rose to 78% during Lent (ibid, 56–7). The Augustinians probably enjoyed a more generous diet than most monastic orders.

The cereals are likely to have been harvested throughout the Merton estate and hinterland, but may also have been imported from other parts of the south-east. References to the priory's barns and granges are made in various leases during the 16th century. One mentions a property called West Barnes in the western part of the estate; in another, 'the Grange' or farm was outside the priory gates (TNA: PRO, SC6/Henry VIII/3463 m 5; Heales 1898, 336–43). The cereals were probably milled within the precinct. Some foodstuffs were imported from the London markets such as marine and estuarine fish and oysters; others came from the Continent like herbs and spices, a rare and expensive commodity. The importance and expense of the latter two to Merton is documented: in the 13th century one priory holding in Southwark was let for a pound of cinnamon, another in 1231 for a pound of pepper and another for potherbs (Jowett 1951, 30). It is also possible that grapes were imported dried (see below).

A proportion of the food would have been grown within the precinct itself. A vineyard and mill are first mentioned in 1117; thereafter Gilbert supplied the brethren with grain, wine, meat, fish and cheeses (Heales 1898, 2–5). A further reference to food production in litigation c 1348 concerning the customs of the manor may also in part refer to production in the precinct. Stephen in the Hale, John Jakes, Richard Est and other men of the prior of Merton complained of his unscrupulous exaction of services and customs such as had not been the case when the king held this demesne. The men alleged they held only by fealty and rent; but the prior exacted one day's forced labour a week, and compelled their services for mending a ditch called Le Brok, shearing the prior's sheep for two days (for which they only received 1/2d a day), mowing his meadows for a day and a half, with pay of 1 1/2d a day, each man also having to find three men for three days to carry the

prior's hay, and for three half-days to take the grain, for nothing. Further, the prior exacted for 12 days a year 24 men to reap his corn with an allowance of 3/4d for four days food, and 1/2d for eight days food. Further, they had to sift the prior's malt from the feast of St Andrew to Christmas, with a 4d fine for any leakages, and to harrow 1 acre (0.4 hectare) for a loaf worth 1/4d; besides which the prior exacted ten eggs a year from each on Good Friday (VCH 1905, 65–6). Stratigraphic evidence suggests that a vineyard or orchard existed (OA5) in the 12th century, while the presence of food waste and 'hatched' chicken and goose eggs hints at food preparation/production there.

How much meat was eaten by the canons or served to guests is unknown. At certain times the canons were allowed meat, principally when ill or at bloodletting. The priory's extensively documented hospitality would require large-scale meal provision for the guests. The eating of meat with guests probably occurred, and restrictions varied from house to house – some adhered to the rules regarding meat only on certain days and partial abstinence appears to have been popular (Burton 1994, 167). Harvey suggests that at Westminster, outside Advent and Lent, the average week comprised four meat days and three fish days (1993, 63). Some idea of the priory's later stores of meat and fish are given when in 1538 Richard Layton reported that at 'Marten Abbey are 18 fat oxen, 40 fat sheep, 200 quarters of malt and £30 in ling and haberdyne [dried and salted fish]' (TNA: PRO, E322/152; L and P Hen VIII, xiii(1), no. 785).

Apart from the foodstuffs recovered from 12th-century deposits, evidence for food and diet derives mainly from the infirmary kitchen (B6), hall (B4a) and cloister garth (OA5), together with the passage (B7) leading to Building 10, from the reredorter (B5), and also from the garden area (OA7) and aisled hall (B11). The main kitchen and refectory lay outside the areas of the excavation. Artefactual evidence for food preparation and consumption is described above (4.7, 'Institutional, religious and personal activities'). The faunal remains form the bulk of the dietary evidence (Tables 3–16; Tables 45–7; Chapter 7.8); the botanical evidence was not particularly abundant and largely restricted to occasional charred cereal grains, legumes and fruit species (Tables 40–4; Chapter 7.6).

The faunal assemblage although abundant (17,617 fragments/c 68kg from periods M1–M4) can only represent a fraction of the food waste produced. At Westminster Abbey during the period c 1495–c 1525, the estimated weights per annum of gadids (cod family) served in the refectory equalled 5255kg, and of beef in the misericord, 1634kg (Harvey 1993, 48, 53). The excavation did not recover the total faunal waste assemblage derived from consumption during the monastic period: the bulk may never have been deposited there but removed, for example for field manuring. The assemblage is probably incomplete in species and relative distribution of carcass parts. For many groups, particularly the smaller passerine and wading birds, identification to species is difficult or impossible. Highly fragmented material from these, such as that at Merton, is very often impossible to identify to even family level. In view of the known consumption of such species throughout the archaeological periods dealt with (Hammond 1995, 130), and their often very specific relationship, in terms of availability, to the status and rank of the consumer, it can be assumed that the faunal dietary component is only very partially revealed. In general the dietary composition remains uniform from the 12th to 14th centuries; the increased abundance and diversity seen from the 13th century onwards is probably a function of larger sample size and increased sampling effort rather than a genuine dietary change (Chapter 7.8).

The assemblage is dominated throughout by cattle, usually adult with a few infants and juveniles; sheep/goat and pig provide lesser although roughly equal components, although the relative proportions of both sheep/goat and pig tends to decrease relative to cattle from the 14th century onwards (Table 21; Table 45; Table 46). Consistent but low-level recovery of foetal/neonate pig bones, and to a much lesser extent sheep/goat, mainly suggest pig rearing, although the diet included pigs and sheep/goats from a range of age-groups – lamb as well as mutton. There was a consistently high fragment count, far higher than that seen at any other London religious house, of domestic chicken, particularly in the 12th to 14th centuries. The consistent but lower level recovery of goose and, to a much lesser extent, mallard/domestic duck also follows this pattern. Recovery of infant and juvenile chicken from the 12th to 14th centuries, and to a lesser extent later, is further evidence that chickens were raised.

More rarely retrieved species indicate consistent low-level consumption of various game species including birds (thrush family – several species including blackbird, dove/pigeon, woodpigeon, common/grey partridge, woodcock, heron, wild duck – unidentified and swan), and mammals (red deer, fallow deer, roe deer, brown hare, and rabbit). The game component of a monastic assemblage can provide a clear indication of the status of a monastic house, as when we compare the almost entirely domesticate composition of the St Mary Spital monastic meat diet (Pipe 1997, 232), and the more obviously luxurious Bermondsey Abbey (plentiful venison, brown hare, waders, swan, crane) (Pipe et al in prep). Heron, swan, partridge, woodcock, and roe deer venison figured prominently on the

menu at, for example, the funeral of the bishop of Bath and Wells in December 1424 (White 1993, 38).

The fish diet shows diversity and abundance derived mainly from marine and estuarine species with a very small component of freshwater species. These would have been available from the Thames estuary and adjacent coasts and are a common component of the medieval diet in London (Wheeler 1979, 83; Hammond 1995, 22). Throughout the monastic period the fish assemblage remains consistent in species-composition and relative abundance. There are five main component groups within the fish assemblage; the clupeids (herring family – marine), gadids (cod family – marine), cyprinids (carp family – freshwater), smelt (estuarine/marine/anadromous), and eel (marine/freshwater/catadromous). All these fish have a long history as commercially exploited species in Britain. The assemblage was numerically dominated by the clupeids (herring family), including herring, from each period except the 15th and 16th centuries (period M4). Gadids, including cod, whiting and haddock, and smelt each contributed roughly a third as many fragments as did the clupeids. Cyprinids (carp family including common bream) and eel provided the bulk of the remainder with small fragment counts also derived from thornback ray, sturgeon, plaice/flounder, conger eel, gurnard and mackerel. There were one or two fragments of salmonid and pike.

The greatest abundance and diversity of fish is seen from the 12th to 14th centuries, but particularly from the 13th century. Salmonids, conger eel, gurnard, mackerel, pike and whiting were only recovered from the 13th and 14th centuries, suggesting a varied, abundant and good quality fish diet, with somewhat more expensive species consumed then.

The general composition of the fish assemblage compares closely with that at St Mary Spital in its overall dominance by clupeids, the general species-composition and the lack of definite high-status indicators (eg turbot and halibut) (Locker 1997, 235). The Merton assemblage does show definite evidence of high-status consumption with the recovery of sturgeon dermal scute fragments from the 13th to 14th centuries (periods M2 and M3). The overall fish menu also resembles that provided for the 'religious men' at the funeral feast for the bishop of Bath and Wells – eels, herring, whiting, gurnard, salmon, pike, plaice, haddock and at least one species of cyprinid (White 1993, 38).

Molluscan dietary evidence is effectively confined to two still commercially important marine species, common/flat oyster (Ostrea edulis) and common whelk (Buccinum undatum) (Tables 48–51; Chapter 7.9). Both the common oyster and whelk are known to have been historically exploited from the outer Thames estuary either by fishing of wild populations (whelk in the mouth of the Thames, oyster off Garrison Point and Sheppey, both in Kent), or by cultivation (oyster at Leigh-on-Sea, Essex) (Wheeler 1979, 83) until the decline in estuarine fisheries because of pollution and interference with the river flow. As they both undoubtedly represent post-consumption refuse and are thoroughly spread but generally in groups of much fewer than 50 shells, this must suggest, as with

Table 21 *Relative percentage representation of the hand-collected major mammalian domesticates (expressed as 100% of the assemblage)*

Species	M1 %	M2 %	M3 %	M4 %	P1 %	P2 %	P3 %
From fragment count							
Cattle	27.5	16.7	31.0	50.3	42.2	39.5	51.4
Sheep/goat	33.3	33.9	30.7	24.3	37.0	32.3	25.1
Pig	39.2	49.4	38.3	25.4	20.8	28.2	23.5
From weight (g)							
Cattle	55.6	43.1	60.6	79.2	80.2	69.8	78.0
Sheep/goat	22.3	24.3	17.1	7.5	13.4	17.0	12.1
Pig	22.1	32.6	22.3	13.3	6.4	13.2	9.9

the animal bone, that the recovered assemblage may represent no more than a trace of the material actually discarded. They were both recovered from a wide range of contexts including floors, ditches, drains, pits, and buildings, before, during and after the functional life of the priory. As a result, it is very difficult to suggest any spatial or temporal patterns of use and disposal beyond evidence for their use at the priory and the conspicuous absence of other commercially valuable species such as cockle and winkle which are known to have been popularly eaten during the medieval period although they were never as popular as oysters (Hammond 1993, 22). This may indicate a deliberate dietary selection or may reflect commercial availability nearby.

The site produced the usual range of cereals: free-threshing wheats (*Triticum* sp), barley (*Hordeum* sp), small amounts of rye (*Secale cereale*) and oat (*Avena* sp), for urban and rural medieval sites and in monastic and secular contexts in England (Greig 1991). In previous excavations of monastic sites in London a similar range has been found at, for example, St Mary Spital (Davis 1997) and St Mary Clerkenwell (Giorgi 1998). The cereal grains may have been used for a variety of purposes. Free-threshing wheat was the preferred grain for making good quality bread although all the cereals could have been used, either alone or together for bread. At Westminster Abbey, wheaten flour was mainly used for bread, with a biscuity form known as 'wastel' being consumed on special occasions (Harvey 1993, 59). Rye bread or maslin bread, made from a mix of rye and wheat flour, was eaten mainly by poor people. The cereal grains may also have been used for biscuits, cakes, pastry and pottages – stews made from a mix of cereals, root vegetables and sometimes meat (Wilson 1991, 191). Barley was the principal grain for malting in the medieval brewing industry (Campbell et al 1993, 25). Indeed, ale consumption was high in religious houses with the ratio of brewing to bread grains sometimes being as high as two to one (ibid, 206). Oats were also sometimes used in brewing although the main use of this cereal was for feeding livestock. Barley was also sometimes used as animal fodder.

Few pulses were found, as has been the case on other monastic sites in London although peas (*Pisum* spp) and lentils (*Lens culinaris*) were identified at St John Clerkenwell (A Davis in Sloane and Malcolm 2004, 368, table 72), and peas and beans (*Vicia faba*) from St Mary Clerkenwell (Davis in prep). Pulses were frequent ingredients of pottage (Wilson 1991, 183) and used for animal fodder. One advantage of pulses was that they could be dried and stored for later consumption.

Few remains of fruits (small amounts of grape (*Vitis vinifera*), apple (*Malus domestica/sylvestris*), plum/bullace (*Prunus domestica*), sloe/blackthorn (*Prunus spinosa*), blackberry/raspberry (*Rubus fruticosus/idaeus*), elder (*Sambucus nigra*), hazel (*Corylus avellana*), and walnut (*Juglans regia*)) were found – mostly from the fill [11252] of a 12th-century drainage ditch (period M1). Historical evidence suggests fresh fruit was not consumed in quantity in the medieval period because it was considered unhealthy and instead mixed with other foods (eg cereals) and cooked as pottage or preserved as jams and jellies (Wilson 1991, 334).

Late 15th- and early 16th-century records from Westminster Abbey suggest that fruit did not play a significant part in the monastic diet, with little spent on mostly dried fruit (Harvey 1993, 35). However it is possible that most households were self-sufficient in some fresh fruit and did not record it in their accounts, while imported raisins, currants, dried figs and prunes played a relatively important part in monastic diets during Lent (Hammond 1995, 74). At Westminster Abbey it was considered a treat and served more frequently at the abbot's table rather than the monks' (Harvey 1993, 61). Few cases of scurvy are known in medieval London, and only two possible cases were identified in the priory population suggesting the minimal dietary requirements to avoid the disease were met for the majority of its inhabitants. Archaeological evidence from other medieval London sites shows that fruit stones and fruit seeds (especially grape, fig (*Ficus carica*), elder and blackberry/raspberry) are frequent finds largely because of the high number of excavated cess and rubbish pits.

The fruits found at Merton may have been used in various ways as food and drink. Elderberries were used as an adulterant of more expensive foreign wines or to disguise English raisin wine (Grieve 1992, 268). English-grown unripe grapes were used for verjuice, that is vinegar used in cooking and pickling. Grapes were also pickled, dried and stored for later consumption and may have been imported as dried fruit from southern Europe. Later customs' records for London between 1480 and 1481 show the import of such from Spain, Portugal and Italy (Cobb 1990, passim). Apples could have been used for making cider and verjuice and were widely cultivated in the medieval period (Greig 1988, 117). The fruit of the wild species of elder and blackberry/raspberry could have been collected from the wild and consumed although both, along with plum/bullace, sloe/blackthorn and hazel, may represent the residues from naturally deposited fruits growing nearby. Plum trees, however, were sometimes cultivated while walnuts may have been either home-grown or imported; shell fragments have been found at a number of sites dating from the early to the late medieval period (ibid, 118).

Pollen samples contributed evidence for diverse habitats in the 16th century within the precinct, not only marsh/wetland and pastoral areas, but also areas of cultivation; borage (*Borago officinalis*), buckwheat (*Fagopyrum esculentum*) and (probably) cannabis (*Cannabis sativa*) were among the crops (Chapter 7.7). There was also some woodland in the vicinity of the precinct, either localised areas or more open park growth. Walnut and two exotics, yew (*Taxus*) and juniper (*Juniperus*), were probably specifically planted.

4.9 The monastic economy

The priory's income was largely derived from the rents of rural and urban (London) property acquired from the foundation onwards, although the priory also farmed some

rural properties itself (Chapter 7.1). Income also came from
the sale of corrodies (above, 4.7, 'Corrodians') and donations
in wills, but little evidence exists for money gained by other
means such as manufacturing or trade. However, it should be
remembered in what follows just how incomplete a record of
the priory's holdings generally survives. This is shown by the
chance survival of a valor, or listing, of the priory's properties
and rents in Surrey, London and Buckingham acquired and
appropriated between 1369 and 1394 (Bodleian, Laud MS 723,
fo 65r). This consisted of assets worth annually a total of £72
10s 8d, more than accounted for by the recorded licences for
alienation in mortmain (see below), and by the £40 pa
additional revenue acquired during these years. The mortmain
licences concern properties not mentioned in the valor and
vice versa.

Some documentary evidence exists for the build-up of the
priory's landholdings in the 12th century. Gilbert's foundation
grants consisted of lands and a mill worth 60s pa, whilst Queen
Matilda's pious deeds probably included further donations, and
Henry I confirmed the grant of the manor, but not the parish
church (given separately to the priory) in 1156–7 (Heales
1898, 26–7). Gilbert is also thought to have given Molesey
(Surrey), while Henry II gave the manor of Ewell with its
members of Kingswood and Selwood (Surrey) in 1156, and
Richard I gave a 100 acres (40.47 hectares) in Ewell. Lordship
of a manor was in itself an important source of income
through the manorial court. Between 1138 and 1157, land in
Wandsworth (Surrey) for fulling mills was exchanged with
Westminster Abbey for other land in Wandsworth near the
granges of Dunsfold (*Westminster Charters*, no. 268), suggesting
holdings along the river and direct farming of the land. By
1177 Merton had gained the church of the manor of Stanstead
(Hertfordshire) (*Early Charters Waltham*, nos 356, 360). Peckham
(Surrey) and the manor of Taplow (Buckinghamshire) were also
acquired in the 12th century. All of this suggests that the priory
had acquired substantial holdings in the vicinity during the
first few decades of its existence.

During the 13th century this pattern of landholding in
Surrey continued, again with suggestions that some land was
farmed directly and some not. Between 1222 and 1230 an
agreement was reached with Waltham Abbey concerning the
tithes of the abbey's newly cultivated land in Stanstead Abbots
(Hertfordshire), of which Merton held the living. As a result,
Merton received 4 acres (1.62 hectares) of meadow in lieu of
the tithe for hay, and 5s payable from the mill for other tithes
(*Early Charters Waltham*, no. 394). In 1274 an agreement was
reached with Bermondsey Abbey concerning the tithes of
Carshalton (Surrey), leased to Merton for 20s pa (*Ann Monast*, iii,
465). An agreement was reached with St Paul's Cathedral in
1234 regarding fisheries in the Thames at Brentford
(Middlesex) and touching upon rights at Sutton and Mortlake
(Surrey), and Chiswick (Middlesex), among other places (*Early
Charters St Paul*, no. 325). However, slightly further afield,
sometime in 1249 to 1252–4 Merton had land at Bishops
Sutton and Ropley (both in Hampshire) (BL, Harley Charter
xxi.25, cited in Heales 1898, 121).

From the middle of the 13th century important
ecclesiastical estates were appropriated to the priory, again
largely in the south-east – Patrixbourne (Kent) in 1258 the
church of Effingham (Surrey) in 1299 worth 20 marks (£13 6s
8d) pa, the church of Cuddington (Surrey) in 1309, and
Kingston church (Surrey) in 1291 valued at £80 pa, mostly via
licence in mortmain (*Cal Pat R*, 1292–1301, 407; 1307–13,
162; *Reg Woodlock*, 374, 445–6; Heales 1898, 150–1, 201, 225,
227–8, 258, 260–3, 275, appendix CXII, cxxxvi; *VCH* 1905,
96, 100–1). Other ecclesiastical holdings included Lower
Hardres (Kent) (*Cal Pat R*, 1377–81, 388) and the distant
Ashcombe in Devon (Heales 1898, 290). Much, perhaps all, of
the secular property acquired or enhanced by the priory in the
14th century came via mortmain, again predominately in
Surrey and the south-east: these included, in 1304, three mills
in Taplow, 15 acres (6.07 hectares) of wood in Upton
(Buckinghamshire), and 8 additional acres (3.24 hectares) of
land there (*Cal Pat R*, 1301–7, 239); in 1305, 16 acres (6.47
hectares) in Upton and 3 acres (1.21 hectares) in Patrixbourne
(ibid, 328, 330); and in 1315 a messuage in Southwark
(Surrey) (ibid, 1313–17, 221). These financial gains may have
allowed the building of the eastern extension in the 14th
century. Other licences related to the loss in 1318 to St
Edmund's chapel, Cambridge (Cambridgeshire), of property
held in part by Merton and Barnwell Priory (Cambridgeshire)
(ibid, 1317–21, 110); 16 acres (6.47 hectares) in Newdigate
(Surrey) in exchange for 16 acres in 'Shelwode' in 1337 (ibid,
1331–8, 520); in 1337 the acquisition of further lands and
rents to an annual value of £10 (ibid, 533); in 1359, a
messuage, 100 acres (40.47 hectares), 2 acres (0.81 hectares)
of meadow and 22½d rent in 'La Legh' and Horley (Surrey)
(ibid, 1358–61, 270); and 10s of the £10 yearly of land and
rent, a toft, 117½ acres (47.55 hectares), 16 acres (6.47
hectares) of pasture and 1 of wood in 'La Legh', Ewell and
Chipstead (Surrey), of the value of 6s 4¾d pa (ibid, 319; *Mon
Angl*, vi(1), 245–8). Two further licences enabled grants to the
priory of £10 pa of land and rent in Surrey in 1372 (*Cal Pat R*,
1370–4, 168) and, accounting for £9 of £10 pa previously
licensed, five messuages, a mill, a carucate and 231 acres
(93.48 hectares), 7 acres (2.83 hectares) of wood and 46s
7½d of rent in Surrey in Southwark, Mitcham, Beddington,
Baudon, Walton, Carshalton, Sutton, Wandsworth and
'Hertyndoncombe', worth £8 11s 2½d pa, in 1373 (ibid,
249). In 1373 lands were purchased in the vills and parishes of
Mitcham and Morden, and, for £186 in 1357, as the discharge
of a debt to the prior (*Cal Close R*, 1369–74, 544). A final 14th-
century licence in 1392 enabled the priory to receive various
properties in Surrey and pasture for 11 plough cattle in Upton
meeting in full the licence granted to them by Edward II to
acquire land and rent to the value of £10 each year (ibid,
1391–6, 127).

Other 14th-century grants, perhaps not associated with
mortmain, include, in 1363, the manor of Wimbledon (Surrey)
with crofts, enclosures, annexes, halls, manors and the great
granges, together with all waifs and strays there pasturing, to be
held with lands, meadows, feedings, pastures, and common of

heath for 300 sheep and easements of all houses (Heales 1898, 257, citing Lambeth Palace Library, Chartae Misc MS 96; *Cal Pat R*, 1361–4, 476), and in 1375 the manor of Banstead (Surrey), with all appurtenances except the park, profit of the warren, knights' fees, wardships, marriage, escheats (the reversion of property to the crown or lord in the absence of legal heirs) and advowsons of churches (*Cal Fine R*, 1369–77, 303).

During the 15th century few acquisitions are recorded via mortmain: one, very minor, in 1408, authorised the purchase for 12 marks (£8) of various properties in Surrey (*Cal Pat R*, 1405–8, 393); another, in 1424, granted the Surrey manor of Combe (*VCH* 1905, 101). There are frequent references to the priory's interests at Patrixbourne, throughout the century. In 1409 the canons were granted an estate in the manor for 60 years for an annual rent of 16s (*Cal Pat R*, 1408–13, 139). Wood and land, including a dilapidated mill at Patrixbourne, were leased by Merton to Sir William Haute, indicating that this land at least was not farmed directly (*Cat Anc Deeds*, vi, B 2874). A lay steward for the priory estates is first referred to on 24 November 1457 with the appointment of Ralph Legh esquire as steward for life of all the priory's manors in Surrey 'and elsewhere within the realm', in return for an annual rent of £4, the costs and expenses of holding courts, and one gown a year of the suit of gentlemen or 10s in lieu (*Cal Close R*, 1454–61, 264).

During the early 15th century there were various disputes involving some priory property along the Thames and its exploitation, particularly the prior's weir (*Cal Plea and Mem R*, 1381–1412, 273); these appear to have been resolved by 1468 (*Cal Pat R*, 1467–76, 111). In 1402 a commission by the archbishop of Canterbury, investigating the mistreatment of tenants, including those of Merton at Feltham (Surrey), discovered that Merton was entitled to receive a pension of 50s pa for a share of the tithes of Effingham (Surrey) (Heales 1898, 295). In 1422–3 Oseney Abbey made over their part of the tithes of Duns Tew (Oxfordshire) to Merton for a fixed annual payment of 26s 8d in perpetuity (*Bodleian Charters*, 325; Heales 1898, 297).

Evidence for priory holdings acquired in the early 16th century is limited. In 1513 the priory received 24 acres (9.71 hectares) of meadow and 116 acres (46.94 hectares) of pasture in 'Cornburgh' [?Canonbury, Surrey] (*VCH* 1905, 101), and before 1529–30 the advowson of the church of Hunsdon (Hertfordshire) (*L and P Hen VIII*, vii(5), no. 923). In 1535 the priory leased out for 40 years their rectory of Tregony (Cornwall) (*Cat Anc Deeds*, iii, D 1226).

The above deals largely with Merton's rural holdings, but the priory also had substantial property in the City of London. In 1291, Merton held property in 31 London parishes, as described in Chapter 7.1. Merton Priory's London holdings and rents at the Dissolution were not included in the *Valor ecclesiasticus*, but four are singled out in ministers' accounts for 1537–8, the first year in which the properties of the recently dissolved priory appear: Holy Trinity parish, 101s 4d; St Margaret Lothbury parish, £10 13s 4d; St Benet Gracechurch parish, £13; St Pancras parish, £11 6s 8d (Heales 1898,

appendix CLII). These properties were probably largely rented out to provide income as happened in 1513 for a tenement and two shops in the parish of All Hallows Bread Street (*Cat Anc Deeds*, iii, D 1043). Further information on these properties and other holdings and rents are listed in Chapter 7.1.

Merton does not feature frequently in the wills of medieval Londoners, whether on account of its known wealth, its relative remoteness from the city, or the survival of the evidence. In 1259 Felicity la Colnere left, on the death of her brother, rents in Westcheap to Merton, along with devises of 'Caponeshors' at Merton and other tenements to Merton and other houses (*Cal Husting Wills*, i, 2–3), and in the same year Andrew Sotesbrok 'his body and his houses' to the church of Meriton (ibid, i, 5). In 1349 John Youn gave his properties to numerous religious houses including Merton (ibid, i, 540). William Wodehall made similar provisions in 1358 (ibid, ii, 6), while in 1391 John Foxton's bequests included a personal one to John Heyford, canon of Merton (ibid, ii, 286). In 1433 Beatrice Hayton of Merton bequeathed to the priory, prior and canons 10 marks (£6 13s 4d), and 10s to the fabric of the church of Merton (TNA: PRO, PROB11/3, fo 143). In 1521 William Clopton gave to the fabric £6 13s 4d, and 6s 8d to every priest, and 3s 4d to every canon (TNA: PRO, PROB11/20, fo 86).

After a period of probable growth in the 12th century and affluence in the 13th century, particularly during the long reign of Henry III, financial problems are suggested in the early 14th century. It is likely that the lavish building works in the 13th century prevented any build-up of capital. Debts recorded as owed to Merton amount to £569 for the period 1337–93, significantly less than the debts of £1000 that the priory itself contracted in the period 1308–51. In so far as the two periods are comparable, with one or two exceptions, the sums advanced by the priory were considerably smaller than those it borrowed. Perhaps the most notable aspect of the comparison is that the period at which the priory began to lend overlaps by only a decade or so the period at which it ceased to borrow. Unless this reflects merely the idiosyncrasies of the Chancery clerks who compiled the Patent and Close Rolls, or more recently those of the Record Office staff who edited them, a revival of the priory's fortunes in mid century would seem to be indicated. This recovery of the priory's fortunes would make sense; archaeological and stylistic evidence both demonstrate that the great eastern extension was approaching completion in the 1350s. The cessation of construction would have allowed the monastic income to be diverted to the repayment of debts and the restoration of credits in the following decades. In this case, the financial gamble usually presented to religious houses by such construction work paid off. However, in 1393 the priory's income amounted to 1345 marks (£896 13s 4d), its outgoings to 1475 marks and 8s (£983 14s 8d), a 130 mark 8s (£87 1s 4d) shortfall, and the prior required a further 440 marks (£293 13s 4d) due to murrain for the last six years; five corrodies were sold to aid the relief of the priory (Heales 1898, 284, citing Bodleian, Laud MS 723, fo 81). Some further evidence of later relative poverty can be seen in the sale to the London Bridgehouse Trust in 1420–1 of small quantities of elm from Kingston, worth 11s and 13s 4d (*Bridge Accounts*, nos 274, 279), while in 1443 the priory was granted protection for ten years in consideration of its poverty and indebtedness (*Cal Pat R*, 1441–6, 159). It contracted no recorded debts at this period, but rigorously pursued small sums owing to itself (ibid, 1476–85, 148, 189). By the Dissolution the priory appears to have recovered financially. Its annual income was assessed at £961 (*Val Eccl*, ii, 48–51), compared with £548 for Bermondsey and £511 for Stratford Langthorne. Merton Priory's London holdings and rents at the Dissolution failed to be included in the *Valor ecclesiasticus* and its income must have therefore exceeded the figure of £961. Its Surrey holdings recorded as worth £20 or more were Canonbury (£53), Merton itself (£50), Chelwood (£32), Molesey (£25), Westbarns (£21), and Carshalton (£20), accounting for £201 out of a total of £471 for the county. In Buckinghamshire the total value was £92, including Upton Coll (£39) and Upton (£20); in Hampshire £87 including Holshott (£36); in Huntingdonshire £78 including the exceptionally valuable rectories of Godmanchester (£50) and Alconbury (£24); while the priory's holdings in the City of London amounted to £59, and those in Kent to £53 including Patrixbourne (£33). Smaller revenues, ranging between £9 and £33, were received from Devon, Hertfordshire, Somerset, Bedfordshire, Oxfordshire, Cambridgeshire, Dorset and Wiltshire. The larger estates, valued together at £403, thus accounted for some 40% of the priory's total income in 1536 of £1039, while the Surrey properties as a whole accounted for 45%.

Merton would have relied on the London markets to supply many of the goods it required and to sell surplus goods from its own lands. Little documentary or archaeological evidence exists for the export of items made by the priory; most non-perishable items are likely to have been for the use of the priory while surplus foodstuffs are likely to have been sold or otherwise exported.

One commodity brought to Merton, probably largely via London and its port, was pottery. The majority was locally produced within the Surrey region but a small quantity came from further afield. Pottery recovered originated in English manufacturing centres, including Stamford (Lincolnshire) and Scarborough (Yorkshire North Riding), and Continental centres like the middle Rhine valley, the Low Countries, France, and Spain. Assemblages dating to the 16th- to 17th-century (period P2) included several noteworthy imports (<P13>–<P15>, Fig 174). Glass vessels were also imported from the Continent such as the pale green *roemer* drinking glass, <S366> (Fig 167); these vessels are uncommon in this country but frequently found on the Continent (Henkes 1994, 255–62).

Commercial transactions are suggested by 11 coins, including one counterfeit penny <S335> and, an unusually high-value single loss for the London area, a groat <S337> (Fig 167) with a total face value of 12³/₄ pence, an uncommon denier of Aquitaine <S343> (Fig 116) issued under the Black Prince during the period of English rule and a fragment of another Continental issue from the Baltic <S344>. There are seven reckoning counters <S345>–<S351>, comprising three English jettons, one 'Anglo-Gallic' <S346> (Fig 167), two Nuremberg issues, and a largely illegible one, possibly French or Low Countries. A touchstone <S352> (Fig 167), an unusual find, implies concern for the quality of gold, whether in the form of coin or other items. This was used to determine the

Fig 167 Groat <S337> and jetton <S346>; touchstone <S352>; and applied 'berry' prunt from a hollow stem imported drinking glass <S366> (scale c 1:1; prunt at 4:1)

purity of gold, including coins, by comparing the colour of scratches from these objects against a series of sample rubbings of known purities retained on the surface – no trace of scratched gold is evident, although two 10th-century touchstones from Winchester have in one instance such marks and in the other traces from gold tested (Biddle 1990, 167, nos 1 and 3, fig 33 and pl IXa).

4.10 Death and burial

The burial areas and population size

The picture of burial customs and cemetery usage is incomplete because many areas where burial took place were not fully excavated; these include the cemeteries and areas within the church and cloister. The central and eastern portion of the church, including much of the choir, the crossing and the area around the high altar, which may have been used for important burials, was not excavated, nor was the central area of the nave. Only the eastern walk of the main cloister walks was excavated; although this only contained one burial (possibly overspill from the chapter house), the remaining walks may have been more intensively used for burial. The chapter house was fully excavated and most probably contained the burials of priors associated with the house. Within the external cemetery areas, nowhere was fully excavated down to the 'natural' (geological) deposits and early burials may have gone undetected. North of the nave (OA6) only the area immediately to the west of the north transept was excavated to any depth; further to the west the cemetery was not excavated. The area immediately outside the 12th- to 13th-century (periods M1–M2) east end of the church, where dense burial would be expected, was not investigated. It is also highly probable that burial occurred well outside the excavation areas; the isolated burial [11203] (period M1–M4; Fig 141) to the east of the infirmary strongly suggests this.

The monastic cemetery was excavated as two separate areas (OA3 south and OA6 north) and analysed as such, although it appears likely that for much of the priory's history, certainly until the 14th century, the monastic cemetery was a single entity, mostly to the east of the church, and regarded as such by the inhabitants. However, even in the 12th and 13th centuries, this may be an oversimplification: sufficient evidence exists to suggest changes in the layout over time. The earliest cemetery phase (period M1; Fig 9) may have been delimited to the north by the wall (S3) but this feature appeared to be short-lived. The cemetery either expanded rapidly beyond its first limits during the 12th/early 13th century, perhaps as far north as the ditch ([3593], OA6), or perhaps the wall may only have defined the canons' initial burial area, with 'laity' buried to the north. This arrangement is paralleled to a certain extent (but at a much later date) at Walsingham where in the 14th–15th century a wall attached to the north side of the presbytery separated the canons' cemetery from the lay cemetery (Robinson 1980, 159).

The cemeteries of the religious were often located to the east or north of the church (Greene 1992, 159; Coppack 1993, 60). If this is the case here at Merton, the removal of the wall might suggest either the removal of any formal division between canon and lay areas or the movement and/or confinement of canons' burials to a different location. The burials to the south of the wall themselves suggest the blurring of any formal division, perhaps even before the wall's removal; these individuals included women and two children [3084] and [3235] to the south of the wall, together with two priests [4593] and [4881], possibly not Augustinian (period M1; Fig 9). There were also adult male 'plank' burials (interments below wooden planks and other timber), three ([4611]; [4893]; [7559]) definitely south of the wall and one [3869] west of the wall. This type of burial is suggested as associated at Cistercian Bordesley Abbey (Worcestershire) with the burial of monastic personnel in the 12th century (Hirst and Wright 1989, 307–8; Astill et al 2004), but the practice is found associated with apparently secular, mixed age and sex burials in London (below, 'Plank burials').

The short presbytery in the 13th century (period M2; Fig 34) and the lack of structures suggesting internal cemetery divisions perhaps indicate that the cemetery was, with the possible exception of a small burial group to the north, north of Road 1, regarded as a single entity at that time. Against the lack of female and child burials to the south (OA3) must be set the smallness of the sample there (22 analysed), and the occurrence to the north (OA6) of further adult male ([4647]; [4649]; [4530]; [4286]), and one female ([4498]), 'plank' burials, and the unusual wooden 'coffin' of an unsexed adult [4673]). However, a greater incidence of burials in stone cists in Open Area 3 may suggest a higher status for burial to the south in all periods.

It is possibly only in the 14th century (period M3; Fig 71), with the eastward extension of the presbytery (and construction of the Lady chapel) that there were, formally, north and south burial areas. Certainly, at this stage, the church layout more closely resembles those monasteries where such a cemetery division occurred (cf Walsingham; Ely: Burton 1994, 147, fig 3). It is tempting to regard the compact group of exclusively male (where sexed) burials immediately to the north (OA3) of the infirmary chapel as canons and perhaps infirmary residents. The five 'plank' burials in the south burial area (OA3) may also be significant. However, the inclusion of two females here argues against complete exclusivity for the whole area. To the north in the 14th century, the apparent lack of 'plank' burials and the inclusion of 12 females and eight children, in what was still predominately a male cemetery, may reinforce this impression, in what is a far larger sample population than previously. A priest [2905] was buried to the north of the nave. The lack of females in the 15th- and 16th-century burial sample (period M4; Fig 129) to the north is offset by the smallness of the sample and the inclusion of two children.

The north burial area (OA6), although at times containing some 'rich' burials, had generally a more mixed burial population than the southern (OA3). The north burial area exhibited a higher incidence of female and immature burials (Fig 168), and a wider range of age at death. However the burial population was, at all times, overwhelmingly male and adult, as would also be true of the living monastic population. The probability that this area was intended for lay individuals associated with the priory but not, generally, for the canons themselves is suggested by the higher incidence of female and immature burials there. These individuals – possibly monastic servants (or members of their families), lay people requesting burial at the priory, or corrodians – would be more likely to be interred in a lay cemetery.

The most popular excavated location for burial within the church was the north transept and its associated chapels. This area exhibited an increasing burial density over time. However, the area around the high altar was not excavated and conceivably had a high or higher density of burial. Daniell (1997, 95) suggests that 'the east end of the church – nearest the high altar

– was the most desirable, followed by the rest of the chancel, and then the nave'. This may be the case at Merton: later burials in the north nave were well spaced and there was a lack of obvious burials in the south aisle, suggesting the nave was not as popular as the north transept (closer to the high altar). Roger Tye in 1428 and Beatrice Hayton in 1433 specifically request burial close to the altar of Holy Trinity within the church (Beatrice because her husband Thomas Hayton rests there), although where this altar was located is unknown.

The human bone assemblage analysed consisted of 664 individuals, although 721 were excavated (not including 15 charnel pits and large amounts of residual human bone). How large a sample of those actually buried this represents is difficult to establish, given the unexcavated areas and lack of defined boundaries. The surface area of the monastic cemetery may have been approximately 2500–3000m². Within the more fully excavated eastern part of Open Area 6 there were

Key:
- 1–6 years
- 7–12 years
- 13–16 years
- female adults
- all other burials

0   25m

Fig 168 Distribution of adult females and children (base plan shows all building-related features including conjecture) (scale 1:500)

approximately 15 burials per 25m². If the burial density were reasonably consistent over Open Area 6 it would suggest at least 1000–1200 individuals interred there. This may be a little high; the burial density at Stratford Langthorne, another largely rural foundation near London, was approximately eight to ten burials per 25m² (Barber et al 2004, 90). To the south (OA3) at Merton, the burial density directly to the north of the infirmary chapel in the 14th century was 20 to 25 individuals per 25m², but this concentration was probably very limited in extent. Assuming instead a density similar overall to the north, Open Area 3 probably had 600–700 interments overall. This would give an estimate of 1600–1900 for Open Area 6 and Open Area 3 combined. Taking into account the church and chapter house and unexcavated areas, a maximum burial population of c 2500–3000 would seem a reasonable figure. Thus the 721 excavated would represent at most 30% and conceivably less of those originally buried. However, any estimate of the actual burial population size is extremely problematic given the limited excavation and probable fluctuations in mortality and catchment size throughout the priory's life, and particularly in the 14th century (Knowles and Hadcock 1953, 490).

The burial population

The burials in the north burial area were, as discussed above, probably a mix of lay and clerical interments. The area to the south-east of the church was probably reserved principally, but not wholly, for the canons and the chapter house for older individuals with a relatively privileged lifestyle – probably priors or higher status laity. The church, with females and children present, held relatively high-status burials compared to the external burial areas.

In the chapter house all the sexed individuals were male (Chapter 7.11; Table 55). This parallels the area to the north of the infirmary chapel in the 14th century and suggests, as was traditional, that it was the main burial place of Merton's priors, although not of all. Some would have been, and were, buried near the high altar or in chapels: Prior William Salyng who died in 1520 was interred near the altar of St Frideswide. Important laymen could also be buried in the chapter house – it is unlikely that the young adult burial found is that of a prior. Only one individual's identity was hinted at, that of prior Michael Kympton who died in 1413 (Fig 136). The 32 graves found appear to have been reused at times. Fifteen graves were cist burials, again suggesting a correlation with high status.

Elsewhere the evidence does not suggest that Merton at any time functioned as a parochial cemetery or church. The sex ratio of males to females in the 12th century (period M1) was 9:1 in the south burial area (OA3) and 10.7:1 in the north burial area (OA6). In the 13th century (period M2) in Open Area 3 all were male, and a greater proportion were now older adults (40.9% compared to 15.3%), while in Open Area 6 there was the same proportion of children as in the 12th century, but the percentage of females had risen to give a ratio of 4.75:1. In the 14th century (period M3) a male:female sex ratio of 33:1 existed to the west in Open Area 3, with a slight majority of

mature adults over older adults, while the area to the north of the infirmary was exclusively male. In Open Area 6 the male:female sex ratio was 8:1 in the 14th century and exclusively male from the 15th century onwards. In the church only five females were found throughout (four in the 14th-century north transept, giving a male:female sex ratio of 6.25:1; one in the 15th-century nave, so 11:1) suggesting similar profiles, but the sample sizes were too small to be of value (Table 54; Table 55). The absence of female burials in the 13th-century church is almost certainly a product of limited excavation and archaeological survival, and need not suggest that their appearance in the 14th century, in the north transept, was in reality new. Nor for the same reasons does their apparent absence in the 14th-century presbytery suggest exclusion, only comparative rarity. Allowing for the vagaries of sample size, archaeological survival and osteological interpretation, the overall male:female sex ratio was 11.2:1 and can be compared with the overall sex ratios of 1.27:1 and 1:1.17 respectively from the 'normal' parish cemeteries of St Nicholas Shambles, London (White 1988), and St Helen-on-the-Walls, York (Dawes and Magilton 1980), and those of 17:1 and 19:1 respectively from the London-region monastic houses of Bermondsey (Connell and White in prep) and Stratford Langthorne (White 2004, 160). Where the sample sizes are largest, in the 14th century, the predominance of males either roughly equals that in the smaller samples or far exceeds it and those of Stratford Langthorne and Bermondsey; even in the other cases the male dominance is greater than those of both the churchyard and church of St Mary Graces (2.8:1 Open Area 9, 2.55:1 the church: Grainger and Phillpotts in prep a). This suggests that no part of Merton was similar to a parish cemetery or church, and more resembled the burial grounds and churches of other monasteries; like those it was overall a burial area to which restricted classes of laity were admitted. The limited information from the church suggests perhaps a greater emphasis on wealthy patrons and senior members of the monastic community. The size of the burial population increases dramatically in the 14th century, both in the cemetery and the church. This may reflect increased mortality or, more likely, a change in the size of the catchment – the canons were simply permitting more of the same types of people to be buried to increase priory revenue.

Stature analysed by period shows little that would differentiate areas within the cemetery or compared to the church (Chapter 7.11, 'Physical appearance'). Considered a possible indicator of status, stature could only be estimated from very small samples. In the 12th century, in Open Area 3, a single male was estimated at 1.78m, in Open Area 6, five males gave an average 1.74m. In the 13th century, the average male stature of 1.78m for Open Area 3 came from only two males, while that of Open Area 6 was 1.74m for six males. In the 14th century the earlier burials in Open Area 3, had an average male stature of 1.76m from two males, the later of 1.71m from seven, and in Open Area 6 1.72m from 15. From the 15th century, only Open Area 6 produced an estimate of 1.71m from three males. The church estimates of male stature are similarly based on poor samples: 1.74m from two burials in the 12th century; 1.72m from nine in the presbytery/Lady chapel and 1.74m from one in the north transept in the 13th century; and no estimates for the 14th century. In the chapter house: 1.79m was estimated from two burials in the 13th century, no estimates for the 14th century, and 1.75m from eight in the 15th century. These, although unreliable, suggest overall no significant difference in stature between those buried in the church and those in the cemetery, and compare favourably with values gained from other London churches for the medieval period: 1.72m for the churches of St Mary Spital (Conheeney 1997, 223) and St Mary Graces (Grainger and Phillpotts in prep a), 1.73m for the church of Stratford Langthorne (White 2004, 173). They are in excess of values for an external cemetery at St Mary Spital (1.69m) and the Black Death burial ground at St Mary Graces (1.67m) both likely to contain better cross sections of the lay population as a whole and/or be drawn from the poorer strata of society, whereas the cemetery of Cluniac Bermondsey produced a value of 1.72m (Conheeney 1997, 223; Grainger et al in prep; Steele in prep). This again perhaps suggests that Merton's cemetery (and that of Bermondsey) had a possibly higher status catchment.

Analysis of the age at death for the various areas over time is also bedevilled by the variety of sample sizes. In the 12th century, Open Area 6, with a far larger sample size, exhibited a slightly more dispersed age range, with a higher proportion of older people, than Open Area 3. In the 13th century both groups were more divergent, but Open Area 3 had a higher proportion of older adults (45+ years). Only three burials within the church were aged for this period – a child, a mature adult (26–45 years) and an older adult male – while two of the three males in the chapter house were older adults. Within the church in the 14th century, the first period with a significant sample size there, it may be significant that there were four young adults (17–25 years) in the main body of the north transept but none in the chapels. The two individuals from the presbytery that could be assigned to a specific age group were both older adults. The one individual in the chapter house was an older male. While in Open Area 3, the group to the west had a slight majority of mature adults over older adults, and those to the north of the infirmary had a slight majority of older adults, and two adolescents. In Open Area 6 there was a spread of age at death with a slight increase in children (1–16 years) over the 13th century (6.2% compared to 2.4%). The proportions in other age groups were very similar to those from this area for both preceding periods. In the 15th century Open Area 6 produced 28 individuals of whom 13 were mature and six older adults. In the nave, of the 12 aged, 10 were mature (including the single female) or older, and all 3 in the north transept were mature males; of the 16 males that could be aged in the chapter house 5 were mature and 10 older adults, with 1 adolescent. All of the above tentatively suggests a tendency towards the burial of mature and older adults (male) and, when allowed, older females in all areas throughout the life of the priory. This compares with the churchyard (OA9) and church of St Mary Graces, where only 14.5% and 8%

respectively of those interred were infants or juveniles, and Bermondsey where only a single individual from the cemetery was subadult (Grainger and Phillpotts in prep a; Steele in prep), whereas the parochial cemetery for instance at St Andrew, Fishergate, York, produced 36% subadults (under 20 years) (Stroud and Kemp 1993, 170).

The status of children in the medieval period at their death was extremely variable, and their burials are generally under-represented in excavated cemeteries. Here, at least four of the few immature burials present suggested they were of reasonably high status (two in the church and two in Caen cists). This may imply that only a limited number of children were admitted for burial and that these were all of relatively high status. No area appears to have been exclusively reserved for children; no areas may have been completely forbidden them either. Although none were buried in the south burial area (OA3) before c 1300, two adolescents aged between 13 and 16 were buried here in the 14th century, and a single young adult was buried in the 15th–16th century in the chapter house. It is unlikely that these interments were of novices; these were theoretically not admitted until the age of 17 (Burton 1994, 174). The burial location of novices unfortunate to meet an early death is at best uncertain. Five young adults (17–25 years), possibly novices or young canons, were interred to the south-east of the church, but suggest no distinct area for such burials.

Other possible indicators of status are certain types of pathology but here again significant differences between the areas were hard to detect, and within the church the sample sizes before the 14th century were too small for any conclusions to be drawn (Chapter 7.11; Table 58). Two types of pathologies found at Merton are to some extent considered indicative of status and occupation. The first is DISH or diffuse idiopathic skeletal hyperostosis which presents itself as bony abnormalities and excessive bone formation, often seen on the vertebrae. This condition is increasingly linked with obesity and late onset diabetes, and originally associated with monastic sites by Tony Waldron based on part of the present sample (1985, 1762–4), it may suggest a high calorie diet. This description could apply to high-ranking clergy or to wealthy laity. The condition was found in all periods and in individuals from all areas (Table 69), but the prevalence rates tended to be lower in the north burial area (OA6), slightly raised in the south burial area (OA3) and possibly in the chapter house (B3b), where sample size was a particular problem, and highest within the church. The general prevalence of DISH for the site was 8.4%, compared, in London, with 7.8% at Bermondsey (Connell and White in prep), 8.2% at St Mary Graces (Waldron in prep), 8.7% at Stratford Langthorne (White 2004, 176), and well below that of St Mary Spital, 20% (Conheeney 1997, 228).

The second possibly indicative pathology comprises the growth of periosteal new bone on the tibia (Table 58). Amongst other pathological conditions, this might be associated with the maintenance of an upright posture for a long period, possibly associated with the choir as described by Harvey for the monks of Westminster (Harvey 1993, 109). The growth of periosteal bone in general was the most common pathology in the majority of the samples from Merton, excluding general degenerative conditions, and the tibia was the most common site for growth in those cases. The prevalence of some enthesopathies (Conheeney 1995) has also been associated with posture but this evidence must be viewed with caution (Chapter 7.11, 'Physical activity').

Given that in both the instances the sample sizes under consideration are comparatively large, it is possible to suggest that both the south burial area (OA3) and the church in general were more likely to contain higher status individuals, either clergy or laity. There were, as noted above, two areas of exclusively male burials – potentially clergy – that is, the chapter house, and north of the infirmary chapel in Open Area 3 suggesting a possible concentration of canon burials here.

In general terms the pathology is of less use in differentiating between the different burial areas. Where physical description was possible in the 12th century, the two external cemetery groups appeared similar. Both had the same femoral and tibial morphology. Both had a high rate of the non-metric trait of supraorbital notch and similar prevalence of most of the other non-metric traits of interest (Table 57). The north burial area (OA6) presented a much wider range of skeletal pathological conditions than the south (OA3), probably because of the larger sample size. Both areas had periosteal new bone as the most frequent skeletal pathology, although those pathology types that did vary, for example osteoarthritis, osteophytosis, cribra orbitalia, healed periosteal bone on the pulmonary surface of ribs and occurrences of periosteal new bone, were more prevalent in Open Area 3 (Table 58; Table 70). Dental pathology was similar between the two samples with females having better dental health in both cases. In the 13th century, the groups were similar to each other and to the 12th-century groups. For the 14th century osteological analysis separated the burials from Open Area 3 into two groups but in most respects, particularly with regard to physique, both these and those of the 13th century were similar where there were sufficient data to allow comparison. Osteological analysis separated the church burials during the 14th century into two groups, those from the new eastern extension and those from the north transept. The individuals from the small, east end sample had periosteal new bone and healed periosteal bone on the pulmonary surface of the ribs as the two most common pathologies, other than osteoarthritis; there are possible similarities with the larger transept group but here these two pathologies had lower prevalence rates than osteoarthritis, osteophytosis and general degenerative conditions. In the 15th- to 16th-century nave and north transept groups there were no significant differences from the 14th-century north transept group, other than the prevalence rates of the relevant pathologies.

Burial practice

A tentative typology of late Saxon and early medieval grave types has already been established for London, from the

evidence of the 11th- to 12th-century parish graveyard of St Nicholas Shambles (Schofield 1988, 18–25). Six types have been identified: I, simple burial, perhaps in a (wooden) coffin; II, with a stone pillow; III, grave with a floor only of chalk and mortar; IV, a cist of mortared stones, or simply lined with chalk and mortar; V, charcoal burial; VI, grave lined with dry-laid tile or stone. The burials on the priory site provide more examples of types I, II and IV, ranging in date from the 12th to the 15th/16th centuries, together with a 14th-century possible 'ash' burial and a number of 'plank' burials.

Grave alignment

All the graves excavated were aligned broadly west–east with the head to the west in line with standard medieval Christian practice. Within the monastic cemetery all graves were roughly aligned to the church and or the infirmary chapel with some variation to the south-west and north-west. A drift in alignment towards the north-east, north-east of the church beyond the guideline of its walls during the 13th century may suggest a number of possible factors: a lack of, or insubstantial/impermanent, grave markers; significant time lapse between interments; an unidentified feature such as a chapel or churchyard cross to which the graves were aligned; or poor cemetery management. Some row structuring was evident, particularly to the north of the Lady chapel and the infirmary chapel during the 14th century and possibly reflecting reorganisation of the burial ground then, which suggests the regulation of popular burial areas.

Within the church, alignments typically followed the axis of the building, with the exception of the grave of an older male [6066] (Fig 129) at the west end of the nave in the 15th–16th century which was aligned slightly north-east–south-west.

Grave cuts

There was considerable variety in grave shape. In the cemetery many grave cuts were not identified and the excavated outline follows the skeleton. The graves were better identified within the church and chapter house and tended to be regular in plan. Reasonably rectangularly shaped graves may suggest coffins or more care on the part of, or just the standard practice of, the gravedigger. Size was largely determined by the size of the individual and/or coffin; double graves required larger cuts, and occasionally graves within the church were wider to insert stone or wood coffins or cist linings.

Graves were both steep sided and shallow and the bases varied in regularity. However, the majority of graves were truncated and generally only approximately 0.30–0.40m deep or less. The deepest recorded burial was [3722] (period M4) at the east end of the north aisle, being 1.14m deep, in a cluster of relatively deep graves that may have been truncated, while some burials within the 14th-century (period M3) north transept ranged in depth between 0.60m and 1.00m. At least two 14th-century cemetery burials may not have been truncated as they had a slab over, which may have been at ground level; burial [2905] in a wooden coffin was 0.63m deep, cist burial [5758] was 0.78m deep.

Body position

The majority of burials were supine with the head to the west. The arms were generally laid by the side but occasionally over the body with the hands on the pelvis, at times crossed. The use of pillows, and head niches in stone coffins, lead coffins and cist burials suggests containment of the head to prevent slippage to the side.

There were three prone burials from the 13th and 14th centuries in the cemetery. Burial [2856], in a multiple burial, was probably thrown in deliberately, without a shroud or coffin; as all three appeared to be casually buried, they all may have been buried in haste having died of communicable disease (or perceived to have done so) and/or been a transient buried out of charity. Prone burial [7098] was in a coffin, while [4503] was probably in a coffin, but no trace of one remained. These two, probably both in coffins, may have been accidentally positioned; there is nothing to suggest that either was deliberately placed prone, and one [7098] from the north side of the infirmary chapel in the 14th century (period M3) is more likely to have been a canon than not. Prone burials, although uncommon, are known elsewhere in London: at least one from Stratford Langthorne (burial population of c 600) (Barber et al 2004, 98); approximately 15–20 at St Mary Spital (burial population of c 10,000) (C Thomas, pers comm), and one in the Black Death burial ground at East Smithfield (burial population of c 750) (Grainger et al in prep).

Shrouds

The majority of the interments were probably shroud burials, but evidence for the shrouds was limited. Possible examples in the church are [2934] (period M3) which may have been dressed or shrouded, and burial [2703] (period M3) in lead coffin <S12> (see below) and [2107] (period M4) buried with the ?hernia belt <S254> which may both have been shrouded (Chapter 7.5). Usually only the body position suggested the corpse had been tightly wrapped and it is uncertain if shrouds were always tight. Calculation of the number of shroud burials was not attempted.

Dressed interments

A number of individuals appeared to be dressed when interred. These occurred in most periods in the church and the cemetery; all were adult males.

Within the church most dressed interments occurred in the 14th–16th centuries and all were in or near the north transept. The 14th-century burials [2402] and [3379] produced gold thread (<S19>, <S21>; below, 'Grave goods'), suggesting rich clothing, possibly ecclesiastical. Textile, possibly worsted and silk, was associated with a mature male [2651], and this individual was also wearing shoes <S18>. Burial [2114] was also possibly wearing shoes, as suggested by shoe buckles <S232>. Burial [2934] discussed below ('Head supports') may also have been dressed (or shrouded).

Several burials had buckles on the pelvic region: [3172] <S208>, [3667] <S209>, [2858] <S206> and <S207> (Fig 23; Fig 101); [7573] <S214> (Fig 107), [7606] <S216> (also strapends <S244> and <S245>), [2531] <S204> and <S205>. Burial [3458] was interred with a belt and seven copper-alloy accessories <S226> (Fig 217), a remarkable combination, probably worn in life. These individuals were probably also dressed when interred rather than in shrouds. In London, the St Mary Graces cemeteries produced 16 such buckles, often in pairs on the pelvis, 12 from victims of the Black Death c 1348–9 and four from the later churchyard, post-1350, all on the balance of probability associated with clothing (Grainger et al in prep; Grainger and Phillpotts in prep a). The ?hernia belt <S254> worn by [2107] has been discussed elsewhere (above, 4.6, and Chapter 7.5).

Stone coffins

Five stone coffins were found: one 13th century, three 14th century, and one unphased (Table 22). Two were in the church and two in the south burial area (OA3) suggesting a higher status for this area than the north (OA6). The fifth was immediately to the north of the north nave wall and was empty, possibly because of early 20th-century excavation or other modern disturbance (Chapter 3.5). The coffins were rectangular, made of Reigate stone, sandstone or ?limestone. Two coffins [2164] and [2933] were carved with head recesses and three ([2933], [5202], [7400]; Fig 44) had drain holes. Coffin [2933] also contained a chalk pillow and the interment

Table 22 Stone coffins from St Mary Merton

Period	Land use	Context no. of coffin	Context no. of skeleton	Stone type	Sex	Age at death (years)
M2	south burial area (OA3)	[7400]	[7401]	sandstone	male	45+
M3	church (B1), presbytery	[2164]	[2381]	?sandstone	male	45+
M3	church (B1), north transept	[2933]	[2934]	?limestone	male	26–45
M3	south burial area (OA3)	[5202]	[5023]	Reigate stone	unknown	unknown
Unphased M1–M4	north burial area (OA6)	[5518]	not analysed	?	-	-

[2934] was possibly dressed (Fig 102). All coffins contained mature males where the skeleton was present and could be sexed, two aged 45 or over.

Cist burials

Thirty-six (definite or possible) stone-lined graves or cists, including a double burial of a male and female, were identified in this study (Table 23). Although the construction method and stone/materials used varied considerably, all suggest higher status burials. Fourteen such burials were in the chapter house, 9 in the south burial area (OA3), 10 in the north (OA6), and 3 (including the double burial) in the church. Most contained adult males, but in the 14th century (period M3) three cists in the cemetery contained possible females, in addition to the female in the double burial in the church, and two 12th-century (period M1) examples in Open Area 6 contained small children (aged 1–6 years).

Some cist burials were disturbed and the overall shape could not be determined, but most cists were rectangular where complete. Of those, at least five had head-shaped niches at their west end. Eighteen cists were constructed exclusively using Reigate stone, either in blocks or part blocks, two from Caen stone, two described as 'sandstone' (Fig 169), and two from chalk blocks. One was a combination of Reigate stone and sandstone blocks and four were a combination of Reigate stone and other materials such flint or chalk (Fig 170). The remainder were composed of chalk fragments or flint, or unspecified stone. The two cist burials from the 13th century in Open Area 3 recorded as constructed from 'sandstone' blocks, were not retained or analysed, but these were most probably Caen stone or limestone.

Of the 18 exclusively Reigate stone cists, 12 were in the chapter house (2 from the 13th century and 10 from the 15th–16th century, out of 32 burials in all), 1 double burial was in the north transept and from the 14th century, and 5

Table 23 *Cist burials from St Mary Merton*

Period	Land use	Context no. of cist	Context no. of skeleton	Stone type	Sex	Age at death (years)
M1	south burial area (OA3)	[5763]	[5762]	Reigate stone	unknown	adult
M1	south burial area (OA3)	[5839]	[5841]	Reigate stone	unknown	unknown
M1	north burial area (OA6)	[3052]	[3084]	Caen stone	unknown	1–6
M1	north burial area (OA6)	[3141]	[3235]	Caen stone	unknown	1–6
M2	chapter house (B3b)	-	[602]	Reigate stone	male	45+
M2	chapter house (B3b)	-	[738]	Reigate stone	unknown	unknown
M2	south burial area (OA3)	[7403]	-	Reigate stone; empty	-	-
M2	south burial area (OA3)	[7429]; [7491]	[7493]	Reigate stone	male	45+
M2	south burial area (OA3)	[7435]	-	Reigate stone, ?sandstone; empty	-	-
M2	south burial area (OA3)	[7449]	[7448]	mortar/flint lining	unknown	adult
M2	south burial area (OA3)	[7457]	[7455]	sandstone	male	45+
M2	south burial area (OA3)	[7509]	[7510]	sandstone	male	26–45
M2	north burial area (OA6)	-	[2537]	mortar/chalk lining	male	26–45
M2	north burial area (OA6)	-	[2577]	chalk, mortar	male	17–25
M2	north burial area (OA6)	[2379]	[2378]	flint	unknown	adult
M2	north burial area (OA6)	[4447]	[4226]	chalk	male	26–45
M3	church, east end (B1)	-	[2387]	Reigate stone, flint, peg tiles	?male	adult
M3	church, north transept (B1)	[2351]	[2352] [2353]	Reigate stone; double burial	female male	26–45 45+
M3	church, north transept (B1)	[2843]	[2844]	chalk	male	26–45
M3	chapter house (B3b)	[575.2/3]	-	unmortared stone cist; empty	-	-
M3	south burial area (OA3)	[5756]; [5809]	[5758]	Reigate stone; cist capped by slab	?female	17–25
M3	north burial area (OA6)	-	[4054]	unmortared flint	male	45+
M3	north burial area (OA6)	[4446]	[4081]	Reigate stone, chalk	?female	26–45
M3	north burial area (OA6)	[6086]	[4039]	Reigate stone, flint, mortar	?female	17–25
M4	chapter house (B3b)	[110.1]	[672]	Reigate stone	male	26–45*
M4	chapter house (B3b)	[324.4]	[622]	Reigate stone	male	45+
M4	chapter house (B3b)	[338.2]	[689]	Reigate stone	unknown	unknown
M4	chapter house (B3b)	[373.2]	[671]	Reigate stone	male	adult
M4	chapter house (B3b)	[380.2]	[623]	Reigate stone	male	45+
M4	chapter house (B3b)	[412]	[325.2]	unmortared stone	male	45+
M4	chapter house (B3b)	[460.3]	[599]	Reigate stone	male	45+
M4	chapter house (B3b)	[534.2]	[601]	Reigate stone	male	45+
M4	chapter house (B3b)	[542.2]	[600]	Reigate stone	male	26+
M4	chapter house (B3b)	[1042]	[105]	Reigate stone	male	45+
M4	chapter house (B3b)	[4702]	[598]	Reigate stone	male	45+
M4	north burial area (OA6)	-	[4032]	Reigate stone, chalk (head/shoulder region)	male	26–45

*: plus disarticulated human bone

Fig 169 'Sandstone' block cist burial [7455] (OA3), looking west (1.0m scale)

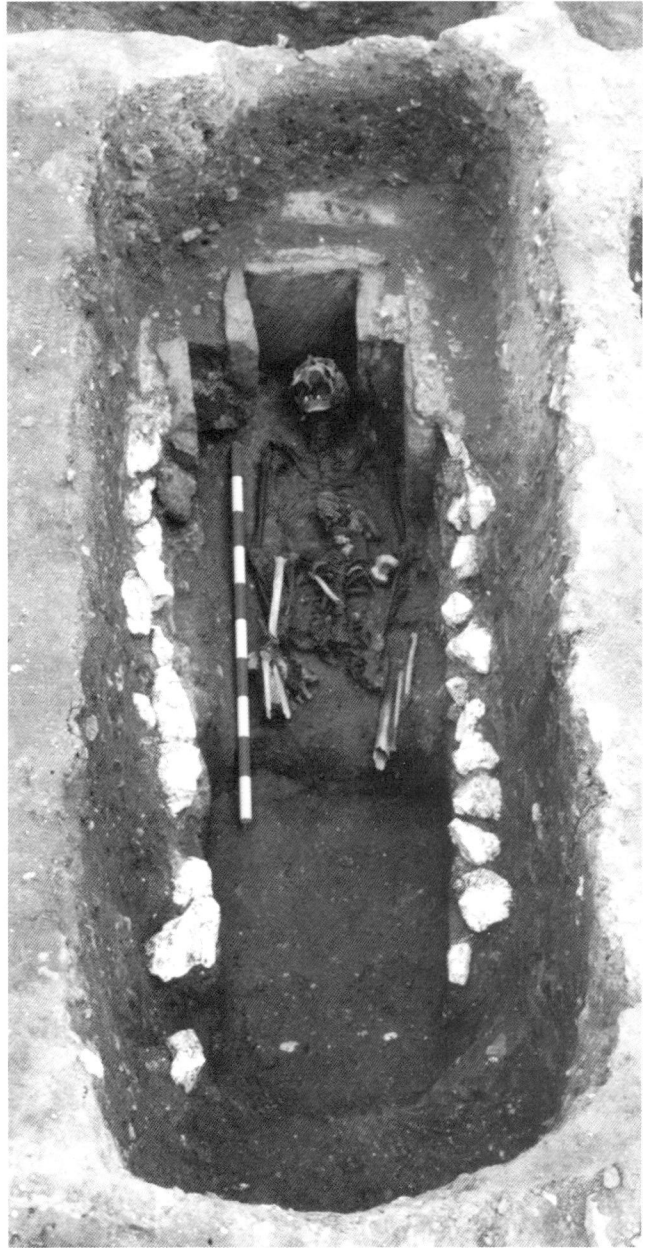

Fig 170 Reigate stone and chalk cist burial [4032] (OA6), looking west (1.0m scale)

were in Open Area 3 (2 12th century, 2 13th century and 1 14th century). One Reigate stone cist was empty and 4 individuals could not be sexed, but the remainder contained 12 males, 1 female (the double burial) and 1 ?female. Of the 12 males, the majority were older adults (45+) at death; 10 of the males were from the chapter house. The Caen stone cists of two small children to the north of the presbytery in the 12th century are unusually opulent for ones so young (Fig 25); they must have been of relatively high status, and their proximity and similarity of burial suggests they were related. This distribution of Reigate stone linings might suggest that it was the most expensive and desirable material, but it would have been readily available as it was such a common building stone on the site (Chapter 7.2, 'Methodology').

The largely unworn paviors used to construct grave linings may, like the plank burials, have come from earlier structures,

perhaps early church or chapel buildings; the use of paviors in a 12th-century grave [5762] may be evidence for this.

Cist burial was in use on the site from the 12th to the 15th century. It was especially popular in the chapter house during the late 14th–15th centuries (period M4), but possibly practised continuously there; some cists may have been reused. Generally, cist burials continued to be used in churches and chapels up to the Dissolution (Thomas et al 1997, 127) but were uncommon in external cemeteries in the later medieval period. At Merton only four external cist burials date to the 14th century, and one (partial) example to the 15th–16th century.

Cist burials accounted for c 5% of the graves excavated (36 out of 721), less apparently than at Bermondsey (20 out of 202) (Steele in prep) but far greater than other London monastic sites such as St Mary Spital (one) (Thomas et al 1997,

153

122) and Stratford Langthorne (none out of 647) (Barber et al 2004, 94–116).

Lead coffins

Three plain 14th-century lead coffins <S12>–<S14> were found, two in the presbytery, the other in the south burial area (OA3) (Table 24). Both church coffins contained adult males; the other individual was unidentified but the coffin was adult size (<S14>, Fig 108).

Both presbytery coffins were 'anthropomorphic', that is moulded around the head and tapered towards the feet. Burial [2701] had been truncated at the legs and only the upper part of the coffin <S13> remained (Fig 100). Burial [2703] in coffin <S12> (Fig 99) appeared to have been wrapped in a shroud: small amounts of a white material were found on the skeleton (not analysed). The lead coffin <S14> (Fig 108) from Open Area 3 was close to the north wall of the infirmary chapel amongst a group of tightly packed burials. The coffin was a trapezoidal box, tapering towards the feet and with a separate lid. This again suggests a higher status for this south burial area. Although relatively rare, medieval lead coffins have been recorded in the London area: four from Stratford Langthorne (Barber et al 2004, 101–2), and two at St Mary Spital (D Bowsher, pers comm).

Wooden coffins

It is probable that the number of wooden coffins positively identified is an underestimate. The survival of timber was rare and the position of nails not recorded in many graves, or the number of nails was low enough to suggest their residuality in the grave fill. It has been estimated that a minimum of a dozen nails is required to construct a coffin (Rodwell 1989, 152; Thomas et al 1997, 38). Additionally, although excavators suggested coffins were present in regularly shaped graves, the lack of other physical evidence to support this means that these are not included in the following minimum estimates.

Definite evidence of coffins in the form of wooden remains and/or nail patterns was found in all areas, and all periods (M1–M4): at least 16 in the north burial area (OA6), 24 in the south (OA3), 1 in the church (B1), and 3 in the chapter house (B3b). There was no obvious significance in their distribution except for a concentration north of the infirmary (B4). Five coffins from Open Area 3 were identified as oak; one was of beech. Dendrochronological samples for four coffined burials

[5293], [7099], [7121], [7635] interred in the 14th century were dated to after 1131, after 1076, after 1128, and after 1096 (Table 71), but none had the heartwood/sapwood boundary (below, 'Plank burials').

Few complete nail patterns were recorded and generally not levelled, so three-dimensional reconstruction is not possible. With burial [2905] nails were found surrounding the grave cut (ten, recorded mainly along the southern and eastern edge), although how the coffin was constructed or sealed could not be established because of the scarcity of nails to the north and west (Rodwell 1989, 152; Thomas et al 1997, 38). However, coffins may have had jointed edges or wooden pegs and only a few nails were required to secure a lid (Thomas et al 1997, 124).

The possible reuse of a wooden object as a coffin was recorded. Individual [4673] in the north burial area (OA6) was interred in a rather large wooden 'coffin' cut to the west by a 15th- to 16th-century buttress extension (period M4) (Fig 49). The coffin was wide in relation to the body and of unusual construction suggesting a different original function. The burial's feet extended beyond the lower end of the 'coffin' suggesting a ?failed attempt to modify this to house the body. The object's original function was unclear although it is similar to one found at Hulton Abbey (Staffordshire) and identified there as a boat (McGrail 1978, 215). However, Damian Goodburn has subsequently suggested that the Hulton example may in fact be a trough, and that the Merton 'coffin' may therefore also be the lower portion of a trough (D Goodburn, pers comm).

Plank burials

Potential plank burials were identified in 20 cases: [3869], [4611], [4860], [4893] and [7559] in the 12th century, [4286], [4498], [4530], [4647] and [4649] (a double burial), [4655] and [4658] in the 13th century, and [4768], [5056], [5080], [7163], [7235], in the 14th century and burials [4567] and [4707] (Fig 141) were unphased (periods M1–M4). Burials [5056], [5080], [5293], [7163], [7235] and [7559] were found in the south burial area (OA3), the rest in the north (OA6) (Figs 47–9). The term 'plank' burial is perhaps slightly misleading; the individuals interred were covered by a variety of timber. In certain cases this involved several timbers and was quite elaborate, for example with supports and/or cross-pieces, or combined with the use of Reigate stone blocks [4530]. Five burials produced dendrochronological dates: [4893] (period M1) after 1009, [4530] (period M2) after

Table 24 Lead coffins from St Mary Merton

Period	Land use	Context no. (catalogue no.) of coffin	Context no. of skeleton	Sex	Age at death
M3	church (B1), presbytery	[2270] (<S13>)	[2701]	male	adult
M3	church (B1), presbytery	[2583] (<S12>)	[2703]	male	adult
M3	south cemetery (OA3)	[7060] (<S14>)	not analysed	-	-

1107, [4567] and [4707] (unphased) after 1091 and after 1036, all without the heartwood/sapwood boundary; one of two samples from [5056] (period M3) however gave a felling date of 1165–1210 (Table 71; cf the wooden coffins above).

At Merton this practice was associated almost exclusively with the burial of adult males (where the age and sex could be established). The double burial may suggest a familial connection, although this was not obvious from skeletal analysis, and does not preclude both being Merton canons. However, one plank burial [4498] was of a female adult. This, and the spatial distribution and variations in detail of the practice as found, may suggest that here the practice does not equate with the burial of canons. The placing of timber over the interments may simply be a 'poor' coffin or have other significance. The planks were usually positioned over the bodies but they may originally have been used to carry the deceased to the grave and subsequently placed in the grave.

This practice, although perhaps purely for reasons of economy or local custom, is reminiscent of that found in the eastern cemetery at Bordesley Abbey where a number of male burials were covered with reused timbers. One timber was dendrochronologically dated to 1150±9, that is only a decade or two after that abbey's foundation, and it is suggested that this may have been the burial of one of the first monks, covered with a timber of special significance, perhaps even saved from the original wooden church (Hirst and Wright 1989, 307–8; Astill et al 2004, 126). Conceivably some of the timber here at Merton could have come from the 12th-century church or even an earlier chapel recently demolished; or perhaps from buildings on the original site, removed and preserved for their symbolic significance (Astill and Wright 1993, 126). But more practical, and secular, interpretations are possible. The lack of sapwood on most of the Merton samples makes these dendrochronological results (where the 'after …' dates all fall into the late 11th and first half of the 12th century) of limited use for dating purposes; radial sections like planks and coffin boards only need to have lost a few centimetres of timber through poor/discontinuous waterlogging to be missing many decades worth of tree-rings (I Tyers, pers comm). Only one sample, from a 14th-century burial, produced a felling date, in the later 12th century/early 13th century. Reuse is a possibility, in particular with regard to the timbers in the 14th-century burials – wood from earlier structures or buildings, possibly only now being demolished or stockpiled timber. (The possible timber and daub building (S1, period M1), for example, was replaced in the 13th century by the infirmary complex.) Burials from the London Guildhall also included plank burials of 11th- to 13th-century date within the parish cemetery. These included children, adolescents and at least one female burial and are more likely to have been entirely secular (Bowsher et al in prep).

Head supports

Two examples of head supports or pillows were recorded: a Reigate stone 'pillow' for an older (45+) male [2434] in the 12th century (OA6) and a chalk 'pillow' in the 14th-century north transept for a mature (26–45) male [2934] in a limestone coffin and with a shroud, or dressed (Fig 102). Daniell suggests this practice was restricted to earlier burials and only exceptionally extended into the 13th century (1997, 160). However at Merton, although rare, it would appear to continue into the 14th century. In cist burial [4032] (period M4, OA6), a mature male was interred with a Reigate stone and chalk head surround; the head did not rest on the stone.

Grave pillows or head supports are recorded on other London sites. Two from Stratford Langthorne, although one of these is a crushed chalk or chalk rubble placed under or around the head, and two from St Mary Spital within the infirmary cemetery (dated to the 13th century) (Barber et al 2004, 104; Thomas et al 1997, 121). Twenty-two cases at St Nicholas Shambles were confined to the 11th and 12th centuries (White 1988, 20–2). The use of a stone head support may be penitential or directly biblical; Jacob used a stone pillow and dreamed of a stairway to heaven (Genesis 28: 10–22).

'Ash' burial

There was a single 14th-century possible ash burial [839] (OA3) of an older adult (45+) male. The charcoal burials of the 9th to 12th century belong to an earlier and perhaps unrelated rite (Daniell 1997, 158), but comparable burials occurred in London at Stratford Langthorne (3, spanning the 13th and 14th centuries: 2 in the church and 1 in the cemetery) and a large number at St Mary Graces (19 in total, 14 from the mid 14th-century Black Death cemetery, 4 from the churchyard and 1 from the church dating to the mid 14th century or later) (Barber et al 2004, 103; Grainger et al in prep; Grainger and Phillpotts in prep a). Three (two definite SPT82 and SRP98, one possible SRP98) burials were excavated at St Mary Spital (D Bowsher, pers comm 2006) and this type of burial was also recorded at St Nicholas Shambles for an infant (White 1988, 24). These later ash burials appear to be a rite principally associated with the London region, and may have the simple practical purpose of soaking up body fluids in coffins or graves. It may also be penitential and related to the laying out of the corpse on sack-cloth and ashes mentioned in documentary sources (Daniell 1997, 30) or, since in some cases (St Mary Graces and St Mary Spital) analysis has shown that the ash used is most likely reused hearth rakings, it may be a reminder of home.

Grave goods

Grave goods were few and ecclesiastical, that is the lead/tin chalices and patens from the 12th century (burial [4881] <S24>, Fig 24, and <S27>; burial [4593] <S25>, Fig 24) and the 14th century ([2905] <S22>, Fig 111; Fig 112) ([3379], <S23> and <S26>); additionally gold thread <S21> was found with [3379]. The presence of the chalice and paten suggests the burial of a priest, the gold thread perhaps someone in higher office. It is uncertain whether the priest burials identified in this way represent the burial of Augustinian canons or secular priests. The small number involved suggests the latter, since all the canons were priests, although the former remains possible if another factor was involved, for example a way of denoting the burial of a canon serving a particular chapel or of a particular rank.

Grave markers

No tombs were recorded *in situ*; however, *ex situ* decorated stonework suggests monuments existed which were intended to show at ground level. A decorated and unweathered grave slab <A64> reused in the 14th-century eastern church extension probably comes from the 13th-century church (Fig 38). Half a Purbeck, or other marble, coffin lid [5647], carved with a cross, was also retrieved from the 13th-century south transept and had presumably originated from a 12th- to 13th-century grave. A carved Reigate stone graveslab capped the cist burial of a young adult (?female) [5758] in the south burial area (OA3) in the 14th century, pre-dating c 1350 (Fig 109). The grave was disturbed leaving only the eastern half of the lid. The design appeared to be a staff or possibly the lower part of a cross. Burial [2905] had a stone slab set in mortar over the western end of the grave (OA6, period M3).

Charnel pits

At least 15 pits thought to be charnel pits were recorded. Most were small, the largest [7061] in the south burial area (OA3, period M3), represented many individuals and was possibly dug to clear the area to the north of the infirmary chapel, prior to the dense group of burials interred during the 14th century.

4.11 The priory in its wider context

Surrey contained relatively few religious houses. At Merton's foundation, the only existing houses were Benedictine Chertsey (refounded by AD 964) 22.5km to the west, and the small alien priory at Tooting (Bec), and another at Lewisham (Kent). The nearest female house, Benedictine Malling (c 1090), lay 40.2km away in Kent, and the first English Cistercian house at Waverley in the far south-west of the county dated to 1128. Other local Augustinian houses to be founded in the future were Newark Priory (Henry II), and the hospitals at Tandridge and Reigate (both in Surrey), founded in the late 12th and 13th centuries respectively. Merton rapidly became a major landowner in Surrey and the south-east (above, 4.9); it was near enough to the main routes between London and the south-west and south coast to be called on frequently for hospitality.

Merton was essentially a rural house, comparable to Newark or rural/sub-urban Stratford Langthorne, but its association with the city and court undoubtedly influenced its structure and life. Within the Augustinian Order Merton's income was only exceeded in 1535 by that of Cirencester Abbey at £1051,

and it could truly be considered one of the wealthiest Augustinian foundations (Robinson 1980, appendix 14, 382). Indeed, although in 1535 Merton's annual income was assessed at £960 (*Val Eccl*, ii, 48–51), the priory's London holdings at the time failed to be included and its income was similar to that of Cirencester in the 1530s. The priory's total income in 1536 was £1039. This figure compares favourably with those of nearby monastic houses, with £474 for Bermondsey and £511 for Stratford Langthorne. The *Valor ecclesiasticus* lists 24 rectories associated with Merton in the 1530s (Robinson 1980, appendix 24, 457). These rectories were widespread, some being 170 miles (273.6km) away. The priory had at one time held property outside the country including a church in Caen (Robinson 1980, 235). It would appear that Merton consistently remained reasonably well off, although happy to solicit assistance when needed, especially (like many other houses) for building campaigns.

The documentary sources also suggest that the priory played an active part in the affairs of the Augustinian Order. Merton aided in the foundation of other houses such as Taunton, Bodmin, Llanthony, Holyrood (Edinburgh, Midlothian), St Gregory Canterbury, Cirencester, and Dover in the 12th century (Burton 1994, 47). In 1145, Prior Robert and subprior Robert witnessed both a grant by St Paul's of the site of Holy Trinity Caddington (Bedfordshire) and adjacent woodland to Christina, the celebrated anchorite of Markyate, and subsequently its consecration (*Early Charters St Paul*, nos 154, 156). As early as 1146–54, William Earl of Chichester, when founding a religious house at his manor of Buckenham, was advised by William Bishop of Norwich to do so according to the Order of St Augustine and the institution of St Mary of Merton (*Cal Chart R*, 1300–26, 368). The prior was clearly considered senior enough to intervene and mediate effectively in the affairs of the Order and occasionally served as arbiter in adjudicating disputes between other religious institutions. Prior Thomas mediated in 1222 between the bishop of London and the abbot of Westminster concerning the church of Stanes (Staines, Middlesex) and the manor of Sunbury (*Chron Majora*, iii, 75) and Prior Walter was employed by the Bishop of Durham in settling a dispute within his diocese at Coniscliffe in 1256–7 (ibid, vi, 326–7, 340).

The priory was actively involved with the Crown, notably during the reign of Henry III. Although not a royal foundation, its founder Gilbert had close connections with the Crown, particularly Queen Matilda, who gave the priory moral and material support. However, royal patronage could be highly selective: Edward I and Edward II were infrequent visitors. The priory dealt financially with the Crown on many occasions, through loans, with a pattern of reciprocal indebtedness. Corrodies continued to be the most regular, and perhaps the most burdensome, service provided by the priory for the Crown. In July 1235 Merton was the collection point for the royal aid levied in Surrey and a council of barons held there in 1236 assented to statutes, concerning among other matters women's dower and wills, taking their name from Merton (*Ann Monast*, i, 249, iii, 144; *Cal Close R*, 1234–7, 191, 353; *Chron*

Majora, iii, 340–3). Also convened at Merton were a royal council of 1255 (*Cal Close R*, 1254–6, 158–9) and a convocation of the church in 1258 summoned by Archbishop Boniface (*Ann Monast*, i, 411–12). The priory continued in its occasional role of agent and creditor to the Crown in the 16th century. In 1513 the prior was appointed as one of the six commissioners for Surrey charged with seizing the property of all known subjects of the king of Scots (*L and P Hen VIII*, i(2), 2222 no. 16). Around the year 1522 the priory was required to lend £133 6s 8d as its contribution to a general loan to be made by the spirituality for the King's personal expenses in the recovery of the French crown; Merton's was a significantly larger contribution than those of St Mary Graces (£66 13s 4d), Bermondsey and Southwark (£100 each), although smaller than that of Waltham Holy Cross (Essex) (£200), Westminster and Reading Abbeys (£1000 each) (ibid, iii(2), 1047 no. 2483).

The increasing scale and pretension of the church in the 13th and 14th centuries suggest huge investment, at times aided by royal patronage. This resulted in a church 110m long at its greatest extent, amongst the largest churches in the Order in England (Robinson 1980, appendix 19, 397) and in the area of what is now Greater London. Belatedly, in the 13th century, adopting a plain Cistercian-type plan, decorative detail nonetheless suggests the house could afford an opulent architectural style. This is illustrated by the decorated and plain-glazed mosaic tiling employed in the 13th-century chapter house and church. The elaborate decoration found on the Merton tiles is not known from elsewhere; such tiles would have been slow and expensive to manufacture and may have been specially made for the priory. Similarities between the worked stone of St Stephen's chapel Westminster and Merton may suggest that at least one of the architects working at St Stephen's also worked on Merton's 14th-century church; equally, similarities with the eastern extension of St Augustine's Bristol suggest more widely travelled masons and influences, including Continental. The high social level of patronage of Augustinian foundations means that regionalism is perhaps of less significance here; only the Cistercians exerted a greater central control over the form of their priories (Cambridge 1977, 286). However, early Augustinian churches were subject to great variability. Although Merton and Newark can be regarded as 'second wave' Augustinian foundations, the general layout of Merton may suggest Augustinian foundations were more flexible in approach here, for example the position of the 13th-century cloister and the changing form of the chapter house. Other Augustinian foundations indicate plans modified as necessary: Haughmond Abbey with its unusual double cloister plan or Llanthony Priory with the dorter in the west range or Bolton Priory (Yorkshire West Riding) with its angled south transept. The full range of Augustinian plan forms is not reflected in surviving examples; peculiar hybrid plans where apsidal side chapels co-exist with square presbyteries existed at St Martin's Priory, Dover and Holy Trinity Priory, Aldgate (Plumptre 1861, 12, pl 3; Schofield and Lea 2005, 24–5).

Burial customs at Merton indicate a large number of higher status interments. Five stone coffins, three lead coffins and 36 cist burials – including the burials of small children – suggest the house attracted requests for burial possibly well beyond those of monastic personnel, servants and the families of local patrons. The church held relatively high-status burials, including females and children, compared to the external burial areas. The higher prevalence of diffuse idiopathic skeletal hyperostosis (DISH) in the church also suggests a privileged lifestyle. The diverse group of game bird species and game in general found indicate high-status consumption. Artefactual evidence suggests the priory mainly relied on London and local markets. The ceramics found come from Surrey and London with occasional imports from Europe. Overall the finds assemblage gives an impression of utilitarian material culture, with exceptions such as the ornate spectacle-frame fragment. There is little suggesting affluence apart from the gold finger ring, the threads from cloth-of-gold, and perhaps the unusually high incidence of coin loss. Dress accessories were usually of base metal, mainly buckles, notably plain, circular versions of copper alloy and iron. However, it should be noted that the artefacts represent a minute percentage of goods that must have originally existed at the priory. The documented presence of royal and other guests within the house is not immediately apparent from the material culture recovered, but Merton's building campaigns were ambitious, its influence considerable and in size and status, although never elevated to an abbey, Merton ranked among the larger houses of the Order. Indeed, one historian of the Augustinian Order (Dickinson 1950, 116–17) described Merton as 'perhaps the most influential of all the English houses of regular canons, certainly one of the very few that could vie in importance with the noblest Continental houses of the order'.

5

The Dissolution and post-medieval period

5.1 Dissolution activity (period P1)

Documentary evidence

In 1535 Sir William FitzWilliam wrote to Cromwell that 'we have done nothing with the abbeys and priories, because Masters Weston and Danaster informed us that you had appointed two of your own auditors for that purpose. Now we are told that your auditors will only meddle with Martyn Abbey, St Mary Overys and Bermondsey, and the Spital in Southwark. Let us know what we are to do' (L and P Hen VIII, ix, no. 4). On 29 September Thomas Legh wrote to Cromwell from Chertsey Abbey that 'at Merton I dismissed two canons; ten more would have been dismissed, but I would not consent until I knew your pleasure, for then only eight would have been left' (ibid, no. 472). In Cromwell's *Valor* of monastic lands in 1535 Merton was valued at £960 16s 6d, considerably higher than Bermondsey (£548), St Mary Overy Southwark (£624), Stratford Langthorne (£511), Holy Trinity Aldgate (£355) and St Mary Clerkenwell (£262) (Val Eccl, ii, 48–51).

On 16 April 1538 John Husee reported to Lord Lisle that 'Martyn Abbey shall be shortly suppressed' (Val Eccl, vi(1), 782). On that day Merton Priory surrendered to the Crown, granting to 'the illustrious prince and lord Henry VIII all the said monastery, house and priory of Merton' and its possessions in 20 counties. Down the left-hand margin of the document appear the signatures of 15 inmates: John Ramsey prior, John Debnam subprior, Thomas Godme'chester sacristan, John Codyngton, Richard Wyndesore precentor, George Albyn succentor; John Hayward, Richard Benese, Thomas Mychell, Edmund Dowman, Thomas Paynell, John Salyng, John Martyn, Robert Knyght and John Page scholar (Heales 1898, pl opp 348, 348–9, cf appendix CLI, cxvii; TNA: PRO, E322/152 (monastic surrenders); L and P Hen VIII, xiii(1), no. 779). Cromwell's commissioners wasted little time, and Richard Layton reported to the lord privy seal on the same day that 'here at Marten abbey are 18 fat oxen, whereof Sir Nicholas Carewe desires part, 40 fat sheep, 200 quarters of malt and £30 in ling and haberdyne. If I shall reserve any of these for your household, please certify me by Mr Belasys' (ibid, no. 785). It was perhaps in connection with arrangements of this kind that Cromwell's accounts for April 1538 include an entry: 'Dr Leyton for things bought at Marten abbey £22' (ibid, xiv(2), 335, no. 782).

A grant of the Court of Augmentation on 25 May 1538 appointed Thomas Cromwell chief steward of lands beyond the Trent belonging to monasteries including Merton (L and P Hen VIII, xiv(1), no. 593). Within a month of the Dissolution Cromwell had arranged for the payment of pensions to the prior and canons half-yearly from Lady Day 1538; that is, from a date some three weeks before the surrender. A memorandum above his signature indicates that John Bowle [sic] the late prior was to receive 200 marks (£133 6s 8d); John Debnaham the subprior £8; Thomas Colson, John

Codyngton, Richard Todde, John Haywarde, George Curson, Thomas Mitchell, John Page scholar, Edmund Honybee, John Meryvale, John Salyng and Robert Knyght £6 13s 4d each (ibid, no. 963). These numbered 13, whereas 15 had signed the surrender only three weeks before, and several of the surnames differ, as in the case of the prior himself. This would suggest the widespread use of bynames, as the Christian names remain largely the same. Two further listings of the canons exist, one dated 9 May 1539 reinstating Richard Benese and Thomas Paynell (ibid, no. 596) who had signed the surrender document; and another, undated but identical (TNA: PRO, E314/20/11, fo 2v).

When providing for the payment of pensions to the former canons less than a month after the Dissolution, Cromwell noted that he had also promised the prior a house and a garden in Trinity Lane, London, for life (L and P Hen VIII, xiv(1), no. 963). On 20 July 1539 John Bowdle prior [sic] was leased a messuage called the Prior's House in Trinity Lane for 20 marks (£13 6s 8d) (ibid, xiii(2), no. 597). Still in the former prior's occupation, this was granted by the Crown to Sir John St John in 1541 with an adjoining messuage and a garden opposite (ibid, xvi, no. 1056.26). The payment of the prior's pension was listed separately in the Court of Augmentation's Book of Payments, as in 1546 (ibid, xxi(1), no. 643) and 1547 (ibid, xxi(2), no. 775).

The demolition of some priory buildings began almost immediately. Paymaster's accounts for the building of Nonsuch Palace for a period ending on 14 September 1538 (L and P Hen VIII, xii(2), no. 342) include the following expenditures:

wages of freemasons (22 April to 20 May) include John Whytakers of Merton 'for uncovering the body of the church at Marten Abbey', 13s 4d; the carriage by land of stone from Merton Abbey to Codynton (Cuddington) at 8d a load, payments to 37 named persons of Wimbledon, Cheam and elsewhere for some 350 loads;
20 May to 17 June: over 500 loads of stone brought 4 miles from Merton Abbey by 47 persons at 2d the mile and 8d the load;
17 June to 13 July: 1300 loads of stone brought from Merton Abbey by 47 persons at 8d the load of 20cwt;
15 July to 10 August: some 500 loads;
12 August to 14 September: 400 loads.

Assuming that all loads conformed to the 20cwt standard of 17 June to 13 July, these figures amount to a total of some 3050 tons removed between 22 April – six days after the suppression of the priory – and 14 September 1538. It would not be easy to define what proportion of the fabric of the priory, or Nonsuch, this represented. Nonsuch was almost complete by 1547 at a cost of £23,000 of which the recorded transport costs from Merton (some £102) account for a modest 0.4% (Dent 1970, 46). The Nonsuch accounts mention only the conventual church, and it is possible that, as elsewhere in the country, the despoliation was confined to that. The earliest ministers' accounts cover the period 16 April to 29 September 1538 and

contain no mention of the former precinct and it is clear from subsequent documents that some priory buildings survived substantially intact. Sir Thomas Heneage's lease of July 1540 refers to the 'house' (domum) and site of the late priory, and excluded the use of all kinds of buildings within the precinct that the king might wish to have 'demolished and removed' (prosterni et auferri), suggesting an intention to preserve them as a quarry for further building work (TNA: PRO, E315/212, fos 186v–7v; L and P Hen VIII, xv, 568). Gregory Lovell's 1587 lease also refers to the 'house' and all houses, building (and) structures within the circuit and precinct (TNA: PRO, C66/1286, m 42). Even a century later, during the civil wars, the site was garrisoned and regarded by parliament as a threat to peace (Manning and Bray 1804, 256).

Heneage's lease also refers to 'all houses buildings barns (orreis) stables dovecotes gardens (orti) orchards gardens (gardinis) mills land and soil existing within the site and precinct', together with property in Merton, Morden, Mitcham and Streatham (Surrey), all of which premises were previously in the hands, cultivation and occupation of the prior and convent, and reserved and occupied to the use of the hospicium at the time of the Dissolution, excepting to the king the great (grossi) trees and woods growing on the premises, and all kind of buildings within the site and precinct of the said later priory (TNA: PRO, E315/212, fos 186v–7v; L and P Hen VIII, xv, 568). As with Bermondsey, but in contrast to St Mary Clerkenwell and Stratford Langthorne, the grant of the whole site to a single lessee precluded the detailed description of individual parts that division between different tenants would have entailed (Barber et al 2004, 121–4; Sloane in prep; Steele in prep).

Ministers' accounts for Michaelmas 1537–8 enumerate a large number of small holdings held by customary tenants, followed by the estates named as: the farm of the grange; the farm of the mills; land called Salying; the farm called Westbarnes; the farm called Holts tenement (or Merton Holts); the farm called Brykehouse; and the farm of the rectory of Merton (TNA: PRO, SC6/Henry VIII/3463 m 5; Heales 1898, 338–43; Chapter 7.1).

Archaeological evidence

Introduction

During the mid 16th century the church (B1) was demolished to provide building stone for Nonsuch Palace, as was perhaps the main cloister (B3a). Much of the site became a demolition yard (OA11). Some of the moulded stone was apparently also used for local building work: a building was constructed from reused moulded stone, possibly from a domestic building at Merton Priory, at the corner of Mill Road and Merton High Street (MIS92) (Fig 3). However, later activity (periods P2 and P3) associated with many of the conventual and domestic buildings suggests that many survived the Dissolution in 1538, and the watermill (B9) appears to have been partially rebuilt in the mid 16th century (Fig 171).

A watermill in the outer court (B9)

During the 16th century – possibly before or soon after the
Dissolution – the mill and the southern abutment forming the
mill head-race were rebuilt with reused roof tiles. The eastern
flint wall was demolished and a tile wall built along the same
alignment. The southern flint abutment was also refaced with
reused roof tiles. Two abutments were found 2.70m apart, both
north–south, forming the mill head-race. These were
constructed of large Reigate stone blocks with a core of flint
overlain by reused roof and floor tiles (Saxby 2005a, 31–4).

A demolition yard (OA11)

The areas between any remaining conventual buildings are
regarded as one large open area (OA11), a demolition yard.
To the north of the church large spreads of crushed Reigate stone,
flint and peg tile suggested that large-scale sorting of demolition
material from the church occured there, probably because the
entrance to the priory was to the north. To the south of the
presbytery, however, demolition deposits contained large amounts
of window glass and pieces of lead not found elsewhere,
suggesting lead culling there. A reasonably large amount of came
material was retrieved including two parts of medieval lights (or
a light) <S52> and <S53> (Fig 172); these retained decayed
window glass and are unusual survivals. Additionally some lead
cames were folded into rough balls, ready for melting. These
survivals represent stages in the recycling process. These demolition
deposits produced much medieval to mid 16th-century material.

Discussion Dissolution activity (period P1)

Much of the stonework from the church was quarried to build
Henry VIII's palace at Nonsuch, therefore, the usual defacement
of the church to prevent future worship (where not taken over
by the parish) was more thorough than usual. Elsewhere in
London, at St Mary Graces, where the Crown also leased the site
to one owner, the church was probably not demolished, only
defaced, until the 1560s, when the Crown reacquired the site
and commenced construction of new buildings elsewhere on it,
also using the medieval buildings to a certain extent as a quarry
(Grainger and Phillpotts in prep b).

Within the inner court, dating evidence from robber fills
and later features suggests that many buildings, including the
chapter house, infirmary hall and chapel and the reredorter,
survived the Dissolution and were not demolished until the
17th century (P2). This concurs with the documentary evidence
from Heneage's lease in 1540 (TNA: PRO, E315/212, fos
186v–7v; L and P Hen VIII, xv, 568).

The rebuilding of the watermill (B9) may have occurred
shortly before the Dissolution or shortly after, and it appears to
have survived until c 1700. In the outer court to the west of the
priory, many buildings apparently survived for centuries after
the Dissolution (Chapter 4.4; Fig 150). As noted above, the
probable 14th-century chapel shown among later buildings in
Fig 149 clearly survived until the early 19th century. To the west

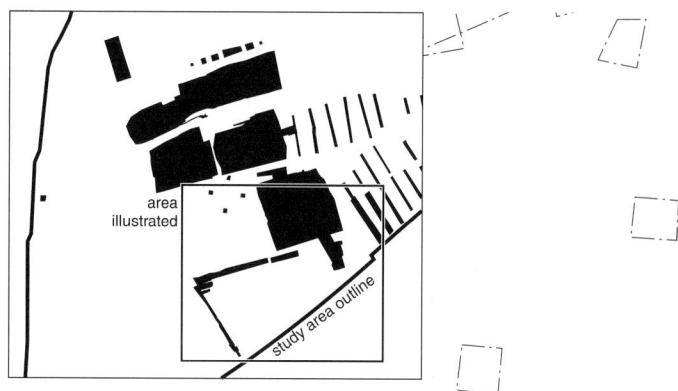

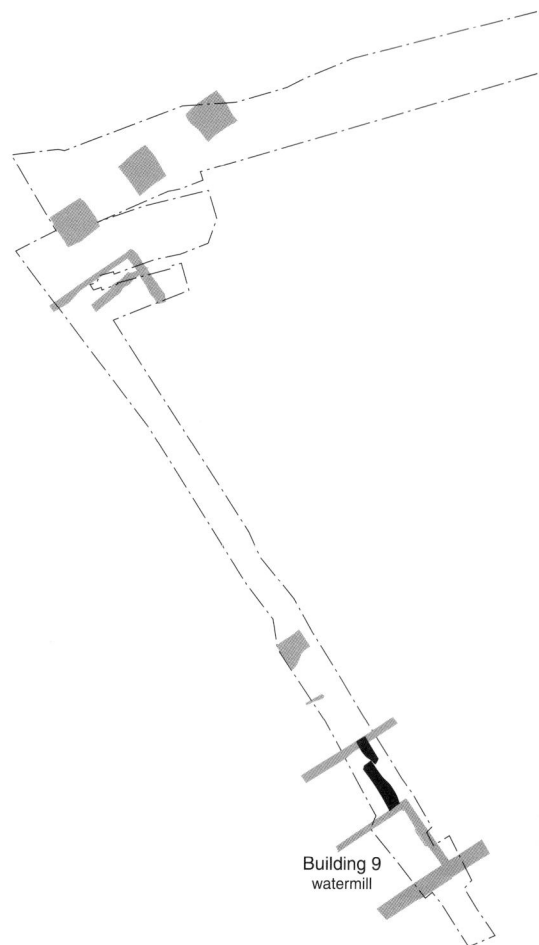

Building 9
watermill

Fig 171 Plan of principal archaeological features in the south part of the precinct,
post-Dissolution (periods P1–P3) (scale 1:500)

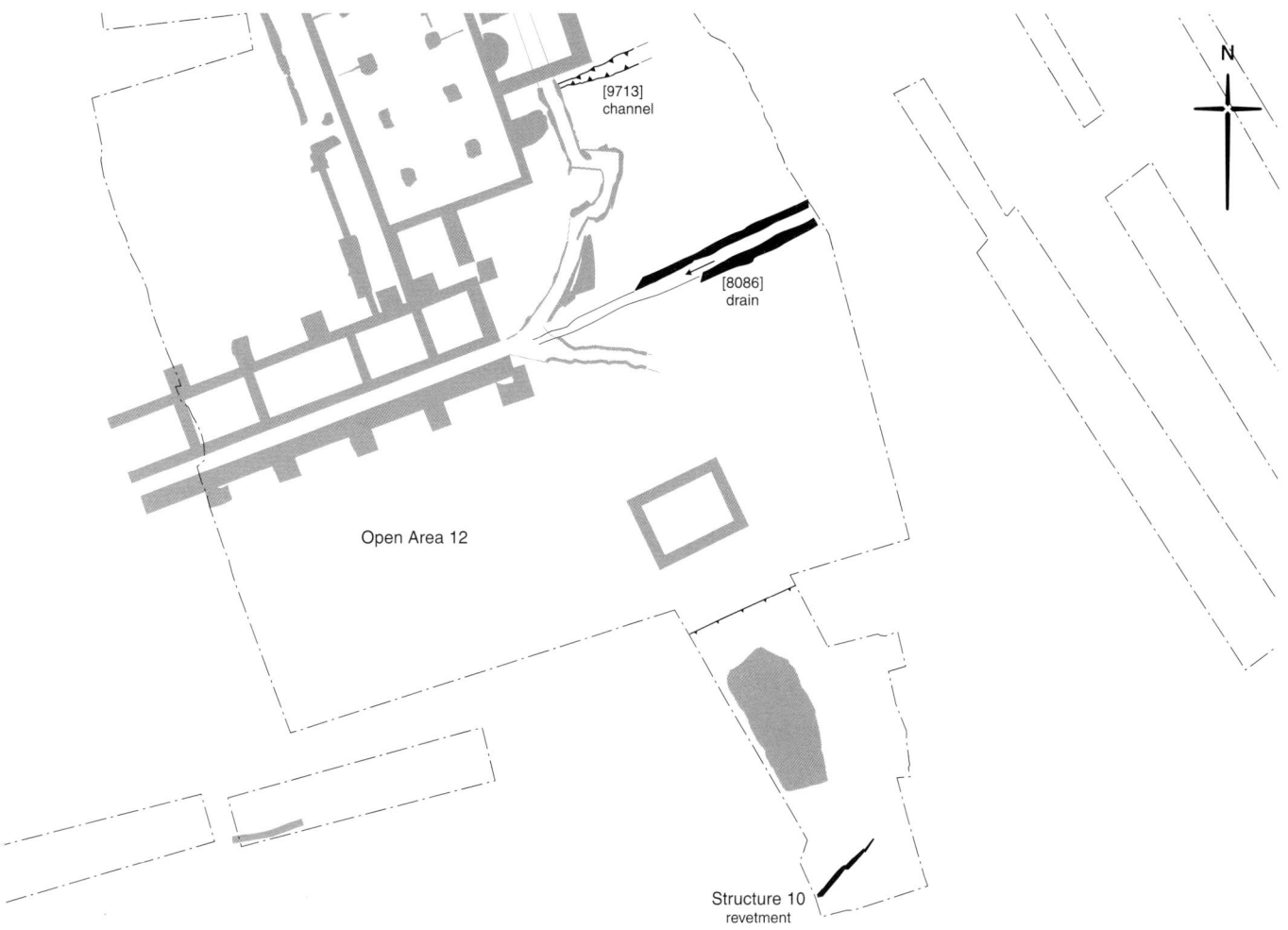

N

[9713]
channel

[8086]
drain

Open Area 12

Structure 10
revetment

0   25m

Fig 172 Lights <S52> and <S53> (scale c 1:4)

of this, the 16th-century and later Abbey House (periods P2 and P3) incorporated a 12th-century arch, while a ?medieval gateway survived until the later 20th century (Fig 151) and was replaced with a replica. Parts of the precinct wall are still extant.

5.2 The 16th to 17th centuries (period P2)

Documentary evidence

Following the Dissolution many surviving buildings, some leased by the priory before 1538, were leased by the Crown to others. In 1554 Mary I granted to Sir Anthony Browne, Master of the Horse, the lordship and manor of Marton, that is Merton (Cal Pat R Philip and Mary, i, 272), and then, in 1558, to the prior and convent of Jesus of Bethlehem at Sheen property described as all her manor of Marton with its rights, members and pertinances in Surrey and lately belonging to the dissolved monastery of Merton 'and also the site of the said late dissolved monastery of Merton and all lands, meadows, pasture, grazing, commons and hereditaments belonging to it or hitherto leased with it, and lately in the tenure and occupation of Sir Thomas Heneage deceased and his assigns' (TNA: PRO, C66/936 m 9; Cal Pat R Philip and Mary, iv, 438). In 1559 the Churchwardens of St Mary at Battersea paid 14s for 'three loads of stone from marten' and 6d to John Tyler for 'digging up the stones we bought' (Jowett 1951, 75), suggesting continued use of the site as a quarry well after the Dissolution. In 1568, Elizabeth I leased to Gregory Lovell, avener of the stable, the house and site of Marten alias Merton Priory and its demesne lands in Merton, Morden, Mitcham, Streatham and Long Ditton (Surrey) (TNA: PRO, C66/1052 m 22; *Cal Pat R Elizabeth*, iv, no. 1866). In 1587, close to the expiry of this first lease, Lovell received a second for a term of 21 years in which the property was described as the site of the late priory (*predictam domum et scitam dicti quondam priorat' de Marton alias Merton*) 'with all houses, buildings structures gardens stables dovecotes gardens orchards gardens mills waters ponds vineyards, fisheries, land fundum soil and hereditaments existing within the site of the circuit and precinct of the same former priory', as well as other Surrey property as first leased to Heneage and subsequently by Elizabeth in 1568; to be held for an annual rent of £26 13s 4d and a fine of £40 (TNA: PRO, C66/1286 m 42). Lovell died on 15 March 1597 (Manning and Bray 1804, 258). By this time, although apparently not earlier, the restriction on the use of priory buildings that the Crown might wish to have demolished and removed (above, 5.1, 'Documentary evidence') was lifted.

St Mary Merton was still held in high regard 50 years after its Dissolution for in a will dated 1587 a John de Lacey directed that his body be buried in Merton Abbey although it is unknown if his request was granted (Manning and Bray 1804). He may have been related to John Lacy, prior of Merton from 1520 until 1530. In the late 16th and 17th century the site of the former priory was commonly referred to as Merton Abbey.

During the Civil War, parliamentarian troops were garrisoned at Merton. In 1648 Merton and many of the strong houses in Surrey required defence against surprise attack by royalist troops, for which Roland Wilson was 'to put such men into it [Merton Abbey] as you shall judge necessary for that purpose' (Jowett 1951, 79). However, a week later, on 10 July 1648, the Derby Houses Committee ordered that 'Merton Abbey, and other such places of strength in Surrey, be rendered indefensible, lest they should endanger the peace of the kingdom. You are hereby authorised to put these places into such condition that no use may be made of them to the endangering of the peace of the kingdom' (Manning and Bray 1804, 256). Little is known about the Civil War activities at Merton. The site was probably used as both a barracks and lookout/defensive site.

From the 1660s Merton Abbey developed into a manufacturing centre, especially textiles. It is possible that the introduction of textile production, which needed vast amounts of water, prompted the diversion and canalisation of the River Wandle. The river was diverted north–south, crossing the site of the current Merton Abbey Mills and continuing to the High Street, before turning east to join the River Pickle at Merton Bridge (Fig 5). A medieval watercourse continued to supply the mill which survived until *c* 1700. By the 1660s the Jacob family were using part of the former priory land as a bleaching ground (Montague 1992b, 74). The works were located to the east of Merton Abbey Mills.

Archaeological evidence

A watermill in the outer court (B9)

In the later 16th century, probably when the priory lands and buildings were sold or rented to various tenants, the mill was at least partially rebuilt in brick (Fig 171). The upper portion of the stone-lined tank (period M4) was rebuilt or repaired with brick and tile and a new in-let inserted into the western part of the south wall (Saxby 2005a, 34–42).

The former chapter house (B3b)

In the chapter house a floor of reused plain-glazed tiles sealed Dissolution deposits. To the east was a small, north–south, brick and reused-stone wall. Similar walls were attached to the northern wall and the east, apsidal wall. The purpose of these is not known (not illustrated).

The former infirmary hall (B4a)

Late medieval or post-medieval, shaped red bricks were found in demolition layers in the infirmary hall. These had one corner cut off and probably decorated a doorway or window opening. A robber trench produced a large amount of copper-alloy waste metal <S311> and <S312>, possibly residual from the recycling of materials at the Dissolution, or associated with metal casting in the vicinity then or later.

The former infirmary cloister (B4c)

Postholes cut, and followed, the northern infirmary cloister wall, perhaps for a fence replacing it.

A riverside revetment (S10)

To the south of the medieval chalk-paved fishpond (S9, period M2) was a north-east to south-west timber riverside revetment. This was constructed from horizontal oak planks, held upright by driven stakes on both sides; it stood to a height of 0.65m (11.35m OD) [11036]. No dating evidence was recovered. This structure probably formed a revetment for a post-medieval, or earlier, watercourse.

?Fields (OA12)

To the south of the former infirmary kitchen (B12) was an east–west channel [9713] cut with a 'V' profile; the base dropped from east to west, from 12.31m to 12.16m OD (Fig 171). A thin layer of tiles [9742] overlay the primary silt fill, possibly the remains of a demolished channel lining. Pottery recovered from this layer included residual medieval wares and London-area early post-medieval redware (PMRE) post-dating *c* 1480. The tile layer was overlain by a dump of flints, [9683], and other large tile fragments [9682], possibly further lining remnants. Pottery from this again post-dated *c* 1480 (PMRE).

Animal bone found included a red deer metarsal (hind foot), roe deer radius, fallow deer antler (not worked) and pig, ox, goose and sheep/goat.

An east–west tile drain [8086] led to the eastern end of the reredorter, sloping downwards from east to west and emptying into the junction of the infirmary and reredorter drains. A smaller north–south ditch (not illustrated) appeared to empty into the north side of this drain. To the north, the infirmary drain (S4b) itself was robbed at some time in this period. Silty fill [9638] produced freshwater snails characteristic of still or slow-flowing weedy water (Table 51). This fill and a secondary robber fill [9078] produced limited botanical remains, dominated by charcoal and elder seeds where the latter may represent residues from use in the textile industry; neither assemblage suggested the drain was still functioning (Table 44; see below). The former drain also produced a large quantity of animal bone fragments including cattle, sheep/goat and pig with smaller components of chicken, goose, rabbit and a single partridge bone. The fish fauna was sparse: occasional fragments of thornback ray, gadids (including cod), clupeid, and cyprinid. Also recovered were a corroded early 16th-century (c 1490–1550) Nuremberg copper-alloy jetton <S351>, and an early Norwich lead cloth seal <S368> (Fig 173), possibly from a worsted, Norfolk's main manufacture from the late 16th century. Two further cloth seals <S369> and <S370> were recovered from the area of the former infirmary and infirmary cloister. This may suggest that the extant priory buildings were used for storage and provides the first evidence of the site's association with the cloth trade, an important industry at Merton during the following centuries.

Samples taken in the area of the former outer court produced seeds of plants with potential industrial/commercial uses, like weld or dyer's rocket (*Reseda luteola*), which produces a yellow dye, and also elder, both used in the textile industry (Chapter 7.6; Table 44). Dyer's rocket in particular is well represented in the sampled fills [10650] and [10855] of a north-east–south-west channel (not illustrated) associated with the timber revement (S10) in Open Area 12; these fills also produced freshwater snails characteristic of still or slow-flowing weedy water (Table 51). Both dyer's rocket and elder, however, are also common waste ground weeds. Seven fragments of an alembic found south of the former reredorter (B5) could date to this period rather than later priory or Dissolution activity (Fig 159, <P9>).

Ditches and pits (not illustrated) dating to the 17th or 18th centuries truncated the walls of the former aisled hall (B11). One, [8706], contained a circular, plano-convex lead weight <S362> (Fig 173), apparently, at 1lb 13^1/$_2$oz (836g) weight, too light, given its nominal 2lb (907g) weight value, for acceptable accurate weighing in the 16th century. A copper-alloy wire dress hook <S361> (Fig 222) may be medieval, but would appear to be a post-Dissolution item.

Open Area 12 produced a small group of London-area early post-medieval redware (PMRE) and London-area post-medieval slipped redware (PMSR) and Surrey-Hampshire border wares

Fig 173 Inscribed lead weight <S362> and lead cloth seal <S368> (scale c 1:1)

(whiteware with green glaze, BORDG; redware, RBOR) suggesting a later 16th-century date for most deposits. Imports included a Raeren stoneware (RAER) jug <P13> (Fig 174), a south Netherlands maiolica (SNTG) Malling-type jug <P14> (Fig 174), and what appears to be a Dutch slipped red earthenware with sgraffito decoration (DUTSG) cooking vessel <P15> (Fig 174). The south Netherlands jug is closely paralleled in a Dissolution group excavated at Mount Grace Priory in Yorkshire (North Riding) (Roebuck and Coppack 1987, 18). Although that group is larger it appears to have been dumped on one occasion and is dominated by a comprehensive range of European imports, only partially reflected in this group.

Later demolition and robber trenches associated with the chapter house, the infirmary hall, the infirmary cloister, the reredorter and the watermill produced a large quantity of animal bone: 5784 fragments/41.21kg hand collected, and, 145 fragments, wet-sieved. Although dominated numerically by unidentified mammal, 'sheep-sized' and 'cattle-sized' mammal fragments, the identified bone consisted mainly of cattle with a substantial group of sheep and goat, and a smaller one of pig. There was a very large group, 290 fragments, of chicken, a smaller one of goose and a few fragments of mallard/domestic duck. There was a very diverse group of wild game species represented by occasional finds of pigeon, woodpigeon, wild duck, blackbird, thrush species, partridge, woodcock, heron, swan, rabbit, brown hare, red deer, fallow deer, roe deer, and

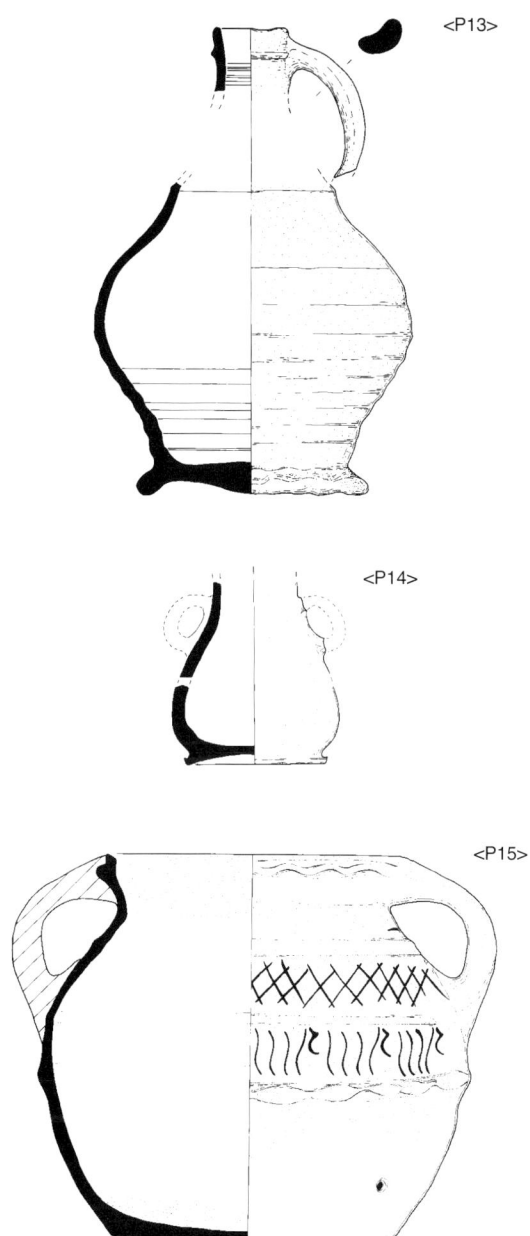

Fig 174 *A Raeren stoneware jug <P13>, a south Netherlands maiolica jug <P14> and a Dutch slipped red earthenware with sgraffito decoration cooking vessel <P15>, from a later 16th-century pottery group in Open Area 12 (scale 1:4)*

porpoise or dolphin. The recovery of rabbit, 121 fragments, was the largest from the whole site assemblage. The fish assemblage was sparse but diverse. It comprised occasional finds of thornback ray, salmonid, clupeids, gadids (including cod), eel, conger eel, cyprinids and plaice/flounder with clupeids providing the largest fragment count. There was also a sparse recovery of corvid, rat, cat and dog. Smaller 'wild' species were confined to frog/toad, mouse or vole (unidentified), common shrew, house mouse and a single recovery of mole.

Discussion 16th–17th centuries (period P2)

Dating evidence from the robber fills of the infirmary hall and reredorter suggest that these buildings were pulled down during the middle to latter part of the 17th century, possibly in 1648 when the site was made 'indefensible' and later during the 1660s when Merton Abbey was developing into a textile manufacturing centre and part of the site was used as bleaching fields. However, the presence of weld or dyer's rocket and a small number of 16th-century cloth seals may perhaps suggest textile manufacture and storage earlier, during the 16th century. The area to the east and south of the infirmary hall may also have been used for small-scale industry, including possibly distilling or fermenting, in the later 16th century, utilising the priory's water and drainage system, as indicated by the rebuilding of the watermill, including the stone-lined tank.

5.3 The 18th to 19th centuries (period P3)

Documentary evidence

The site became a major calico manufacturing centre in the 18th century (Lysons 1792, 345; Harris 1992; Montague 1992b). In 1724 a calico manufactory was established along the east bank of the Wandle, probably including the chapel at the Abbey Mills (Fig 150). The calico works probably adapted existing priory buildings: in 1752 a second calico works was established 'within the walls' of the priory (ie within the precinct; located to the north along Merton High Street). Much of the site was open grassland used as bleaching fields during the 18th century, containing parallel, water-filled ditches used to wash the cloth before it was laid out in the sunlight to bleach.

By the end of the 18th century the Abbey Mills print works were occupied by Newton, Hodgson and Leach (Lysons 1792, 345). The 1805 estate map of Merton Abbey indicates that the works had expanded (SHC, Zs/261). Around 1801–2 a third calico works was established at Merton Abbey by John Leach, located to the south and west. Leach cut a new mill pond and tail-race which ran in an easterly direction (now part of 'Bennett's Ditch'). By 1820 the works were in the hands of Leach's son-in-law, Thomas Bennett, for the production of colourful handkerchiefs and other goods. The Merton Abbey works, as they had now become known, were taken over by Edmund Littler in 1831 for the production of silks and fine fabrics. Two years later, Littler also acquired Bennett's print works and the site became one large printing manufactory (Harris 1992, 10; Montague 1992b, 85). In 1881 William Morris acquired the 1752 print works. The works stood until 1940. In 1904 Littler's print works were acquired by Liberty and Co. Ltd, who pulled down a number of the old buildings and replaced them with workshops. Only two of the early buildings survived Liberty's modernisation, the Colour House and the Wheelhouse, although the Coles Shop dates from the later 19th century. Liberty and Co. Ltd continued production until 1977, after which the works were occupied by a number of printers until closure in 1982. The buildings of the Abbey Mills survived and are currently principally a craft market known as Merton Abbey Mills (Saxby 1995).

Archaeological evidence

A bleaching ground (OA13)

A series of east–west 18th-century ditches (not illustrated), used for the bleaching of cloth, crossed the site. The fills produced little evidence of textile production, apart from a large number of pins. An east–west fence line of large postholes crossed the site of the chapter house, and related to a property boundary shown on the 1805 estate map dividing the two calico manufactories (SHC, Zs/261).

In the area of 'Bennett's Ditch' was a series of ditches. The first [10776], north-east to south-west, 4.16+m by 1.96m wide, by 0.72m deep, with near vertical sides and a flat base, was filled with silts, peats and clay, which contained clay tobacco pipe stems. A second north-east to south-west ditch [10748], 3.88+m by 0.82m wide, by 0.44m deep, had cut the underlying riverine deposits and was filled with a sequence similar to the first.

This period produced a substantial hand-collected animal bone assemblage, 853 fragments/10.79kg. The identifiable material was dominated numerically by cattle, and to a lesser and equal extent by sheep/goat (including sheep) and pig, with small components of chicken, goose and one find of mallard/domestic duck. A diverse game assemblage was represented by occasional finds of thrush species, red deer, fallow deer, rabbit and brown hare; there were occasional finds of rat, dog and horse. Fish recovery was confined to single finds of thornback ray and cod.

Discussion 18th–19th centuries (period P3)

This period saw the expansion of the textile industry along the banks of the new course of the Wandle. This continued in the former monastic precinct from the 17th century until the 19th century when the last of the major manufactures were William Morris and, later, Arthur Liberty. During the 18th century much of the site was used for the bleaching of cotton cloth and many of the associated ditches were briefly recorded during the archaeological excavation.

6

Conclusions and future research

The excavations at Merton Priory collectively represent one of the most extensive and detailed modern archaeological investigations of a large medieval monastic house in the London region, comparable to others presented in the MoLAS Monograph Series (eg St Mary Spital, St Mary Stratford Langthorne, St John Clerkenwell; Chapter 1.1). Furthermore, in Merton we have a rarity in this country – a large-scale archaeological study of a pre-eminent establishment of the Augustinian Order, comparable to that at Norton Priory, St Gregory's Canterbury, and, in London, at Holy Trinity Priory, Aldgate – and including here its cemetery. The project thus potentially gave a chance to elucidate the spatial organisation and zoning of the priory, its building methods, and to reconstruct the appearance of selected buildings and the lifestyle of the inhabitants, in particular their medical care, health, diet and hygiene, and the manner of their death and burial. The large body of data retrieved from Merton contrasts in the London region with that from Holy Trinity Aldgate and the nunnery of St Mary Clerkenwell, where reconstruction of the church and other buildings relies heavily on architectural and documentary sources, with only limited remains excavated, particularly with regard to cemeteries.

Of necessity the fulfilment of any of this potential was restricted almost entirely to the areas excavated, which have so far centred largely on the inner court: the church, cemetery areas and conventual buildings. Although various buildings and open areas beyond the main conventual buildings were investigated, these tended to be as isolated entities, and the description of the Augustinian precinct as a whole, comparable to the work at Thornholme (Coppack 1989), is here incomplete. What the investigation of the inner precinct does show is a willingness to adopt and adapt on the part of the Augustinians from the earliest days of the priory. Parallels for the late 12th-century and subsequent churches can be found in the Cistercian Order, whether disseminated directly by the Cistercians or via other Augustinian houses. The use of a space, separating the cloister from the nave hints at an adaptation to local circumstances (most probably a large resident guest population worshipping in the nave) paralleling particularly friaries, and a lack of formal guidelines governing the monastic layout for the Order. In other respects the ground plan of the conventual buildings was perhaps typical of many monasteries regardless of order, but not necessarily entirely so. The excavations so far have failed to determine much of the conventual layout in the 12th and early 13th centuries. They suggest, but do not prove, that much of the priory beyond the church was still in timber before the early 13th century. Even for the period from c 1230 onwards the excavations have not determined the size and shape of the cloister, and the certain, rather than implied, positions in each period of the dormitory and refectory. The excavated remains, including the *ex situ* architectural fragments, however, have allowed detailed reconstruction of the changing appearance of the church and, to a lesser extent, the cloister, the chapter house – rebuilt in the 14th century in an archaic apsidal form apparently for entirely practical reasons – and the extremely large infirmary complex rivalling that of bigger Cistercian houses. A certain amount of reconstruction has been possible with regard to the monastic water system and exploitation of the Wandle. Merton's extensive excavated rebuilding campaigns emphasise a general, although not necessarily continuous, prosperity unlike that of many other foundations within the Augustinian and other orders.

If the Merton project has one contribution above all others to make to the understanding of monastic archaeology and the Augustinians in particular, it is in the excavation of a large and generally well-phased burial population. This, although again only the product of partial excavation and incomplete, permits attempts to track changes in both the layout of the monastic cemetery and the burials within it over time. A number of suggestions have been made with regard to the likely burial areas for the canons and their monastic superiors, and changes in these and the pattern of their burial within a burial population that clearly included some laypersons. The study of the burials within both the cemetery and the church has confirmed and amplified work on other monastic sites, indicating the restriction of burial rights to select, if only broadly defined, predominantly male, lay groups. It is in the diversity, frequency and to some extent richness of Merton's burial customs and artefacts that the site makes a real contribution to the study of the types and distribution of higher status burial – for instance, the extensive but frequently localised use of cist burial and to a lesser extent lead and stone coffins, in the church, chapter house, and to the north and south in the cemetery, and the concentration of individuals interred (apparently) clothed in or near the north transept. The site also makes a significant contribution to the study of 'plank' burials (ie covered with timbers), suggesting several interpretations for this enigmatic practice, almost exclusively associated with adult male interments at Merton.

The second area in which the Merton excavation significantly advances the study of monastic archaeology is the infirmary complex. As noted in Chapter 4.5, few such complexes have been investigated thoroughly using modern archaeological techniques. In many ways the results here contain few surprises, given the more flexible layout of monastic infirmaries in general. The earlier large, open plan hall and its subdivision in the 14th century are attested to elsewhere, and the position and layout of the adjacent chapel to the north is not unusual. Yet the excavation has suggested many details about the use of such buildings, and the size of the complex as a whole does perhaps surprise, particularly with regard to the cloister, suggesting a large number of residents in what was traditionally the most comfortable part of a monastery. This, coupled with the other excavated remains, such as the large aisled hall, possibly for guests, and the possibly smaller main cloister and open space to the south of the nave, suggests a shifting of focus to the infirmary area at Merton in order for the canons to cope with Merton's well-documented and extensive hospitality. If the excavation of the infirmary demonstrates well one further aspect of monastic archaeology, it is the difficulty in identifying buildings from fragmentary remains in the absence of a known formal plan or documentary evidence. The identification of the other buildings in the infirmary is tentative at best, each having several possibilities.

The osteological study of the burial population, and the artefacts and environmental material have much to tell about the health and lifestyle of the inhabitants. The distribution of diffuse idiopathic skeletal hyperostosis (DISH) in the church and chapter house suggests a number of privileged individuals resident in or connected to the priory, and is increasingly being noted in skeletal assemblages from monastic houses. However, the occurrence of individuals exhibiting pathologies potentially connected to a monastic vocation, vitamin deficiencies associated with the monastic diet (Chapter 7.11, 'Diet'), or infectious diseases associated with the communal life is far less frequent in such assemblages. The majority of Merton artefacts and environmental material suggest a monastic institution similar to others in material culture, but some objects, such as the possible hernia belt and bone spectacles, are rare and unusual, and the inscribed gold ring also points toward a high standard of living on the part of a number of individuals.

Merton was one of a select group of larger Augustinian houses and, although never attaining the rank of abbey, could easily be considered of a similar status to such houses as the abbeys of St Augustine at Cirencester, Waltham and Bristol. Architecturally, the evidence for the church has greatly elaborated the comparatively simple model of development initially set out by Bidder (Bidder and Westlake 1930, 58) although our debt to his work remains large. The first church – testified to by ex situ stone – remains an unknown, but the lost remains of the church from Merton's 'daughter house' St Martin's in Dover, founded in 1130 and recorded in the 1860s (Plumptre 1861, 6), could provide a clue. The large scale of the Dover church suggests that the abandonment of the first Merton church was due to its over-ambitious scale (as suggested by the documentary evidence); whether the few heavily robbed foundations excavated north-east of the later church are part of this first church remains to be proven. The design of the second church commenced in the 1170s or so indicates a specifically Augustinian layout of intermediate size. The simple cross plan departs little from the featureless but hugely influential 'first generation' plans of the Cistercian Order, with the exception of the two large chapels in each transept. Despite documented royal interest, the design goes nowhere near the scale and complexity of the great royal foundations of Waltham Abbey or St Andrews (Fife). Only the aisled presbytery can be said to reflect the special needs of the Order. After the collapse of the crossing tower in 1222, the opportunity was taken to upgrade the church with a transept arm and nave comparable to Henry II's expanded Waltham Abbey, although, strangely, the c 1170s presbytery was retained; perhaps the intention was to also expand it. The financial health of the priory was finally equal to that task in c 1290. It is likely that masons from the royal works at St Stephen's chapel Westminster were involved in the jewel-like eastern extension, raised unwittingly on the marshy verge of a Roman road. The prior was able to call on the services of the finest 'marbrers' of the West Country and, perhaps, the enigmatic William the

Geometer, the possible architect of the east arm of St Augustine's Bristol (Harvey 1987, 115). High level geometrical skills were used at Merton to cut the huge blocks of Purbeck marble required and the new east arm would have employed the finest of everything then available. These works caused Merton financial distress for several decades. Any plans to reconstruct the remainder of the church were possibly abandoned after the Black Death. The new work must have started to tear away from the old almost immediately, and all subsequent work consisted only of running repairs. The church, destroyed in 1538, was distinguished by its degrees of mismatching, elaboration and disrepair, and it is likely that even without Henry VIII's intervention it would have only survived to this day in a greatly reconstructed form.

Today very little trace of the priory of St Mary Merton survives to testify to its position as a large and important Augustinian house during the medieval period. The church was destroyed at the Dissolution and much of the rest followed in later centuries, leaving, by the 20th century, few standing remains. Fortunately, the excavations of that century recovered a substantial portion and indeed preserved a small part, the chapter house foundations (Fig 175), which are still on the site today and accessible to the public. Yet despite the extensive excavations reported here, and excavation between 1999 and 2004 to the south of Merantun Way, large areas of the precinct remain unexcavated, and although the research aims of the current project have been largely attained a number of further questions were revealed during this analysis. These include the following.

· Where was the early documented church?
· What was the internal layout of the choir, crossing and nave of the church?
· What was the layout and development of the cloister? Little of this area was open for excavation and the evidence recovered

so far allows for a number of interpretations.
· What did the infirmary complex consist of? Further excavation could help identify the function of ancillary buildings, and combined with an examination of other infirmary complexes assist in a comparison of monastic infirmaries and hospitals.
· What other buildings existed within the priory precinct? Recent archaeological evaluation carried out from 2001 has shown that other buildings survive between the conventual buildings and the River Wandle. Further excavation of these could allow a more detailed landscape of the outer precinct to be drawn.
· Are further burials located to the east of the infirmary and if so what are that burial area's boundaries?

The human bone assemblage should be the subject of further, more detailed study. The data presented and analysed here represent a small fraction of the archived data and the assemblage has massive potential for future research on disease/pathology and demographic studies. The viability of several such projects has already been evaluated and these are listed below, but the potential of the assemblage to support other such research is inestimable and will grow as the synthesis, development and refinement of the techniques of archaeology and science continues. For this reason the Merton Priory assemblage has been recorded in detail on to the Wellcome Osteological Research Database, making available a very extensive amount of data, in addition to that offered in this volume, online through the Museum of London website. Future research projects could include the following.

· Further differences from other monastic orders
The various religious orders in England conducted their liturgical life in different ways and differences are to be observed in the division of labour, health, in-house treatment of disease (or lack of treatment) and lifespan. *How do the*

Fig 175 *The chapter house foundations as they are preserved today, looking west*

monastic dead from Merton Priory differ from contemporary lay people or other religious orders, with regard to age-at-death, stress indicators and health?

· The canons at Merton Priory underwent bleeding up to eight times per year to improve them spiritually, mentally and physically. *Were the Augustinian canons more anaemic or otherwise less healthy than the lay people buried at the same site or than members of other monastic orders?*

· Isotopic and other scientific analysis

Isotopic analysis can identify the general categories of food eaten (Keegan 1989) and the proportion of the diet that they represented. The St Mary Merton sample as a whole has confirmed the relationship between monastic sites and DISH suggested by Waldron (1985). *Can stable isotope analysis of skeletal material from the specimens exhibiting DISH establish a positive link between diet and this condition?*

· Tuberculosis (TB) and leprosy

Novices of most orders were required to be free of disease when they entered the convent. It is known that some nevertheless would go on to develop debilitating disease as the result of previous exposure. This is true of leprosy and tuberculosis, although the latter could also be acquired within the crowded establishment itself. Genetic and chemical analysis has been used to confirm cases of such diseases and also to detect them in individuals who were infected, yet show no skeletal manifestations. *Can submicroscopic evidence for TB and leprosy be found in preclinical stage skeletons using ancient DNA analysis or specific mycolic acids (Gernaey et al 1998), especially in those that show a potential TB condition in characteristic rib lesions?*

7

Specialist appendices

7.1 Property held by Merton Priory

Tony Dyson

Merton Priory had numerous and extensive properties in the City of London, the south east and England in general. The documentary evidence for these holdings, presented below, consists principally of two sources for the properties outside the City: Edward IV's charter of confirmation of 2 August 1468, and the ministers' accounts for Michaelmas 1537–8.

Priory property in 1468

Listed in Edward IV's charter of confirmation of 2 August 1468 (Heales 1898, 300–3)

Manors of Merton, Dunsford in Wandsworth, Mitcham, Fetcham, Ashstead, Mulsey in Surrey
Villata and hamlets of Thames Ditton, West Molsey, Thorpe Lane, Apse, Walton on Thames, Haverycchesham, members of the said manors of Mulsey as alleged
Manor of Kingston upon Thames
Villata of Hertyngton, Hacche, Hamme, Berewelle, members of the said manor of Kingston as alleged
Manor of Ewell
Villata of Shelwode, Legh, Horlegh, Cherlewode, Newdegate, Langeshot, Kyngeswode, Pachenesham, Codyngton, Tullesworth, Hoke, members of the said manor of Ewell as alleged
Assise of the manor of Patrikesbourne, Kent
Villata of Brigg, which is a member of the manor of Patrikesbourne as is alleged
Manor of Upton co Bucks
Villata of Chalvey Michelmylwardsey, Sloo, Legh, Wexham, Horton, Colbroke members of the manor of Upton as alleged
Assise within the manor of Holshot, Hants
Villata and hamlets of Mattinglegh, Heysell, Bromshill, Heghfeld, Hartlegh, Puccham, Stratfeld Turgeys, members of the manor of Holshot as is alleged
also within all other manors, lands and feuds within his (the king's) vill of Windsor etc …

Property in the ministers' accounts for Michaelmas to Michaelmas 1537–8

Merton grange

A parcel of the demesne of Merton belonging to the grange ('Graung') there, situated outside the gates of the late priory of Merton and leased for £23 pa to John Hyller by the priory on 20 April 1533. This included fields called 'Lyon' estimated at 49 acres (19.83 hectares), 'le vyne [10 acres, 4.05 hectares], the twenty acres, Oxenlese [22 acres, 8.90 hectares], Marlese [Marelease, 10 acres], grete Bykworth [47 acres, 19.02 hectares], Orchard [16 acres, 6.47 hectares]'; a rabbit warren ('warren cunicul'); fields called 'grete Waterden [24 acres, 9.71

hectares] lytill Waterden [18 acres, 7.28 hectares] hokelandis' and 'oke busshes [26 acres, 10.52 hectares], Blaklandis [60 acres, 24.28 hectares]'; 2 acres of arable lying between 'Marlye' and Mordon on the north side and land of the abbot of Westminster on the south side; fields called 'Redland [14 acres, 5.67 hectares], Holowe mede' with another field adjacent [in all 12 acres, 4.86 hectares]; a meadow ('prati') called 'grete brassemore [9½ acres, 3.84 hectares]'; a marsh or meadow called 'lytell brassmore'; a meadow called 'pyppis mead'; together with a grove ('groua') called 'pypis grove' and closes ('claus') called 'Shepehouse close' and 'mychelle close [3½ acres, 1.42 hectares]', with all buildings and curtilages belonging to the Grange with a certain house with garden [½ acre, 0.20 hectare] in which the (tenant) farmer ('firmar') lives, reserving to the prior of Merton and his successors a dovecote, fishpond, wood and undergrowth and all other commodities and profits by reason of free entrance and exit for access and for view of frankpledge within the grange as often as necessary; to be held for 21 years from the following Michaelmas, John repairing and maintaining. The lease was renewed on 4 November 1534 with the stipulation that all hedges and ditches of the grange were to be repaired and maintained (Heales 1898, 336–8; information in square brackets derived from the lease of June 1553; see below).

Hyller's lease of 'Merton grange, parcell of Merton manor' was renewed by the Court of Augmentation on 28 August 1546 on the surrender of his old 21-year lease from the priory (L and P HenVIII, xxi(2), 438 no. 774). On 4 June 1553 the grange, now in the occupation of William Tirrell, was granted to John Earl of Warwick, Master of the Horse; the property was as described in 1533 except for the addition of Sheapelease (5 acres, 2.02 hectares) and Lytle Byckworth (10 acres, 4.05 hectares) and the subtraction of half the coneywarren (24 acres, 9.71 hectares), and was to be held at fee farm as of the manor of East Greenwich, rendering £20 pa (Cal Pat R Edward VI, v, 242–3). Following the earl of Warwick's attainder and the forfeiting of half of the property to Queen Mary, it was granted on 13 May 1564 to Sir Henry Sydney, President of the Council in the Marches of Wales (Cal Pat R Elizabeth, iii, no. 359). By 1629 it was among the possessions of Richard Burroll who sold it to Robert Bromfield for £2100 (VCH 1912b, 67).

Two mills

Two mills lying in the parish of Merton called 'Amery mills' together with a tenement belonging to them and a garden called le Amery gardeyn leased by priory indenture to William Moraunt on 4 November 1534; to be held by him, heirs and executors from the Christmas following for a term of 22 years at a farm of 116s 8d, and being responsible for all charges at the mills. According to Sir Thomas Heneage's grant of 6 July 1540, there were mills actually within the priory precinct (L and P HenVIII, xv, no. 568). On 26 November 1568 the queen granted to Robert Beaumont, one of her musicians, a 21-year lease of mills and lands (named) in Merton, once of the monastery and late of the priory of Jesus of Bethlehem of

Sheen, with reservations, which with other property was to be held from the expiry of a lease of the Court of Augmentations dated 1 April 1550 to Robert Pakenham, then clerk of controlment of the household, inter alia, at a rent of £5 16s 8d, for a term of 30 years from the expiry of the 22-year lease from the following Christmas granted to William Morant [Moraunt] on 4 November 1534 (Cal Pat R Elizabeth, iv, no. 2365).

From May 1557 Morant also held a close of 40 acres (16.19 hectares) in Wimbledon that lay before 'the mill of Merton called Saunders' and had formerly belonged to St Thomas's Hospital, Southwark (Cal Pat R Philip and Mary, iii, 417). The proximity of the priory to lands in Wimbledon is also shown by Queen Mary's grant of 13 March 1556 to Cardinal Pole of land previously granted by Queen Catherine to Sir Robert Tyrwhitt, including the 'mansion house of the manor of Wimbledon' and excepting 'Greatefield' adjacent to the late monastery of Merton (ibid, 76).

The land called Salyngs

A tenement in Merton called Salyngs, together with all lands, meadows, grazings and pastures and the assize of lands and pastures pertaining to it, in which John Randolf lately dwelt, with barn adjoining and 4 acres (1.62 hectares) of arable land by the chapel of Blessed Mary there, reserving to the priory the mansion or tenement of the said John Randolph with the adjoining croft, was leased by the priory to John Clerk on 1 June 1536, to be held from Michaelmas 1537 for 40 years for £10 5s pa rent, payable to the keeper (custos) of the said chapel of the Blessed Virgin Mary (TNA: PRO, SC6/Henry VIII/3463 m 5). On 21 April 1567 the tenement called 'Salinges' [Salyngs] in Merton, now or late in the tenure of John Clerke [Clerk], parcel of the manor of Merton, late of the house of Jesus of Bethehem of Sheen, and formerly of the monastery of Merton, was leased for 21 years to William Bartilmewe, groom of the scullery, and Thomas Spenser, child of the same, with reservations; to be held from the expiry of the former lease, for an annual rent of £10 5s and a fine of £20 (TNA: PRO, C66/1037 m 27; Cal Pat R Elizabeth, iv, no. 583).

Along with the renewal of his lease of the priory site on 7 January 1587, Gregory Lovell, gentleman and cofferer of the household, also received land in Merton that had been leased to William Barthilmew [Bartilmewe], groom of the scullery, and Thomas Spenser, boy of the scullery, on 21 April 1567; to be held for 21 years from the previous Michaelmas for an annual rent of £10 5s (TNA: PRO, C66/1286 m 42). On 27 February 1590 Salings was leased to John Browne valet and John Somelawe, for 21 years commencing on the expiry of the current lease to Gregory Lovell, renewed on 17 February 1590 for 21 years to commence on the expiry of the existing lease (ie in 1608) (TNA: PRO, C66/1353 m 43; TNA: PRO, E147/2/11). By June 1616 Henry Downer was tenant of both Salings and the manor of Merton under Thomas Hunt (TNA: PRO, C78/249, item 3). On 10 January 1617 the manor was granted to Thomas Ford of London gentleman with a tenement called Salyngs (Manning and Bray 1804, 244).

West Barnes

A certain mansion called 'Westbarnes' with all houses, barns, stables, curtilages and gardens belonging to it, seven little adjacent closes next to it and containing about 31 acres (12.5 hectares), and also a certain parcel of meadow and woodland, viz one close containing about 33 acres (13.35 hectares) called 'bromsell', a close of meadow and wood containing 45 acres (18.21 hectares) called 'hoppyng mede'; a close containing 55¹/₂ acres (22.46 hectares) called 'hoppyng'; another containing 25 acres (10.12 hectares) called 'pules'; another containing 106 acres (42.9 hectares) called 'Estfeld'; another called 'canondownhyll'; a field containing 33 acres (13.25 hectares) called 'Twyryfeld'; and a parcel of land likewise lying in three closes called 'Westfeld' and 'blaldenys' and containing 188 acres (76.08 hectares) and with all tithes within in the said farm; leased by priory indenture to Thomas Bedle and Geoffrey Bedle on 31 August 1536, excepting the tithes of growing wood within the farm and also all manner of wood, trees etc, for 40 years from Michaelmas next at an annual rent of £18 10s, the lessees being responsible for all repairs at their own expense.

On 12 September 1545 property including a farm called Westbarnes and numerous closes in the tenure of Thomas and Geoffrey Bedell [Bedle] in Merton parish was granted in fee to Sir Richard and Sir John Gresham of London and William Gresham, mercer of London (*L and P Hen VIII*, xx(2), no. 496.25), supplemented on 27 January 1547 by rents reserved by the earlier grant (ibid, no. 771.35). On 28 November 1556 John Gresham, son of Sir John Gresham who died on 23 October last, was pardoned at the cost of £33 6s 8d for his trespass in property including a farm and lands called Westbarnes in Merton, lately purchased of Sir Edward North, Lord North, and which John was to hold on the decease of North's widow Katharine (*Cal Pat R Philip and Mary*, iii, 338). On 2 January 1567 Thomas and Elizabeth Gresham were licensed to alienate the same property to Sir Thomas Gresham (TNA: PRO, C66/1038 m 11) (*Cal Pat R Elizabeth*, iv, no. 647), while on 16 December the same year Catherine, widow of Sir John Gresham, late alderman, William Gresham and John Gresham were licensed to alienate it to John Carpenter of Merton yeoman (TNA: PRO, C66/1041 m 28; *Cal Pat R Elizabeth*, iv, no. 961). On 25 February 1574 John Gresham mercer was licensed to alienate lands in Merton to Thomas Randall citizen and mercer and his eldest son Thomas (ibid, vi, no. 1837), but it was sold by the Gresham family to John Carpenter in 1612, Robert Carpenter holding it in 1660. It was sold to the Budgen family in 1732 (*VCH* 1912b, 67).

Merton Holts

A tenement in Merton called Merton Holts, formerly Holts, with closes and pastures but reserving to the prior and convent all wood, underwood and trees; granted on 12 October 1532 by priory indenture to William Lok for 32 years from the previous Michaelmas, at an annual rent of £4 13s 4d, William

covenanting to thatch and to repair all walls from the ground to a height of 8ft, and to make good all injuries done by him or his tenants or cattle, and to keep in order all ditches and enclosures.

Brickhouse close

Two closes in the vill of Merton called Brykhouse closes, with other closes containing 1 acre (0.4 hectare), and a barn pertaining to it, and reserving all wood and trees; leased by priory indenture to William Lok on 14 March 1521 for a term of 55 years from Michaelmas last for an annual rent of 40s.

Merton Holts and Brickhouse close

On 10 July 1547 Sir Richard Lee was leased property including the messuage in Merton called 'Martynholltes' in the tenure of William Lock [Lok], the lands leased with it and two closes in Merton called Bryckehouse Closes in Lock's tenure, all late of Merton monastery, for a rent of 9s 4s for Martyn holtes and 4s for the enclosures called Bryckhouse Closes (*Cal Pat R Edward VI*, i, 109).

Merton rectory

The rectory of Merton with a tenement and parcel of land lying on the west side of the parish church of Merton and a barn and close there called 'le parsonage barn', as well as all tithes, oblations, mortuaries, profits, commodities and advantages belonging to the rectory, were leased by priory indenture dated 4 October 1537 to William and Thomas Saunder for a term of 40 years from Michaelmas for an annual rent of 40s; William and Thomas being responsible for finding a suitable priest to celebrate in the church, and also wine, bread, wax and all necessaries required by ancient law for the church, and all other burdens ordinary and extraordinary of the rector.

General

Sir Thomas Heneage's lease of the priory site 6 July 1540 also included much property adjacent to the precinct, and some of it was involved in the leases reviewed above: three meadows 'apud Bakers' (40 acres, 16.19 hectares), two meadows called 'Russhe mede' (12 acres, 4.86 hectares), a meadow called 'le Southmede' (16 acres, 6.47 hectares), a meadow called 'le Twyryemede' (20 acres, 8.09 hectares), a meadow called 'le Sandepytte mead' (26 acres, 10.52 hectares), a meadow called 'Combstrowede mede' (30 acres, 12.14 hectares), first covering (*primam vesturam*) of a meadow called 'Hobboldys mede' (24 acres, 9.71 hectares) and of a meadow called 'Flemyng mede' (7 acres, 2.83 hectares), a pasture at 'Bakers iuxta Merton common' (30 acres), a pasture called Hyllfelde (8 acres, 3.24 hectares), a pasture called 'Okefelde' (30 acres), a close of pasture on 'cannonsdownehylle' (7 acres) and a pasture called 'Cannondownehylle' (60 acres, 24.28 hectares) (TNA: PRO, E315/212, fos 186v–7v; *L and P Hen VIII*, xv, 568). A close called 'canondownhyll' and a field called 'Twyryfeld' containing 33 acres (13.35 hectares) were leased to Thomas Bedle and Geoffrey Bedle as part of West Barnes in August 1536.

The City of London properties

In 1291, Merton held property in 31 London parishes: All Hallows Bread Street, All Hallows Honey Lane, St Antonin, St Benet Fink, St Benet Paul's Wharf, St Dionis Backchurch, St Edmund Lombard Street, St Giles Cripplegate, St John Zachary, St Lawrence Pountney, St Magnus Martyr, St Margaret Lothbury, St Martin Ludgate, St Martin Orgar, St Martin Pomary, St Martin Vintry, St Mary Abchurch, St Mary Aldermary, St Mary Axe, St Mary Bothaw, St Mary le Bow, St Mary Magdalene Old Fish Street, St Michael Bassishaw, St Michael le Querne, St Nicholas Cole Abbey, St Nicholas Shambles, St Pancras Soper Lane, St Peter Paul's Wharf, St Peter Westcheap, St Sepulchre, St Thomas the Apostle; and at other times in St Olave Old Jewry, St Benet Gracechurch Street and Holy Trinity the Less (Keene and Harding 1985, 186).

Each of those described below, and one other in St Giles Cripplegate, is recorded as being sold off subsequent to the Dissolution.

The prior's house, Trinity Lane, Holy Trinity parish

Property including the messuage formerly called the 'Prior's House' in Trinity Lane and the garden opposite it, in the tenure of John Bowle, late prior of Merton, and the messuage adjoining the said Pryours House. It was sold to Sir John Saint John on 4 July 1541 (L and P Hen VIII, xvi, no. 1056.26).

A month after the Dissolution, Cromwell had promised the prior a house and a garden in Trinity Lane for life (L and P Hen VIII, xv(1), no. 963), and on 20 July 1539 John Bowdle (Bowle; alias Ramsey, see Chapter 4.7, 'Priors and other office holders') was granted a messuage called the Prior's House in Trinity Lane (ibid, xiii(2), no. 597), that is his own former town-house. It is not clear how the sale to Saint John in 1541 affected Bowle, who was still alive in 1547, but Saint John's interest there was eventually replaced by that of the Painters' Company. A 'Rental of parcels of lands and possession of various monasteries, abbeys and priories' dating later than 1541 includes, under the heading 'Merton', the item: 'Farm of parcel of land in the tenure of the Painters' Company (Societatis pictorum) in the parish of Holy Trinity, in Hog Lane, 13s 4d' (TNA: PRO, SC12/37/7).

The prior's house, its location unfortunately not noted, was the subject of an assize of nuisance on 10 April 1310, when the prior of Merton defended himself against William Amys's demand that the party wall of the prior's house should be demolished on the grounds that it did not stand straight but leaned towards his own land, and that, after he had laid the foundations of a new wall in stone at his own expense, the prior should find the timber to complete it. The assize found that Amys must meet the entire cost of the building, the wall remaining to the prior (Chew and Kellaway 1973, 149).

St Margaret Lothbury parish

Property including a messuage etc in the parish of St Margaret Lothbury in the tenure of Thomas Archer. Sold to John Pope and Anthony Foster of London on 26 September 1544 (L and P Hen VIII, xix(2), no. 340.45).

Property including the 'Sarson's Head', St Benet Gracechurch parish

A tenement in St Benet Gracechurch in the tenure of William Chamber. Sold to Ralph Clarvys of London on 18 March 1541 (L and P Hen VIII, xvi, no. 678.50); Clarvys was also licensed on 18 June to alienate to James Hall, in the same parish, a messuage and tenement or hospice called 'the Sarson's Head' in the tenure of Richard Hudson, and messuages and tenements in the tenure of Bertram Jaxson and Avicia Banks widow (ibid, no. 947.37).

A 'Rental of parcels of lands and possession of various monasteries, abbeys and priories', dating after 1541 includes under 'Merton': 'Tithe of divers tenements and messuages St Benet Gracechurch in letters patent Ralph Clarves, 26s' (TNA: PRO, SC12/37/7).

St Pancras Soper Lane parish

Two messuages in the parish of St Pancras in the tenure of William Abbott and Philip Yorke. Sold to Edward Bowland of London for £113 6s 8d on 27 September 1544 (L and P Hen VIII, xix(2), no. 340.52). On 27 May 1532 a dispute had arisen between the prior of Merton, plaintiff, and the parson and church wardens of St Stephen Walbrook, defendants, concerning a building and ground in St Pancras and adjoining the parsonage of that parish (London Viewers, no. 95).

Whitecross Street, St Giles Cripplegate parish

Messuages in Whitecross Street, St Giles Cripplegate, formerly in the tenure of John Gyles and now of the fellowship of Clerks of London. Described as lying between the street to the east, gardens formerly of Richard Esterly, William Jurdan and Sir Edmund Momforde to the west, the lordship of Finsbury to the north and the land of Richard Frende to the south (dimensions given). Sold to John Howe on 27 August 1544 (L and P Hen VIII, xix(2), no. 166.72).

The garden of the prior and convent of Merton is referred to in a deed of 9 July 1415 as adjoining to the east a property on the eastern side of Golden Lane ('Goldynglane') (Cal Close R, 1413–19, 279).

All Hallows Bread Street

Acquittance by the priory and convent of Merton of 10s 4d received from the prior and convent of Charterhouse, London, for a yearly quitrent of a tenement and two shops in All Hallows Bread Street on the north side of the highroad called Watlyngstrete, 20 October 1513 (Cat Anc Deeds, iii, D 1043).

All Hallows Honey Lane

On 11 December 1338 an inquest *ad quod damnum* on William de Elsyng's proposed hospital found that no problems arose from two messuages in All Hallows Honey Lane which pay quitrents to the canons of Merton and others (*Cal Plea and Mem R, 1323–64*, 183).

St Antholin

After 11 June 1311 the prior of Merton, presented by Friar William de Eytone, came before John de Gysors, mayor, in 1312–13 and claimed 1 mark pa quitrent charged on a tenement in the parish; his claim was upheld by a subsequent inquiry (*Cal L Book D*, 190).

St Dunstan in the East

The Fishmongers' Company owes 10s from messuages and Crown Quay in St Dunstan's parish, owed to the late priory of Marteyn [Merton], c 1550 (*Cal Pat R Edward VI*, iii, 392).

St Martin Orgar

Grant by Serlo the mercer to the new hospital without Bishopsgate of land in St Lawrence Pountney in St Martin's Lane, paying 5s pa to the canons of Merton [c 1197–c 1225] (*Cart Holy Trinity*, no. 397).

St Martin Vintry

On 13 February 1368 a royal writ was sent to the mayor and escheator of London concerning a 20s pa quitrent paid to the prior and convent of Merton from tenements in St Martin Vintry bequeathed in mortmain by Henry de Hereford, whose net annual value, allowing for this rent and repairs, was 46s 8d (*Cal Inq Misc, 1348–77*, 686).

St Mary le Bow

Geoffrey Buscy, a usurer, held land in the City of London which came into the hands of King Richard as an escheat. The king gave it to William of Southwark, whose son and heir afterwards gave it to the prior of Merton, who gave it to Andrew Trentemars, whose heirs now hold it. Let it be taken into the king's hands. The heirs are to come and show their warrant, if they have any, etc. Thereupon the prior of Merton comes and proffers a charter of King Richard attesting that the same king gave, granted and confirmed to his beloved and faithfull William of Southwark, for his service, all the land that belonged to Ralph de Buscy in the Cordwainery in the parish of St Mary le Bow. He also proffers a charter of Luke, son and heir of William of Southwark, which attests that Luke gave to God and to the church of St Mary Merton and the canons there serving God all the aforesaid land with its appurtenances [etc]. Therefore it is adjudged that they hold it in peace, and the

sheriffs are ordered to cause them to have their seisin [etc] (*Eyre 1244*, no. 212).

St Mary Staining

On 6 March 1253 Henry III granted to Merton Priory houses which Mr Nicholas of St Albans had in 'Stanigelane' in London, and which the abbot and canons of Waltham, executors of his will, sold to Merton; that neither they nor those inhabiting the said houses nor their chattels shall be tallaged in any tallage of London more than ? mark (*Cal Pat R, 1247–58*, 181; 1254–6, 262).

? St Mary Woolnoth

Grant of Robert son of John Cherunburt to Holy Trinity of a certain stone house in the parish of St Mary Wulnoth, paying 1d to the king for soke and 2s to the monks of Moroton [?Merton] [1193–1212] (*Cart Holy Trinity*, no. 1022).

St Michael Bassishaw

Sale and quitclaim by Richard de Flit and Alice daughter of Alfred the Mercer to the prior and convent of Holy Trinity of lands in Basinghaw, between the land of Andrew Neuel(im) held of the canons and the land of the canons of Merton, and Aldermanbury [1193–1212] (*Cart Holy Trinity*, no. 1023).

St Michael le Quern

The Grocers' Company owes 6s 8d pa from messuages in St Michael le Quern (ad Bladum) to the late priory of Marten [Merton] c 1550 (*Cal Pat R Edward VI*, iii, 393).

St Thomas Apostle

In 1227 x 37 the canons of Merton reserved 3s pa from lands in the parish of St Thomas Apostle, granted by the chaplain and rector of St Magnus [?Martyr] to Nicholas of Warwick, skinner, for 1 mark pa (*Cart St Mary Clerkw*, no. 353).

Other holdings and rents in unspecified or multiple parishes

1160: In this year Gozo, a vintner of London, gave the house a return or rent of 60s pa (Heales 1898, 20, citing [Parker Library] Corpus Christi College, MS 59).

Grant by Thomas de Haverille to St Bartholomew's hospital of various rents from property in Ironmonger Lane, west of the *piscaria* [fisheries], land in Holborn, St Nicholas Shambles and the *aurifabria* [goldsmiths' shop or quarter], as well the grant of a house and land in Wood Street bought from John Cosin. 5s pa payable to the canons of Merton, although from which property is not stated. c 1210 (*Cart St Bart*, no. 866).

They say that other land which belonged to [Richard] Russel the usurer is opposite the lands which belonged to Martin Boydin which Andrew Trentemars held of the convent of

Merton and it is worth 1 mark pa, now however the convent of
Merton holds it and the prior comes and proffers the king's
charter (*Eyre* 1244, no. 282).

Felicia la Colnere, by her will undated but proved on this
day left rents in Westcheap London to her brother Roger for life
and then to the priory for pious uses; also a house in St Mary
Somerset. She also devised her tenement of 'Caponeshors' at
Merton and other tenements, to the houses of Haliwell, Merton
and St Helen. Undated, proved 10 March 1259 (*Cal Husting Wills*,
i, 2–3).

Andrew Sotesbrok gives and assigns his body and his houses
to the church of Meriton (interpreted by R R Sharpe as
Merton). No date; proved 16 June 1259 (*Cal Husting Wills*, i, 5).

Nichol Pike and Niel Drury, sheriffs of London concerning
£32 14s 10d levied of the rent which was of Adam de Stratton,
among other debts of the king: re raising of a rent for Merton
Priory from a void place in Cheapside once of Sir John
Banquell. Response: go to Exchequer for remittance, 1308–9
(*Rot Parlt*, i, 274a, no. 7).

28 May 1309: grant after inquisition *ad quod damnum* to
Hamo de Rothyng of the reversion of a yearly rent of £32 15s
3d in the City of London, late of Adam de Stratton, which the
late king, into whose hands the estate escheated, had assigned
to the prior and convent of Merton until his indebtedness to
them be discharged (*Cal Pat R*, 1307–13, 160).

3 June 1316: guardianship of Ralph son of Robert le
Chaundeler entrusted to Amicia his mother, relict of the said
Robert, by the mayor and aldermen, together with a tenement
formerly belonging to Adam le chaundeler, which Ralph
recovered from Roger de Evere by assise of novel dissseisin, the
tenement being charged with certain payments to the prior of
Merton and others (*Cal L Book E*, 67–8).

The Fishmongers' Company owes 7s from a messuage called
le lambe on the Hope, formerly due to the late priory of
Martyn, Surrey, *c* 1550 (*Cal Pat R Edward VI*, iii, 393).

Non-priory property leased by Merton

A single instance is recorded of Merton Priory leasing property
belonging to another religious house: during the reign of
Edward I the canons of Merton are recorded as tenants of Holy
Trinity Aldgate in land in 'St Martin' parish for a rent of 7s (*Cart
Holy Trinity*, nos 385–6).

7.2 The moulded stone

Mark Samuel

Introduction

No published excavation in the Greater London area has
produced so vast a range of *ex situ* medieval moulded stones.
Many can be linked to the excavated remains of the church and

claustral complex. Excavation by the Museum of London of a
number of monasteries in the London area permit direct
comparison of worked stone assemblages from foundations of
very different date, history and affiliation across the region. The
architectural history of the church and the construction phases
can be linked to a documented key event, the fall of the tower
in 1222 (Chapter 3.2, 'Documentary evidence'). Recorded
antiquarian interest in Merton commenced when a 'marble
head of a royal or noble personage' was found in 1797 (Society
of Antiquaries cat. no. 148). 'Stones of one of the crux piers (?)
… dug up at Merton Abbey Station' were preserved by the
Guildford Museum (Guildford, Surrey) in the early part of the
20th century (Johnston 1914, 136–7), possibly derived from
the water main trench in 1891 (Bidder and Westlake 1930, 54).

At the Dissolution the church was pulled down and the
materials taken away to build Nonsuch Palace (Chapter 5.1). An
excavation of Nonsuch Palace in 1959 revealed many hundreds of
fragments, recorded by Terry Ball (unpublished) in the early
1960s. Tracery fragments were removed to the Museum of
London and re-identified by Anne Webster in 1992. Some
fragments were left in the Mansion House at Ewell and recorded
by Richard K Morris and Geoff Quilley (then of Warwick
University) during 1992; 66 substantial fragments have thrown
additional light on buildings of the priory extant in 1538. Not all
the building material from the priory was reused at Nonsuch.
Andrew Skelton identified the 'King John's pillar' that stands
outside Kingston Library as part of St Mary Merton; the stones
had been found near Clattern Bridge (Kingston) and re-erected
c 1929 (Finny 1929, 104). Guildford Museum may still have the
unrecognised 'crux' (crossing) blocks, found in possibly the
1890s (Johnston 1914, 136–7). This museum also holds a
collection of minor fragments excavated in 1962–3 which have
been the subject of geological study (Turner 1967, 44–6) and the
conclusions are therefore relevant here.

The excavations at Merton 1986–90 produced 607
recognisable mouldings and elements, found reused in later
rebuilding phases of the priory or recovered from Dissolution
deposits. Statistical analysis shows that the majority of datable
fragments date from before *c* 1270. Even when the datable
fragments are broken down into recognisable classes of major
element, the same sharp fall in numbers at *c* 1310 is apparent.
These figures should be treated as indicators of survival,
however, rather than an accurate reflection of the priory's
building history. Excavation in 1992 on a site within the
northern part of the priory complex at Mill Road, Merton
(MIS92) produced a small number of mouldings, including an
important fragment of the 14th-century cloister arcade only
otherwise known from Nonsuch Palace.

Methodology

The moulded stones were dated by three methods: moulding
pattern, tooling techniques and petrology. A corpus of major
12th-century London monastic assemblages exists in paper and
on the MoLAS ORACLE database, available through the Museum
of London archive.

A pattern-based system of relating developed by R K Morris 'breaks up' each moulding into its constituent elements (patterns) and these elements rather than the entire moulding form the basis of comparison. Complete parallels are so rare as to not be expected, and the occurrence of a rare pattern in otherwise dissimilar mouldings may be of greater significance. Published parallels can provide dates more accurate than medieval pottery dates when associated with documented monuments (Stocker 1993, 19). Occasionally, a close date range can be argued when dealing with those periods of architectural experimentation and flux such as the 'transitional' period. A 50-year date span, however, is 'good' in normal circumstances (R Lea, pers comm).

Tooling marks form a rough means of dating. This method has been used extensively at Merton; the criteria are summarised elsewhere in a report on St Gregory's Canterbury (Hicks and Hicks 2001, 153–4).

The identification at Merton of 'Reigate stone' and Purbeck marble as opposed to generic 'greensand' and other English 'marbles' is based on general characteristics and F G Dime's (Geological Museum) report on the stone fragments found in the 1962–3 excavations at Merton (Turner 1967, 44–5); Caen stone was likewise confirmed at that time (ibid, 45). Identification of Taynton stone is based on, again, general characteristics and limited scientific analysis made for the present report. Samples of oolitic limestone were identified by D F Williams (Southampton University) as from the Taynton or Burford beds of Oxfordshire and described as follows:

a buff-coloured shelly oolitic limestone which contains frequent, generally well-sorted, ooliths. This stone is most probably from the Great Oolite series, in particular the Taynton stone of the Middle Jurassic of Oxfordshire. The Taynton stone formation covers a wide area and quarrying during the medieval period was principally carried out at Taynton, the largest quarry, and also at Burford, Barrington, Sherborne and Windrush (Arkell 1947, 54–78 and fig 27). There is a little variation in texture within the four pieces from Merton Priory which might suggest that they did not necessarily all come from the same location.

Reigate stone played a very important role at St Mary Merton, but Taynton was extensively employed in the mid 12th-century phase. Convenience of access to quarries obviously was a factor and the choice of stone also varied over time. Although there is evidence that Reigate stone was quarried from the immediate pre-Conquest era (Tanner and Clapham 1933, 234), it has been suggested that the loss of Normandy in the reign of John may have intensified the exploitation of the North Downs quarries at Reigate and elsewhere (Tatton-Brown 1990, 76). The effects of medieval warfare on trade can be over-stated and do not explain the fall-off in the use of Taynton stone after c 1200 at Merton.

Interpretable isolated stones and the best examples of duplicated stones were categorised as 'typestones'. Typestones were grouped according to demonstrable relationships into stone groups (see the archive catalogue) and these were then placed in build and construction phases. The published catalogue of illustrated stone, <A1>–<A99>, is ordered chronologically by construction phase (CP1–CP8) and build number (eg CP1.1).

Chronological catalogue of typestones

All stone is 'Reigate stone' unless specified otherwise. Descriptions here are summary where a detailed discussion appears in the relevant period section in Chapter 3.

Construction phase 1 (early part of period M1) or possibly construction phase 2 (later part of period M1)

FRAGMENTS POSSIBLY DERIVED FROM THE FIRST CHURCH

This relatively small group of stones is tentatively identified with the first unlocated church commenced in the second quarter of the 12th century (CP1) (Chapter 3.1, 'Archaeological evidence', 'Ex situ evidence for a mid 12th-century stone church'). The stones were cut with boasters and hafted adzes in a typically 'Norman' manner. Surfaces which were meant to be seen were more neatly finished with diagonal striations. Masons' marks are rare. Reigate stone was the building stone used for dressings. Taynton stone was rarely used. The later (period M1) church (B1) was largely dressed with Taynton stone, but it would be unwise to try and date typestones by no more than their building stone.

Other mouldings which may derive from a mid 12th-century church include part of a string course with Romanesque-style palmette ornament, found reused in the infirmary (<4482> [8722]; CP1.7; not illustrated), which may originally have formed the capital of an ornamental strip pilaster flush with the wall face.

<A1> Scalloped respond capital (cover illustration; Fig 7)
<3066>, [7302]; CP1.1
Vault, or possibly arcade pier, respond in Reigate stone; construction phase 1 (CP1) or 2 (CP2).

<A2> Vault ribstone (Fig 176)
<607>, [4251]; CP1.9
A hemispherical ribstone in Reigate stone was recut as a quoin and used in the late 12th- to early 13th-century church (period M1). Derived from vaults closely resembling those of the mid

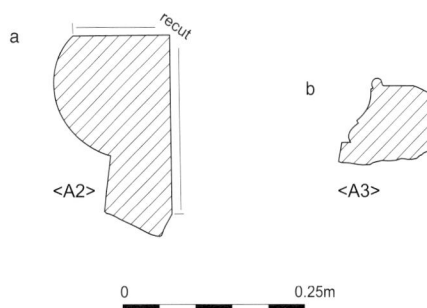

Fig 176 *Cross sections of mouldings possibly from the mid 12th-century church: a – vault ribstone recut as quoin <A2>; b – pilaster base <A3> (scale 1:10)*

12th-century crypt at St John Clerkenwell, but larger; that is, a quadripartite vault employing a soffit roll, possibly associated with scalloped rectilinear respond capitals (eg <A1>) (Chapter 3.1).

<A3> Small fragmentary base mould (Fig 176)
<3676>, [7424]; CP1.9
This base mould in Taynton stone could have many applications. It consisted of a round base mould on a polygonal base with sloping sides. The lost shaft it supported was c 0.18m wide and was held in place by a dowel. The base mould is paralleled by that used at East Meon church (Hampshire). Rigold dates this form to the later 1130s outside East Anglia (1977, fig 5 no. 126). This would make the colonnette base the earliest accurately dated architectural element from the site. The use of Taynton stone, however, is characteristic of the construction phase 2 church.

<A4> Column base with tall square plinth (Fig 8)
<602>, [4251]; CP1.9
This skilfully dressed column base in Taynton stone represents part of a blind arcade; the base was cut on setting to place the shaft directly against the wall. The modified-attic moulding of 'reduced upper roll form' resembles those used in the choir at Chichester after 1114 (Rigold 1977, fig 4 no. 77) and so would be a highly conservative moulding for the late 12th-century church (period M1, B1).

FRAGMENTS DERIVED FROM AN EARLY CLOISTER
Mouldings like capitals from a ?cloister (Chapter 3.1, 'The claustral area (OA4)') were carefully cut.

<A5> and <A6> Coupled capital and coupled column base, cloister (Fig 19; Fig 177)
<A5>, <4808>, [10983]; CP1.9
<A6>, <1007>, [5905]; CP1.9
A scalloped, coupled capital <A5>, initially painted in shades of orange and brown, but later whitewashed (Fig 177). A

Fig 177 Coupled capital <A5>, painted and then whitewashed over, from a possible masonry cloister (Fig 19a–b)

fragmentary, coupled column base <A6> with coupled shafts c 104mm wide and a stylobate (the continuous base supporting the columns) c 0.45m wide; iron dowels held the shafts to the base.

Construction phase 2 (later part of period M1)

This comprises fragments derived from the church and claustral complex (Chapter 3.1, 'Archaeological evidence', 'The late 12th-/early 13th-century church (B1)' and 'The claustral area (OA4)'). The 1130+ dressings and those of the 1170s church are not always distinguishable. The tooling shows the increased use of the boaster chisel although the striated surfaces continued to be diagonally oriented. The boaster was probably used more than is recognised (Stocker 1993, 23). Distinctive lens-shaped dents show that an adze was used to quickly dress the beds or jointing surfaces between dressings. A boaster chisel was used to finish the surfaces of mouldings, ashlars and curved surfaces. On ashlars, the striations are always diagonal.

<A7> Vault rib (Fig 178)
<2895>, [+]; CP2.1

<A8> Plinth moulding (Fig 178)
<5427>, [+]; CP2.5
A wave moulding indicates that this formed the top of a plinth moulding; the severe weathering of the Reigate stone moulding shows it formed part of an external plinth. The moulding capped a plain vertical course, with a chamfered course below it just above ground level. At Lesnes such a moulding was used internally at the south-west pier of the tower (Clapham 1915, pl xii); this must date to the foundation of Lesnes in 1178.

<A9> Sculpture (Fig 63)
<5488>, [10957]; CP2.6
Only the left side of the stylised mane and one eye survives but it can be recognised as a lion's head in a recognisably Romanesque style. The treatment suggests an internal label stop; unabraded, it was perhaps located in the infirmary kitchen.

<A10> ?Wall respond abacus (Fig 178)
<574>, [2034]; CP2.11
Finely cut from Caen stone, this was of rectilinear section with an engaged round shaft. Scribe lines on the impost indicate a soffit-roll rib with a rectilinear dosseret 0.51m wide. The complete abacus was c 0.59m wide.

<A11>–<A15> Aumbries (Fig 20; Fig 21)
<A11> <2421>, [4260]; CP2.14
<A12> <717>, [4284]; CP2.14
<A13> <2466>, [+]; CP2.14
<A14> <913>, [2034]; CP2.14
<A15> <5437>, [+]; CP2.14

<A16> Base of coupled shafts from a ?cloister (Fig 178)
<958>, [5793]; CP2.15

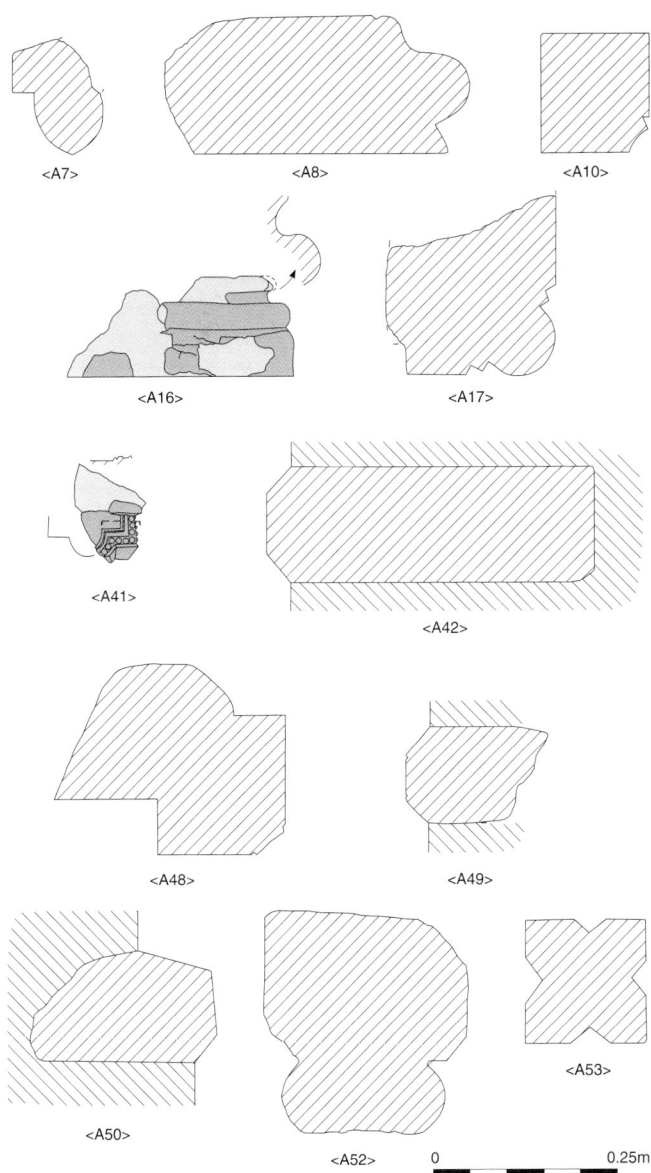

Fig 178 Stone mouldings from construction phase 2: <A7>, <A8>, <A10>, <A16>, <A17>, <A41>, <A42>, <A48>–<A50>, <A52> and <A53> (scale 1:10)

A weathered and abraded single base broken up for reuse. A stylobate 15in wide (0.38m) is indicated. The shafts were 4in (104mm) wide and fastened with iron dowels to the base. The 'simplified' neo-attic base moulding is paralleled by one at Darenth, Kent (Rigold 1977, fig 7 no. 227). This indicates a date between c 1180 and c 1210.

<A17> Rear arch voussoir (Fig 178)
<993>, [5905]; CP2.21
The Reigate stone voussoir forms the moulded junction between the main wall face and a rear arch at right angles to it. The heavy angle-roll is flanked by arrises but other ornament is absent. The opening was c 0.72m wide; it could have been part of a small door or derive from a cloister arcade. This stylistically isolated arch form shows the use of a type of ornament otherwise absent at Merton Priory. The use of flanking arrises to

an angle roll can be seen in the hall at Christchurch Castle which Wood dates to c 1160 (Wood 1965, fig 117 no. xiii); there, paired rather than single flanking arrises are used.

<A18>–<A21> ?West portal arch (Fig 15; Fig 16)
<A18> <889>, [2034]; CP2.33
<A19> <571>, [2034]; CP2.33
<A20> <5454>; CP2.33
<A21> <843>; CP2.33
Two vertical mouldings, one a door jamb, and two voussoirs probably derive from the same multiple-order portal. Their association is suspected rather than proven, being based on derivation from the same complex of foundations. To restore the portal in too much detail would be a mistake as more than one may be represented. The CP2.33 portal did not use shafts but employed a variant of saw-tooth chevron, 'an exclusively late phenomenon' dated after c 1174 at Broadwell church (Borg 1967, 136). Saw-tooth chevron in Peterborough Cathedral (Conway Library, Courtauld Institute of Art, negative no. A94/308), probably dates c 1170–80. The association of billet and chevron is quite normal in this period (eg Canterbury Cathedral 1174–85).

This portal had an ?internal opening c 2.5m wide and may have stood at the west end. Like many features from this church, Taynton and Reigate stone were employed interchangeably.

<A22>–<A32>Architectural features (windows) employing quirk-and-hollow ornament (Fig 12; Fig 13)
<A22> <2843>, [4259]; CP2.35
<A23> <846>, [2034]; CP2.35
<A24> <722>, [4248]; CP2.35
<A25> <2845>, [2034]; CP2.35
<A26> <704>, [4258]; CP2.35
<A27> <702>, [4258]; CP2.35
<A28> <706>, [4248]; CP2.35
<A29> <2929>, [2034]; CP2.35
<A30> <721>, [4258]; CP2.35
<A31> <865>, [2034]; CP2.35
<A32> <701>, [135]; CP2.35
A common moulding form occurred in two sizes, hollow-chamfered with a fillet (Fig 12; Fig 13). Taynton stone was used although not exclusively. The embrasures were in some cases ornamented with a shallow roll (Fig 12b; Fig 13c) but were normally plain. The windows were presumably glazed although little direct evidence for this survived. It is usual in such windows for the iron saddlebars to be socketed into the inner of the two reveals, but only one such socket was seen. The cames were probably fastened to the bars by twisted wire. Some embrasures and other features employed a distinctive chevron-forming-lozenge ornament, and although it was not possible to determine their exact relationship to the windows, they certainly formed part of the same build.

The largest opening (Fig 12) was 0.61m wide (2ft) and was set in a wall only 0.58m thick. It might be that shallow buttresses between the windows increased the effective thickness of the wall. The arched head was slightly pointed (two-centred). The height of the lancet is unknown, but such windows could be very tall. The frequency of fragments was remarkable, enough to indicate the existence of several examples of this window.

Slight differences in geometry indicate the co-existence of a slightly smaller lancet (0.50m wide) set in a thinner wall (0.49m thick) (<A28>–<A32>, Fig 13). Several examples of this lancet are indicated. The simple window moulding can be compared to windows in White Ladies Priory (Shropshire) (Chapter 3.1, 'Archaeological evidence', 'The late 12th-/early 13th-century church (B1)'). The use of a large external rebate for the glass and the incorporation of the sills in a continuous string are notable features.

<A33>–<A35> Lancet sill and string courses (Fig 14)
<A33> <5461>, [+]; CP2.35
<A34> <848>, [2034]; CP2.35
<A35> <874>, [2034]; CP2.35
A third and rarer variety of window employed a heavier moulding with a frontal fillet. Although the arch was not recorded, the lower part of the window articulated with a 'standard' 5in (127mm) string course block to form a sill.

The 'standard' string course blocks survived in large numbers and the window sill illustrates relationship to the windows, entirely typical of the period. The string was cut from Reigate and Taynton stone and was used internally and externally. Some blocks were roughly cut to form window sills (see above) or adapted to hold the lower border of thief-proof window grills.

<A36>–<A40> Architectural features (portals) employing chevron-forming-lozenge ornament (Fig 17; Fig 18)
<A36> <5411>, [+]; CP2.35
<A37> <802>, [4251]; CP2.35
<A38> <586>, [4254]; CP2.35
<A39> <803>, [4251]; CP2.35
<A40> <587>, [140]; CP2.35
Two unweathered (?internal) arches are highly ornate, being cut with chevron-forming-lozenge ornament. They are apparently rear arches but show almost no splay on the reveal and, as such, cannot be associated with any surviving external mouldings. The larger (<A36>, Fig 17) is likely to be associated with a portal, otherwise unknown, while the smaller <A37>–<A40> can be reconstructed in detail as an embrasure c 865mm wide. The arch shows evidence for a hinge pintle (Fig 18b) but lacks a door rebate. This type of ornament, relatively unusual, occurs in loose material from St Gregory's Priory, Canterbury (Hicks and Hicks 2001, 162–3).

<A41> Colonnette capital (Fig 178)
<668>, [3353]; CP2.35
The provenance of this fine square colonnette capital is uncertain. The interior of each main face was sunk to create a rectangular field with a semicircular pendant and pelletal surround. The motif is paralleled in the capital responds of the

north nave arcade at Augustinian Dunstable Priory (Bedfordshire), which is thought to post-date c 1150 (Conway Library, Courtauld Institute of Art, negative no. 520/11 (20); VCH 1912a, 364). Oddly, this fragment was recut, apparently to form part of a blind arcade in the late 12th-century church (period M1, B1) – it was found in a period M2 robber trench fill in the north transept – but it may originally have been freestanding.

<A42> String course (Fig 178)
<989>, [4260]; CP2.38
A massive version (183mm thick) of the basic polygonal string, but far rarer.

<A43>–<A46> Large lancet window variant (with plain rebate) (Fig 11)
<A43> <708>, [4258]; CP2.40
<A44> <777>, [4251]; CP2.40
<A45> <932>, [2034]; CP2.40
<A46> <707>, [4248]; CP2.40
This type of window had an external opening 0.75m wide with a plain external rebate being otherwise unadorned. This window displayed a peculiarity observed on many other fragments: a groove was cut into the rear arch after the window was built. This may have held some form of ephemeral fixture, such as a fabric screen. All found reused in the period M2 north transept foundations; <A44> Taynton stone, the rest were Reigate stone.

<A47> Polygonal pier (Fig 179)
<2753>, [4926]; CP2.49
The provenance of this important but enigmatic element apparently was not recorded during the excavation. The use of Taynton stone suggests that it derives from the 1170s church and it can be reconstructed to form one course of a polygonal pier. The sheer size suggests that it was part of the basal sub-plinth rather than the shaft. The 'unadjusted' reconstruction would have one long axis slightly longer than the other but there is no evidence for this other than the position of the

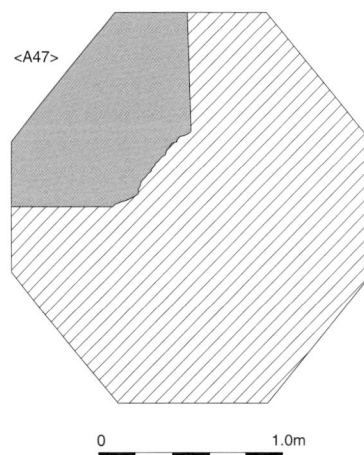

Fig 179 Polygonal pier <A47>: profile (scale 1:40)

median joints. It was more probably 6ft (1.82m) square. The pier may derive from the church of this period although it was not aisled. One possible location for such a pier would be between the presbytery and the inner pair of chapels (Fig 145).

<A48> Door jambstone (Fig 178)
<738>, [4254]; CP2.51
Some stones used in the 1170s church (M1) were initially cut to serve other purposes: a window jambstone was reversed and recut leaving a chamfered door jamb <A48>. This stone was either reused from the putative 1130s church or there was an accidental excess of window jambstones cut when the 1170s (M1) church was being built.

<A49> Polygonal string course (Fig 178)
<2834>, [+]; CP2.55
This element was cut to fit round a corner and as such could have had a variety of applications. It is elaborated by 'nicks' (quirks) above and below the fascia.

<A50> Caen stone ?ground table (Fig 178)
<775>, [4251]; CP2.57
A heavier (158mm) string was used on the exterior employing blocks of Caen stone 17in and 18in (432mm and 457mm) long. The decorative potential of this expensive building stone was deliberately exploited by marking an offset; perhaps at ground table level.

<A51> ?Buttress string course (Fig 180)
<2425>, [4260]; CP2.62
This angled string course may derive from a buttress and is shown in such a role. It marks an offset in the wall and may therefore derive from near its base. It differs fundamentally from the other string courses used in this period, and may derive from construction phase 3.

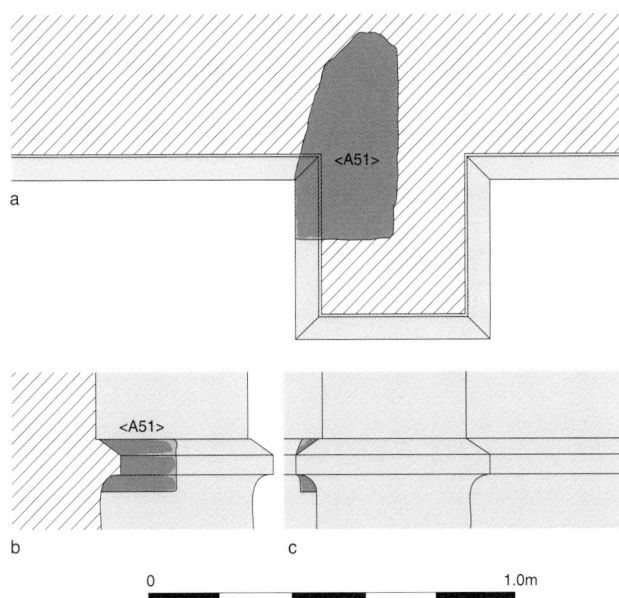

Fig 180 ?Buttress string course <A51>: a – plan, b – transverse section, c – section (scale 1:20)

<A52> ?Rib voussoir fragment (Fig 178)
<2458>, [+]; CP2.63

<A53> Roof finial (Fig 178)
<4181>, [7000]; CP2.74
This fragment was probably a decorative roof finial; it seems to derive from very near the tip of the finial and was brought to a high polish. The use of Taynton stone may indicate a pre-1222 date. The absence of weathering (despite its occurrence in a period P2 demolition layer) is surprising.

Construction phase 3 (rebuilding of the church after 1222: period M2)

This was the oldest part of the church demolished in 1538 and little moulding evidence survives, in contrast to the 1170s church (period M1). On the other hand documentary, stratigraphic and structural (foundation) evidence is well represented and it is on that basis that a separate phase was distinguished. The fragmentary mouldings were recovered from general destruction deposits but are distinguished on stylistic and technical grounds. The vertical tooling is characteristic of a general change of tooling that occurred c 1220. It is therefore a very useful indication of date throughout Britain (Clapham 1934, 116).

Reigate stone was used exclusively, apart from shafting. The flat faces of mouldings are striated parallel to the 'path' of the moulding. A distinctive reeded effect was created on flat surfaces with a very sharp chisel blade about 30mm wide. Distinct bands of parallel marks overlap slightly at the ends to cover the surface. Rolls and moulding details were finished or even polished using abrasive stones, presumably of varying grades. The mortar keying between blocks was enhanced by keying the beds at regular intervals with a pick; this was presumably carried out before the moulding was completed to reduce the risk of damage.

Poured molten lead was used to secure the structurally demanding features that become more common in this period, such as finials. Round channels were drilled through components while they were 'test fitted' on the bank. The molten lead was poured through the channels at the time of setting. Other narrow channels allowed air to escape.

Vaulting fragments confirm that the nave aisles were not built until this time. The observed similarities with Hexham (Northumberland) and Salisbury Cathedral place work squarely in the 1220s and the following decades. The basic form of the nave ?aisle vault rib profile is probably widespread, resembling, for example, the ribs used in the choir aisles at Hexham (Sharpe 1848, 'Vaulting-ribs'), but the use of a beaked roll axial termination is closely indicative of date; these are employed in the main arcades at Salisbury after c 1220 (Morris 1992, 4). This indicates at Merton a nave reconstruction whose date is in close agreement with the documentary record, where reconstruction of the church appears to be under way in 1225 (Chapter 3.2, 'Documentary evidence'). The wave-like lateral rolls of <A63> are however more teardrop-shaped than round in profile, and in this respect the rib has a greater overall affinity to mouldings used at the directly contemporary Salisbury, such as those in the east end of the main arcade (Morris 1992, 4–5). The presbytery at Boxgrove Priory (Sussex) with its lavish use of marble shafting is directly contemporary and may well convey the appearance of the new nave. Enough fragments of Purbeck marble shafting (eg <2185> [5490]; CP3.8; not illustrated) occurred to establish the widespread use of this shafting in the new nave and transepts.

Three stones (<2151> [5466]; <2155> [3798]; <2317> [2151]; CP3.9; not illustrated) represent three courses from the same plain, sloping base course. This can only be approximately dated by the tooling, but technically it was similar to the choir base course at Rievaulx Abbey (Yorkshire North Riding) (Sharpe 1848, 'Base courses'). It hints at the complexity of the external base course that was probably present in the post-1222 church.

Very little evidence survives to show the style of the church's fenestration. Grouped lancets are indicated by two fragments, one of which was reused at Nonsuch Palace. The presbytery at Chetwode (Buckinghamshire), once an Augustinian priory, hints at the appearance of the lost transepts. Minster Abbey, Thanet (Kent), a house for Benedictine nuns, also gives a good idea of Merton church's appearance at this time.

<A54> String (Fig 181)
<5419>, [+]; CP3.1
Only one form of 'five-inch' string can be identified from this building campaign and the survival of four examples suggests it was extensively employed in the church interior. The mould is comparable to a scroll mould but is not paralleled by any published example.

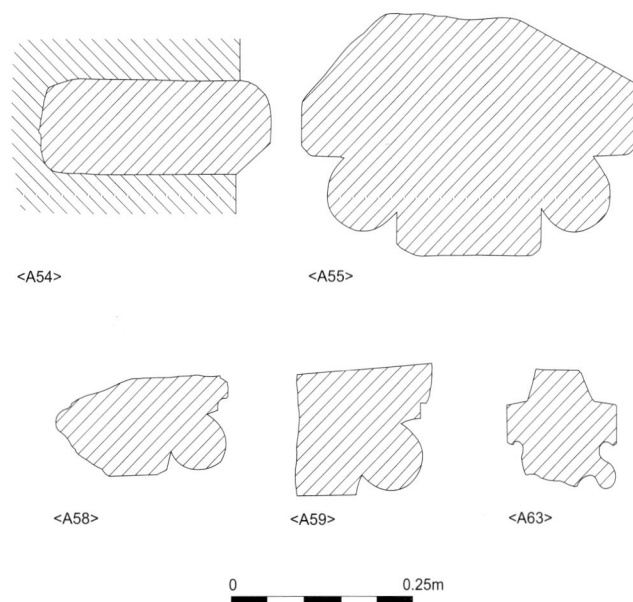

Fig 181 Mouldings <A54>, <A55>, <A58>, <A59> and <A63> from construction phase 3 (scale 1:10)

<A55> ?Transverse rib, from the ? aisle vaulting (Fig 181)
<826>, [5157]; CP3.2
This voussoir may be a transverse rib from the aisle vaulting but could alternatively be the minor order of an arcade or crossing arch. It has a simple rectilinear profile with angle rolls. The profile of the crossing arch at Lindisfarne Priory (Northumberland) c 1120 is a good parallel (Clapham 1934, fig 42 v), but such a simple profile could easily recur.

<A56> and <A57> Vaulting from the aisles of the nave (Fig 36)
<A56> <1029>, [+]; CP3.4
<A57> <5479>, [+]; CP3.4
No labelling survived on the springer block <A57> but it is likely to derive from the nave of this period. An elaborate quadripartite vault was built with moulded diagonal ribs 'dying' into chamfered transverse ribs as at Boxgrove while a simple label mould formed the wall rib. The segmental diagonal rib had a centre about 3.16m distant. The transverse rib was sharply pointed and must have either died away into the wall or been supported by a corbel.

Because the angle between the diagonal rib and the wall is known, a bay division c 5m long and an aisle width of 3.1m can be inferred. This is compatible with the known distance between the nave north wall (M2) and the aisle arcade sleeper wall (Fig 34).

The vault rib profile resembles the ribs used in the choir aisles at Hexham but the use of a beaked roll axial termination parallels the main arcades at Salisbury after c 1220 (see above).

<A58> Lancets (Fig 181)
<836>, [+]; CP3.5
The window moulding rear arch is represented on the site and at Nonsuch Palace. A row of small uniform rear arches, probably from a row of lancets, is indicated. It may have derived from the south transept extant in 1538. This type of window survives in the presbytery of the church of St Mary and St Nicholas at Chetwode which originated as an Augustinian house. There the window is dated c 1250 (RCHM 1913, 85).

<A59> Moulded arch (Fig 181)
<5455>, [+]; CP3.7
The near-complete angle-roll voussoir is likely, because of its large size, to derive from the nave arcade. Differentials in tooling on the soffit show that it formed the major order of the arch.

<A60>–<A62> External superstructure (Fig 182)
<A60> <2928>, [4379]; CP3.10
<A61> <2261>, [4379]; CP3.10
<A62> <2832>, [+]; CP3.10
A severely weathered structure of uncertain purpose. The weathering drip <A61> formed the end of a weathering (Fig 182a). A much larger ?sill block <A60> went above the weathering, and may have related to it in the manner depicted. The lowest block <A62> shared the profile of the weathering block. Tooling is the only indication of date.

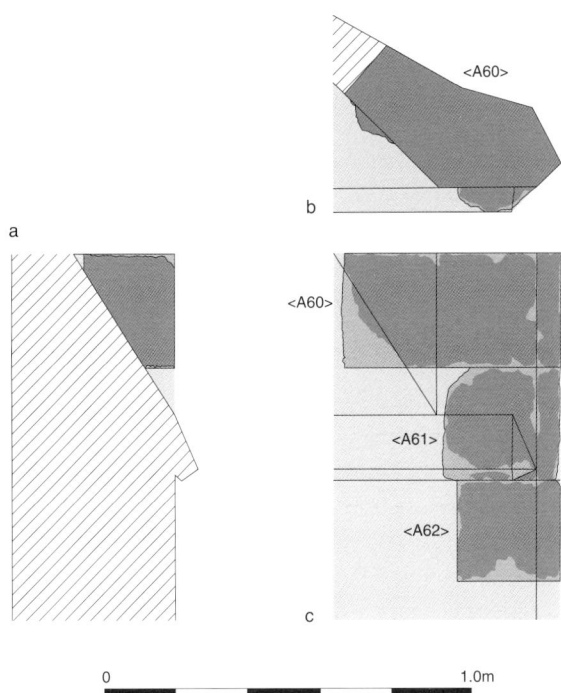

Fig 182 External superstructure <A60>–<A62>: a – transverse section, b – plan, c – elevation (scale 1:20)

This structure, and a stair turret (Chapter 3.2, 'Archaeological evidence', 'The later 13th-century church (B1)'), may derive from part of the ?tower, which may have had to be rebuilt during repairs in the late 14th century.

<A63> Vault rib (Fig 181)
<2903>, [+]; CP3.11
This rib moulding is derived from a substantial vault, which probably covered the south transept or perhaps the chapter house (one piece <2992> of this group was recovered from the south transept robbing). A 'keel' provided keying for the vault web.

<A64> Grave slab (Fig 38)
<507>, [2121]; CP3.12
This Purbeck marble slab, broken into five major pieces, is 1.69m long, tapered and stood about 0.12m proud of the floor. The borders were heavily hollow-chamfered, leaving only a narrow flat strip in the middle occupied by a staff and 'pill box' design, with a barely recognisable cross formed from four circles with raised margins. The design was used on most surviving gravestones of this type in parish churches in, for example, Cambridgeshire and Huntingdonshire (Butler 1956, fig 1). The 'four-circle' cross derives from the floral 'round-leaf' pattern introduced into East Anglia in the early 13th century (ibid, 92) and a mid 13th-century example from Spaldwick (Huntingdonshire) (ibid, fig 1 iv) could be a prototype for the Merton form, although the Merton slab is more stylised. Sally Badham identified this slab as an example of a type found both locally to the originating quarry workshops at Corfe (Dorset) and further afield, including churches in Buckinghamshire, Kent and Lincolnshire; the crosshead is of a voided bracelet type with pointed buds, the stem has a rounded knop, but, very unusually, no mount, and again unusually there is no moulding round the edge of the top surface of the slab. The closest parallel is a broken slab at Cobham (Kent) and the Merton coffin lid is of likely early 13th-century date (S Badham, pers comm).

<A65> ?Processional marker (Fig 183)
<4480>, [8722]; CP3.13
This Reigate stone, cut down for reuse in a foundation in the infirmary hall (B4a, period M3), had a stylised nine-petalled daisy cut into the ashlar face. This may have derived from the infirmary chapel and is tooled in a manner indicative of the 13th century.

Fig 183 Part of a decorated stone ?processional marker <A65>, reused in foundations in the infirmary hall (B4a, period M3) (0.2m scale)

Construction phase 4 (building of claustral structures after c 1222 period M2)

Many fragments were found reused in the period M3 reredorter; these included chamfered ribs and springers from the period M2 undercroft (eg <2898> [+]; <5264> [8361]; <5272> [8361]; CP4.1; not illustrated; Chapter 3.2, 'Archaeological evidence', 'The reredorter (B5)') and window pieces (below).

<A66>–<A68> Windows in reredorter (Fig 67)
<A66> <5273>, [8361]; CP4.2
<A67> <5459>, [+]; CP4.2
<A68> <5275>, [8361]; CP4.2
At least four lancet windows are represented by numerous fragments; all parts being represented (Fig 67). The tooling was unusually rough and each head was cut 'freehand' from a single block. The wall thickness was only 0.34m which would suggest the lancets were set within larger embrasures. The sill <A68> has a whitewashed embrasure. The internal splays were whitewashed. The windows were presumably externally shuttered although no direct evidence for such an arrangement was seen. The tooling can be broadly dated c 1200–75.

Construction phase 5 (the eastern extension of the church) equates approximately to period M3

This phase provides novel insights about medieval building technology and the structural use of Purbeck marble. The methods of cutting, finishing and assembly of this unforgiving material demanded the special skills of 'marbrers' from the West Country. The eastern extension's complexity required the best design skills in the kingdom, perhaps provided by the master who may have built the presbytery at Bristol Cathedral, 'Villam le [G]eometer' (Harvey 1987, 115). Michael of Canterbury was another mason whose responsibility for the new chapel of St Stephen at Westminster Palace suggests a possible involvement. His purchases of marble in the 1290s suggest that he was likely to have been a participant, at least as a middleman (Harvey 1987, 45).

Quarried blocks of Purbeck marble were transported to the site and prepared by masons with special experience of this stone. More confident guesses can be made about them. In 1290 Edward I built a magnificent series of crosses for his dead wife, Queen Eleanor, the Purbeck marble being supplied by Robert Blund and William Canon of Corfe (Salzman 1952, 134). The Canon family seem to have exerted considerable control over the trade and it was probably William or his son who supplied the great unworked blocks used at Merton. They would have been familiar with the great transport difficulties that had to be overcome. Stylistically, apart from slight elaboration of the window mouldings towards the end of the campaign, the eastern extension followed a close design over ?30 years of building; in parallel with the great royal project down the river.

The partial destruction of one important building in the priory seems to have occurred during period M3 in tandem with repairs to the reredorter. A massive Reigate stone block (<4842> [10983]; CP5.1; not illustrated) formed part of a base course like that of Howden (Yorkshire East Riding) (Sharpe 1848, 'Base courses'). The sloping weathering formed a drip which directed rainwater on to a chamfered ground table. The block may alternatively have been released during repairs to the eastern arm in the 15th century. The badly weathered base course was of some age when destroyed. Howden's late 14th-century date (Webb 1956, pl 141) fits in with the general date of the eastern extension.

The church's main parapet coping (of which many Reigate stone fragments were preserved in the later buttress extensions: eg <2179>, <2731>; CP5.15; not illustrated) was apparently uncrenellated and its asymmetrical profile tends towards the stereotyped roll-and-weathering coping used in the London Perpendicular style of the 15th century. It was completely different from the contemporary decorative crenellation used on the gable (<A80>, Fig 97) and the coping of the flying buttresses (over the aisle; see below, <A80>) because it formed part of a wall-walk with a proper parapet.

A probable stair tread from a newel (<2404> [3775]; CP5.4; not illustrated) may have derived from stair turrets at the re-entrants between the Lady chapel and ambulatory.

<A69> Window tracery (Fig 184)
<5449>, [+]; CP5.2
The tip of a large cusp from a ?trefoliated window opening was connected by a web to the surrounding (missing) major order archlet. The cusp is formed by a continuation of the entire minor order. The window glass was secured by a groove. Despite its high finish the window was noticeably irregular and was of no great age when destroyed.

Despite the fragmentary nature of the window, the Decorated style (1280–1377) is detectable. The polygonal form of the axial termination stems from work at Amiens Cathedral (Picardy, France) which dates after 1236 (Morris 1979, 12, fig 13 n). This window may therefore reflect direct influence from Picardy, where the form is thought to have originated (ibid, 12). In this period, the architecture of both lands was closely linked.

<A70>–<A72>, Purbeck marble arcade: minor pier (Fig 81)
<A70> <1921>, [3440]; CP5.3
<A71> <2985>, [3440]; CP5.3

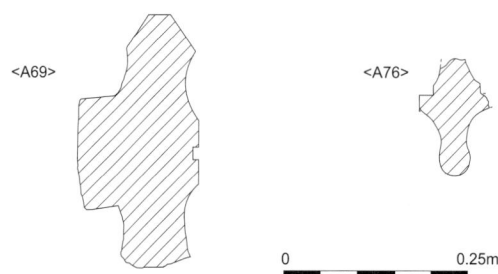

Fig 184 *Tracery mouldings <A69> and <A76> from construction phase 5 (scale 1:10)*

<A72> <2940>; CP5.3

Elements of the annulet course of the minor pier were reused in the foundations of reinforcing buttresses of the Lady chapel thus escaping the general demolition at the Dissolution. This reuse was fortunate because they form part of the superstructure that was otherwise removed to Nonsuch Palace at the Dissolution. Not all were reused at Nonsuch, a series of related blocks were re-erected outside Kingston Library c 1929. They had been reused elsewhere being discovered near Clattern Bridge when digging foundations of new buildings (Finny 1929, 104). These throw important light on the form of the capital and base and are therefore described here, although not excavated on site.

These 'free piers' probably stood immediately east of the crossing. They have severely weathered: this stone, despite its hardness, crumbles badly in outside use.

The moulding of the pier had two-way symmetry with four axial triple-rolls-in-echelon separated by hollows. Each course was split into two blocks (Fig 81) but care was taken to constantly vary the position of the joint. The course height of 265mm was constant.

An assembly letter was deeply cut into the bed of each block (Fig 192, <MM35>, <A71>, and <MM36>, <A72>). The slight striations remaining on the polished surfaces reveal that shaped abrasive tools of granite or some very hard stone were used for polishing.

Scribe lines and compass points on the upper bed of the annulet course provide indirect evidence of the design process (Fig 81b). The moulding was created with a square of exactly 2 feet collinear with the flat fillets flanking the rolls. The corners of the square correspond to the centres of the quadrant hollows. The square had only to be rotated through 45° to form the remainder of the design. This rotation provides the underlying framework of the chamfered shafts, only the slight adjustments of the flanking shafts depart from the geometrical ideal.

The design could be quickly reproduced with burin and compass, as seen on the annulet course <A70>. The majority of the blocks were probably cut with the aid of a template but it is apparent that some exceptional blocks such as the annulet course demanded individual redesign. The scribelines on this block served an additional role: they allowed the exact positioning of the blocks in relation to survey points on the walls. The plain pier blocks lack these setting-out lines, which suggests that the checks were only made at important levels. The changeover to annulets, bases or capitals would be a logical time to make such checks. The appearance of the complete annulet course is modelled according to the geometry in the AutoCAD view (Fig 84).

For the Kingston Library capital and base (Fig 86; Fig 88) a single three-unit capital moulding was used, sweeping around the shaft without variation. Weathering has removed detail but the capital has been reconstructed on the lines of the corbel used on the contemporary Purbeck marble piscina (<A75>, Fig 98; Fig 185).

The upper course of the base survived at Kingston (Fig 86). It formed a double bell base that sharply overhung a polygonal sub-base. The stylistic probability is that the sub-base 'died' into a square plinth. A single surviving block, perhaps from a polygonal respond (not illustrated), supports this assumption.

The masterly 'crowding' of the continuous mouldings on bases (Fig 86) and capitals (Fig 88) is not readily paralleled. One occurrence of this demanding technique is at Bayham Abbey where the outstanding east end (1260s) is 'hard to match precisely in England or elsewhere' (Rigold 1985, 16). The use of 're-entrant arcs' as well as 'intersecting arcs' in the setting out of the capitals and bases is no more easily explained than executed (ibid). It allowed however a constant base or capital moulding on the most sinuous of shafts.

As with the capital, the double-bell moulding swept around the plinth shaft without interruption. Between the triple rolls, the mouldings of the capital and base did not sweep round the centres from which the mouldings were 'struck', as one would expect. The masons instead 'shifted in' each unit of the moulding along a radiant line as required. The intersections of the curves were thereby controlled, producing a harmonious effect and continuous base and capital moulding best appreciated in three dimensions (Fig 87; Fig 89). The same geometric techniques are recorded in the surviving details of the chapter house plinths at St Paul's Cathedral, which Harvey dates c 1332 (Harvey 1961, fig 8.3).

The minor piers were set at a diagonal to the arcade: the 'flint concrete' foundations of the eastern pair of arcade bases were 'diamond-shaped at ground-level' (Bidder and Westlake 1930, 63). These foundations flanked the reredos. Bidder's records make it clear that the reredos and side screens (probably containing an elaborate Easter sepulchre as well as the piscina) were built as a single entity. No shaft/reredos 'bridging' pieces or any part of the reredos superstructure were found (piscina aside), but something of its nature can be predicted from the foundations.

<A73> Arcade voussoir (Fig 90)
<2752>, [4296]; CP5.3

The similarity between this unfinished moulding (Fig 90a) and the minor arcade pier identifies it as part of the same arcade (Fig 90b). The unfinished block allows the moulding of two arcade arches to be reconstructed at the point they met the capital. The 3-D reconstruction of the arcade arch (Fig 91) is based upon the known bay interval of the presbytery (5.94m). The geometry of the arch is otherwise unknown other than it was probably two-centred. The thickness of the arcade wall was about a metre.

This sole surviving voussoir was apparently flawed by overcutting (Fig 90a) but the block throws light on the techniques of the craftsmen. The block was roughed out on the bench with repeated blows of a jadd pick or racer. Once the approximate thickness of the voussoir was reached, the initial cutting of the moulding was carried out using a sharply pointed punch which was repeatedly hit creating a coarsely grooved surface. The next stage was chipping off the ridges between the grooves. This stage was reached in one of the hollows but the craftsman then accidentally spalled off one of the arrises, probably giving rise to some choice words of Middle English.

The moulding is shown in its simplest form. It is possible however that double ogees were cut into the angled faces.

<A74> Purbeck marble arcade: major pier (Fig 82; Fig 84)
<2841>, [3774]; CP5.3

The major arcade piers of the eastern extension repeat the basic triple-rolls-in-echelon theme, but no part of the mould is common to the minor and major forms. Four identical blocks were ingeniously pieced together to form a pier moulding with four-way symmetry (Fig 82b). This 'modular' assembly is based on a grid square with sides 4ft long (1.22m) (Fig 82a). The entire design and jointing system follows this grid rigidly (see below).

Unobserved assembly letters and scribe lines are probably present but the blocks were too heavy to fully inspect. The moulding was cut with a high degree of uniformity, revealing the use of a template. The block is thickest at the visible face but diminishes slightly with distance from it. This would allow a mortar bed while minimising the visible joint. Variable course lifts of c 0.34, 0.28 and 0.58m shows that even the largest quarried blocks were used without wastage.

The geometric basis of the pier was a grid of 16 square feet – the square of the minor pier (Fig 82a). Examination of Fig 82 shows how this grid was used to determine the portion of every compass point from which the moulding was 'struck'. The relation of the grid to the minor pier was determined by the rotated square, the intermediate square representing the square root of 2 (1:1.4142). The mason experimented with the positions of the arc centres, moving them along their respective lines of the grid until satisfied with the result; no centres however were placed in complete independence of the grid.

The use of a foot grid based on the rotated square speeded up the design of the pier by presenting a limited but harmonious choice of designs. The unknown designer responded aesthetically to the very rigidity of this geometry. The grid also helped divide the pier course into its constituent elements. A 'minimalist' template was devised to trace out blocks with a 'swastika' jointing system (Fig 82b) deriving from the grid. This division placed joints at the centres of the hollows. In some cases the entire hollow and its flanking fillet were included on a single block to hide the joint (Fig 82b, broken lines). This was however wasteful of stone. At least one pier was whitewashed but there is no doubt that the polished surfaces were originally bare.

How does this pier fit the excavated foundations? The western of four solid foundations of flint concrete were '6 feet 6 inches' square (Bidder and Westlake 1930, 62). The long axis of the pier as reconstructed is 1.88m or slightly more than 6 feet, but the size of the missing base must be allowed for. It is therefore likely that the pier sat 'squarely' on this foundation. Any 'excess' was taken up by the unknown pier base.

The major pier was probably adorned with annulets like the minor pier. The reconstructed 3-D view (Fig 84) shows the appearance of the putative annulet course from above. Each triple roll probably had a separate capital, in this respect differing from the treatment of the minor pier. It is likely that the north- and south-facing median triple rolls formed wall shafts that rose to the vault springing without interruption.

<A75> Purbeck marble piscina (Fig 98; Fig 185)
<5433>, [2152]; CP5.3

A finely cut basin of the highest quality would have fitted an alcove 2ft (0.61m) wide. This probably owes its survival to reuse in one of the buttress extensions. A drain hole ran through the centre of the basin. The alcove was flanked by three-quarter shafts resting on delicately carved corbels with elegant swirling foliage pendants. The piscina at Great Bedwin (Wiltshire) (Fletcher 1943, 460), gives a good idea of its complete state. This piscina perhaps derived from a chapel in the aisle/ambulatory or from the south side of the presbytery. The break across it may have led to its removal in the late 14th-century repairs. The basin's projecting lip was carved in the form of a capital that survives in outline. A three-unit capital can be reconstructed but the bell and necking are conjectural. The remainder of the alcove may have taken the form of an ogival arch ornamented with crockets. The Merton basin capital terminated with either a pendant or an engaged shaft; the second possibility is shown (Fig 98b).

The 'capitals' are 0.13m across and are typical of fashionable works of the south-east in the Decorated period (Morris 1979, 23). The pattern occurs in, for example, the Meopham tomb at Canterbury Cathedral dated to 1333 (ibid, fig 16 j: ii). The 'swept-over' foliage pendants are paralleled at Bayham Abbey (S Hurman, pers comm) in the work of the east end, which Rigold dates to not much later than the 1260s (1985, 16).

<A76> Traceried window (Fig 184)
<2954>, [7395]; CP5.6

Many small fragments deriving from the destruction of a traceried window were found within a Dissolution demolition layer to the east of the Lady chapel. Unfortunately no substantial element survives; the remaining fragments represent no more than the 'reject' material – the minor order tracery too small to be of use. It can be roughly dated to the Decorated period (c 1280–1377). This may have been a window (? the great east

Fig 185 Fragment of piscina <A75>, for a 2ft-wide (0.61m) alcove

window) in the Lady chapel (and every bit as odd as its Bristol counterpart) but the small scale and irregular craftsmanship suggests it derived not from the eastern extension but from another structure such as the infirmary chapel.

<A77> Foliate capital/finial (Fig 186)
<241>, [3217]; CP5.7

A fragmentary ?finial still displays the lead fixing that secured it to another dressing above it; this is a rare survival. The lead was poured down a central channel in the abacus to radiate out along star-like patterns of grooves, carefully cut in opposite beds to match, thus improving the bond.

<A78> Window tracery (Fig 79; Fig 80; Fig 187)
<5298>, [7395]; CP5.9

This window was on a scale suitable to a great abbey church. Two-handed elements derive from either side of a great oculus with a timber frame provided from the start. The other lights were conventionally glazed. The major-order oculus was flanked by a minor-order septfoil archlet, level with the centre of the oculus.

The major and minor order were set out on parallel lines 67.5mm apart scribed on the beds (Fig 79a). The major order was twice the width of the minor order.

The toolkit and technology are characteristic of the early 14th century. A high finish left no tooling marks but regular diagonal marks on the bed show a chisel was used. The tracery elements were held together by lead, which was poured down channels cut into the connecting beds. These channels radiate from the glazing groove (Fig 187); the lead entry hole would be concealed when the cames were set. The spread of the lead in the joint was encouraged by sloping all the joints including those that would normally be horizontal (Fig 80).

The window was destroyed when major structural work was carried out to cure movement (period M4). The oculus probably held a pivoting window to allow fumes to escape during major religious festivals. Like the even larger ?aisle window (CP5.12, <A83>–<A86>) this had a timber-framed oculus. Both were reused in close proximity suggesting they came from the same area of the eastern extension, probably the crossing.

The flanking keeled rolls existed in the crypt of St Stephen's chapel, Westminster (Mackenzie 1844, pl xii). The axial termination at Westminster employed a roll and fillet flanked by quirks; similar to the axial termination of the diagonal vault rib of the central vessel of the Merton church. The beak mould (Fig 79; Fig 93) points to a common building campaign for these windows and the vault. On this basis, the window is probably from the clerestory.

<A79> Flying buttress (Fig 96)
<5453>, [+]; CP5.10

The possible construction of flying buttresses over the aisles in this period is indicated by the survival of a solitary abutment (<A79>, Fig 96) and by copings (<2270>, <2273>; not illustrated) probably from a second, wider and curved flying

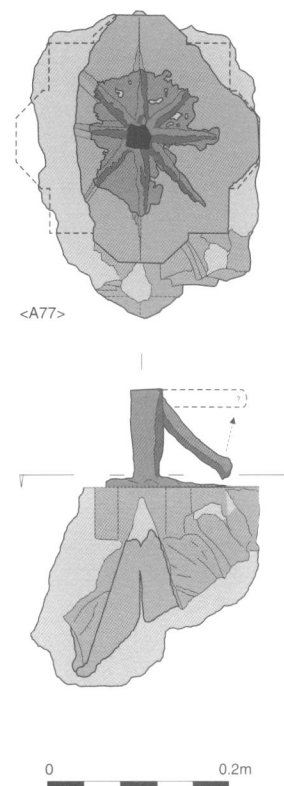

Fig 186 *Foliate capital/finial <A77> (dark tone denotes lead fixing) (scale 1:8)*

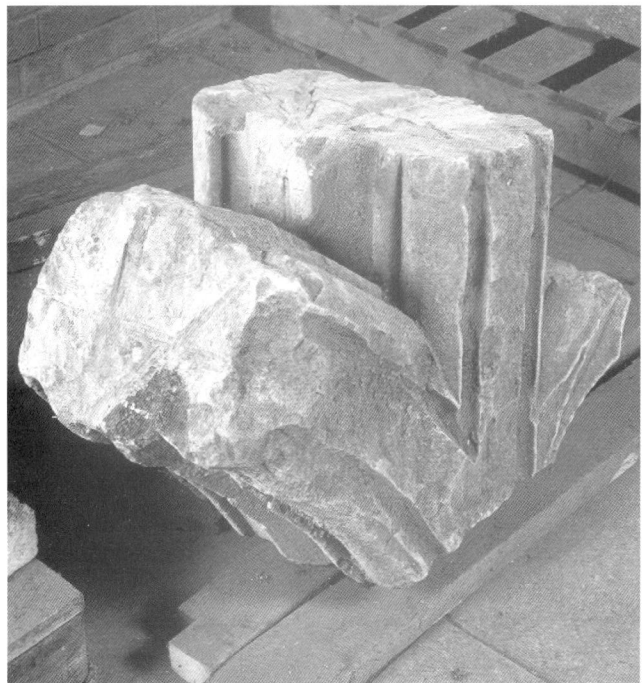

Fig 187 *Window tracery <A78> (maximum height c 0.49m)*

buttress. The moulding of the latter is very similar, but larger, to that employed on the crenellation <A80>. The similarities in tooling and the use of a notably friable Reigate stone confirm that these fragments derive from the very end of the building of the eastern extension.

187

<A80> Crenellated gable (Fig 97)

<2276>, [4260]; CP5.10

The solitary crenellation fragment <A80> is sole testament to the presence of a sharply pointed gable, making it improbable that the eastern extension was a hall church. The uniform moulding formed a symmetrical coping stone with stepped weatherings (Fig 97a); it had a central 'handrail' and was exactly 2ft (0.61m) in wall depth.

The crenellation moulding meets at an obtuse angle of 137.4°. The most probable location of the coping is on a steeply pitched crenellated gable apparently pitched at 42.6° (Fig 97b). The angle at the base of the merlon is close to the more regular 45° (the diagonal of a square) and it is likely that 45° was the true roof pitch.

<A81> and <A82> Buttress weatherings (Fig 94; Fig 95)

<A81> <2290>, [3026]; CP5.11

<A82> <2291>, [3026]; CP5.11

Kentish ragstone.

<A83>–<A86>Window tracery (Fig 77; Fig 78)

<A83> <2136>, [4926]; CP5.12

<A84> <2837>, [+]; CP5.12

<A85> <3903>, [7395]; CP5.12

<A86> <5300>, [7395]; CP5.12

The fragments of tracery from the ?aisles of the eastern extension owe their survival to repairs made to the eastern extension in the late 14th century. The footings of buttress extensions on the north and south aisles produced several examples. They may derive from a single window severely damaged by the structural instability of the church. Alternatively, the fragments are failed tracery elements that had to be individually replaced at the same time that the buttresses were strengthened.

Unlike the ?clerestory window (CP5.9, <A78>), this window was represented by nine typestones. This window was the larger of the two (the width of the strong mullion was 319mm as opposed to 271mm).

The four fragments <A83>–<A86> form a supermullion/oculus complex and a separate openwork trefoil/dagger complex. The first fragment can be recognised as a cusp of an openwork trefoil and <A84> archlet. A sharp vertical cusp subdivided the base of an inverted dagger over <A83> may associate with it as illustrated (Fig 77).

It is not possible to relate the two areas of tracery <5296> [7395] and <A86>. The supermullion <A86> incorporates a minor archlet. It is possible that the two fragments <A85> and <A86> relate as depicted in Fig 78.

A ?central round oculus c 1.51m (?5ft) across was hinged for ventilation (Fig 78). The width probably corresponds to two standard light widths plus one mullion. This indicates that a standard light width of 595mm (?2ft) was used (not illustrated). The known aisle module would accommodate four-light windows.

The oculus was provided with a timber frame at the outset. This presumably held a pivoted circular shutter.

The tracery is similar to the subarcuated and intersecting tracery of the east window of St Ethelreda's, Ely Place, London, which contains complete trefoils and inverted daggers of this form.

Glass was held in this window employing three different techniques and it may be that while some lights were glazed at the point of assembly, other tracery openings had to wait for the completion of stained glass. It was therefore necessary to make the subsequent insertion of completed cames possible, rather than delay construction. The trefoil fragment <A83> (Fig 77) shows the use of two separate techniques on the same moulding. Undercut external rebates rather than grooves were used on the supermullions. A V-shaped channel held the timber frame of the oculus in position.

Technically, the window was broadly similar to the ?clerestory window (CP5.9) but a different 'fist' is detectable in the chisel marks. All joints were lead-bound. The horizontal bed of <A86> showed a 'fishbone' pattern of lead grooves, the lead being presumably poured in at the glazing groove. Different cutting as well as moulding preferences are represented; these changes probably were introduced over a building campaign lasting decades.

The use of openwork trefoils seems to originate in the late Rayonnant style (literally 'radiating', a French style of Gothic architecture, characterised by distinctive rose windows) as exemplified in such buildings as in Troyes, St-Urbain: where they were employed at some date after 1262 in the inner layer of tracery within the tracery of the apse of the south chapel (Wilson 1990, fig 85). The 'Kentish' St Ethelreda's, Ely Place, is dated by Harvey (1987, 45) to the incumbency of Bishop Louth (1290–8). This is in good accord with the remainder of the stylistic dating for the eastern extension.

Dating by these methods is never exact, for mouldings employed in Gloucester Cathedral have similar axial terminations and are dated c 1331 and c 1337 (Harvey 1961, fig 8.1). A date in the early years of the 14th century seems the most balanced assessment.

<A87>–<A89> Vault ribs and boss (Fig 92; Fig 93)

<A87> <2917>, [2507]; CP5.13

<A88> <2977>, [2507]; CP5.13

<A89> Nonsuch; CP5.13

The vault boss <A89> from Nonsuch throws much light on the vaulting system used at Merton.

Eight ribs converged at the boss (Fig 92), which in its original form was probably a yard (914mm) long; the angles of abutment show that the heavier ribs were diagonal while the light ribs formed the ridges. The diagonal rib abutments were 16.25° from the vertical. The diagonal ribs were a foot (305mm) from web to soffit and about 9½in wide (242mm). Abutments on the boss are the only evidence for the ridge ribs but fragments of diagonal ribs occurred both on site and at Nonsuch. The ridge ribs were 7½in deep (0.19m) and roughly 8in wide (208mm). The four diagonal rib fragments have a barely detectable curve (Fig 93).

An extremely sharp chisel allowed a very fine finish. The jointing beds of the boss and horizontal ridge ribs were cut and fixed with poured lead as with the windows. The diagonal (arch) ribs did not require such lead reinforcement. Two of the diagonal rib joints and one of the ridge rib joints are recut. Documented repairs probably involved the reconstruction of the vault.

The reverse of the boss and the ridge ribs formed a continuous level walkway in the roof space. The 'triangulation point' (not illustrated) played an important role in the correct construction of the vault. The angle between the diagonal and ridge ribs was 28.38°, showing the vaulting compartment to

have been very elongated in relation to its width. It is therefore possible to reconstruct the proportions of the vaulting compartment through tan 28.375 as 1:1.85. The ridge rib joints were cut with an 'arrow head' pattern. The 'arrow point' formed a hole on the reverse of the rib, where the lead was poured in.

The compartment long axis ran north–south across the central vessel of the church (Fig 188). The 'standard' eastern extension bay was 5.93m x 10.69m as measured from the midline of the arcades. This proportion was 1:1.80, a close

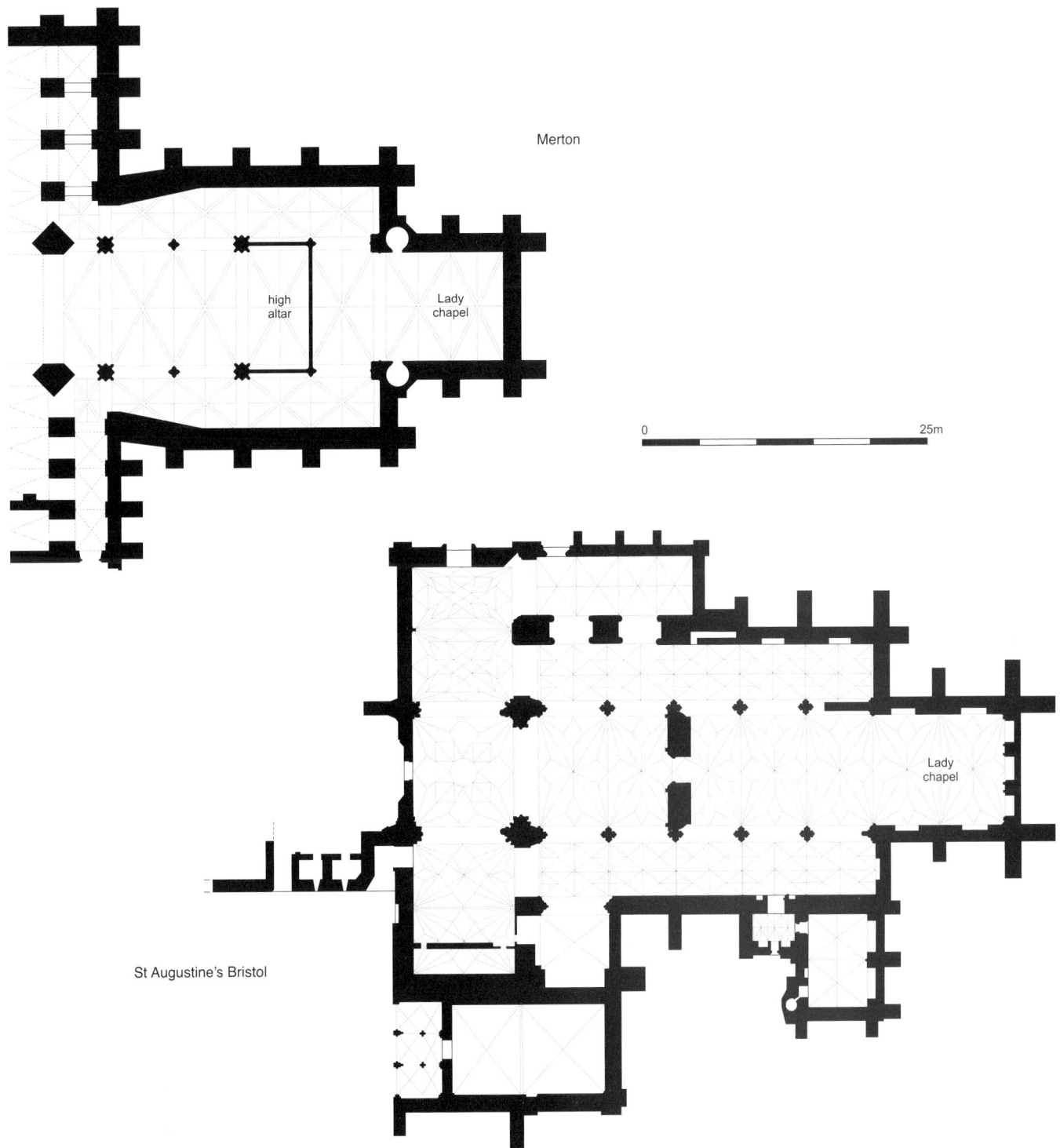

Fig 188 Comparative reconstructed plans of (upper) Merton's eastern extension and (lower) the pre-restoration presbytery of St Augustine's Bristol (Bristol Cathedral), showing vaulting compartments (after Britton 1836) (scale 1:500)

enough, if not perfect, fit with the Merton boss, that does not allow however for the arcade wall thickness. Compartments at Bristol are 1:1.58 (Fig 188). The limited evidence at Merton (see below) suggests it had a fairly conventional vault, unlike Bristol. At Bristol level ridge ribs are absent and lierne ribs are employed (Pevsner and Metcalf 1985, 38). The presence of liernes at Merton cannot however be ruled out.

A possible explanation can be advanced for the disparity in compartment proportion. At Merton, the alternating pier system forced a different vaulting solution to the Bristol pattern. The median wall shafts on the major piers may have continued upwards to support moulded transverse arches that crossed the central vessel at every second bay. Three separated pairs of quadripartite vaulting compartments fitted between the three putative transverse arches that rested on the major piers. There are grounds for seeing both Merton and Bristol as part of an enquiry into novel architectural solutions on much the same plan.

The stylistic links between some windows and the vault are apparent. The mouldings of the major rib form important dating evidence. They are closely paralleled in the cloisters of Norwich Cathedral (1279 sqq: Morris 1979, fig 15 e) and the church of St Mary in Beverley (Yorkshire East Riding) (Fletcher 1943, 454). The minor form is very similar to those used in the cloister at Lincoln (1295 and later; Morris 1979, fig 14 d). A simple hollow chamfered rib is known from the Nonsuch assemblage (Morris type 28; eg <1028>; CP5.13; not illustrated). It resembles the rib moulding used in the choir aisles of York Minster after 1361 (Morris 1979, fig 14 m). The arch centre was c 4.6m; such geometry is compatible with the Merton eastern extension aisle vaulting. The toolmarks are characteristic of the decades following the Black Death and a separate building campaign is apparently represented.

Construction phase 6 (building of structures in the 14th century, period M3)

This phase represents works and alterations to priory buildings. Although such activity is very poorly represented on the main excavation, it is significant that the destruction of a single post-medieval building (MIS92) produced an important group probably deriving from one or more priory buildings of this period. Such buildings are likely to have survived the initial demolitions only to fall to a later and local demand for stone.

A ?undercroft vault corbel (<5492>; CP6.5; not illustrated) found at MIS92 may come from a rebuilding of the north wall of the reredorter. This new wall [8145] was built over the central partition wall [11254] of the 13th-century undercroft. The reredorter superstructure was extensively rebuilt in the mid 14th century. The corbel's apparent date range is compatible with such use.

<A90>–<A93> 'Freehand' two-light window (Fig 127)
<A90> <4821>; CP6.9
<A91> <4828>; CP6.9
<A92> <4829>; CP6.9
<A93> <5457>, [10983]; CP6.9

The tracery of a two light-window was cut from a single block. It illustrates a 'freehand' approach, normally avoided, and suggests the work of an inadequately trained mason. A more carefully thought-out window would have been pieced together from several elements. The two lights were conventionally glazed but the oculus and falchions presented the glazier with serious problems, so that the glazing panels had to be nailed on to the exterior!

The tooling techniques are those used prior to the Black Death. The tracery pattern is very widespread and can be seen in such domestic buildings as Bampton Castle (Oxfordshire), where it was used in the gatehouse range which is dated to 1315 (Wood 1965, pl LV, a). The absence of weathering shows that this window was nearly new when destroyed. The alterations to the reredorter that destroyed the window probably came not later than 1450.

Construction phase 7 (rebuilding of cloister, period M3)

<A94>–<A99> Cloister arcade (Fig 104; Fig 105)
<A94> NON59 <1006>, [-]
<A95> NON59 <1010>, [-]
<A96> NON59 <1011>, [-]
<A97> NON59 <1015>, [-]
<A98> NON59 <1021>, [-]
<A99> MIS92 <11>, [1]; CP7.1

The Nonsuch excavation produced 23 important inter-related tracery fragments, probably from at least one large window. (These moulding variants were named as part of a system devised by Richard K Morris; this system is used here.) The mouldings recovered in 1959 were so well preserved as to suggest the intention to reuse the structure at Nonsuch, but they were eventually reused in foundations (M Biddle, pers comm). The MIS92 excavation produced a single fragment (Morris's type 11; <A99>, Fig 104a–c) confirming that the Nonsuch tracery derives from Merton.

Six key elements <A94>–<A99> survive. The tracery scheme had four lights, each 2ft (0.61m) wide with cinquefoil heads. Four supermullions, each 8in (0.2m) wide, rose from the apices of the cinquefoils. A fifth supermullion rose from the central divisions. 'Sub-reticulation' describes these round openings with trefoliated cusping. The remaining gaps were filled by quatrefoiled eyelets. The tracery was uniform apart from slight rearrangements in the sub-reticulations and their capping straight pieces.

The MIS92 minor mullion <A99> incorporates small capitals at the springing line and glazing grooves are absent. Such capitals are used in cloisters at, for example, the west cloister at Westminster (Harvey 1978, pl 25). An Ewell fragment is dated to the mid to late 14th century (R K Morris, pers comm). An unrecorded reconstruction of the main cloister about this time seems to have occurred. This seems to have been the last major work of any kind in the priory.

Two types of arcade tracery differ only in minor details, one variant being illustrated (Fig 105). A 'strong mullion' known from Nonsuch (Morris's type 6: Fig 104d) would logically be employed as the division between bays (not illustrated), but this would have made the wall no more than 0.45m thick at that point. The capital <A99> known from MIS92 was certainly absent from the 'type 6' mullion – another problem. The best explanation is that variants of the window existed, some of which were glazed and without capitals, or with glazing restricted to the tracery and employing capitals. The absence of glazing grooves on the capital mullion (Fig 104a) indicates a cloister. Some of the Nonsuch fragments held at Ewell also lack this feature. The foundation to the west of the chapter house hints at buttressed piers in an arcade (the interval being c 3.87m).

There is no evidence for a stone vault over the cloister. The opening was 10ft wide (3.05m) measured from reveal to reveal.

Construction phase 8 (miscellaneous unprovenanced works from c 1366–1538, late period M3 and M4)

It would be misleading not to make some further mention of material from Nonsuch Palace. Thirty-two separate builds can be distinguished from fragmentary material deriving from the main excavation, MIS92 and the Nonsuch excavation (NON59). Fourteen of these builds are only known from NON59 and it is possible that some of this late medieval material derives from a parish church at Nonsuch swept away by Henry VIII. It would therefore be unwise to draw too many hard conclusions from the assemblage.

A collective view of the assemblage shows both the difficulty in dating material of the Perpendicular style while conveying how the priory encountered in 1538 was, at least in its appearance, a collegiate structure of the late medieval period. Only certain parts of the church and claustral structures were older. At least four ?domestic windows and a fireplace can be distinguished as well as seven windows of a more ornate nature. The latter perhaps indicate late refenestration of the church but could equally well derive from the more important buildings of the priory. It must be remembered that a large number of the excavated fragments represent buildings removed before the Dissolution.

Two of the three survivals of sculpture derive from Nonsuch Palace. A fine standing figure of a ?canon (CP8.13) and the head of a lion (CP8.16) at Ewell suggest the destruction of monuments within the church that probably occurred immediately after the Dissolution (R K Morris, pers comm; Dent 1970, pl 3a).

Masons' marks

The great majority of the ashlars recovered were reused in cist graves, possibly stockpiled for reuse after the destruction of the late 12th/early 13th-century (period M1) church in 1222. Many are scribed on their visible surfaces with masons' marks (Fig 189; Table 25); these are generally thought to be a form

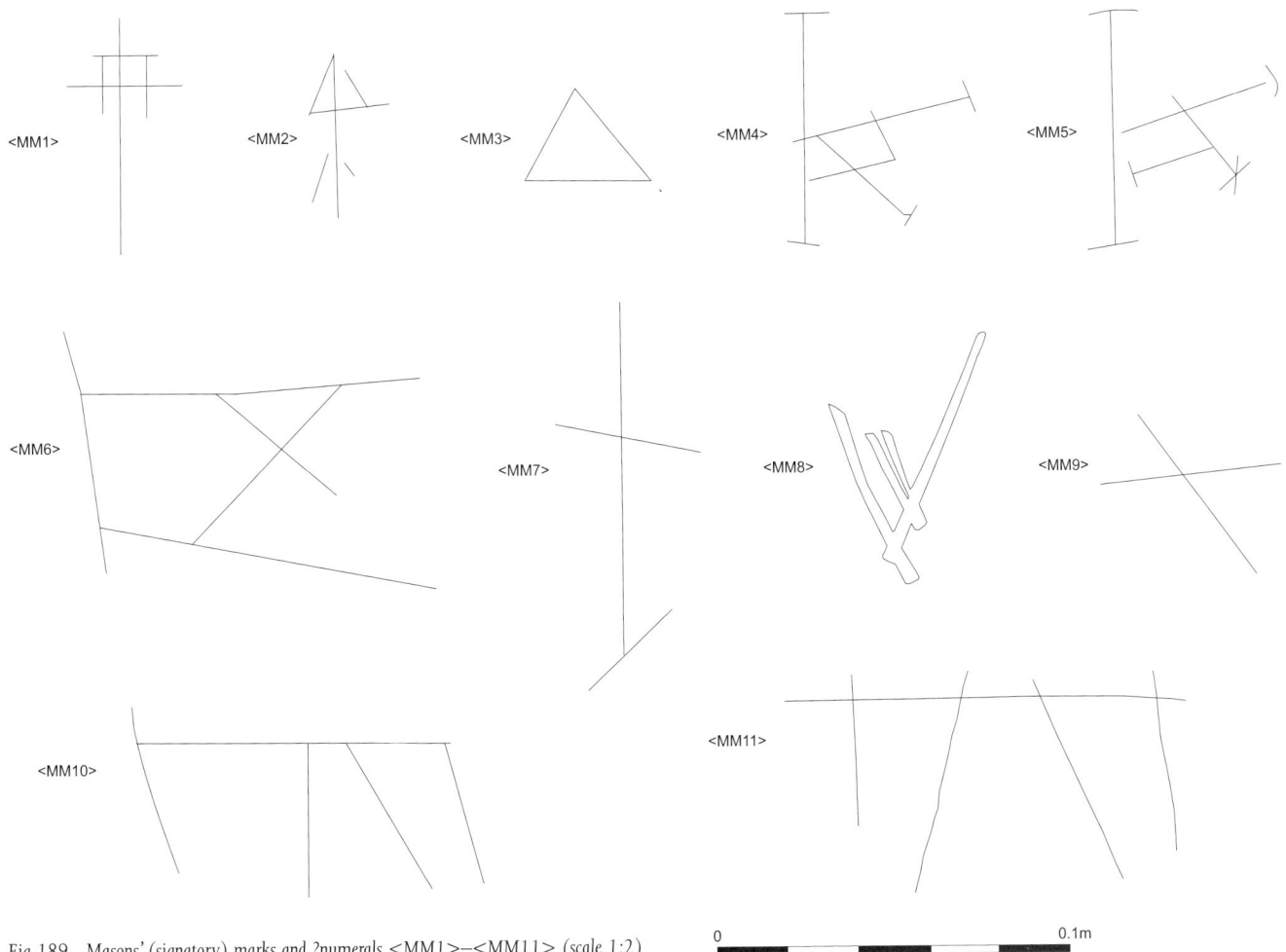

Fig 189 Masons' (signatory) marks and ?numerals <MM1>–<MM11> (scale 1:2)

Table 25 Illustrated masons' marks

Masons' mark no.	Accession no.	Stone type, description	Ashlar course height (mm)	Ashlar course width (mm)	Fig no.
Masons' (signatory) marks and ?numerals on exposed surfaces of dressings					
<MM1>	<3640>	moulding: window jamb hollow chamfer, c 1350+	-	-	189
<MM2>	<3064>	moulding: arcade soffit, c 1350+	-	-	189
<MM3>	<5462>	moulding: flying buttress, c 1350+	-	-	189
<MM4>	<2067>	ashlar: 'K' mark (9 strokes); Reigate stone	225	310	189
<MM5>	<2069>	ashlar: 'K' mark (10 strokes); Reigate stone	217	265	189
<MM6>	<2833>	ashlar: (5 strokes); Reigate stone	155	222	189
<MM7>	<2927>	ashlar: (3 strokes); Reigate stone	225	310	189
<MM8>	<2784>	ashlar: 'flail' mark (3 strokes); Reigate stone	202	188	189
<MM9>	<2921>	ashlar: 'X'	200	193	189
<MM10>	<1955>	pavior: ?numeral; orientation unknown; Reigate stone	-	-	189
<MM11>	<2780>	pavior: ?numeral; orientation unknown; Reigate stone	-	-	189
?Non-signatory marks, purpose unknown					
<MM12>	<5467>	moulding/voussoir: c 1200–75; temporary mark, scribe line, orientation unknown	-	-	190
<MM13>	<715>	moulding/voussoir: c 1150–c 1250; temporary mark, scribe line, orientation unknown	-	-	190
<MM14>	<2871>	moulding/voussoir: c 1150–c 1250; temporary mark, scribe line, orientation unknown	-	-	190
<MM15>	<5461>	moulding/voussoir <A33>: c 1170–c 1200; temporary mark, scribe line, orientation unknown	-	-	190
<MM16>	<5474>	moulding/voussoir: c 1150–c 1225; temporary mark, deep cut, oriented to wall face	-	-	190
<MM17>	<766>	moulding/voussoir: c 1200–c 1300; temporary mark, deep cut, oriented to wall face	-	-	190
<MM18>	<779>	moulding/voussoir: c 1170–c 1200; temporary mark, deep cut, oriented to wall face	-	-	190
<MM19>	<3440>	ashlar: c 1225–c 1300; very large visible mark	-	-	190
<MM20>	<5482>	ashlar: stairwell, c 1225–c 1300; four concentric circles , ?graffito; Reigate stone	180	253	190
<MM21>	<837>	ashlar: c 1150–c 1225; ?quarry mark	323	216	190
Temporary bed marks, associated with ? survey/regulation					
<MM22>	<2919>	ashlar: 'N' mark	240	184	191
<MM23>	<806>	vousoir: 'N' mark	-	-	191
<MM24>	<->	voussoir: 'set square' indicating arch centre	-	-	191
<MM25>	<5407>	voussoir: numeral	-	-	191
<MM26>	<2776>	ashlar: survey control mark, concealed triangle for ? plumb bob, ? survey point, oriented to wall face; Caen stone	178	233	191
<MM27>	<765>	voussoir: survey control mark, corner-indicating arrow, oriented to wall face	-	-	191
Temporary ?setters' marks, on bed and oriented to wall face					
<MM28>	<2856>	ashlar: 'T' mark; Reigate stone	194	206	192
<MM29>	<2525>	ashlar: concealed 'intersecting tramline' or 'hourglass', occupying entire surface	223	>385	192
<MM30>	<2865>	ashlar: concealed 'crossed z' or 'hourglass', occupying entire surface; oolitic limestone	195	275	192
<MM31>	<2054>	ashlar: c 1150–c 1225; concealed pentangle; ?Caen stone	199	249	192
<MM32>	<2844>	ashlars: c 1225–c 1300; concealed 'arrowhead' marks on both upper and lower beds; Reigate stone	170	202	192
<MM33>	<2777>	ashlar: concealed 'flail' mark; ?Caen stone	197	232	192
<MM34>	<2593>	ashlar: concealed 'R'; Reigate stone	160	320	192
Assembly letters					
<MM35>	<2985>	pier element <A71>; Purbeck marble	-	-	192
<MM36>	<2940>	pier element <A72>; Purbeck marble	-	-	192

of individual signature. The assemblage however allows a variety of 'concealed markers' to be studied (Figs 190–2; Table 25), an impossibility in a surviving building. These raise a series of questions, but were presumably connected with assembly. Very few were seen on mouldings (Fig 189, <MM1>–<MM3>).

The significance of masons' marks remains uncertain. The great majority appear to pre-date 1222 and throw particular light on concealed markers. Some 'normal' masons' marks also occur and show the elaboration of individual signatory marks (Fig 189, <MM4>, <MM5>) that is a recognised practice

(Samuel 1999, 165–7). The purpose of the deeper marks roughly cut with a boaster chisel is less clear (eg Fig 190, <MM16>, <MM17>, <MM18>). These deep marks occur on the beds of both ashlar and mouldings.

The heavy concealed marks include a very heavy reversed 'N', occurring several times on both plain rear-arch (the arch on the inside of a wall that encloses a window or door) voussoirs and ashlars (Fig 191, <MM22>, <MM23>). In one instance, a 'W' masons' mark is lightly inscribed on the visible face of the same voussoir, suggesting the 'N' served another purpose. In other cases, 'arrows' seem to draw attention to

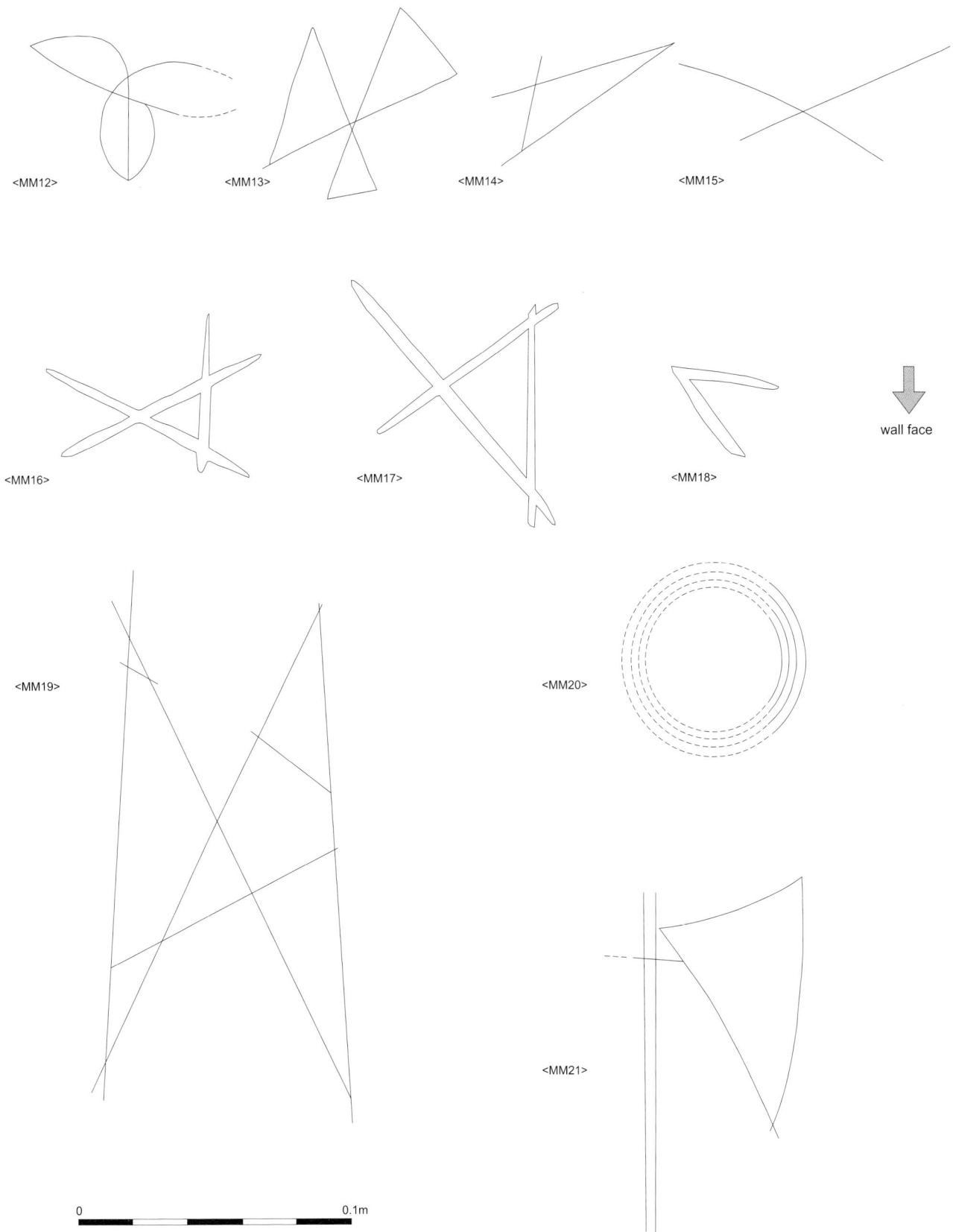

<MM12>

<MM13>

<MM14>

<MM15>

<MM16>

<MM17>

<MM18>

wall face

<MM19>

<MM20>

<MM21>

0   0.1m

Fig 190 Masons' ?non-signatory marks <MM12>–<MM21>, of unknown purpose (scale 1:2)

some feature (eg Fig 191 <MM27>), while in one instance an 'L' or ? set square seems to be placed to assist in the alignment of a voussoir (Fig 191 <MM24>). One mark resembles a plumb bob mark familiar today (Fig 191

<MM26>). A mark roughly cut into a voussoir (Fig 191 <MM25>; from CP2.68) bears a close resemblance to numerals on the reverse of medieval *opus sectile* tiles used in Prior Crauden's chapel at Ely Cathedral.

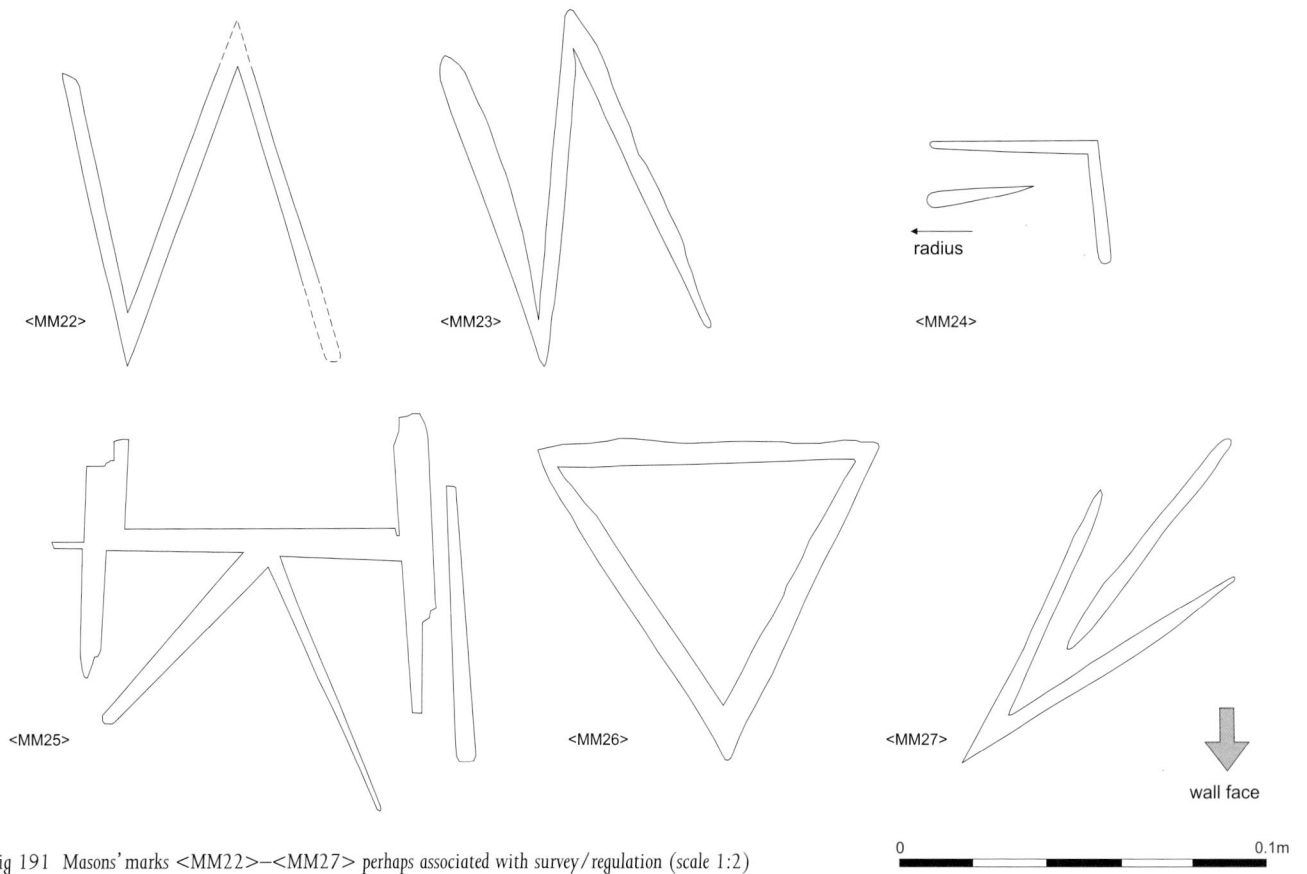

Fig 191 *Masons' marks <MM22>–<MM27> perhaps associated with survey/regulation (scale 1:2)*

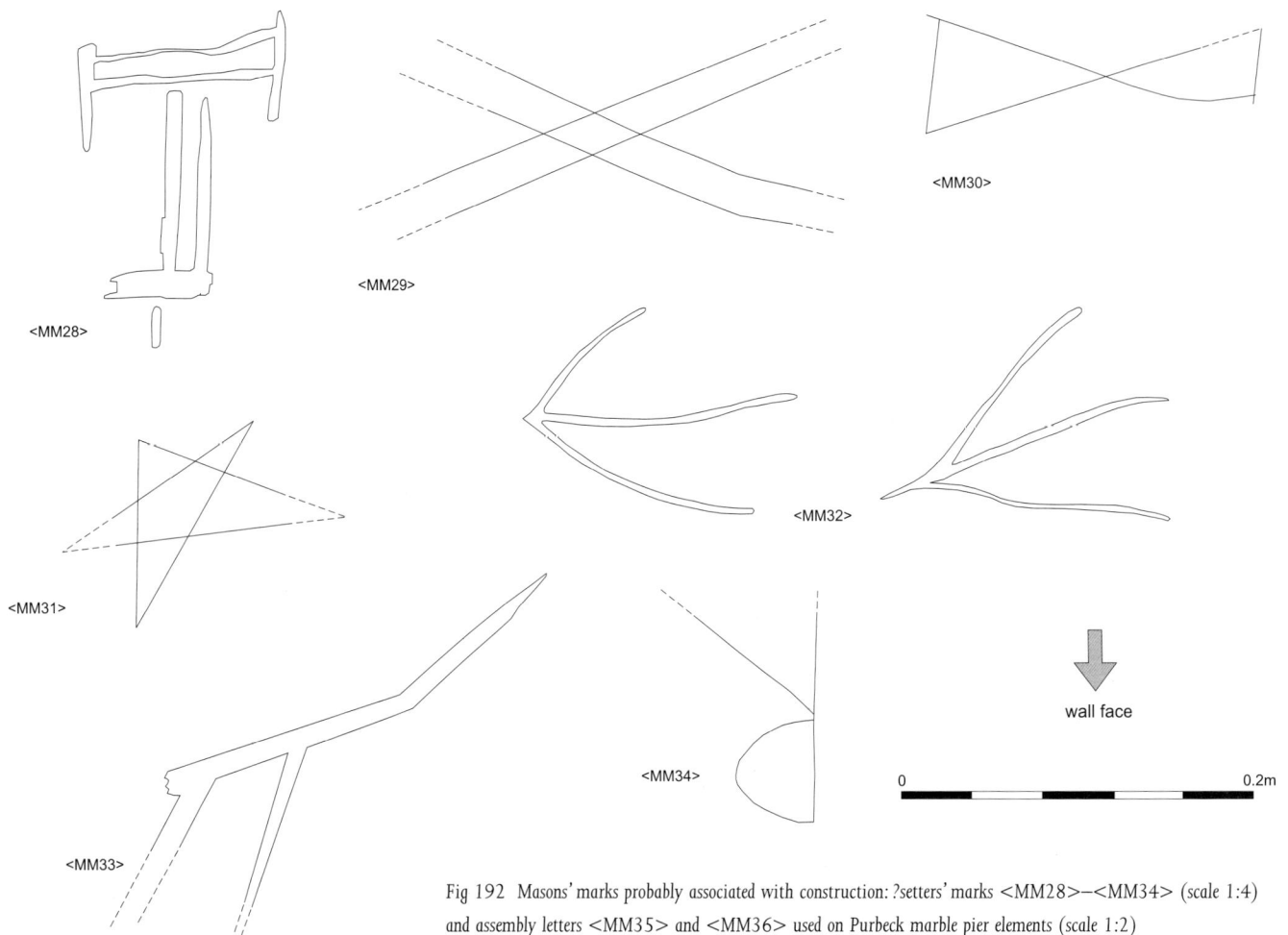

Fig 192 *Masons' marks probably associated with construction: ?setters' marks <MM28>–<MM34> (scale 1:4) and assembly letters <MM35> and <MM36> used on Purbeck marble pier elements (scale 1:2)*

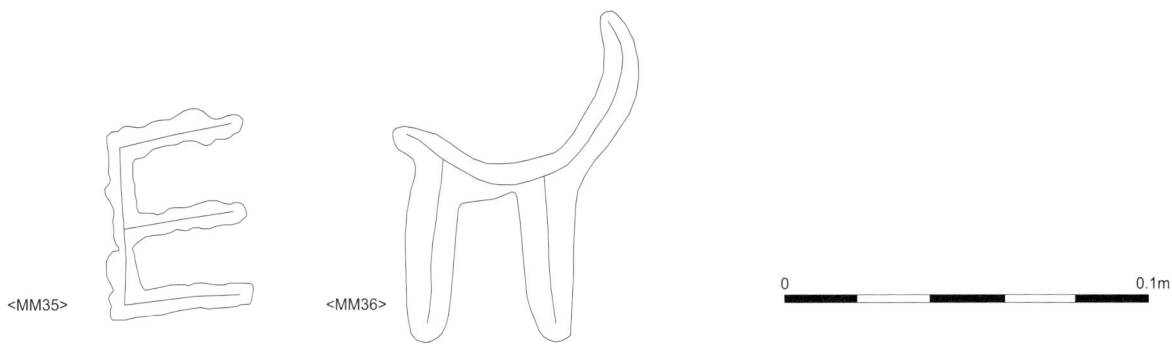

<MM35>   <MM36>

0   0.1m

Fig 192 (cont)

7.3 Ceramic and stone building material

Ian Betts

Introduction

The Merton project produced an enormous quantity of ceramic items, the vast majority from Dissolution demolition and later deposits, but only a fraction of this material could be examined. Resources were directed to the more important ceramics namely the floor tiles and early 13th-century moulded bricks. All the decorated and plain mosaic floor tiles have been fully recorded, as have c 85% of the remaining plain-glazed floor tiles. Most of the bricks have been examined, particularly the 13th-century moulded bricks and later yellow medieval types.

The biggest single class of building material encountered was roofing tile, an estimated 250 large sacks from the 1988 excavation alone. However only a fraction of this assemblage (less than 5%) could be examined, the remainder was discarded. The roofing tile was very quickly scanned to extract individual items of importance such as complete tiles, tiles with marks and rarer types such as hip tiles. All these were then fully recorded. Full descriptions of the fabric types, together with contextual information, are in the archive (Betts 1997); type numbers refer to the Museum of London fabric reference collection.

Floor tile

The excavations produced over 1000 decorated and plain mosaic floor tiles. In addition, there are many hundreds of plain-glazed and unglazed floor tiles. Large areas of the priory were probably paved with decorated and plain floor tiles from the 13th century onwards.

The majority of floor tiles fall into a number of discrete groups, based on the different clays (fabric type) used in their manufacture and, in the case of the decorated tiles, the design. The plain mosaic tiles have been classified by shape and fabric type. What is not altogether certain is the date of some of these groups, particularly those with decorative designs not found on tiles used in London.

Decorated floor tile identification

The decorative designs at St Mary Merton have been identified by reference to tiles published elsewhere. The principal source of published medieval floor tile designs in Britain is by Eames (1980). In the various tables of designs listed below, tiles illustrated in Eames have the letter E preceding the design number.

A number of 14th-century Penn tiles are included in a catalogue published by Hohler (1942). The design numbers given by Hohler have also been included in the section on Penn tiles for completeness (these have the letter P preceding the design number). For 13th-century 'Westminster' tiles the design numbers published by Betts (2002) are given (these have the letter W preceding the design number). Where tiles are not illustrated by Eames, Hohler or Betts, reference is made to drawings in other publications.

A small number of decorative tiles from the priory, found before the excavations in 1976, have been published previously. The current location of many of these tiles is unknown, but most designs are represented in the groups discussed below.

Plain floor tile identification

These are mainly classified by size and fabric type, although other features such as keying and the presence of nail holes is equally important. Certain plain tiles are from the same source as some of the decorated floor tiles, so it makes sense to discuss these together. Others are probably also from the same source as certain of the decorated tiles, but which plain tiles group goes with which decorated group is not always altogether clear. These tiles have therefore been discussed separately. Other plain floor tiles are from different sources to the decorated examples, notably the large number of plain-glazed tiles from the Low Countries (often referred to as 'Flemish' tiles) and tiles made from a distinct clay type characterised by numerous very small black iron oxide grains. Again these are discussed separately.

Building material fabric type and sources

Analysis of fabric has revealed that various floor tile groups were made using the same clay type, which would suggest that they all originate from the same tilery or tilemaking area.

What is particularly significant is that at St Mary Merton there are Chertsey tiles, made at Chertsey Abbey itself around c 1290–c 1300. They were produced using the same clay (fabric type 2894) as that used to make a number of other floor tile groups, notably a set of mosaic tiles and decorated square tiles with thick white and pink slip. Whether these were also made at Chertsey is not known, although the distance from Merton to Chertsey (22.5km) is not too great. What it does indicate is these floor tiles were probably made somewhere in Surrey.

The presence of different types of floor tile made using the same clay suggests that the priory was supplied with tiles from a settled community of tile makers over a prolonged period. Floor tiles in fabric type 2894 seem to have first arrived after the priory church was rebuilt after 1222 and continued to be used until at least the end of the 13th century.

Many of the roofing tiles are made from similar clay to the floor tiles in fabric type 2894 (roof tile fabric type 2586). This would suggest that the Surrey tile makers may well have supplied Merton with its ceramic roofing tile, at least during the 13th century. It may also be significant that many of the thin glazed bricks, perhaps used as wall decoration, are also made from similar clay.

1222–c 1300 (period M2)

DECORATED AND PLAIN MOSAIC GROUP

Fabric type: 2894

The most spectacular floor tiles used at the priory in this period are the series of large, plain-glazed and decorated tiles which formed a mosaic paving within the chapter house (<T1>–<T24>, Fig 40; <T25>–<T34>, Fig 41). Regretably, the white slip on the decorated tiles was only thinly applied with the result that many tiles are very badly worn, as well as being very fragmentary. Later floor tiles used at the priory from the same tilemaking area, had a much deeper decorative clay inlay.

A total of 30 plain mosaic shapes and 85 decorated tiles are present (Table 26) ranging in thickness from 25mm to 33mm (but mostly 30–33mm). The plain tiles are glazed, usually yellow, black or various shades of green or brown, although light green glaze on white slip tiles are also present. These tiles seem to be slightly thicker than the decorated examples, although this may be because many seem less worn.

There seem to be two slightly different versions of one design, perhaps made using slightly different templates (<T27> and <T28>). Certain decorated tiles seem to have been made to the same shape as certain plain-glazed examples, such as decorated <T16> and plain <T34>, suggesting they were used in the same area of pavement. How the various mosaic shapes fitted together is far from certain, as it is apparent that there must have been other tile shapes that have not been found. In certain areas larger plain yellow tiles and decorated tiles seem to have been bordered by smaller dark green and brown coloured tiles. Designs <T26> and <T33> seem to fit together (<T35>, Fig 193) as may designs <T27> and <T28>, <T15> and

Table 26 *Decorated and plain mosaic tiles from St Mary Merton*

Tile no.	No. of tiles	Fig no.
Decorated tiles		
<T1>	2	40
<T2>	4	40
<T3>	4	40
<T4>	22	40
<T5>	1	40
<T6>	2	40
<T7>	4	40
<T8>	1	40
<T9>	1	40
<T10>	5	40
<T11>	9 (includes 3 uncertain examples)	40
<T12>	2	40
<T13>	2	40
<T14>	1	40
<T15>	1	40
<T16>	9	40
<T17>	5	40
<T18>	1	40
<T19>	1	40
<T20>	1	40
<T21>	1	40
<T22>	4	40
<T23>	1	40
<T24>	1	40
Plain mosaic		
<T25>	4	41
<T26>	5	41
<T27>, <T28>	4	41
<T29>	4 (includes 2 uncertain examples)	41
<T30>	7 (includes 1 uncertain example)	41
<T31>	2	41
<T32>	1	41
<T33>	2 (includes 1 uncertain example)	41
<T34>	1	41
Uncertain	37	
Total	152	

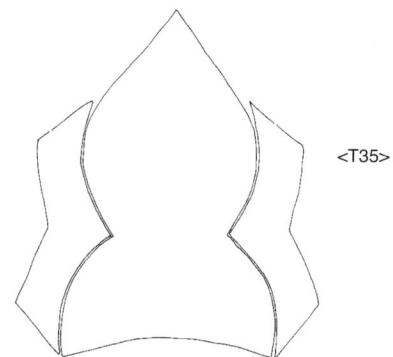

Fig 193 *The mosaic tile reconstruction <T35> (scale 1:6)*

<T30>. There also seem to have been panels of decorated square tiles (designs <T2>, <T3>, <T7>, <T8>, <T10>) bordered by plain-glazed triangular tiles <T32>. The tiled floor at Byland Abbey has panels of different styles of mosaic together with areas of square tiles with triangular tiles at the edge.

THINNER DECORATIVE TILE

Two further tiles (<T36> and <T37>, Fig 194) have designs in a similar decorative style to that found on the mosaic tiles. This suggests that they are either contemporary or were made a short time after, perhaps to pave another area of the priory. Both were made using the same type of clay as the tiles in the mosaic group. Where they differ is in their thickness, being only 19–26mm thick. Too little survives of either tile to say whether they formed part of a mosaic pavement although both tiles seem to be square in shape.

KEYED, WHITE SLIP, PLAIN-GLAZED AND UNGLAZED GROUP
Fabric type: 2894

The decorated tiles in this group (Fig 195; Table 27) are characterised by the application of a thick layer of white slip below the glazed surface. The majority of these tiles have a single large central keying mark in the base, although one tile (design 4, <T43>) has two such holes. The use of a thick white slip, which would have made these tiles expensive to produce, suggests they are of early date. They are probably 13th century, the date given by Eames (1980) for design E2457. A large

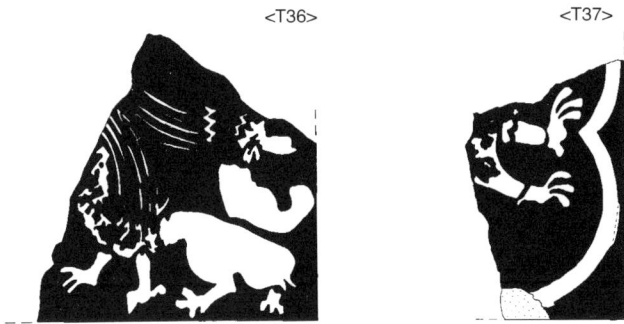

Fig 194 Thinner decorative floor tiles <T36> and <T37> (scale 1:3)

Fig 195 Decorated keyed, white slip floor tiles <T38>–<T49> (scale 1:3)

Table 27 Decorated keyed white slip tiles from St Mary Merton

Design no.	No. of tiles	Tile no. (Fig 195)
E1880	6	<T38>
E2457	23 (includes 1 uncertain example)	<T39>
1	2	<T40>
2	3	<T41>
3	8	<T42>
4	8 (includes 1 uncertain example)	<T43>
5	5	<T44>
6	1	<T45>
7	7	-
8	9	-
7 & 8	1	<T46>
9	1	<T47>
10	1	<T48>
11	1	<T49>
Uncertain	8	-
Total	84	

Table 28 Complete plain keyed tiles from St Mary Merton, by size

Size group	Length/breadth (mm)	Thickness (mm)	Glaze type
1	141–142	?	glazed
2	168–172	30–33	unglazed
3	216	30	unglazed

number of decorated white slip tiles were found dumped in burials in the north transept. There seems little doubt that these were used on the floor of the priory church, probably with those decorated with a thick pink-coloured slip (discussed below).

Certain tiles of design E2457 (<T39>) have been scored and cut into four smaller tiles. These have either the flower petal or fleur-de-lis parts of the decoration. Designs 7 (flower) and 8 (star) are cut down from larger tiles, although only one half-complete tile, which has both the flower petal and star designs, has survived (<T46>). These smaller cut-down tiles measure around 70–73mm square. There are also two triangularly shaped tiles both decorated with design 5 (<T44>).

The central key seems to have weakened the complete tiles in this group so that relatively few survive intact. Those that do measure 141–146mm square, by 25–30mm in thickness, apart from the solitary tile with design 10 (also keyed; <T48>) which measures just 101mm square by 24–25mm thick.

Two decorated white slip group tiles were published by Eames (1980, designs 1880, 2457; <T38>, <T39>) from Merton, although there is no indication where they were made or where either tile was found. It is possible that the decorated white slip and other keyed tiles may have been close to the priory itself. Certainly, the use of large amounts of white slip on each tile would have made them expensive to produce; it is unlikely such tiles would have been mass-produced for a commercial market. If they were indeed made close to the priory, perhaps by the priory itself, this would account for the presence of a very bloated and over-fired decorated tile (design E2457) which cannot be anything other than a kiln waster.

The distinctive central keying, along with fabric type, can be used to identify plain examples which appear to have been made at the same tilery. Some of these have yellow-, brown- and light green-glazed colours whilst others are unglazed. The

use of unglazed tiles is rather odd as floor tiles lacking glaze were not introduced into the City of London until they were first imported from the Low Countries in the late 16th or early 17th centuries.

Plain keyed tiles were made in three sizes, the smallest of which corresponds with the majority of complete decorated examples. Table 28 shows that the smaller sized tiles are glazed whilst the larger tiles are unglazed, although this observation is based on only a very small number of complete examples.

The thickness of the incomplete glazed examples is 23–31mm (similar to the decorated tiles) which compares with 26–36mm for the unglazed tiles. In general the unglazed tiles tend to be slightly thicker than the glazed examples indicating they formed part of tiles of slightly larger size. This suggests that the division in size between glazed and unglazed types in Table 28 is probably correct.

The glazed tiles were probably used with the decorated tiles in the same floor area, whilst the unglazed tiles are more likely to have paved a less prestigious part of the priory. One light green-glazed tile is unusual in having been made with a central key but then diagonally scored and broken into two triangular fragments after firing.

There is no reason to think that the glazed tiles are any later in date than the unglazed examples. Indeed, one unglazed tile has glaze splashes on its base, suggesting both types were fired in the same kiln.

PINK SLIP GROUP
Fabric type: 2894

The glazed tiles in this group (Fig 196; Table 29) are very similar to the thick white slip group discussed above, and are even made from the same distinctive sandy clay. There are, however, two important differences, firstly the thick slip used to create the decorative designs has a pink tinge and secondly none of the tiles have keyed bases, many are also of different size.

The use of the same clay and the decorative design made using thick slip would indicate that these pink slip group tiles originate from the same tilery as the white slip group. The difference in design and lack of keying, on the other hand, suggests that they are unlikely to be contemporary, although it is far from certain whether they were made earlier or later than the white slip group, although both are probably 13th century in date.

Only one design in the pink slip group has been previously published by Eames (1980, design 2431; <T50>) from an

Table 29 Decorated pink slip tiles from St Mary Merton

Design no.	No. of tiles	Tile no. (Fig 196)
E2431	13	<T50>
1	6	<T51>
2	2	<T52>
3	4	<T53>
4	1	<T54>
Uncertain	2	-
Total	28	

Fig 196 Decorated pink slip group tiles <T50>–<T54> (scale 1:3)

unknown site. Most of the tiles in this group measure 111–120mm square by 28–33mm in thickness. An exception are the two tiles of design 3 (<T53>) which measure 147mm square by 28–30mm in thickness, which is similar to certain decorated and plain-glazed tiles in the white slip group.

As with the white slip group certain tiles were cut down to a smaller size by the normal practice of scoring the clay and then breaking the tile after firing. One tile with design E2431 has been cut to a breadth of only 42mm. Another similarity with the white slip group is that there is evidence for tile manufacture, in the form of a tile with glaze over the broken edge which may have been discarded as a 'waster'.

There are a number of plain-glazed floor tiles, discussed later, which may have been made around the same time as the pink slip tiles, as they use the same clay and lack keying.

'WESTMINSTER' TILE

Fabric types: 2199, 2892

Tiles of 'Westminster' type are so-called because they were first recognised in the floor of the muniment room at Westminster Abbey. They are the only floor tiles known with certainty to have been made in London as a tile kiln making 'Westminster' tiles was uncovered at Farringdon Road in the 19th century (Price 1870, 32). Both plain-glazed and decorated tiles of 'Westminster' type are very common in London, occurring on many church and monastic sites. They are also found in Bedfordshire, Berkshire, Buckinghamshire, Herfordshire, Essex, Surrey and north Kent. The 'Westminster' tile makers also travelled north to establish a separate tile-manufacturing centre

in the Midlands (Betts 2002, 16–20).

The dating of 'Westminster' tiles is still somewhat problematic, the earliest securely dated tiles are those laid in the floor of the muniment room at Westminster Abbey in the late 1250s or early 1260s. How long 'Westminster' continued to be made in London is uncertain, although the number of decorative designs, which presently stands at over 160, suggests manufacture over a considerable period of time. Production had almost certainly ceased by the beginning of the 13th century when floor tiles of the Eltham Palace/Lesnes Abbey group were being used to pave the priory.

A large number of both plain and decorated 'Westminster' tiles have been found at St Mary Merton. Table 30 provides a concordance with the Westminster (W) numbers used in Betts (2002); a selection of the designs found at Merton are illustrated in Fig 197 (ie the designs which, when this report was originally written, were unpublished but were subsequently included in Betts 2002).

'Westminster' tiles were used in the rebuilt priory church during the 13th century, and a number of plain and decorated examples were found in situ in the west aisle (room 3) of the infirmary hall (B4a). Other 'Westminster' tiles were found in floor layers within the slype of the chapter house and in the apse of the building itself.

The plain lead-glazed 'Westminster' floor tiles from the priory are normally various shades of brown, yellow and dark green, although a small number of plain black tiles are present. On a small number of tiles this lead glaze does not cover the whole of the upper surface.

<T55>   W3

<T56>   W136

<T57>   W83

<T58>   W153

<T59>   W107

<T60>   W53

<T61>   W59

<T62>   W11

<T63>   W139

<T64>   W111

<T65>   W102

<T66>   W94   <T67>   W151

<T68>   W130

<T69>   W70

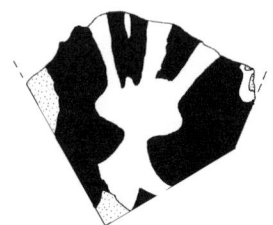

<T70>   W73

Fig 197 'Westminster' decorated floor tiles <T55>–<T70> (scale 1:3)

It is common at Merton for plain 'Westminster' tiles to have been scored diagonally and then, after firing, split into two triangular-shaped fragments. Decorated triangular tiles are not present, although one decorated square tile (W49) was cut into this shape at a later date. Some of these triangular tiles would have been used along the edge of panels of decorated tiles if the square tiles were set at a 45° angle to the walls, as in parts of the muniment room, Pyx chamber and St Faith's chapel at Westminster Abbey (Betts 2002, 32–5). Others may have been used for other purposes, at Seal House in London a pavement of 'Westminster' tiles had decorative bands of triangular and square tiles (Schofield 1995, 112, fig 126). These decorative bands may have contained a type of smaller sized triangular tile found at the priory. These were produced by scoring square tiles in both directions diagonally, which could then be broken into four smaller triangular tiles.

The square decorated and plain tiles measure 102–115mm square (most are 108–110mm) by 21–28mm in thickness. The only exception is a solitary plain, dark green-glazed example which measures 133mm in breadth by 29–30mm in thickness.

Certain tiles (from [1114], OA3, period M2) show evidence of over-firing, having cracked and become distorted during the firing process. There is no evidence that these tiles were made at Merton so presumably such tiles arrived at Merton, along with the properly fired examples, for other uses such as hard-core or rubble infill. The same may be true of another 'Westminster' tile (from [1057], B4a, period M4) which has green glaze covering a partly broken top surface.

A number of plain-glazed tiles have been cut to shape after firing so allowing them to fit a particular floor area. This reshaping takes the form of the removal of one corner. Of more significance is the shaped decorated tile with Betts design W73 which has had one corner deliberately removed before firing (<T70>, Fig 197). It is possible that this tile may have been made especially for St Mary Merton to fit a specific area of floor. A similar tile has been found at Bermondsey Abbey (Betts 2002, 7, fig 1 no. 4).

A distinctive feature at Merton is the presence of small mosaic tiles made using similar clays to the 'Westminster' tiles although not necessarily made at the same location. They were found in building rubble containing Coggeshall-type brick of c 1220 and Kingston ware pottery dated after c 1230. They clearly pre-date the main 'Westminster' series discussed earlier, so it would seem likely they were installed in the 1230s or 1240s. This would place them in a similar date range as other mosiac pavements such as Fountains Abbey (1220–47) and Salisbury Cathedral (c 1225 and c 1240).

Seven mosaic shapes (A–G) are present (<T71>–<T78>, Fig 198; Table 31), mostly measuring 19–29mm in thickness. All were made by scoring, firing and then breaking what were presumably originally square tiles. Of particular interest in this respect is a square tile <T78> which has been deeply scored in order to make smaller square mosaic tiles like <T75>, although for some reason this was never carried out. Similarly, two examples of a diamond shape tile <T71i> have been scored to make other mosaic shapes <T71ii> and <T71iii>, but again this

Table 30 Decorated 'Westminster' tiles from St Mary Merton

Design no. (Betts 2002)	No. of tiles	Tile no. (Fig 197)
W2	1	-
W3	10	<T55>
W11	4	<T62>
W19	1	-
W46	1	-
W47	3	-
W48	7 (includes 1 uncertain example)	-
W49	13	-
W53	9	<T60>
W55	14	-
W59	7	<T61>
W62*	1	<T80>**
W65	2	-
W70	1	<T69>
W71	1	-
W73	14 (includes 2 uncertain examples)	<T70>
W74	16 (includes 3 uncertain examples)	-
W80	1	-
W82	6	-
W83	7	<T57>
W88	1	-
W94	1	<T66>
W95	3	-
W99	8	-
W102	1	<T65>
W103	7	-
W107	6	<T59>
W111	1	<T64>
W121	2	-
W130	32	<T68>
W133	7 (includes 3 uncertain examples)	-
W136	7	<T56>
W139	7	<T63>
W143	2	-
W148	2	-
W149	1	-
W151	1	<T67>
W153	4	<T58>
Uncertain	27	-
Total	238	

*: related industry
**: illustrated Fig 199

was not carried out. Using the information from mosaic floors elsewhere in England it is possible to reconstruct how the 'Westminster' tiled floor would have been arranged in the priory (<T79>, Fig 37). Laurence Keen has drawn attention to certain similarities between the Merton mosaic tiles and those used in the Medway area, especially the pavements in Rochester Cathedral (Kent) which have tiles of almost exactly the same size and more importantly the same arrangement, although set at a 45° angle to the reconstruction shown in Fig 37 (Keen 2002).

RELATED 'WESTMINSTER' INDUSTRY
One of the most intriguing tiles from the priory was found in 1986 (OA13, period P3). This tile has a 'Westminster' design (the only example of W62 from Merton) (<T80>, Fig 199) but was made using a different clay (fabric 2894 near 1810) from all the

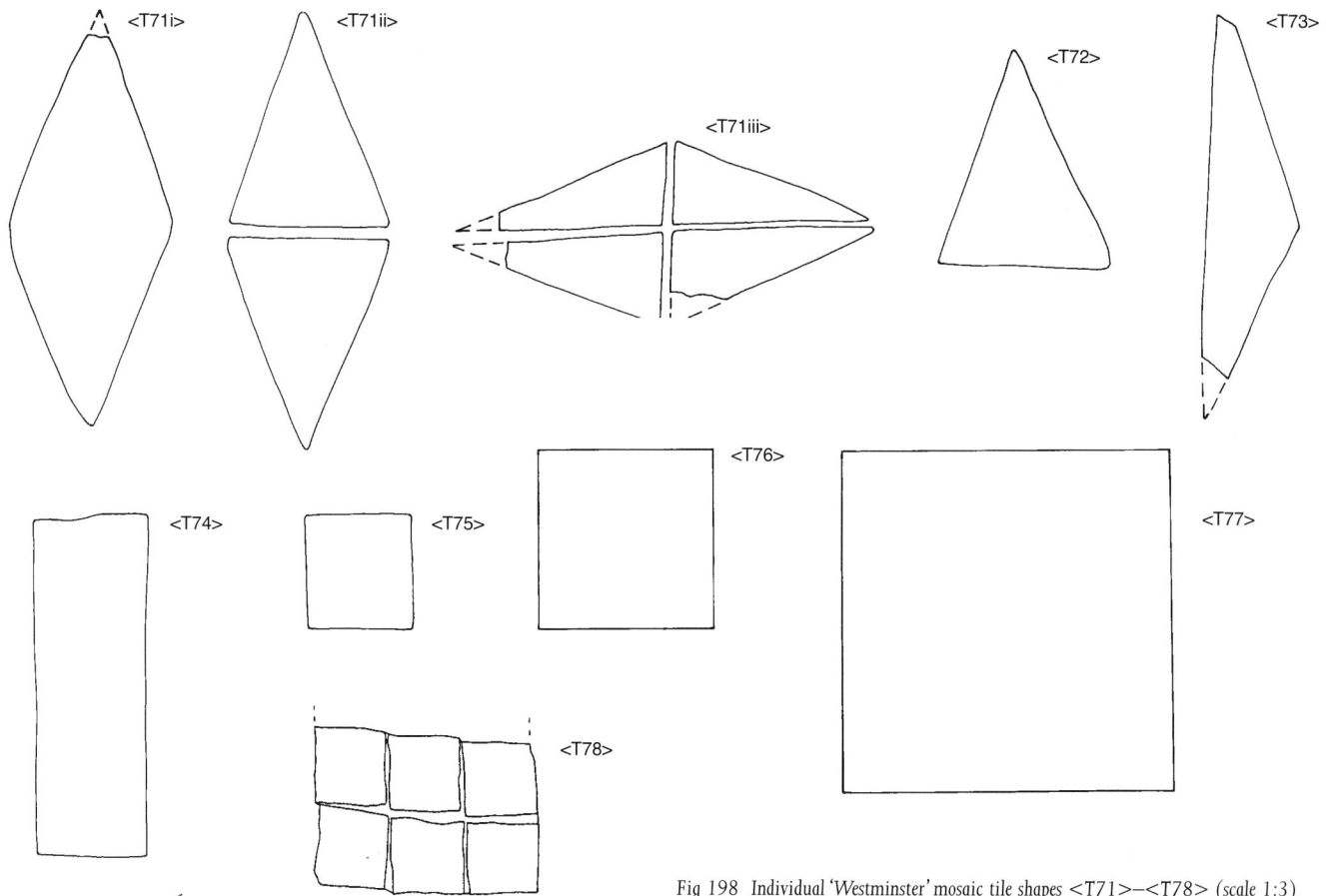

Fig 198 *Individual 'Westminster' mosaic tile shapes <T71>–<T78> (scale 1:3)*

Table 31 *'Westminster' mosaic tiles from St Mary Merton, by shape type*

Shape type (Betts 2002, 40–1)	No. of tiles	Tile no. (Fig 198)
A1	5	<T71i>
A2: A1 scored to make 2 triangles (shape B)	4	<T71ii>
A3: A1 scored to make 2 (shape C) or 4 triangles	4	<T71iii>
B	1	<T72>
C	2	<T73>
D	4	<T74>
E	5	<T75>
F	1	<T76>
G	1	<T77>
Uncertain (G or F)	1	-
G scored to make smaller squares (shape E)	1	<T78>
Total	29	

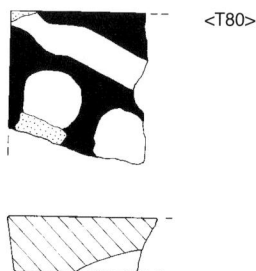

Fig 199 *Related 'Westminster' industry: decorated floor tile <T80> (scale 1:3)*

other 'Westminster' tiles found at the priory. It also has a keyed base, a feature found only on a 'Westminster' tile with the same design in Guildford Museum (Eames 1967, 47, fig 6 no. 65).

There seems little doubt that this tile was made at a different tilery from the other 'Westminster' tiles found at Merton, and it is almost certainly of slightly different date. The stamp used to make the tile must, however, have come with the 'Westminster' tilers when they moved to a new location. A small number of other tiles believed to have been made at this same location have also been found at the priory of St John Clerkenwell, Bermondsey Abbey and at Guildhall Yard in the City of London (Betts 2002, 12). Their rarity suggests that production was short-lived.

CHERTSEY TILE
Fabric type: 2894
These tiles were made at Chertsey Abbey in Surrey where a kiln used for the manufacture of floor tiles was excavated in 1922 (Eames 1992, 48). All six examples found at Merton are of the same design (Eames design 1286) (<T81>, Fig 200), which dates to *c* 1290–*c* 1300 (Eames 1980). The tiles are rectangular in shape, none are complete but the surviving fragments measure 57–59mm in breadth by 23–30mm in thickness. Complete examples with the same design in the British Museum have a length of 163–165mm (ibid, 513, 576).

What is rather puzzling is why these rectangular tiles were the only floor tiles certainly of Chertsey manufacture used at the priory. Perhaps other tile makers in the late 13th century

Fig 200 *Chertsey Abbey decorated floor tile <T81> (scale 1:3)*

did not produce the rectangularly shaped tiles that the priory required. Such tiles were presumably used as borders around plain or decorated tiles of other type. Certainly tiles of this shape were not made by the Eltham Palace/Lesnes Abbey tile makers (discussed below) who were making floor tiles around the same period.

OTHER PLAIN-GLAZED AND UNGLAZED TILES

?Source

Fabric type: mainly 2894, some 2324

This group comprises a number of tiles which are similar in appearance to the plain tiles belonging to the keyed white slip group. Where they differ is not having any keying in their base. Most tiles are glazed, but a small number of unglazed tiles are also present. The glazed tiles measure 139–148mm square by 23–30mm in thickness, whilst the two unglazed tiles with surviving length measurements are of the same size (143mm square by 27–29mm thick). One of the latter has been scored and then broken in half after firing, as have a number of the glazed examples. There are also a few plain-glazed triangular-shaped tiles.

The glaze colours used are yellow, various shades of green, brown and black. A few tiles are a yellow colour in the centre and light green on the outside, whilst others are green and brown. One apparently unglazed tile has glaze spots on the top, suggesting both may have been fired together in the same kiln.

The tiles in this group are clearly related to the keyed plain-glazed and unglazed tiles discussed earlier. Their fabric is the same and their size is similar to glazed keyed examples. It seems reasonable to suppose that they were made at the same tilery or at least in the same geographical area. There is no indication of date, so it is not certain whether they preceded or succeeded the manufacture of keyed tiles, although the latter would seem more likely. The lack of keying suggests that they may have been made around the same time as the decorated tiles in the pink slip group, which are themselves unkeyed.

MISCELLANEOUS OTHER PLAIN-GLAZED TILES

There are a number of other plain-glazed tiles, in a variety of fabric types, which are too small or undiagnostic to allocated to any sort of group. Most of these are probably English, although no kiln sources are known. Tiles from at least three different groups are present.

1) A dark green-glazed tile measuring ? x 113mm x 24mm (OA6, period M2) associated with pottery dated c 1230–c 1350. This is made from a similar clay (fabric 2324) to the Eltham Palace/Lesnes Abbey group but is significantly smaller in size. There are also no nail holes present.

2) Two tiles (OA12, period P2) of approximately the same size which may belong to one of the groups discussed earlier. The first (fabric 2317) has a green and yellow glaze and measures ? x 230mm x 32–33mm. The second (fabric 1813), which is unglazed, measures ? x 235mm x 32mm). Other tiles in the same fabrics (plus 2199, 2324), glazed green and brown, were unstratified.

3) An unglazed tile (OA13, period P3) in fabric 2505 measuring 36–40mm thick.

c 1300–c 1390 (period M3)

ELTHAM PALACE/LESNES ABBEY GROUP

Fabric type: 2324

Tiles in this series were first identified at Eltham Palace in Kent where they were used to pave Anthony Bek's hall sometime around c 1300–5 (Eames 1982, 238). The tilery supplying these tiles is not identified, but the rarity of such tiles elsewhere suggests production was for a shorter period than that of 'Westminster' tiles. Of the eight different designs found at Eltham Palace no less than seven are also found at Merton (Fig 201; Table 32). This would suggest a firm late 13th- to early 14th-century date for the Merton examples. Two tile designs in this group have also been found at Lesnes Abbey (designs E1528 and EP8). Eames has already drawn attention to the close similarity between many of the designs found at Lesnes and Eltham, which are less than 8km apart. Certain designs are so similar that she believes that both were probably made by the same tile makers. This is supported by examination of the fabric of the St Mary Merton examples. Tiles decorated with designs used on both Lesnes Abbey and Eltham Palace tiles are made using what appears to be the same clay source. This would support the suggestion by Eames that both were made at the same tile manufacturing site. Other features such as size, glaze colour and style of decoration are all consistent with production from a single source. Tiles in this group seem to have been used in the priory church where most of these tiles have been found. An Eltham Palace/Lesnes Abbey tile was found in a debris deposit in the Lady chapel.

Many of the tiles decorated with fleur-de-lis design (EP4) were scored diagonally allowing them to be split into two triangular shapes after firing. Decorated triangular tiles with both the left and right sides of design EP4 are present, as are a number of plain-glazed examples. Plain triangular medieval floor tiles are fairly common in the London area, particularly those of 'Westminster' type, but decorated examples are far more rare.

Both the decorated and plain floor tiles in the Eltham Palace/Lesnes Abbey group are all similar in size, ranging from

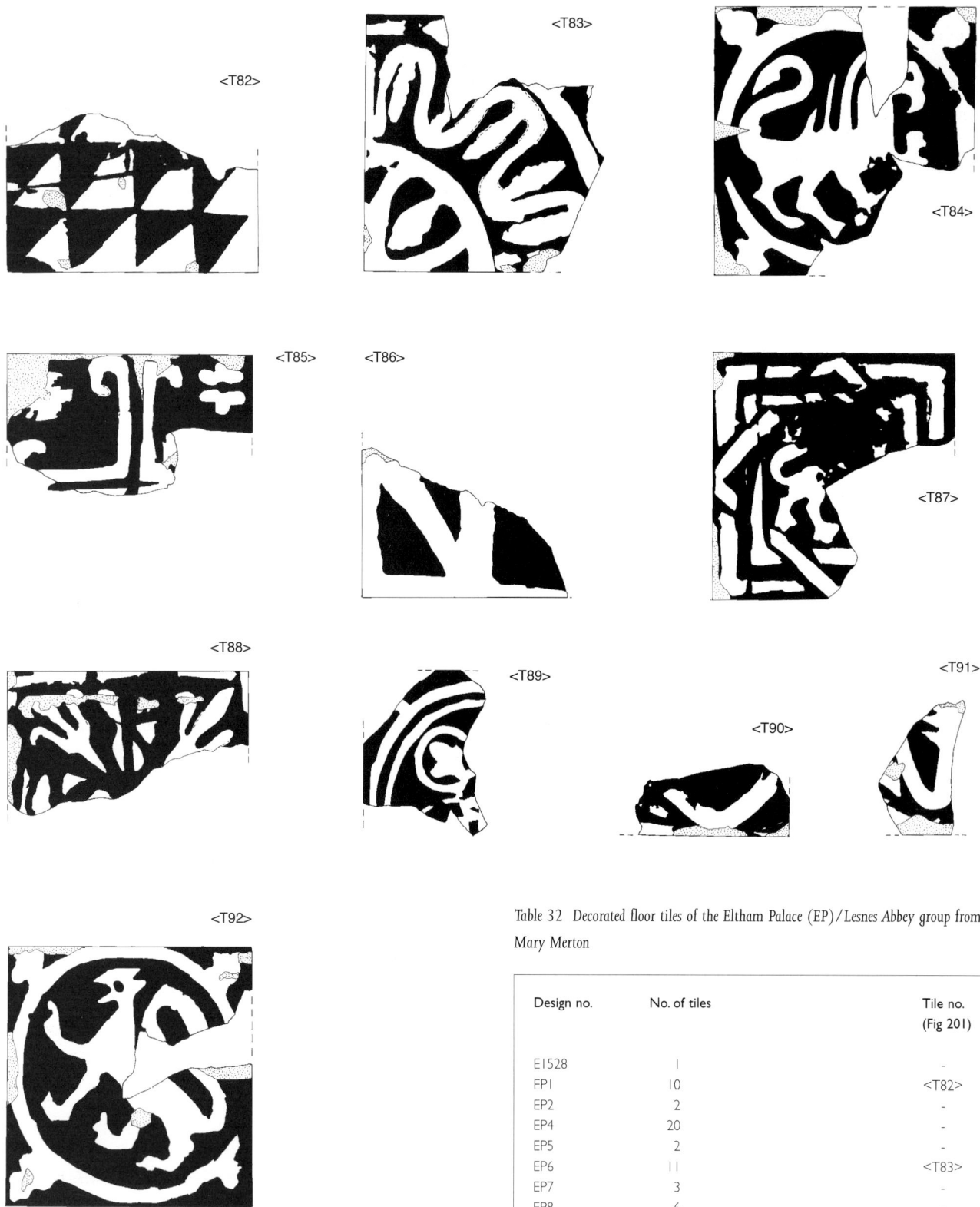

Fig 201 Decorated floor tiles of the Eltham Palace/Lesnes Abbey group <T82>–<T92> (scale 1:3)

Table 32 Decorated floor tiles of the Eltham Palace (EP)/Lesnes Abbey group from St Mary Merton

Design no.	No. of tiles	Tile no. (Fig 201)
E1528	1	-
FP1	10	<T82>
EP2	2	-
EP4	20	-
EP5	2	-
EP6	11	<T83>
EP7	3	-
EP8	6	-
1	11 (includes 1 uncertain example)	<T84>
2	4	<T85>
3	1	<T86>
4	2	<T87>
5	4	<T88>
6	8 (includes 1 uncertain example)	<T89>
7	2	<T90>
8	1	<T91>
9	9	<T92>
Uncertain	8	-
Total	105	

127mm to 136mm square, with a thickness of 20–27mm. The plain tiles are normally covered with yellow, brown or dark green glaze, although one black tile and a number of brown- and yellow-glazed tiles are also present along with a mottled green and brown example. The quality of the glazing is not always of a high standard, on certain tiles the glaze is in the form of splashes, or is absent altogether from parts of the top surface.

A very unusual feature of the plain-glazed examples is the presence of round, oval, square and rectangularly shaped nail holes in their top surface. Each tile would have had two such holes, one each in diagonally opposite corners. One tile has a square nail hole measuring 2mm x 2mm. The oval shapes were probably made by round nails, the holes being distorted when the nail board was removed. Nail holes are normally a feature used to identify tiles of Low Countries origin, so perhaps the English tilery making these tiles employed foreign craftsmen. Another distinguishing feature of tiles in the Eltham Palace/Lesnes Abbey group is the fine-sized moulding sand attached to their bottom surface.

PENN TILE

Fabric types: 1811, 1810, 2894, 3246

Penn in Buckinghamshire was the location of one of the most successful commercial tileries making floor tiles known in medieval England. The main period of production occurred after the Black Death when large quantities of predominantly decorated tiles arrived in London from the 1350s until just before 1390. It is to this period that the large number of St Mary Merton examples belong (Table 33; Fig 202).

The larger number of uncertain examples is due to the presence of many small fragments which are very hard to identify. Identification of Penn tiles is often very difficult due to

Table 33 Decorated Penn (P) floor tiles from St Mary Merton

Design no.	No. of tiles	Tile no. (Fig 202)
E1398/P123	4 (includes 3 uncertain examples)	-
E1398/P123 or E1399/P121	6	-
E1803	77 (includes 2 uncertain examples)	<T97>
E1833	9 (includes 4 uncertain examples)	-
E2027 or E2030	4	-
E2028 or E2029	1	-
E2037	52 (includes 1 uncertain example)	-
E2200/P69	16 (includes 2 uncertain examples)	-
E2220/P51 or E2221	2	-
E2231/P54	2	-
E2286 or E2287	1	-
E2353/P58	1	-
?E2388/?P64	1	-
E2390/P63	10	-
E2394/P62	1	-
E2395	7 (includes 1 uncertain example)	-
E2460/P107	1	-
?E2551	1	-
E2552/P85	1	-
E2842/P134	6 (includes 1 uncertain example)	-
1	34	<T93>
2	1	<T94>
3	1	<T95>
4	1	<T96>
Uncertain	81 (includes 1 possible E1455)	-
Total	321	

the production of tiles with very similar designs.

Most Penn tiles used in London are very similar in size, the plain and decorated St Mary Merton tiles are all between 106mm and 116mm square with a thickness of 19–25mm. One decorated Penn tile (design E1803; <T97>, Fig 202) is of particular note, this has the central animal design picked out by a thin line around the edge. Whether this was meant to be deliberate or represents an idle doodling of the tile maker is uncertain, although no other decorated Penn tiles known to the writer have this feature.

The number of plain Penn tiles is relatively small in comparison with decorated examples. These tiles are normally either plain green or plain yellow, whilst others are glazed brown or yellow and brown together. Many plain tiles were probably used along the wall edge or as plain strips to break up panels of decorated tiles. One tile has been split in two rectangular shapes after firing to fit the available floor space. A few triangularly shaped plain tiles are also present including an unusually small example measuring 50mm x 35mm x 35mm with a thickness of 20mm.

OTHER DECORATED TILES

In this category are four tiles decorated with Eames design 2801 (<T98>, Fig 203) which cannot be placed in any of the groups discussed earlier. These tiles, which measure 134mm square by 25–27mm in thickness, were all made from the same sandy clay (fabric 1813). The origin of these tiles is unknown, although a tile decorated with the same design has been found at Godstow Abbey in Surrey (Eames 1980, 499) dated to the 14th century. One recovered from post-Dissolution demolition might represent part of the reredorter floor.

Mention must also be made of ten tiles which are so worn the design cannot be identified with any certainty. Four may belong to the decorated and plain mosaic group, one is possibly

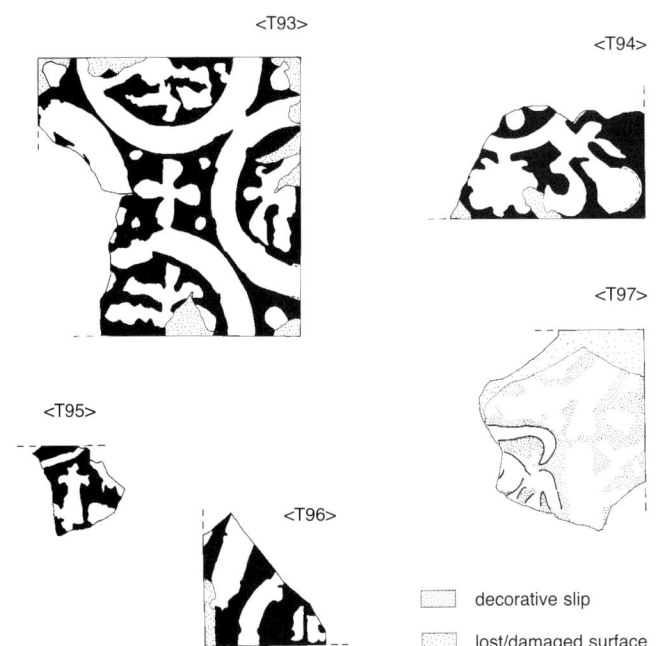

Fig 202 Decorated floor tiles of Penn type <T93>–<T97> (scale 1:3)

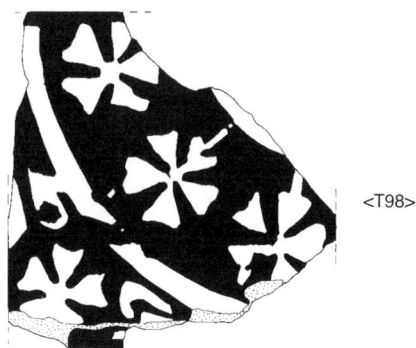

Fig 203 Floor tile <T98> of uncertain source (scale 1:3)

Table 34 Low Countries floor tiles from St Mary Merton, by size

Size group	Length/breadth (mm)	Thickness (mm)	Nail holes
1	91–94	18–22	2; 5; round
2	112–121	22–28	5 (1 may have 4); round
3	125–129	25–31	?5; round
4	186–190	38–41	2; round
5	212–217	28–31	?2/?4; oval
6	over 156–228	28–35	?; round, square

from the Eltham Palace/Lesnes Abbey group, whilst the others cannot be identified.

c 1300–1538 (periods M3–M4)

LOW COUNTRIES ('FLEMISH') PLAIN FLOOR TILE

Fabric types: 1678, 2323, 2497, 2504, 3083 (calcium carbonate fabric types); 2850, 3075 (silty fabric types)

Plain-glazed tiles from the Low Countries (also known as 'Flemish' tiles) can be identified by nail holes in their top surface and their distinctive fabric types. The date when these floor tiles were first imported into London is uncertain, but it is unlikely to be much earlier that c 1300 when English plain-glazed 'Westminster' tiles seem to have been readily available. Plain-glazed tiles continued to be imported from the Low Countries until at least the mid 16th century.

Many later imported tiles can be distinguished by their larger size and their silty clay fabric. Earlier tiles are generally made from calcium carbonate-rich clays; Low Countries tiles made from silty clays did not appear in London until around c 1480. By the late 16th or early 17th century such tiles were no longer glazed.

The Low Countries floor tiles at Merton have either a yellow glaze or are various shades of brown or dark green, although a few tiles have a light green colour where the green glaze has been applied above a covering of white slip. They would have been laid in a chequerboard pattern with yellow coloured tiles alternating with brown or dark green examples. A floor of Low Countries tiles laid in this decorative pattern was found in situ in the north transept. Further tiles were found in situ in the west aisle of the infirmary hall (B4a) and many other tiles have been found in the northern part of the infirmary chapel (B4b). Other Low Countries tiles have been found in floor layers inside the infirmary kitchen (B6). In certain buildings these floor tiles must have been subject to heavy wear as a number of tiles have been worn to a thickness of only 14–17mm.

There are at least six sizes of Low Countries floor tile present (Table 34), there may have been more but all of the larger size tiles (size group 6) are no longer complete. Of particular interest are the very small Low Countries tiles in group 1, there are no other examples of Low Countries tiles of this small size from the City of London.

The tiles in size groups 1–5 are all made using calcium carbonate-rich clays, whilst the incomplete large fragments in size group 6 are a mixture of both calcium carbonate and silty fabric varieties. The vast majority of smaller size tiles have five nail holes in the top surface, one near each corner and one in the centre. Larger tiles tend just to have two nail holes, set in diagonally opposite corners, although one of the very small tiles in group 1 seems to have just two holes.

The majority of tiles in size groups 1 and 2 are of five round nail hole type, although on certain tiles less than five holes are visible. This may well be because they are completely filled with glaze or were smoothed over before the glaze was applied. Alternatively, only certain nails may have been in contact with the clay if the nail board was only lightly pressed into the clay surface. The tiles in size group 3 are almost certainly also of five nail hole type, although only four holes are clearly visible on the one surviving complete tile.

In the small tiles the nail hole shape is usually round (normally 1.0mm to 1.5mm diameter), although they are sometimes distorted to an oval shape. This was caused when the nail board, used as a template to cut around the sides of the tile, was twisted as it was lifted from the clay during manufacture. The nail holes on the larger tiles are either round or, more frequently, square in shape, the latter measuring around 3mm x 3mm square.

The dating of plain-glazed Low Countries floor tiles is very difficult. All that can be said with any confidence is that the smaller sized tiles (sizes 1–3) are the earliest in date, probably 14th to mid/late 15th century, whilst the larger tiles probably date from around the late 15th century to the Dissolution. The latter include the in situ Low Countries tiles laid in a chequerbroad pattern in the north transept (size 5). There is a solitary unstratified unglazed Low Countries tile which may be post-Dissolution.

A number of individual Low Countries tiles have unusual features. A deep groove in the base of one tile is probably accidental damage. Another tile has an odd dent in the corner as well as the nail hole in an unusual position (<T99>, Fig 204), the purpose of this dent is not clear. A third tile seems to have had one edge cut off to fit in a particular place in the floor. A number of other tiles have also been scored diagonally across the surface ready to split into triangular shapes after firing. Surprisingly this never occurred and they were shipped to England still square.

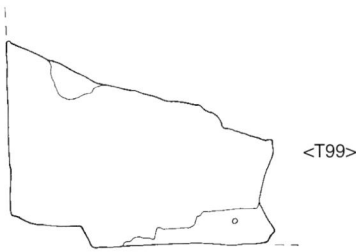

Fig 204 *Low Countries tile <T99> (scale 1:3)*

OTHER PLAIN-GLAZED TILES
?Source
Fabric type: 2505
These tiles can be identified by their distinct fabric type which comprises numerous small black iron oxide grains (best seen under x10 magnification) in a fairly sandy matrix. They have a yellow, brown, green or greenish-yellow glaze and a thickness of between 23mm and 28mm. Regrettably there are no tiles with surviving lengths, although there is an incomplete length of 139mm.

There is no indication as to either source or date, although the clay used would suggest English manufacture.

Dissolution activity/16th century (period P1/P2)

PLAIN SANDY TILES
Fabric types: mainly 1813, one 2191
The tiles can be distinguished by their frequent quartz sand in the clay matrix. Most are covered by a brown, green or yellow glaze, although on certain tiles just a splash glaze is present. They have a length of 192–207mm and a thickness of 28–37mm. A larger size may also be present as there is an incomplete tile measuring 210mm. A ?yellow tile in sandy fabric 2194 may come from the same unknown source. These tiles are probably English.

PLAIN VERY SANDY TILE
Fabric type: 3084
There is a single very worn brown-glazed tile in very sandy fabric type 3084 from the robbing of the priory church (OA11, period P1) measuring 28mm in thickness. Tiles of this type have been found at St Mary Spital and at Bishopsgate, where they may be post-Dissolution in date (Crowley 1997, 199). Again their source is unknown. Probably English.

Decorated floor tiles from earlier excavations

Additional information concerning the types of decorated floor tiles used at the priory comes from earlier excavations on the site. Included under this heading are the decorated floor tiles published by Bidder and Westlake (1930) from their excavations in the 1920s whilst further excavations near the priory in 1962–3 produced a further 34 fragments which were examined by Elizabeth Eames (1967).

1920s excavations

Bidder and Westlake (1930) published five tile designs of which only the Eltham Palace/Lesnes Group designs were found in the 1976–88 excavations. These may have been some of the tiles found in *situ* in the priory church along with stone paving (it is not entirely clear from the text where they were found).

FRAGMENTARY TILE WITH RUNNING DOG, VERY SIMILAR TO MOSAIC GROUP DESIGN 7
Uncertain source
The border is very similar to one of the thin square tiles <T37> believed to be linked with the mosaic group.

ELTHAM PALACE/LESNES ABBEY GROUP
EP7
Design 1

PENN
E2220/P51 or E2221
Found in the nave of the church, along with stone paving, are two varieties of floor tile. These are described by Bidder and Westlake (1930, 64) as 'a band of patterned tiles' (133mm square) and 'red flooring tiles' (178mm square). The smaller size corresponds with those of the Eltham Palace/Lesnes Abbey group whilst the larger type may refer to the plain unglazed tiles in the keyed white slip group. Mention is also made of 'tiling' in the chapter house; presumably these are floor tiles although no details are given.

1960s excavations

Although Eames lists some 34 decorated floor tiles, regrettably only nine designs are drawn, these drawn examples are listed below. The illustrated tiles are in Guildford Museum where they have been re-examined by the author. It is extremely difficult to identify the designs which have only written descriptions. However, it is possible to positively identify certain designs and make suggestions as to others. The number in brackets is the catalogue number given by Eames in 1967.

The majority of floor tiles examined are from either topsoil or destruction deposits. Only one decorated floor tile came from a sealed context. This was a 'Westminster' floor tile (W130) in a clay layer beneath a Reigate stone floor. This was also the location of a number of plain tiles belonging to the keyed white slip group. These were around 152–202mm square by 26–29mm thick and at least one had traces of brown glaze. Numerous other plain-glazed floor tiles were found in destruction deposits, including a complete dark blue-green coloured tile measuring around 102mm square probably of 'Westminster' type.

THICK WHITE SLIP GROUP
Design 7 (no. 35)

'WESTMINSTER'

W3 (nos 54–6)

W74 (no. 46)

W99 (no. 53)

W130 (nos 48–9)

W149 (no. 57, but missing pattern wrongly reconstructed)

RELATED 'WESTMINSTER' INDUSTRY

W62 (no. 65)

A tile with the same design and from the same source as a tile from the 1976–88 excavations.

PENN

E1803 (no. 41)

E2390/P63 (no. 42)

E2392? (no. 62)

E2842/P134 (no. 44)

Design 1 (no. 45, but missing pattern wrongly reconstructed)

Probably Hohler P66 (no. 63)

Perhaps Hohler P106 (no. 43)

Similar pattern to Hohler P120 (nos 52, 64)

PERHAPS MOSAIC GROUP

Design ? (no. 38)

Roofing tile

1222–c 1300 (period M2)

FLANGED AND CURVED ROOFING TILE

Fabric type: 2273

Some of the earliest buildings probably had tiled roofs. At least one building had a roof comprising flanged and curved tiles, used in the same manner as Roman tegula and imbrices. In London these tiles date from the early/mid 12th to the early 13th century, which is almost certainly when they were used at Merton (Betts 1990, 221–3; in prep a). The Merton examples are made from the same distinctive sandy clay as the London examples, which would suggest that they were brought in from the London area. There is evidence that tiles of this date were made at a kiln at Nibblet Hall, Temple Lane, just west of the city walls (Geoquest 1993, 3).

PEG ROOFING TILE

Fabric types: mainly 2586, with smaller amounts of 2271, 2273, 2276, 2816, 3097 and 3201

In London such tiles first appear in the late 12th century and continued to be the principal form of ceramic roof covering throughout the medieval period (Betts 1990, 223). When such tiles were first used at Merton is not certain, although it seems unlikely to have been much later than the start of the 13th century. Vast quantities of roofing tile were recovered from the priory, which clearly indicates that most buildings would have had peg tiled roofs with plain ridge tiles running along the roof crest.

In addition to roofing, peg tiles were used for other functions, such as walling, flooring and as hearths. Peg tiles were, for example, used as flooring in the infirmary hall (B4a) and the infirmary kitchen (B6), whilst they were used in the priory church (B1) in wall foundations and possibly as flooring; the kitchen (B6) had a hearth made out of peg tiles set on end.

The peg tiles used at Merton occur in a variety of different sizes (Fig 205), which probably reflect different dates of manufacture. In Table 35 the different sizes of rectangular flat peg tile have been grouped into those believed to be medieval in date and those thought to be late medieval or post-medieval. Not all size groups can be dated with any certainty, although tiles in size groups 2 to 4, and possibly 5, occur in both periods M2 and M3 and are clearly 13th century. The two incomplete tiles in size group 1, found in post-Dissolution demolition deposits in the infirmary, are most probably of similar date.

The tiles in fabric type 2276 (size groups 10–13), which have fine moulding sand attached and a variety of different nail hole types, are almost certainly either late 15th century or post-medieval in date. The two nail holes found on these and earlier peg tiles were needed for attachment by means of either wooden pegs or iron nails.

The peg tiles of 13th-century date are much larger than many of the peg tiles used in London at this period. This suggests that they may have been made at a tilery situated somewhere close to the priory, perhaps at a tileworks operated by the priory itself. St Mary Clerkenwell nunnery made roofing tiles for its own use, and perhaps for sale, sometime during the mid 14th–late 15th century (Betts in prep b). In contrast, from the late 15th century onwards many tiles are of identical type to those used in London, both having the same fine moulding sand on their base, the same variety of nail hole shapes and the same variations in size. It would seem that it was the commercially run tileries operating around London which supplied the priory's roofing tile needs during the last 50 or so years of its life.

Two peg tiles (fabric types 3097 and 3201) are from outside the London area, they were presumably brought in for minor repair work. They differ slightly in the amount of quartz present, but both probably came from the same tilery. This was probably located somewhere in north Kent where roof tiles in the same fabrics have been found on a number of sites (Betts in prep c; Betts and Smith in prep). One fragment, broadly dated 1200–1450 elsewhere, was found associated with the infirmary hall (B4a, period M3), whilst the other came from post-Dissolution demolition debris associated with the infirmary hall. There is no indication of size or nail hole type.

There are two tapered peg tiles from the priory. The complete example, which has splash glaze, measures 149mm at the base narrowing to 133mm at the top (unstratified). The other, more tapered tile has just the complete top edge remaining, which measures 112mm (Fig 205, <T100> [2024]). These tapered tiles, both of which are of two round nail hole type, may have been used on a curved roof. There may be other tapered peg tiles from the priory as it is often difficult to distinguish small fragmentary examples from normal straight-sided peg tiles.

On certain 13th-century peg tiles the edges have been carefully knife trimmed, as have the nail holes on the sanded underside. Splash glaze is present on certain of these tiles, but is absent on others. Why only certain tiles had glaze added during manufacture is rather puzzling. Other tiles, probably also of 13th-century date, have a more uniform covering of lead glaze. Later tiles, made from the late 15th century onwards, no longer have glaze present.

Perhaps the most unusual peg tile found at Merton was found in a demolition deposit in the vicinity of the former infirmary cloister garth (OA5). This tile has both a slip and splash glaze on its sanded base, rather that its top surface. Perhaps the bottom surface was slipped and glazed in error. A number of other peg tiles have the remains of paw prints or hoof prints on their upper surface, indicating they were laid out on the ground to dry at the tilery, prior to being fired. Certain peg tiles have finger marks near their top edges which are believed to be batch marks. Two of these marks are of a type not seen previously on medieval peg tile

Fig 205 Peg roofing tiles of different sizes and dates <T100>–<T104> (scale 1:4)

Table 35 Rectangular flat peg tiles from St Mary Merton, by size

Group (illustrated tile no.) (Fig 205)	Fabric	Length (mm)	Breadth (mm)	Thickness (mm)	Nail hole type
Medieval					
I	2586	-	227–229	14–18	-
2 (<T101>)	2586	340–350	190–199	14–18	R
3	2271/2586	327–333	199–212	11–16	R
4 (<T102>)	2273/2586	311–319	184–204	12–19	R
5	2273/2586	293–302	178–196	13–15	R
6	?2271	280–282	161–163	12	R
7 (<T103>)	2271	279	147–149	11–14	?R
8	2586	c 273	c 171	14–16	R
9	2271/2586	250–264	133–149	8–14	-
Late medieval/post-medieval					
10	2816+	285	174–176	12	H
11	2276	-	176–185	13–15	R, S
12*	2276	262–278	157–165	11–13	R, S, D
13* (<T104>)	2276	259	140–155	13–16	R, S, D, H
?Date					
14	2271/2586	c 295	169–185	13–14	S, D
15	2586	-	161–177	12–16	R
16	2271/2586	266	150–154	11–15	R, D
17	2816	-	143	13–15	R

*: there is no clear division between groups 12 and 13, although their breadth suggests moulds of at least two sizes were employed
+: near fabric type 2276
Nail hole type: R – round; S –square; D – diamond (square hole at 45° angle); H – hexagonal

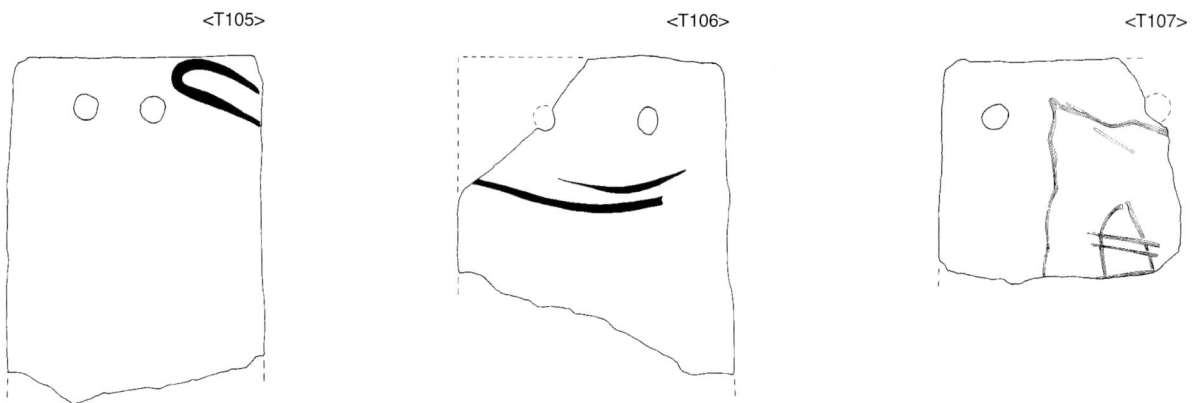

Fig 206 Peg tiles with markings <T105>–<T107> (scale 1:4)

from the London area <T105> [7016] and <T106> [8519] (Fig 206). One further peg tile <T107> [7281] has graffiti made by a sharp stick (Fig 206).

YELLOW GLAZE ?ROOF TILE
Fabric type: 2586
From the demolition deposits of the priory church came three small fragments of what appear to be flat glazed roofing tile. Unlike normal roofing tile, these are partly covered by a white slip which in turn is partly covered by a yellow and green or plain yellow coloured glaze. They are also thicker than most

peg roofing tiles, measuring 18–21mm.

Tiles belonging to the same group have also been found in post-Dissolution deposits. These are of similar thickness (18–23mm) and have the same white slip and plain yellow glaze. Another yellow-glazed tile which may belong to the same group was found in the south burial area (OA3, period M2). This has both mortar and glaze on the broken edge suggesting it was a reject which was used for some other function. A tile in period M1 was found with pottery dated c 1150–c 1300, suggesting these yellow-glazed tiles are probably 13th century in date.

Certain tiles have partly knife-trimmed edges, but there are no fragments with nail holes, hence it is not absolutely certain that they are roof tiles. There are no complete tiles either, but one has an incomplete length/breadth of 125mm. The presence of yellow glaze gives these tiles the appearance of floor tiles, but their uneven top surface and the lack of any signs of wear shows that they were not used for paving. It would seem most likely that these are specially made roofing tiles (none have been found elsewhere), which were made for a porch or some other prominent position where their yellow colour would have been readily visible.

c 1300–c 1390 (period M3)

HIP TILE
Fabric types: 2276, 2586
The earliest hip tile was found associated with the infirmary hall (B4a) with pottery dated c 1230–c 1400. It is certainly of medieval date as splash glaze is present. This tile is very unusual in having twin round nail holes, 10mm diameter, situated near the apex of the tile; normally only one is present. A second hip tile found in the post-Dissolution destruction debris of the same building has the same feature, although this time the two nail holes are 8mm square.

Three further hip tiles, one probably medieval as there appears to be the remains of glaze, the others of late medieval or early post-medieval date (fabric 2276), were found associated with the former infirmary drain (S4b) (OA12, period P2).

There may well be other hip tiles from the priory which have not been recognised. It is very difficult to distinguish small fragments of hip tile from other types of ceramic roofing tile.

RIDGE TILE
Fabric types: 2273, 2276, 2586
Curved ridge tiles are found from the 13th century onwards. It would seem highly likely that all the buildings which had tiled roofs had undecorated ridge tiles running along the crest of the roof. These tiles would have been made at the same tileries which supplied the flanged and curved, peg and hip tiles. Only one ridge tile has survived intact, a late medieval or early post-medieval example (fabric 2276) measuring 312mm in length by 11–16mm in thickness ([2000] <T108>, Fig 207).

A very odd fragment of what may be a decorated ridge tile, although this is far from certain, was recovered from the north burial area (OA6, period M3). This has been cut to shape with a white slip on the smoothed side and what may be decoration in white and red slip on the other, sanded, side ([2639] <T109>, Fig 207). The tile is fairly thick, measuring 20–23mm.

GUTTER TILE/DRAIN
Fabric types: 2273, 2586
A large fragment of very thick drain or gutter tile (fabric 2586) was found with mid 13th- to mid 14th-century pottery in the infirmary cloister garth (OA5, period M3). This has a brown

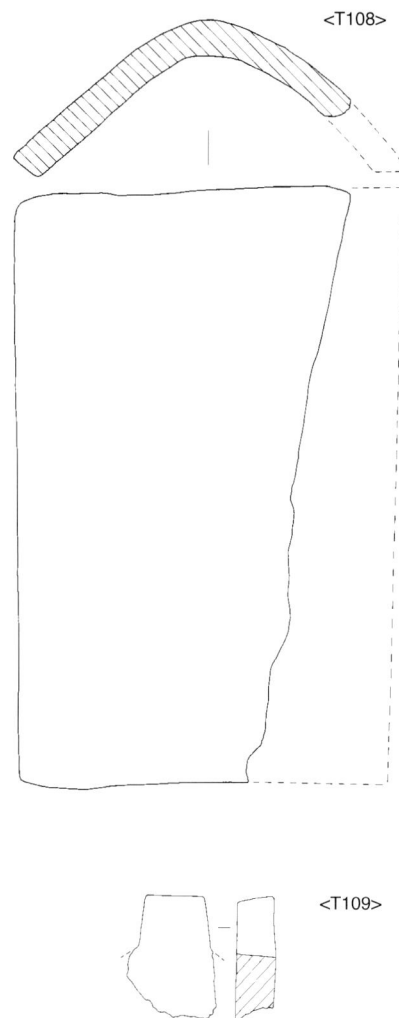

Fig 207 *Ridge tiles <T108> and <T109> (scale 1:4)*

glaze on the sloping inside edge ([10164] <T110>, Fig 122) and is over 200mm in length with a thickness of 34–42mm. This may have been used around the edge of the infirmary cloister to catch and channel away rainwater running off the roofs.

A second example of what may be either a gutter tile, or semicircular drain (fabric 2273), was recovered from a levelling dump for a post-medieval hearth [354] (OA11, period P1). Again the curved inside, which is also sanded, has been deliberately glazed. This tile is, however, considerably thinner, measuring just 21–22mm in thickness.

Brick

? late 12th/early 13th century–c 1300 (periods M1–M2)

COGGESHALL-TYPE BRICKS
Fabric type: 2273
A special type of thin, shaped brick occurs in period M1 onwards. These are brown in colour frequently with a grey core and made with a fairly coarse sandy clay. The bricks would originally have been rectangular in shape, although none are

now complete, and are characterised by having a quadrant missing from one corner. Bricks of this shape were used at Coggeshall Abbey in Essex where they date to c 1220 (Gardner 1955, pl XIII). Other bricks, probably surplus stock, were used in various churches, mostly within 19km of Coggeshall. Ryan has identified Coggeshall bricks in various Essex churches dating from the late 12th century to c 1230 (1996, 26–7, map 3). Bricks of similar date were also used at Stratford Langthorne Abbey (Smith 2004, 143–4).

The Coggeshall-type bricks at St Mary Merton are the first examples to have been found outside Essex, but the Merton bricks are in a different fabric to the Coggeshall examples so it is highly unlikely that they were brought in from Essex. In the City of London there are various types of early/mid 12th- to early 13th-century roofing tile made from a similar clay (discussed earlier) but it would also seem unlikely that the Coggeshall-type bricks were brought in from London. The clay used for the Merton bricks lacks the calcium carbonate inclusions which are commonly found in the clay used to make these early roofing tiles. More importantly, there is no evidence that Coggeshall-type brick was ever used in buildings in the City of London or the immediate surrounding area.

It seems far more probable that the bricks were made close to the priory site, as there is roofing tile made from the same fairly coarse sandy clay (fabric 2273) which seems unlikely to have moved far. At Coggeshall Abbey the bricks are believed to have been made either at a kiln located about 1.6km to the north, or possibly next to the abbey itself (Ryan 1996, 28). The similarity in the shape and form of these bricks does imply however that the same skilled craftsmen were involved in brickmaking at both Coggeshall and at the brickyard situated somewhere close to Merton.

The Coggeshall-type bricks from Merton are just 25–35mm in thickness (average 31mm). Although none of the Merton bricks are complete, brick of two sizes can be identified (Table 36). It is also significant the Coggeshall-type bricks were produced in more than one size (Fig 208).

At Coggeshall brick was used as quoins, decoration around window openings and to form a decorative arch in walls constructed of flint and pebble rubble. The Merton bricks would have been used in a similar manner in the 13th-century flint rubble walls of the priory. The presence of semicircular corner areas suggests that their principal use would have been around window and door openings, although others may have been used as quoins.

Two Coggeshall-type bricks have single glaze splashes, but these would appear to be accidental rather than deliberate. They may have been fired with other products which had a lead glaze, perhaps peg roofing tile. Another brick differs from the rest in being slightly tapered. This, however, was made using a slightly finer sandy clay (fabric 2586) so may be from a different kiln source.

THIN BRICK (?WALL TILE)
Fabric types: 2271, 2586 (some near 2273)
A second type of thin tile or brick occurs at Merton from period M2. The earliest examples were found associated with the reconstruction of the priory church (B1) after 1222 and in a make-up layer of the infirmary chapel (B4b).

Most of these thin bricks are made with the slightly finer, sandy clay mentioned above and many have glaze on their top surface. The glaze colour is normally a greenish-brown applied as either a uniform covering or, more commonly, a splash glaze. This gives them a similar appearance to floor tiles but they do not have the knife-cut edges characteristic of tiles used as flooring, instead the sides are straight with moulding sand attached. Regrettably all these thin Merton bricks are highly fragmentary. Only one has a complete breadth of 157mm, the others have a thickness of between 22mm and 34mm (average 29mm).

Certain tiles have the appearance of Roman bricks which have been glazed, although there is no evidence that

Table 36 Coggeshall-type bricks from St Mary Merton, by size

Size group	Breadth (mm)	Thickness (mm)	Tile no. (Fig 208)
Larger	221	30–35	<T111>
Smaller	142	27–30	<T112>

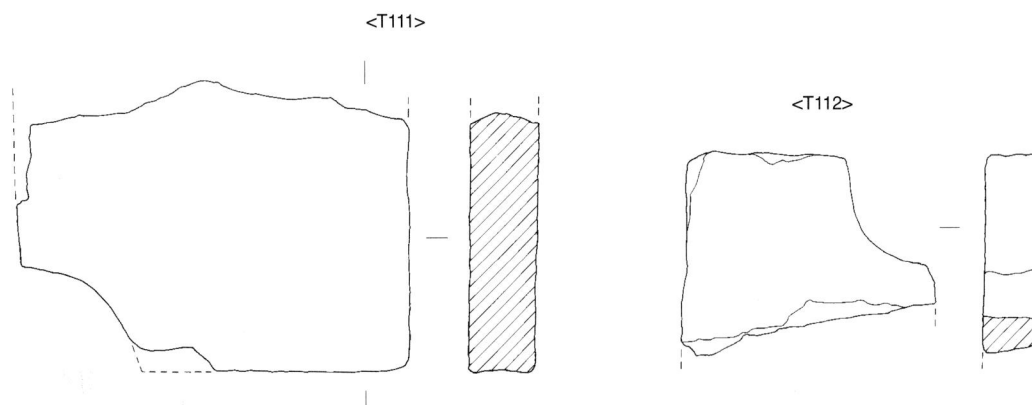

Fig 208 Coggeshall-type bricks: <T111>, larger size, and <T112>, smaller size (scale 1:4)

Roman bricks were ever reused in this manner. They are also similar in certain respects to tiles used as decorative walling during the 11th century at Westminster Abbey and in the City of London (Betts 1996, 19–24). The St Mary Merton examples normally lack the more complete glaze covering of the London and Westminster examples, but could have been used for a similar purpose in the earliest priory church.

c 1300–1538 (periods M3–M4)

REDDISH COLOURED BRICK

Fabric types: 3042, 3043, 3046, 3065, 3206, 3208

Bricks were not used in any great quantity for building work at St Mary Merton. Most of the bricks which are present are probably no earlier than the mid to late 15th century. Very little brick was used before this date, although a few earlier bricks have been identified. Found in the infill of the former infirmary drain (S4b) (OA12, period P2) is a possible Low Countries import (fabric 3043) of 13th- or 14th-century date. This measures ? x 105mm x 43mm in size. There are two bricks in rare fabric type 3208 from Open Area 12, period P2, which measure 179mm x 86mm x 47–9mm in size. The date and origin of these bricks is not known, although their odd size would suggest a medieval date.

Brick dating from the mid to late 15th century to the Dissolution is scattered across the site of the priory. It is not certain which buildings contained structural elements in brick although fragments were found in the vicinity of the infirmary hall (B4a), the infirmary cloister walk (B4c, period M3), the priory church (B1) and the chapter house (B3b). All these bricks probably originated from brickyards situated around the outskirts of London making use of local brickearth deposits. Bricks were being produced at Deptford, for use in London, as early as 1404 (Schofield 1984, 129) and by the 17th century there were a number of centres involved in brick manufacture such as Islington, Spitalfields and Moorfields (Ray 1965).

Most reddish coloured bricks are in either sandy fabric type 3065 or in less sandy type 3046. Fabric 3206 is similar to both types but is characterised by more calcium carbonate inclusions whilst fabric 3042 is similar to 3046 but has a more lumpy clay texture. All are of similar size indicating that they may have originated from the same brickyards, the difference in fabric reflecting variation in local brickearth deposits.

Red bricks made during the mid/late 15th to mid 16th century vary little in size, the Merton examples are between 50mm and 58mm thick and have a width of 108–117mm. Certain examples have indented borders, a feature frequently found on bricks of this date. Only one complete brick has been examined, which measures 225mm x 113mm x 53mm in size. This came from the disuse (period P1–P2) of the infirmary hall (B4a) and was found with pottery dated c 1500–c 1550. This has been especially shaped, having one corner absent ([8969] <T113>, Fig 209) so that it could be used in a door or window opening, very much in the same manner as the Coggeshall-type bricks. Another shaped brick was recovered from demolition deposits (OA11, period P1; [1015] <T114>, Fig 209); this probably formed part of a decorative plinth.

Deliberate markings on brick are very rare, but one of the bricks from the infirmary drain (B4b) infill (OA12, period P2) has a mark in the top surface ([9915] <T115>, Fig 209). This would seem to be some sort of batch mark.

YELLOW BRICK

Fabric type: 3031

There are a small number of yellow-coloured medieval bricks. These bricks seem to have been frequently used as paving, as at St Mary Clerkenwell nunnery (Betts in prep b), as well as walling. It is not certain what the Merton yellow bricks were used for, although two cut and shaped fragments may have formed part of a decorative hexagonally shaped chimney.

These yellow bricks are also found in Essex where they are believed by Ryan (1996, 33–4) to be imports from the Low Countries. At Merton bricks of two sizes are apparent, a smaller size measuring ? x 101mm x 47–48mm and a larger size, which includes the probable chimney bricks, which measure ? x 111–113mm x 54–58mm.

The earliest yellow bricks were found in the north burial area (OA6) and the garden area in the ? outer court (OA7). The contexts in which they occur have been allocated to period M3, but the building material present suggests they more probably belong to period M4. Evidence from elsewhere in London suggests that these bricks were brought in from the Low Countries from the 14th to the late 15th century.

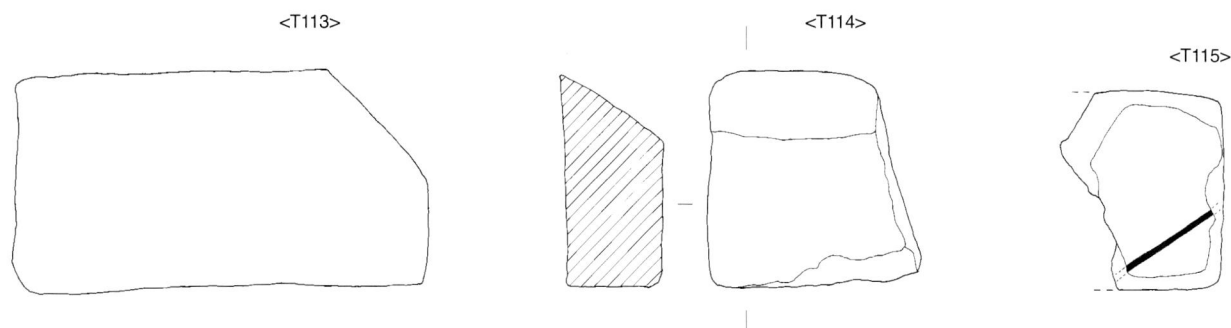

Fig 209 Shaped red brick: <T113> window/door opening; <T114> cornice; and <T115> possible batch mark (scale 1:4)

16th–19th centuries (periods P2–P3)

Certain of the bricks found in Period P2 relate to post-Dissolution activity, particularly the bricks in fabric type 3032 which were not used in London until after the Great Fire of 1666. These bricks are similar to those in the previous group but are characterised by a greater percentage of flint, pebble and ash inclusions. Two incomplete post-Fire bricks from Merton have been examined, one of which has a frog indicating a probable 18th-century date. These bricks measure 98–106mm in breadth by 59–64mm in thickness.

Stone building material

The worked stone, stone rubble and stone flooring are discussed in more detail above (7.2) and in Chapter 3.

1222–1538 (periods M2–M4)

STONE ROOFING

There are a small number of fine-grained, laminated sandstone roofing tiles, of uncertain quarry source, from the priory. As with ceramic roofing tiles, these were attached to the roof by means of nails or wooden pegs. Round nail holes, 11mm in diameter, still survive on two tiles (eg [2344] <T116>, Fig 210). These roofing tiles may have been large as one has an incomplete length of 449mm.

The earliest fragment of stone roofing came from the cloister (B3a/e) in period M2. Other later fragments are scattered across the priory site. None were found concentrated near any specific building, so it is not certain where they were used.

STONE PAVING

Part of the priory church was paved by Reigate stone blocks (B1, period M2), and blocks were used, or reused, elsewhere in the priory in, for example, foundations or cists. The two blocks retained for analysis measure 265mm x 206mm x 80–90mm and 243mm x 229mm x 80mm.

Thicker fragments of the fine-grained, laminated sandstone used for roofing may have also been used as paving. One

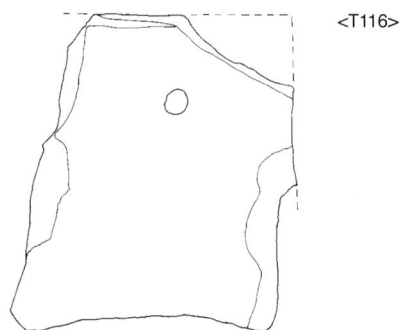

Fig 210 Stone roofing tile with nail hole <T116> (scale 1:4)

fragment, measuring 23–24mm thick, was found in the ? outer court (OA7, period M2), and another in a demolition layer (period P2) in the area of the former infirmary (B4a).

7.4 The pottery

Roy Stephenson, with residue analysis by John Evans

Methodology

All of the pottery from Merton Priory was recorded initially within the Department of Greater London Archaeology (DGLA) system. This recorded the size of assemblage and the presence and absence of fabric and form types within individual contexts, from which a spot date could then be calculated. These records are accessible in an EXCEL format. Selected contexts have been quantified using sherd count, EVE (estimated vessel equivalent) and weight for further analysis and publication. These assemblages have been recorded using standard MoLSS terminology (Table 37) and are entered on the MoLAS Oracle database using the site code MPY86. Illustrated vessels are catalogued in Table 38.

A chronological summary of the ceramic assemblage

Pre-monastic settlement at Merton is represented by Saxon chaff-tempered ware (CHAF) and late Saxon shelly ware (LSS), which occur residually in period M1 features but are significant as an indication of earlier settlement on this site.

Mid 12th to early 13th-century assemblages, associated with the priory foundation and development (period M1), are illustrated by several large assemblages, such as from the secondary fills, [9531], [9889], of the eastern ditch [11318] in Open Area 5 (Table 2). These groups produced large quantities of early medieval shell-tempered ware (EMSH) and early Surrey ware (ESUR); 90% in context [9531] and 62% in context [9889]. The presence of substantial quantities of slightly later Stamford-type ware (STAM), coarse London-type ware (LCOAR) and calcareous London-type ware (LCALC) dates these assemblages to c 1080–1200. An early 13th-century date is confirmed by the presence of Kingston-type ware (KING), Limpsfield-type ware (LIMP) and Earlswood-type ware (EARL). These assemblages therefore date the filling within the ditch as c 1200–30.

Thirteenth-century (period M2, after 1222) assemblages from the area of the infirmary contain predominantly Limpsfield-type ware (LIMP), Kingston-type ware (KING), London-type ware (LOND), coarse London-type ware (LCOAR) and Earlswood-type ware (EARL) which conform to the north Surrey typology. These are associated with a group of fabric types; early Surrey ware (ESUR), early medieval shell-tempered ware (EMSH) and early medieval sand- and shell-tempered

Table 37 Medieval and post-medieval pottery fabric codes

Fabric	Expansion	Date range AD (approximate)
Medieval		
ASHT	Ashstead ware	1200–1400
BLGR	blue-grey ware (possibly from 1000)	1000–1200
CBW	coarse Surrey-Hampshire border ware	1270–1500
CHAF	chaff-tempered ware	400–750
CHEA	Cheam whiteware	1350–1500
DENM	Denham-type ware	1150–1300
EARL	Earlswood-type ware	1200–1400
EMFL	early medieval flint-tempered ware	970–1100
EMS	early medieval sandy ware	970–1100
EMSH	early medieval shell-tempered ware	1050–1150
EMSS	early medieval sand- and shell-tempered ware	1000–1150
ESUR	early Surrey ware	1050–1150
KING	Kingston-type ware	1230–1400
KINGSL	Surrey medieval slipware	1250–1400
LCALC	calcareous London-type ware	1080–1200
LCOAR	coarse London-type ware	1080–1200
LIMP	Limspfield-type ware	1150–1300
LIMP COAR	coarse Limpsfield-type ware	1150–1300
LIMP SHEL	Limpsfield-type shell-tempered ware	1150–1300
LOGR	London-area greyware	1050–1150
LOND	London-type ware	1080–1350
LOND NFR	London-type ware with north French-style decoration	1180–1270
LSS	late Saxon shelly ware	900–1050
MG	Mill Green ware	1270–1350
SAIG	Saintonge ware with even green glaze	1280–1350
SHER	south Hertfordshire-type greyware	1140–1300
SIEG	Siegburg stoneware	1300–1500
SSW	shelly-sandy ware	1140–1220
STAM	Stamford-type ware	1050–1150
TUDG	'Tudor Green' ware	1350–1500
Post-medieval		
BORDG	Surrey-Hampshire border whiteware with green glaze	1550–1700
CHEAR	Cheam redware	1480–1550
DUTSG	Dutch slipped red earthenware with sgraffito decoration	1450–1550+
PMBL	post-medieval black-glazed ware	1580–1700
PMBR	London-area post-medieval bichrome redware	1580–1700
PMRE	London-area early post-medieval redware (formerly TUDB)	1480–1600
PMSR	London-area post-medieval slipped redware	1480–1660
RAER	Raeren stoneware	1480–1550
RBOR	Surrey-Hampshire border redware	1580–1800
SNTG	south Netherlands maiolica	1480–1550+
STGW	miscellaneous Spanish tin-glazed ware	1480–1700

ware (EMSS), which appear to continue beyond their anticipated span at Merton, as is illustrated in the assemblage from the infirmary kitchen (B6) (Fig 211). In the infirmary hall (B4a) assemblage there are no particular fabrics or forms which could be regarded as being specifically utilised in the care of the sick, although vessels such as a Kingston-type ware (KING) bowl could be indicative of individual food serving. The infirmary kitchen (B6) assemblage produced a larger range of pottery and included cooking pots and jugs. One possible indicator of food preparation and service is the presence of three fragments of blue-grey ware (BLGR) ladles. Blue-grey ware comes from a variety of sites in the middle Rhine valley and is found in the City of London until c 1200. The occurrence of blue-grey ware ladles in this area at Merton may be

indicative of these fragments being residual, or like some of the earlier fabrics have a different ceramic sequence at Merton. A number of regional and Continental imports, for example Stamford-type ware (STAM), blue-grey ware (BLGR) and Spanish tin-glazed ware (STGW), occur in small quantities, underlining that Merton is of sufficient importance to receive ceramics from further afield than the immediate environs.

Ceramic assemblages from the 14th-century phase of the priory (period M3) are dominated by the presence of Kingston-type ware (KING) and London-type ware (LOND), with an increasing and significant quantity of Cheam whiteware (CHEA) and coarse Surrey-Hampshire border ware (CBW), illustrated by the assemblage from the infirmary hall (B4a) (Fig 212). Cheam whiteware and coarse Surrey-Hampshire border

Table 38 Catalogue of illustrated pottery (for fabric codes see Table 37)

Catalogue no.	Context	Fabric	Form	Pottery date range (approx)	Period	Land use	Fig no.
Medieval pottery from period M2 (?M1)							
<P1>	[10393]	EARL	jug handle	1200–1400	M2	OA5	58
<P2>	[10536]	BLGR	ladle	1000–1200	M2 (?M1)	S4a (phase 1)	60
<P3>	[9974]	LCOAR	jug	1080–1200	M2 (?M1)	S4a (phase 2)	60
<P4>	[10016]	EMSH	cooking pot	1050–1150	M2 (?M1)	S4a (phase 2)	60
<P5>	[10016]	LIMP	cooking pot	1150–1300	M2 (?M1)	S4a (phase 2)	60
<P6>	[9974]	LIMP COAR	cooking pot	1150–1300	M2 (?M1)	S4a (phase 2)	60
<P7>	[7924]	KING	alembic	1230–1400	M2	OA9	159
Medieval to 16th-century pottery in demolition and post-Dissolution deposits							
<P8>	[9394]	PMRE	alembic	1480–1600	P1	OA11 (infirmary drain S4b)	159
<P9>	[9742]	PMRE	alembic	1480–1600	P2	OA12 (south of reredorter B5)	159
<P10>	[8068]	LOND	jug	1080–1350	P2	OA12 (south east of infirmary hall B4a, east of reredorter B5)	159
<P11>	[10136]	SSW	cooking pot	1140–1220	P2	OA12 (infirmary cloister B4c/OA5)	161
<P12>	[1015]	LOND	sprinkler	1080–1350	P1	OA11 (north of church B1)	164
<P13>	[8146]	RAER	drinking jug	1480–1610	P2	OA12 (reredorter B5)	174
<P14>	[8146]	SNTG	jug	1480–1575	P2	OA12 (reredorter B5)	174
<P15>	[8146]	DUTSG	cooking pot	1480–1550	P2	OA12 (reredorter B5)	174
<P16>	[8009]	LIMP	cooking pot	1150–1300	P3	OA13 (pit in infirmary area)	213
<P17>	[9770]	EARL	jug spout	1200–1400	P1	OA11 (infirmary drain S4b)	213
<P18>	[2406]	EARL	jar	1200–1400	P1	OA11 (north of church B1)	214

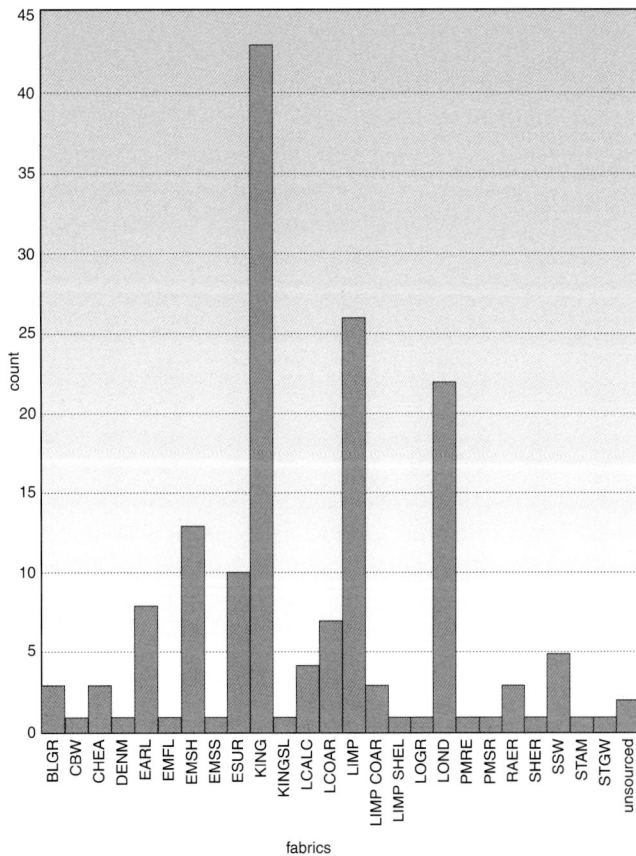

Fig 211 A summary of fabric types by estimated vessel equivalents (EVEs) in the infirmary kitchen (B6, period M2), c 1222–c 1300 (for fabric codes see Table 37)

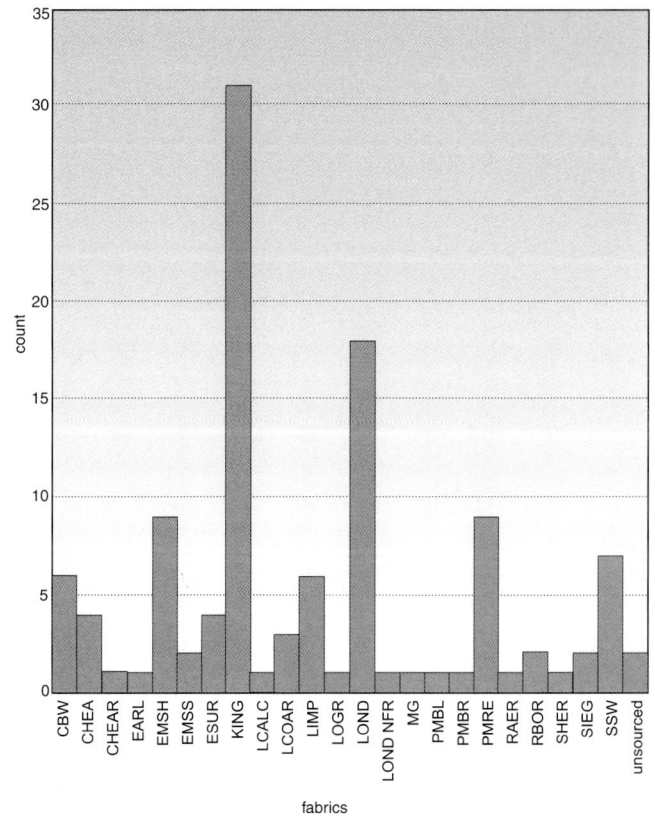

Fig 212 A summary of fabric types by estimated vessel equivalents (EVEs) in the infirmary hall (B4a, period M3), c 1300–c 1390 (for fabric codes see Table 37)

ware start to come to prominence in the 14th century and to supersede Kingston-type ware and Limpsfield-type ware (LIMP). The presence of Cheam whiteware, Siegburg stoneware (SIEG) and 'Tudor Green' ware (TUDG) corroborates the change in the composition of these assemblages and supports the coin evidence for a date in the 1360s–70s for changes to the infirmary hall.

Post-Dissolution, 16th- to 17th-century (period P2), assemblages from the area of the former reredorter (B5) include London-area early post-medieval redware (PMRE), London-area post-medieval slipped redware (PMSR) and Surrey-Hampshire border whiteware with green glaze (BORDG), and a number of noteworthy imports – a Raeren stoneware (RAER) jug <P13>, a south Netherlands maiolica (SNTG) Malling-type jug <P14>, apparently coated externally in a blue cobalt glaze, and a Dutch slipped red earthenware with sgraffito decoration (DUTSG) cooking vessel <P15> with possible inscription (Fig 174). The south Netherlands maiolica jug is closely paralleled in a Dissolution group excavated at Mount Grace Priory (Roebuck and Coppack 1987, 18). The Mount Grace assemblage is a larger discrete group that appears to have been dumped on one occasion shortly after suppression of the house. There is no clear evidence that the Merton material was deposited in the same way, but there are certain parallels that suggest that it may be a similar discrete group of pottery.

Sources of north Surrey ceramic types and their chronological sequence at Merton

The ceramic assemblages from Merton are a hybrid between the types of wares found in Surrey and the types of assemblages recovered in the City of London. There is an opportunity, therefore, to examine if there are differences in the sources and the trade patterns involved in the acquisition of pottery between the two areas.

There are a number of well documented sources of local whitewares in the immediate area within Surrey, for example the 13th- to 14th-century kilns at Kingston-upon-Thames (Pearce and Vince 1988; Miller and Stephenson 1999) and later at Cheam from the mid 14th century (Pearce and Vince

1988). The source of mundane greywares (Limpsfield-type ware) and coarsewares (early Surrey ware) is not so clear, as kiln sites are scarce in the area. Early Surrey ware is known to have been in circulation in the city, in significant quantities, and is assumed to be from Surrey on account of some similarities with the later medieval whitewares produced in the Surrey-Hampshire border region (ibid, 11). From the mid 12th century the major source and suppliers of pottery in north Surrey were in the Limpsfield area some 27km to the south-west of Merton. A number of sites have produced waster pottery in the area (Prendergast 1974). Limpsfield-type ware is generally characterised as a quartz- tempered unglazed reduced greyware, although the waster material has produced a vast number of variations in colours from light grey to brown as well as occasionally red. Vessel forms include cooking pots, jugs and to a much lesser extent dishes. There are parallel examples in the waster material to vessels found at Merton, for example cooking pots with applied strip decoration <P16> (Fig 213).

Limpsfield-type wares are also found in assemblages in the city of London, but regrettably not always distinguished from the products of the south Hertfordshire greyware industry. It is not, therefore, possible to quantify the extent to which the Limpsfield products managed to penetrate the lucrative city market. It is, however, possible to gauge the quantities of greywares in contemporary groups of ceramics. For example, in the fill of the sluice at St Mary Spital (Thomas et al 1997, 56) greywares account for 30% of the group by EVEs, consisting mostly of cooking pots and to a lesser extent jugs. In the assemblage excavated from the city ditch at Ludgate (Vince 1985), dated to the first quarter of the 14th century, greywares constitute 23% by EVEs. In all likelihood the greater portion of these groups are the products of south Hertfordshire, but a portion must be derived from the Limpsfield industry. Other known sources of locally made wares includes Ashstead ware (ASHT) (Frere 1941), which is a coarse gritty pink-grey ware, and Earlswood-type ware (Turner 1974) which is a sandy orange-pink fabric, the products of which include jugs covered with a white slip and green or clear lead glazes. Many of these jugs have bands of white slip arranged horizontally or in a cross pattern

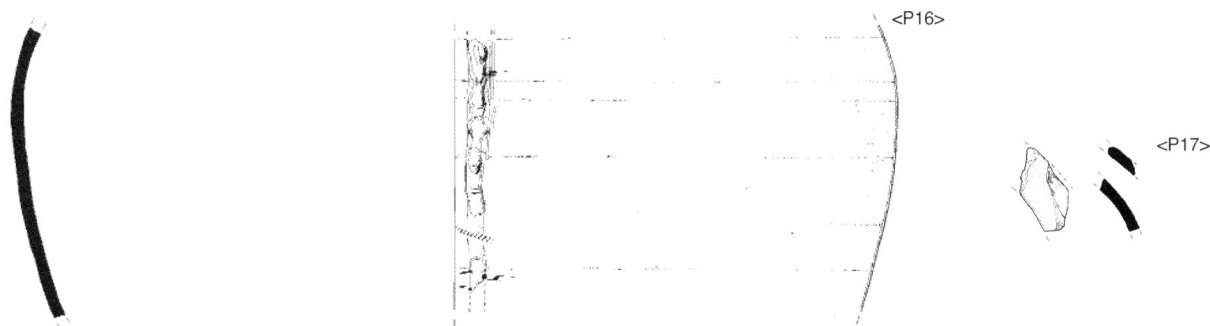

Fig 213 A Limpsfield-type ware cooking pot with applied decorative strips <P16>; and the spout from an Earlswood-type ware jug <P17> (scale 1:4)

(McCarthy and Brookes 1988, 310).

The pottery from Merton appears to share some of the same characteristics as assemblages from the city, as illustrated by the large groups in the eastern ditch [11318] (Table 2), but with some variation in the dating of early medieval shell-tempered ware (EMSH) and early Surrey ware (ESUR). These assemblages date the last infilling of the ditch to the first half of the 13th century, as demonstrated by the association of 13th-century wares in both groups, such as Kingston-type ware dating from c 1230 and Limpsfield-type ware from c 1150. Also present, however, are significant quantities of both EMSH and ESUR, which constitute 90% and 60% of the groups by weight. These are significant percentages by comparison with city assemblages where EMSH amounts to only 8% by weight of ceramic phase 4 (Vince and Jenner 1991, 64) and suggests that these wares continue in circulation at Merton longer than the mid 12th century and quite possibly well into the 13th century. This is partially borne out by the presence of EMSH in the ceramic assemblage at Elmwood Playing Fields in Wallington (Stephenson 2004), which produced moderate amounts of EMSH in contexts dating from the late 13th or early 14th century.

The ceramic supply patterns at Merton appear to differ from the norm, the gap between the early medieval hand-made tradition, and the later wheel-thrown industries such as London-type ware, the Limpsfield greyware tradition and Kingston-type ware is usually spanned by wheel-thrown shelly-sandy ware (SSW). Shelly-sandy ware is a pottery fabric that shares some characteristics with both early medieval shell-tempered ware (EMSH) and London-type ware (LOND). This fundamental change from hand-made to wheel-thrown pottery may have been caused by the arrival of immigrant potters (Vince and Jenner 1991, 42). Shelly-sandy ware is not entirely absent from deposits at Merton, but it occurs very infrequently.

A tentative supply pattern can therefore be postulated. From c 1050, and probably before, the prominent wares are early medieval shell-tempered ware (EMSH) and early Surrey ware (ESUR), which continue well beyond the conventional date of c 1150 and possibly up to c 1230 where early medieval shell-tempered ware (EMSH) is found in association with Kingston-type ware (KING). However, the possibility that KING is being produced and is in circulation prior to c 1230 should not be dismissed. The presence or absence of KING in city waterfront sites (Pearce and Vince 1988, 16) creates Kingston-type ware's nominal starting date of c 1230. There is some slight evidence that KING may have been in circulation prior to this. Small quantities have been found on the Horsefair site in Kingston-upon-Thames in association with one of the bridge piers, known to date from the 1190s from documentary evidence (G Potter, pers comm). There is, therefore, a strong probability that KING was in circulation, locally, prior to 1230.

The supply of early Surrey ware (ESUR) obviously tails away rapidly after c 1150, leaving early medieval shell-tempered ware (EMSH) and the 'new' products to fill the gap. The rise of Limpsfield-type ware (LIMP) is apparent in the ditch group (Table 2), and is a predominant proportion of other groups on this site after 1150. The same pattern is found at other sites such as Elmwood Playing Fields in Wallington (Stephenson 2004), where LIMP is a major portion of the assemblage, amounting to 95% of the group dating to the late 13th century or early 14th century. It is clear therefore that LIMP ware is a major portion of the north Surrey groups.

Early medieval shell-tempered ware (EMSH) and the related fabrics; early medieval sandy ware (EMS) and early medieval sand- and shell-tempered ware (EMSS), are assumed to derive their materials from outcrops of the Woolwich Beds, which are found in north-west Kent and extend as far as north Southwark (Vince and Jenner 1991, 63). The exact production location is therefore unknown. The large quantities of EMSH continuing into the 13th century at Merton may suggest a point of manufacture close to the site, particularly as these large quantities appear to be a localised phenomena.

Contexts dating to the 13th and 14th century produced small, but significant, quantities of Earlswood-type ware (EARL), which is rarely found on city sites, and only occasionally on sites on the periphery of the city. Merton Priory produced EARL in relative abundance. Most notable among which is the slip-decorated jar <P18> (Fig 214). Little is known about the Earlswood industry. The excavated kiln site at Bushfield Shaw (Surrey) was thought to have been fired only for one season (Turner 1974, 49), although the surrounding area of worked out brick fields must also have been the site of more kilns and waster heaps, now destroyed. The waster assemblage from Bushfield Shaw has no immediate parallel for the jar from Merton, which is decorated with broad chevrons in white slip, embellished with lines of red slip and green glaze, although the waster material did produce jug fragments with chevrons with white slip and spots of green glaze. Clearly this vessel is a 'one off' and possibly a special commission, and what its precise function is can only be guessed at. One further point of interest is a number of EARL sherds from jugs including an elaborately stabbed handle <P1> (Fig 58) and a spout <P17> (Fig 213).

Pottery residue analysis

John Evans

A small number of sherds were examined in 1999 for organic residues (the methodology is described in the archive report: Evans 1999). Interpretation was based on both the detection of characteristic compounds and by comparison with the analyses of various 'standards'. The fact that all the sherds gave positive, interpretable results shows clearly that the pottery fabrics have not absorbed any organic soil components to any practical extent (ie: any such contamination had only penetrated the outer 1–2mm at most, and hence was removed prior to extraction).

Fig 214 Earlswood-type ware, lavishly slip-decorated jar <P18> as found (0.5m scale)

Table 39 Organic residues in pottery samples

Period of deposition	Land use	Context no.	Pottery type	Pottery date range (approx)	Contents
M1	OA5 (fill of the eastern ditch [11318])	[9531]	LCOAR jug	1080–1200	fats/oil, complex pattern
M1	OA5 (fill of the eastern ditch [11318])	[9889]	LIMP cooking pot (base)	1150–1300	fats/oil + complex mixture
M2 (?M1)	S4a (phase 2)	[10016]	LIMP cooking pot (base)	1150–1300	fats/oil, meat, cereal (?barley)
M2 (?M1)	S4a (phase 1)	[10536]	BLGR ladle <P2>	1000–1200	fats/oil, cereal (?wheat)
P1	OA11 (north of church B1)	[2406]	EARL slip-decorated jar (base) <P18> jar	1200–1400	fats/oil, cereal (?barley)
P2	OA12 (south of reredorter B5)	[9742]	PMRE alembic <P9>	1480–1600	beer (?barley) or similar fermented product

Fatty acids were found in all samples (Table 39). This was not entirely unexpected as the pottery matrix absorbs oils/fats (triglyceride systems) preferentially. The complexity of the mixtures detected in the two samples from contexts [9531] and [9889], from the eastern ditch, may indicate secondary usage, or possibly a stew or casserole of some type. The interpretation of the presence of fermented system (ie beer) in alembic <P9> [9742] also requires a note of caution. As beers and wines are produced by fermentation processes they are essentially the result of natural decomposition. Consequently it is possible that the presence of 'beer' traces could have been produced by the natural decomposition, via fermentation initiated by wild yeast spores, of other types of food remains. However, its occurrence in this study appears to make archaeological sense, as it is associated with a sherd that has lead glaze on both surfaces. This would have made the pot relatively waterproof; the acidity of beer would not have been insufficient to attack the lead, thus making it a health hazard.

7.5 The non-ceramic finds

Geoff Egan, with a contribution on the possible hernia belt by Helen Ganiaris and Christie Pohl

Introduction

While most materials survive in a recognisable state, the iron is generally in poor condition – most of these finds having advanced corrosion and in many instances being in danger of breaking up or having already actually fragmented. In extreme cases this means the label description and X-radiographic record are the only information usable for cataloguing. A few waterlogged deposits, on the other hand, have ensured the survival in good condition of a small number of wooden and leather objects. Many medieval items occurred in contexts assigned to demolition and post-Dissolution phases.

A selection of the catalogued items <S1>–<S370> are illustrated. Catalogue entries are arranged as follows: (first line) catalogue number, brief description, and (where illustrated) Fig no.; (second line) accessioned find number (inside angled brackets) and context number (inside square brackets), followed by period in which item was found, and lastly land use. Accession numbers are prefixed by the excavation year. X-ray fluorescence (XRF) analysis was carried out by the Museum of London conservation department (MoLC). The following abbreviations are used:

Diam	diameter
estd	estimated
H	height
L	length
Th	thickness
W	width
Wt	weight

Saxo-Norman

The small number of finds assignable to this period were all residual as discovered. They are too limited and diverse to permit any focused comment beyond that together they suggest some kind of permanent settlement in the locality. Despite the limitations they include evidence of bone/antler working and a couple of high-quality items – a pin made of an exotic material and a piece of fine metalwork – which hint at a relatively affluent late Saxon/early Norman presence.

<S1> Ivory 'hipped' pin (Fig 6)
88 <3734>, [8083]; period P3, OA13
L 41mm; head is in form of a bird with open wings, W 10mm, its head being pierced centrally, the pin shaft and point representing an elongated beak (not all of which would have been visible when worn). Bone pins of this form (with various heads) are assigned to the 11th–12th centuries, although versions in copper alloy are known from the 8th century onwards (Margeson 1982, nos 23–46, fig 47; 1993, 9–10, nos 24–5, fig 4; MacGregor 1985, 116 and 121).

<S2> Antler comb (Fig 6)
88 <4423>, [9597]; period M3, B9
Double-sided, composite form, 71mm x 47mm, with slightly concave ends emphasised by grooves widthways; graded fine and coarse teeth 9 // 4 per 10mm (most of the former are broken off or missing); connecting strips have paired grooves lengthways along each side and are held by three rusted iron rivets.

<S3> Antler comb (Fig 6)
88 <4772> and <5800>, [10697]; period M1, OA5
Fragments (18 extant) of two distinct components from a comb or comb case: D-section pieces with edge grooves lengthways, 10mm x 4mm in section, and flattish, triangular-section pieces with two series of circle-and-dot motifs flanked by lengthways grooves (two along the central spine); part of an iron-stained rivet hole on one piece of the former is an indication of fixture.

<S4> Copper-alloy mount (Fig 6)
88 <4000>, [9154]; period P1, OA11
Cast, possibly incomplete, 32mm x 19mm; voided oval flanked by stylised leaf-like forms, narrowing at the other end to a stylised duck-like head (holed for a rivet or tack) and extending to a flat terminal (similarly holed). The foliate motifs could perhaps (although not to scale) be seen as the spread wings of a bird in flight. ? From a casket etc.

<S5> Antler needle (Fig 6)
88 <5228>, [9037]; period M2, B5
L 55mm.

<S6> Antler needle
88 <3833>, [8833]; period M3, B5
Incomplete, L 24mm.

<S7> Bone bodkin
88 <4536>, [8720]; period P2, OA12
Head only; made from pig tibia; surviving L 43mm; D-shaped hole.

ANTLER/BONE-WORKING WASTE

<S8> Implement
88 <4807>, [10399]; period M3, OA5
Pointed end of roughly trimmed implement, surviving L 53mm. Uncompleted bone pin or needle etc.

<S9> Trimmed bone
88 <6124>, [9531]; period M1, OA5
Bone: three pieces cut/broken from long bone shafts, with evidence of rough trimming.

<S10> Offcut
88 <4604>, [9804]; period M1, OA5
Red/fallow deer antler; two tine points transversely cut off, one holed from one side at proximal end, the other blade-trimmed at the point.

<S11> Offcut
88 <4577>, [9531]; period M1, OA5
Red/fallow deer antler; triangular section, cut probably at junction of tines.

Monastic (periods M1–M4)

The assemblage is unmistakably from a religious foundation. While lead coffins <S12>–<S14> (see also <S360>) are unusual among excavated objects (at least in the London area) several finds listed below are of categories that regularly feature in assemblages from the sites of religious houses (cf Egan 1997a, 109 table 104), 11 or arguably 12 of these categories being present among the Merton finds and others can probably now be added. There is equipment for the basic institutional needs of lighting (glass and stone lamps <S259>–<S261>) and water management (lead piping <S190>), fine metalwork (here in the form of cloth-of-gold from burials <S19>–<S21>, and hinted by mount <S256>), tomb inscriptions (two letters and part of a plaque <S15>–<S17>) and two rosary beads <S48> and <S49>. Four base-metal chalices and three patens <S22>–<S27> from burials are priests' grave goods. Music at the priory is represented by a tuning peg from a stringed musical instrument, a jew's harp and a buzz bone <S29>–<S31>, but it is uncertain that the latter two would have been used at services, as opposed to informally. Four shell palettes <S33>–<S35> still holding paint may also be counted. Clerkly skills of writing and reading are heavily represented, with nine writing implements – one bone stylus and eight of lead <S37>–<S45> – book mounts <S46> and <S47> and a fragment <S253> from the most ornate spectacle frames so far known from the medieval period, with its delicate carving. A bone die <S32>, indistinguishable from those used for gaming may perhaps, in the context of the religious house, take on a religious significance. This is more certain for two sacring bells <S50> and <S51>.

The bulk of individually listed finds are from windows: cames <S52>–<S70> (including sizeable portions of two lights) and glass fragments <S71>–<S188> (some of them decorated with stylised foliate motifs, some with fragmentary lettering from inscriptions and there are a few hints of figurative painting – ? an angels' wing, a clothed leg and some ashlar stonework – while three crown-edge pieces seem to be waste from the insertion or repair of windows).

Security, as at many religious houses seems from the finds to have been a preoccupation, with a slide-key padlock <S191> and 11 rotary keys <S192>–<S202>, which include a possible hint of a particular tradition in the detail of manufacture of some of the lock mechanisms not recognised elsewhere from multiple finds). Caskets, which would have been lockable, are suggested by copper-alloy and iron mounts <S256> and <S258> and a bone panel may be part of an early version. Dress accessories <S203>–<S252>, all but one of base metals, have a heavy emphasis on buckles with 41 finds, notably plain, circular versions of copper alloy (including one from a burial) and of iron (including six from burials, among which there are two pairs). A few more-decorative copper-alloy buckles of various styles include a plate engraved with the Lamb of God <S223>, and one burial had a unique and important group of seven belt accessories <S226>, some of these of types previously unknown. There is one unusual clasp <S247>, of a cheap lead/tin. There is also a part of a low-quality brooch of copper alloy <S248> and another of lead/tin <S249>, a couple of purse bars <S250> and <S251> of forms which probably post-date a purse hanger <S239>, and an enamelled gold finger ring <S252>, which, anomalously for an object from a religious institution, carries an amatory inscription. The earliest of three knives <S262>–<S264> retains its wooden handle with simple, turned decoration and a leather scabbard <S265> with foliate ornament is another organic survival. Kitchen equipment includes part of a sizeable cast copper-alloy cauldron, a fragment of another and part of the rim of a sheet vessel (<S273>–<S275>), the first, along with a stone mortar <S295>, being an expensive item appropriate for an institution, and there are six wooden bowls <S289>–<S294>, three of them with ownership marks. Glassware comprises three bottles <S276>–<S278> and the fragmented remains of probably upwards of half a dozen urinals <S279>–<S288>. Industries within the precinct included textile or leather working from finds of two needles <S296> and <S297>, and two thimbles <S298> and <S299>. Metal-working waste from copper alloy casting <S300>–<S312>, iron processing <S313>–<S327> and lead casting etc <S328>–<S331>, each forms a smallish assemblage; there is a possible concentration of the first (which is unusual in religious houses in the

London area so the rural context may well be significant) but all are somewhat scattered, both chronologically and spatially. The presence of horses is indicated by part of a horseshoe <S353>, three spurs <S354>–<S356>, a snaffle bit <S357> and two pendants <S358> and <S359>. Some level of outward-looking commercial concerns are attested by 11 English coins, <S332>–<S342>, including one counterfeit penny and a groat, an unusually high-value single loss for the London area (total face value 12^3/$_4$ pence), along with an uncommon denier of Aquitaine issued under the Black Prince during the period of English rule and a fragment of another Continental issue from the Baltic, <S343> and <S344>. There are seven jettons or counters <S345>–<S351>, comprising three English, one 'Anglo-Gallic', two Nuremberg issues, and a largely illegible one, possibly French or Low Countries. An unusual find is a touchstone, <S352>, which implies concern for the quality of gold, in the form of coin or of other items.

There is a wider than usual range of objects from human burials: three occurrences of threads from cloth-of-gold, several buckles (unusually these include some for shoes, which the particular corpses were presumably wearing at the time of interment – as attested by the soles <S18> from a different burial) and other girdle accessories (notably the truss group), and the four combinations of patens and chalices (one together with a fragment of cloth-of-gold).

The Dissolution was probably responsible for the discarding of most but not all of the large amounts of cames and fragmented window glass. Pieces from earlier deposits will relate to window assemblage and repairs. The lead cames from the 1983 excavations alone (the second largest assemblage) amount to almost a kilogram in weight. It is possible that a somewhat inaccurate 2lb lead weight <S362> (from a post-Dissolution deposit) may perhaps have been cast from this source during the recycling process, which may not have been quite as effective here as at other religious houses in the London area.

The assemblage from the religious house considered as a whole, while unusually prolific in terms of burial goods and dress accessories, overall gives an impression of utilitarian material culture, with ornament largely confined to items with spiritual connotations like the window glass – the extraordinary spectacle-frame fragment excepted. There is little directly suggestive of affluence apart from the finger ring (which seems out of place) and perhaps the unusually high incidence of coin loss (including a relatively high denomination) whilst the Continental issues may have come in among small change in general circulation), and also – indirectly – the touchstone. The jettons, indicative of accounting, are found at most religious house sites, while the horse equipment looks to travel and concerns beyond the precinct (the two gilded harness pendants were probably not particularly expensive, certainly not when set against the value of the horses they went on). Production evidence, aside from the commonly encountered needles and thimbles that indicate some level of textile/leather working, is confined to metalworking. The copper alloy casting could have given the institution its major bells, although even such a modest iron-working assemblage is unusual at religious houses in the central London area (Merton's rural location may have meant cheaper transportation), while lead working is universally attested at religious institutions.

Items relating to instutional use

LEAD COFFINS

Details of the three items listed are taken from records (Bruce and Mason 1993, 20; Chapter 4.10, 'Lead coffins').

<S12> Lead coffin (Fig 99)
86 <109> and <211>, [2583]; period M3, B1
The former is described as complete; the second is a series of small sheet fragments, presumably deriving from the first. Contained burial [2703].

<S13> Lead coffin (Fig 100)
86 <108>, [2270]; period

M3, B1
Described as three-quarters complete. Contained burial [2701].

<S14> Lead coffin (Fig 108)
88 <3156>, [7060]; period M3, OA3
(No details given in records; photograph suggests complete; individual not analysed.)

TOMB INSCRIPTIONS

Individual letters like the two below are not uncommon among excavated finds from ecclesiastical sites (Blair 1987, 140), but the panel is a more unusual survival in the ground.

<S15> Copper-alloy panel (Fig 136)
86 <333>, [1]; period P3, OA13
Incomplete panel with three straight edges and one broken at the left, surviving 78mm x 63mm, Th 4mm; bevelled edge at right; deeply engraved blackletter legend in two lines: '[…] /…[?m, n or u]pton qu…/…puletur…'; there is a roughly tooled ?hexagon at the top; hole for attachment at break; roughly scratched saltire on back. The legend seems to refer to a named individual, who is buried … (…pton qu[i]… [se]puletur); presumably reused turned over, as one of the smooth

edges cuts through the inscription.

<S16> Copper-alloy letter I (Fig 103)
86 <120>, [2792]; period M3, B1
H 40mm, W 13mm, Th 2.5mm. Blair's (1987, 140) main group size II.

<S17> Copper-alloy lombardic letter A
86 <162>, [3020]; period M3, B1
H 35mm, W 31mm, Th 2.5mm. Blair's (1987, 140) main group size III.

SHOES

The remains of two leather shoes found in a human burial were in a position that suggested the corpse was interred wearing them. The shoe buckles from several other graves (below, 'Dress accessories') are presumably differentially surviving evidence of the same phenomenon.

<S18> Leather shoes
86 <116>–<117>, [2651]; period M3, B1
Two partly decayed, waisted

soles (neither toe survives), respectively L 168mm, W 61mm and L 115mm, W 48mm (? no indication of left versus right).

As the most distinctive part, the toe, is in each case missing, the form of this pair of shoes

is uncertain (there is no indication that these ones were buckled). From burial [2651].

TEXTILES

A number of fragments of cloth found in burials (Bruce and Mason 1993, inside back cover) but only precious-metal threads, suggesting important personages in the religious community, are dealt with here.

The following fragments presumably derive from ecclesiastical dress in burials (cf Egan 1997a, 109, table 114, category D):

<S19> Gold thread
86 <75>, <77>–<81> and <90>, [2253]; period M3, B1
Scraps, including some parallel threads.

<S20> Gold thread
86 <170>, [2357]; period P1, B1
Single thread.
<S21> Gold thread

86 <281>, <290>, <297> and <6049>, [3311]; period M3, B1
Several scraps, among which only some of <290> shows obvious coherence from a woven form; <6049>, a single thread surviving from a tiny group, was found beside paten <S26> from burial [3379].

CHALICES AND PATENS

Base-metal (lead/tin, none were analysed) vessels of these two categories are sometimes found in the graves of priests, where they were to hand for religious use at the final resurrection (Egan 1997a, 109, table 14, category D, with references to comparable discoveries). The three sets of chalice and paten, together with a fourth chalice, are a sizeable group. The lifting of these fragile items in soil blocks is described by Jones (1992, 29–33).

<S22> Lead/tin chalice and paten (Fig 111; Fig 112)
86 <141>, [2904]; period M3, OA6
Corroded and incomplete: large chalice with flaring base Diam c 145mm, broad stem W c 55–72mm and round cup – Diam at surviving top (possibly the original cup rim) c 130–140mm; standing on remains of paten, Diam c 170mm; consolidated together in plaster – overall has surviving H c 85mm. Paten not separately numbered. From burial [2905].

<S23> Lead/tin chalice
86 <301>, [3311]; period M3, B1
Corroded and distorted: collar at base of round cup; original H c 100mm, Diam of cup rim ? c 140mm, Diam at flaring base c 100mm; base appears to have been angled near stem and

perhaps bevelled at rim; consolidated in plaster. Found with paten <S26>, from burial [3379].

<S24> Lead/tin chalice (Fig 24)
86 <6010>, [4880]; period M1, OA6
Corroded; flaring base, Diam 100mm, with slight bevel at rim, grooved knop and part of cup survive; H to cup base c 60mm. Found with paten <S27>, from burial [4881].

<S25> Lead/tin chalice (Fig 24)
86 <484>, [4592]; period M1, OA6
Corroded and incomplete; part of flaring base with bladed knop and bevelled collar to traces of cup; fragments of rim survive, probably from base.

From burial [4593].

<S26> Lead/tin paten
86 <302>, [3311]; period M3,
B1
Corroded and incomplete,
consolidated in plaster; Diam
c 140mm. Found with chalice
<S23> and with gold thread

<S21>, from burial [3379].

<S27> Lead/tin paten
86 <481>, [4880]; period M1,
OA6
Corroded and incomplete;
Diam c 130mm. Found with
chalice <S24>, from burial
[4881].

POSSIBLE CASKET

<S28> Possible bone casket
(Fig 166)
86 <231>, [3164]; period P1,
OA11
Corroded; rectangular antler
panel, 74mm x 27mm (material
identified by Alan Pipe); three
sides are bevelled, the two
shorter ones each with a pair
of holes obliquely for bone
dowels (parts of two of which
survive) and one of the long

sides with a single hole also
obliquely; the other long side
has a lengthways groove.
Presumably an end from a
prestigious casket (MacGregor
1985, 200–3), the groove
perhaps being to accommodate
an adjoining part or perhaps a
sliding lid; the unusual material
suggests it was for holding a
liturgical item or a valued
writing implement.

TUNING PEG

<S29> Bone tuning peg
(Fig 154)
88 <4135>, [9054]; period P2,
OA12
L 40mm, Diam at end 5mm,
rectangular head 8mm x 4mm
has a hole for string and is
stained green, presumably

from copper-alloy wire. These
pegs from stringed instruments
are regularly found at the sites
of religious houses (Egan
1997a, 109, table 14, category
U) as well as more generally
(Wardle 1998, 285–7, fig
218).

JEWS HARP

<S30> Copper-alloy Jews harp
(Fig 166)
88 <5398>, [7796]; period P3,
OA13
Incomplete (both prongs

broken short); surviving
L 34mm, oval head W 21mm;
remains of iron tongue
(Wardle 1998, 284–5, nos
933–8).

BUZZ BONE

<S31> Buzz bone (Fig 59)
86 <6121>, [10257]; period
M2, S4a
Pig metapodial with rough,
transverse hole centrally and
slightly trimmed towards distal
end; L 57mm; no sign of
sustained wear from use.
Bones of this type were put on

a string, which was then
twisted, and made to produce
a whirring sound when held
between two hands and
alternately pulled and relaxed
(MacGregor 1985, 103–4;
Lawson and Brown 1990;
Lawson 1995; Willemsen 1998,
112).

DIE

<S32> Bone die (Fig 118)
88 <5226>, [9416]; period M3,
B4a
8mm x 7mm x 7.5mm; the

numbers are indicated by circle-
and-dot motifs, in the 'regular'
pattern (ie opposite sides add up
to seven) – configuration 4 in

Potter's system (Egan 1997b).
See Biddle (1990, 698) for the
possible use of dice at religious

institutions, drawing on divine
guidance to select an
appropriate course of action.

PALETTES

Containers for paint used in mural or manuscript painting.
These are becoming regular finds at the sites of religious
houses; in most other instances oyster shells similar to
<S33> and <S34> were used.

<S33> Two oyster shell palettes
86 <2687>, [5381]; period M1,
OA3
Containing remains of red
pigment; mercury (MoLC, XRF) –
presumably natural cinnibar or
artificial vermilion.

<S34> Oyster shell palette
88 <4473>, [9622]; period M2,
B5
Containing traces of purplish-red
pigment; lead (MoLC, XRF) –
probably red lead.

<S35> Shell palette
88 <5275> [9883]; period P2,
OA12
Two small fragments of

nacrous, bivalve shell(s) (not
oyster) with traces of purplish-
red pigment; lead (MoLC,
XRF) – presumably red lead.
Presumably pieces of one or
two palettes (as found,
residual from the religious
house).

<S36> Sample
86 <6119>, [3500]; period M2,
OA6
Sample of reddish material;
titanium, iron, zinc and lead
(MoLC, XRF) – could be
titanium white, zinc white and
red lead – the iron could be
haematite (red iron oxide) or
from iron in the soil.

WRITING IMPLEMENTS

Bone styli are common, almost ubiquitous finds at the sites of
religious houses (Egan 1997a, 109, table 14, category H) and
lead styli, of which eight are listed here, are also regular finds
at these institutions (ibid, category I).

<S37> Bone stylus
(Fig 163)
88 <4008>, [9101];
period P2, OA12
Turned; incomplete, surviving
L 50mm; terminal knop has
double collar (cf Egan 1998,
272–3, nos 899–911, fig 210;
Egan in prep). See Turner
(1965, 146) for another found
during earlier excavations at
Merton.

<S38> Lead stylus
76 <7570>, [41]; period P1,
OA11
Wedge-shaped end and trimmed
point at other end; L 125mm,
Diam 6mm.

<S39> Lead stylus
76 <7577>, [41]; period P1,
OA11
Incomplete (two fragments);
wedge-shaped surviving end,

surviving L 53mm, Diam 6mm.

<S40> Lead stylus
77 <7618>, [382]; period P1,
OA11
Distorted, possible stylus; L
123mm, Diam 5mm.

<S41> Lead stylus (Fig 163)
83 <7582>, [1005]; period P1,
OA11
L 52mm, Diam 6mm; plain top,
bifacially facetted point (Egan
1998, 270–1, fig 209).

<S42> Lead stylus (Fig 163)
83 <7147>, [1015]; period P1,
OA11
As preceding item but L 74mm.

<S43> Lead stylus
83 <7480>, [1040]; period M3,
B4
Shaft only of possible incomplete
stylus; surviving L 51mm,

Diam 6mm.

<S44> Lead stylus
88 <4450>, [8558]; period M3, B4a
Incomplete; pointed end survives, other broken off; surviving L 44mm, Diam 6mm.

<S45> Lead stylus
88 <4590>, [10250]; period M3, OA5
Possible stylus; wedge-shaped and pointed ends; hole in one side near centre; L 74mm, Diam 5mm. The significance of the hole is unclear.

BOOK MOUNTS

Copper-alloy book mounts and clasps frequently turn up at the sites of religious houses (Egan 1997a, 109, table 14, category L).

<S46> Copper-alloy mount (Fig 163)
83 <43>, [1025]; period P2, OA12
Flared mount consisting of two sheets, front one 36mm x 31mm and with engrailed long edge and engraved motif of two compass-made, concentric circles and central dot with three lines radiating from opposite sides, and narrowed, hooked tab; this is held by three rivets to a smaller sheet underneath.

<S47> Copper-alloy book clasp
88 <664>, [1]; period P3, OA13
Probable book clasp; 26mm x 19mm, square with curving flange that is broken off; engraved with foliate motifs (cf sycamore) in four-square grid, with pair of grooves along flange; three iron rivets.

BEADS

Beads, presumably from rosaries, are also frequent finds at the sites of religious houses (Egan 1997a, 109, table 14, category B).

<S48> Bone bead (Fig 215)
88 <3996>, [8555]; period M3, OA7
Turned; L 5.5mm, max Diam 5mm, hole Diam c 1.5mm; central bulge is flanked on both sides by a groove.

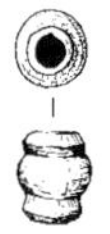

<S49> Bone bead (Fig 118)
88 <3730>, [8558]; period M3, B4a
Presumably a bead; turned; asymmetrical lenthways; L 12mm, max W 6mm, Diam of hole c 1.25mm; one end has two reels on a main cylindrical length, the other has a thicker collar with four turned grooves and obliquely scored cuts, and there is a turned terminal groove here too. The asymmetry is unusual.

Fig 215 Turned bone bead <S48> (scale 1:1)

SACRING BELLS

These bells were rung when the host was elevated at Mass (Biddle and Hinton 1990, 725–7, fig 202).

<S50> Copper-alloy sacring bell (Fig 52)
83 <7600>, [1081]; period M2, B4a
Incomplete; cast, open-mouth form, H 42mm, Diam at base c 34mm; three circumferential bands at base; loop at top for suspension.

<S51> Copper-alloy sacring bell
88 <4645>, [10536]; period M2, S4a (item missing)
As preceding item but complete and with plain base; H 55mm, Diam at base 32mm.

Structural items

Almost all the glass, by far the most prolific of the non-ceramic finds, is corroded and fragmentary, unless otherwise indicated. Most pieces appear to have been pale green or colourless where the original colour can be determined (other colours that are definite are stated); paint is now red unless indicated otherwise. The condition is such that few of the painted motifs can be made out in their entirety and many are currently completely unidentifiable. Grozing indicates that the dimensions, generally given where three or more edges survive, are original ones (where edges are broken and hence unlikely to represent the state as originally used, no details of size are given). A few pieces of window glass retain their surrounding cames of the medieval tradition (<S89>, <S136>, <S178> and <S179>; not individually catalogued here). Only <S52>, a substantial, although very distorted survival of a single light, gives any real indication of the configuration of more than a single quarry.

Of the painted devices that can be made out to a greater or lesser extent, most can be categorised as foliate-scroll motifs on fields of cross hatching, and there is a limited amount with restrained, highly stylised, spiky, sub-foliate designs on broad, completely plain fields. A small minority of figurative work has been recognised – a possible leg under clothing on <S80>, a wing on <S163> (both on blue glass), perhaps drapery on <S154>, a rose on roundel <S166>, fragments with an acorn and a more stylised rose, and others with possible ashlar masonry <S148> and <S152> (cf <S99>). Other ?colourless and blue pieces, both strips and lens shaped, have grids with annulets or running ?border motifs of roundels etc, for example <S83>, <S147> and <S153>. Fragments <S110>, <S124> and <S182> feature inscriptions in black letter and <S102> has ? black letter or lombardic script. Among the coloured pieces, durable blue appears fairly prominent in the listing, probably because it is readily recognised as well as having survived in good condition, and there are a couple of olive-brown pieces, several different shades of green and some fragments of flash ruby. Two pieces from the edges of crown-spun colourless/pale green sheets and a similar one of flash ruby have no evidence for use (<S75>, <S183> and <S170>) and so may – like a number of fragments found at the site of Bermondsey Abbey (Egan in prep) – have been discarded as waste.

CAMES

All those examined are in the medieval cast tradition (ie not milled and so non-reeded).

Each year of excavation produced a number of pieces of cames – modest assemblages for 1976, 1977 and 1986 but hundreds of pieces in 1988. Limited resources, along with no significant variation in the bulk of this material, mean that only the medium-sized assemblage from 1983 is considered in detail below, along with two exceptional survivals from 1988.

Two substantial but distorted survivals of parts of lights or a light (bent over into one or more layers), both retaining some (by no means all) decayed glass, were lifted in soil blocks. It is not possible without considerable further work (considered too risky by conservators) attempting to unfold the tangled cames to gain a clearer indication of the overall configuration of these unusual survivals.

<S52> Lead came (Fig 172)
88 <5760>, [8771]; period P1, OA11
Bent into area *c* 450mm x 300mm; upwards of a dozen quarries survive complete or substantially so (mainly quadrangular), with seven of these contiguous in area *c* 210mm x 170mm giving the fullest indication available of the configuration of part of any of the priory's lights.

<S53> Lead came (Fig 172)
88 <5761>, [8771]; period P1, OA11
Bent into two main areas of survival, with upwards of 17 quarries altogether, *c* 180mm and 175mm x 120mm respectively, mainly quadrangular quarries with a couple of triangular ones (a loose,

colourless fragment is not necessarily from the main light); the configuration of the surviving areas appears to differ from that of <S52> but only a relatively small area of either light survives.

The exceptional survival of <S52> and <S53> aside, as well as individual pieces, there were several finds of grouped, used cames of medieval form – some folded into rough balls, presumably in anticipation of the melting pot. The largest group of these, <S55>, weighs *c* 0.95kg; the total weight of medieval-type cames recovered comes to *c* 2.3kg (this is with some soil still adhering).

<S54>–<S70> Lead cames
A full catalogue is available in the research archive.

WINDOW GLASS

A full catalogue of the window glass <S71>–<S188> can be found in the research archive, a selection highlighting the more interesting and the illustrated items is presented here.

<S71> Roundel (Fig 135)
76 <7061>, [3]; period P3, OA13
Durable-blue roundel, Diam 31mm.

<S73> Painted glass
76 <7059>, [13]; period P2, OA12
Two painted fragments; one with ?foliate motif on cross-hatched field and grid of lozenges with central pellets all in reserve.

<S74> Roundel (Fig 135)
76 <7069>, [13]; period P2, OA12
Durable-blue roundel, Diam 30mm.

<S77> Fragments (Fig 135)
76 <7111>, [37]; period P2, OA12
Three fragments of two different greens.

<S80> Painted fragments

(Fig 39)
77 <7074>, [838]; period M3, OA3
Several fragments, including one almost complete, durable-blue quarry of complex outline, 62+mm x 32mm, painted with ?drapery around flexed knee and lower leg. Cf <S163>.

<S82> Quarry (Fig 39)
77 <7913>, [845]; period M3, OA3
Olive-brown quarry, 35mm x 21mm, complex outline.

<S84> Painted fragments
(Fig 138)
83 <7014>, [1]; period P3, OA13
Two durable-blue fragments with paint; one irregular lentoid, 47mm x 19mm, having traces of grid of lozenges with central annulets. Cf <S147> (also <S155>) for the first.

<S90> Painted fragments

83 <7910>, [1]; period P3, OA13
Two fragments with paint; corner with cross hatching and ?foliate motif, and ?grid in reserve.

<S91> Quarry (Fig 135)
83 <7915>, [1]; period P3, OA13
Incomplete, flash-ruby, sub-lozenge-shaped quarry, 53mm x 40+mm; even colour.

<S93> Painted fragment
(Fig 138)
83 <7464>, [1003]; period P1, OA11
Four-sided fragment, surviving 52mm x 50mm with one concave side; painted with leaf (cf hazel) and ? large bud.

<S99> Painted fragment
(Fig 138)
83 <7868>, [1003]; period P1, OA11
Right-angled fragment painted with right-angled lines and rectangular blocks of colour (possibly including a column capital).

<S104> Painted fragments
(Fig 138)
83 <7000>, [1005]; period P1, OA11
Five fragments painted with spiky foiliate motifs.

<S109> Painted fragment
(Fig 138)
83 <7838>, [1005]; period P1, OA11
Fragment with right angle, painted with ornate, radiating motif.

<S113> Quarry fragment
(Fig 137)
83 <7844>, [1005]; period P1, OA11
Fragment of amethyst quarry of complex shape.

<S117> Painted quarry
(Fig 216)
83 <7863>, [1005]; period P1, OA11
Fragment of curving ?sub-rectangular quarry 36+mm x 18mm; reserve-painted scroll with ? buds and leaves.

<S120> Painted fragments
83 <7007>, [1014]; period P1,

OA11
Five fragments with paint: include part of black letter legend, foliate motif on cross-hatched field and ?rectangular quarry 52+mm x 46mm with (?border) row of roundels with paired annulets between in reserve.

<S121> Painted fragment
(Fig 138)
83 <7848>, [1014]; period P1, OA11
Fragment painted with ?trefoil in angled border.

<S123> Painted fragments
(Fig 138)
83 <7941>, [1014]; period P1, OA11
Several painted fragments, including foliate motifs; one on cross-hatched background and one ?border with circles alternating with paired annulets in reserve.

<S130> Painted quarry
(Fig 137)
83 <7859>, [1015]; period P1, OA11
Incomplete lozenge-shaped quarry, surviving 107mm x 69mm; painted with restrained quatrefoil and spiky foliate motif.

<S141> Quarry fragment
(Fig 137)
83 <7851>, [1025]; period P2, OA12
Green fragment of quarry of irregular outline.

<S147> Quarry (Fig 137)
83 <7870>, [1025]; period P2, OA12
Durable-blue lens-shaped quarry, 60mm x 23mm; painted with oblique grid with annulets in the centres, and part of another. Cf <S84> (also <S155>) with the first.

<S148> Painted fragment
(Fig 138)
83 <7918>, [1025]; period P2, OA12
Fragment painted with ? ashlar stonework.

<S153> Quarry (Fig 137)
83 <7013>, [1028]; period M4, OA5
Durable-blue rectangular quarry,

Fig 216 Coloured and painted glass fragments <S117>, <S156>, <S166> roundel, <S170> and <S184> corroded quarry (scale c 1:1)

78mm x 15mm; grey painted row of roundels in reserve, flanked by narrower line (?border).

<S156> Quarries and fragments (Fig 216)
83 <7857>, [1028]; period M4, OA5 [?four+]
Several (four+?, three illustrated) durable-blue quarries and fragments, including complex-subrectangular 94mm x 37mm, trapezoid 51+mm x 22mm, curving 64mm x 20mm, and strips 41+mm x 16mm and 52+mm x 8mm.

<S160> Painted fragment
83 <7018>, [1034]; period M3, B4
Fragment apainted with cross hatching and foliate motif.

<S161> Painted fragments
83 <7019>, [1040]; period

M3, B4
Two painted fragments; one with row of roundels alternating with lozenges with paired annulets between, all in reserve, flanked by single line.

<S162> Fragment
83 <7858>, [1040]; M3, B4
Green fragment.

<S163> Painted quarry (Fig 54)
83 <7037>, [1042]; period M3, B4
Durable-blue quarry of complex shape, 42mm x 27mm; traces of painted ?wing. Cf <S80>.

<S164> Painted quarry (Fig 54)
83 <7022>, [1046]; period M3, B4
Almost complete rectangular quarry, 56mm x 46mm; painted foliate motif in reserve.

<S165> Painted fragments
83 <7023>, [1046]; period

M3, B4
Two fragments with paint, one with ?foliate motif.

<S166> Roundel (Fig 216)
83 <7004>, [T2, B]; period P3, OA13
Roundel, Diam 25mm, painted with six-petalled rose.

<S170> Fragment (Fig 216)
86 <6179> [2163]; period P3, OA13
Corroded, flash-ruby (streaked) fragment; no evidence for use; possible edge piece from crown sheet.

<S172> Painted fragment
86 <694>, [5380]; period M3, B4
Fragment painted with field of lozenges with central annulets.

<S176> Painted fragments (Fig 138)
88 <3001>, [7023]; period P1,

OA11
Two fragments with paint; one with trefoil motif, the other's ?paint corroded to white.

<S182> Painted fragment (Fig 138)
88 <5812>, [8285]; period P2, OA12
Fragment painted with vertical row of three voided lozenges in front of black letter legend ([?]*himis*… or similar).

<S184> Quarry (Fig 216)
88 <4235>, [9339]; period M2, B5
Very corroded, ?rectangular quarry, 103mm x 22mm; divided by zigzag into triangles with central annulets, all in negative relief. Presumably the decoration was originally painted, and that surface has come off, taking with it some of the glass underlying the painted lines.

Fittings

SETTINGS

<S189> Lead setting
83 <7580>, [1005]; period P1,
OA11
Rectangular form, 50mm x
24mm x 19mm, catering
for a rectangular bar *c* 39mm
x 18mm x 10mm; cut flat at
top. Presumably to secure an
iron bar in masonry.

WATER PIPE

This is another category of find regularly encountered on the
sites of institutions like religious houses (Egan 1997a, 109,
table 14, category F). The following fragment may well have
gone with a larger piece of piping removed from nearby
context [8871] (object not traced).

<S190> Lead water pipe
88 <3487>, [8102]; period P2,
OA12
Slightly distorted, cut section,
original Diam estd *c* 24mm.

Security equipment

Eleven rotary keys and an incompatible single surviving lock
were recovered. The warding on <S192>, <S197> and <S201>
is similar to the extent that they all feature a triple-branched
cleft (cf Ward Perkins 1940, pl 31, nos 55 and 57) – possibly
an indication of a common maker. Two small keys may be for
caskets. Most are described from X-ray plates.

<S191> Iron padlock
88 <4673>, [8808]; period P2,
OA12
Slide-key form (described from X-
ray plate); case 60mm x 31mm has
lengthways ribs and at least one
end plate appears to survive.

<S192> Iron key
86 <278>, [2163]; period P3,
OA13
(Described from X-ray plate)
overall L 71mm, kidney-shaped
bow 26mm x 20mm, symmetrical
bit 10mm x 20mm.

<S193> Iron key
88 <3561>, [7000]; period P2,
OA12
Incomplete, robust key (described
from X-ray plate); surviving L
99mm (bow broken off),
?asymmetrical bit ? 22mm x
32mm.

<S194> Iron key
88 <3165>, [7797]; period P3,
OA13
L 99mm, kidney-shaped bow
32mm x 24mm; bit 20mm x
28mm has complex, asymmetrical
warding.

<S195> Iron key
88 <3612>, [8089]; period P2,
OA12
Incomplete (described from
X-ray plate); overall L 91mm,
oval bow 35mm x 31mm (bit
broken off).

<S196> Iron key
88 <5634>, [8114]; period
M2, OA5
?Shank and bit only survive
(complete according to X-ray
plate, from which the
description is taken); L 45mm,
circular bow Diam 14mm has
rectangular loop at top and
?pierced-quatrefoil motif; L of
hollow shaft 26mm, bit 5mm
x 8mm has two clefts. A small
key possibly for a casket.

<S197> Iron key
88 <3806>, [8296]; period P2,
OA12
Incomplete (described from
X-ray plate); surviving L 138mm,
L of shaft 135mm,
symmetrically warded bit 25mm
x 34mm (most of bow broken
off); protruding part of pin
possibly narrowed.

<S198> Iron key
88 <3569>, [8523]; period M3,
OA6
(Described from X-ray plate)
overall L 120mm, circular bow
Diam 32mm, asymmetrically
warded bit 24mm x 32mm has
traces of non-ferrous coating.

<S199> Iron key
88 <3814>, [8691]; period P2,
OA12
Incomplete (described from X-ray
plate); surviving L 48mm,
symmetrical bit, 13mm x 18mm,
has cruciform and two other clefts
(bow broken off).

<S200> Iron key
88 <5737>, [8842]; period P2,
OA12
(Described from X-ray plate)

<S201> Iron key
88 <4160>, [9100]; period P2,
OA12
Incomplete (described from X-ray
plate); overall L 100mm, kidney-
shaped bow *c* 23mm x 24mm,
symmetrically warded bit 14mm
x 24mm.

<S202> Iron key
88 <4704>, [9778]; period P2,
OA12
(Described from X-ray plate)
overall L 48mm, circular bow
Diam 18mm, has decorated
shoulders, bit 13mm x 10mm,
?hollow shank. A small key
possibly for a casket.

overall L 124mm, circular bow
Diam *c* 40mm, asymmetrical bit
21mm x 31mm, hollow stem.

Dress accessories

The copper-alloy buckles catalogued are mainly notable for those
from burials – <S204> and <S205>, <S206> and <S207>,
<S208>, <S209>, <S210>, <S214>, <S216>, <S226> (cf
Egan 1997a, 109, table 14, category D), which give a rare
oppportunity to define the sex and age of the wearers (cf Clay
1981, 133, 135, fig 48; 138 fig 50 for eight copper-alloy
buckles and one of iron excavated on burials at the Austin Friars
in Leicester). Plain circular buckles like <S205> have been
found in burials elsewhere in London at St Mary Graces
(Grainger and Phillpotts in prep a) and a pair was excavated in
similar circumstances at Waterford in Ireland (Lightbown 1997,
520–1, nos 7 and 9, fig 15.20 – mistakenly regarded as
brooches). Presumably the iron accessories <S227>–<S238> –
buckles, some from burials, including shoe fasteners – include
the 'iron boot studs' noted in Bruce and Mason (1993, 22).

BUCKLES

<S203> Copper-alloy buckle
86 <158>, [2041]; -, -
Circular, Diam 35mm; bent-rod
pin is slightly worn from contact
with frame.

<S204> Copper-alloy buckle
86 <87>, [2531]; period M3,
OA6
Found to inside of right femur
near top end in burial, circular,
Diam 39mm; iron corrosion
around (obscures ?pin). From
burial [2531].

<S205> Copper-alloy buckle
86 <86>, [2531]; period M3,
OA6
Similar item and position to

preceding, but partly
corroded on left leg. From
burial [2531].

<S206> Copper-alloy buckle
(Fig 101)
86 <136>, [2858]; period
M1–M4, OA6
Circular, Diam 34mm; pin has
plain grip at base; no obvious
wear. From same context as
following item and <S231>.
Cf Egan and Pritchard 1991,
57 and 115, buckle pins nos
541 etc. From burial [2858].

<S207> Copper-alloy buckle
(Fig 101)
86 <151>, [2858]; period

M1–M4, OA6
Similar to preceding item from same context, but Diam 37mm and pin is bent. From burial [2858].

<S208> Copper-alloy buckle
86 <232>, [3172]; period M3, B1
Similar to preceding item, Diam 39mm. From burial [3172].

<S209> Copper-alloy buckle
(Fig 23)
86 <381>, [3667]; period M1, OA6
Similar to preceding item, but Diam 35mm and pin worn by frame. From burial [3667].

<S210> Copper-alloy buckle
86 <159>, [2951]; period M1, B1
Circular, Diam 35mm; cast pin has grip by loop. From burial [2951].

<S211> Copper-alloy buckle
86 <469>, [4500]; period P2, OA12
Circular, Diam 45mm; cast pin has triply-grooved grip by loop; traces possibly of leather noted by conservator.

<S212> Copper-alloy buckle
(Fig 120)
86 <728>, [5387]; period M3, B4c
Oval with folded plate, 23mm x 20mm (40mm x 16mm); offset bar and triple grooves flanked by knops on thicker outside edge of frame; plate has holes for missing pin and three missing rivets, and engraved zigzags along sides.

<S213> Copper-alloy buckle
88 <4797>, [7000]; period P2, OA12
Double-oval frame, 22mm x 14mm; trace of rust from missing pin.

<S214> Copper-alloy buckle
(Fig 107)
88 <3129>, [7572]; period M3, OA3
D-shaped frame, 45mm x 33mm; cast pin is transversely grooved; mineralised textile remains noted by conservator. From burial [7573].

<S215> Copper-alloy buckle

(Fig 45)
86 <95>, [2318]; period M2, OA6
Rectangular with heavy, bevelled frame, 16mm x 21mm, and narrowed bar, all with traces of white-metal coating; frame and sheet pin (which has two transverse grooves near loop) are worn from contact with each other.

<S216> Copper-alloy buckle
88 <3141>, [7606]; period M3, OA3
Corroded and incomplete; rectangular frame, ? 18mm x 21mm, with thicker, transversely grooved outside edge; parts of folded sheet plate and iron pin survive. From burial [7606] (also strapends <S244> and <S245>).

<S217> Copper-alloy buckle
88 <3204>, [7790]; period P1, OA11
Incomplete, cast pin; surviving L 41mm; grip at base; part of loop broken off.

<S218> Copper-alloy buckle
(Fig 165)
88 <3193>, [7816]; period P2, OA12
Rectangular frame ? of sheeting, 10mm x 8mm (16mm x 6mm), transversely ?cut in outside edge, with incomplete, folded sheet plate having holes for missing pin and retaining

two rivets. Presumably a buckle, despite its small size and flimsiness – it is difficult to imagine where this might have gone in costume.

<S219> Copper-alloy buckle
(Fig 165)
88 <4149>, [8409]; period P2, OA12
Slightly trapezoidal frame 13mm x 11mm (24mm x 8mm) with thicker, transversely grooved outside edge, folded sheet plate with holes for wire pin and single rivet.

<S220> Copper-alloy buckle
(Fig 165)
88 <3930>, [8616]; period P1, OA11
Oval frame, 18mm x 13mm (20mm x 14mm), with offset bar, notched lip for cast, flanged pin and folded sheet plate having slot for pin and retaining two rivets. A second, incomplete sheet (19+mm x 16mm, folded over at one end and with one surviving rivet) is probably from another strap accessory.

<S221> Copper-alloy buckle
(Fig 165)
88 <3727>, [8680]; period P2, OA12
Double-oval frame, 34mm x 30mm, with projecting spur at each corner and edges thickened to angled lips; sheet pin; folded sheet plate 22+mm

x 15mm is incomplete.

<S222> Copper-alloy buckle
88 <4089>, [8873]; period P1, OA11
Sheet fragment ? from buckle plate; surviving corner, 15mm x 14mm, has engraved zigzags along straight sides and further tooled motifs (cf quatrefoil overall); three small piercings.

<S223> Copper-alloy buckle
(Fig 165)
88 <3659>, [9000]; period P2, OA12
Front sheet from composite buckle, surviving part 35mm x 24mm; holes for two rivets; engraved with Lamb of God with cross and banner, moon and sun above and over panel with IHC.

<S224> Copper-alloy buckle
88 <4453>, [9573]; period M3, B4c
Probable buckle frame; circular, Diam 24mm.

<S225> Copper-alloy buckle
88 <4790>, [9865]; period M3, B4
Corroded, cast pin only, surviving L 42mm; worn from frame near tip; broken at loop; pin has plain grip at base as on eg <S206>.

<S226> Seven copper-alloy accessories (Fig 217)

Fig 217 Copper-alloy belt accessories <S226> from older adult male burial [3458] buried in the north-east corner of the aisle crossing (B1, period M4) (scale c 1:1)

86 <344>, [3458]; period M4, B1

Buckle, with oval and rectangular double-loop frame, 31mm x 39mm, bar notch and frame groove for pin (of which no trace survives); three sheet sexfoil mounts, Diam 24mm, each with a central hole and a pair of separate rivets; ? sliding strap loop, with oval and rectangular double-loop frame, 37mm x 20mm; sheet contiguous paired-crescents mount, 29mm x 10mm, with pair of separate rivets (one of which survives) – this was found in a position behind the body, suggesting it was a strapend; sheet rectangular mount (plate), 30mm x 21mm, with central hole – front and back plates held on strap by four separate rivets (three of which survive); some of these items retain traces of textile from the strap, which would have been c 20mm wide (judging from the smaller loop of the buckle).

The central holes in the sexfoil mounts (Egan and Pritchard 1991, 187–9, nos 950 etc, and 229, fig 143) may well have been to accept the buckle pin (one of the mounts was found very close to the buckle (cf ibid, 102–3, no. 472) but not in a position reconcilable with attachment in this way. This remarkable combination of varied accessories, among which the ?strapend cannot readily be paralleled and this form of ? sliding loop (with the same basic design as the buckle it accompanies) has not otherwise been recognised, is presumably a suite of items as worn in life by contemporaries. The rectangular plate's specific function (if there was one – in several parallels the hole is roughly worn) is not elucidated, save to indicate that these were for human wear rather than from book covers (cf ibid, 225–7, nos 1205, 1207 and 1215–16, fig 141).

MOUNTS, CLASPS AND BROOCHES

<S239> Copper-alloy purse hanger (Fig 166)
86 <686>, [5451]; period P2,

From burial [3458].

<S227> Iron buckle
86 <129>, [2774]; period M1–M4, OA6
Circular, Diam 37mm; lacechape in adhering corrosion. From burial [2774].

<S228> Iron buckle
86 <374>, [3666]; period M1, OA6
Incomplete; ?circular frame, Diam c 32mm.

<S229> Iron buckle
86 <514>, [4187]; period M3, OA6
Circular, Diam 43mm.

<S230> Iron buckle
86 <515>, [4290]; period M3, OA6
D shaped, 36mm x 41mm.

<S231> Iron buckle
86 <152>, [2858]; period M1–M4, OA6
Rectangular, 21mm x 29mm; ?tin coating suggested by X-ray plate. From same context as <S206> and <S207> of copper alloy. From burial [2858].

<S232>–<S238> are plain, small circular iron buckles probably standard-form, late medieval shoe fasteners, and a full list is available in the research archive (cf Egan and Pritchard 1991, 60–2, nos 60–113). Several were recorded as coming from burials including <S232> (three or four) from burial [2114] (B1 north transept, period M3) and <S235> from burial [2856] (from 'hand') (OA6, period M3); the rest were from unphased burials (not discussed in detail in this publication) in the north burial area (OA6): <S233> (two) from burial [2774] (see also <S227>), <S234> (two) from burial [2801], <S236> from burial [2919], <S237> from burial [2937], <S238> (two) from burial [2938].

OA12
Cast; single-arched purse hanger; 45mm x 9mm; U-bent

ends have terminal knops (cf Egan and Pritchard 1991, 223–4, fig 140 lower right, from Oxfordshire).

<S240> Copper-alloy strap loop
88 <4460>, [9861]; period M3, B4a
Cast, pentagonal strap loop with rivet internally; 19mm x 13mm (15mm). Cf Egan and Pritchard 1991, 231–2, nos 250–3. See also <S226>.

<S241> Copper-alloy strapend (Fig 165)
86 <192>, [3160]; period P1, OA11
Incomplete front sheet probably from strapend; 27+mm x 13mm; trilobed terminal has engraved line longitudinally down the middle and possibly a transverse one at the point of breakage, compass-engraved circles with three central holes, and two further, less prominent ones. The tooling (or part of it) may have been intended for a crude animal-head motif (none of the holes was obviously for attachment).

<S242> Copper-alloy strapend (Fig 45)
86 <456>, [4269]; period M2, OA6
Composite; 22mm x 14mm; two shield-shaped sheets with concave inside edges and tapered strip surviving on one side; single rivet.

<S243> Copper-alloy strapend
86 <177>, [2507]; period P1, OA11
D-shaped sheet, 19mm x 10mm; hole for single rivet. From a composite strapend.

<S244> Copper-alloy strapend
88 <3145>, [7606]; period M3, OA3
Corroded and incomplete; round-ended, composite accessory of two sheets joined by strip; surviving L 21mm, W 10mm. See <S245> from same deposit. From burial [7606].

<S245> Copper-alloy strapend
88 <3146>, [7606]; period M3, OA3
Corroded and incomplete; surviving rectangular sheet with

two rivets, 29mm x 11mm; possibly a strapend. Despite the similar scale to the preceding item from the same context, this is unlikely to be part of it, although it could well have come from the same strap. From burial [7606].

<S246> Copper-alloy clasp
86 <660>, [5269]; period P1, OA11
Folded sheet plate, 26mm x 12mm; recessed for missing frame; single rivet.

<S247> Lead/tin clasp (Fig 160)
88 <4613>, [10030]; period P1, OA11
Sub-circular frame with trapezoidal aperture, lengthways recess in outside edge to channel strap, and integral with plate, which consists of front and back sheets only (rather than the more familiar sleeve); 18mm x 16mm (15mm x 9mm); the outside edge has on the front an uneven lozenge-shaped motif with a central band and two curving lines; single rivet of same metal as frame survives.

<S248> Copper-alloy brooch (Fig 166)
88 <3625>, [7000]; period P2, OA12
Incomplete, cast, ?circular frame, Diam estd c 10mm, with knops having drilled holes in fours and pairs; wire pin survives.

<S249> Lead/tin brooch (Fig 140)
88 <3415>, [8352]; period M4, OA7
Presumably a brooch frame with the narrowing for the pin broken off; 'star'-like outline, max Diam 27mm; motif of two intersected squares indicated in relief.

<S250> Iron purse bar
88 <3323>, [8146]; period P2, OA12
Incomplete (described from X-ray plate); central suspension loop, Diam 27mm, on swivel with terminal rove, and one incomplete arm of bar L 93mm, survive.

<S251> Iron purse bar

88 <3803>, [8683]; period P2, OA12
(Described from X-ray plate); L 105mm; central suspension loop, at least three rivets and one separate terminal survive.

Items relating to other activities

<S252> Gold finger ring
(Fig 153)
88 <4170> [9294]; period P2, OA12
Diam 17mm; engraved with flowers and French black letter legend: [Je] ne weil [= ?veille] aymer autre que vous ('I am not seeking to love anyone but you') (J Cherry pers comm); traces of enamel remain around the letters. The amatory inscription makes this seem a somewhat anomalous item to come from the precinct of a religious house. Previously published as 15th century in Murdoch (1991, 93 no. 113), and Bruce and Mason (1993, inside backcover).

<S253> Bone spectacles
(Fig 157)
88 <4354> [9638]; period P2, OA12
Fragment of bridge side of frame for one of the lenses; surviving portion 23mm x 16mm; groove along curved edge to hold missing lens; transverse fine grooves, with periodic deeper ones, along outer edge; upper motif of five comma-shaped cut-outs around central round one, all in two concentric compass-cut grooves, and lower motif of triple elongated, round-headed cut-outs below three ovals and with concave-sided, triangular cut-out above. Presumably residual from the priory (cf Egan 1997a, 109, table 14, category N). Previously illustrated in Egan (1998, 277, fig 213).

<S254> Iron ?hernia belt
(Fig 134; Fig 156)
86 <52>, [2107]; period M4, B1

Helen Ganiaris and Christie Pohl

One individual [2107] was found with what appears to be a hernia belt. The assemblage was lifted on a soil block along with the pelvis and the base of the vertebral column for further work by conservators (Jones 1992, 27–9). It remained on its soil block for investigation and has been inverted for further examination. This description is an interim report, based on the information curently available from work in progress.

The iron component of the belt lies across the front of the pelvis and consists of one piece with two finished ends, indicating that this metal part of the belt did not continue around the body (approximately 410mm long, 50mm wide). To the right of centre over the pelvis is a flap or downward extension (95mm) which is identical to the belt in thickness and texture. This component appears to be made of a thin iron sheet over which lies a fibrous material which has been preserved by corrosion from the iron.

The iron sheet, which is obscured by the organic covering and corrosion, was made apparent by X-radiography and then confirmed by investigative cleaning. The X-radiographs show that it is a continuous sheet with no indication of rivet holes or joins (Lang 1999); interim work shows evidence of holes at one end and these may have been to receive a tie or cord.

Samples of the fibrous material overlying the belt were examined by scanning electron microscopy. The orientation of the fibres suggests a woven textile and although very degraded, the scale pattern on the fibres indicates animal fibre, possibly sheep. No remains of leather were found (Cameron 1999).

Above the right end of the belt is a copper-alloy buckle of a type often found in burials, and in two places, below the left end and the centre, there are in total three lacechapes. In the corrosion surrounding the copper-alloy buckle, traces of organic material were also found; scanning electron microscopy showed that these were fibres that may have belonged to a yarn of some sort but are too degraded to identify further.

We here follow the interpretation of the find as a hernia belt, rather than as an item of metal penitential clothing (belts or girdles) of the kind that are attested for medieval Europe or other cultures. Both hernia belts and penitential clothing are fully described in a report on a 5th-/6th-century iron girdle found at excavations at Llandough (Glamorganshire) conducted by the Cotswold Archaeological Trust and now at the National Museum of Wales (Redknap 2005, who also suggests that such belts might serve both purposes). Few other examples have been found in the United Kingdom but on the Continent in burials a number have been found which have been positively identified as hernia belts. These are in fact more similar to the Merton Priory example than to the one found at Llandough; they do not extend fully around the body, and there is an extension which is placed either on the left or right side. Most seem to have been found on male skeletons but some have been found with female burials. The belts are generally reported to be made of iron and usually have traces of leather and/or textile. Similarly some have associated copper-alloy fittings and buckles (Joffroy 1974, 38–9).

The low position of the Merton Priory strap seems to indicate that it served as a scrotal rather than an inguinal hernia belt (C Knüsel, pers comm). The latter were more common and sited higher on the body. With the Merton Priory belt and the Continental examples, it appears likely that the iron element was attached to the body with another material to give sufficient pressure to contain the hernia. The traces of woven fibre found on the belt and the buckle, the holes at one end and the presence of lacechapes are likely to be evidence for this. Further work to examine the back of the belt and the skeleton as a whole is planned.

<S255> Copper-alloy tweezers
88 <4733>, [10389]; period M2, OA5
Sheet strip bent into tweezer configuration; L 41mm, W 4.5mm.

Furnishings

MOUNTS

<S256> Copper-alloy mount
(Fig 120)
86 <726>, [5387]; period M3, B4c
Cast octofoil, Diam 10mm; single, integral rivet; traces of gilding. Probably from an ornate casket or chasse etc. Cf Egan 1997a, 109, table 14, category A.

<S257> Copper-alloy mount
(Fig 113)
88 <3587>, [8518]; period M3, OA6
Sheet, serrated, lanceolate leaf, 43mm x 21mm, with veining indicated by hammered tool lines. Perhaps from a religious furnishing.

<S258> Iron mount
88 <4563>, [9778]; period P2, OA12
(Described from X-ray plate) incomplete strapping, W 10mm, with terminal fleur-de-lis-like motif (incomplete) surviving c 40mm x 40mm; traces of white-metal coating. Probably from a chest. Cf Brenan 1998, 78–80, nos 195 and 203.

LAMPS

<S259> Glass lamp (Fig 218)
86 <450>, [2105]; period M4, B1
Thimble-shaped base from pendent lamp of overall funnel form; max surviving Diam 27mm, surviving H 12mm.

<S260> Glass lamp
88 <3855>, [8863]; period

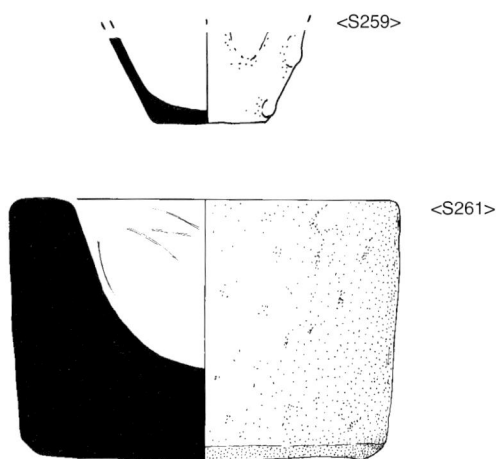

Fig 218 The base of a glass lamp <S259> (scale 1:1) and a stone lamp <S261> (scale 1:2)

M3, OA6
Corroded; similar to preceding item. Cf Keys 1998, 129–30, nos 344–5, fig 97.

<S261> Stone lamp (Fig 218)
88 <5789>, [10320]; period P1, OA11

Incomplete; pale grey Reigate stone (identified by Ian Betts); round drum, Diam estd 110mm, H 65mm, with horizontal rim and conical central well; no clear trace of burning. Perhaps an adapted building block.

Tools

KNIVES

<S262> Iron knife (Fig 22)
86 <673>, [5381]; period M1, OA3
Whittle-tang knife; blade L 85mm, tapering from W 25mm; turned wood handle, L 72mm, Diam 27mm, with nine bands of grouped, circumferentially turned lines (four to eight – progressively more towards top end).

<S263> Iron knife
88 <3170>, [7797]; period P3, OA13
Incomplete, expanding scale-tang handle; surviving L 83mm, max W 14mm; one of at least two rivets survives; sheet terminal plate with central knop.

<S264> Iron knife
88 <4107>, [8351]; period P2, OA12
Incomplete, surviving overall L 88mm; part of blade is broken off; worn bone handle with ornate end has fragment missing, surviving L 68mm, blunted-oval section, and one of two original holes drilled near the end has worn right through. The holes may have been for suspension at the waist (this implement seems to have continued in use long after the break meant this was no longer possible, at least not as securely as may originally have been envisaged); the advanced wear evident is difficult to parallel among London finds and implies many years of sustained use.

<S265> Leather knife scabbard (Fig 114)
88 <3579>, [8522]; period M3, OA6
L 140mm, W 36mm, decorated with impressed lines; handle part, L 60mm, has ?bird motif in rectangular border; highly stylised foliate motif in triangular border on blade part; leather tie for suspension in square configuration survives around top; slight wear.

HONES

<S266> Stone hone
83 <7628>, [1088]; period M3, B4
Incomplete; blackish, slate-like stone; rectangular with slightly rounded end; 34mm x 12mm, surviving L 69mm; neatly shaped; white, mortar-like material adhering to one main face.

<S267> Stone hone
86 <1031>, [1]; period P3, OA13
Norwegian schist: broken off at both ends; surviving L 72mm, 25mm x 10mm.

<S268> Stone hone (Fig 72)
86 <69>, [2254]; period M3, OA6
Norwegian schist; neat, rectangular form; broken off at both ends; surviving L 54mm, 8mm x 5mm; hole (drilled halfway from each side) and trace of another, not completed, at top (smoothed by wear). The first attempt at a hole for suspension presumably

resulted in breakage.

<S269> Stone hone
86 <1943>, [3063]; period M4, OA6
Pale grey micaceous schist (identified by Ian Betts); irregular but smoothed from use; broken off at both ends; surviving L 57mm, 18mm x 12mm.

<S270> Stone hone
88 <5732>, [7000]; period P2, OA12
Norwegian schist; surviving L 85mm, roughly rectangular section, 30mm x 22mm. Presumably residual as found.

<S271> Stone hone
88 <5720>, [9998]; period M2, S4a
Sliver of Norwegian schist.

<S272> Stone hone
88 <5724>, [10920]; period M3, B6
Sliver of Norwegian schist. Stone tools: see also touchstone <S352>.

Vessels

<S273> Copper-alloy vessel (Fig 161)
86 <734>, [5527]; period P1, OA11
Cast; sub-triangular section, longitudinally ribbed foot, tapering from 53mm x 27mm, H 83mm, with part of thin walling from round vessel (Th c 1.1mm at some points); Wt just over 0.5kg; foot abraded from use, and this and outside are soot blackened. From large, institutional-scale cooking vessel, Diam perhaps c 300mm; the very robust foot is at odds with the thinness of the walling.

<S274> Copper-alloy vessel
88 <4796>, [8880]; period M4, S4b
Flaring, plain-rim fragment of thin-walled, cast vessel; Diam at rim c 180mm. Probably from a cauldron, as preceding, larger item.

<S275> Copper-alloy vessel
88 <4489>, [9774]; period

M2, B7
Rim from sheet vessel, Diam c 500mm; two holes for rivets.

<S276>–<S278> are very corroded probable glass bottle fragments.

<S279>–<S288> are fragments of glass urinals, also decayed to greater or lesser extents. A full list can be consulted in the research archive; two are illustrated.

<S280> Glass urinal (Fig 158)
88 <3694>, [7000]; period P2, OA12
Fragment of horizontal rim, Diam c 60mm.

<S284> Glass urinal (Fig 158)
88 <4222>, [9351]; period P2, OA12
Fragment of splayed rim and wide neck, Diam c 140mm.

<S289> Wooden bowl (Fig 162)
86 <1056>, [4531]; period

M3, OA6
Fragment of bowl, Diam at plain rim c 220mm, Diam at base c 92mm, H c 44mm; the base is defined by a groove and has part of a central cut mark, probably of ownership; paired grooves on outside wall; the central part of the surviving piece retains a roughly cut profile on the outside – perhaps either because the turning was ill-judged relative to the cut rough-out form and had removed too much wood elsewhere (this seems unlikely in that the inner well could have been adapted), or possibly because a handle or some other side feature was cut off prior to deposition; the inside is stained dark from use.

<S290> Wooden bowl (Fig 162)
86 <1019>, [4531]; period M3, OA6
Incomplete; Diam at plain rim (beaded internally) c 180mm, Diam at base c 75mm, H 45mm; burned crozier-shaped mark for ?owner on base (possibly made by a heated U staple applied at a slight angle); a knot in the wall has become lost.

<S291> Wooden bowl
86 <1953>, [4531]; period M3, OA6
Fragment of splayed rim, Diam c 220mm.

<S292> Wooden bowl (Fig 162)
86 <404>, [4531]; period M3, OA6
?Bowl or plate, most of base only; Diam 75mm, defined by turned groove; most of carved cross potent mark for ?owner survives. Previously published by Bruce and Mason (1993, inside back cover).

<S293> Wooden bowl
88 <3055>, [7242]; period M1, OA3
Fragments, Diam at plain, bevelled rim c 220mm, Diam at base c 80mm.

<S294> Wooden bowl (Fig 162)
88 <3581>, [8518]; period M3, OA6
Fragments of bowl: rounded well; Diam at flat, horizontal rim c 100mm, Diam at base c 60mm, H c 25mm. The elegant shape may well derive from pewterware.

<S295> Stone mortar (Fig 161)
88 <3921>, [8353]; period M2, S7
Incomplete mortar – about a third of the vessel: Reigate stone (identified by Ian Betts); Diam at rim c 260mm, Diam at base c 210mm, H 186mm; round baluster with angled roll at shoulder; round well.

Items relating to production

TEXTILE OR LEATHER WORK

<S296> Copper-alloy needle (Fig 219)
86 <176>, [2756]; period P1, OA11
L 76mm, punched eye and triple-facetted point.

<S297> Copper-alloy needle (Fig 219)
86 <288>, [3222]; period M3, OA6
L 78mm, punched eye and triple-facetted point.

<S298> Copper-alloy thimble
88 <4667>, [8893]; period

Fig 219 Copper-alloy needles <S296> (right) and <S297> (scale c 1:1)

M3, OA7
Corroded; top broken off; light duty, stamped thimble; Diam at base c 16mm, surviving H 10mm; drilled pits in vertical rows; engraved line around base. Cf Egan 1998, 266–7, no. 821.

<S299> Copper-alloy thimble
88 <4469>, [9778]; period P2, OA12
Corroded; cast, heavy duty thimble; Diam at base 20mm, H 22mm; spiral of drilled pits from apex. Cf Egan 1998, 266–7, nos 829–31.

Evidence for metalworking

Evidence for copper alloy casting <S300>–<S312> is scattered in distribution (with a possible focus in the north burial area, OA6, and a large weight of waste metal found within the demolition deposits of the infirmary hall, B4a) and by phasing through the period of the religious house and beyond (the finds in the latest phases probably as residual material); this may perhaps indicate more than one phase of activity. Scientific analysis of <S306> indicates the piece examined is bronze (further work might give more detailed indications of overall homogeneity or of diverse alloys; bronze is not a common alloy in the medieval period, except for bells, which have c 20% tin). No obvious mould fragment, waster or other hint of the end product(s) has been recognised (strange if this is evidence for bell casting, as this usually generates a large amount of broken moulds).

Iron-working waste <S313>–<S327> was widely scattered, both spatially and chronologically through the priory-period sequence – this may be what is referred to as 'iron smelting' by Bruce and Mason (1993, 4). The evidence apparently begins in the earliest phase of the priory and (as with copper alloy casting waste) there seems to have been a focus in the north burial area (OA6). Again, no clear indication of the product(s) of these efforts has emerged from the finds. Several lumps of what could be poor-quality iron ore, although they are more likely to be locally occurring iron concretions, were retrieved.

As on most occupied medieval sites, lead waste <S328>–<S331> was not uncommonly present in the form of runnels and sheet offcuts and trimmings, which may relate to routine maintenance and repair, as well as initial building construction and in the present case of recycling at the Dissolution.

A full list for <S300>–<S329> can be consulted in the research archive.

The two following items come close to obvious weight standards but the deviations are enough to call into question whether either of them was intended for accurate weight measurement (cf Egan 1997a, 109, table 14, category S). It is possible they are ingots cast to approximate standards (see <S362>, which with its scratched indication plainly was intended as some kind of weight).

<S330> Lead weight or ingot
77 <7563>, [81]; period M3, B3
Irregular, plano-convex oval, 103mm x 71mm, max Th 21mm, Wt just under 700g (c 1¹/₂lb); scratch marks on flat face. Probably an ingot, but perhaps respecting a standard weight.

<S331> Lead weight or ingot
88 <3842>, [8863]; period
M3, OA7
Plano-convex disc,
incorporating small lumps of
charcoal; rectangular hole near
centre; Diam 65mm, max Th
15mm, almost 425g (c 15oz).
Similar to weight <S362> but
rougher.

Items relating to trade

(Coins marked * were already identified by M Hammerson –
? and others unknown – when examined by the writer.)

<S332> Penny
77 <7586>, [348]; period P2,
OA12 *
Silver; some wear; clipped; York
post-treaty penny of Edward III,
1369–77.

<S333> Penny
77 <7588>, [433]; period M3,
B4c *
Silver; very worn, clipped;
Canterbury penny of Edward I
or II: ?Fox class X, issued
c 1302–10.

<S334> Penny
77 <7589>, [522]; period M4,
B3b *
Silver; little evident wear; worn
and clipped (fragment missing
since retrieval); Durham penny
of Edward IV, initial mark pansy,
1473–6 (Bishop Lawrence
Booth). Found with <S335>, in
grave fill of burial [539]; grave
badly disturbed.

<S335> Penny
77 <7590>, [522]; period M4,
B3b *
Silver; corroded; clipped;
counterfeit York penny of
Edward IV, 1465–76 (Archbishop
George Neville) – poor style.
Found with <S334>.

<S336> Penny (Fig 220)
77 <7591>, [541]; period M3,
B3b *

Silver; little wear (although
residual in context); Ipswich
penny of John, c 1205–10,
moneyer Johan; Lawrence
class Vb.

<S337> Groat (Fig 167)
86 <70>, [1]; period P3, OA13 *
Silver; some wear; slightly
clipped; London groat of Edward
III, 1351–61. Published in Bruce
and Mason 1993, 6 (wrongly
captioned as no. 340).

<S338> Penny
86 <99>, [2471]; period M3,
OA6
Silver; no wear evident
(although residual in this
context, a grave fill); cut short-
cross farthing of Henry II or III,
1180–1247 (probably the
former, 1180–9).

<S339> Penny
86 <725>, [5384]; period M1,
OA3
Silver; worn; cut short-cross
halfpenny of Henry II or III,
1180–1247.

<S340> Penny
86 <685>, [5451]; period P2,
OA12 *
Silver; some wear; London long-
cross penny in name of Henry
III (with sceptre), moneyer
(Ren)aud, 1251–72. Cf North,
pl XVI, no. 38, in Bruce and

Mason 1993, 6 (wrongly
captioned as no. 337).

<S341> Penny
88 <4556>, [10042]; period
M3, B6
Silver; clipped, worn and
corroded; long-cross penny,
probably Edward I–III,
1279–1377.

<S342> Penny
88 <4786>, [10417]; period
M1, OA5
Silver; 'Watford'-type penny
of Stephen or derivative
baronial issue, 1134–54 (poorly
struck as is usual for these
issues).

<S343> Denier (Fig 116)
83 <7595>, [1046]; period
M3, B4a *
Silver; worn ? and clipped;
irregular flan, part of which has
broken off; half-length, draped
figure of Edward the Black
Prince crowned [with circlet],
facing right and holding sword,
(?EDW…) REG ANGL around
// cross and pellets, [?PRC]PS
A(GITA)[?E or L] around.
Aquitaine sterling (denier) of
the Black Prince, c 1362–76.
? Limoges mint possibly
indicated by the final letter. It
has not proved possible to locate
any other find in London of
these late 14th-century issues
for France under English rule
(J Clark, pers comm).

<S344> Coin
88 <4302>, [9567]; period
M3, B4a
Silver; torn fragment; Diam
c 20mm; shield with ?cross or
pale triply stranded, (?on)
cross potent lacking left arm
M…E(?R)AL·IS around //
cross, …RVM:PRV… around
(lombardic lettering) Vierling
of Winrich von Königsrode
(Grand Master of the Teutonic
Order of Prussia). Königsberg
mint (identified by Barrie
Cook, British Museum); issued
1351–82 (J Baker, Ashmolean
Museum, pers comm).

<S345> Jetton
83 <7594>, [1007]; period P1,
OA11 *
Copper alloy; corroded (parts of
edge missing); Diam 20+mm;
octofoil // cross [moline] with

pellets in angles, border of
pellets. English; cf Mitchiner
1988, 115, nos 228–9 (there
dated to c 1280–1350).

<S346> Jetton (Fig 167)
86 <623>, [1]; period P3,
OA13
Copper alloy; Diam 24mm;
shield with arms of England,
+ME·ME(N)·TO·DOMINE·MEI·
around // doubly stranded
arcuate cross fleurdelisée around
fleur-de-lis, AVE·MARIA·PG·:·
around (lombardic lettering).
'Anglo-Gallic'; cf Mitchiner
1988, 133, parallels described
following no. 328 (there dated
to c 1330–1450): no precise
parallel.

<S347> Jetton
86 <1>, [619]; period M2, B4c
Copper alloy; corroded (parts of
edge missing); Diam 22mm;
large orb in tressure // ?five-
petalled rose, crowns and fleurs
around (legends illegible).
Nuremberg; cf Mitchiner 1988,
377–86 (there dated to c 1500–
50). Intrusive as found.

<S348> Jetton (Fig 166)
88 <3614>, [7032]; period P3,
OA13
Copper alloy; Diam 22mm; one
side as <S345>, the other with
cross fleurdelisée, trefoils in
angles, border of pellets
between fleurs-de-lis. English;
cf Mitchiner 1988, 117, nos
250–1 (there dated to c 1345–
55): no precise parallel.

<S349> Jetton
88 <3257>, [8102]; period P2,
OA12
Copper alloy; corroded (parts
of edge missing); Diam 26mm;
illegible main device in multiply
arched border, … SVIS… around
// (?plain) cross etc. No obvious
parallel for the very limited
survival.

<S350> Jetton
88 <3913>, [8250]; period P2,
OA12
Copper alloy; corroded; Diam
20mm; both sides as second on
<S345>. English; cf Mitchiner
1988, 116, nos 238–41 (there
dated to c 1280–1350).

<S351> Jetton
88 <4557>, [9778]; period P2,

Fig 220 Obverse and reverse views of an Ipswich silver penny of King John <S336>
(scale c 2:1)

233

OA12
Copper alloy; corroded (several holes); Diam 25mm; (?ship on sea), (?G)PVA(?O)E(?P)S...(VPA) around (lombardic lettering, underlined character retrograde) // lozenge with fleurs-de-lis, (legend illegible). Nuremberg; early 16th-century 'ship' issue; cf Mitchiner 1988, 372ff (there dated to *c* 1490–1550).

For further jettons found at the priory see Turner (1965,

145–6, nos 1 and 2).

<S352> Touchstone (Fig 167)
88 <5721>, [9193]; period M1, OA3
Incomplete black rectangular fine-grained ?phyllite (material identified by Ian Betts) with subtly curving sides, broken off at one end; surviving L 86mm, 11mm x 10mm; remains of sheet copper-alloy sheath, L 9mm, on two sides at surviving end.

Catalogued horse equipment

<S353> Iron horseshoe
88 <4579>, [9648]; period M2, B6
Corroded (described from X-ray plate); part of heel of ?wavy-outline shoe. Cf Clark 1995, 86 and 92 type 2A, assigned to *c* 1050–1150.

<S354> Iron spur
86 <223>, [2555]; period P1, OA11
Corroded (identified from X-ray plate).

<S355> Iron spur
86 <381>, [3667]; period M1, OA6
Corroded (identified from X-ray plate).

<S356> Iron spur
86 <749>, [5389]; period M2, OA6
Corroded (described from X-ray plate); biconically bevelled prick L 25mm; overall L 105mm, span between branches 76mm; paired holes for leathers on each side; white-metal coating is decoratively applied on prick. Cf Ellis 1995, 131, no. 319, fig 90, dated to the 12th century.

<S357> Iron snaffle bit
88 <3408>, [7035]; period P2, OA12

Corroded (described from X-ray plate), parts of both D-looped cheek pieces (original L *c* 90mm) and most of the looped, one-part mouthpiece (surviving L 67mm) were recovered. Cf Clark 1995, 47 C for the cheek piece and I for the mouthpiece (none of the bits catalogued there has a one-part mouthpiece, which Ward Perkins (1940, 81) says occurs sparingly at all periods).

<S358> Copper-alloy harness mount (Fig 113)
86 <100>, [2594]; period M3, OA6
Dished, scallop-shell form pendent, 25mm x 16mm, centrally pierced and with folded, two-armed attachment to broken off single loop of missing suspension mount; engraved chevrons; traces of gilding. Cf N Griffiths in Clark 1995, 67–9, nos 72 and 73–6, figs 50 and 52, the hole may have been to hold a missing knop etc.

<S359> Copper-alloy harness mount (Fig 128)
88 <4071>, [9159]; period M3, S7
Pendant cross with lobed arms, 38mm x 34mm; gilded.

Miscellaneous

<S360> Lead (Fig 221)
88 <4521>, [9864]; period P2, OA12
Robust, ingot-like form, tapering from L 89mm, 18mm x 14mm; herringbone-like pattern flanked by

grooves along one face; cut off along one side, possibly broken off at both ends. Ornamental flange, possibly from pipework (or possibly a coffin), residual as found from the priory.

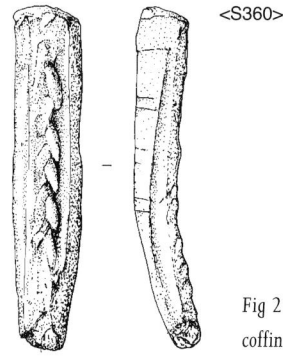

Fig 221 *Lead pipework or possibly a coffin fragment <S360> (scale 1:2)*

Dissolution and post-Dissolution, 16th to 19th centuries (periods P1–P3)

Some of these items may be residual from the religious house: dress hook <S361> was a long-lived fashion, weight <S362> could be either post-Dissolution or residual, pin <S363> is of a 16th-century form, key <S364> may be late medieval, glass vessel fragments <S365> and <S366> are in different post-medieval traditions, and the three cloth seals <S368> to <S370> (one identifiable Norfolk issue and the two others probably Continental) are likely all to be of 16th-century date, but it is not possible to say which side of the Dissolution they belong. All three seals are the two-disc form (see Egan 1995; and Endrei and Egan 1982 on cloth seals in general).

<S361> Copper-alloy dress hook (Fig 222)
88 <3052>, [7000]; period P2, OA12
Wire; L 37mm, max W 7mm; consists of three lengths – two thicker ones which are bent into hooked ends (giving paired hooks at both ends of the

complete object – one hook is bent back) and a thinner one running between these and multiply wound around all three lengthways strands to bind the entire object together. These vicious-looking double hooks are known from the medieval period perhaps into the 16th century; there seems to have been no concession to their potential to gash the wearer or anyone else who came into close contact, nevertheless their most likely function was as some kind of fastener for clothing (they may be the ancestors of the varied single-hooked clasps of the late 15th/early 16th century, as, for example, Egan 2005, 42–7, nos 151–70).

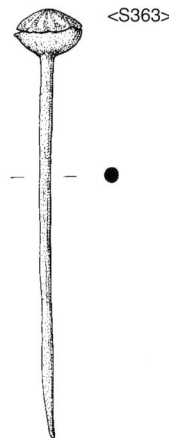

<S362> Lead weight (Fig 173)
88 <3796>, [8706]; period P2, OA12
Circular, plano-convex, Diam 85mm, max Th 18mm, Wt *c* 850g; inscribed :II: over L= on flat side. About 1lb 13?oz in today's terms, compared with the apparent indication of 2lb (*librae*) in the inscription (ie *c* 4.7% light of the specified

Fig 222 *Copper-alloy wire dress hook <S361> and pin <S363> (scale 1:1)*

standard – a deviancy probably too large to have been acceptable at the time for accurate weighing in the 16th century).

<S363> Copper-alloy pin (Fig 222)
83 <7596>, [1114]; period M2, OA3
Flattened-disc head of two sheets, Diam 9mm, soldered together with lead/tin (MoLC), the upper one with a relief eight-rayed asterisk motif; L 57mm. Sixteenth-century (intrusive as found), presumably for a woman's headdress (cf Egan and Forsyth 1997, 222–4).

<S364> Copper-alloy key
88 <3005>, [7000]; period P2, OA12
Corroded; L 44mm, circular bow, Diam 36mm; narrowed pin; asymmetrical bit c 33mm x 23mm.

<S365> Glass vessel
88 <4804>, [7000]; period P2, OA12
Crystal latticinio ?wall fragment, Diam c 120mm; made from contiguous, spirally threaded rods, the white slightly decayed. Probably from a drinking vessel; ? English (London) product.

<S366> Glass vessel (Fig 167)
88 <4877>, [7000]; period P2, OA12
Applied 'berry' prunt from hollow stem Diam c 55mm, of pale green roemer drinking glass. These vessels are not very common in this country but are extremely frequently excavated in parts of the Continent (cf Henkes 1994, 255–62).

<S367> Glass vessel
88 <3697>, [8592]; period P1, OA11
Colourless (undecayed) fragment of folded foot with vertical moulded ribbing, Diam 70mm, from drinking vessel or bowl.

<S368> Lead cloth seal (Fig 173)
88 <5373>, [9864]; period P2, OA12
Diam 16mm // 18mm (connecting strip missing); castle over (lion passant) (rough engraving) // large, lombardic N, with rosette of beading in centre. The first disc has the arms of Norwich and the second re-emphasises this origin with the city's initial. This is one of the earliest Norfolk/Norwich seals known; the relatively small, lightweight flan suggests it may have been from a worsted, the fabric which was to become the county's main manufacture from the late 16th century. Cf Egan 2001, nos 21–2.

<S369> Lead cloth seal
88 <3238>, [8102]; period P2, OA12
Diam 16mm // incomplete disc; two rivets: (scratched) line with three shorter ones transversely // (illegible apart from beaded border). The scratched lines seem to be a convention for denoting a specification – here 5 (long line) + 3 (short lines) = 8.

<S370> Lead cloth seal
88 <4779>, [10389]; period M2, OA5
Missing disc // Diam 19mm; holes for two rivets: illegible (?lettering) (?intrusive).

information on the nature of economic and/or human activities and the character of the local environment, both on a spatial and temporal basis. This number of samples, however, was substantially reduced before assessment on the basis of archaeological information. Details on this selection process are presented in the assessment report (Gray-Rees 1997). A total of 59 samples were assessed with the report available for consultation in the Museum of London Archive.

Sampling and processing methods

The samples were processed according to the potential level of preservation of biological remains. Samples, which appeared to contain well-preserved organic remains (by survival in an anoxic environment), were subsampled (500g) and the soil wet-sieved to 0.25mm with the resultant material being stored in industrial methylated spirits (IMS). The remaining part of these and all other samples were processed in a flotation machine using sieve sizes of 0.25mm and 1.00mm for the recovery of the flot and residue respectively. The flots and residues from flotation were dried with the residues being sorted for biological and artefactual material.

Assessment and analysis

The samples were initially assessed to establish the range, frequency and diversity of the various forms of biological remains present. On the basis of the assessment, 32 of the 59 assessed samples were selected for further analysis of the plant remains. The number of samples by feature type and period is summarised in Table 40, which shows that the majority of the samples came from periods M2 (1222–c 1300) and M3 (c 1300–c 1390) and from a range of feature types.

Identification and recording methods

The flots were separated into different size fractions for ease of sorting and scanning and the plant remains identified using a binocular microscope, the MoLSS seed reference collection and standard seed reference manuals (Beijerinck 1947; Berggren 1981). Virtually all the flots were sorted and examined wet.

7.6 The plant remains

John Giorgi

Introduction

Methodology

Almost 500 bulk environmental soil samples from a range of features were collected for the recovery of biological data. This included the retrieval of archaeobotanical remains for

Table 40 Number of samples analysed for plant remains by feature and period

Period	MI	M2	M3	P2	Total
Feature					
Ditch/drain fills	3	I	–	3	7
Pit fills	2	2	I	–	5
Floor, occupation and miscellaneous deposits	–	5	4	–	9
Alluvial, channel and peat/clay deposits	–	3	6	2	11
Total	5	11	11	5	32

Charred plant remains were extracted and quantified in absolute numbers while waterlogged and mineralised material was only scanned and abundance of individual species recorded using the following system:

+: 1–10 plant items

++: 11–50 plant items

+++: 51–250 plant items

++++: 251+ plant items.

Identifications were entered in the MoLAS computer database and tables of results generated. Ecological information is based mainly on Clapham et al (1987) and Stace (1991). The results are shown in (Tables 41–4) and are ordered by period and land use (indeterminate plant material – buds, leaves, stems, thorns, wood, plant tissue – is omitted). Taxonomic order and nomenclature follows Clapham et al (1987).

General characteristics of the material

The individual samples produced variable amounts of plant remains, most of which were preserved by 'waterlogging'; seeds and fruits were the most common and easily identifiable remains while moss, wood and stem fragments were present in some samples with leaf, bud and thorn fragments in several other richer organic deposits. There were much smaller amounts of charred plant remains in 16 samples with identifiable remains (other than charcoal) consisting mainly of small numbers of cereal grains in 14 samples, cereal chaff fragments in 2 samples and weed seeds in 5 samples. Charred remains of fruits (grape (*Vitis vinifera*), hazelnut (*Corylus avellana*)) were found in the sample from the ditch fill [11252] (period M1). Flecks and small fragments of charcoal were present in most samples.

The waterlogged plant remains consisted mainly of a range of wild plants with a high frequency and species diversity of plants of wetland (aquatic and bankside/marshland) and disturbed (including cultivated) ground and waste places. Grassland and woodland/hedgerow plants were presented by smaller amounts of remains. Food plants preserved by 'waterlogging' were generally poorly represented and consisted mainly of fruits, with most of the cultivated species being found in a single deposit [11252] from period M1. The other periods only contained wild fruits, some of which, for

example, plum/bullace (*Prunus domestica*), however, may have been cultivated from time to time. Black mustard (*Brassica nigra*) seeds definitely appear to have been used either as a flavouring or for its medicinal values, dominating the plant assemblage from the alluvial deposit [7924] (period M2) and well represented in several other samples. Some of the other wild plants may have been also exploited for their medicinal properties (Chapter 4.6) while ?hemp (cf *Cannabis sativa*) and dyer's rocket (*Reseda luteola*), recovered in several samples, could have been used in textile production, the first for fibres and the second for dye.

The interpretation of the plant assemblages was carried out on a sample by sample basis taking account of habitat information for individual species and the potential uses of the different plants. Other biological and artefactual remains in the individual samples were also considered in the interpretation of the plant assemblages. Details on the plant assemblages from individual samples may be found in the archive report (Giorgi 1999) while botanical information from the most interesting plant assemblages has been integrated into the chronological text and the thematic sections. There follows a summary of the botanical remains by period.

1117–1222 (period M1)

Five samples were analysed from this period from ditch and pit fills within the garden or orchard area (OA5) and the north burial area (OA6). The results by sample are shown in Table 41.

The two samples from pit fills, [8538] and [8540], in the north burial area (OA6) produced only very small botanical assemblages with a small range of wild plants, characteristic of a range of habitats although mainly waste/disturbed ground, for example, blackberry/raspberry (*Rubus fruticosus/idaeus*), elder (*Sambucus nigra*), and nettles (*Urtica dioica*). The brambles and elder may have been exploited for their fruits. Damp conditions in the pits are suggested by the presence of sedges (*Carex* spp) and ?hemlock (*Conium maculatum*). The botanical evidence suggests disturbed damp ground conditions in the vicinity of and within the pits; the fruits may either suggest a hedgerow or represent food debris.

The vast majority of the plant remains from period M1 were from the fills [10818], [11252], [10635] of ditches

Table 41 *Plant remains from selected samples from period M1*

Species					Land use	OA5	OA5	OA5	OA6	OA6
					Context	[10635]	[10818]	[11252]	[8538]	[8540]
					Sample	{4181}	{4227}	{4364}	{3616}	{3618}
Latin name	Common name	Plant/part	Habitat/use	Preservation						
Triticum aestivum L sl	bread/club wheat	-	Fl	C	2		3		
Triticum spp	wheat	-	Fl	C	I		2		
Triticum/Secale sp	wheat/rye	-	Fl	C			I		
Hordeum sativum L	barley	-	Fl	C	I	2	7		
Avena sp	oat	-	AFl	C		I			
Cerealia	indeterminate cereal	-	Fl	C	3		3		

Table 41 (cont)

Latin name	Common name	Plant/part	Habitat/use	Preservation	OA5 [10635] {4181}	OA5 [10818] {4227}	OA5 [11252] {4364}	OA6 [8538] {3616}	OA6 [8540] {3618}
Vitis vinifera L	grape	-	FI	C			2		
Corylus avellana L	hazel	-	CF	C			+		
Anthemis cotula L	stinking mayweed	-	ABGH	C			2		
Indeterminate	charcoal	WD	-	C	+++	+	+++	+++	+
Characeae	-	-	E	W	+++		+		
Ranunculus acris/repens/bulbosus	buttercups	-	ABCDEG	W	+	++	+		
R sceleratus L	celery-leaved crowfoot	-	E	W			+		
Ranunculus spp	-	-	ABCDEG	W		+			
Papaver somniferum L	opium poppy	-	BGHI	W		+			
Fumaria sp	fumitory	-	ABC	W		+			
Brassica nigra (L) Koch	black mustard	-	BFHI	W	+++				
B cf *nigra*	?black mustard	-	BFHI	W			+		
Brassica/Sinapis spp	-	-	ABFGHI	W			+		
Hypericum sp	cat's ear	-	BD	W			+		
Silene spp	campion/catchfly	-	ABCDF	W			+		
Chenopodium spp	goosefoot etc	-	ABCDFH	W	+	+	+		
Atriplex sp	orache	-	ABFGH	W		+	+		
Vitis vinifera L	grape	-	FI	W			+		
Rubus fruticosus/idaeus	blackberry/raspberry	-	CFGH	W			+	+	
Prunus spinosa L	sloe/blackthorn	-	CFG	W			+		
P domestica L	plum/bullace	-	CFI	W			+		
Prunus spp	-	-	CFGI	W			++		
Malus domestica/sylvestris	apple/crab apple	-	CFHI	W			+		
Oenanthe fistulosa L	water dropwort	-	E	W			+		
Aethusa cynapium L	fool's parsley	-	A	W			+		
Conium maculatum L	hemlock	-	CEG	W		+	++	+	
Apiaceae indeterminate	-	-	-	W			+		
Bryonia dioica Jacq	bryony	-	CG	W		+			
Euphorbia helioscopia L	sun spurge	-	AGI	W		+	+		
Polygonum lapathifolium L	pale persicaria	-	ABE	W		+			
Fallopia convolvulus(L) A Love	black bindweed	-	ABF	W			+		
Rumex sp	dock	-	ABCDEFG	W		+	+		
Urtica dioica L	stinging nettle	-	BCDEFGH	W		+++	++++	++	
Juglans regia	walnut	-	FHI	W			+		
Corylus avellana L	hazel	-	CF	W			++		
Hyoscyamus niger L	henbane	-	BDG	W	+	+	+		
Solanum nigrum L	black nightshade	-	BF	W			++		
Verbena officinalis L	vervain	-	BG	W			+		
Mentha sp	mint	-	ABCEFGI	W	+				
Lycopus europaeus L	gipsy-wort	-	EH	W		+	+		
cf *Stachys* sp	?woundwort	-	ACEG	W		+			
Ajuga reptans L	bugle	-	CDE	W		+	+		
Labiatae indeterminate		-	ABCFEFI	W			+		
Sambucus nigra L	elder	-	BCFGH	W	+	+	+	+	
Carduus/Cirsium spp	thistles	-	ABDEG	W		+	+		
Sonchus oleraceus L	milk-/sow-thistle	-	AB	W		+			
S asper (L) Hill	spiny milk-/sow-thistle	-	AB	W			+		
Alisma sp	water-plantain	-	E	W		++			
Juncus spp	rush	-	ADEH	W	++	+++			
Sparganium erectum L	branched bur-reed	-	E	W			+		
Eleocharis palustris/uniglumis	spike-rush	-	E	W			+		
Schoenoplectus lacustris (L) Palla	bulrush	-	E	W			+		
Carex spp	sedge	-	CDEH	W		+++	++	+	
Carex spp	sedge	UT	CDEH	W			+		
Cyperaceae indeterminate	-	-	ABCDEFI	W	+		++		
Poaceae	grass	-	ABCDEFHI	W	+				
Bryophyta indeterminate	moss	-	-	W	+++	++	++		

Plant part: R – rachis; WD – wood; UT – utricle

Preservation: C – charred remains; W – waterlogged remains

Habitat/use codes: A – weeds of cultivated land; B – ruderals, weeds of waste places and disturbed ground; C – plants of woods, scrub, hedgerows; D – open environment (fairly undisturbed); E – plants of wet/damp environment; F – edible plants; G – medicinal and poisonous plants; H – commercial/industrial use; I – cultivated plants

Frequency: + = 1–10 plant items; ++ = 11–50 plant items; +++ = 51–250 plant items; ++++ = 250+ plant items

[10817], [10050], [10636] within the garden area (OA5). The ditch fills produced the greatest amount of remains particularly in [11252] which contained a wide range of food debris with small numbers of cereal grains, free-threshing wheat (*Triticum* spp), barley (*Hordeum sativum*) and with a very wide range of fruit remains including grape (*Vitis vinifera*) (charred and waterlogged seeds), apple (*Malus domestica*), sloe/blackthorn (*Prunus spinosa*), plum/bullace (*P domestica*), elder (*Sambucus nigra*), blackberry/raspberry (*Rubus fruticosus/idaeus*), and fragments of hazel (*Corylus avellana*) and walnut (*Juglans regia*) shell. A small number of black mustard (*Brassica nigra*) seeds were also identified.

The wild plants included a large number of species typical of disturbed ground and waste places with a number of plants characteristic of nitrogen-rich soils, for example, stinging nettle (*Urtica dioica*), black nightshade (*Solanum nigrum*), henbane (*Hyoscyamus niger*), goosefoots (*Chenopodium* spp); some of the disturbed ground plants could represent arable weeds imported on to the site with the cereal remains, particularly when found charred, for example, stinking mayweed (*Anthemis cotula*). Wetland plants (bankside/marshland and aquatic) were also well represented, particularly sedges and rushes (*Juncus* spp) with others including water-plaintain (*Alisma* sp), stoneworts (Characeae), celery-leaved crowfoot (*Ranunculus sceleratus*) and gypsy-wort (*Lycopus europaeus*). Some of these species may have been growing in or on the margins of water within the ditch [10050].

The botanical remains suggest a damp environment with possible bodies of standing or slow moving water within the ditch, with a wet habitat also indicated by the presence of freshwater molluscs (OA5, Table 48) and water flea eggs (*Cladoceran ephippia*) in the samples. There also appears to be some debris from food preparation and consumption in this feature, with not only botanical material but also mammal, bird and fish bones, marine shell for example, oyster, in the sample residues.

The fill [10635] sample from the garden area was significantly different, producing only a small range of botanical remains with just a few charred cereal grains and a few wild plants but dominated by the remains of aquatic freshwater algae (stoneworts), plus large numbers of black mustard seeds, suggesting the presence of standing bodies of water (albeit possibly temporary) within this feature into which a little food debris had been deposited.

1222–*c* 1300 (period M2)

Eleven samples were analysed from this period from six different areas of the site and from a range of feature types; from ditch and channel fills, alluvial deposits, pit fills, floors/occupation deposits and an external deposit. Table 40 shows the breakdown of the samples by area and feature type for this period while the results from each sample are shown in Table 42.

Most of the remains from these samples represent wild plants of disturbed ground, waste places and wetland environments. The botanical material was mainly from the drain, channel and alluvial deposits with very little such material in the other feature types, pit fills, floor deposits and an external deposit.

Economic plants were limited to small assemblages of charred grains in nine samples with free-threshing wheat, barley and oat (*Avena* sp), while rye (*Secale cereale*) was identified on the basis of two rachis fragments. These grains reflect background debris from the final stages of crop processing and food preparation.

The only other definite evidence of a used plant was the extraordinary amount of black mustard seeds found in alluvial deposit [7924] in the marshy area east of the infirmary (OA9), probably representing a spillage. There were also a large number of black mustard seeds in a floor deposit [9636] within the kitchen (B6); these may have been for cooking although there was very little other evidence for food debris in the two analysed samples from this area other than a few grains and a large amount of charcoal (presumably spent fuel from heating/cooking). Indeed, the only other botanical remains from the samples in the kitchen area were from a few aquatic and bankside/marshland species, which may represent material collected accidentally along with flooring materials from ditches and riverbanks, although these samples only included a few rushes and no sedges, common flooring materials at the time.

Several samples contained elder seeds, while there were a few blackberry/raspberry seeds in two samples, both potential food plants. Hemp (*Cannabis sativa*) was tentatively identified in another sample [7924]. However, all three of these plants may have been growing wild with the seeds accumulating naturally.

There was a large wetland component, as would be expected in the channel deposits [9251] (OA8), alluvial deposits [7921] and [7924] (OA9) and in the infirmary cloister garth drain [10255] (S4a in OA5), but also in an occupation deposit in the reredorter [9469] (B5). This consisted of a wide range of both aquatic species (particularly in the marsh area OA9) and bankside/marshland species, for example, stoneworts, pondweeds (*Potamogeton* spp), water-plantain, horned-pondweed (*Zannichellia palustris*), rushes, sedges, duckweed (*Lemna* sp) (especially in the infirmary cloister garth drain [10255]), branched bur-reed (*Sparganium erectum*) and gypsy-wort. This evidence points to the presence of slow-flowing or static bodies of water (albeit possibly temporary in some cases). Other biological evidence in some of the samples supports this interpretation, for example, water flea eggs (*Cladoceran ephippia*) in the infirmary drain.

Species typical of disturbed ground and waste places were not so well represented but included a number of plants characteristic of nitrogen-rich soils, for example, stinging nettle, henbane, goosefoots and oraches (*Atriplex* spp), while some may have been imported on to the site as arable weeds together with the cereal grain; for example, fumitory (*Fumaria* sp), milk-/sow-thistle (*Sonchus oleraceus*), particularly when found charred. For instance, a small range of charred weed seeds, including bedstraw (*Galium* spp), dock (*Rumex* sp) and stinking

Table 42 Plant remains from selected samples from period M2 (see Table 41 for key to plant parts, preservation, habitat and frequency codes)

Species					Area	B4a	B5	B5	B5	B5	B6	B6	S4a/OA5	OA8	OA9	OA9
					Context	[10918]	[9331]	[9469]	[10491]	[10496]	[9636]	[10277]	[10255]	[9251]	[7921]	[7924]
Latin name	Common name	Plant part	Habitat/use	Preservation	Sample	{4291}	{3976}	{3851}	{4119}	{4120}	{4269}	{4064}	{4082}	{3782}	{3293}	{3287}
Triticum aestivum L sl	bread/club wheat	-	FI	C									2		I	
Triticum spp	wheat	-	FI	C									2			I
Secale cereale L	rye	R	FI	C				I							I	
Hordeum sativum	barley	-	FI	C				3				2				
cf *H sativum*	?barley	-	FI	C			I					I				
Avena sp	oat	-	AFI	C					I	I						
cf *Avena* sp	?oat	-	AFI	C							3			I		
Cerealia	indeterminate cereal	-	FI	C		I		9	5	9		I	5			
Vicia/Lathyrus sp	vetch/tare/vetchling	-	ACDEFI	C									I			
Fabaceae indeterminate	legume fragments	-	-	C				2					I			
Rumex sp	dock	-	ABCDEFG	C				I								
Galium spp	bedstraw	-	ABCDE	C				2								
Anthemis cotula L	stinking mayweed	-	ABGH	C				I						I		
Lolium sp	rye-grass	-	BDI	C				I		I						
Indeterminate	charcoal	WD	-	C		++	++	+++	++	+++	++++	+++	+++	+		++
Characeae	-	-	E	W				++	++						++++	++
Ranunculus acris/repens/bulbosus	buttercups	-	ABCDEG	W				++					+			
R sceleratus L	celery-leaved crowfoot	-	E	W								+++	+++			
R subgen Batrachium (DC) A Gray	crowfoots	-	E	W										++		
Ranunculus sp	-	-	ABCDEG	W				+		+						
Ceratophyllum demersum L	rigid hornwort	-	E	W											+	
Chelidonium majus L	greater celandine	-	BC	W									+++			
Fumaria sp	fumitory	-	ABC	W				+		+			++			
Brassica nigra (L) Koch	black mustard	-	BFHI	W				+			+++					++++
Brassica/Sinapis spp	-	-	ABFGHI	W				+								
Stellaria media gp	chickweeds	-	ABCDE	W										+		
Chenopodium spp	goosefoot etc	-	ABCDFH	W				++								++
Atriplex spp	orache	-	ABFGH	W				+								++
Rubus fruticosus/idaeus	blackberry/raspberry	-	CFGH	W				+					+			
Prunus sp	-	-	CFGI	W				+								
Conium maculatum L	hemlock	-	CEG	W				++								+
Rumex sp	dock	-	ABCDEFG	W				+								
Urtica dioica L	stinging nettle	-	BCDEFGH	W			+++	+++					+	+++		+
cf *Cannabis sativa* L	?hemp	-	BGHI	W												+
Betula sp	birch	-	CDH	W				+							+	
Hyoscyamus niger L	henbane	-	BDG	W		+	+	++						+		
Solanum nigrum L	black nightshade	-	BF	W				+								
Mentha sp	mint	-	ABCEFGI	W				+					+		+	+
Lycopus europaeus L	gipsy-wort	-	EH	W				+			++	+	+++			+
Lamium purpurem	red dead nettle	-	AB	W												
Ajuga reptans L	bugle	-	CDE	W												++
Labiatae indeterminate	-	-	ABCFEFI	W				+					+			
Sambucus nigra L	elder	-	BCFGH	W		+		+					+++	++		
Sambucus sp	elder	-	BCFGH	W									+			
Carduus/Cirsium spp	thistles	-	ABDEG	W				+								++
Lapsana communis L	nipplewort	-	BCF	W												++
Leontodon sp	hawkbit	-	BDF	W		+										
Sonchus cf *oleraceus*	? milk-/sow-thistle	-	AB	W				+								
S asper (L) Hill	spiny milk-/sow-thistle	-	AB	W				+							+	++
Sonchus sp	milk-/sow-thistle	-	ABE	W		+										
Taraxacum officinale Weber	dandelion	-	BDFGH	W											+	
Alisma sp	water-plantain	-	E	W				+					+++			
Potamogeton spp	pondweed	-	E	W											++	
Zannichellia palustris L	horned pondweed	-	E	W											+++	+
Juncus spp	rush	-	ADEH	W		++	++		+	+			++	+		
Lemna sp	duckweed	-	E	W				++			++		+++			
Sparganium erectum L	branched bur-reed	-	E	W											++	++
Schoenoplectus lacustris (L) Palla	bulrush	-	E	W											+	
Carex spp	sedge	-	CDEH	W				++					+	+	++	++
Cyperaceae indeterminate	-	-	ABCDEFI	W												++
Poaceae	grass	-	ABCDEFHI	W												
Bryophyta indeterminate	moss	-	-	W		++	++	++	++	++	++	++	++	+	++++	+++

mayweed were identified in the reredorter deposit [9469], the seeds possibly burnt as tinder following processing.

c 1300–c 1390 (period M3)

Eleven samples were analysed from this period from four different areas of the site, with six of the samples being from channel and alluvial deposits (OA9). Another three samples were from a pit fill and occupation deposits in the infirmary (B4a) while there were single samples from an occupation deposit in the aisled hall (B11) and an external garden deposit (OA7). The results by sample are shown in Table 43.

The majority of the botanical remains were from wild plants, again mainly from disturbed ground and waste places and wetland environments. The few food plants were limited to small assemblages of charred grains in four samples from the infirmary (B4a), aisled hall (B11) and garden (OA7), with free-threshing wheat, barley and oat being identified. These grains reflect background debris that may have been blowing around the site from the final stages of crop processing and food preparation.

Small quantities of black mustard seeds were found in two samples from an occupation deposit [9595] in the aisled hall (B11) and channel deposit [8385] in the marsh area (OA9). A few blackberry/raspberry seeds and slightly more elder seeds were present in six samples (mainly in OA9) while there were a few plum/bullace stones and hazelnut shell fragments in alluvial deposit [8315] from this area; this material may have been deposited from plants growing close by rather than representing food residues.

The botanical remains in the samples from the infirmary (B4a), the garden area (OA7) and aisled hall (B11) consisted mainly of very fragmented charcoal, occasional grains and a small range of wild plants (including a few charred weed seeds, corn cockle (*Agrostemma githago*), stinking mayweed, possibly used as tinder). These assemblages provide little information on either economic activities or the environment within these areas. There were a fairly large number of seeds of rushes in pit fill [10657], which may be discarded flooring materials from the infirmary floor (B4a).

The samples from the marsh deposits (OA9), however, produced some very rich wild plant assemblages with by far the richest assemblage (both in terms of species diversity and item frequency) being in the sample from the alluvial deposit [8315]. A wide range of wetland plants (both aquatic and bankside/marshland) and indicative of the immediate environment, included the following well-represented plants: celery-leaved crowfoot, gypsy-wort, water-plantain, horned pondweed, rushes, yellow iris (*Iris pseudacorus*), duckweed, branched bur-reed and sedges. There was a significantly smaller number of plants of disturbed ground and waste places represented by fewer seeds including stinging nettle, dock, *Polygonum* species, spiny milk-/sow-thistle (*Sonchus asper*), corn spurrey (*Spergula arvensis*) (the seeds of which were sometimes used for their oil), and the hedgerow species elder and blackberry/raspberry, which may have been from drier areas close by.

16th–17th centuries (period P2)

The plant remains in five samples from period P2 contexts were analysed, two from natural channel fills [10650], [10855] associated with riverside revetment (S10), and three from Open Area 12: two fills [9078], [9638] of the former infirmary drain (S4b) and ditch fill [8002] in the former marshy area (OA9). The results are presented in Table 44.

Both channel samples produced a range of mainly wild plants although the greatest species diversity and item frequency was in the sample from [10855]. The only food plants were represented by a single charred wheat or rye grain and possibly by small numbers of elder seeds and plum/bullace stones although the latter may simply be from plants growing close by. There was also a very large number of dyers rocket seeds in [10650], which may be from the residues of the plant used for dyeing although it is also a common weed. Fairly large quantities of charcoal were found in both samples, indicative of human activities.

The wild plants were mainly from disturbed ground and waste places and wetland environments with a fairly equal

Table 43 Plant remains from selected samples from period M3 (see Table 41 for key to plant parts, preservation, habitat and frequency codes)

					Area	B4a	B4a	B4a	B11	OA7	OA9	OA9	OA9	OA9	OA9	OA9
					Context	[8558]	[10633]	[10657]	[9595]	[8798]	[8315]	[8326]	[8328]	[8328]	[8385]	[8466]
Species					Sample	{4145}	{4170}	{4192}	{3910}	{3659}	{3576}	{3554}	{3538}	{3539}	{3597}	{3604}
Latin name	Common name	Plant part	Habitat/use	Preservation												
Triticum aestivum L. sl	bread/club wheat	-	Fl	C						3						
Triticum spp	wheat/rye	-	Fl	C						2						
Triticum/Secale sp	wheat/rye	-	Fl	C					l							
Hordeum sativum L	barley	-	Fl	C								l				
cf *Avena* sp	?oat	-	AFl	C					l							
Cerealia	indeterminate cereal	R	Fl	C						3		l				
Cerealia	indeterminate cereal	-	Fl	C							6					
Agrostemma githago L	corn cockle	-	AB	C					l							
Trifolium sp	clover calyx	-	ABDI	C								l				
Rumex sp	dock	-	ABCDEF	C								l				

Table 43 (cont)

Species — Latin name	Common name	Plant part	Habitat/use	Preservation	B4a [8558] {4145}	B4a [10633] {4170}	B4a [10657] {4192}	BII [9595] {3910}	OA7 [8798] {3659}	OA9 [8315] {3576}	OA9 [8326] {3554}	OA9 [8328] {3538}	OA9 [8328] {3539}	OA9 [8385] {3597}	OA9 [8466] {3604}
Anthemis cotula L	stinking mayweed	-	ABGH	C				I							
Indeterminate	charcoal	WD	-	C	++++	++++	+++	+++	+++		+				+
Characeae	-	-	E	W			+								
Ranunculus acris/repens/bulbosus	buttercups	-	ABCDEG	W	++	++	+			++					+
R flammula L	lesser spearwort	-	EG	W								+			
R sceleratus L	celery-leaved crowfoot	-	E	W						+++			+		
R subgen *Batrachium* (DC) A Gray	crowfoots	-	E	W								+	+		
Ranunculus spp	-	-	ABCDEG	W					+	+		+		+	
Ceratophyllum demersum L	rigid hornwort	-	E	W											+
Chelidonium majus L	greater celandine	-	BC	W			+	+							
Brassica nigra (L) Koch	black mustard	-	BFHI	W				++						+++	
Brassica/Sinapis sp	-	-	ABFGHI	W				+							
Raphanus raphanistrum L	wild radish/charlock	-	A	W						+					
Stellaria media gp	chickweeds	-	ABCDE	W										+	
Spergula arvensis L	corn spurrey	-	ADF	W						++++					
Chenopodium sp	goosefoot etc	-	ABCDFH	W				+				+			
Rubus fruticosus/idaeus	blackberry/raspberry	-	CFGH	W				+		++	+	+	+		+
Potentilla sp	cinquefoil/tormentil	-	BCDEFGH	W								+	+		
Prunus domestica L	plum/bullace	-	CFI	W						+					
Conium maculatum L	hemlock	-	CEG	W					+						
Polygonum persicaria L	persicaria	-	ABEH	W						++		+			
P lapathifolium L	pale persicaria	-	ABE	W						+		+			
P hydropiper/mite	water-pepper	-	E	W						+					
Fallopia convolvulus (L) A Love	black bindweed	-	ABF	W											+
Polygonum sp	-	-	ABCDEFG	W						+					
Rumex acetosella agg	sheep's sorrel	-	AD	W						+					
Rumex spp	dock	-	ABCDEFG	W					+	+++					+
Urtica dioica L	stinging nettle	-	BCDEFGH	W						+		++	++	+++	++
Betula sp	birch	-	CDH	W					+					+	
Corylus avellana L	hazel	-	CF	W						+					
Hyoscyamus niger L	henbane	-	BDG	W		+				+	+				
Solanum nigrum L	black nightshade	-	BF	W				+							
Mentha spp	mint	-	ABCEFGI	W						+		+			
Lamium pupurem	red dead nettle	-	AB	W				+							
Lycopus europaeus L	gipsy-wort	-	EH	W						+++					+
Prunella vulgaris L	self-heal	-	BCDG	W								+			+
Stachys palustris L	marsh woundwort	-	AE	W										++	
Ajuga reptans L	bugle	-	CDE	W						+					
Labiatae indeterminate	-	-	ABCFEFI	W				+			+				
Sambucus nigra L	elder	-	BCFGH	W	+			+		+++	+		+		+
Sambucus sp	elder	-	BCFGH	W							+				
Eupatorium cannabinum L	hemp agrimony	-	E	W											+
Carduus/Cirsium spp	thistles	-	ABDEG	W				+		++					
Lapsana communis L	nipplewort	-	BCF	W								+			
Leontodon sp	hawkbit	-	BDF	W				+							
Picris echioides L	bristly ox-tongue	-	BC	W								++			
Sonchus oleraceus L	milk-/sow-thistle	-	AB	W								+			
S asper (L) Hill	spiny milk-/sow-thistle	-	AB	W					+	+		++	++		
Taraxacum officinale Weber	dandelion	-	BDFGH	W								+			
Alisma sp	water-plantain	-	E	W						++					
Alismataceae indeterminate	-	-	E	W						++					+
Zannichellia palustris L	horned pondweed	-	E	W						+					+++
Juncus spp	rush	-	ADEH	W				+++		++		+			
Iris pseudacorus L	yellow iris yellow flag	-	E	W						++++					
Lemna sp	duckweed	-	E	W						+++					
Sparganium erectum L	branched bur-reed	-	E	W						++					
Eleocharis palustris/uniglumis	spike-rush	-	E	W										+	
Carex spp	sedge	-	CDEH	W						++++		+	+		+++
Carex spp	sedge	UT	CDEH	W						++					++
Cyperaceae indeterminate	-	-	ABCDEFI	W						++					++
Poaceae indeterminate	grass	-	ABCDEFHI	W						+	+				
Bryophyta indeterminate	moss	-	-	W	++	+++	+	+++		+++	+	+++	+++	+++	+++

Table 44 Plant remains from selected samples from period P2 (see Table 41 for key to plant parts, preservation, habitat and frequency codes)

					S10/OA12 [10650] {4186}	S10/OA12 [10855] {4287}	S4b/OA12 [9078] {3950}	S4b/OA12 [9638] {3902}	OA12 [8002] {3308}
Species				**Area Context Sample**					
Latin name	**Common name**	**Plant part**	**Habitat/use**	**Preservation**					
Triticum/Secale sp	wheat/rye	-	FI	C	I				
Indeterminate	charcoal	WD	-	C	++	+++	+++	+++	++
Characeae	-	-	E	W	+				
Ranunculus acris/repens/bulbosus	buttercups	-	ABCDEG	W	+	++++			+++
R arvensis L	corn crowfoot	-	A	W		+			
R sardous Crantz	hairy buttercup	-	ABE	W					+++
R cf *parviflorus*	? small-flowered buttercup	-	CD	W					+
R sceleratus L	celery-leaved crowfoot	-	E	W	+	+++			
Ranunculus spp	-	-	ABCDEG	W	+	++			++
Chelidonium majus L	greater celandine	-	BC	W			+		
Fumaria sp	fumitory	-	ABC	W	+	++		+	
Brassica sp	wild cabbage/turnip/mustard	-	ABFI	W					+
cf *Raphanus raphanistrum*	? wild radish/charlock	-	A	W					+
Nasturtium officinale R Br	watercress	-	EFI	W		+			
Reseda luteola L	weld/dyer's rocket	-	ABGHI	W	++++	++			
Viola spp	violet	-	ABCDG	W	+			+	
Silene sp	campion/catchfly	-	ABCDF	W		+			
Agrostemma githago L	corn cockle	-	AB	W					+
Stellaria media gp	chickweeds	-	ABCDE	W					+++
S graminea L	lesser stitchwort	-	CD	W					+
Chenopodium album gp	fat hen	-	ABFH	W					+
Chenopodium spp	goosefoot etc	-	ABCDFH	W		+++		+	++
Atriplex spp	orache	-	ABFGH	W	+	++			+
Potentilla spp	cinquefoil/tormentil	-	BCDEFGH	W	+				+
Prunus domestica L	plum/bullace	-	CFI	W		+			
Torilis sp	hedge-parsley	-	ACD	W		+			
Apiaceae indeterminate	-	-	-	W		+			
Euphorbia peplus L	petty spurge	-	AB	W		+++			
Polygonum aviculare agg	knotgrass	-	ABG	W					+
P persicaria L	persicaria	-	ABEH	W		+++			
P lapathifolium L	pale persicaria	-	ABE	W					+
P hydropiper/mite	water-pepper	-	E	W		+			
Polygonum spp	-	-	ABCDEFG	W	+				
Rumex spp	dock	-	ABCDEFG	W		++			+
Urtica urens L	small nettle	-	AB	W		+			
U dioica L	stinging nettle	-	BCDEFGH	W	++++	+++			++
Betula sp	birch	-	CDH	W			+		
Hyoscyamus niger L	henbane	-	BDG	W		++		++	
Solanum nigrum L	black nightshade	-	BF	W		+		+	
Solanaceae indeterminate	-	-	-	W				+	
Lycopus europaeus L	gipsy-wort	-	EH	W	+	++	+		
Stachys sp	woundwort	-	ACEG	W		+			
Lamium purpurem	red dead nettle	-	AB	W		++			
Labiatae indeterminate	-	-	ABCFEFI	W		+			
Sambucus nigra L	elder	-	BCFGH	W	+	++	+++	+++	
Eupatorium cannabinum L	hemp agrinomy	-	E	W		+			
Carduus/Cirsium spp	thistles	-	ABDEG	W		+			
Centaurea sp	knapweed/thistle	-	ABDGH	W					+
Lapsana communis L	nipplewort	-	BCF	W	+				+
Sonchus cf *oleraceus*	? milk-/sow-thistle	-	AB	W					
S asper (L) Hill	spiny milk-/sow-thistle	-	AB	W		+			+
Potamogeton sp	pondweed	-	E	W		++			
Zannichellia palustris L	horned pondweed	-	E	W		++			
Juncus spp	rush	-	ADEH	W		+	+	+++	
Lemna sp	duckweed	-	E	W					+++
Sparganium erectum L	branched bur-reed	-	E	W		+			
Carex spp	sedge	-	CDEH	W	+	++			
Carex spp	sedge	UT	CDEH	W		+			
Cyperaceae indeterminate	-	-	ABCDEFI	W					+
Poaceae indeterminate	grass	-	ABCDEFHI	W	++				+
Bryophyta indeterminate	moss	-	-	W	++	+++	++	+++	+++

representation of both. The wetland plants (aquatic and bankside/marshland species) included celery-leaved crowfoot, gypsy-wort, pondweed, horned pondweed, branched bur-reed and sedges while well-represented disturbed ground plants included fumitory, goosefoots, oraches, petty spurge (*Euphorbia peplus*), persicaria (*Polygonum persicaria*), dock, stinging nettle and henbane, with also a large number of seeds of buttercups (*Ranunculus acris/repens/bulbosus*), a plant that may grow in a range of habitats. The wetland plants indicate a damp environment within the channels although the fairly high number of other weeds suggests that there was drier land close by, or possibly infilling or temporary drying out of the area.

The sample from a ditch fill [8002] in the marshy area (formerly OA9) produced botanical remains from a range of wild plants mostly from disturbed (including cultivated) ground and waste places with well-represented species including hairy buttercup (*Ranunculus sardous*), chickweed (*Stellaria media*), goosefoots/oraches and stinging nettle. Buttercups were again well represented. Wetland plants were surprisingly poorly represented with the exception of duckweed. There was little evidence from the plants for human activities except for a small amount of charcoal. The paucity of wetland plants suggests that the ditch had dried out or was being backfilled by this period.

The two drain fills [9078] and [9638] were fairly similar with both producing only very small plant assemblages with charcoal and a small range of wild plants (mainly from disturbed ground and waste places) with the only moderately well-represented species being henbane, elder and rushes. The rush seeds are the only possible indication of a damp environment with the assemblages suggesting that the drain (S4b) was not functioning as such by this time.

In addition to the plant remains discussed here, samples from sediments presumed to be of 16th-century date in the chalk-based fishpond (S9) were analysed and contained substantial numbers of well-preserved pollen and spores (below, 7.7). The pollen spectra provide evidence for several habitats – marsh/wetland, pastoral, cultivated areas and background woodland, including exotic introduced trees (notably juniper (*Juniperus*)) – and also a diverse range of herb pollen types.

7.7 The pollen analysis

Rob Scaife

Introduction

Six pollen samples have been assessed for their pollen and spore content, preservation and potential for environmental reconstruction. These samples {4247}–{4252} were taken from 600mm of organic silts/silty peat ([10641]; [10659]; [10773]; [10660]; [10317]; [10319]), part of the lower fill of the chalk-paved fishpond (S9); the lowest silt possibly of medieval date, the upper deposits presumed to be 16th century in date. It was anticipated that if pollen was preserved at this site, data on the character of the local environment of the priory would be forthcoming. This proved to be the case with recovery of a diverse range of tree, shrub and herb pollen from all of the samples examined. This report provides the results of the pollen analysis (Scaife 2000).

Methodology

A total of six samples was examined for sub-fossil pollen and spore content. Standard techniques were used for the extraction of the microfossils (Moore and Webb 1978; Moore et al 1991). Samples of 2ml volume were used and absolute pollen frequencies were calculated using an exotic marker/spike (Stockmarr 1971, *Lycopodium* tablets) to the measured volume of sample. Although samples provided were only as an assessment, the relatively high pollen absolute frequencies allowed larger pollen counts than normal for such an assessment. Totals of *c* 300 grains of dry land taxa plus extant marsh/wetland and spore taxa have been counted at each level. The resulting data were calculated and plotted using Tilia and Tilia Graph. Percentage calculations were as a percentage of the sum of total dry land pollen (tdlp) with marsh/aquatic and spores as a percentage of these categories plus the basic sum. Thus marsh = %tdlp + marsh; spores = %tdlp + spores. Taxonomy in general follows that of Moore and Webb (1978), Moore et al (1991) modified according to Bennett et al (1994). These procedures were carried out in the Department of Geography, University of Southampton.

The pollen data

Well-preserved pollen and spores were obtained from these organic sediments with absolute pollen frequencies ranging from 47,000 grains/ml at 50cm to highest values of 194,000 grains/ml at 40cm. Overall, the pollen spectra of the six levels obtained from the 60cm of stratigraphy are broadly similar and thus, no pollen zonation has been carried out. The principal characteristics of the assemblages are as follows (Fig 223).

Tree and shrub total pollen values are small and attain a maximum of 25% at 400mm although there is a relatively diverse range of taxa. *Quercus* and *Corylus avellana* type are the most important taxa (20% and 15% respectively). In addition there are sporadic occurrences of wind pollinated types including *Betula*, *Pinus*, *Alnus* and *Populus*. Less well-represented taxa include *Fagus*, *Fraxinus* and *Ulmus*. Interesting occurrences of *Juglans*, *Juniperus* and *Taxus* occur. With regard to herbs, Poaceae (to 50%) is dominant along with Cyperaceae (in the marsh/wetland category). The remaining, diverse assemblages of herbs comprise a mixture of taxa which are referable to growth in pastoral, arable and waste/disturbed ground habitats. Evidence of cultivated crops include the pollen of *Fagopyrum esculentum Cannabis* type (*Humulus* and *Cannabis*) and cereals-*Triticum* type/undifferentiated, *Secale cereale* and *Avena/Hordeum* type.

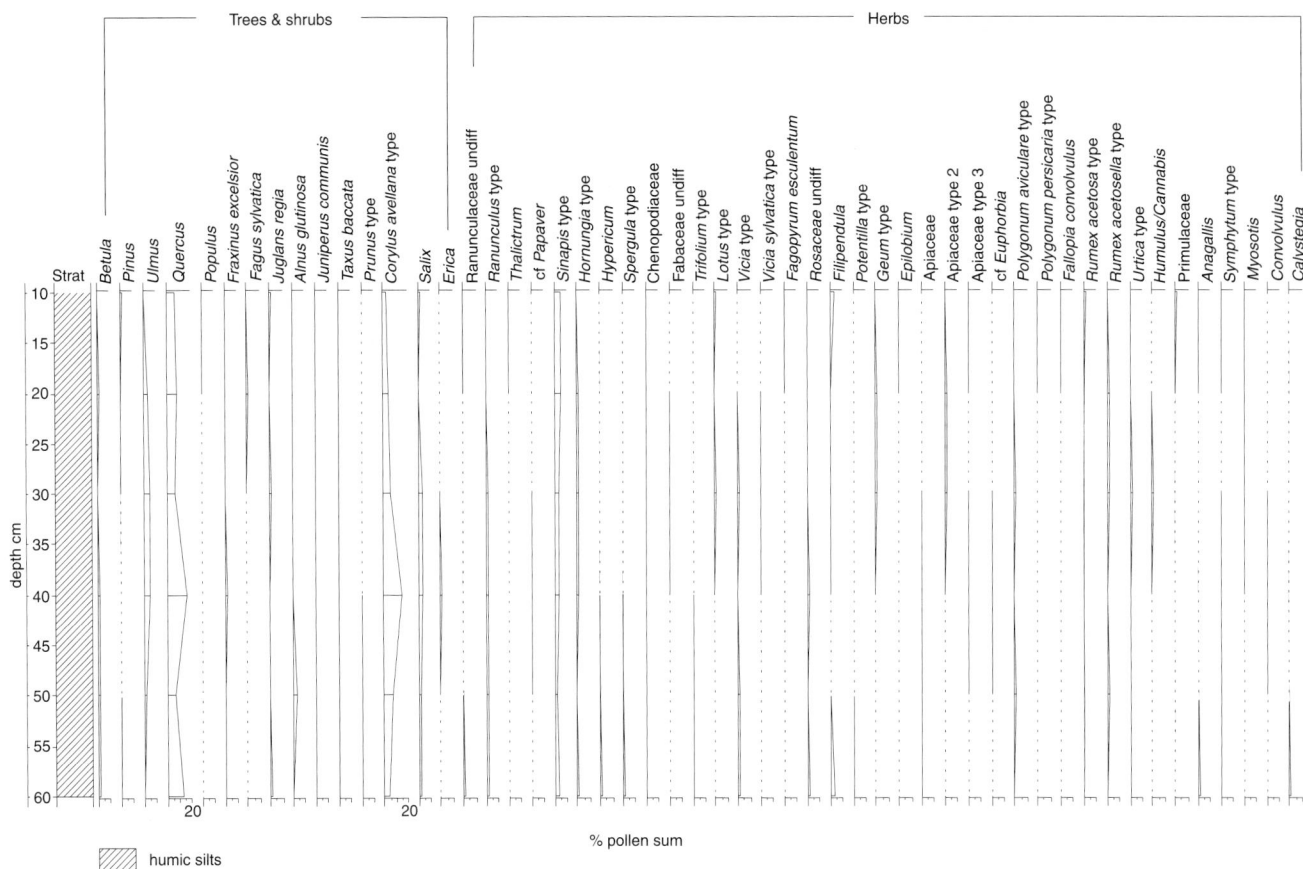

Fig 223 *Pollen analysis of samples from the lower fill of the chalk-paved fishpond (S9)*

Weeds of arable cultivation are present including *Sinapis* type/ Brassicaceae, Chenopodiaceae, *Convolvulus* type, *Polygonum convolvulus, Persicaria maculosa* type, *Fallopia convolvulus, Spergula* type and *Centaurea cyanus*. It is possible that other taxa which are not identifiable to a lower taxonomic level are also from this habitat. Conversely, those noted may also come from other disturbed ground habitats (eg *Plantago media/major*, Cirsium type).

Pastoral habitats are less easy to differentiate as pollen types typical of grassland may also come from marsh habitats. However, taxa such as *Ranunculus* type, *Thalictrum, Trifolium* type, *Lotus* type, *Vicia* type, *Filipendula, Rumex* sp, Scrophulariaceae, *Plantago lanceolata, Centaurea scabiosa, C nigra* type may all be referable to pastoral habitats. The herb *Borago officinalis* was recorded at 600mm and may have been a weed of waste ground or cultivated for culinary purposes. Mire or aquatic habitats are characterised by high relative values of Cyperaceae (to 38%) but with occurrences of *Myriophyllum, Lemna, Callitriche* and *Potamogeton*. There are also small numbers of algal *Pediastrum*. Some taxa within the main sum could also relate to damp/wet areas of grassland in proximity to this marshland habitat (eg Poaceae, *Thalictrum, Valeriana officinalis*).

Overall, there are only small numbers of spores of ferns with *Pteridium aquilinum* (6%) and sporadic occurrences of *Polypodium vulgare* and *Equisetum*.

Discussion

The predominance of herb pollen types reflects the diversity of habitats associated with the wetland area and the proximity of the priory and human occupation. Many of the pollen taxa are indistinguishable to species or generic level due to similar pollen morphologies and may be from plants of catholic distribution or ecology. Thus, it is in such cases of diverse assemblages difficult to assign types to specific ecologic communities. However, it is clear from the pollen data that a number of habitats can be distinguished. These include the background, regional vegetation: essentially trees and shrubs, wind pollinated (anemophilous), and more local communities of cultivated plants and associated weeds and the marsh habitat itself.

The depositional environment of the site is clearly illustrated by the dominance of Cyperaceae (to 38%) and monocot remains present within the sediments. The presence of aquatic and marginal aquatic taxa suggests that there were also areas of free-standing water with *Lemna* (duckweed), *Myriophyllum spicatum* (water milfoil) and *Potamogeton* (pondweed). This was possibly fringing reed swamp with *Typha latifolia* (bulrush), *Typha angustifolia/sparganium* (lesser bulrush/bur-reed), Iris and *Lythrum salicaria* (purple loosestrife).

There are relatively small percentages of arboreal and

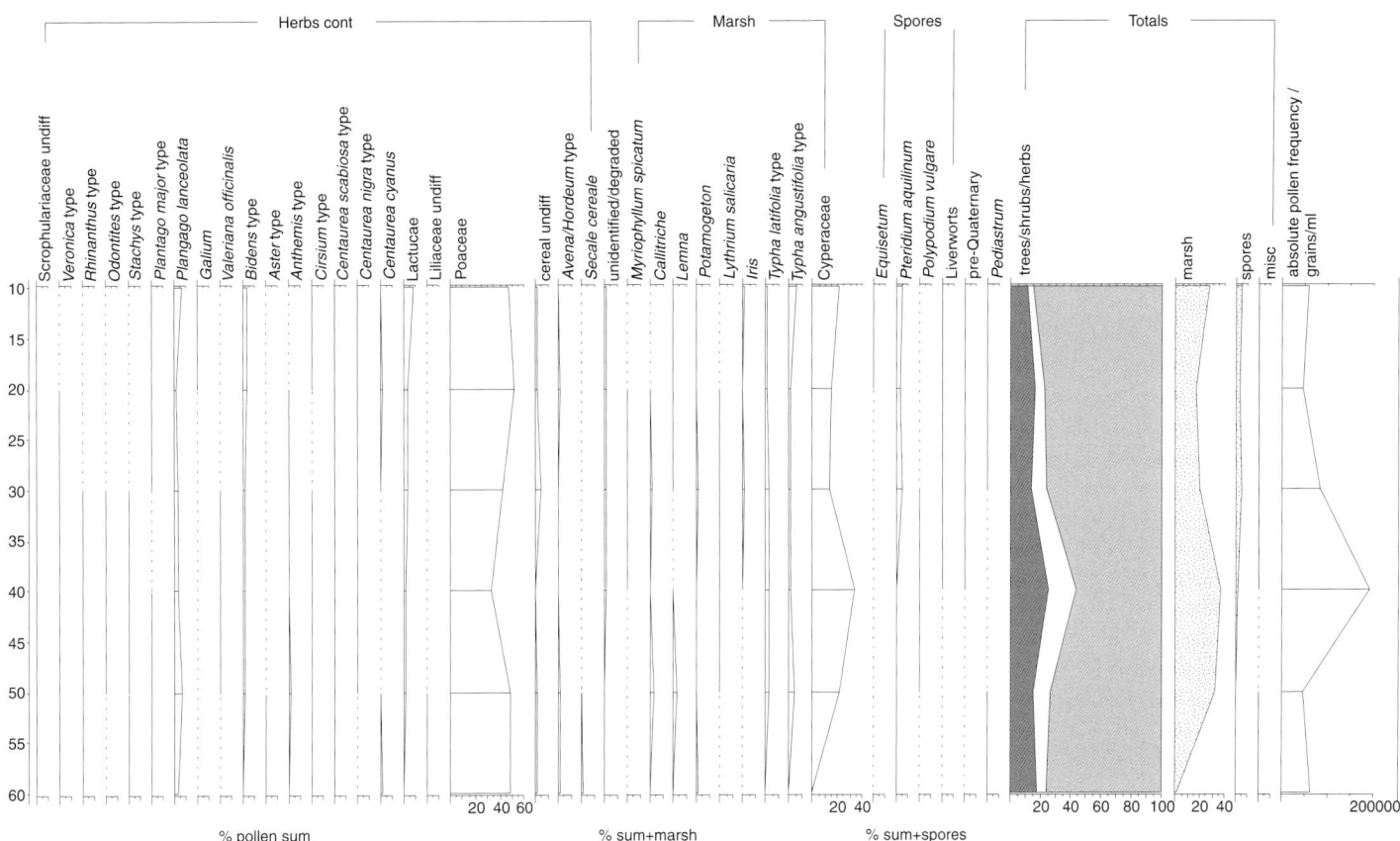

shrub types, yet a broad diversity is a characteristic of pollen data from historic London. This reflects the fact that *Quercus* (oak) and *Corylus avellana type* (hazel) remained the principal woodland types within the broad region, these taxa being readily wind disseminated. Other taxa noted are, however, less well transported. The presence, albeit in small numbers, of *Fagus* (beech) and *Fraxinus* (ash) and to some extent *Ulmus* (elm) attests to their growth close to the site. Whether this pollen was from localised areas of woodland or from more open park growth is unclear. Of interest are the occurrences of *Juglans* (walnut), *Juniperus* (juniper) and *Taxus* (yew). It seems likely that these were specifically planted. The former is well documented as a Roman introduction into western Europe. It seems that once introduced by the Romans into London, where it has been found at the Temple of Mithras (Scaife 1982a), it remained throughout the historic period. From these later periods its pollen has been recorded at the Tower of London (Scaife 2004), Broad Sanctuary Westminster (Scaife 1982b), Hampstead Heath (Greig 1992) and sites along the Jubilee Line extension (Sidell et al 2000). Yew and juniper, however, may be associated with the priory grounds/gardens and the latter is an unusual occurrence for this period and locality.

Evidence for cultivation of crops in such an area was expected along with the diverse range of herbs recovered and is typical of post-Roman London with pollen assemblages associated with human activity. Although quantities of cereal-type pollen (*Avena/Hordeum*, *Triticum*, *Secale cereale*) are not high, they do attest to the use of these crops and possibly local cultivation. The taphonomy of cereal pollen may be complex with pollen being derived from not only areas of cultivation but also from faecal material, floor coverings/bedding and that liberated during crop processing (threshing and winnowing). Apart from the cereals noted, cannabis (*Cannabis sativa*) and buckwheat (*Fagopyrum esculentum*) are the only other cultivated plants found. Both are likely to have been grown within the priory. The former was not unfortunately differentiable from hop (*Humulus lupulus*), which has a similar pollen morphology. Both hop and cannabis are possible although the latter was perhaps more likely. The presence of buckwheat is a scarce and important pollen record and must relate to cultivation of this introduced crop for production of buckwheat flour.

A similarly interesting and rare pollen record is that of borage (*Borago officinalis*); although only a single pollen grain/record, the pollen is very distinguishable and must reflect growth locally of this culinary herb. This may have been deliberately grown or derived from escaped plants. It was, however, a plant used as a culinary herb and also an additive to 'wine cups' and cider.

7.8 The vertebrate remains

Alan Pipe, with a contribution on eggshell by Jane Sidell

Introduction

Methodology

Vertebrate bones were recovered by hand collection and by wet-sieving of bulk environmental samples. Faunal remains from the residue and flot fractions were bagged and labelled as sample groups divided into overall broad taxonomic groups, that is insects, mollusc shell, bird eggshell, and animal bone (grouped into fish, amphibian, bird and mammal components). A record sheet was completed for each processed sample in summary of the floral, faunal and artefactual assemblages; these data are archived and are available for consultation on request. The hand-collected and wet-sieved animal bones were then recorded directly on to the MoLAS/MoLSS Oracle 7 animal bone post-assessment database in terms of context/sample number, species, skeletal element, fragment count, fragmentation, weight (g), body side, fusion state or tooth wear stage if applicable, modification (burning, gnawing, working, pathology), and measurements (if applicable). All measurements were taken to the nearest 0.1mm using manual Vernier calipers and following the sequences and techniques given by von den Driesch (1976). In view of the very low weights, often below 0.1g, of bone recovered from each sample group, this material was recorded in terms of fragment count only.

A total of 20,206 fragments, 127.95kg, of animal bone was recovered from stratified contexts by hand collection. Period assemblages for periods M1 to P3 varied between 704 and 5784 fragments, and 7.5 and 41.2kg. A total of 5294 fragments was recovered from stratified contexts by wet-sieving.

Eggshell was recovered from 17 environmental samples and analysed by Jane Sidell. The methodology is described in Sidell (1993) and the full report is available in the archive.

Preservation

For both the hand-collected and wet-sieved material, a consistent feature of the site assemblage as a whole was the excellent surface condition of the material allowing detailed identification of species and skeletal element in the majority of cases. For this reason, it was generally possible to determine fusion stages, tooth wear stages, bone modification effects (butchery, burning, gnawing, working, pathological changes), and measurement points.

Fragmentation

A further characteristic of the hand-collected material was the consistently small fragment size; the calculated mean fragment weight of 6.3g being far less than that seen at any other London religious house. Although this reflects the skill

of the excavators, it also has implications for on-site activity in terms of waste disposal practice and subsequent trampling; indeed the high fragment count and weight for 'unidentifiable mammal' fragments from periods M1–P3 (17.0–37.7% of period fragment count/2.1–6.4% of period weight) implies that the material received far more physical damage than that associated with mere butchery, consumption and disposal.

Discussion

Information from the most interesting individual assemblages and from the overall period-based breakdown has been integrated into the chronological text (Chapter 3, including Tables 3–16) and the thematic sections (Chapter 4, including Table 21 which shows the representation of the major mammalian domesticates). Table 45 and Table 46 summarise species representation by period for the hand-collected assemblage and Table 47 for the wet-sieved assemblage.

Although much of the hand-collected and wet-sieved faunal evidence is of obvious value for interpretation of dietary preference and availability (Chapter 4.8), on-site activity and waste-disposal practices, the species present are mainly there as a direct result of deliberate human activity and consequently this does not allow any interpretation of local habitats. Some of the smaller animal species, usually most commonly recovered by wet-sieving, are components of local 'wild' non-exploited faunas, and may be used as indicators of local conditions in the light of their specific ecological requirements (Gray-Rees and Pipe 1999).

Throughout all periods there was consistent but infrequent recovery of local fauna associated with the local environs. The material recovered included a large component of small bird and mammal material unidentifiable to genus or species due to excessive fragmentation and therefore grouped into such approximate categories as 'passerine bird', 'small passerine bird', 'small mammal', mouse/vole, vole (unidentified), and 'small rodent' (ie smaller than rat). The potential value of this material for interpretation of the site is very limited and, of the range of passerine birds present, many of the species are probably dietary components and therefore not of direct significance in terms of the local environment. The recovery of small species derived from the true local fauna depends to a considerable extent on the physical character of the site – open features can effectively act as pit-fall traps and include ground-living species in pit and well deposits. The retrieval of such potential indicator species was disappointing throughout all periods in terms of both abundance and diversity (Tables 45–7). This fauna derived from frog/toad (probably common frog *Rana temporaria*/common toad *Bufo bufo*), common shrew (*Sorex araneus*), mole (*Talpa europaea*), field vole (*Microtus agrestis*), house mouse (*Mus domesticus*), black/brown rat and black rat (*Rattus rattus*). Common frog and common toad are both ubiquitous throughout Britain (Arnold 1995, 8–9, 14–15) and active on land for most of the year. They are commonly recovered from archaeological sites either as a result of chance

Table 45 *Species representation from the hand-collected assemblages by period, by fragment count (%)*

	Period	M1 %	M2 %	M3 %	M4 %	P1 %	P2 %	P3 %
Species								
Common name	Latin name							
Fish								
Fish unidentified		0.3	0.3	0.3	-	1.0	<0.1	-
Thornback ray	*Raja clavata*	-	<0.1	<0.1	-	0.2	<0.1	0.1
Sturgeon	*Acipenser sturio*	-	-	<0.1	-	-	-	-
Salmon family	Salmonidae	-	-	<0.1	-	-	<0.1	-
Cod	*Gadus morhua*	0.2	0.2	0.2	-	0.2	<0.1	0.1
Cod family	Gadidae	0.3	0.2	0.1	0.1	0.1	<0.1	-
Cod-sized		0.6	<0.1	0.1	0.3	0.2	<0.1	-
Haddock	*Melanogrammus aeglefinus*	0.2	<0.1	-	-	0.2	-	-
Conger eel	*Conger conger*	<0.1	<0.1	<0.1	-	-	<0.1	-
Plaice/flounder	Pleuronectidae	-	-	<0.1	-	-	<0.1	-
Amphibian								
Frog/toad	Ranidae	0.4	<0.1	0.1	-	-	<0.1	-
Birds								
Bird unidentified		0.5	2.7	0.8	0.8	0.6	0.9	2.3
Chicken	*Gallus gallus*	4.2	8.4	5.1	1.6	3.2	5.0	1.6
Chicken-sized		0.2	0.2	0.8	0.3	0.1	0.5	-
Goose, domestic	*Anser anser*	1.2	1.7	1.7	1.3	2.1	1.6	1.1
Goose-sized		0.1	0.4	0.2	-	0.1	0.2	0.2
Mallard/domestic duck	*Anas platyrhynchos*	0.2	<0.1	0.2	-	0.2	0.2	0.1
Duck unidentified	Anatidae	<0.1	<0.1	<0.1	-	-	<0.1	-
Swan unidentified	*Cygnus* sp	-	-	-	-	-	<0.1	-
Heron	*Ardea cinerea*	-	-	<0.1	-	-	<0.1	-
Partridge, grey	*Perdix perdix*	-	<0.1	<0.2	-	0.2	<0.1	-
Woodcock	*Scolopax rusticola*	-	-	<0.1	-	-	<0.1	-
Wood pigeon	*Columba palumbus*	-	-	<0.1	-	-	<0.1	-
Rock/stock dove	*Columba livia/C oenas*	-	-	0.2	<0.1	-	<0.1	-
Blackbird	*Turdus merula*	-	-	-	-	-	<0.1	-
Crow unidentified	Corvidae	-	-	<0.1	-	-	<0.1	-
Carrion crow	*Corvus corone*	<0.1	<0.1	<0.1	-	-	-	-
Buzzard	*Buteo buteo*	-	-	<0.1	-	-	-	-
Thrush species	Turdidae	-	<0.1	<0.1	-	-	<0.1	0.1
Passerine bird		-	-	-	-	0.2	<0.1	-
Mammals								
Mammal unidentified		33.8	22.7	26.2	35.8	37.7	21.6	17.0
Cattle	*Bos taurus*	6.9	4.8	8.0	13.8	9.9	10.9	19.3
Cattle-sized		7.8	6.6	9.8	15.8	12.1	14.2	21.8
Sheep/goat	*Ovis aries/Capra hircus*	8.0	9.3	7.5	6.7	8.6	8.6	9.3
Sheep	*Ovis aries*	0.3	0.3	0.4	-	-	0.3	0.1
Sheep-sized		24.0	26.6	25.3	14.9	11.6	23.6	15.5
Goat	*Capra hircus*	-	<0.1	-	-	-	<0.1	-
Pig	*Sus scrofa*	9.8	14.2	9.9	7.0	4.9	7.8	8.8
Horse	*Equus caballus*	0.1	<0.1	<0.1	0.1	-	0.2	0.2
Dog	*Canis familiaris*	<0.1	<0.1	0.1	-	0.8	0.2	0.2
Cat	*Felis catus*	-	0.1	0.5	0.1	0.1	0.5	-
Porpoise/dolphin	Cetacea	-	-	-	-	-	<0.1	-
Red deer	*Cervus elaphus*	-	-	0.1	-	-	<0.1	0.3
Fallow deer	*Dama dama*	0.5	<0.1	0.1	0.1	-	0.2	0.2
Roe deer	*Capreolus capreolus*	<0.1	<0.1	0.1	-	-	<0.1	-
Deer unidentified	Cervidae	0.1	<0.1	<0.1	-	-	-	-
Hare, brown	*Lepus europaeus*	0.1	0.4	0.2	0.1	0.1	0.2	0.6
Rabbit	*Oryctolagus cuniculus*	0.1	0.2	1.3	1.0	5.3	2.1	0.6
Mole	*Talpa europaea*	-	-	-	-	-	<0.1	-
Rat, black	*Rattus rattus*	-	-	-	-	0.2	-	-
Rat unidentified	*Rattus* sp	-	<0.1	-	-	-	<0.1	0.2
Total no. of frags (20179)		2651	4377	4907	704	903	5784	853

Table 46 *Species representation from the hand-collected assemblages by period, by weight (Wt %)*

	Period	M1 Wt %	M2 Wt %	M3 Wt %	M4 Wt %	P1 Wt %	P2 Wt %	P3 Wt %
Species								
Common name	Latin name							
Fish								
Fish unidentified		<0.1	<0.1	<0.1	-	<0.1	<0.1	-
Thornback ray	*Raja clavata*	-	<0.1	<0.1	-	<0.1	<0.1	<0.1
Sturgeon	*Acipenser sturio*	-	-	<0.1	-	-	-	-
Salmon family	Salmonidae	-	-	<0.1	-	-	<0.1	-
Cod	*Gadus morhua*	0.1	<0.1	<0.1	<0.1	<0.1	<0.1	-
Cod family	Gadidae	0.1	<0.1	<0.1	-	<0.1	<0.1	<0.1
Cod-sized		0.1	<0.1	<0.1	<0.1	<0.1	<0.1	-
Haddock	*Melanogrammus aeglefinus*	<0.1	<0.1	<0.1	-	-	<0.1	-
Conger eel	*Conger conger*	-	-	<0.1	-	-	<0.1	-
Plaice/flounder	Pleuronectidae	0.2	<0.1		-	<0.1	-	-
Amphibian								
Frog/toad	Ranidae	<0.1	<0.1	<0.1	-	-	<0.1	-
Birds								
Bird unidentified		<0.1	2.7	<0.1	<0.1	<0.1	<0.1	<0.1
Chicken	*Gallus gallus*	0.1	1.5	1.0	<0.1	<0.1	1.0	0.2
Chicken-sized		<0.1	<0.1	0.1	<0.1	<0.1	<0.1	-
Goose, domestic	*Anser anser*	0.4	<0.1	0.6	0.3	0.7	0.6	0.2
Goose-sized		<0.1	<0.1	<0.1	-	<0.1	<0.1	<0.1
Mallard/domestic duck	*Anas platyrhynchos*	0.1	<0.1	<0.1	-	<0.1	<0.1	<0.1
Duck unidentified	Anatidae	<0.1	<0.1	<0.1	-	-	<0.1	-
Heron	*Ardea cinerea*	-	-	-	-	-	<0.1	-
Swan	*Cygnus sp*	-	-	<0.1	-	-	<0.1	-
Partridge, grey	*Perdix perdix*	-	<0.1	<0.1	-	<0.1	<0.1	-
Woodcock	*Scolopax rusticola*	-	-	<0.1	-	-	<0.1	-
Wood pigeon	*Columba palumbus*	-	-	-	-	-	<0.1	-
Rock/stock dove	*Columba livia/C oenas*	-	-	<0.1	0.3	-	<0.1	-
Blackbird	*Turdus merula*	-	-	-	-	-	<0.1	-
Crow unidentified	Corvidae	-	-	<0.1	-	-	<0.1	-
Carrion/hooded crow	*Corvus corone*	<0.1	<0.1	<0.1	-	-	-	-
Buzzard	*Buteo buteo*	-	-	<0.1	-	-	-	-
Thrush species	Turdidae	-	<0.1	<0.1	-	-	<0.1	<0.1
Passerine		-	-	-	-	<0.1	<0.1	-
Mammals								
Mammal unidentified		6.1	4.2	4.0	6.4	2.8	3.5	2.1
Cattle	*Bos taurus*	35.9	29.6	42.4	53.3	61.4	44.9	58.8
Cattle-sized		13.2	12.8	14.0	19.8	15.8	21.2	17.3
Sheep/goat	*Ovis aries/Capra hircus*	13.2	15.7	10.8	5.1	10.3	10.4	8.9
Sheep	*Ovis aries*	1.2	0.8	1.1	-	-	0.5	0.1
Sheep-sized		9.5	9.0	7.9	4.1	2.3	6.1	2.8
Goat	*Capra hircus*	-	0.4	-	-	-	<0.1	-
Pig	*Sus scrofa*	14.2	22.4	15.6	8.9	4.9	8.5	7.4
Horse	*Equus caballus*	<0.1	1.5	0.5	1.6	-	1.4	0.9
Dog	*Canis familiaris*	<0.1	0.1	0.2	-	0.4	0.3	0.1
Cat	*Felis catus*	-	0.1	0.2	<0.1	<0.1	0.2	-
Porpoise/dolphin	Cetacea	-	-	-	-	-	<0.1	-
Deer, red	*Cervus elaphus*	-	-	0.3	-	-	0.2	0.9
Deer, fallow	*Dama dama*	2.3	0.3	0.3	<0.1	-	0.5	0.1
Deer, roe	*Capreolus capreolus*	<0.1	0.1	0.2	-	-	<0.1	-
Deer unidentified	Cervidae	<0.1	0.1	0.1	-	-	-	-
Hare	*Lepus europaeus*	<0.1	0.2	<0.1	<0.1	<0.1	<0.1	0.1
Rabbit	*Oryctolagus cuniculus*	<0.1	<0.1	0.2	<0.1	0.7	0.3	0.1
Mole	*Talpa europaea*	-	-	-	-	-	<0.1	-
Rat, black	*Rattus rattus*	-	-	-	-	<0.1	-	-
Rat unidentified	*Rattus sp*	-	<0.1	-	-	-	<0.1	<0.1
Total weight (g) (127413.3)		13076.7	21881.8	27784.6	5146.1	7519.6	41210.2	10794.3

Table 47 Species representation from the wet-sieved assemblages by period, by fragment count (%)

Species Common name	Latin name	Period	MI %	M2 %	M3 %	M4 %	PI %	P2 %
Fish								
Fish unidentified			1.1	0.5	1.0	2.4	-	0.7
Ray/shark			-	<0.1	<0.1	-	-	-
Thornback ray	Raja clavata		0.3	<0.1	0.2	2.4	-	-
Sturgeon	Acipenser sturio		-	<0.1	-	-	-	-
Smelt	Osmerus eperlanus		15.3	9.9	6.3	-	-	-
Salmon family	Salmonidae		-	<0.1	<0.1	-	-	-
Herring	Clupea harengus		1.9	2.2	1.8	-	1.2	-
Herring family	Clupeidae		13.4	21.6	24.4	10.6	5.8	9.7
Pike	Esox lucius		-	-	<0.1	-	-	-
Cod family	Gadidae		13.9	8.5	6.2	2.4	3.5	2.8
Cod	Gadus morhua		1.6	-	0.2	-	-	-
Haddock	Melanogrammus aeglefinus		0.3	<0.1	<0.1	-	-	-
Whiting	Merlangius merlangus		-	<0.1	0.2	-	-	-
Conger eel	Conger conger		-	<0.1	0.2	-	-	-
Eel	Anguilla anguilla		2.2	4.5	3.8	-	0.6	0.7
Plaice/flounder	Pleuronectidae		3.5	1.5	0.6	0.8	-	-
Plaice	Pleuronectes platessa		-	<0.1	-	-	-	-
Carp family	Cyprinidae		3.3	2.8	6.1	-	1.2	0.7
Bream	Abramis brama		-	<0.1	<0.1	-	-	-
Gurnard family	Triglidae		-	0.8	0.1	-	-	-
Mackerel	Scomber scombrus		-	<0.1	0.3	-	-	-
Amphibian								
Frog/toad	Ranidae		-	0.5	0.8	0.8	-	2.1
Birds								
Bird unidentified			4.3	4.6	7.9	4.1	5.3	6.9
Chicken	Gallus gallus		3.2	3.0	3.1	-	1.2	2.8
Chicken-sized			2.8	4.0	5.9	3.3	1.2	9.0
Goose, domestic	Anser anser		-	0.1	0.2	-	1.8	-
Goose-sized			-	<0.1	0.3	-	-	-
Mallard/domestic duck	Anas platyrhynchos		-	-	0.2	-	-	-
Duck unidentified	Anatidae		0.2	<0.1	0.2	-	-	-
Partridge, grey	Perdix perdix		-	0.1	<0.1	-	-	-
Woodcock	Scolopax rusticola		-	<0.1	-	-	-	0.7
Wood pigeon	Columba palumbus		-	-	<0.1	-	-	-
Rock/stock dove	Columba livia/C oenas		-	<0.1	0.2	-	-	-
Crow family	Corvidae		-	-	<0.1	-	-	-
Small corvid	Corvidae		0.2	-	-	-	-	0.7
Thrush species	Turdidae		-	0.1	0.1	-	0.6	-
Large thrush	Turdidae		0.8	0.2	0.3	-	-	-
Small thrush	Turdidae		-	0.5	0.2	-	-	-
Large passerine			0.2	<0.1	-	-	-	-
Small passerine			0.6	3.4	0.7	0.8	1.2	1.4
Mammals								
Mammal unidentified			14.0	13.0	9.1	43.1	56.7	23.4
Cattle	Bos taurus		0.2	-	0.3	0.8	0.6	2.1
Cattle-sized			0.2	0.6	0.6	8.9	1.2	2.1
Sheep/goat	Ovis aries/Capra hircus		1.1	1.4	1.7	4.1	1.2	2.1
Sheep	Ovis aries		-	-	0.1	-	-	-
Sheep-sized			10.0	9.4	9.5	7.3	1.8	17.2
Pig	Sus scrofa		4.1	2.0	2.6	4.9	1.8	0.7
Dog	Canis familiaris		-	0.1	<0.1	-	-	-
Cat	Felis catus		-	-	0.3	-	0.6	1.4
Hare, brown	Lepus europaeus		0.3	<0.1	0.4	-	0.6	-
Rabbit	Oryctolagus cuniculus		-	0.3	0.1	2.4	2.3	3.4
Small mammal unidentified			1.3	0.7	1.8	-	4.7	3.4
Shrew, common	Sorex araneus		-	<0.1	0.3	-	-	0.7

Table 47 (cont)

	Period	M1 %	M2 %	M3 %	M4 %	P1 %	P2 %
Species							
Common name	Latin name						
Rodent unidentified	Rodentia	-	<0.1	0.7	-	-	0.7
Rat unidentified	*Rattus* sp	-	<0.1	0.2	-	-	-
Mouse/vole	Muridae	-	0.2	0.2	-	1.2	2.1
Vole, field	*Microtus agrestis*	-	<0.1	<0.1	-	2.9	-
Vole unidentified		-	<0.1	0.4	0.8	1.2	2.1
Mouse	Muridae	-	-	0.4	-	-	-
Mouse, house	*Mus domesticus*	-	-	0.1	-	-	0.7
Total no. of fragments (5294)		634	2232	1989	123	171	145

casualties in pit-fall features or as inclusions in owl pellets. Common shrew is also extremely widespread throughout mainland Britain apart from some of the highest uplands; they can occur almost anywhere amongst vegetation and leaf litter (Arnold 1993, 27), a habitat preference shared by some of the mollusc assemblage (Gray-Rees and Pipe 1999; below, 7.9). Moles occur throughout mainland Britain where there is sufficiently deep soil and sufficient invertebrates. Although originally a woodland species, they now occur in open pasture, arable land and even mountain moorland (Arnold 1993, 25). Field vole is slightly less ubiquitous; it occurs throughout the bulk of mainland Britain, except for the highest uplands, and has a definite preference for open grassland but also hedgerows and young forestry plantations (ibid, 81). Analysis of the molluscan fauna suggests the presence of open grassland and hedgerows at Merton (Gray-Rees and Pipe 1999). Finally, house mouse and rats are ubiquitous throughout Britain both in and out of doors although mainly associated with human activity (Arnold 1993, 93).

In summary, the wet-sieved local fauna tends to indicate what would be expected to derive from a site of human habitation, activity, food storage and waste disposal in proximity to grassland and hedgerows, possibly with other habitats such as woodland in the vicinity.

7.9 The molluscs

Lisa Gray and Alan Pipe

Introduction

This report is intended to quantify, describe, and interpret the terrestrial, freshwater and marine molluscan assemblages from Merton and environs in order to allow comment on the economy and local habitats of the complex, and to detect any patterns of spatial and temporal change.

Methodology

The molluscan samples derive from the processing of bulk soil samples (above, 7.8, 'Introduction'). The molluscan material, mainly shells and shell fragments, was identified to genus and species using a binocular microscope and following Ellis (1969; 1978), Hayward et al (1996), Macan (1977) and Kerney and Cameron (1979). The identifications were then interpreted using Ellis (1978), Hayward et al (1996), Kerney and Cameron (1979) and Kerney (1999). Table 48 includes a key to the codes used to describe the habitat preference(s) of each recorded species. For each sample group the estimated abundance of each species was expressed using a three-point scale:

+ (1–10 shells)
++ (11–50 shells)
+++ (51–150 shells).

Each identified molluscan species was interpreted in the light of habitat preference and known distribution, and thereby effectively considered as an indicator of past conditions at and around the priory.

Results

A diverse and abundant molluscan fauna was recovered from processed bulk samples. The results are given in tabular form (Tables 48–51) in terms of species and estimated abundance for each sample group. The assemblage from each period/land-use group invariably consisted of three components: 1) edible marine species; 2) freshwater species; 3) terrestrial species. Each assemblage is summarised in terms of habitat preference and distribution in the chronological narrative. The implications of the recovered molluscan fauna for interpretation of the priory and environs are summarised in Chapter 4.

Discussion

All the freshwater and terrestrial molluscs identified are ubiquitous throughout south-east England in suitable habitats. They include species associated with ditches, waterside

Table 48 Mollusc species from selected samples from period M1

Taxon	Common name	Habitat	OA3 [7773] {3240}	OA5 [10635] {4181}	OA5 [10818] {4227}	OA5 [11252] {4364}	OA5 [9531] {3903}
		Land use / Context / Sample					
Lymnaea truncatula	dwarf pond snail	FuTm				+	
Bithynia leachii/B tentaculata	leach's/common Bithynia	Fsmo			+++	++	++
Bithynia spp	common Bithynia	Fsmo		++			
Bathyomphalus contortus	twisted ramshorn	Fsv		+	++		+
Planorbis carinatus	keeled ramshorn	Fsv				+	+
Anisus leucostoma	button/white-lipped ramshorn	Fsv		+++	++	++	+
Sphaerium corneum	horny orb mussel	Ffs			+	+	+
Sphaerium sp	freshwater mussel	F		+			
Valvata cristata	flat valve snail	Fcmosv			+++		
Valvata piscinalis	common valve snail	Fms	+++	+++		+++	+++
Carychium minimum	herald/sedge snail	Tms					+
Cecilioides acicula	blind/agate snail	Tbd	+	+	+	+	
Cochlicella acuta	pointed snail	Tdo		+			+
Cochlicopa lubrica	slippery moss snail	Tms	++	+	++	+	
Columella edentula	toothless chrysalis snail	T		+			
Discus rotundatus	rounded snail	Ts				+	+
Euconulus fulvus	tawny glass snail	Tms				+	
Helix aspersa	garden/common snail	TEsw		+	+		
Cepaea nemoralis	grove/brown-lipped snail	Tmo			+		
Helicella caperata	wrinkled snail	Tdow					+
Oxychilus helveticus	glossy/Swiss glass snail	Thms			+		+
Aegopinella nitidula	smooth/dull glass snail	Thms	++				
Truncatellina cylindrica	cylindrical whorl snail	Tdow			+++		
Vallonia excentrica	eccentric grass snail	Tdow				++	
Vallonia pulchella	smooth/beautiful grass snail	Tmo		+++		+	++
Vallonia spp	grass snail	Tmo/dow	+++	++	+++	+	+
-	Operculae	-			++++		
Buccinum undatum	common whelk	ME	+	+	++	+	+
Ostrea edulis	common/flat oyster	ME			+	++	+

Habitat codes: F – freshwater; u – ubiquitous, wide ranging preferences; s – slow current; f – fast current; c – clean; o – well oxygenated; m – mud/silt substrate; v – well vegetated; T – Terrestrial; b – burrowing/subterranean; d – dry/well-drained; o – open; s – shelter/woodland; h – tolerates/prefers human activity; m – moist; w – walls; M – marine; E – edible
Frequency: + = 1–10 shells; ++ = 11–50 shells; +++ = 51–150 shells

Table 49 Mollusc species from selected samples from period M2 (see Table 48 for key to habitat and frequency codes)

Taxon	Common name	Habitat	B4a [10890] {4261}	B4a [10918] {4291}	B5 [8052] {3779}	B6 [10277] {4064}	B6 [10957] {4317}	S4a/OA5 [10176] {4052}	S4a/OA5 [10255] {4082}	OA5 [10648] {4028}
		Land use / Context / Sample								
Bithynia tentaculata	common Bithynia	Fmos	+		+			++		
Bathyomphalus contortus	twisted ramshorn	Fsv		+						
Lymnaea peregra	common pond snail	Fu	+					++		
Pisidium spp	pea shell	F								+
Planorbis carinatus	keeled ramshorn	Fsv		+						
Anisus leucostoma	button/white-lipped ramshorn	Fsv		+			+		+	
Sphaerium sp	freshwater mussel	F		+					+	
Valvata piscinalis	common valve snail	Fms	+++	+++	+	++	+++		++	++
Carychium minimum	herald/sedge snail	Tms		+						
Cecilioides acicula	blind/agate snail	Tbd	+	+	+	+				+

Table 49 (cont)

Taxon	Common name	Habitat	B4a [10890] {4261}	B4a [10918] {4291}	B5 [8052] {3779}	B6 [10277] {4064}	B6 [10957] {4317}	S4a/OA5 [10176] {4052}	S4a/OA5 [10255] {4082}	OA5 [10648] {4028}
Cochlicella acuta	pointed snail	Tdo		+						
Cochlicopa lubrica	slippery moss snail	Tms	+		+				+	+
Columella edentula	toothless chrysalis snail	To								+
Discus rotundatus	rounded snail	Ts	+	+	+	+	+		+	
Ena obscura	lesser bulin	Ths			+					
Helix aspersa	common/garden snail	TEsw		+						
Oxychilus helveticus	glossy/Swiss snail	Thms					+		+	
Pupilla muscorum	moss chysalis snail	Tdo			+					
Aegopinella nitidula	smooth/dull glass snail	Thms		+	+	+				
Aegopinella pura	clear/delicate glass snail	Tms	+							
Vallonia costata	ribbed grass snail	Tdo			+					
Vallonia excentrica	eccentric grass snail	Tdow							+	
Vallonia pulchella	smooth/beautiful grass snail	Tmo	+	+					++	+
Vallonia sp	grass snail	To	++	+++		+	+		+	+
Euconulus fulvus	tawny glass snail	Tmsu						+		
Succinea putris	large amber snail	Tmv						+		
-	Operculae	-			+					
-	slug plates	-					+			
Buccinum undatum	common whelk	ME						++		
Ostrea edulis	common/flat oyster	ME	+		+	+	+	+++	+	+

Table 50 Mollusc species from selected samples from periods M3 and M4 (see Table 48 for key to habitat and frequency codes)

Taxon	Common name	Habitat	M3 B4a [10682] {4189}	M3 B4a [10777] {4199}	M4 OA7 [8970] {3700}
Bithynia tentaculata	common Bithynia	Fmos			+
Valvata piscinalis	common valve snail	Fms	+++		
Lymnaea peregra	common pond snail	Fu	++		
Acroloxus lacustris	lake limpet	Fc			+
Pisidium spp	freshwater mussel	F		+	
Cecilioides acicula	blind/agate snail	Tbd	+	+	
Cochlicopa lubrica	slippery moss snail	Tms	+++		+
Discus rotundatus	rounded snail	Ts	+		+
Helix aspersa	garden/common snail	TEsw	+	+	
Cepaea nemoralis	grove/brown-lipped snail	Tmo	+		
Pomatias elegans	round-mouthed snail	To		+	
Pupilla muscorum	moss chrysalis snail	Tdo	+		
Aegopinella pura	clear/delicate glass snail	Tms			+
Vallonia costata	ribbed grass snail	Tdo		+	
Vallonia pulchella	smooth/beautiful grass snail	Tmo	++		+
-	Operculae	-	+		
-	slug plates	-	++		
Buccinum undatum	common whelk	ME		+	+
Ostrea edulis	common/flat oyster	ME			

Table 51 *Mollusc species from selected samples from period P2 (see Table 48 for key to habitat and frequency codes)*

Taxon	Common name	Habitat	Land use Context Sample	S4b/OA12 [9348] {5864}	S4b/OA12 [9638] {3902}	OA9 [10791] {4206}	S10/OA12 [10855] {4287}
Acroloxus lacustris	lake limpet	Fcsv		+		++	
Lymnaea truncatula	dwarf pond snail	FuTm				+	
Bithynia spp	Bithynia	Fmso		+	+++	+++	+++
Planorbis carinatus	keeled ramshorn	Fsv		++	+	++	
Bathyomphalus contortus	twisted ramshorn	Fsv			+		
Anisus leucostoma	button/white-lipped ramshorn	Fsv			+	++	
Sphaerium sp	freshwater mussel	F			+		
Valvata piscinalis	common valve snail	Fms			+++	+++	
Cecilioides acicula	blind/agate snail	Tbd		+	+	++	
Cochlicella acuta	pointed snail	Tdo			+	+	+
Cochlicopa lubrica	slippery moss snail	Tms		+			
Columella edentula	toothless chrysalis snail	T					+
Discus rotundatus	rounded snail	T		++	+++	++	+
Helix aspersa	garden/common snail	TE			+	+	+
Oxychilus helveticus	glossy/Swiss glass snail	Tmsh			+		+
Oxychilus spp	glass snail	Tmsh					+++
Pomatias elegans	round-mouthed snail	To			+		
Aegopinella nitidula	smooth/dull glass snail	Thms			++	+	
Aegopinella pura	clear/delicate glass snail	Tms		++			
Vallonia excentrica	eccentric grass snail	Tdow				+++	
Vallonia pulchella	smooth/beautiful grass snail	Tmo		+++	+++	+++	
Vallonia sp	grass snails	To		++	++	++	++
Buccinum undatum	common whelk	ME			+++	++	++
Ostrea edulis	common/flat oyster	ME		+	+	+	+

vegetation, hedgerow bases, walls and leaf-litter, together with those of damp or dry calcareous grassland and those able to exploit gardens and live under human rubbish. Although the assemblages vary between each land-use group they indicate the predominantly rural and uncontaminated character of the priory and its surroundings. Retrieval of freshwater and water margin species from occupation layers and floors strongly suggests the use of rushes and sedges, possibly from nearby ditches and marshes, as floor covering.

After the Dissolution the few available samples are mainly derived from ditches and reflect no significant change in the character of the water bodies or their associated vegetation (Table 51).

7.10 The Coleoptera (beetles)

David Smith

Introduction

Two samples were analysed for insect remains: [7921] (period M2) and [8466] (period M3) both derived from

alluvial deposits in the marshy area (OA9) to the east of the infirmary. It was hoped that an examination of the insect remains might be informative on indications of fresh or tidal waters present, the range of aquatic environments and water conditions present, the surrounding landscape and its possible land use and adjacent settlement or the dumping of settlement materials.

Processing and analysis

This material was processed using the standard method of paraffin flotation as outlined in Kenward et al (1980) to extract any insect remains that it contained. The fragments were sorted from the flot using a binocular microscope at a magnification of x20 and identified by direct comparison to modern specimens housed in the Gorham and Girling collections of British Coleoptera, Department of Ancient History and Archaeology, The University of Birmingham.

The faunas recovered

The insect taxa recovered consisted of the remains of Coleoptera (beetles) with small numbers of Caddis flies (Tricoptera). The Coleoptera are listed in Table 52. The nomenclature used follows that of Lucht (1987).

Table 52 Coleoptera remains recovered from periods M2 and M3 from St Mary Merton

Period	M2	M3
Land use	OA9	OA9
Context	[7921]	[8466]
Carabidae		
Elaphrus riparius (L)	1	-
Clivina fossor (L)	1	-
C ?contracta (Fourcr)	-	1
Bembidion spp	3	-
Bradycellus spp	2	-
Pterostichus sp	-	1
Calathus sp	-	1
Agonum sp	1	-
Haliplidae		
Haliplus spp	2	8
Dytiscidae		
Hydroporus palustris (L)	1	-
H sp	1	-
Stictotarsus duodecimpustulatus (F)	1	-
Potamonectes depressus (F)	-	1
Noterus clavicornis (Geer)	1	-
Colymbetes fuscus (L)	1	2
Gyrinidae		
Gyrinus spp	-	1
Hydraenidae		
Hydraena spp	1	2
H testacea Curt	-	1
Ochthebius spp	5	-
Limnebius spp	1	2
Heloporus spp	5	8
Hydrophilidae		
Coelostoma orbiculare (F)	-	1
Cercyon impressus (Sturm)	4	-
Cercyon spp	4	1
Megasturnum boletophagum (Marsh)	1	-
Hydrobius fusipes (L)	2	1
Laccobius spp	1	1
Enochrus spp	1	1
Cymbiodyta marginella (F)	-	1
Histeridae		
Hister spp	1	1
Catopidae		
Choleva sp	-	1
Orthoperidae		
Corylophus cassidoides (Marsh)	-	1
Orthoperus sp	-	1
Staphylinidae		
Lesteva longelytrata (Goeze)	1	1
Omalium sp	-	1
Oxytelus rugosus (F)	2	1
O sculpturatus Grav	9	1
O nitidulus Grav		1
Stenus spp	2	2
Lathrobium spp	1	1
Xantholinus sp	1	-
Philonthus spp	2	-
Staphylinus sp	1	-
Quedius sp	1	-
Bolitobius sp	-	1
Aleocharinidae gen and spp indeterminate	1	1
Elateridae		
Agroites spp	1	1
Buprestidae		
Trachys pumilus III	-	1
Helodidae		
Helodidae gen and spp indeterminate	1	3
Dryopidae		
Oulimnius spp	4	10
Elmis aenea (Müll)	-	1
Esolus parallelepipedus (Müll)	-	1
Riolus subviolaceus (Müll)	1	-
Nitidulidae		
Meligethes sp	-	1
Brachypterus sp	1	-
Cucujidae		
Monotoma sp	-	1
Cryptophagidae		
Cryptophagus sp	-	1
Atomaria sp	-	1
Phalacridae		
Phalacrus corruscus (Panz)	1	-
P caricis Sturm	1	1
Olibrus aeneus (F)	1	-
Lathridiidae		
Lathridius minutus (Group)	-	2
Corticaria spp	1	1
Ptinidae		
Ptinus sp	-	1
Anthicidae		
Anthicus antherinus (L)	1	-
Scarabaeidae		
Aphodius spp	4	1
Chyrsomelidae		
Donacia crassipes F	1	-
D marginata Hoppe	1	1
Plateumaris sericea (L)	27	2
P affinus (Kunze)	-	2
Prasocuris phellandri (L)	-	1
Phyllotreta sp	1	-
Chalcoides sp	1	-
Chaetocnema spp	3	-
Bruchidae		
Bruchus sp	1	-
Scolytidae		
Hylesinus oleiperda (F)	-	1
Pteleobius vittatus (F)	-	1
Cuculionidae		
Apion cerdo Gerst	2	-
A sp	-	1
Phyllobius sp	-	1
Barypeithes sp	-	1
Sitona lineatus (L)	1	1
S sp	2	-
Bagous sp	1	-
Notaris sp	1	-
Sitophilus granarius (L)	-	1
Limnobaris pilistriata (Steph)	1	-
Ceutorhynchus contractus (Marsh)	1	-
C sp	1	1
Mecinus pyraster (Hbst)	-	1
Rhynchaenus sp	-	1

Discussion

The majority of the species present in both faunas are water beetles, or species that are associated with waterside and emergent vegetation.

The majority of the water beetles, such as Hydroporus palustris, Noterus clavicornis, Colymbetes fuscus, Hydreana testacea and the Gyrinus 'whirligig' beetle are typical of slow flowing and well vegetated waters such as ponds and freshwater swamps (Hansen 1987; Nilsson and Holmen 1995). Many of the species of hydrophilids present, such as Coelostoma orbiculare and Cymbiodyta marginella, are also found at the shallow edges of such waters.

There are clear indications in both samples for the presence of a relatively rich flora of emergent plants. The large numbers of Plateumaris sericea and P affinus beetles indicates a dominant presence of Carex or Cladium sedges (Koch 1992). This area also apparently contained the large bur-reed Sparganium ramosum that is the foodplant for Donacia marginata (ibid). Also present are a number of phalacrid species of beetle. These feed on a range of smuts and moulds that develop on such waterside plants.

Perhaps the single discordant note is that a number of

species of water beetle indicative of faster flowing waters, often running across sands or gravels, are also present. As such they are normally associated with larger rivers or active streams. Amongst these are the two dytiscid beetles *Stictotarsus duodecimpustulatus* and *Potamonectes depressus* and the elmids *Esolus parellelepipedus* and *Riolus subviolaceus* (Holland 1972; Nilsson and Holmen 1995). The other elmids present are also found in faster channel conditions but are thought to perhaps have a higher tolerance for slower waters and silts than other species in this family. A possible explanation for the presence of these species in an area of apparently slow flowing water is that they may have been carried in from a larger and active river during times of floods.

What is clear is that this body of water was not, to any extent, saline or tidal. There are a wide range of beetle and insect species that exploit these conditions but none of these were recovered here.

A limited number of the species may perhaps suggest the nature and land use of the surrounding ground. There is a suggestion that grassland or rough ground was present. This is suggested by the presence of beetles that feed on plants commonly found as weeds in these conditions. For example, *Mecinus pyraster* feeds on ribwort plantain (*Plantago lanceolata*), *Sitona lineatus* on clovers (Koch 1992) and *Apion cerdo* feeds on vetches (*Vicia* spp). A few individuals of *Aphodius* dung beetles may suggest that herbivores were present in the area. There is also some evidence for nearby scrub or woodland which is suggested by the leaf minor *Rhynchaenus* sp and the two scolytid 'bark beetles' *Hylesinus oleiperda* and *Pteleobius vittatus*, which are associated with ash (*Fraxinus*) and elm (*Ulmus*).

There are a few species such as the cryptophagid, lathridiid and ptinid species that, although present in the natural environment, are also commonly associated with human settlement. *Sitophilus granarius*, the granary weevil, is a pest of stored grain that does not occur in the wild in Britain and is the only species found at Merton that is dependent on human settlement.

In summary, the insects present suggest that this area of the site contained slow water and marsh plants. There are suggestions of either rough ground or grassland in the area. What is clear is that during the period of the formation of these deposits there is no evidence for any tidal influence.

7.11 The human bone

Jan Conheeney

The assemblage

In total 664 burials were available for analysis, making this one of the largest and, therefore, most valuable monastic assemblages excavated to date. It was possible to assign 83% of the burials to four phases within the time span, something often not possible with material from London due to the density of burials, thus further increasing the research value of the assemblage (Waldron 1994, 10–27). The size of the sample has meant that even with subdivision by period and area of the site, subsamples of sufficient size for meaningful analysis still remain (Table 53).

Table 53 The human bone assemblage subsamples with area descriptions and sample numbers

Period	Land use and sub-area	Description	No. of individuals analysed	Subsample no. (archive)
M1	OA3	south burial area	12	3
M1	OA6	north burial area	82	2
M2	B1n	church – north transept	2	4
M2	B1s	church – south transept	3	5
M2	B3b	chapter house	3	24
M2	OA3	south burial area	22	7
M2	OA6	north burial area	83	6
M3	B1n	church – north transept	36	8 + 9
M3	B1e	church – eastern extension	6	23
M3	B3b	chapter house	1	13
M3	OA3	south burial area – main body of cemetery	78	11
M3	OA3i	south burial area – burials in rows near infirmary	31	12
M3	OA6	north burial area	129	10
M4	B1ac	church – aisle crossing	1	15
M4	B1n	church – north transept	3	14
M4	B1nn	church – north nave	12	16
M4	B3b	chapter house	19	17 + 18
M4	OA6e	north burial area – east of church	2	19
M4	OA6w	north burial area – west of church	26	20
Unphased M1–M4	B1	church	31	22
Unphased M1–M4	OA6	north burial area	82	21
Total			664	

Integrity of the sample

There was a certain amount of disturbance of burials during the life of the priory accounting for the disarticulated bone and charnel pits (Conheeney 1995). This material has not been included in the analysis and the burials reported on were on the whole intact and undisturbed although highly fragmented. The low levels of intrusive material included in the burial contexts corroborate this level of integrity. A small amount of intrusive human bone is a common occurrence in densely used burial sites.

Methods

Data were recorded on to the MoLAS Oracle 7 database (with the exception of the chapter house burials: see below). The age of immature individuals was estimated using dental development, state of epiphyseal fusion and diaphyseal lengths (Ferembach et al 1980; Brothwell 1981; Ubelaker 1984; Bass 1995). Adults were aged by tooth wear, morphology of the pubic symphysis and degree of fusion of cranial sutures (Brothwell 1981; Meindl and Lovejoy 1985; Brooks and Suchey 1990). Individuals were assigned to an age group on the basis of the estimate, and it is these groups that are compared in the report in an effort to avoid the danger of regarding age estimates as absolute ages rather than a summary of relative age (Table 54; Table 63). The most probable sex of an adult was decided on the basis of the dimorphic characteristics of the pelvis and skull, tooth crown dimensions and several measurements of the post-cranial skeleton (Phenice 1969; Ferembach et al 1980; Brothwell 1981; Roesing 1983; Bass 1995). Most weight was given to the pelvic data as these are the most reliable indicator of sex, but as many characteristics or measurements as possible were considered to arrive at an overall consensus of the sex of an individual (Table 55; Table 63). This proved especially good practice in this instance, as the sciatic notch alone proved a very poor indicator of sex.

Standard cranial and post-cranial measurements were taken (Brothwell 1981; Bass 1995). Stature was calculated using the regression formulae of Trotter and Gleser (1952; 1958); lower limb lengths were used for this as lower limbs tend to give a more accurate estimate than upper limbs (Buikstra and Ubelaker 1994). Handedness was considered by comparing left and right humeral length with the supposition that the dominant hand usually corresponds with the side of the longest humerus. Cranial, femoral and tibial measurements were used in the calculation of a series of indices, the interpretation of which is open to debate, but which do appear to reveal variability within and between groups (Mays 1998, 96–100). The severely fragmented nature of the sample meant that an impression of the shape of very few skulls could be derived by measurement. A selection of enthesopathies were recorded as a possible indicator of variation in physical activity between groups, bearing in mind the cautionary note of Stirland (1991). The majority of these were present in a similar order of magnitude between the sexes and between the subsamples

formed by consideration of area and period, and the data are available from the MoLAS archive. The prevalence of enthesopathies that indicated some possible variation between groupings was noted.

Cranial, dental and post-cranial non-metric traits were recorded (Berry and Berry 1967; Finnegan 1978; Hillson 1986). Those traits of interest, which appeared to indicate some variation in prevalence between subsamples, are included in the report (below and Table 56 dental, Table 57 skeletal). Data on the remainder are available from the archive.

Dental and skeletal pathology were recorded in detail for each individual (in archive). Again, only those results of interest are presented here (below and Tables 59–62 dental; Table 58 and Tables 64–70 skeletal).

Subsamples with no cases are omitted from the tabulated data; the total number of individuals from all the subsamples is 664. The chapter house burials had been examined and reported on previously by Tony Waldron (n d [1977]) and were not re-recorded as part of this post-excavation project; they are discussed here, but are generally not included in the detailed tabulated datasets.

Preservation

Preservation was defined in two ways: the proportion of the skeleton present and the condition of the remains. Condition was scored on a scale of 1–3, where the majority of required data was recoverable from a grade 1 skeleton and very little from a grade 3. Over a third of the sample had more than 80% of the skeleton present (34.7%) and there was a general trend towards completeness of the skeleton rather than a normal distribution, with 68.2% of the sample with more than 50% of the skeleton present. However, the great majority of the sample fell into condition grade 2, namely that the bone surface itself was in reasonable condition, but owing to fragmentation, some of the metrical data would not be recoverable. Only 27.1% were classified as condition grade 1, and 4.2% as grade 3.

Characteristics of the skeletal material

c 1117–1222 (period M1)

SOUTH BURIAL AREA (OA3)

Twelve individuals were available for analysis (Table 54; Table 55). All of the 12 were adults, predominantly males (six mature adult males, two older adult males, an adult male otherwise not aged), together with a mature adult female and two adult individuals of indeterminate sex. The stature of the female and a single male could be estimated as 1.62m and 1.78m respectively. The cranial index of a single male could be calculated and this indicated he was mesocranial. The female could be assessed in terms of femoral form or flattening, and both her femurs were eumeric. Seven males could be measured and the most common form bilaterally was eumeric. The female could be assessed also for tibial flattening and proved to be

Table 54 Age composition of the human bone assemblage as a percentage of the subsample

Subsample: land use, period	No. in subsample	Age composition (%)								
		Child 1–6 years	Child 7–12 years	Child 13–16 years	Young adult 17–25 years	Mature adult 26–45 years	Older adult 45+ years	Adult not aged	Unknown age	Child not aged
B1 church										
M2 north transept	2	-	-	-	50.0	-	-	-	50.0	-
M2 south transept	3	-	33.3	-	-	33.3	33.3	-	-	-
M3 north transept	36	-	-	-	11.1	52.8	27.8	8.3	-	-
M3 eastern extension	6	-	-	-	-	-	33.3	66.7	-	-
M4 north transept	3	-	-	-	-	100.0	-	-	-	-
M4 aisle crossing	1	-	-	-	-	-	100.0	-	-	-
M4 north nave	12	-	-	8.3	-	50.0	33.3	8.3	-	-
Unphased	31	-	3.2	-	3.2	45.2	25.8	22.6	-	-
Total no.	94		2	1	6	43	26	15	1	
B3b chapter house										
M2	3	-	-	-	-	33.3	66.7	-	-	-
M3	1	-	-	-	-	-	100.0	-	-	-
M4	19	-	-	-	5.3	26.3	52.6	10.5	5.3	-
Total no.	23				1	6	13	2	1	
OA3 south burial area										
M1	12	-	-	-	-	58.3	16.7	25.0	-	-
M2	22	-	-	-	-	40.9	40.9	18.2	-	-
M3 main body	78	-	-	-	5.1	48.7	33.3	11.5	1.3	-
M3 burials in rows	31	-	-	6.5	6.5	38.7	41.9	6.5	-	-
Total no.	143			2	6	66	50	18	1	
OA6 north burial area										
M1	82	2.4	-	-	1.2	43.9	29.3	22.0	1.2	-
M2	83	1.2	1.2	-	6.0	43.4	28.9	14.5	3.6	1.2
M3	129	-	2.3	3.9	9.3	46.5	24.0	13.2	0.7	-
M4 (east)	2	-	-	-	50.0	50.0	-	-	-	-
M4 (west)	26	-	7.6	-	7.7	46.2	23.1	15.4	-	-
Unphased	82	-	3.7	3.7	6.1	40.2	13.4	26.8	4.9	1.2
Total no.	404	3	9	8	26	178	96	73	9	2
	664	3	11	11	39	293	185	108	12	2

eurycnemic on both sides. Five males could be measured and the most common form was eurycnemic on the right side and split between eurycnemic and mesocnemic on the left. Dental non-metric traits present in the subsample included crowding, unusual wear and enamel pearls (Table 56). The skeletal non-metric traits that were of interest as they revealed some variation in prevalence between the subsamples are presented in Table 57 (all other traits recorded were of a similar order between sexes and subsamples). Males of this subsample scored a high rate of supraorbital notches compared to many of the other subsamples.

NORTH BURIAL AREA (OA6)

The skeletal material from 82 individuals was analysed and comprised 80 adults and two children (aged 1–6 years). The adults included 64 males (31 mature adults, 22 older adults, 10 only classifiable as adult and 1 not assignable to an age group) and six females (1 young adult, 3 mature adults and 2 older adults). The sex of ten individuals could not be determined (two mature adults and eight could not be aged more precisely than adult). Stature could be estimated for only five of the

males and an average of 1.74m (within the range 1.66–1.78m) was indicated. The cranial index could be calculated for three male skulls, two of which were brachycranial and one was dolichocranial, that is the two extremes of skull form were present. The femoral shape of six females and 50 males could be measured and the femurs of both sexes were most commonly eumeric on both sides. Similarly, the tibial form of two females and 43 males could be calculated, and this was eurycnemic on both sides. Several dental non-metric traits were present: crowding, malformation of teeth, additional roots, rotation, unusual wear, and spacing (Table 56). The males of the subsample had a slightly high rate of supraorbital notch compared to the majority of the subsamples, but there was nothing of particular note amongst the skeletal non-metric traits (Table 57).

1222–*c* 1300 (period M2)

THE CHURCH (B1)

Two individuals were available for analysis from the north transept (B1n). One was a young adult male; the other was

Table 55 *Sex composition of the human bone assemblage as a percentage of the subsample*

Subsample: land use, period	No. in subsample	Sex composition (%) Child (not sexed)	Male adult and male child (13–16 years)	Female adult	Uncertain sex adult or unknown age	Sex ratio male:female
B1 church						
M2 north transept	2	-	50.0	-	50.0	-
M2 south transept	3	33.3	66.7	-	-	male
M3 north transept	36	-	83.3	13.9	2.8	6.0:1
M3 eastern extension	6	-	83.3	-	16.7	male
M4 north transept	3	-	100.0	-	-	male
M4 aisle crossing	1	-	100.0	-	-	male
M4 north nave	12	-	91.7	8.3	-	11.0:1
Unphased	31	3.2	83.9	6.5	6.5	12.9:1
Total no.	94	2	79	8	5	
B3b chapter house						
M2	3	-	100.0	-	-	male
M3	1	-	100.0	-	-	male
M4	19	-	94.7	-	5.3	male
Total no.	23		22		1	
OA3 south burial area						
M1	12	-	75.0	8.3	16.7	9.0:1
M2	22	-	81.8	-	18.2	male
M3 main body	78	-	84.6	2.6	12.8	32.5:1
M3 burials in rows	31	6.5	83.9	-	9.7	male
Total no.	143	2	119	3	19	
OA6 north burial area						
M1	82	2.4	78.0	7.3	12.2	10.7:1
M2	83	2.4	68.7	14.5	14.5	4.8:1
M3	129	5.4	74.4	9.3	10.9	8.0:1
M4 (east)	2	-	100.0	-	-	male
M4 (west)	26	7.7	84.6	-	7.7	male
Unphased	82	4.9	68.3	6.1	20.7	11.2:1
Total no.	404	17	297	35	55	
	664	21	517	46	80	

Table 56 *Dental non-metric traits: number of dentitions affected (see Table 53 for key to land use abbreviations)*

Subsample (period: land use)	Sex	No. of individuals with dentition	Crowding	Hypercementosis	Hypocementosis	Malformation	Peg tooth	Additional roots
M1: OA3	M	5	5	0	0	0	0	0
M1: OA6	F	5	3	0	0	0	0	0
M1: OA6	M	38	8	0	0	1	0	1
M2: B1n	M	1	0	0	0	0	0	0
M2: B1s	M	2	9	0	0	0	0	0
M2: OA3	M	14	15	1	0	0	1	1
M2: OA6	F	4	0	4	0	1	2	0
M2: OA6	M	39	4	2	0	3	2	0
M3: B1e	M	4	0	0	0	0	0	0
M3: B1n	M	27	12	0	0	8	1	0
M3: OA3	F	2	1	0	0	0	0	0
M3: OA3	M	52	22	0	1	2	3	1
M3: OA3i	M	15	4	1	0	0	0	1
M3: OA6	F	5	8	2	0	0	0	2
M3: OA6	M	61	9	2	0	5	0	3
M4: B1n	M	3	0	0	0	0	0	0
M4: B1nn	M	10	6	0	0	0	0	0
M4: OA6e	M	2	6	0	0	0	0	0
M4: OA6w	M	17	6	0	0	0	0	0
Unphased: B1	F	1	0	0	0	0	0	0
Unphased: B1	M	17	9	0	0	4	0	0
Unphased: OA6	F	4	0	0	0	0	0	0
Unphased: OA6	M	39	24	0	0	1	0	1

severely truncated and age and sex could not be determined. Both his femurs were eumeric and both his tibias were eurycnemic. The only dental non-metric trait was a Carabelli's cusp and there were too few individuals to comment on the skeletal non-metric traits present (Table 57), or on the most frequent skeletal pathology present (Table 58).

The site records describe a group of four individuals in the south transept (B1s). Three of these survived to analysis stage. The average stature of the two males present was 1.74m (1.79m and 1.68m). The femoral shape of both adults could be calculated and both were eumeric on both sides. Most common tibial form for both adults was eurycnemic on both sides. There are too few individuals in this subsample on which to draw any valid observations.

The only notable difference between the groups from the two transepts was the high rate of alveolar resorption and periodontal disease in those from the south transept compared to all other subsamples (Table 61), and an absence of the two conditions in those from the north transept. This is most likely simply a product of the very small sample size and, as both can be age related conditions, the presence of the older individual in the south transept.

THE CHAPTER HOUSE (B3B)
Of nine burials interred within the chapter house (B3b), only three complete or near-complete skeletons, all male, survived for analysis: one mature adult and two older adults. Stature could be estimated for two of the skeletons: 1.83m and 1.74m. None had surviving dentition. The prevalence of skeletal pathology is to be found in Table 58. Individual [602] (not shown on period plan) had mild diffuse idiopathic skeletal hyperostosis (DISH).

SOUTH BURIAL AREA (OA3)
Twenty-two individuals were available for analysis: 18 males (9 mature adults, 9 older adults) and four whose sex could not be determined (all aged as adult). The stature of two males was estimated at 1.8m and 1.75m. The skull of a single male could be measured in order to calculate the cranial index; it was brachycranial. Fourteen males could be included in an assessment of femoral flattening; the most common shape of the femur on both sides was eumeric. The tibial form of ten males could be assessed, and this was most commonly eurycnemic on both sides. A number of dental non-metric traits were present including crowding, hypercementosis, a peg tooth, additional roots, rotation; unusual wear and Carabelli's cusp (Table 56). With regard to skeletal non-metric traits, the subsample had high rates of acetabular crease; double calcanear facet; posterior condylar canal; and supraorbital notches relative to the other subsamples, and low rates of hypotrochanteric fossa and supraorbital foramen (Table 57). The prevalence of skeletal pathology is to be found in Table 58 and dental pathology in Tables 59–62. The subsample had a high rate of ante-mortem tooth loss (Table 59) and low prevalence of alveolar resorption and periodontal disease relative to the other subsamples (Table 61).

NORTH BURIAL AREA (OA6)
Eighty-three individuals were available for analysis: 2 children (1–6 years and 7–12 years); 57 males (4 young adults, 30 mature adults, 19 older adults and 4 adults); 12 females (6

Hypodontia	Rotation	Unusual wear	Deciduous retention	Spacing	Enamel pearl	Carabelli's cusp	Taurodontism	Shovel shape
0	0	2	0	0	1	0	0	0
0	0	0	0	0	0	0	0	0
0	7	8	0	5	0	0	0	0
0	0	0	0	0	0	2	0	0
0	0	0	0	0	0	0	0	0
0	2	13	0	0	0	2	0	0
0	0	0	0	0	0	0	0	0
0	8	1	6	4	0	3	0	0
0	0	0	0	0	0	0	0	0
1	8	0	1	3	1	0	1	0
0	0	0	0	0	0	0	0	0
1	15	0	0	4	1	8	0	0
0	2	0	0	2	0	0	0	1
1	1	7	0	0	0	0	0	0
0	4	1	0	27	0	2	0	6
0	2	0	0	0	0	0	0	0
0	2	0	0	0	0	1	0	0
0	0	0	0	0	0	2	0	0
1	5	0	0	0	0	1	0	0
1	0	0	0	0	0	0	0	0
0	2	0	0	5	0	2	0	0
0	0	0	1	0	0	0	0	0
0	5	5	0	0	0	0	0	0

Table 57 *Skeletal non-metric traits of interest: prevalence rates expressed as a percentage of the observable number in the subsample (see Table 53 for key to land use abbreviations)*

Subsample (period: land use)	Sex	Acetabular crease		Atlas double facet		Calcaneal double facet		Coronal wormians		Hypotrochanteric fossa		Lambdoid wormians	
		No.	%	No.	%	No.	%	No.	%	No.	%	No.	%
M1: OA3	F	2	100.0	0	-	2	100.0	0	-	2	100.0	0	-
M1: OA3	M	0	-	0	-	0	-	2	100.0	8	25.0	6	83.3
M1: OA6	F	0	-	0	-	5	80.0	2	100.0	5	20.0	6	66.7
M1: OA6	M	73	11.0	56	14.3	58	53.5	24	66.7	85	36.5	26	80.8
M2: Bln	M	0	-	0	-	0	-	0	-	2	100.0	2	100.0
M2: OA3	M	21	28.6	21	28.6	14	78.6	13	69.2	21	19.1	14	85.7
M2: OA6	F	15	33.3	6	16.7	9	44.4	4	100.0	15	20.0	5	20.0
M2: OA6	M	82	11.0	51	15.7	47	44.7	43	67.4	85	20.0	44	93.2
M3: Bln	M	37	7.5	28	8.2	41	42.7	25	87.7	34	20.6	21	100.0
M3: Ble	M	8	12.5	0	-	8	87.5	9	66.7	7	28.6	6	100.0
M3: Bln	F	3	100.0	0	-	0	-	0	-	0	-	0	-
M3: OA3	F	0	-	0	-	0	-	0	-	0	-	0	-
M3: OA3	M	70	15.7	71	8.5	49	51.0	31	61.3	79	13.9	39	84.6
M3: OA3i	M	36	13.9	26	23.1	22	50.0	18	94.4	35	28.6	18	61.1
M3: OA6	F	16	25.0	12	8.3	13	38.5	6	33.3	19	5.3	6	66.7
M3: OA6	M	131	13.0	97	9.3	96	57.1	53	83.0	137	29.2	52	61.5
M4: Blac	M	0	-	0	-	1	100.0	0	-	0	-	0	-
M4: Bln	M	0	-	4	25.0	6	33.3	6	66.7	0	-	5	60.0
M4: Blnn	F	0	-	0	-	0	-	1	100.0	0	-	1	100.0
M4: Blnn	M	18	33.3	14	14.3	15	73.3	15	73.3	18	38.9	18	72.2
M4: OA6e	M	0	-	0	-	4	75.0	4	100.0	4	100.0	2	100.0
M4: OA6w	M	23	4.3	26	30.8	21	52.4	11	54.6	27	40.7	13	100.0
Unphased: Bl	F	2	100.0	0	-	2	50.0	0	-	4	100.0	1	100.0
Unphased: Bl	M	33	9.1	24	25.0	27	48.2	26	76.9	31	16.1	26	96.2
Unphased: OA6	F	5	20.0	6	33.3	0	-	0	-	6	50.0	0	-
Unphased: OA6	M	69	20.3	53	9.4	52	50.0	30	80.0	77	27.3	39	82.1

Table 58 *Prevalence rates of skeletal pathology expressed as a percentage of the number of individuals in the subsample with the relevant part of the skeleton present (see Table 53 for key to land use abbreviations)*

Subsample (period: land use)	No. in subsample	Anomalies (%)	Bunions (%)	Malignant cancer (%)	Benign cancer (%)	Cribra orbitalia (%)	DISH* (%)	Fractures (%)	General degenerative conditions (%)	Gout (%)	Haematoma (%)
M1: OA3	12	16.7	-	-	-	20.0	8.3	-	41.7	-	-
M1: OA6	82	11.0	-	1.2	1.2	-	8.5	19.5	45.1	2.6	3.7
M2: Bln	2	-	-	-	-	-	-	-	-	-	-
M2: Bls	3	-	-	-	33.3	33.3	33.3	-	33.3	-	33.3
M2: B3b	3	-	-	-	-	-	33.3	-	66.7	-	-
M2: OA3	22	-	-	-	-	-	18.2	4.5	50.0	-	-
M2: OA6	83	4.8	1.2	-	4.8	4.1	1.2	13.3	47.0	-	1.2
M3: Ble	6	-	16.7	-	-	16.7	16.7	-	16.7	-	-
M3: Bln	36	13.9	2.8	5.6	5.6	11.1	8.3	13.9	36.1	-	2.8
M3: B3b	1	100.0	-	-	-	-	100.0	-	-	-	-
M3: OA3	78	10.3	-	1.3	7.7	6.2	11.5	9.0	44.9	-	1.3
M3: OA3i	31	12.9	3.2	-	3.2	10.0	12.9	12.9	38.7	-	-
M3: OA6	129	7.8	-	1.6	5.4	6.1	9.3	19.4	41.9	-	1.6
M4: Blac	1	-	-	-	-	-	100.0	-	-	-	-
M4: Bln	3	33.3	-	-	-	-	33.3	-	66.7	-	-
M4: Blnn	12	-	-	-	16.7	-	16.7	16.7	75.0	-	-
M4: B3b	19	21.1	-	-	-	-	10.5	-	5.3	-	-
M4: OA6e	2	-	-	-	-	-	-	-	-	-	-
M4: OA6w	26	7.7	-	-	-	19.2	-	11.5	38.5	-	-
Unphased: Bl	31	19.4	-	-	6.5	12.0	6.5	12.9	51.6	-	-
Unphased: OA6	82	14.6	-	-	2.4	-	4.9	9.8	36.6	-	-

*: diffuse idiopathic skeletal hyperostosis
**: healed periosteal bone on pulmonary surface of ribs

Lateral squatting facet		Mastoid foramen		Parietal foramen		Posterior condylar canal		Pterygoid spurs		Septal aperture		Supraorbital foramen		Supraorbital notch	
No.	%	No.	%	No.	%	No.	%	No.	%	No.	%	No.	%	No.	%
0	-	0	-	0	-	0	-	0	-	0	-	0	-	0	-
0	-	5	40.0	6	33.3	0	-	6	66.7	0	-	3	33.3	4	75.0
4	25.0	8	62.5	8	37.5	5	40.0	0	-	7	42.9	5	20.0	5	60.0
41	19.5	62	41.9	44	56.8	16	18.8	68	35.3	72	1.4	39	30.8	39	71.8
0	-	0	-	0	-	1	100.0	0	-	0	-	2	100.0	0	100.0
12	8.3	22	45.5	13	30.8	13	46.2	22	36.4	18	11.1	19	10.5	19	79.0
5	40.0	5	80.0	6	16.7	3	100.0	8	25.0	10	20.0	6	50.0	6	33.3
41	19.5	58	58.6	44	34.1	22	22.7	57	28.1	68	4.4	40	42.5	44	45.5
31	16.0	41	35.5	32	56.1	16	17.2	43	26.7	0	-	43	35.2	42	52.5
0	-	9	44.4	6	50.0	6	16.7	6	66.7	0	-	8	25.0	7	57.1
0	-	1	100.0	4	50.0	0	-	0	-	0	-	0	-	1	100.0
0	-	2	100.0	0	-	0	-	0	-	0	-	0	-	4	50.0
33	12.1	86	53.5	42	50.0	29	27.6	77	23.4	77	2.6	46	30.4	46	52.2
18	5.6	30	43.3	16	68.8	15	53.3	30	20.0	31	6.5	19	10.5	19	57.9
11	27.3	18	22.2	12	8.3	2	50.0	12	8.3	16	18.8	6	33.3	7	71.4
81	13.6	104	53.9	69	49.3	49	34.7	112	28.6	113	3.5	63	33.3	64	67.2
0	-	0	-	0	-	0	-	0	-	0	-	0	-	0	-
0	-	5	60.0	4	50.0	6	33.3	6	33.3	0	-	0	-	4	100.0
0	-	0	-	0	-	0	-	0	-	0	-	0	-	2	100.0
8	12.5	19	47.4	15	73.3	11	36.4	16	25.0	0	-	12	25.0	14	57.1
0	-	0	-	4	50.0	4	25.0	0	-	0	-	0	-	0	-
0	-	25	64.0	16	12.5	18	11.1	25	24.0	0	-	18	61.1	20	35.0
0	-	0	-	0	-	0	-	0	-	1	100.0	0	-	0	-
21	9.5	33	57.6	22	50.0	11	27.3	28	64.3	0	-	21	23.8	22	68.2
0	-	5	20.0	0	-	0	-	8	25.0	5	20.0	2	50.0	2	50.0
30	10.0	58	34.5	43	55.8	23	8.7	58	34.5	0	-	31	16.1	32	68.8

Hyperostosis frontalis interna (%)	Infection (%)	Osteoarthritis (%)	Osteophytosis (%)	Osteochondritis dissecans (%)	Osteoporosis (%)	Paget's disease (%)	Periosteal new bone (%)	Rib lesions** (%)	Scurvy (%)	Spondylolysis (%)
-	-	41.7	41.7	-	-	-	58.3	25.0	-	-
-	7.3	30.5	28.0	7.3	1.2	2.4	28.0	17.1	1.2	-
-	-	-	-	-	-	-	-	25.0	-	-
-	-	33.3	-	33.3	-	-	33.3	33.3	-	-
-	-	-	-	33.3	-	-	-	-	-	-
-	-	45.5	36.4	18.2	-	-	40.9	18.2	-	-
2.0	-	37.3	16.9	8.4	1.2	1.2	31.3	10.8	1.2	-
-	16.7	50.0	16.7	-	-	-	33.3	33.3	-	-
2.8	-	69.4	30.6	8.3	-	2.8	16.7	13.9	-	-
-	-	-	-	100.0	-	-	-	-	-	-
-	1.3	33.3	26.9	9.0	-	2.6	39.7	28.2	-	-
-	-	29.0	16.1	3.2	-	3.2	32.3	9.7	-	3.2
-	1.6	37.2	29.5	17.1	1.6	2.3	26.4	16.3	-	2.4
-	100.0	-	-	-	-	-	100.0	-	-	-
-	-	-	-	-	-	-	33.3	-	-	-
-	-	16.7	16.7	16.7	-	8.3	16.7	8.3	-	-
-	-	5.3	10.5	-	-	-	5.3	-	-	-
-	-	-	-	50.0	-	-	-	-	-	-
-	-	46.2	23.1	15.4	-	-	19.2	23.1	-	3.8
4.0	-	45.2	12.9	9.7	-	-	35.5	35.5	-	3.2
1.8	2.4	25.6	14.6	4.9	1.2	2.4	29.3	13.4	-	2.4

Table 59 Prevalence of post-mortem and ante-mortem tooth loss and unerupted teeth for female and male adults and children, expressed as a percentage of surviving bone sockets (see Table 53 for key to land use abbreviations)

Period: land use	Sex	No. of sockets	Post-mortem loss (%)	Ante-mortem loss (%)	Unerupted teeth (%)
Adults					
MI: OA3	F	24	-	-	12.5
MI: OA6	F	126	4.8	13.5	2.4
M2: OA6	F	97	12.4	10.3	1.0
M3: BIn	F	24	25.0	41.7	-
M3: OA3	F	58	-	10.3	-
M3: OA6	F	129	4.7	3.9	0.8
M4: BInn	F	28	12.1	25.0	3.6
Unphased: BI	F	12	8.3	33.3	-
Unphased: OA6	F	91	11.0	14.3	3.3
MI: OA3	M	93	9.7	20.4	3.2
MI: OA6	M	704	9.9	11.9	2.4
M2: BIn	M	14	-	14.3	14.3
M2: BIs	M	59	5.1	6.8	3.4
M2: OA3	M	382	12.6	20.4	2.9
M2: OA6	M	789	6.3	10.6	2.0
M3: BIe	M	89	33.7	21.3	1.1
M3: BIn	M	677	8.9	10.2	2.4
M3: OA3	M	1003	11.9	9.2	3.7
M3: OA3i	M	308	9.4	12.0	1.3
M3: OA6	M	1448	13.7	13.0	2.0
M4: BIn	M	88	25.0	20.5	2.3
M4: BInn	M	166	15.1	9.0	4.2
M4: OA6e	M	64	-	4.7	-
M4: OA6w	M	378	9.3	7.7	2.6
Unphased: BI	M	400	10.8	4.3	3.8
Unphased: OA6	M	699	8.7	12.6	2.3
Children					
M3: OA6	-	16	-	25.0	-
M4: BInn	-	32	-	-	6.3
Unphased: OA6	-	29	-	17.2	-

Table 60 Prevalence of hypoplasia, caries and calculus for female and male adults and children expressed as a percentage of the teeth present (see Table 53 for key to land use abbreviations)

Period: land use	Sex	No. of teeth	Hypoplasia (%)	Caries (%)	Calculus (%)
Adults					
MI: OA3	F	21	4.8	-	95.2
MI: OA6	F	115	3.5	7.0	90.4
M2: OA6	F	76	13.2	11.8	135.5
M3: BIn	F	8	-	50.0	462.5
M3: OA3	F	56	3.6	-	100.0
M3: OA6	F	125	24.8	18.4	133.6
M4: BInn	F	13	-	23.1	107.6
Unphased: BI	F	10	-	-	110.0
Unphased: OA6	F	72	12.5	9.7	93.1
MI: OA3	M	66	7.6	3.0	95.5
MI: OA6	M	652	7.8	14.0	88.7
M2: BIn	M	19	-	5.3	100.0
M2: BIs	M	50	2.0	10.0	92.0
M2: OA3	M	253	5.1	9.1	86.2
M2: OA6	M	735	7.5	5.2	89.7
M3: BIe	M	42	7.1	7.1	95.2
M3: BIn	M	560	7.0	13.9	90.0
M3: OA3	M	918	13.9	7.3	99.8
M3: OA3i	M	276	6.5	4.3	99.6
M3: OA6	M	1143	11.7	9.7	100.7
M4: BIn	M	46	8.7	32.6	60.9
M4: BInn	M	137	2.9	23.6	78.8
M4: OA6e	M	61	31.1	1.6	72.1
M4: OA6w	M	331	10.0	11.2	105.1
Unphased: BI	M	359	8.9	8.4	88.0
Unphased: OA6	M	645	11.6	9.6	97.5
Children					
M3: OA6	-	13	-	7.7	76.9
M4: BInn	-	30	6.7	23.3	80.0
Unphased: OA6	-	27	-	-	85.2

The percentage affected by calculus is sometimes more than 100% as calculus is scored more than once for a tooth when it occurs on different aspects of that tooth

mature adults, 5 older adults and 1 not aged); 12 individuals of indeterminate sex (1 young adult, 8 adults, 1 immature, 2 not aged). Stature could be estimated for six males; the average was 1.74m the range being 1.69m to 1.83m. The skulls of a single female and eight males could be measured for calculation of the cranial index. The female was brachycranial and the most common skull type amongst the males was mesocranial. The degree of flattening of the femur could be calculated in six females and this was eumeric on both sides, as was the case for the 50 males that could be assessed. Similarly, tibias tended to be rounded with nine females and 35 males most commonly being eurycnemic on both sides. Dental non-metric traits present included crowding, hypercementosis, malformation, peg tooth, rotation, unusual wear, deciduous retention, spacing and Carabelli's cusp (Table 56). Males and females presented differing rates of acetabular crease, coronal and lambdoid wormians, lateral squatting facets, mastoid foramen, parietal foramen, posterior condylar canal and septal aperture (Table 57). Females were amongst the highest scoring subsamples for acetabular crease, coronal wormians, mastoid foramen and septal aperture. Males were amongst the highest for lambdoid wormians. The most frequent skeletal pathological condition, excluding general degeneration, was periosteal new bone (Table 58), and in this subsample the females tended to have worse dental health than the males (Tables 60–2), but they were a small sample.

c 1300–c 1390 (period M3)

THE CHURCH (B1)

The north transept provided 36 individuals for analysis, all adult: 30 male, 5 female and 1 not sexed. Females comprised three mature and two older adults. Of the males, 4 were young adults, 16 mature adults, 8 older adults, 2 could only be identified as adults. The stature of a single male could be estimated; this was 1.74m. The skulls of five males could be measured in order to calculate the cranial index; the most common type was mesocranial. Three females and 22 males

Table 61 *Prevalence of alveolar resorption and periodontal disease in female and male adults as a percentage of bone sockets present (see Table 53 for key to land use abbreviations)*

Period: land use	Sex	No. of sockets	Alveolar resorption (%)	Periodontal disease (%)
MI: OA3	F	24	70.8	62.5
MI: OA6	F	126	50.0	42.1
M2: OA6	F	97	87.6	64.9
M3: BIn	F	24	70.8	66.7
M3: OA3	F	58	24.1	22.4
M3: OA6	F	129	61.2	53.5
M4: BInn	F	28	25.0	25.0
Unphased: OA6	F	91	33.0	36.3
Unphased: BI	F	12	33.3	33.3
MI: OA3	M	93	38.7	34.4
MI: OA6	M	704	40.2	47.9
M2: BIn	M	14	-	-
M2: BIs	M	59	62.7	57.6
M2: OA3	M	382	32.2	30.9
M2: OA6	M	790	39.9	41.6
M3: BIe	M	89	27.0	28.1
M3: BIn	M	677	29.8	27.2
M3: OA3	M	1003	33.3	35.3
M3: OA3i	M	309	38.8	39.8
M3: OA6	M	1448	43.7	43.0
M4: BIn	M	88	22.7	19.3
M4: BInn	M	166	34.9	31.9
M4: OA6e	M	64	43.8	42.2
M4: OA6w	M	378	37.3	45.5
Unphased: BI	M	400	38.3	37.0
Unphased: OA6	M	699	34.6	31.6

No children affected

Table 62 *Number of female and male adults with abscesses (see Table 53 for key to land use abbreviations)*

Period: land use	Sex	No. of individuals with dentition	No. of individuals affected
M2: OA6	F	4	3
M3: OA6	F	5	2
Unphased: OA6	F	4	1
MI: OA3	M	5	1
MI: OA6	M	38	19
M2: BIs	M	2	1
M2: OA3	M	14	5
M2: OA6	M	39	7
M3: BIn	M	27	5
M3: OA3	M	52	3
M3: OA6	M	61	25
M4: BIn	M	3	5
M4: BInn	M	10	4
M4: OA6w	M	17	10
Unphased: BI	M	17	6
Unphased: OA6	M	39	12

No children affected

could be included in an assessment of femoral flattening; the most common femoral form on both sides was eumeric. Eighteen males could be assessed for degree of flattening of the tibia; most commonly both sides were eurycnemic. Several types of dental non-metric traits were present in the subsample (Table 56). These included crowding, malformation, peg tooth, hypodontia, rotation, deciduous retention, spacing, enamel pearls and taurodontism. There were too few females to allow comment on the skeletal non-metric traits present amongst them, but amongst the males there were low rates of atlas double facet, mastoid foramen, posterior condylar canal and septal aperture, and high rates of coronal wormians and lambdoid wormians relative to the other subsamples (Table 57). The most frequently occurring skeletal pathological conditions for the whole subsample, excluding osteoarthritis, osteophytosis and general degeneration, were periosteal new bone, rib lesions and fractures (Table 58). Females apparently had much higher rates of ante-mortem tooth loss, dental caries, alveolar resorption and periodontal disease than males and no females suffered from hypoplasia compared to 7.0% of males (Tables 59–61). It is possible, however, that this apparent variation is a product of the much smaller size of the female sample.

Finally within the church, from seven burials from the eastern extension another six skeletons were recovered: five were male and the sex of one undetermined; two were older adults, but the remaining four could not be refined beyond adult. The stature of a single male could be estimated at 1.72m from the left femur. A single skull provided the requisite measurements for calculation of the cranial index, and this indicated that the skull was mesocranial. The degree of femoral flattening could be calculated for five right femurs and four left, and all were eumeric. Tibial flattening could be calculated for three right and three left tibias; all the latter were eurycnemic, but two of the three right were mesocnemic (the third was eurycnemic). There were no dental non-metric traits present in the four individuals with surviving dentition, and the subsample was too small for a detailed discussion of skeletal non-metric traits, although there did appear to be high rates of calcaneal double facet and lambdoid wormians, and low rates of atlas double facet, posterior condylar canal and septal aperture (Table 57). The most common skeletal pathology, excluding osteoarthritis, was periosteal new bone and healed periosteal bone on the pulmonary surface of the ribs (Table 58). The subsample had a relatively low rate of caries and hypoplasia which may be offset by the relatively high rate of ante-mortem tooth loss (Table 59).

THE CHAPTER HOUSE (B3B)
The single intact burial from the chapter house in period M3 was an older adult male [716]. He suffered from DISH, osteochondritis dissecans (Fig 224; Table 58), and a congenital anomaly of a bifid odontoid process to his axis. Dental pathology included seven teeth lost ante-mortem, massive carious lesion on a surviving upper lateral incisor, and slight calculus and periodontal disease (Waldron nd [1977]).

Fig 224 *An example of osteochondritis dissecans on the left femoral medial condyle of individual [4716] (period M3, OA6) (scale c 1:1)*

SOUTH BURIAL AREA (OA3)

Of the 120 burials, 109 individuals were available for analysis. Two groups were distinguishable: 78 burials that formed the main (western) body of the cemetery and a further 31 that were arranged in rows, to the north of and possibly associated with the infirmary building.

The 78 in the first group, all adult, comprised 66 males (3 young adults, 34 mature adults, 25 older adults, 3 only identifiable as adult and 1 not aged), 2 females (1 young and 1 mature adult) and 10 whose sex could not be determined (3 mature adults, 1 older adult and 6 aged as adult). Only two of the males provided data for estimation of stature: 1.73m and 1.8m. The cranial index could be calculated for three male skulls, and all three were brachycranial. The most common femoral form amongst 53 males was eumeric on both sides; two females also had eumeric femurs on both sides. The most common tibial form in 38 males was eurycnemic on both sides and again two females had eurycnemic tibias on both sides. A wide range of dental non-metric traits were present: crowding; hypocementosis; malformation; peg teeth; additional roots; hypodontia; rotation; spacing; enamel pearls; and Carabelli's cusp (Table 56).

The 31 individuals in the second group were all male where sex could be determined: 26 males (2 young adults, 12 mature and 12 older adults) and three adults who could not be sexed (1 older adult and 2 adults). There were two immature individuals aged between 13 and 16 years. Estimated stature could be calculated for seven of the males; average stature was 1.71m and the range was 1.65m to 1.77m. The cranial index could be calculated for three male skulls and all were mesocranial. The degree of femoral flattening of 19 males could be calculated and the most common form was eumeric on both sides. The most common tibial form amongst 14 males was eurycnemic on both sides. Dental non-metric traits present included crowding, hypercementosis, additional roots, rotation, spacing and shovel shaping (Table 56). Skeletal non-metric traits

included high rates of atlas double facet, coronal wormians, parietal foramen and posterior condylar canal; and a low rate of supraorbital foramen relative to the other subsamples. The most common skeletal pathological condition present, excluding general degenerative conditions, was the occurrence of periosteal new bone (Table 58). Dental pathology present included a low rate of caries and a high rate of periodontal disease relative to the other subsamples (Table 60; Table 61).

NORTH BURIAL AREA (OA6)

In period M3 this area provided the largest subsample with 129 individuals available for analysis. This group was made up of 8 children (3 aged 7–12 years, 5 aged 13–16 years), 120 adults and 1 individual who could not be aged, broken down by age and sex as follows: 96 males (3 children 13–16 years, 9 young adults, 50 mature adults, 30 older adults and 4 defined only as adult); 12 females (2 young adults, 8 mature adults, 1 older adult and 1 adult); 14 of indeterminate sex (1 young adult, 2 mature adults, 10 adults and 1 not aged). The stature of two of the females could be estimated at 1.63m and 1.66m, giving an average of 1.65m. The average stature of 15 of the males was 1.72m within a range of 1.65m to 1.80m. The cranial index could be calculated for a single female and three males. The female and two of the males were brachycranial, the third male was mesocranial. The most common femur type amongst ten females and 82 males was eumeric on both sides, and the most common tibial form amongst nine females and 64 males was eurycnemic on both sides. Certain dental non-metric traits presented at different rates in males and females, but this could be a product of the small sample size for females. Dental non-metric traits included crowding, hypercementosis, malformation, additional roots, hypodontia, rotation, unusual wear, spacing, Carabelli's cusp and shovel shape (Table 56). Males had higher rates of coronal wormians, hypotrochanteric fossae, mastoid and parietal foramina, and pterygoid spurs than females. Females had higher rates of lateral squatting facet and septal aperture than males. Relative to the other subsamples, females had the highest rate of lateral squatting facet and the lowest rate of pterygoid spurs. Males had amongst the highest rates of coronal wormians (Table 57).

c 1390–1538 (period M4)

THE CHURCH (B1)

Of 17 burials in the north aisle of the nave, aisle crossing and north transept, 16 were available for analysis.

The three individuals from the north transept comprised two mature adults [2181] and [2126], the former male, the latter probably male, and a probable mature adult male [2107]. The cranial index of [2107] could be calculated and indicated the skull was mesocranial. The most common form of femur amongst the three was eumeric on both sides, and the most common form of tibia was eurycnemic on the right and between eurycnemic and mesocnemic on the left. Male [2107] was buried wearing a possible hernia belt (<S254>; above 7.5 and Chapters 3.4 'Archaeological evidence', 'The 15th- and

16th-century church (B1)', 4.6). This (very small) sample had a high rate of ante-mortem tooth loss (Table 59), the highest rate by a large margin of dental caries, yet the lowest rates of calculus, alveolar resorption and periodontal disease of all the burials apart from the two in the north transept of the church in period M2 (Table 60; Table 61).

The burial in the north-east corner of the aisle crossing, near the transept, was an older adult male [3458]. Both femurs were eumeric in form and his right tibia was mesocnemic (the left was missing). He had no dental non-metric traits and the only skeletal non-metric trait included amongst those of special interest was a double facet to the calcaneus. He exhibited the classic characteristics of DISH, and had periosteal new bone affecting his tibiae, possibly as a reaction to an infection of the overlying soft tissue.

Of 12 individuals available for analysis from the north nave 11 were males (1 aged 13–16 years, 5 mature adults, 4 older adults, and 1 adult) and one a mature adult female. The cranial index, calculated for five males, indicated a split between brachycranial and mesocranial, with a single male presenting as dolichocranial. Again a single female could be assessed for degree of femoral flattening and, unusually for this sample, both her femurs were platymeric or flattened. Six males could be measured and these were most commonly eumeric on both sides. The most common tibial form amongst six males was eurycnemic, as were both tibias of a single female. Dental non-metric traits present included crowding, rotation and Carabelli's cusp (Table 56). There were too few instances of skeletal non-metric traits to observe any variation in frequency relative to other subsamples; those present are listed in Table 57. There was an even spread between a range of skeletal pathologies once general degenerative conditions were excluded (Table 58). The subsample had the second lowest rate of hypoplasia, the second highest rate of caries (Table 60) and average rates of alveolar resorption, periodontal disease (Table 61) and ante-mortem tooth loss (Table 59) relative to the other subsamples.

THE CHAPTER HOUSE (B3B)

Nineteen individuals were available for analysis from this phase of the chapter house: 18 were male and included 1 young adult, 5 mature, 10 older adults and 2 that could not be aged other than as adult; 1 was an uncertain sex adult. (A possible female adult [771] was initially identified (Waldron nd [1977]) and described as female in previous studies (Waldron 1985, 1762), but the burial was severely truncated and the sex was assessed from a single sciatic notch; it has been recognised subsequently that the sciatic notch is a very poor indicator of sex for the Merton sample and this individual has been reclassified as an adult male.) Stature could be estimated for eight males, with an average of 1.75m and a range of 1.63m to 1.82m. Dental pathology present included wear ranging from slight in two cases to severe in nine; slight to moderate calculus; very variable expressions of severity of periodontal disease; and only two individuals with caries, although a further nine dentitions had suffered from ante-mortem loss

and/or abscesses (Waldron nd [1977]). The most common skeletal pathology excluding general degenerative conditions was DISH, with two of the 19 individuals, definitely or possibly, affected (Table 58; Table 69).

NORTH BURIAL AREA (OA6)

There were two distinct groupings amongst the burials from Open Area 6 during period M4: one group to the east of the church and one to the west.

The former group provided two individuals for analysis, both male (a young adult and a mature adult). The cranial index indicated that the skull of the only assessable male was mesocranial. The degree of femoral flattening of a single male could be assessed and this individual was bilaterally eumeric. The same male was eurycnemic, with regard to tibial form, on both sides. Dental non-metric traits present were crowding and Carabelli's cusp, and although there were skeletal non-metric traits present, these were too few to comment on their frequency relative to other subsamples (Table 56; Table 57). The skeletal pathology present is given in Table 58. The subsample had the highest rate of hypoplasia, a very low rate of caries and amongst the higher rates of alveolar resorption and periodontal disease compared to other subsamples (Table 60; Table 61), but as this was based on only two individuals, the observation is of no significance.

The second group to the west of the church included 26 individuals: 22 male adults and 2 adults of indeterminate sex (2 young adults, 12 mature, 6 older and 4 aged as adult); and 2 children (aged 7–12 years). Three of the males provided an estimate of stature with an average of 1.71m and a range of 1.69m to 1.73m. The cranial index could be calculated for two males: one was brachycranial, the other mesocranial. The most common femoral form amongst 14 males was eumeric on both sides, and the most common tibial form for 13 males was eurycnemic on both sides. Dental non-metric traits present included crowding, hypodontia, rotation and Carabelli's cusp (Table 56). With regard to skeletal non-metric traits, the subsample had a low rate of acetabular crease, coronal wormians, parietal foramen, septal aperture and supraorbital notch relative to other subsamples, and a high rate of atlas double facet, lambdoid wormians, mastoid foramen and supraorbital foramen (Table 57). The most frequent skeletal pathology present, when general degenerative conditions were excluded, was healed periosteal bone on the pulmonary surface of ribs (Table 58). There was nothing of particular note amongst the rates of dental pathology relative to other subsamples (Tables 59–62).

Unphased medieval burials (periods M1–M4)

This catch-all group could be split into two subgroups despite the lack of stratigraphic data; those in the north burial area (in OA6) outside the (period M3) eastern extension of the church, and those from the church within the area of the eastern extension. The former area provided a large subsample of 82 individuals. These included seven children: 1 not aged,

3 aged 7–12 years and 3 aged 13–16 years. Two of the latter could also be identified as male. Counting these individuals, there were 56 males, 5 females and 17 individuals of indeterminate sex. None of those of indeterminate sex could be aged with any accuracy; 13 were adult and four provided no indication of age. Amongst the females were two mature adults and two older adults. The males included 5 young adults, 31 mature, 9 older and 9 identifiable as adult, in addition to the 2 aged 13–16 years.

An estimate of stature could be made for four of the males; the average was 1.69m and the range was 1.61m to 1.74m. The cranial index could be calculated for four male skulls and these were all brachycranial. The degree of femoral flattening could be calculated for four females and 44 males; the most common male form was eumeric on both sides, the females were most commonly eumeric on the right and split between eumeric and platymeric on the left. Most common tibial form was eurycnemic on both sides amongst 33 males, but much more erratic between the two assessable females with one eurycnemic and one mesocnemic right, and one platymeric left (the second left was missing). Dental non-metric traits present included crowding; malformation; additional roots; rotation; unusual wear; and one case of deciduous retention in a female (Table 56). The only skeletal non-metric traits of any note were low rates of posterior condylar canal; septal aperture and supraorbital foramen relative to other subsamples (Table 57). The most frequent type of skeletal pathology present, with the exception of general degenerative conditions was the occurrence of periosteal new bone (Table 58). Males and females had very similar levels of dental pathology of all types.

The second group from within the church consisted of 31 individuals. There was a single child of age 7–12 years, 26 males, 2 females and 2 of indeterminate sex. The males included 1 young adult, 13 mature, 8 older adults and 4 classified as adult. The females included one mature adult and one who could not be aged more precisely than adult, as was the case with both those of indeterminate sex.

The cranial index could be calculated for two males; one was mesocranial, the other was brachycranial. Two females and 23 males could be examined for degree of femoral flattening. The most common form amongst the males was eumeric on both sides and the two females were both eumeric on the right but one was eumeric and one was platymeric on the left. The tibial form of 21 males could be assessed and the most common form was eurycnemic on both sides. Dental non-metric traits present included crowding, malformation, hypodontia, rotation, spacing and Carabelli's cusp (Table 56). There were too few females to discuss the prevalence of skeletal non-metric traits, but amongst males, there was a low prevalence of acetabular crease, hypotrochanteric fossa, lateral squatting facet and septal aperture relative to other subsamples, and a high rate of lambdoid wormians and pterygoid spurs (Table 57). The most frequent skeletal pathology present was the occurrence of periosteal new bone and healed periosteal bone on the pulmonary surface of ribs, when general degenerative conditions and osteoarthritis were excluded (Table

58). The subsample had a very low rate of ante-mortem tooth loss, but in all other aspects of dental pathology was unremarkable (Tables 59–62).

Demography

Six hundred and sixty-four skeletons were recorded as the overall sample from Merton Priory. Adults accounted for the great majority of this total at c 94%. There were very few children present, only three under 6 years of age, and only slightly more older children (Table 63). Thus immature individuals less than 17 years of age made up only 4.1% of the overall sample. The remainder were very fragmented and/or truncated and no age estimate could be assigned. There was a marked male bias amongst the adults, with 77.2% male and 6.9% female; a male:female sex ratio of 11.2:1 (Table 63).

Several things were immediately apparent from this age and sex profile. The composition of the Merton sample was markedly different from that expected if the assemblage was drawn from a 'normal' population. In the latter, approximately even proportions of males and females could be expected, and a high proportion of immature individuals. Examples of such assemblages are St Nicholas Shambles, London, with a male:female sex ratio of 1.27:1 (White 1988, 29–30), St Helen-on-the-Walls, York, at 0.86:1 (Dawes and Magilton 1980, 11, 65); and the pre-monastic cemetery at St Andrew, Fishergate, York at 1.4:1 (Stroud and Kemp 1993, 170–1). At the latter, subadults (under 20 years of age) made up c 36% of the total sample. The youngest age group could be expected to account for the majority of immature individuals, typically the ratio of those of less than 1 year of age to those under 20 years is between 4:1 and 4:3 (Brothwell 1971a; 1971b). Here, the youngest age group (1–6 years) accounted for only 0.5% of all

Table 63 *Age and sex composition of the human bone assemblage: summary*

Age composition	No.	% of sample
Children 1–6 years	3	0.5
Children 7–12 years	11	1.7
Children 13–16 years	11	1.7
Children not aged	2	0.3
Young adults 17–25 years	39	5.9
Mature adults 26–45 years	293	44.1
Older adults 45+ years	185	27.9
Adults not aged	108	16.3
Unknown age	12	1.8
	664	
Sex composition*		
Males	517	77.2
Females	46	6.9
Indeterminate sex	80	11.9
Children	27	4.1
	670	

*: total number in sample is 664, but six individuals aged 13–16 years could be sexed (as male) and so are included twice; overall male:female ratio is 11.2:1

burials, with 3.3% spread between the remaining immature age groups, 7–12 years and 13–16 years (and note that the youngest age group in this analysis includes children up to 6 years of age emphasising the disparity still further) (Table 63).

One slight note of caution is necessary here. Over 500 contexts of disarticulated bone were excluded from the analysis on the basis that the time necessary to extract the data they could provide, relative to that available from over 600 intact burials, was not justified. However, in more than one case the bones of a very young infant were observed amongst these contexts. It is possible that such individuals were buried in shallow graves relative to larger adults (note the post-medieval custom in poorer cemeteries of London of cramming infants towards the top of stacks of coffins as if to utilise every available bit of space, as at St Brides lower churchyard: Miles and Conheeney in prep). In such an arrangement, the occupants of these shallow graves may have suffered more from clearances and so forth than the more protected deeper burials. The only way to rule out this possibility would be to make a rapid scan of the disarticulated contexts, to identify the proportion of young individuals and to establish if they would alter significantly the demographic structure described above. On the other hand, low percentages of immature individuals have been recorded from other monastic sites.

Assuming that the disarticulated bone contexts would not have a significant effect and the composition described is roughly correct, it is not surprising, given the documentary and archaeological evidence firmly associating the burials with the life of the priory, that the comparison of the Merton sample to a 'normal' population confirms the specialist nature of the former. Perhaps of more note was that the male:female sex ratio for the overall Merton sample at 11.2:1 falls between the values obtained for those monastic assemblages thought to represent principally the monastic community such as St Mary, Stratford Langthorne, and St Saviour, Bermondsey, both London religious establishments at 19:1 and 17:1 respectively (White 2004, 160; Connell and White 1998) and those samples drawn from monastic houses but thought to include individuals from outside the monastic community for a variety of reasons. For example St Mary Spital, London, a religious house and hospital with an overall ratio of 1.15:1 (Conheeney 1997, 222); St Andrew, Fishergate, York, a group of lay and monastic burials, at 3.2:1 (Stroud and Kemp 1993, 170–1) and urban friaries where the samples are believed to include lay benefactors and priors and/or friars, such as the Blackfriars, Oxford, at 5:1 (Lambrick 1985, 203), the Whitefriars, Ipswich (Suffolk), at 3.67:1 (Mays 1991a), or the Blackfriars, Ipswich, at 2.36:1 (Mays 1991b); and the leper hospital of St James and St Mary Magdalene, Chichester, at 5:4 (Lee and Magilton 1989, 279) subsequently revised after further excavation to 2.5:1 (F Lee, pers comm 2006). The underlying explanation of this became apparent when the demographic composition of individual areas of the Merton complex were considered. In summary, the demographic structure observed in the chapter house and south burial area (OA3), almost exclusively male and very few children, suggested areas set aside predominantly for the

brethren. The more mixed composition of the burials made within the church and north burial area (OA6) were more likely to be mixed areas of clerical and lay burials (Table 54; Table 55). This apportionment of areas was very reminiscent of the organisation of the monastic period cemetery at St Andrew, Fishergate, York (Stroud and Kemp 1993, 252–6). It is impossible to state with certainty who the lay burials represent, but the wider range of age and sex apparent in the north burial area (OA6) in Table 54 and Table 55, compared with the narrower range of types (biased towards males and adults) in the church, may suggest it was harder to achieve burial within the building than without. A selection process in any setting suggests the strongest candidate wins through, and in this context high rank in the church or the most wealth with which to secure burial in the 'holiest' parts of the complex are the two most likely selection criteria. This would certainly agree with the archaeological evidence that the richest grave goods and burial types were found within the church and with documentary evidence for the type of person buried within, and the organisation of, the monastic cemetery. Priors from the monastic community and wealthy benefactors from the outside community would most obviously fit these descriptions, and although women and children were not excluded from the church and, therefore, must have had access to status in some form, they were relatively few in number, suggesting that status was a predominantly male prerogative. This argument is supported by the predominance of males in the transepts, thought to be a more sought-after location than other parts of the church. If this assumption is correct, the greater number of women and children in the north burial area (OA6) may suggest that there was some other reason than status for their inclusion. Most likely explanations may be that they were lay servants, or family of male servants, or corrodians in their own right.

Amongst the adults, the most common age at death was in the mature adult group (44.2% of the overall sample); next most common older adults (28.3%), and least common young adults (5.7%). The age structure for mature and older adults was similar in the church, south (OA3) and north (OA6) burial areas, but differed in the chapter house. Not surprisingly, perhaps, given the documentary evidence that the chapter house would be reserved for burial of the priors, the older age group is the most common age at death in all three periods of this area, presumably rank taking time to achieve and those surviving into old age most likely to have achieved the position (Table 54). The proportion of older aged individuals in the sample as a whole was comparable to a number of monastic sites but large relative to several of London's religious houses, such as St Saviour Bermondsey with 18.1% surviving over 45 years (Connell and White 1998), St Mary Stratford Langthorne with 22.7% (White 2004, 173) and St Mary Spital with 9.0% (Thomas et al 1997, 112). The low rate at St Mary Spital can be explained by the inclusion of hospital inmates, presumably more likely to have a lower average age of death. The slightly higher proportion of older individuals at Merton than at the other two sites is harder to explain. One possible factor may be geographical location. All three sites were prone to flooding; perhaps this was more of a problem with the risk of associated disease in the centre of the city for St Saviours Bermondsey, or to the relatively industrialised east for St Mary, Stratford Langthorne than to the more rural west and Merton. All three sites had a lower proportion of older individuals than Westminster Abbey (66.8% were older), and this structure was reflected at St Andrew, Fishergate, York (65.9%; Stroud and Kemp 1993, 256). Perhaps this is an indication that the more important point is the cause of the lower proportion of older individuals at these three sites compared to Westminster and what this may reveal about life at the institutions, rather than the slight variation in rates between the three sites themselves. Of interest in this respect were the much lower proportions of young adults in the three areas possibly associated with monastic burials or high status at Merton, the church, the chapter house and south burial area (OA3), in the majority of periods, compared to the continuous presence of young adults in the north burial area (OA6) (Table 54). This may suggest that those buried in the north burial area (OA6) were not enjoying the same benefits in lifestyle contributing to longevity as those to which individuals in the other areas had access. Again this may support the suggestion that the lay people buried in Open Area 6 were more likely to be in a servile role than included as corrodians or some mark of privilege. Unfortunately, one of the possible indicators of status – high relative values for stature – was of little use in this sample as estimates of stature were possible for so few individuals, given the fragmentary nature of the sample. There was some variation in pathology and possibly physical activity that may be relevant, and these are discussed below. An alternative explanation could be that some of the children and young adults in Open Area 6 represent the intake of the priory into its almonry. Harvey (1993, 138), using Westminster as an example, makes the point that young monks fared well in most years and experienced a low death rate, but in 'crisis' years, such as plague years, they were most vulnerable and would have a higher death rate. Merton must have had a similar intake and as these do not feature in the first two periods of Open Area 3, assuming it to be the most likely candidate as the canon's cemetery, they must be buried elsewhere, most logically in Open Area 6. Interestingly, Harvey (1993, 143) says that in the later years of Westminster's history, the age of profession had to be lowered to keep numbers in the monastery up, and these young cloister monks were especially vulnerable to disease as they had less time in the almonry to prepare them for urban diseases.

Two groupings, possibly familial amongst other explanations, have been suggested on archaeological grounds: a double burial [2352] and [2353] within the north transept, and in Open Area 6, three burials [2712], [2855] and [2856] apparently thrown into a grave. The double burial was that of a mature probable female and an older probable male. The group of three included two older males and a child in the 7- to 12-years age group. Non-metric traits and pathology present were of no help in interpreting these arrangements. Black marking on the skeletons of the triple burial had been questioned as

possible burning. This black, soot-like deposit was quite common across the site. It was not the result of burning, and was most probably a by-product of a mould (T Waldron, pers comm) and as such part of the natural process of decomposition. Elsewhere, non-metric traits have suggested the possibility of family groups: St Andrew, Fishergate (York), Austin friars, Leicester, and Guildford friary (Surrey) (Stroud and Kemp 1993, 253–4), so this possibility cannot be ruled out. Non-metric traits have also been used to suggest the possible biological distinctiveness of a monastic population from the wider population of the period at Bermondsey Abbey (Connell and White 1998). In the St Mary Merton sample there were generally low prevalence rates of all dental non-metric traits (Table 56).

Physical appearance

Unfortunately, the interpretation of physical appearance was the aspect of the osteological analysis that suffered most from the highly fragmented nature of the remains. Although it was possible to carry out many measurements elsewhere on the skeleton, the measurements and observations of most use in reconstructing physical appearance rely on the availability of complete skulls and long bone lengths, and these two features fared particularly badly with very few uncrushed skulls and complete long bones, given the size of the sample.

Overall, three female and 43 male skulls survived sufficiently to allow calculation of the cranial index. This index expresses the maximum breadth of the skull as a proportion of its maximum length, effectively quantitatively describing the roundness or long, narrow shaping of a skull, and although of questionable significance, have been used traditionally to assess variability within and between populations (Mays 1998, 96–100). The three female skulls were brachycranial. Of the male skulls, 19 were brachycranial, 21 mesocranial, and three dolichocranial, where brachycrani effectively indicates roundness and dolichocrani suggests a long, narrow skull anterioposteriorly. Comparative sites mostly tend to brachycranial, although a few, notably the Ipswich samples, were mesocranial (Mays 1991a; 1991b). Stroud (1994, 437) also states that the most common later medieval skull shape was brachycranial. Interestingly, the 11th- and 12th-century St Nicholas Shambles assemblage was mesocranial (White 1988, 30). Could the almost even split in male skull shape between mesocrani and brachycrani be a product of the time span of the Merton sample from the 12th century through to the 16th century? This was not borne out in the discussion by phase above, where the two skull shapes occurred throughout the periods. An alternative explanation suggested by Molleson (Farwell and Molleson 1993) is that a mix of cranial indices is indicative of a heterogeneous population drawn together from many origins rather than of local origin. She suggested that such a population would also be sexually dimorphic. For instance, there would be a large difference between male and female average statures. This was not necessarily the case here as there was a difference of approximately 80mm, but the average statures were very similar to those of the comparative medieval sites. The most likely explanation of this difference from other sites, rather than a biological cause, is that this author prefers to look at most frequent occurrence of skull type rather than the more usual practice of taking the average value of the index across the sample. On the whole then, the sample had average to round heads, considering breadth relative to length.

Average male stature was 1.72m with a range of 1.61m to 1.83m. The average for females was 1.64m, with a range of 1.62m to 1.67 m. However, these figures were calculated from only 3 females and 44 males, a disappointing number as elsewhere, at St Mary Spital (Conheeney 1997, 223) and St Mary Graces, London (Waldron 1993; in prep), extremes of stature for the period had been used to support the case for differences in status between groups of individuals. The small number of individuals for whom stature could be calculated, once subdivided by area and period, meant that a similar discussion was not possible here.

Indices exist to describe the degree of flattening of the femur anterioposteriorly and the tibia mediolaterally. Again, there is debate concerning the significance and cause of such variation in the long bones. Merton was unusual in that the overwhelming female and male most common femoral shape was eurymeric (meric index 85.0 to 99.9; Brothwell 1981, 88), that is not flattened to any degree, whereas the majority of the available comparative sites had platymeric, or flattened, femurs. The tibial form at St Mary Merton was more usual for the period with both sexes eurycnemic.

Finally, based on the assumption that handedness corresponds to the side of the longest humerus, three of 37 assessable males may have been left handed. At 8.1%, this is not dissimilar to the rate in modern Britain (c 10%), as compared with greater proportions of left-handed individuals present at St Saviour Bermondsey (16.7%) or at St Mary Stratford Langthorne (19.1%) (White 2004, 173).

Physical activity

Repetitive activity of a strenuous nature may promote the development of enthesopathies, or bony spurs, at the sites of muscle insertion into bones. However, extreme caution is required in interpreting their prevalence as many other factors probably play a part in their development, such as age, sex, genetic factors, trauma and so forth. Stirland (1991) makes the case that there are so many potential contributory factors that comparisons should only be made within extremely homogenous groups and are invalid between populations. In addition, a particular enthesopathy cannot be linked to a particular activity or occupation, instead it must be taken simply as an indication of the type of movement to which the muscles at that particular site contribute.

Bearing these limitations in mind, and consequently drawing comparisons between the subsamples here rather than comparing the overall sample to that from other sites, a few possible trends did seem apparent as regards enthesopathies

associated with the iliac crest, the ischial tuberosity and the soleal line (Conheeney 1995). Males and females were possibly involved in different activities, based on the differences between individuals in periods M1 and M2 from the north burial area Open Area 6. Females had no marked muscle markings, but males may have been involved with something that involved flexing the fingers and either walking or standing still for long periods. Similarly, in the south burial area Open Area 3, differences in enthesopathies between the males buried in rows north of the infirmary in period M3 and those from the remainder of Open Area 3 in this period and Open Area 3 in period M2, possibly indicate that those associated with the infirmary were also involved in something that required the maintenance of an upright posture. These were the only two possible patterns picked up, and should be viewed with considerable caution; it is important to note that there was much variation in the enthesopathies listed between all the subsamples (ibid).

The type of fractures present in a sample can be another very useful indicator of patterns of activity. Fractures recorded for the sample are presented in Table 64 and the state of healing of those fractures in Table 65. Thirteen per cent of individuals in the overall sample had suffered at least one fracture of some sort. This was a little higher than the 5.6–8.8% range quoted for five comparable medieval sites in Connell and White (1998). Judd and Roberts (1998) suggest that an increased rate at St James and St Mary Magdalene, Chichester, is because the site was a leper hospital, with increased fracture rate due to sensory impairment associated with the condition. At Merton, one contributory factor may be the larger proportion of elderly individuals than at some of the comparative sites, with the joint implication of more time for people to accumulate fractures and the increased fragility of older bones. In many cases, individuals had multiple fractures that they had received at varying times, judging from the degree of healing and remodelling that had taken place. Subsamples from Open Area 6 did appear to have slightly higher prevalences of fractures in most periods than burials from other areas (Table 64), and it has been suggested elsewhere (Stroud and Kemp 1993, 258) that servants would have a higher prevalence of fractures than monks because of differences in activity.

The most frequent site for fracture was the ribs, with 41 cases (Table 64). Fracture of the ribs and the clavicle, of which there were nine cases, are suggestive of falls. In addition there were five cases of possible Colles fracture of the distal radius, typical of falling with the hands out to save oneself. None of the rib and Colles fractures occurred in the same individuals.

It has been suggested that this type of injury, combined with fractures of the lower leg (Fig 225 and also in situ Fig 158), of which there were nine cases, is indicative of a rural population engaged in more physical activity than an urban sample (Farwell and Molleson 1993, 199).

There appears to have been an element of violence in the lives of some of the people, not unusual for monastic sites, with evidence of violence from St Mary Stratford, Langthorne (White 2004, 178), St Mary Graces, London (Waldron in

Table 64 The numbers and types of fractures present (see Table 53 for key to land use abbreviations)

Subsample (period: land use)	No. in subsample	No. of individuals affected	% of individuals affected	Ribs*	Scapula	Humerus	Radius	Ulna	Hand	Vertebra	Femur	Lower leg	Foot	Clavicle	Skull
M1: OA6	82	16	19.5	7	0	2	0	0	4	0	0	2	0	0	0
M2: OA3	22	1	4.5	1	0	0	0	0	0	0	0	0	0	0	0
M2: OA6	83	11	13.3	6	0	0	1	0	3	0	0	1	0	1	1
M3: B1n	36	5	13.9	2	1	0	0	0	1	0	0	0	0	1	0
M3: OA3	78	7	9.0	3	0	1	1	0	1	0	0	1	1	0	0
M3: OA3i	31	4	12.9	3	0	0	0	0	0	0	0	0	0	1	1
M3: OA6	129	25	19.4	14	0	0	3	2	2	0	2	3	0	4	2
M4: B1nn	12	2	16.7	1	0	0	0	0	0	0	0	1	0	0	0
M4: OA6w	26	3	11.5	1	0	0	0	0	0	0	1	0	0	1	0
Unphased: B1	31	4	12.9	0	0	0	0	1	0	0	1	1	0	0	1
Unphased: OA6	82	8	9.8	3	0	0	1	2	2	1	0	1	0	1	2
Total	664	86	13.0	41	1	3	6	5	13	1	4	9	2	9	7

*: the rib fractures are counted in the table as rib cages affected; frequently more than one rib was affected for each one counted

Table 65 The state of healing of the fractures present in the sample (see Table 53 for key to land use abbreviations)

Subsample (period: land use)	No. in subsample	No. of individuals affected	% of individuals affected	Healed	Unhealed	Well aligned	Misaligned	Drainage hole	Crush fracture	Infected
M1: OA6	82	16	19.5	4	1	5	6	1	4	2
M2: OA3	22	1	4.5	1	0	1	0	0	0	0
M2: OA6	83	11	13.3	11	0	8	4	0	0	1
M3: B1n	36	5	13.9	3	0	2	2	0	0	1
M3: OA3	78	7	9.0	8	0	4	3	0	0	0
M3: OA3i	31	4	12.9	5	0	4	2	0	0	2
M3: OA6	129	25	19.4	31	4	16	11	0	0	0
M4: B1nn	12	2	16.7	1	0	2	1	0	0	0
M4: OA6w	26	3	11.5	3	0	0	3	0	0	0
Unphased: B1	31	4	12.9	5	0	3	1	0	0	0
Unphased: OA6	82	8	9.8	10	0	6	3	0	0	0
Total	664	86	13.0	82	5	51	36	1	4	6

prep), and St Andrew, Fishergate, York (Stroud and Kemp 1993, 232–41). All seven cases of trauma to the skull appeared to have been the result of violence. They included slice, puncture and depression wounds, all very well healed indicating the individual had survived the incident. Five cases were from different periods of Open Area 6, one from Open Area 3 and one from an unphased burial within the church. All but one of those affected were males. The exception, [4998], an older possible female, had a possible puncture type lesion, with a 3mm diameter hole surrounded by a 20mm depression. There was no sign of infection, the edges of the lesion had healed and she had survived. Interestingly, the depression fracture to the right parietal and frontal of [2988] was accompanied by a parry fracture of the right ulna; a typical defensive wound resulting from raising the forearm to ward off a blow. There were three other cases of such a fracture, in one instance, [2383], accompanied by a fractured second metacarpal, or

hand bone, which one could imagine being injured at the same time as a blow to the forearm, especially if the thumb was tucked into the palm at the time leaving the second metacarpal exposed at the upper edge of the hand.

Spondylolysis, where the neural arch fails to fuse to the vertebral body, has been linked to trauma as a result of overuse or excessive strain on the back in adolescence. There were eight cases altogether, five bilaterally, three with single sides affected. All cases occurred in the north (OA6) and south (OA3) burial areas, except for one case from an unphased burial within the church (Table 58). Similarly Schmorl's nodes, a lesion on the vertebral body surface caused by herniation of the intervertebral disc, also are thought to have their cause in some cases in excessive load bearing in childhood. The most common site affected was the thoracic spine, not unusually (Table 66). Males were more severely affected than females in all mixed sex subsamples, perhaps

Fig 225 Healed spiral fracture of the left tibia of individual [2817] (periods M1–M4, OA6) (scale c 1:4)

suggesting that males were undertaking either heavier physical work, or from an earlier age than females. Virtually all subsamples were affected. The prevalence rates from OA3 appeared slightly higher than most although not significantly so.

Finally, the distribution of osteoarthritic changes throughout the skeleton have been suggested as indicators of frequent weight bearing, and the difference in prevalence between the sexes used to suggest different work roles. However, once again, many factors contribute to the onset and nature of progression of the condition, making the association of particular patterns with specific activities very tenuous (Rogers and Waldron 1995, 32–3). The spines of both sexes were extensively affected, not surprising in a predominantly adult assemblage with a large proportion of elderly individuals (Table 67). There was no clear distinction between male and female distributions or rates. The cervical vertebrae tended to be worse affected; 33.6% of all individuals were affected by the condition elsewhere in the skeleton, with the sites most frequently affected in decreasing order: the shoulder, rib necks, ankle, hip, wrist, knee, elbow plus a few instances in other joints (Table 68). Both the frequency and distribution differed from that observed at St

Table 66 Types of vertebral pathology present expressed as a percentage of the number of each type of vertebra present within the subsamples (see Table 53 for key to land use abbreviations)

Subsample (period: land use)	Sex	No. of vertebrae present	Osteoarthritis No. affected	%	Fusion No. affected	%	Schmorl's nodes No. affected	%	Intervertebral disc disease No. affected	%	Osteophytosis No. affected	%	Ossification of the ligamentum flavum No. affected	%
M1: OA3	F	24	5	20.8	0	-	4	16.7	2	8.3	5	20.8	9	37.5
M1: OA3	M	89	12	13.5	0	-	19	21.3	18	20.2	15	16.9	3	3.4
M1: OA6	F	113	51	45.1	0	-	0	-	8	7.1	24	21.2	3	2.7
M1: OA6	M	885	252	28.5	0	-	79	8.9	149	16.8	472	53.3	169	19.1
M2: B1n	M	25	0	-	0	-	0	-	0	-	0	-	4	16.0
M2: B1s	M	43	0	-	0	-	4	9.3	5	11.6	24	55.8	19	44.2
M2: OA3	M	290	133	45.9	0	-	57	19.7	38	13.1	159	54.8	52	17.9
M2: OA6	F	160	78	48.8	0	-	7	4.4	12	7.5	87	54.4	29	18.1
M2: OA6	M	926	168	18.1	2	0.2	116	12.5	66	7.1	276	29.8	165	17.8
M3: B1e	M	78	18	23.1	0	-	12	15.4	31	39.7	61	78.2	17	21.8
M3: B1n	F	17	9	52.9	0	-	0	-	7	41.2	0	-	0	-
M3: B1n	M	568	41	7.2	0	-	38	6.7	30	5.3	137	24.1	107	18.8
M3: B3b	M	18	0	-	0	-	0	-	0	-	0	-	0	-
M3: OA3	F	44	1	2.3	0	-	2	4.5	1	2.3	11	25.0	0	-
M3: OA3	M	1177	168	14.3	2	0.2	187	15.9	102	8.7	401	34.1	234	19.9
M3: OA3i	M	368	90	24.5	0	-	60	16.3	60	16.3	150	40.8	117	31.8
M3: OA6	F	212	38	17.9	0	-	11	5.2	9	4.2	49	23.1	44	20.8
M3: OA6	M	1639	338	20.6	11	0.7	144	8.8	180	11.0	751	45.8	285	17.4
M4: B1ac	M	13	0	-	0	-	4	30.8	2	15.4	0	-	1	7.7
M4: B1n	M	65	1	1.5	0	-	7	10.8	0	-	13	20.0	24	36.9
M4: B1nn	F	25	0	-	0	-	0	-	0	-	0	-	2	8.0
M4: B1nn	M	191	25	13.1	0	-	13	6.8	9	4.7	33	17.3	38	19.9
M4: B3b	M	190	5	2.6	0	-	11	5.8	0	-	13	6.8	0	-
M4: OA6e	M	49	0	-	0	-	9	18.4	0	-	0	-	7	14.3
M4: OA6w	M	402	15	3.7	0	-	74	18.4	18	4.5	90	22.4	78	19.4
Unphased: B1	F	16	0	-	0	-	0	-	3	18.8	2	12.5	1	1.2
Unphased: B1	M	419	124	29.6	0	-	32	7.6	31	7.4	76	18.1	67	16.0
Unphased: OA6	F	86	22	25.6	0	-	0	-	7	8.1	13	15.1	16	18.6
Unphased: OA6	M	914	170	18.6	2	0.2	141	15.4	72	7.9	367	40.2	131	14.3

271

Table 67   Prevalence of vertebral osteoarthritis expressed as a percentage of the number of each type of vertebra present within the subsamples (see Table 53 for key to land use abbreviations)

Subsample (period: land use)	Sex	Cervical vertebrae			Thoracic vertebrae			Lumbar vertebrae			Sacral vertebrae			Total no. present	Total no. affected	Total % affected
		No. present	No. affected	%	No. present	No. affected	%	No. present	No. affected	%	No. present	No. affected	%			
M1: OA3	F	7	3	42.9	12	2	16.7	5	0	-	0	0	-	24	5	20.8
M1: OA3	M	16	8	50.0	46	4	8.7	24	0	-	3	0	-	89	12	13.5
M1: OA6	F	37	21	56.8	56	24	42.9	18	6	33.3	2	0	-	113	51	45.1
M1: OA6	M	254	124	48.8	422	120	28.4	184	44	24.0	25	2	8.0	885	290	32.8
M2: Bln	M	7	0	-	12	0	-	5	0	-	1	0	-	25	0	-
M2: Bls	M	8	0	-	23	0	-	10	0	-	2	0	-	43	0	-
M2: OA3	M	94	71	75.5	136	39	28.7	52	21	40.4	8	2	25.0	290	133	45.9
M2: OA6	F	30	6	20.0	83	39	47.0	39	30	76.9	8	3	37.5	160	78	48.8
M2: OA6	M	223	79	35.4	431	69	16.0	236	18	7.6	36	2	5.6	926	168	18.1
M3: Ble	M	24	6	25.0	36	7	19.4	16	4	25.0	2	1	50.0	78	18	23.1
M3: Bln	F	4	2	50.0	12	6	50.0	0	0	-	1	1	100.0	17	9	52.9
M3: Bln	M	154	21	13.6	284	13	4.6	114	7	6.1	16	0	-	568	41	7.2
M3: B3b	M	6	0	-	12	0	-	0	0	-	0	0	-	18	0	-
M3: OA3	F	12	0	-	24	0	-	7	1	14.3	1	0	-	44	1	2.3
M3: OA3	M	322	112	34.8	587	47	8.0	235	9	3.8	33	0	-	1177	168	14.3
M3: OA3i	M	49	30	61.2	201	49	24.4	103	11	10.7	15	0	-	368	90	24.5
M3: OA6	F	60	13	21.7	99	16	16.2	46	9	19.6	7	0	-	212	38	17.9
M3: OA6	M	466	153	32.8	773	155	20.1	349	29	8.3	51	1	2.0	1639	338	20.6
M4: Blac	M	0	0	-	7	0	-	5	0	-	1	0	-	13	0	-
M4: Bln	M	19	1	5.3	31	0	-	14	0	-	1	0	-	65	1	1.5
M4: Blnn	F	7	0	-	11	0	-	6	0	-	1	0	-	25	0	-
M4: Blnn	M	49	10	20.4	89	7	7.9	48	8	16.7	5	0	-	191	25	13.1
M4: B3b	M	69	0	-	78	5	6.4	32	0	-	11	0	-	190	5	2.6
M4: OA6e	M	14	0	-	23	0	-	11	0	-	1	0	-	49	0	-
M4: OA6w	M	117	6	5.1	207	6	2.9	67	2	3.0	11	1	9.1	402	15	3.7
Unphased: Bl	F	4	0	-	3	0	-	9	0	-	0	0	-	16	0	-
Unphased: Bl	M	130	65	50.0	176	53	30.1	103	5	4.9	10	1	10.0	419	124	29.6
Unphased: OA6	F	26	7	26.9	40	9	22.5	18	4	22.2	2	2	100.0	86	22	25.6
Unphased: OA6	M	263	84	31.9	444	6	1.4	182	9	4.9	25	0	-	914	99	10.8

Table 68   Prevalence and distribution of cases of osteoarthritis other than in the vertebrae (see Table 53 for key to land use abbreviations)

Subsample (period: land use)	No. of individuals in subsample	No. affected as % of no. of individuals	Rib neck	Wrist	Hip	Elbow	Shoulder	First metatarsal	Ankle	Knee
M1: OA3	5	41.7	1	0	0	0	1	0	2	1
M1: OA6	25	30.5	9	6	7	0	10	4	3	5
M2: Bls	1	33.3	0	0	0	0	1	0	0	0
M2: OA3	10	45.5	2	0	0	0	8	0	2	0
M2: OA6	31	37.3	11	0	4	4	13	0	5	5
M3: Ble	3	50.0	1	0	1	0	2	0	2	0
M3: Bln	15	41.7	5	0	1	1	5	0	5	2
M3: OA3	26	33.3	12	8	4	1	11	0	7	2
M3: OA3i	9	29.0	2	2	0	1	4	0	4	1
M3: OA6	48	37.2	14	12	14	6	25	0	9	4
M4: Blnn	2	16.7	1	1	0	0	1	0	0	0
M4: OA6w	12	46.2	2	2	3	0	6	0	3	0
Unphased: Bl	14	45.2	4	2	0	1	8	0	2	1
Unphased: OA6	21	25.6	11	2	2	2	5	0	5	0
Total (664)	222	33.4	75	35	36	16	100	4	49	21

Saviour Bermondsey and St Mary Stratford Langthorne, where prevalence was described as infrequent (Connell and White 1998; White 2004, 176–7). As the same criteria were employed in scoring for the condition (Rogers and Waldron 1995), the most likely explanation would be the larger proportion of older individuals at Merton.

Diet

One possible indication of a deficiency in the diet may be related to morbus in tibia (Harvey 1993, 109), a multi-complaint of the shin bone, attributed to the effect of circulatory conditions (Harvey suggests prolonged standing still to sing the office as a contributory factor – see above, 'Physical activity', for possible supporting evidence), or reflecting a deficiency in vitamin C. In general, such periostitis can be the result of trauma, infection by common bacteria or systemic disease. In the skeleton vitamin C deficiency may present as periosteal new bone on the surface of the tibia. In all 158 individuals were affected on one or both tibias by this condition out of 484 individuals with tibias (32.6%). This was a very similar frequency to that observed at St Saviour Bermondsey (Connell and White 1998). Harvey (1993, 63) makes the point that the monastic diet, although excessive in some components, namely dairy produce and meat and fish, was probably deficient in vitamins A, C, and sometimes D when large amounts of fish were not available.

Interestingly, there were two possible cases of scurvy, perhaps lending support to the presence of a vitamin C deficiency. Both came from the north burial area (OA6) from periods M1 and M2 (Table 58). Individual [3891] had changes to the sphenoid (Fig 226) in keeping with those described by Ortner and Ericksen (1997) and very severe tooth wear which perhaps led to some difficulty later in life in eating foods so a tendency to eat sloppy, cooked or processed foods. Individual [2758] exhibited the same changes to the sphenoid and widespread periosteal bone on the femoral and tibial shafts. Less conclusively, there were five cases of severe alveolar osteitis extending over the palate which Molleson (Farwell and Molleson 1993, 185) has also attributed to vitamin C deficiency. Four of the five cases were again from Open Area 6, the fifth from an unphased burial within the church.

On the other hand, Harvey (1993, 63) also suggested a likely deficiency in vitamin D. The common manifestation of such a deficiency is rickets, but there was no evidence for this condition at Merton.

Cribra orbitalia is considered another indicator of stress. The porotic bone lesions in the roof of the orbit are often attributed to iron deficiency anaemia possibly as the result of dietary deficiency (Stuart-Macadam 1986). However, they could also be part of the body's response to fighting infection, and thus reflect levels of disease in the population (Goodman et al 1988). The Merton sample had an overall prevalence of 6.1% of all possible skulls affected either unilaterally or bilaterally. This was very similar to the rate observed at St Saviour Bermondsey (5.2%), but much lower than the 18.8% of cases at St Mary Stratford Langthorne (Connell and White 1998; White 2004, 176).

Low male stature has been attributed to a diet low in protein (Farwell and Molleson 1993, 184). This is probably not relevant in this analysis as many of the monastery inmates would have been at least in their teens before joining the community and therefore not as affected by this deficiency as someone who had lived with it all their lives.

There does appear to be limited evidence for some dietary deficiency. To balance this, evidence of excess should be considered. Gout is an affliction that comes to mind. However, only one questionable case was present, with characteristic lesions undercutting the articular surface of both first metatarsal head, and this individual was from period M1 of Open Area 6, perhaps the least likely area to manifest excesses if all the previous discussion is correct. Another possibility is diffuse idiopathic skeletal hyperostosis or DISH. Although the aetiology of this condition is still not known, increasing evidence links it to obesity and possibly late onset diabetes. It could, therefore, serve as a potential indicator of a high calorie diet. The overall prevalence at Merton was 8.6% of all individuals compared to a modern day rate of around 3%. The prevalence rate using clinical criteria was 5.7% but the other cases were clearly cases of DISH in a palaeopathological sense (Rogers and Waldron 1995, 51). A fascinating distribution became evident when the prevalence rates of individual subsamples were considered, even using only clinical cases (Table 69). The lowest prevalence rates were found habitually in Open Area 6, the possible mixed lay and clerical cemetery (although OA6 contained the highest number of definite and possible cases); rates were raised (about twice as high) in Open Area 3, the possible canon's cemetery,

Fig 226 Individual [3891] (period M1, OA6) sphenoid and maxilla with indications of scurvy (scale c 1:1)

Table 69 *Prevalence of cases of diffuse idiopathic skeletal hyperostosis (DISH) (see Table 53 for key to land use abbreviations)*

Subsample (period: land use)	No. in subsample	No. of definite cases	No. of possible cases	Bone-former	Total cases excluding bone-formers	Prevalence of definite cases %	Prevalence of possible cases %	Overall prevalence %
M1: OA3	12	1	0	0	1	8.3	-	8.3
M1: OA6	82	4	3	1	7	4.9	3.7	8.5
M2: B1s	3	0	1	0	1	33.3	-	33.3
M2: B3b	3	1	0	0	1	33.3	-	33.3
M2: OA3	22	2	2	1	4	9.1	9.1	18.2
M2: OA6	83	1	0	0	1	1.2	-	1.2
M3: B1e	6	1	0	0	1	16.7	-	16.7
M3: B1n	36	2	1	0	3	5.6	2.8	8.3
M3: B3b	1	1	0	0	1	100.0	-	100.0
M3: OA3	78	5	4	0	9	6.4	5.1	11.5
M3: OA3i	31	4	0	2	4	12.9	-	12.9
M3: OA6	129	7	5	2	12	5.4	3.9	9.3
M4: B1ac	1	1	0	0	1	100.0	-	100.0
M4: B1nn	12	2	0	0	2	16.7	-	16.7
M4: B1n	3	0	1	0	1	-	33.3	33.3
M4: B3b	19	1	1	1	2	5.3	5.3	10.5
Unphased: B1	31	2	0	1	2	6.5	-	6.5
Unphased: OA6	82	3	1	0	4	3.7	1.2	4.9
Total	664	38	19	8	57	5.7	2.7	8.6
M1–M4 B1	94	8	3	1	11	8.5	3.2	11.7
M1–M4 B3b	23	3	1	1	4	13.0	4.3	17.4
M1–M4 OA3	143	12	6	3	18	8.4	4.2	12.6
M1–M4 OA6	404	15	9	3	24	3.7	2.2	5.9

and in the church, with the highest rate of all in the chapter house, a likely location of privileged individuals.

Other characteristics of the diet are reflected by the dental pathology present in the sample. There must have been a coarse element to the diet as all adult age groups experienced tooth wear to some extent, and to a severe degree in the older age group (tabulated data in the archive). Dental caries may reflect sugar content in the diet (and hygiene levels). Males, females and children had similar prevalences at Merton with 10.1%, 10.9% and 11.4% of all teeth present affected respectively (Table 60). This was not dissimilar to the prevalence of 12.1% in the monastic period at St Andrew, Fishergate, York, but higher than that at St Saviour Bermondsey of 6.5% and St Mary, Stratford Langthorne (Stroud and Kemp 1993, 257; Connell and White 1998; White 2004, 178). The Merton caries prevalence showed an increase over earlier medieval rates of around 5%, and this probably reflects the increase in sugars in the diet, both in the form of fruits and honey, and in imported sugar cane from the 13th century. Caries prevalence varied between the areas of the complex, but no clear pattern emerged to suggest that any section of the sample was worse affected. It was also the case that sometimes the lowest caries prevalence occurred in subsamples with the higher rates of ante-mortem tooth loss, such as the males from period M1 Open Area 3 (Table 59). In these cases severely carious teeth may have been lost ante-mortem thus giving a deceptively low caries prevalence. Again

there is no set pattern to this distribution across the subsamples with some having high ante-mortem loss and caries, and some having low prevalence of both.

Calculus, calcified deposits of plaque on the teeth, was a widespread, severe problem (Table 60). Given the high rates present, the lower rates of alveolar resorption and periodontal disease present were of note. No children were affected (Table 61). Male and female rates of alveolar resorption were 34.5% and 40.2% of all bone sites available affected respectively, and of periodontal disease 35% and 32.9% respectively.

The similarity of the prevalences for the two conditions is not surprising given their inter-relatedness. All three conditions, calculus deposits, alveolar resorption and periodontal disease are cumulative with age and reflect hygiene levels. Poor hygiene allows a build-up of calculus over time and the irritant by-products of the bacteria which live in plaque deposits can contribute to the progression of periodontal disease (Fig 227). The high calculus prevalence, therefore, suggests that poor oral hygiene was practised. Harvey (1993, 135), in her survey of Westminster, concludes that personal hygiene standards were low. Something must, therefore, be off-setting this poor hygiene to explain the lesser periodontal disease prevalence. This could well be the coarse element to the diet suggested by the tooth wear rates, as this would stimulate the gums during mastication and help to keep them healthy.

Fig 227 Example of gum disease in individual [2741] (periods M1–M4, OA6) (scale c 1:2)

Hygiene

In addition to oral health, the presence of parasites can be an indication of the general standard of hygiene in the establishment. A pilot study on 20 samples found such a low presence of parasitic nematode eggs that a more extensive examination was not thought worthwhile.

Stress in childhood

Other types of stress, other than dietary deficits, can affect the skeletal and dental development of children. With only three children under 6 years of age, it was not surprising that few data emerged about this age group. There were, however, many cases of dental hypoplasia (Table 60), an interruption of the normal formation of the enamel of the tooth in response to stress in childhood. This stress may be nutritional, psychological, or due to severe illness. In children, 2.9% of all deciduous teeth were affected, 11.5% of adult female teeth and 10.2% of males. The sexes did not appear to have received differing treatment in childhood based on the similarity of these rates. Again there did not appear to be a discernible pattern in the varying rates between subsamples (Table 60).

Evidence of overcrowding

Tuberculosis is often associated with conditions of poverty and overcrowding. There were only four possible cases identifiable in the sample using traditional characteristics, such as Pott's spine, three from periods M3 and unphased burials of Open Area 6 and one from period M3 Open Area 3. The spine was implicated in all four cases, and other parts of the body in two. Whilst this would not seem to indicate marked levels of either poverty or overcrowding, it is interesting that the majority of cases again come from Open Area 6, the most likely area to include lay personnel other than the upper classes.

It is possible that a much larger number of cases was present based on less conventional characteristics. Nearly a fifth of all individuals (a minimum figure) exhibited periosteal new bone formation on the visceral surface of ribs (Fig 228; Table 70). In two instances there may also be associated active erosive lesions. Right and left ribs were more or less equally affected,

and the impression was gained that all ribs could be involved. It is difficult to be more specific than this as the majority of ribs were fragmentary and pieces could not be sided. There appeared to be no pattern to their distribution between the subsamples (Table 70). Roberts et al (1994), in a survey of the Terry collection, found that such rib lesions were more common in individuals dying from tuberculosis (61.6%) than in individuals dying from other causes (15.2%). At the least, rib lesions suggest a pulmonary infection. Merton's environment is known to have been marshy and wet, certainly to the west of the claustral complex. Perhaps such damp conditions promoted

Fig 228 Examples of rib lesions: a – on the surface of the right rib of individual [2984] (period M3, OA6) (scale c 1:1); b – two right rib lesions with periosteal bone of individual [4196] (period M2, OA6) (scale c 1:2)

Table 70 Prevalence of cases of healed periosteal bone on the pulmonary surface of ribs (see Table 53 for key to land use abbreviations)

Subsample (period: land use)	No. of individuals affected	No. in subsample	Left	Right	Unsided	Prevalence %
M1: OA3	3	12	2	1	0	25.0
M1: OA6	14	82	11	7	2	17.1
M2: BIn	1	2	1	1	0	25.0
M2: BIs	1	3	1	1	0	33.3
M2: OA3	4	22	3	3	0	18.2
M2: OA6	9	83	4	7	1	10.8
M3: BIe	2	6	1	1	1	33.3
M3: BIn	5	36	1	3	1	13.9
M3: OA3	22	78	17	18	0	28.2
M3: OA3i	3	31	3	3	0	9.7*
M3: OA6	21	129	15	11	1	16.3
M4: BInn	1	12	1	1	0	8.3
M4: OA6w	6	26	5	4	0	23.1
Unphased: BI	11	31	11	10	0	35.5*
Unphased: OA6	11	82	8	10	0	13.4
Total	114	635**	84	81	6	18.0***

*: includes a possible active erosive lesion
**: excludes 29 burials: M2, M3, M4: B3b; M4: BIac; M4: BIn; M4: OA6e
***: an overall prevalence rate for the total population of 664 of 17.2%

widespread affliction with chronic pulmonary infections of some kind. The work of Gernaey et al (1998), identifying the presence of tuberculosis by means of mycolic acids, could be of great use in ascertaining which of the two was the most likely scenario. Although the lifestyle of a medieval monk could not be said to be one of poverty, the cloister monks lived, prepared food and slept communally (Harvey 1993, 143), meaning that infectious disease could be spread very easily. These cloister monks tended to be young and, therefore, perhaps more vulnerable to infection, and they made up about a third of the monastic community. The fact that the majority of lesions were examples of healed periosteal new bone suggests that whatever the complaint it was probably chronic and the sufferers were often sufficiently fit to survive, or live with, the infection.

The prevalence rate of the rib lesions for each subsample was compared to that for DISH, the reasoning being that those individuals suffering from DISH often produce large amounts of bone in association with other conditions as a by-product of DISH. High prevalence of these rib lesions has not been reported frequently from other monastic sites, so there was a remote possibility that the high rate of DISH at Merton was leading to individuals being more prone to build-up deposits of periosteal bone.

There was no correlation between the prevalence rates for the two conditions within each subsample suggesting that the high rate of rib lesions relative to other monastic sites is a genuine feature.

Support from the community

There were five cases of spina bifida occulta, four with the sacral canal open for its entire length. Three were from Open Area 6, one from Open Area 3 and one (unphased, M1–M4) from the church. The sufferer would probably be unaware of this condition in life, except in one case from period M1 Open Area 6, where the laminae of the first and second thoracic vertebrae were unfused perhaps indicating a case of true spina bifida (Fig 229). If so the individual is likely to have needed some degree of help and support from the community.

Sufferers of certain other pathologies may have required assistance if and when their condition became sufficiently disabilitating. For example, [4735] in period M1 Open Area 6 may have suffered from a sero-negative arthropathy which would deteriorate over time; an individual with probable diaphyseal aclasia (Fig 230), [3878] buried in Open Area 6 period M3, was grossly malformed and would have almost certainly required care; another individual from the same subsample, [2532] had possible chondromalacia affecting both patellae which would have caused pain whilst climbing stairs for example and perhaps needed the use of a stick when walking; [3811] in period M4 Open Area 6 may have had a neuropathic left foot, with disuse atrophy affecting the metatarsals and severe secondary infection to the metatarsals, indicating some condition which has caused sensory deprivation with secondary infection such as polio, diabetes or leprosy, though there were no signs of the latter elsewhere in the

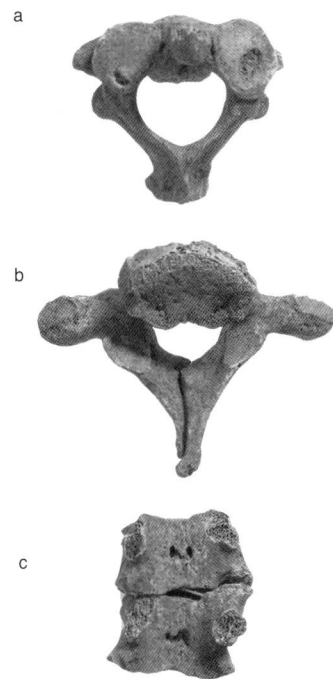

Fig 229 Defects to vertebrae: a – subchondral bone defects to both sides of C2, b – spina bifida to T1, disc disease, and c – congential fusion for two thoracic vertebrae, by pedicals, individual [5194] (period M3, OA6) (scale c 1:2)

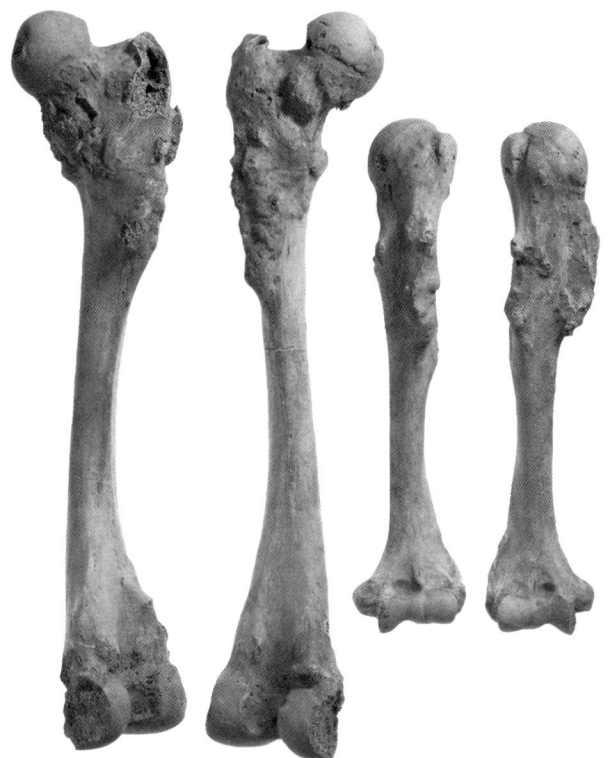

Fig 230 Evidence of diaphysial aclasia, individual [3878] (period M3, OA6) (scale c 1:4)

skeleton. It was interesting that all these examples came from Open Area 6, perhaps suggesting that some of the people buried there may have been under the protection of the monastery.

Pathology of old age

Certain conditions are indicative of the presence of an older aged component in the sample. The high prevalence of DISH has already been mentioned, and this tends to afflict males over 45 years of age. There was only one case of a possible sero-negative arthropathy; these can reflect the presence of older adults or familial relationships or even environmental pollution. One case is not sufficient to interpret in such a way. Degenerative joint disease tends to accumulate with age. The rates of osteoarthritis have already been discussed. Conditions classed as general degeneration, often the early stages of osteoarthritis but not satisfying the diagnostic criteria for the latter (that is pitting and or enlargement of a joint surface), were widespread and frequent with an overall prevalence of 41.9% of individuals affected (Table 58). Prevalence of osteophytosis was somewhat lower at 22.9% of all individuals affected. There was a very low prevalence (0.8% of all skulls present compared to 4% in modern populations) of hyperostosis frontalis interna. This condition generally affects post-menopausal women, thus accounting for the low prevalence in this sample, which contains relatively few females. Osteoporosis (loss of bone mass) is another condition that affects females more frequently than males in modern society. There were only five individuals affected. Finally Paget's Disease tends to affect predominantly males over 65 years of age today at a rate of about 7%. Thirteen individuals were possibly affected in all, an overall prevalence of 2% of all individuals.

Remaining pathology

Neoplasms

Neoplasms are abnormal masses of tissue commonly referred to as tumours. Benign types such as button osteomas on the skull are not uncommon in archaeological material, but examples of malignant cancer are more unusual. The overall prevalence for all neoplastic disease was 5.1% of all individuals affected, not dissimilar to modern rates. In summary, 4.2% of all individuals were affected by the benign button osteomas and 0.9% (six cases) by malignant varieties. These were drawn from all areas of the site and included two cases of meningiomas, one odontoblast, one possible leukaemic reaction, one possible osteoma on a left femur and one metastatic carcinoma in a female.

Bunions (hallux valgus)

These lesions to the first metatarsal and proximal foot phalange are often taken to indicate the wearing of tight footwear. There was evidence that 0.6% of all individuals had the right foot affected and 0.3% had the left affected.

Haematoma

Damage to soft tissue can result in tearing of ligaments and tendons and ossification of any associated haematoma (blood clot). The tibia, femur, fibula and rib were affected at Merton with an overall prevalence of 1.3% of individuals affected.

Congenital and developmental disorders

A variety of congenital disorders were present in small numbers: palatal torus (one case); mandibular torus (one); mid and distal foot phalanges fused (eight); bipartite navicular (two); bipartite first cuneiform (two); unfused thoracic laminae (one); flattened head to first right metacarpal (ten); flattened head to first left metacarpal (seven); hamate hook absent (nine); six lumbar vertebrae (one); lumbarised S1 (two); sacralised L5 (one); fusion of carpals (two); accessory facet on sacrum (one).

Other pathology

A number of single cases of probable pathological variation that do not easily fit into any of the above categories are listed in the archive.

7.12 The dendrochronological analysis

Gretel Boswijk and Ian Tyers

A total of 35 samples from Merton Priory were originally submitted for dendrochronological spot-dating. These samples were derived from excavations undertaken many years ago and were not in particularly good condition. No sample is complete to bark-edge. Where a sample has some sapwood, but is not complete to the bark-edge a felling date range is obtained by applying the maximum and minimum numbers of rings of sapwood normally seen in English oaks, to the relevant samples. All oak material has been reinterpreted using sapwood estimates 10–46 (I Tyers, pers comm 2006). Where no sapwood survives a *terminus post quem* date is obtained by adding the minimum number of sapwood rings likely to have been lost to the date of the latest surviving ring. This type of date is very much less useful than the other two types since a very great number of rings could have been lost either through ancient carpentry practise, or poor site preservation, and thus the felling date of such material may be considerably later than the tree-ring date.

The results for 15 timbers found to date successfully are summarised in Table 71.

Table 71 Dendrochronological results for timber from St Mary Merton (periods M1—M4)

Period	Land use	Context no.	Description	Associated skeleton	Sample no.	Species	No. of rings	Type of end rings	Date of sequence (AD)	Interpretation
M1	OA6	[4836]	plank burial	[4893]	86 {2659} timber B	oak	68		932–99	after 1009
M1	OA8	[9237]	wattle-lined ditch	n/a	88 {3811 087} sample 1	oak	133		980–1112	after 1122
M1	OA8	[9237]	wattle-lined ditch	n/a	88 {3811 087} sample 2	oak	80		1033–1112	after 1122
M1	OA8	[9264]	wattle-lined ditch	n/a	88 {3815 093}	oak	144	?h/s	949–1092	1102–?47
M2	OA6	[4582]	plank burial	[4530]	86 {2638}	oak	156		942–1097	after 1107
M3	OA3	[5256]	plank burial	[5056]	86 {2662} timber A	oak	150	h/s	1006–1155	1165–1210
M3	OA3	[5256] timber B	plank burial	[5056]	86 {2662} timber B	oak	125		1052–1176	after 1186
M3	OA3	[5293]	coffin	[5077]	86 {2663} timber B	oak	151		971–1121	after 1131
M3	OA3	[7099]	coffin	[7098]	88 {3256 033}	oak	120		947–1066	after 1076
M3	OA3	[7121]	coffin	[7116]	88 {3034 010} sample 1	oak	83		1036–1118	after 1128
M3	OA3	[7635]	coffin	[7634]	88 {3211 028}	oak	102		985–1086	after 1096
M1–M4	OA6	[4587]	plank burial	[4567]	86 {2646} timber A	oak	102		980–1081	after 1091
M1–M4	OA6	[4781]	plank burial	[4707]	86 {2660} timber A	oak	105		922–1026	after 1036
M1–M4	OA6	[4955]	coffin	[4942]	86 {2661} timber A	oak	157		971–1127	after 1137
M2–M4	S9	[10319]	fishpond	n/a	88 {4378 161}	oak	119		969–1087	after 1097

h/s: heartwood/sapwood boundary
?h/s: possible heartwood/sapwood boundary

FRENCH AND GERMAN SUMMARIES

Résumé

Le prieuré augustinien de Notre-Dame de Merton (Surrey) fut fondé en 1117 par Gilbert, bailli du Surrey. Les fouilles conduites de 1976 à 1990 mirent au jour une large partie de l'établissement médiéval situé à environ 11 km au sud-ouest de Londres, sur les bords de la rivière Wandle. Merton, l'une des maisons de chanoines réguliers les plus influentes d'Angleterre, reçut au XIIIe siècle la faveur d'Henri III, qui y séjourna fréquemment.

Les recherches permirent de restituer la topographie et l'évolution du prieuré du XIIe siècle jusqu'à la Dissolution (chapitres 2 et 3). Les fouilles révélèrent les vestiges d'une église en pierre, commencée vers 1170 et probablement achevée vers 1200, située sur une plate-forme au-dessus de la plaine alluviale et des marais. Cependant, des fragments architecturaux déplacés et des données stratigraphiques et textuelles suggèrent qu'il ne s'agissait pas de la première église de pierre mais qu'un édifice plus précoce avait été construit à proximité, au milieu du XIIe siècle. La deuxième église fut reconstruite au XIIIe siècle, probablement après la chute de la tour attestée en 1222. Au sud de la nouvelle église, plusieurs bâtiments du XIIIe siècle furent identifiés à la fouille : une partie du cloître et des ailes est et sud, y compris une salle de chapitre rectangulaire (présentant des carreaux de pavement vernissés unis et décorés), séparée du bras sud du transept par un passage couvert ou peut-être un vestiaire ; le soubassement des latrines et, au sud-est, une vaste infirmerie dotée de son propre cloître et d'une chapelle. Le cloître principal, au sud de l'église, était apparemment séparé de la nef par un espace ouvert, un élément inhabituel dans une maison augustinienne. Une porterie, un moulin et ce qui a pu être une vaste hôtellerie à bas-côtés furent aussi identifiés à l'intérieur de l'enclos. Dans le courant du XIVe siècle, la construction d'un nouveau chevet et d'une chapelle mariale donna à l'église une longueur d'environ 110 m, tandis que la salle capitulaire fut reconstruite avec une extrémité absidale. A la même époque, la grande salle de l'infirmerie fut compartimentée pour créer des espaces privés. Des édifices secondaires adjacents à l'infirmerie ont pu remplir des fonctions domestiques et médicales. Certains des bâtiments prieuraux, en particulier l'église, furent largement détruits après la Dissolution et de grandes quantités de pierres furent utilisées pour construire le palais d'Henri VIII de Nonsuch, près d'Ewell (Surrey). Des éléments de construction – notamment des moulures, des fragments de verres à vitres et des carreaux – récupérés dans les couches de démolition ont permis de mieux restituer l'apparence des bâtiments.

Une série de sections thématiques (chapitre 4) concerne les points majeurs de la recherche. La fondation et l'histoire précoce du prieuré, ainsi que la topographie monastique, sont analysées. Une restitution architecturale est proposée des transformations de la salle capitulaire et de l'église dans son état du XIVe siècle, correspondant à l'une des réalisations majeures de la « période Décorée » dans le sud-est de l'Angleterre. L'ensemble de l'infirmerie a été largement fouillé et offre un grand intérêt. Destinés au soin de la communauté monastique, la grande salle, la chapelle, le cloître et les lieux de stockage formaient un ensemble indépendant, dont les bâtiments doublaient les fonctions de l'ensemble principal et où les serviteurs, les « corrodians » (c'est-à-dire des laïcs qui ont mérité le droit de logement gratuit dans l'enclos monastique) et autres laïcs pouvaient parfois être admis. Les indices témoignant de traitements médicaux (dont un éventuel bandage herniaire et des plantes médicinales), la nourriture et le régime alimentaire, la culture matérielle et la vie quotidienne ainsi que l'économie monastique sont considérés, de même que l'identité des occupants du prieuré et de ceux qui furent inhumés dans différents secteurs de l'enclos. Le grand nombre de tombes fouillées (721 inhumations, dont 664 analysées, compte non tenu des ossuaires et des grandes quantités d'ossements erratiques), provenant du cimetière, de l'intérieur de l'église, du cloître et de la salle capitulaire, est d'une importance nationale. La diversité des pratiques funéraires ainsi que la courbe démographique et l'état sanitaire des individus sont étudiés. Une dernière section considère la place de Merton dans l'Ordre des Augustiniens et l'importance du patronage royal.

Les conséquences de la Dissolution et l'histoire du site jusqu'au XIXe siècle sont résumées dans le chapitre 5. La location des bâtiments subsistants, le cantonnement de troupes pendant la Guerre Civile et le développement à partir des années 1660 de « Merton Abbey » comme centre de production, en particulier d'une manufacture de textiles, sont présentés. Les conclusions et l'exposé des recherches à venir constituent le chapitre 6 tandis que le dernier chapitre réunit les rapports de spécialistes y compris les catalogues de mobilier.

Zusammenfassung

Das Augustinerpriorat St. Maria (Merton, Surrey) wurde 1117 von Gilbert, dem Sheriff von Surrey, gegründet. Ausgrabungen zwischen 1976 und 1990 förderten viel des kleinen mittelalterlichen Klosters zutage, das 11,3 km südwestlich von London am Flußufer des Wandle lag. Merton stellte eines der einflußreichsten englischen Häuser von Ordenskanonikern dar; während des 13. Jhs. wurde es von Heinrich III. besonders geschätzt und häufig besucht.

Die Untersuchungen erlauben es, Elemente des Grundrisses und der Entwicklung des Klosters vom 12. Jh. bis zu seiner Säkularisierung im 16. Jh. zu verfolgen (Kapitel 2 und 3). Die Ausgrabung erbrachte die Reste einer steinernen Kirche auf einer Plattform oberhalb von Überschwemmungsebene und Sumpf; ihr Bau hatte ca. 1170 begonnen und war möglicherweise bis 1200 fertig gestellt worden. Nicht mehr in ihrer ursprünglichen Lage gefundene Architekturfragmente sowie stratigraphische Beobachtungen und historische Dokumentation legen allerdings nahe, daß dies nicht die erste Steinkirche am Ort war und ein früherer Bau in der Nähe existiert haben muß, der um die Mitte des 12. Jhs. errichtet worden war. Die Kirche des späten 12. oder frühen 13. Jhs. wurde im 13. Jh. wiedererrichtet, wahrscheinlich nach dem historisch überlieferten Einsturz des Turms im Jahre 1222.

Gebäude aus dem 13. Jh., die südlich von der neuen Kirche identifiziert wurden, beinhalten Teile des Kreuzganges und des Ost- und Südflügels, inklusive eines quadratisch abschließenden Kapitelsaales mit Schmuckfußboden aus großen sowohl einfarbig glasierten als auch verzierten Fliesen. Der Kapitelsaal war vom südlichen Querschiff durch einen überdachten Gang oder möglicherweise ein Vestiarium getrennt. Es gab außerdem eine Latrinenkrypta und im Südosten ein großes Klosterkrankenhaus mit eigenem Kreuzgang und eigener Kapelle. Zwischen dem Hauptkreuzgang südlich der Kirche und dem Seitenschiff lag offenbar ein freier Platz, was ein ungewöhnliches Element in einem Augustinerkloster darstellt. Eine Torhalle, eine Mühle und möglicherweise eine große mehrschiffige Gästehalle wurden darüber hinaus auf dem Klostergelände identifiziert. Im 14. Jh. kam es durch den Bau eines Presbyteriums und einer Marienkapelle zur Verlängerung der Kirche auf 110 m, und auch der Kapitelsaal wurde erneuert und mit einem apsidialen Abschluß versehen. Im Krankenhaus entstanden zu dieser Zeit Unterteilungen, um private Unterbringungen zu schaffen. Nebengebäude nahe des Krankenhauses könnten ähnliche häusliche und medizinische Funktionen erfüllt haben. Einige der Klosterbauten, besonders die Kirche, wurden nach der Säkularisierung weitgehend zerstört, und große Mengen geraubter Steine fanden beim Bau des Palasts von Nonsuch, nahe Ewell (Surrey), durch Heinrich VIII. als Spolien Verwendung. Baumaterial – vor allem Architekturplastik, Fensterglas und Fliesen – wurden insbesondere aus den Abbruchschichten geborgen und ermöglichen eine detailliertere Rekonstruktion des Erscheinungsbildes der Klostergebäude.

Eine Anzahl von Beiträgen (Kapitel 4) behandelt wichtige Forschungsthemen. Die Gründung und frühe Geschichte des Priorats sowie die Gestaltung der voll entwickelten Anlage werden beschrieben. Es wird versucht, die sich verändernde Form des Kapitelsaales und der Klosterkirche zu rekonstruieren, was in der Osterweiterung des 14. Jhs., einem verlorenen Hauptwerk des „Decorated" Stils in Südostengland seine Vollendung fand. Dem großflächig ausgegrabenen Krankenhauskomplex von Merton gilt besonderes Interesse. Krankenhaushalle, -kapelle, -kreuzgang und -nebengebäude, in ihrer Funktion den Gebäuden des eigentlichen Klaustrumkomplexes vergleichbar, bildeten eine eigenständige Anlage für die Pflege des Klosterpersonals und gelegentlich auch der Dienerschaft, der „corrodians" (d.h. Laien, die das Recht auf Unterkunft und Verpflegung im Klosterbezirk verdient oder gekauft hatten) und anderer Laien. Die Nachweise für medizinische Versorgung und Behandlung (inklusive eines möglichen Bruchbands und medizinischer Pflanzen), Nahrung und Ernährung, Gegenstände des täglichen Lebens und die klösterliche Wirtschaft werden besprochen sowie die Identität der Klosterbewohner und derjenigen, die an verschiedenen Stellen des Klostergeländes begraben waren. Die hohe Anzahl der freigelegten Bestattungen (721 Körpergräber, 664 davon untersucht, ausgenommen Beingruben und große Mengen menschlicher Knochen aus dem Siedlungsareal ohne Grabzusammenhang) aus dem Kirchhof, dem

Kircheninnenraum, dem Kreuzgang und dem Kapitelsaal besitzt nationale Bedeutung. Eine Bandbreite an Bestattungssitten, das demographische Profil sowie Gesundheit und Krankheit sind Gegenstand weiterer Betrachtung. Das Kapitel „The priory in its wider context" („Das Priorat in seinem breiteren Zusammenhang") beschäftigt sich mit Mertons Rolle und Stellenwert im Augustinerorden und mit der Bedeutung des königlichen Patronats.

Die Auswirkungen der Säkularisierung und die Geschichte des Fundplatzes bis ins 19. Jh. werden in Kapitel 5 behandelt. Die Vermietung der überlebenden Gebäude, die Stationierung von Truppen während des Bürgerkrieges der 1640er und die Entwicklung von „Merton Abbey" als Produktionszentrum speziell für Textilien seit den 1660ern kommen hier unter anderem zur Sprache. Schlußergebnisse und zukünftige Forschungsthemen werden in Kapitel 6 dargelegt. Den letzten Teil bilden die Beiträge der Spezialisten samt Fundkatalogen in Kapitel 7.

BIBLIOGRAPHY

Manuscript sources

Bodleian Library, Oxford (Bodleian)

Laud MS 723 Merton Priory miscellany

British Library, London, manuscripts department (BL)

Cotton MS Cleopatra C.vii cartulary of charters and deeds for Merton Priory

College of Arms, London

MS 28 *Historia fundationis prioratus de Merton*

Conway Library, Courtauld Institute of Art, University of London

Photographs of Dunstable Priory and Peterborough Cathedral

Merton Library and Heritage Service, Morden (MLHS)

Pictorial and other material: photographs, plans etc, including H F Bidder's plan of the 1920s excavation and J P Malcolm's engraving of *c* 1800

The National Archives (TNA): Public Record Office (PRO)

CHANCERY
C66 patent rolls
C78 Chancery decree rolls

EXCHEQUER CLASSES
E147 particulars for grants and leases
E314 Augmentations miscellanea
E315 miscellaneous books of the Court of Augmentations
E322 monastic surrenders

MINISTERS' ACCOUNTS
SC6/Henry VIII rentals and surveys
SC12 rentals and surveys

MINISTRY OF WORKS
WORK 14/740 case file for Merton Priory, 1914

PREROGATIVE COURT OF CANTERBURY WILLS
PROB11/3 wills of Roger Tye of Merton, 1428, and Beatrice Hayton of Merton, 1433
PROB11/18 will of Thomas Salyng, 1517
PROB11/20 will of William Clopton, 1521

Surrey History Centre, Woking (SHC)

Zs/261 estate map of Merton Abbey, 1805

Warwick University, History of Art Department, Coventry

LSP 1017 example of architectural fragment from St Paul's, London, in reference collection of moulding records

Printed and other secondary works

Abdy, C, and Bierton, G, 1997 A gazeteer of Romano-British archaeological sites in Ewell, *Surrey Archaeol Collect* 84, 123–41

Ann Monast Annales Monastici (ed H R Luard), Rolls Series, 5 vols, 1864–9, London

Arkell, W J, 1947 *Geology of Oxford*, Oxford

Arnold, H R, 1993 *Atlas of mammals in Britain*, Inst Terrestrial Ecol Res Publ 6, London

Arnold, H R, 1995 *Atlas of amphibians and reptiles in Britain*, Inst Terrestrial Ecol Res Publ 10, London

Astill, G, and Wright, S M, 1993 Perceiving patronage in the archaeological record: Bordesley Abbey, in Carver, M, *In search of cult: archaeological investigations in honour of Philip Rahtz*, 125–37, Woodbridge

Astill, G, Hirst, S, and Wright, S M, 2004 The Bordesley Abbey project reviewed, *Archaeol J* 161, 106–58

Aston, M, 1993 *Monasteries*, London

Aston, M, 2000 *Monasteries in the landscape*, Stroud

Aubrey, J, 1718 *A perambulation of the county of Surrey; begun 1673, ended 1692*, London

Barber, B, Chew, S, Dyson, T, and White, B, 2004 *The Cistercian abbey of St Mary Stratford Langthorne, Essex: archaeological excavations for the London Underground Limited Jubilee Line Extension project*, MoLAS Monogr Ser 18, London

Bass, W M, 1995 (1971) *Human osteology: a laboratory and field manual*, 4 edn, Missouri Archaeol Soc Spec Pap 2, Columbia

Bazely, R, 1989a King's College sports ground (west), unpub MoL rep

Bazely, R, 1989b King's College sports ground (east), unpub MoL rep

Beijerinck, W, 1947 *Zadenatlas der Nederlansche Flora: I–II*, Veenman and Zonen, Wageningen

Bennett, K D, Whittington, G, and Edwards, K, 1994 Recent plant nomenclatural changes and pollen morphology in the British Isles, *Quaternary Newsl* 73, 1–6

Berggren, G, 1981 *Atlas of seeds and small fruits of north-west European plant species: Part 3, Salicaeaea-Cruciferae*, Stockholm

Berry, A C, and Berry, R J, 1967 Pigenetic variation in the human cranium, *J Anat* 101, 361–79

Betts, I M, 1990 Building materials, in Medieval buildings in the vicinity of Cheapside, London (eds J Schofield, P Allan and C Taylor), *Trans London Middlesex Archaeol Soc* 41, 220–9

Betts, I M, 1996 Glazed 11th-century wall tiles from London, *Medieval Ceram* 20, 19–24

Betts, I M, 1997 Merton Priory, ceramic and stone building material, unpub MoL rep

Betts, I M, 2002 *Medieval 'Westminster' floor tiles*, MoLAS Monogr Ser 11, London

Betts, I M, in prep a Building materials, in Bowsher et al in prep

Betts, I M, in prep b Building materials, in Sloane in prep

Betts, I M, in prep c Painted wall plaster, ceramic and stone building material from Thurnham Roman villa, in Booth in prep

Betts, I M, and Smith, T P, in prep Medieval ceramic and stone building material from Parsonage Farm, Westwell, in Booth in prep

Bidder, H F, 1934 Some new material for the determination of the course of Stane Street 17th century, *Surrey Archaeol Collect* 42, 11–25

Bidder, H F, and Westlake, M V O, 1930 Excavations at Merton Priory, *Surrey Archaeol Collect* 38(1), 49–66

Biddle, M, 1990 *Object and economy in medieval Winchester: artefacts from medieval Winchester*, Winchester Stud 7(2) (2 vols), Oxford

Biddle, M, and Hinton, D, 1990 Copper-alloy bells, in Biddle 1990, 725–7

Bilson, J, 1909 The architecture of the Cistercians, *Archaeol J* 64, 185–280

Blair, J, 1987 English monumental brasses before 1350: types, patterns and workshops, in *The earliest English brasses: patronage, style and workshops, 1270–1350* (ed J Coales), 133–74, London

Bodleian Charters Calendar of charters and rolls preserved in the Bodleian Library (eds W H Turner and H O Coxe) 1878, Oxford

Bond, J, 2001 Monastic water management in Great Britain: a review, in *Monastic archaeology: papers on the study of medieval monasteries* (eds G Keevill, M Aston and T Hall), 88–136, Oxford

Booth, P (ed), in prep Ceramics from section one of the Channel Tunnel Rail Link, Kent, *CTRL scheme-wide specialist report series*, CTRL digital archive, Archaeology Data Service, http://ads.ahds.ac.uk/catalogue/projArch/ctrl

Borg, A, 1967 The development of chevron ornament, *J Brit Archaeol Ass* 30, 123–40

Bottomley, F, 1995 *The abbey explorer's guide*, Otley

Bowsher, D, Dyson, T, Holder, N, and Howell, I in prep *The London Guildhall: an archaeological history of a neighbourhood from early medieval to modern times*, MoLAS Monogr Ser, London

Brenan, J, 1998 Furnishings, in Egan 1998, 65–87

Bridge Accounts London Bridge: selected accounts and rentals, 1381–1538 (eds V Harding and L Wright), London Rec Soc 31, 1995, London

Britton, J, 1836 *Cathedral antiquities: Vol 5, Peterborough, Gloucester, and Bristol*, London

Britton, J, 1997 (1828) *The history and antiquities of Peterborough Cathedral*, repr, Glossop

Brooks, S T, and Suchey, J M, 1990 Skeletal age determination based on the *os pubis*: comparison of the Ascadi-Nemeskeri and Suchey-Brooks methods, *J Hum Evol* 5, 227–38

Brothwell, D R, 1971a Medieval human remains from the Coventry Cathedral site, in Hobley, B, *Excavations at the cathedral and Benedictine priory of St Mary Coventry*, 130–9, Oxford

Brothwell, D R, 1971b Palaeodemography, in *Biological aspects of demography* (ed W Brass), 111–29, London

Brothwell, D R, 1981 *Digging up bones*, 3 edn, London

Bruce, P, and Mason, S, 1993 *Merton Priory*, London

Buikstra, J E, and Ubelaker, D H, 1994 *Standards for data collection from human remains*, Washington DC

Burton, J, 1994 *Monastic and religious orders in Britain 1000–1300*, Cambridge

Butler, L, 1956 Medieval gravestones of Cambridgeshire, Huntingdonshire and the soke of Peterborough, *Proc Cambridge Antiq Soc* 50, 89–100

Butler, L, and Given-Wilson, C, 1979 *Medieval monasteries of Great Britain*, London

Byard, S, 2001 English hospitals from the Conquest to the Dissolution, unpub PhD thesis, Courtauld Institute of Art

Cal Chart R *Calendars of charter rolls* (6 vols), 1903–27, London

Cal Close R *Calendars of close rolls*, 1892–1975, London

Cal Fine R *Calendars of fine rolls*, 1911–63, London

Cal Husting Wills *Calendar of wills proved and enrolled in the Court of Husting, London, AD 1258–1688* (ed R R Sharpe), 2 vols, 1889–90, London

Cal Inq Misc *Calendars of inquisitions miscellaneous*, 1916–69, London

Cal L Book D *Calendar of letter books of the City of London: letter book D, AD 1309–14* (ed R R Sharpe), 1899–1912, London

Cal L Book E *Calendar of letter books of the City of London: letter book E, AD 1314–37* (ed R R Sharpe), 1899–1912, London

Cal Pat R *Calendars of patent rolls* (65 vols, 1291–1509, 1547–63), 1893–1948, London

Cal Pat R Edward VI *Calendar of the patent rolls preserved in the Public Record Office: Edward VI* (6 vols: 1547–8; 1548–9; 1549–51; 1550–3; 1553, appendix 1547–53; index), 1924–9, London

Cal Pat R Elizabeth *Calendar of the patent rolls preserved in the Public Record Office: Elizabeth* (9 vols: 1558–60; 1560–3; 1563–6; 1566–9; 1569–72; 1572–5; 1575–8; 1578–80; 1580–2), 1939–, London

Cal Pat R Philip and Mary *Calendar of the patent rolls preserved in the Public Record Office: Philip and Mary* (4 vols: 1553–4; 1554–5; 1555–7; 1557–8), 1936–9, London

Cal Plea and Mem R *Calendar of plea and memoranda rolls preserved among the archives of the Corporation of the City of London: Vols 1–4, 1323–1437* (ed A H Thomas), 1926–43, Cambridge; *Vols 5–6, 1437–82* (ed P E Jones), 1953–61, London

Cambridge, E, 1977 The early building history of St Andrews Cathedral, Fife, and its context in northern transitional architecture, *Antiq J* 57, 277–88

Cameron, E, 1999 Merton Priory strap – report on fibre samples, unpub Institute of Archaeology Oxford rep

Campbell, B M S, Galloway, J A, Keene, D, and Murphy, M, 1993 *A medieval capital and its grain supply: agrarian production and distribution in the London region c 1300*, Hist Geogr Res Ser 30, London

Cart Holy Trinity *The cartulary of Holy Trinity, Aldgate* (ed G A J Hodgett), London Rec Soc Publ 7, 1971, Leicester

Cart St Bart *Cartulary of St Bartholomew's Hospital founded 1123* (ed N J Kerling), 1973, London

Cart St Mary Clerkw *The cartulary of St Mary Clerkenwell* (ed W O Hassall), Camden Soc 3 ser 71, 1949, London

Cat Anc Deeds *A descriptive catalogue of ancient deeds in the Public Record Office* (6 vols), 1900, London

Cherry, B, and Pevsner, N, 1991 *The buildings of England: Devon*, 2 edn, repr with corrections, Harmondsworth

Chew, H M, and Kellaway, W (eds), 1973 *London assize of nuisance 1301–1431: a calendar*, London Rec Soc 10, London

Chron Majora *Matthaei Parisiensis, monachi Sancti Albani, chronica majora* (ed H R Luard), Chronicles and memorials of Great Britain and Ireland during the Middle Ages (7 vols), 1872–80, London

Clapham, A R, Tutin, T, and Moore, D, 1987 *Flora of the British Isles*, 3 edn, Cambridge

Clapham, A W, 1915 *Lesnes Abbey in the parish of Erith, Kent*, London

Clapham, A W, 1934 *English Romanesque architecture: after the Conquest*, Oxford

Clark, A J, and Simmonds, P H, nd Archaeomagnetic dating report … Merton measurement, unpub Engl Heritage Ancient Monuments Lab rep 840509

Clark, J (ed), 1995 *The medieval horse and its equipment, c 1150–c 1450*, HMSO Medieval Finds Excav London 5, London

Clark, J (ed), 1897 *The observances in use at the Augustinian priory of St Giles and St Andrew at Barnwell*, Cambridgeshire

Clay, P, 1981 The small finds, in Mellor and Pearce 1981, 130–44

Cobb, H S (ed), 1990 *The overseas trade of London: exchequer customs accounts 1480–1*, London Rec Soc Publ 27, London

Coldstream, N, 1987 The kingdom of heaven and its architectural setting, in *The age of chivalry: art in Plantagenet England* (eds J Alexander and P Binski), 92–7, London

Coldstream, N, 1991 *Medieval craftsmen: masons and sculptors*, London

Colker, M L, 1970 Latin texts concerning Gilbert, founder of Merton Priory, *Studia Monastica* 12, 241–71

Conheeney, J, 1995 Merton Priory 1986–8 human bone assessment, unpub MoL rep

Conheeney, J, 1997 The human bone, in Thomas et al 1997, 218–31

Connell, B, and White, W, 1998 The human bones from the priory of St Saviour, Bermondsey, Southwark, unpub MoL rep

Connell, B, and White, B, in prep The human bone, in Steele in prep

Cook, G H, 1960 *The English cathedral*, London

Coppack, G, 1989 Thornholme Priory: the development of a monastic outer court, in Gilchrist and Mytum 1989, 185–22

Coppack, G, 1990 *English Heritage book of abbeys and priories*, London

Coppack, G, 1993, *Abbeys and priories*, London

Coppack, G, Harrison, S, and Hayfield, C, 1995 Kirkham Priory: the architecture and archaeology of an Augustinian house, *J Brit Archaeol Ass* 3 ser 148, 55–135

Crowley, N, 1997 Ceramic building material, in Thomas et al 1997, 195–201

Culpeper, N, 1653 *Culpeper's complete herbal*, Foulsham

Daniell, C, 1997 *Death and burial in medieval England, 1066–1550*, London

Davis, A, 1997 The plant remains, in Thomas et al 1997, 234–45

Davis, A, 2004 The plant remains, in Sloane and Malcolm 2004, 376–82

Davis, A, in prep The plant remains, in Sloane in prep

Dawes, J D, and Magilton, J R, 1980 *The cemetery of St Helen-on-the-Walls, Aldwark*, The Archaeology of York 12/1, London

Dent, J, 1970 *The quest for Nonsuch*, London

Dickinson, J C, 1950 *The origins of the Austin canons and their introduction into England*, London

Dickinson, J C, 1961 *Monastic life in medieval England*, London

Didron, A, 1845 *Un grand monastère au XIIe siècle: Tome 3, Annales archéologiques*, Paris

Domestic Intelligencer, 1680 [advertisement, description of Merton Abbey to let], 5 March

Driesch, A von den, 1976 *A guide to the measurement of animal bones from archaeological sites*, Peabody Mus Bull 1, Cambridge, Mass

Dyer, C, 1989 *Standards of living in the later Middle Ages: social change in England c 1200–1520*, Cambridge

Eames, E S, 1967 Patterned floor tiles, in Turner 1967, 46–50

Eames, E S, 1980 *Catalogue of medieval lead-glazed earthenware tiles in the Department of Medieval and Later Antiquities British Museum*, London

Eames, E S, 1982 The tile pavements, in Woods, H, Excavations at Eltham Palace 1975–9, *Trans London Middlesex Archaeol Soc* 33, 238–44

Eames, E S, 1992 *Medieval craftsmen: English tilers*, London

Early Charters St Paul The early charters of the cathedral church of St Paul, London (ed M Gibbs), Camden Soc 3 ser, 58, 1939, London

Early Charters Waltham The early charters of Augustinian canons of Waltham Abbey, Essex, 1062–1230 (ed R Ranford), Stud Hist Medieval Religion 2, 1989, Woodbridge

Egan, G, 1995 *Lead cloth seals and related items in the British Museum*, British Museum Occas Pap 93, London

Egan, G, 1997a Non-ceramic finds, in Thomas et al 1997, 201–15

Egan, G, 1997b Dice, Finds Res Group 700–1700 Datasheet 23, Oxford

Egan, G, 1998 *The medieval household: daily living c 1150–c 1450*, HMSO Medieval Finds Excav London 6, London

Egan, G, 2001 Cloth seals, in *Salisbury and South Wiltshire Museum medieval catalogue: Part 3* (ed P Saunders), 43–86, Salisbury

Egan, G, 2005 *Material culture in London in an age of transition: Tudor and Stuart period finds c 1450–c 1700 from excavations at riverside sites in Southwark*, MoLAS Monogr Ser 19, London

Egan, G, in prep Reports on finds from the site of Bermondsey Abbey, London

Egan, G, and Forsyth, H, 1997 Wound wire and silver gilt, in *The age of transition: the archaeology of English culture 1400–1600* (eds D Gaimster and P Stamper), Soc Medieval Archaeol Monogr Ser 15/Oxbow Monogr 98, 215–38, Oxford

Egan, G, and Pritchard, F, 1991 *Dress accessories – medieval finds from excavations in London*, London

Ellis, A E, 1969 *British snails – the non-marine gastropoda of Great Britain and Ireland*, Oxford

Ellis, A E, 1978 *British freshwater bivalve mollusca*, London

Ellis, B, 1995 Spurs and spur fittings, in Clark 1995, 124–50

Endrei, W, and Egan, G, 1982 The sealing of cloth in Europe, with special reference to the English evidence, *Textile History* 13, 47–75

English Heritage, 1991 *Management of archaeological projects*, London

Evans, J, 1999 Merton Priory pottery project – residue analysis, unpub MoL rep

Eyre 1244 The London eyre of 1244 (eds H Chew and M Weinbaum), London Rec Soc 6, 1970, London

Farwell, D E, and Molleson, T I, 1993 *Poundbury: Vol 2, The cemeteries*, Dorset Natur Hist Archaeol Soc Monogr Ser 11, Dorchester

Ferembach, D, Schwidetzky, I, and Stloukal, M, 1980 Recommendations for age and sex diagnosis of skeletons, *J Hum Evol* 9, 517–49

Fernie, E C, 1985 Anglo-Saxon lengths: 'the northern system', the perch and the foot, *Archaeol J* 142, 246–54

Ferris, I, 2000 *Haughmond Abbey, Lilleshall Abbey, Moreton Corbet Castle, Shropshire*, London

Finnegan, M, 1978 Non-metric variation in the infra-cranial skeleton, *J Anat* 125, 23–37

Finny, W E St L, 1929 A 14th-century column from Kingston, *Surrey Archaeol Collect* 38, 104

Fitznells Cart Fitznells cartulary: a calendar of Bodleian Library MS Rawlinson B 430 (eds C A F Meekings and P Shearman), Surrey Rec Soc 26, 1968, Guildford

Fletcher, B, 1943 (1896) *A history of architecture on the comparative method*, 11 edn, London

Foyle, J, 2004 Syon Park, rediscovering medieval England's only Bridgettine monastery, *Current Archaeol* 16(192), 550–5

Frere, S S, 1941 A medieval pottery at Ashtead, *Surrey Archaeol Collect* 47, 58–66

Gallagher, D M B, 1994 The planning of Augustinian monasteries in Scotland, in *Meaningful architecture: social interpretation of buildings* (ed M Locock), Worldwide Archaeol Ser 9, 167–87, Aldershot

Gardner, J S, 1955 Coggeshall Abbey and its early brickwork, *J Brit Archaeol Ass* 18, 19–32

Geoquest, 1993 Archaeomagnetic study of a tile kiln at Niblett Hall, City of London, unpub Geoquest Associates rep

Gerard, J, 1994 *Gerard's herbal: the history of plants* (ed M Woodward), London

Gernaey, A M, Minnikin, D E, Copley, M S, Power, J J, Ahmed, A M S, Dixon, R A, Roberts, C A, Robertson, D J, Nolan, J, and Chamberlain, A, 1998 Detecting ancient tuberculosis, *Internet Archaeol* 5, York

Gilchrist, R, and Mytum, H, 1989 *The archaeology of rural monasteries*, BAR Brit Ser 203, Oxford

Gilchrist, R, and Mytum, H (eds), 1993 *Advances in monastic archaeology*, BAR Brit Ser 227, Oxford

Gilchrist, R, and Sloane, B, 2005 *Requiem: the medieval monastic cemetery in Britain*, London

Gilmour, B J J, and Stocker, D A, 1986 *St Mark's church and cemetery*, The Archaeology of Lincoln 13/1, Lincoln

Gilyard-Beer, R, 1972 (1959) *Abbeys*, London

Gilyard-Beer, R, and Coppack, G, 1986 Excavations at Fountains Abbey, North Yorkshire, *Archaeologia* 108, 147–88

Giorgi, J, 1998 The environmental evidence, in Excavations at the former Allied Brewery, 148–180 St John Street, London, EC1 (ed K Tyler), *Trans London Middlesex Archaeol Soc* 49, 121–7

Giorgi, J, 1999 The plant remains from Merton Priory (MPY86), unpub MoL rep

Godfrey, W, 1959 Medieval hospitals in Sussex, *Surrey Archaeol Collect* 97, 130–7

Goodman, A H, Thomas, R B, Swedlund, A C, and Armelagos, G

J, 1988 Biocultural perspectives on stress in prehistoric, historical and contemporary population research, *Yearb Phys Anthropol* 31, 169–202

Grainger, I, and Phillpotts, C, with Mills, P S, in prep a *The abbey of St Mary Graces, East Smithfield, London*, MoLAS Monogr Ser

Grainger, I, and Phillpotts, C, in prep b *The Royal Navy victualling yard, East Smithfield, London*, MoLAS Monogr Ser

Grainger, I, Hawkins, D, and Waldron, T, in prep *The Black Death cemetery at East Smithfield, London*, MoLAS Monogr Ser

Gray-Rees, L, 1997 Assessment of the plant remains in environmental samples from Merton Priory (MPY88), unpub MoL rep

Gray-Rees, L, and Pipe, A, 1999 Mollusc remains from the priory of St Mary Merton, Surrey, unpub MoL rep

Green, L, 1977 Merton Priory: 12th-century extension, *Surrey Archaeol Collect* 71, 95–100

Greene, J P, 1989, *Norton Priory: the archaeology of a medieval religious house*, Cambridge

Greene, J P, 1992 *Medieval monasteries*, Leicester

Greig, J, 1988 Plant resources, in *The countryside of medieval England* (eds G Astill and A Grant), 108–27, Oxford

Greig, J, 1991 The British Isles, in van Zeist, K, Wasylikowa, W, and Behre, K, *Progress in Old World palaeoethnobotany. A retrospective view on the occasion of 20 years of the International Work Group for Palaeoethnobotany*, 299–334, Rotterdam

Greig, J, 1992 The deforestation of London, *Rev Palaeobot Palynol* 73, 71–86

Grieve, M, 1992 *A modern herbal*, Harmondsworth

Hall, J, 1979 (1974) *Hall's dictionary of subjects and symbols in art*, rev edn, London

Hammond, P W, 1993 *Food and feast in medieval England*, Stroud

Hammond, P W, 1995 (1993) *Food and feast in medieval England*, reprinted with corrections, Stroud

Hansen, M, 1987, *The Hydrophiloidae (Coleoptera) of Fennoscandia and Denmark, Fauna Entomologica Scandinavica* 18, Leiden

Harris, P D, 1992 *The historic River Wandle: the mills in pictures, the Merton section*, Merton Hist Soc in conjunction with Merton Library Service [privately printed]

Harvey, B, 1993 *Living and dying in England 1100–1540: the monastic experience*, Oxford

Harvey, J H, 1961 The origin of the Perpendicular style, in Jope, E M, *Studies in building history*, 135–65, London

Harvey, J H, 1978 *The Perpendicular style, 1330–1485*, London

Harvey, J H, 1987 *English mediaeval architects, a biographical dictionary down to 1550*, Gloucester

Hayward, P, Nelson-Smith, A, and Shields, C, 1996 *Seashore of Britain and Europe*, London

Heales, A C, 1898 *The records of Merton Priory in the county of Surrey, chiefly from early and unpublished documents*, London

Henkes, H, 1994 *Glass without gloss*, Rotterdam Pap 9, The Hague

Hicks, M, and Hicks, A, 2001 *St Gregory's Priory Northgate, Canterbury: excavations 1988–91*, The Archaeology of Canterbury ns 2, Canterbury

Hills, G M, 1866 Hardham Priory of canons of St Augustine, *Sussex Archaeol Collect* 18, 54–9

Hillson, S, 1986 *Teeth*, Cambridge

Hirst, S M, and Wright, S M, 1989 Bordesley Abbey church: a long term research excavation, in Gilchrist and Mytum 1989, 295–312

Historia Minor Matthaei Parisiensis, monachi sancti albani, historia Anglorum, sive, ut vulgo dicitur, historia minor (ed F Madden), Rolls Series, 3 vols, 1866–9, London

Hoey, L R, 1997 The articulation of rib vaults in the Romanesque parish churches of England and Normandy, *Antiq J* 77, 145–77

Hohler C, 1942 Medieval paving tiles in Buckinghamshire, *Rec Buckinghamshire* 14, 33–42

Holland, D G, 1972 *A key to the larvae, pupae and adults of the British species of elminthidae*, Freshwater Biological Ass Scientific Publ 26, Ambleside

Horn, W, and Born, E, 1979 *The plan of St Gall* (3 vols), Berkeley

Joffroy, R, 1974 Bandages herniaires, in *Le Mobilier funeraire*, in *Le Cimetière de Lavoye, nécropole mérovingienne*, 38–9, Paris

Johnston, P M, 1914 A discovery at Merton Priory, *Surrey Archaeol Collect* 27, 136–40

Jones, H, 1992 The retrieval of grave goods from medieval and Roman cemeteries in London, in Payton, R, *Retrieval of objects from archaeological sites*, 27–37, London

Jowett, E M, 1951 *An illustrated history of Merton and Morden*, London

Judd, M A, and Roberts, C A, 1998 Fracture patterns at the medieval leper hospital in Chichester, *American J Phys Anthropol* 105, 43–55

Keegan, W F, 1989 Stable isotope analysis of prehistoric diet, in *Reconstruction of life from the skeleton* (eds M Y Iscan and K A R Kennedy), 223–36, New York

Keen, L, 2002 Review of Medieval 'Westminster' floor tiles, *J Brit Archaeol Ass* 155, 316–19

Keene, D, and Harding, V, 1985 *A survey of documentary sources for property holding in London before the Great Fire*, London Rec Soc 22, London

Kenward, H K, Hall, A R, and Jones, A K G, 1980 A tested set of techniques for the extraction of plant and animal macro-fossils from waterlogged archaeological deposits, *Sci Archaeol* 22, 3–15

Kerney, M P, 1999 *Atlas of the land and freshwater molluscs of Britain and Ireland*, Colchester

Kerney, M P, and Cameron, R A D, 1979 *Land snails of Britain and north-west Europe*, London

Keys, L, 1998 Hanging lamp, in Egan 1998, 129–30

Knowles, D, and Hadcock, R N, 1953 *Medieval religious houses: England and Wales*, London

Knüsel, C J, Kemp, R L, and Budd, P, 1995 Evidence for remedial medical treatment of a severe knee injury from the Fishergate Gilbertine monastery in the city of York, *J Archaeol Sci* 22, 369–84

Koch, K, 1992 *Die Käfer Mitteleuropas, katalog 2*, Krefeld

L and P Hen VIII Letters and papers, foreign and domestic, of the reign of Henry VIII (eds J S Brewer, J Gairdner and R H Brodie), 22 vols in 35, 1864–1932, London

Lambrick, G, 1985 Further excavations on the second site of the Dominican priory, Oxford, *Oxoniensia* 50, 131–208

Lang, J, 1999 Radiographic examination of the Merton Priory

pelvis, unpub British Museum rep 7106

Lawrence, C L, 1984 *Medieval monasticism: forms of religious life in western Europe in the Middle Ages*, Harlow

Lawson, G, 1995 *Pig metapodial 'toggles' and buzz discs: traditional musical instruments*, Finds Res Group 700–1700 Datasheet 18, Oxford

Lawson, G, and Brown, D, 1990 Toggles, in Biddle 1990, 589–91

Lee, F, and Magilton, J, 1989 The cemetery of the hospital of St James and St Mary Magdalene, Chichester: a case study, *World Archaeol* 21(2), 273–82

Lewis, J, Wiltshire, P E J, and Macphail, R, 1992 A Late Devensian/Early Flandrian site at Three Ways Wharf, Uxbridge: environmental implications, in *Alluvial archaeology in Britain* (eds S P Needham and M G Macklin), Oxbow Monogr 27, 235–47, Oxford

Lightbown, R W, 1997 The jewellery, in Hurley, M F, and Scully, O M B, *Late Viking age and medieval Waterford excavations 1986–1992*, 518–23, Waterford, Ireland

Lilley, J M, Stroud, G, Brothwell, D R, and Williamson, M H, 1994 *The Jewish burial ground at Jewbury*, The Archaeology of York 12/3, York

Little, B, 1979, *Abbeys and priories in England and Wales*, London

Lloyd, N, 1983 (1925) *A history of English brickwork*, repr, Woodbridge

Locker, A, 1997 The fish bones, in Thomas et al 1997, 234–5

Lockwood, S, 1993 Reigate stone: geology, use and repair, *Structural Survey* 12(5), 18–22

London Viewers *London viewers and their certificates, 1508–58* (ed Janet S Loengard), London Rec Soc 26, 1989, London

Lucht, W H, 1987 *Die Käfer Mitteleuropas: Katalog*, Krefeld

Lyne, M, 1997 *Lewes Priory: excavations by Richard Lewis, 1969–82*, Lewes

Lyon, J, 2007 *Within these walls: Roman and medieval defences north of Newgate, at the Merrill Lynch Financial Centre, City of London*, MoLAS Monogr Ser 33, London

Lysons, D, 1792 *The environs of London: Vol 1*, London

Macan, T T, 1977 *A key to the British fresh- and brackish water gastropods*, 4 edn, Freshwater Biological Ass Scientific Publ 13, Ambleside

McCarthy, M R, and Brookes, C M, 1988 *Medieval pottery in Britain AD 900–1600*, Leicester

McGrail, S, 1978 *Logboats of England and Wales with comparative material from European and other countries*, BAR Brit Ser 51, Oxford

MacGregor, A, 1985 *Bone, antler, ivory and horn*, London

Mackenzie, F, 1844 *The architectural antiquities of the collegiate chapel of St Stephen, Westminster: the late House of Commons*, London

Manning, O, and Bray, W, 1804 *The history and antiquities of the county of Surrey: Vol 1*, London

Margeson, S M, 1982 Worked bone, in Coad, J G, and Streeten, A D F, Excavations at Castle Acre Castle, Norfolk 1972–7, *Archaeol J* 139, 241–55

Margeson, S M, 1993 *Norwich households: the medieval and post-medieval finds from Norwich survey excavations 1977–8*, E Anglian Archaeol Rep 58, Norwich

Martin, G H, and Highfield, R, 1997 *A history of Merton College, Oxford*, Oxford

Mays, S, 1991a The burials from the Whitefriars friary site, Buttermarket, Ipswich, Suffolk (excavated 1986–8), unpub Engl Heritage Ancient Monuments Lab rep 17/91 part 1

Mays, S, 1991b The medieval burials from the Blackfriars friary, School Street, Ipswich, Suffolk (excavated 1983–5), unpub Engl Heritage Ancient Monuments Lab rep 16/91 part 1

Mays, S, 1998 *The archaeology of human bones*, London

Meindl, R S, and Lovejoy, C O, 1985 Ectocranial suture closure: a revised method for the determination of age based upon the lateral anterior sutures, *American J Phys Anthropol* 68, 57–66

Mellor, J E, and Pearce, T, 1981 *The Austin friars, Leicester*, CBA Res Rep 35, London

Miles, A, and Conheeney, J, in prep, *Excavations in the St Bride's lower churchyard*

Miller, P, and Stephenson, R, 1999 *A 14th-century pottery site in Kingston upon Thames, Surrey: excavations at 70–76 Eden Street*, MoLAS Archaeol Stud Ser 1, London

Mitchiner, M, 1988 *Jettons, medalets and tokens: Vol 1, The medieval period and Nuremberg*, London

Mon Angl Dugdale, W, 1970 (1830) *Monasticon Anglicanum: Vol 6, Part 1* (eds J Caley, B Badinel and H Ellis), London

Montague, E N, 1992a *The archaeology of Mitcham*, Merton

Montague, E N, 1992b *A study of the textile bleaching and printing industry in Mitcham and Merton from 1590 until 1870*, Stud in Merton Hist, Merton Hist Soc in conjunction with Merton Library Service [privately printed]

Montague, E N, in prep *History of Colliers Wood*

Moore, P D, and Webb, J A, 1978 *An illustrated guide to pollen analysis*, London

Moore, P D, Webb, J A, and Collinson, M E, 1991 *Pollen analysis*, 2 edn, Oxford

Morris, R K, 1979 The development of later Gothic mouldings in England, *Architect Hist* 21, 21–57; 22, 1–48

Morris, R K, 1992 An English glossary of medieval mouldings, *Architect Hist* 35, 1–16

Murdoch, T (ed), 1991 *Treasures and trinkets: jewellery in London from pre-Roman times to the 1930s*, London

Musty, J, 1978 Exploratory excavations within the monstic precinct, Waltham Abbey 1972, *Essex Archaeol Hist* 10, 127–73

Nielsen, R, 1993 Deen City Farm grazing, Varley Way, Mitcham London Borough of Merton: an archaeological evaluation, unpub MoL rep

Nilsson, A N, and Holmen, M, 1995 *The aquatic Adephaga (Coleoptera) of Fennoscandia and Denmark: 2, Dytiscidae*, Fauna Entomologica Scandinavica 32, Leiden

Norton, C, 1996 The decorated pavements of Salisbury Cathedral and Old Sarum, in Keen, L, and Cocke, T, *Medieval art and architecture at Salisbury Cathedral*, Brit Archaeol Ass Conference Trans 17, 90–105, Leeds

Orme, N, and Webster, M, 1995 *The English hospital 1070–1570*, London

Ortner, D J, and Ericksen, M F, 1997 Bone changes in the human skull probably resulting from scurvy in infancy and childhood, *Int J Osteol* 7, 212–20

Paul, R W, 1898 Newark Priory, *The Builder* [November], 474–7

Paul, R W, 1913 Plan of the church and monastery of St

Augustine, Bristol, *Archaeologia* 63, 231–50

Pearce, C M H, 1932 An account of the buildings at Newark Priory, *Surrey Archaeol Collect* 40, 1–39

Pearce, J, and Vince, A G, 1988 *A dated type series of London medieval pottery: Part 4, Surrey whitewares*, London Middlesex Archaeol Soc Spec Pap 10, London

Pearce, J, Vince, A G, and Jenner, M A, 1985 *A dated type series of London medieval pottery: Part 2, London-type ware*, London Middlesex Archaeol Soc Spec Pap 6, London

Peers, C 1986 (1967) *Rievaulx Abbey, Yorkshire*, London

Pevsner, N, and Metcalf, M, 1985 *The cathedrals of England*, Harmondsworth

Phenice, T W, 1969 A newly developed visual method of sexing the *os pubis*, *American J Phys Anthropol* 30, 297–302

Philp, B, 1968 *Excavations at Faversham, 1965: the royal abbey, Roman villa and Belgic farmstead*, Kent Archaeol Res Group Res Rep 1, Bromley

Pipe, A, 1997 The animal bone, in Thomas et al 1997, 231–4

Pipe, A, Rielly, K, and Ainsley, C, in prep The animal bone, in Steele in prep

Plumptre, F C, 1861 Some account of the remains of the priory of St Martin's, and the church of St Martin-le-Grand, at Dover, *Archaeol Cantiana* 4, 1–26

Prendergast, M D, 1974 Limpsfield medieval coarseware: a descriptive analysis, *Surrey Archaeol Collect* 70, 57–77

Prescott, E, 1992 *The English medieval hospital 1050–1640*, London

Price, J E, 1870 Medieval kiln for burning encaustic tiles discovered near Farringdon Road, Clerkenwell, *Trans London Middlesex Archaeol Soc* 3 (for 1866–70), 31–6

Ray, Y, 1965 The sources of London's bricks, unpub dissertation, Morley College

RCHM(E), 1912 Roy Comm Hist Monuments (Engl), *An inventory of the historical monuments in Buckinghamshire: Vol 1, South*, London

RCHM(E), 1913 Roy Comm Hist Monuments (Engl), *An inventory of the historical monuments in Buckinghamshire: Vol 2, North*, London

Reading Cart Reading Abbey cartularies (ed B R Kemp), 2 vols, Camden Soc 4 ser, 31, 33, 1986–7, London

Redknap, M, 2005 An early medieval girdle from burial 631, in Holbrook, N, and Thomas, A, An early medieval monastic cemetery at Llandough, Glamorgan: excavations in 1994, *Medieval Archaeol* 49, 53–64

Reg Wolsey Registrum Thomae Wolsey, cardinalis ecclesie Wintoniensis administratoris (eds H Chitty and F T Madge), Canterbury York Ser 32, 1926, Oxford

Reg Woodlock Registrum Henrici Woodlock diocesis Wintoniensis 1305–16 (ed A W Goodman), Canterbury York Ser 43–4, 1940–1, Oxford

Rigold, S E, 1977 Romanesque bases in and south-east of the Limestone belt, in *Ancient monuments and their interpretation: essays presented to A J Taylor* (eds M Apted, R Gilyard-Beer and A D Saunders), 99–137, London

Rigold, S E, 1985 (1974) *Bayham Abbey*, London

Roberts, C, Lucy, D, and Manchester, K, 1994 Inflammatory lesions of ribs: an analysis of the Terry collection, *American J Phys Anthropol* 95, 169–82

Robinson, D, 1980 *The geography of Augustinian settlement in medieval England and Wales*, BAR Brit Ser 80, Oxford

Robinson, D (ed), 1998 *The Cistercian abbeys of Britain: far from the concourse of men*, London

Rodwell, W, 1989 *The English Heritage book of church archaeology*, rev edn, London

Rodwell, W, 2001 *Wells Cathedral: excavations and structural studies, 1978–93* (2 vols), London

Roebuck, J, and Coppack, G, with Hurst, J G, 1987 A closely dated group of late medieval pottery from Mount Grace Priory, *Bull Medieval Pottery Res Group* 11, 15–24

Roesing, F W, 1983 Sexing immature human skeletons, *J Hum Evol* 12, 149–55

Rogers, J, and Waldron, T, 1995 *A field guide to joint disease in archaeology*, Chichester

Rot Parlt Rotuli parliamentorum: ut et petitiones, et placita in parliamento (ed J Strachey), 6 vols, 1767–77, London

Round, J H, 1899 *The commune of London*, Westminster

Ryan, P, 1996 *Brick in Essex, from the Roman conquest to the Reformation*, Chelmsford

St John Hope, W H, 1884 Repton Priory, Derbyshire, *Archaeol J* 41, 349–63

St John Hope, W H, and Brakspear, H, 1909 Haughmond Abbey, Shropshire, *Archaeol J* 66, 2 ser 16, 281–311

Salzman, L F, 1952 *Building in England down to 1540: a documentary history*, Oxford

Samuel, M W, 1999 The use and significance of the masons' marks: how these and other technical features throw light on the craft traditions of the waterfront masons, in Thurley S, *Whitehall Palace: an architectural history of the royal apartments, 1290–1698*, 164–8, London

Samuel, M W, 2004a Worked stone, in Barber et al 2004, 132–8

Samuel, M W, 2004b The moulded stone, in Sloane and Malcolm 2004, 280–97

Samuel, M W, in prep Worked stone, in Steel in prep

Saxby, D, 1991 An archaeological evaluation at Streatham House, Merton, unpub MoL rep

Saxby, D, 1995 *William Morris at Merton*, London

Saxby, D, 1997 Land bordered by High Street Colliers Wood, Christchurch Road and the Pickle: an archaeological desktop assessment, unpub MoL rep

Saxby, D, 1998 Land bordered by High Street Colliers Wood, Christchurch Road and the Pickle: a post-excavation assessment, unpub MoL rep

Saxby, D, 2001 Furnitureland, Merton High Street, London, SW19, an archaeological excavation report, unpub MoL rep

Saxby, D, 2004 1–11 High Street Colliers Wood an archaeological evaluation, unpub MoL rep

Saxby, D, 2005a Colliers Wood, 2CW, land bordered by Bennett's Ditch, the River Wandle and Merantun Way: a post-excavation assessment and updated project design for residential block C within trench 31 (MMY99), unpub MoL rep

Saxby, D, 2005b Colliers Wood, 2CW, land bordered by Bennett's Ditch, the River Wandle and Merantun Way: a post-excavation assessment of excavation trench 3 and evaluation trenches 28 and 29 (MMY99), unpub MoL rep

Saxby, D, in prep *Recent work on the site of Merton Priory*, MoLAS Stud Ser

Scaife, R G, 1982a Pollen analysis of Roman peats underlying the temple of Mithras, London, unpub Ancient Monuments Lab rep os 3592

Scaife, R G, 1982b Pollen analysis of urban medieval sediments, in Mills, P, Excavations at Broad Sanctuary, Westminster, *Trans London Middlesex Archaeol Soc* 33, 360–5

Scaife, R G, 2000 Merton Priory: pollen analysis, unpub MoL rep

Scaife, R G, 2004 The pollen, in Keevill, G, *The Tower of London moat, archaeological excavations 1995–9*, Oxford

Schofield, J, 1984 *The building of London from the Conquest to the Great Fire*, London

Schofield, J, 1988 Burial types and practices, in White 1988, 18–27

Schofield, J, 1995 *Medieval London houses*, London

Schofield, J, and Lea, R, 2005 *Holy Trinity Priory, Aldgate, City of London: an archaeological reconstruction and history*, MoLAS Monogr Ser 24, London

Sharpe, E, 1848 *Architectural parallels: the progress of ecclesiastical architecture in England, through the 12th and 13th centuries*, London

Sidell, E J, 1993 *A methodology for the identification of archaeological eggshell*, Museum Applied Science Centre for Archaeology (MASCA), University of Pennsylvania, Philadelphia

Sidell, J, Wilkinson, K, Scaife, R, and Cameron, N, 2000 *The Holocene evolution of the London Thames: archaeological excavations (1991–8) for the London Underground Limited Jubilee Line Extension Project*, MoLAS Monogr Ser 5, London

Sloane, B, in prep *Excavations at the nunnery of St Mary de fonte clericorum, Clerkenwell, London*, MoLAS Monogr Ser

Sloane, B, and Malcolm, G, 2004 *Excavations at the priory of the Order of the Hospital of St John of Jerusalem, Clerkenwell, London*, MoLAS Monogr Ser 20, London

Smith, T P, with Betts, I, 2004 Ceramic building material, in Barber et al 2004, 138–46

Stace, C, 1991 *New flora of the British Isles*, Cambridge

Steele, A, in prep *Excavations at the monastery of St Saviour Bermondsey, Southwark*, MoLAS Monogr Ser

Stephenson, R, 2004 The pottery, in Howe, E, A medieval timber building at London Road, Wallington, *Surrey Archaeol Collect* 91, 223–7

Stirland, A, 1991 Diagnosis of occupationally related pathology: can it be done?, in Ortner, D T, and Aufderheide, A C, *Human palaeopathology: current synthesis and future options*, 40–7, Washington, DC

Stocker, D, 1993 Recording worked stone, in Gilchrist and Mytum 1993, 19–26

Stockmarr, J, 1971 Tablets with spores used in absolute pollen analysis, *Pollen et spores* 13, 614–21

Stratford, N, 1992 Les Bâtiments de l'abbaye de Cluny à l'époque medievale, *Bulletin Monumental* 150, 383–411

Stroud, G, 1994 The population, in Lilley et al 1994, 424–49

Stroud, G, and Kemp, R L, 1993 *Cemeteries of the church and priory of St Andrew, Fishergate*, The Archaeology of York 12/2, York

Stuart-Macadam, P, 1986 Health and disease in the monks of Stratford Langthorne Abbey, *Essex J* 21, 67–71

Tanner, L E, and Clapham, A W, 1933 The Confessor's church, *Archaeologia* 83, 227–36

Tatton-Brown, T W T, 1990 Building stone in Canterbury, in Parsons, D, *Stone quarrying and building in England, AD 43–1525*, Rochester, 70–82

Thomas, C, Sloane, B, and Phillpotts, C, 1997 *Excavations at the priory and hospital of St Mary Spital, London*, MoLAS Monogr Ser 1, London

Thorne, J, 1876 *Handbook to the environs of London …: Part 2*, London

Trotter, M, and Gleser, G C, 1952 Estimation of stature from long bones of American whites and Negroes, *American J Phys Anthropol* 10, 463–514

Trotter, M, and Gleser, G C, 1958 A re-evaluation of estimation of stature based on measurements of stature taken during life and long bones after death, *American J Phys Anthropol* 16, 79–123

Turner, D J, 1965 Excavations at Merton Priory, Merton, Surrey, *London Natur* 44, 139–46

Turner, D J, 1967 Excavations near Merton Priory 1962–3, *Surrey Archaeol Collect* 64, 35–70

Turner, D J, 1974 Medieval pottery kiln at Bushfield Shaw, Earlswood, *Surrey Archaeol Collect* 70, 47–55

Ubelaker, D H, 1984 *Human skeletal remains: excavation, analysis, interpretation*, Washington, DC

Val Eccl Valor ecclesiasticus, tempore Henrici VIII, auctoritate regia institutus (eds J Caley and J Hunter), 2, Rec Comm 9, 1814, London; 6 (2 parts), 1834, London

VCH, 1905 *Victoria History of the county of Surrey: Vol 2*, London

VCH, 1911 *Victoria History of the county of Surrey: Vol 3*, London

VCH, 1912a *Victoria History of the county of Bedfordshire: Vol 3*, London

VCH, 1912b *Victoria History of the county of Surrey: Vol 4*, London

Vince, A G, 1985 Kingston-type ware, *Popular Archaeol* 6(12), 34–9

Vince, A G, and Jenner, A, 1991 The Saxon and early medieval pottery of London, in *Aspects of Saxon and Norman London: Vol 2, Finds and environmental evidence* (ed A G Vince), London Middlesex Archaeol Soc Spec Pap 12, 19–119, London

Waldron, T, nd [1977] A report on the human bones from Merton Priory, unpub Ancient Monuments Lab rep 4483

Waldron, T, 1985 DISH at Merton Priory: evidence for a 'new' occupational disease?, *Brit Med J* 291, 1762–4

Waldron, T, 1993 The human remains from the Royal Mint site, unpub MoL rep

Waldron, T, 1994 *Counting the dead: the epidemiology of skeletal populations*, Chichester

Waldron, T, in prep The human bone, in Grainger and Phillpotts in prep a

Walford, E, 1895 *Greater London: a narrative of its history, its people and its places* (2 vols), London

Ward Perkins, J B, 1940 *Museum of London medieval catalogue*, London

Wardle, A, 1998 Musical instruments, in Egan 1998, 284–7

Watkin, A (ed), 1956 The great cartulary of Glastonbury, *Somerset Rec Soc* 64, 627–9

Weaver, O J, 2001 *Boscobel House and White Ladies Priory*, London

Webb, E A, 1913 The plan of St Bartholomew's, West Smithfield, and the recent excavations, *Archaeologia* 64, 165–76

Webb, G F, 1956 *Architecture in Britain: the Middle Ages*, Harmondsworth

Westlake, H F, 1923 *Westminster Abbey: the church, convent, cathedral and college of St Peter, Westminster* (2 vols), London

Westminster Charters Westminster Abbey charters, 1066–c 1214 (ed E Mason), London Rec Soc Publ 25, 1988, London

Wheeler, A, 1979 *The tidal Thames*, London

White, E, 1993 The measure of meat: monastic diet in medieval England, in *Food for the community: special diets for special groups* (ed C A Wilson), 5–42, Edinburgh

White, W, 1988 *Skeletal remains from the cemetery of St Nicholas Shambles, City of London*, London Middlesex Archaeol Soc Spec Pap 9, London

White, W, 2004 Human skeletal remains, in Barber et al 2004, 158–79

Willemsen, A, 1998 *Kinder delijt: middeleeuws speelgoed in de Nederlanden*, Nijmeegse Kunsthistorische Studies 6, Nijmegen

Wilson, C, 1990 *The Gothic cathedral: the architecture of the great church 1130–1530*, London

Wilson, C, 1991 (1976) *Food and drink in Britain: from the Stone Age to recent times*, repr, London

Wilson, C, Physick, J, Tudor-Craig, P, and Gem, R, 1986 *Westminster Abbey*, London

Wood, M E, 1965 *The English medieval house*, London

Wymer, J J, 1968 *Lower Palaeolithic archaeology in Britain as represented by the Thames valley*, London

INDEX

Compiled by Ann Hudson

Page numbers in **bold** indicate illustrations and maps
All street names and locations are in Merton/Colliers Wood unless specified otherwise
County names within parentheses refer to historic counties
Artefacts are medieval unless otherwise stated
In Section 7.1 (pages 171–6) only information in headings is indexed

Index